The
Vital Records
of
KINGSTON, NEW HAMPSHIRE

1694–1994

by

Judith Lane Arseneault

CLEARFIELD

Printed for
Clearfield Company, Inc. by
Genealogical Publishing Co., Inc.
Baltimore, Maryland
1995

Reprinted for
Clearfield Company, Inc. by
Genealogical Publishing Co., Inc.
Baltimore, Maryland
2002

International Standard Book Number: 0-8063-4552-7

Made in the United States of America

This book is dedicated to my husband Donald
for all his support and encouragement.

I would also like to thank Bettie, Holly and
Eleanor for all their assistance.

TABLE OF CONTENTS

INTRODUCTION

This book contains a transcription of the birth, marriage, and death records of Kingston, New Hampshire for the 300 years from 1694 to 1994. The information was taken from the original Kingston vital records for the years 1694–1900, and from the official Town Reports for the years 1901–1994. In most cases, the data were transcribed verbatim, except that a few obvious errors were corrected.

In all records, parents' names appear in parentheses. In the early records, towns given in parentheses refer to birthplaces. In later years the information varied, and the town referred to may have been a birthplace or place of residence at the time of record. In a few instances, birthplace/residence at the time of record are listed in that order. Thus, in "Hampstead/Kingston" the first town is the birthplace, the second the town of residence. Some records give birthplace or residence and age at the time of record, for example, "Kingston/33." Unless otherwise noted, all towns listed are in New Hampshire.

The following is a list of towns (with their abbreviations) which appear in the text in parentheses:

Atkinson	A	Hampton Falls	H/F	Nottingham	Not
Brentwood	B	Haverhill, Ma.	Hav.	Plaistow	P
Danville	D	Kensington	Ken.	Portsmouth	Ports.
Dover	D/O	Lawrence, Ma.	Law.	Raymond	R
East Kingston	E/K	Manchester	M	Rochester	Roch.
Exeter	E	Newton	N	Salem	S
Fremont	F	Newton	N/J	Sandown	San
Hampstead	Ham.	No. Danville	N/D	Stratham	Strat.
Hampton	H	Northwood	Nor.	Westville	W

The following is a list of cemeteries referred to in the death records. All cemeteries are located in Kingston.

Plains Cemetery	P/C	Mill Stream Cemetery	M/S
Village Cemetery	V/C	So. Kingston Cemetery	S/K
Greenwood Cemetery	G/C	Kingston Cemetery	K/S
Pine Grove	P/G		

BIRTHS
1694-1900

ABBOTT: Peter & Phebe Spratt: Edmand, 11 Nov 1782; Peter Gragg, 05 Dec 1785
Peter Abbott & Elizabeth Gilmon: Betty, 07 Jun 1762; Betty, 15 Dec 1766;
Daniel, 07 Jun 1762; Epraim, 16 Dec 1764
ADEMS: William & Hannah: Male, 27 Oct 1880
ADISON: William & Hannah: William M, 16 Oct 1879
ALLEN: Robert (New Brunswick) & Charity (New Brunswick): Male, 25 Jan 1892
AVERY: Frank & Addie(Mary) Davis: Alfred J, 02 Apr 1878; Frank A J, 25 Jun
1876; Grace E, 04 Jul 1880
BALL: Albert H & Ida: Olive Ida, 13 Sep 1887
BALONGER: Frank Balonger: Male Child, 06 Feb 1880
BACHELDER: Ebenezer & Dorety Boynton: Nathan, 23 Oct 1734
Elisha & Theodate Smith: Josiah, 06 Mar 1752; Sarah, 18 Aug 1756; Zebelen,
20 Apr 1757
Josiah & Abigel Lampriel: Abigel, 06 Jun 1732; Deborah, 01 Feb 1733/4; Beniman,
11 Sep 1736
Nathan & Mary Darbon: Anna, 29 Jan 1731; Elisabeth, 03 May 1728; Mary, 26 May
1733; Nathaniel, 04 Jan 1725
Phienes & Elizabeth Gilmon; John, 28 Feb 1730/1; Mary, 13 Apr 1729; Stephen,
21 Apr 1727
BADGER: Benjamin & Sally Wadleight: Daniel, 25 Dec 1803; John, 13 Sep 1799; Joseph,
01 Dec 1811; Samuel, 31 Mar 1814; Stephen, 20 May 1802
Stephen & Doley Webster: Benjamin, 15 Mar 1774; Hanah, Jul 1770; Joseph, 28
Aug 1783; Molly, 01 Apr 1791; Sarah, 06 Mar 1779; Stephen, 02 Apr 1777;
William, 26 Dec 1786
BAILY: George E & Sarah A Cram: Mabel Louise, 04 Oct 1896
BAKIE: Daniel J (So Boston) & Nellie J Sanborn (Kingston): Male, 15 Sep 1889
William A (Kingston)& Flora A Gordon (Danville): Florence, 17 Mar 1897; Warren
Gordon, 20 Oct 1899; William A, Jr, 20 Oct 1899
BALL: Albert H (Haverhill,Ma) & Ida M (Laconia): Annie R, 18 Feb 1894; Emma B, 24 Apr
1891; Lucy Delia, 14 Nov 1889; Male, 12 Dec 1889; Olive Ida, 13 Sep 1887
BALLANGER: Frank G (Canada) & Mary A (Epping): Female, 15 Nov 1890
BARBER: Robert & Penelope Hunt: Easther, 12 Mar 1764; Elisabeth, 08 Oct 1750;
Hannah, 28 Dec 1743; Jethro, 04 Mar 1762; Mary, 10 Oct 1745; Peter, 05 Dec 1760;
Robert, 09 Oct 1759
BARNARD: Steven & Mary Colins: Alic, 15 Apr 1756; Easter, 21 Apr 1744; Mary,
17 Apr 1753; Sarah, 9 Jan 1759
BARRETT: James & Mary: ----, 20 Apr 1852
John Ellsworth (Kingston) & Lizzie Simpson Trafton (York,Me): Earl Benny, 19 Jul

1899; Raymond H, 11 Dec 1894; Ruth Freeman, 25 Sep 1892

Thomas (Ireland) & Ellen (Ireland): Catherine F, 15 Jul 1881; Female Child, 11 Jul 1873; John James, 27 Apr 1886

BARTLETT: Benjamin & Susanna Ladd: Benjamin, 15 Jan 1788; Peter, 13 May 1789

Francis & Mary A Rowe: Clarence E, 10 Mar 1879; Albert, 11 May 1869; Walter W, 27 Mar 1873

George A & Sophia D: George F, 15 May 1868

Hosea B & Ann: Gracie P, 22 Aug 1870; Roscoe L, 07 Aug 1873

John (Bartelot) & Mary Quimbe: Elisebath, 12 Jan 1743; Hannah, 30 Dec 1749; John, 24 Dec 1789; John, 20 Feb 1813; Joseph Charles, 09 Aug 1794; Judith, 13 Apr 1811; Sarah, 23 May 1792; Seth, 24 Nov 1784

John (Brentwood) & Philena (Kingston): Female, 23 Mar 1886

Joshua, Jr & Sarah Badger: Hannah, 01 Jul 1760

Dr Josiah & Maray: Ezra, 13 Sep 1770; Hannah, 31 Aug 1762; Hanah, 13 Dec 1766; Josiah, 20 Aug 1765; Josiah, 29 Aug 1768; Levi, 02 Sep 1763; Lois, 02 Jun 1756; Maray, 28 Dec 1754; Meriam, 19 Jun 1758; Rhoda, 22 May 1760; Sarah, 29 Jul 1773

Hon Levi, Esq & Abigail Stevens: Juina Loret, 01 Jun 1810; Levi Steven, 03 Dec 1811; Luella Julia, 30 Dec 1807

Levi & Aroline E Sanborn: ----, 14 Sep 1851; Aroline, 13 Feb 1846; Junia L, 01 Mar 1850; Levietta, 14 Sep 1851

Levi S (E Kingston) & Grace Sanborn (Fremont): Female Child, 04 Nov 1887; Gertrude E, 26 Aug 1885; Junia L, 04 Nov 1887; Levi L, 14 Mar 1884; Lottie Mary, 12 Sep, 1893

Mattias & Elizabeth Davis: Abigail, 12 Jun 1769; Abigail, 12 Jan 1775; Anna, 03 Oct 1779; Elisabeth, 08 Nov 1778; Elisabeth, 12 Oct 1770

Matthias & Tamesin Harbert: Matthias, 07 Nov 1778

Nathan & Jonnah Flanders: Ebenezer, 23 Apr 1750; Jeremiah, 06 Dec 1757; John, 31 Jul 1743; John, 31 Dec 1747; Jonnah, 04 Jan 1742; Mary, 05 Sep 1745; Nathan, 25 Feb 1752; Sarah, 19 Apr 1761; Zeprah, 06 Mar 1754

Nathan, Jr & Mary Blasdel: Jomia, 03 Mar 1773; Sarah, 22 Mar 1777

R. Benson (Kingston) & Medora Stevens (Kingston): Frank, 08 Sep 1887; Laura, 15 Aug 1890; Male Child, 08 Sep 1887

Richard Bartlett & Lora R: Male Child, 20 Dec 1880

Richard Bartlett & Anna: Stephen, 16 May 1801

William J Bartlett & Lettie M Crane: Female Child, 19 Apr 1870

BATCHELDER: George W & Harriet D Merrill: Winnifred Weld, 09 Nov 1871

BAUBIN: John & Ida: Male Child, 16 Aug 1879

BEAN: Daniel & Abigal Clifford: Bathsheba, 03 Jul 1746; Daniel ----; Mary, 03 Sep 1747; Mary, 26 Jun 1753; Samuel, 22 Apr 1749; Sarah, 23 Apr 1751

James & Sarah Brady; Benjamin, 05 May 1699; Catharan, 22 Aug 1714; Jeremiah, 09 Apr 1707; Jeremiah, 09 Apr 1707; Margrett, b 06 Apr 1702; Sammell, b 11 Jan 1710/11

Joseph & Meriam Folsum: Daniel, 30 Sep 1745; Jonathan, 31 Aug 1741; Joseph, 13 Nov 1734; Mary, 08 Aug 1741; Miriam, 01 Jul 1749; Nathanal, 10 Nov 1739

Joseph & Haner Davies: Joseph, 30 Sep 1742; Margret, 12 Aug 1738; Peter, 28 Jan 1744; Sarah, 19 Apr 1740

BEEDE: Ebenezer & Mehitabel: Thomas, 01 Jun 1732
   Hezekiah & Hephzibah Smith: Azariah, 29 Nov 1768; Bazaeleel, 22 Aug 1759;
   Deborah, 26 Sep 1766; Hephzibah, 12 Mar 1772; Jososheba, 15 Jan 1762; Phinehas,
   24 Sep 1749; Rezia, 06 Jul 1764
   Hezekiah & Judeth Beede: Jeremiah, 19 Dec 1774; Seth, 08 Apr 1736
   John & Sarah: Male Child, 27 Mar 1878
   Oscar & Hannah Webster: Male Child, 12 Jul 1877
BEEN: Samuel & Sarah: Elles, 09 Nov 1736
BELDEN: Zacharie & Jennie Shelden: Female Child, 21 Jun 1871; Female Child, 16 Feb
   1872
BLACK: Sarvent of Eben Stevens, Esq: Dinah Black, Nov 1752; Seser Black, 17 Aug 1754
BLAISDEL: Ralph & Merream Rowel: Judith, 21 Nov 1749; Mary, 13 Feb 1753;
   Nemiah, 28 Feb 1756; Samuel, 06 Mar 1750
BLAKE: Jonathan & Lucy Robinson:David, 24 Apr 1780; Lucy, 06 Jul 1778; Samuel,
   29 Nov 1782
BLASDELL: Ralfe & Mary: Mary, 04 Feb 1724/5
BLYE: Daniel H (Haverhill,Ma) & Ida (Haverhill,Ma): Male, 26 Aug 1887
BOOTMAN: Amos & Sarah Webster: Mary, 11 Nov 1750; Thomas, 25 Sep 1758;
   Webster, 03 Feb 1755
BOWHORNE: Androw & Tabathey; Sarah, 23 Jan 1736
BRAGDON: Fred L Bragdon (Brentwood) & Emma F Prescott (Kingston): John Augustus, 23
   May 1897; Ernest Prescott, 08 Jul 1895
   George L (Milton)& Martha Knox (Lebanon,Me): Dorria L, 22 Jan 1896; Female Child,
   05 Aug 1877; George Raymond, 07 Aug 1880; Lewis Albert, 04 May 1884
BRICKETT: John & Prudence: Susana, 29 Jun 1777
BRIDGES: Luther W (Windham) & Clara B Colcord (Kingston): Gladys Viola, 19 Jun 1893
BRON: Joseph & Elesebeth Sayer: Isac, 24 May 1761; Joseph, 31 Mar 1759
BROWN: Amos T & Abigail Brown: Dorothy, 05 Feb 1777; Hannah, 31 Dec 1774;
   Samuel, 22 Aug 1785; Sarah, 20 Apr 1781; Simeon, 22 Apr 1779
   David & Ruth Morrel: Abigal, 13 Aug 1746; Daniel, 10 Dec 1750; Ezekel, 10
   Aug 1756; Lydia, 29 Aug 1744; Meriam, 23 Mar 1753; Ruth, 01 Nov 1748;
   Sarah, 13 Feb 1758
   Edward E (Kingston) & Bertha (Kingston): Arthur F, 16 Jan 1894
   James & Rosanna: ----, 27 Oct 1851
   Joshua & Johaner: Abigal, 18 Sep 1746; Nathanal, 29 Oct 1748; Nathaniel Tredwill,
   May 1744
   Nathaniel G & Peace Ann (Annie) Chase: Clara,16 Apr 1885; Edward E, 13 Jan 1871
   Dr. Simen & Hannah Young: Henery, 19 Oct 1730; Joseph, 01 Jul 1735; Sarah, 31 Jul
   1737
BUCKLEY: Sylvester (Haverhill,Ma) & Agnes (Woodstock,Vt): John, 31 Mar 1891
BUSIEL: Wiliam & Juda Davies: Joseph, 08 Jul 1725; Mehetibol, 10 Mar 1723; Sarah, 17
   Apr 1718; William, 08 Dec 1720; Cornelios, 05 May 1777
BUSSEL: Daniel & Hannah Rummels: Abigal, 05 May 1777; Hanna, 03 Jan 1781; James,
   31 May 1798; John, 16 Feb 1793; Lydia, 23 Jul 1782 ; Lydia, 21 Nov 1790; Phebe,

13 Jan 1785; Polly, 09 Aug 1795; Stephen, 21 Sep 1788; True, 31 Jan 1802; William, 22 Nov 1788

BUSWEL: James & Elisaebath Clough: Abigal, 02 Feb 1765; Elisabeth, 04 Sep 1761; Mary, 09 Nov 1763; Sarah, 17 Feb 1767

Samuel & Mary Winslo: Cornelos, 18 Nov 1759; Elisha, 10 Nov 1757; Juda, 08 Oct 1763; Juda, 14 Jun 1768; Mary, 08 Feb 1762; Mary, 17 Dec 1771 Mary, 08 Jan 1776; Mehibebal, 15 Jan 1771; Samuel, 01 Mar 1766; Sarah, 20 Nov 1755

Simons & Cattorn Been (Bean): Hannah, 27 Apr 1746; Joseph, 25 Dec 1742; Mehetabel, 15 Jan 1748/9; David (Buriel-Buswell), 28 May 1753; Jean (Buriel-Buswell), 11 Mar 1750/1

William, Jr & Abegel Thorn: Abigel, 03 Sep 1749; Daniel, 03 May 1746; Haner, 16 May 1732; James, 10 Apr 1740; Phebe, 16 Jun 1736; Sarah, 20 Mar 1752

BUSWELL: Calob & Mary Badger: John, 28 Mar 1761; Richard, 28 Mar 1761; Walker, 04 May 1763

Samuel & Mary Worthen: Anna, 07 Nov 1737; Deliverance, 28 Dec 1729; Isaac, 31 Aug 1738; Mary, 17 Jun 1736

William, Jr & Judah Davies: Samuel, 14 Apr 1729

William, 3rd & Elisebath Wenslow: Elisebath, 12 Jul 1760; Hanah, 28 Jan 1758; Huldah, 19 Aug 1747; Joseph, 30 Aug 1770; Juda, 07 Feb 1744; Moses, 13 Jul 1768; Martha, 25 May 1752; Sarah, 03 Dec 1749; Sarah, 06 Mar 1766

CALCORD: Sammell & Elizebeth Folsom: Benjamen, 10 Jan 1713/4; Elizebeth, 13 Jun 1708; Mary, 01 Jan 1714/5; Peter, 27 Jun 1705; Sammell, 22 Aug 1710

CALEF: John & Jude Chalies: Amos, 01 Jul 1769; Hanah, 04 Mar 1760; John, 1762; Joseph, 05 May 1756; Mary, 19 Jan 1758; Robert, 26 Feb 1772; Samuel, 11 Dec 1764

Joseph & Hannah Pettingell: Benjamin, 22 Jun 1783; Benjamin, 13 Jul 1786; Dorothy, 24 Apr 1781; Elisebath, 01 Oct 1767; Joseph, 03 Jan 1773; Joseph, 04 Nov 1774; Judeth, 03 Jan 1777; Loes, 04 Dec 1770; Nathaniel, 26 Oct 1769; Rebecca, 26 Jan 1779

Joseph & Miriam Bartlett: Josiah, 21 May 1782; Miriam, 20 May 1784

Joseph & Molly Hook: Molly, 09 Oct 1790

Samuel & Mary Ann Berry: George Everett; Horace Berry (dates unknown); Mary E, 16 Jul 1844

CALFE: William & Lowis: Doley, 20 Jun 1762; Joseph, 12 Dec 1742; Lidea, 30 Jul 1745; Lowis, 04 Jan 1739; Mary, 23 Sep 1758; Sarah, 15 Sep 1749

CALLE: Darbe & Sarah Honton: Edward, 18 Jul 1731; Philep, 12 Jun 1735; Sammel, 25 Aug 1733

CALLINGS: Joseph (Collins) & Sarah Bagley: Joseph, 17 Mar 1763; Mary, 09 Sep 1770; Moses, 06 Aug 1761; Sarah, 29 Sep 1767

CAMIT: Silas & Cattern Judkins: Ane, 10 Dec 1753; John, 30 Dec 1749; Jonathan, 29 Feb 1747; Silas, 23 Dec 1751

CAMPBELL: Alfred H & Hattie: Arthur W, 12 Sep 1878

Buel C (N Fairfax,Vt) & Esther L (Fairfield,Vt): Buel C, 01 Aug 1889

CARNIS: Rev James: Female Child, 28 Jun 1876

CARLTON: William M (Kingston)& R.J. Emery (Newton Jct): Wilbur George, 09 Sep 1897

CARR: James & Sarah: Betty, 22 Feb 1756; Hanah, 08 Mar 1754
    Sanders & Elisebeth Pick: Ane, 19 Sep 1749; Bettey, 14 Nov 1741; Elias, 17 May 1757;
    Elias, 26 Feb 1761; Johana, 04 Nov 1741; Lydia, 09 Jul 1745; Mary, 27 Jun 1758;
    Pirssala, 09 Sep 1757; Solomon, 20 Feb 1743
    Sanders & Sarah Page: Nome, 24 Sep 1760
CURRIER: Magloire & Mary Ann Remillard: Mary Rosanna Lillian, 17 Aug 1897
CARTER: Charles & Mary B Page: Harry C, 04 Mar 1880
    George F (E Kingston) & Mary Etta (Andover,Ma): George F, 24 Jan 1891; Harry
    L, 07 Jun 1886; Minnie, 24 Jan 1891
    Horrace W & Ellen: Lewis N, 11 Jul 1876
    John & .....: Male Child, 26 Nov 1880
    Thomas & .....: Miriam, 03 Mar 1760
CHALIES: Timothey & Elisebeth Brown: John, 22 Jan 1765; Nathaniel Brown, 18 Oct 1762
CALLIS: Ezekiel & Elizabeth Challis: Polly, 08 May 1785; Seth, 24 Jul 1786; William, 24
    Dec 1787
    William & Mary Colbey: David, 16 Jun 1769; Dolly, 31 Jan 1776; Ezekiel, 22 Jul
    1765; Judeth, 03 Sep 1773; Nanne, 14 Apr 1767; Sarah, 01 Oct 1771
CHAMBERLIN: Charles & Abbie Fifield: Female Child, 11 Sep 1878; Female Child,
    11 Aug 1876
    Harry P (Strafford) & Maud B Hoyt (Peabody,Ma): Beverly Sterling, (date unknown)
CHASE: Amos & Hannah Hook: Amos C, 10 Mar 1833; Isaac H, 18 Oct 1843; Josiah H,
    15 Sep 1830; Sarah E, 06 Oct 1835; William, 09 Jun 1828
    Amos & Emily A Belden: Charles A, 03 Sep 1870; Male Child, 29 Apr 1879; Male
    Child, 01 Nov 1876
    Charles (Kingston) & Mary Calef (Litchfield): Amos, 02 Apr 1801; Anna, 03 Apr 1794;
    Charles, 26 Jan 1780; Mary, 21 Mar 1790; Miriam, 22 Jul 1787; Nathaniel, 15 Nov
    1798; Samuel, 05 Nov 1796; Sarah, 08 Jul 1785; William, 26 Feb 1792
    Samuel & Mary A: ----, 10 Sep 1851
CHELLIS: Timothy: Timothy, 30 Jul 1767
CHENEY: Albert N & Mary L Silloway: Albert, 09 Dec 1880; Hattie M, 04 Sep 1883
    Edward L & Nancy L Strout: David, 14 Apr 1891
    William A & Estella A Page: Christie Blanche, 30 Aug 1892; Hayden E, 16 Nov
    1897; Lenora Belle, 02 Nov 1896; Roland Woodbury, 08 Jun 1888
    Edward L (Kingston)& Nancy L (Millbridge,Me): David, 14 Apr 1891
CHOAT: Benjamin & Ruth Edwards: Annie, 15 Sep 1742; Benjamin, 19 Oct 1744;
    Benjamin, 08 Aug 1754; Joseph, 17 Jan 1747; Ruth, 01 Aug 1750; Semion, 14
    Jan 1748
    Jonathan & Elizebeth Moodey: Abigel, 26 May 1747; Anne, 20 Dec 1751;
    Elizebeth, 11 Dec 1749; Jeremiah, 19 Aug 1739; Jonathan, 04 Nov 1741;
    Jonathan , 06 Nov 1743
CHOATE: Benjamen & Abigaill Burnnum: Abigel, 27 Mar 1723; Abigail, 16 Sep 1711;
    Abigaill, 02 Jun 1710; Benjamin, 30 Dec 1713; Benjamen, 07 Aug 1715;
    Jerimah, 12 Aug 1721; Jonathan, 31 May 1708; Luse, 23 Dec 1717; Ruhame,
    22 Dec 1718
    Joseph L & Hattie Webster: Male Child, 11 Oct 1876

CILLEY: Clarence & Annie L Towle: Laburton, 25 Sep 1880
   George B & Lela M Bartlett: Helen May, 13 Jul 1899
CLARK: Charles L & Mary J: Laburton, 25 Sep 1880
   Charles H (Bangor,Me) & Nellie R Little (Portland,Me): Lois E, 02 Feb 1894; Male, 09 Jul 1899
   Herbert W & Blanche: Herbert W, 08 Feb 1878
   J. T. Clark & S. E. Clark: Mary A, 26 Sep 1873
   Simeon L C & Johannah Eastman: Alsina F, 09 Oct 1838; Charles B, 31 Mar 1829; Elizabeth L, 24 Dec 1830; Ellen R, 27 Jan 1848; John Tyler, 24 Jul 1844; Leon Allen, 24 Sep 1846
   Simeon P & Mary Etta Fellows: Henry Howard, 08 Apr 1892; Wilbur John, 20 Jan 1896
   Walter S (Kingston) & Abbie Sanborn (Lawrence,Ma): Edward Bird, 28 Dec 1890; Ernest D, 23 Jul 1894; Harry S, 15 Dec 1887; Helen A, 07 Jul 1880; Kate Chase, 22 Jan 1878; Marion, 26 Aug 1883; Walter Otis, 19 Oct 1885
CLARKE: Ward & Mary Frost: John, 22 Jul 1730
CLEMENT: Obediah & Sarah Flanders: Abigal, 21 Mar 1741; Abraham, 11 Aug 1738; Ezekiel, 22 Jun 1739; Jonathan, 14 Jan 1753; Obediah, 19 Feb 1743; Philip, 29 Apr 1745; Ruben, 09 Jul 1746; Ruben, 25 Jan 1749; Sarah, 23 Aug 1748
CLIFORD: Richard & Mehibisia Cliford: Elisabeth, 07 Jun 1731
   William & Sarah Towle: Anteny, 13 Oct 1743; Beniman, 26 Apr 1738; Jacob, 14 Apr 1749; John, 01 Jan 1741; Joseph, 04 Jun 1736; Margret, 27 Dec 1747; Mehetibal, 10 Apr 1752; Richard, 12 Mar 1740; Sarah, 11 Sep 1745; Zackriah, 31 Oct 1734
CLIFFORD: Isaac & Sarah Taylor: Elisabeth, 21 Aug 1735; David, 17 Dec 1725; Isaac, 01 May 1721; Isrel, 21 Feb 1728; Joseph, 17 Jun 1718; Sarah, 13 Feb 1723; Tristrum, 04 Mar 1738; William, 31 Oct 1727; Zachrias, 21 May 1730
   Joseph & Mary Healey: Zachrias, 21 May 1730; Daniel, 28 Nov 1761; Jeremiah, 08 Jan 1755; John, 11 Sep 1743; Joseph, 21 Mar 1745; Joseph, 11 Jun 1750; Mary, 07 Jan 1747/8; Sarah, 17 Nov 1757
   Joseph & Lydea Perkens: John, 13 Aug 1719; Joseph, 09 Dec 1721
   Joseph & Sarah French: Joanah, 12 Nov 1711; Sarah, 06 Dec 1714
   William & Abigal Gove: Abigal, 14 Feb 1746; Isaac, 03 Dec 1750; Samuel, 12 Nov 1752; William, 04 Nov 1748
CLOUGH: Benjamin & Mary Sanborn: Comelos, 19 Jan 1755; Mary, 13 Aug 1763
   Benjamin & Mary Levit: Jemima, 09 Aug 1771; Jonna, 31 May 1768; Rebecke, 18 Apr 1773
   Cornelos & Mary Levit: Benjamin, 26 May 1777; Benjamin, 02 Mar 1782; Dorothy Stevens, 13 Mar 1775; Sarah, 22 Oct 1779
   Daniel & Sarah Baker; Meream, 24 Mar 1741
   Elisha & Mary Welch: Elisabeth, 18 Sep 1741; Mary, 13 Jun 1743; Richard, 01 Sep 1747
   Isaac (Plaistow) & Mary Louise (Topsfield,Me): Forest L, 25 Dec 1893
   Joseph & Mary Jennes: Ezra, 24 Jun 1709; Joseph, 17 May 1713; Joseph, 04 Jul 1717; Mary, 03 Jul 1719; Maxey, 15 Apr 1711; Moses, 13 Feb 1714/5; Moses, 30 Sep 1720; Obodiah, 01 Feb 1722; Ruben, Nov 1720

Isaac & Mary Louise: Forest L, 25 Dec 1893

Obediah & Sarah Wadleh: Jude, 13 Aug 1748; Mary, 22 Mar 1753; Sarah, 24 Jan 1750

CLOW: Benjamin H & Mary L Perley: Benjamin H, 26 Aug 1882

COATS: Margrat Clark Coats: Hanah , 03 Mar 1743

COLBE: Orlando (Calbe) & Kisiah: Dorret, 17 May 1749; Enos, 16 Apr 1746; Thomas, 16 Apr 1746

COLBY: Joseph & Sarah Thuriel: Elisebath, 02 May 1763; Nones, 22 Jun 1761

Thomas Elet & Susana: Benjamin, 15 Feb 1756; Susana, 31 Oct 1759;

COLCOARD: Ebenezener Colcoard & Haner Fellows: Abigel, 18 May 1733; Ebenezener, 05 Jan 1726; Haner, 19 Mar 1727; Mary, 01 Aug 1735; Peter, 19 Mar 1727; Peter, 22 Apr 1732

COLCORD: Daniel & Doley Clifford: Doley, 11 Jan 1771; Hannah, 28 Mar 1774; Louis, 21 Oct 1772; Peter, 13 Aug 1775

Elihu T & Lucy A Frost: ----, 25 Jun 1825; ----, 24 Dec 1827

Monroe & Hannah Webster: Daniel, 23 May 1850; Monroe, Jr, 20 May 1847

Samuel C & Mary: Clarabel, 14 Jun 1875; Female Child, 24 Jan 1872

Samuel & Sarah: ----, 02 Feb 1852

Samuell & Mehetuball Lad: Daniel, 16 Oct 1747: Elisabeth, 19 Dec 1733; Elisabeth, 25 Feb 1739; Hannah, 13 Mar 1754; Mary, 06 Feb 1744; Peter, 20 Jan 1736; Samuell, 23 Jul 1741; Samuell, 30 Mar 1749; Susana, 01 Apr 1758; Hannah, 28 Mar 1751; Mehitabel, 28 Mar 1751

COLINGS: Ebenezener & Affier Meriel: Elisabeth, 02 Jul 1731; Jonathan, 28 Apr 1728; Marcy, 17 Mar 1733; Mary, 02 Apr 1730; Richard, 12 Mar 1733; Sarahzer, 28 Jun 1726

COLLINS: Andrew J & Anna M Collins: Elmer A, 13 Sep 1870; Female Child, 08 Oct 1868; Female Child, 15 Apr 1874

Benjamin: Benjamin, 13 Mar 1763

Benjamin & Ruth: Lida, 26 Jul 1760; Mary, 05 Sep 1757; L Nathan, 01 Jan 1762; Ruth, 22 Apr 1755; Tristram, 15 Jun 1751

Elmer Andrew & Susie Anna Nason: Charles Elmer, 23 Jan 1895; Clarence Edwin, 17 Jan 1897; Leon E, 28 Jan 1902; Oral Walter, 28 Aug 1899; Viola Edith, 05 Jan 1892

Henry P (Kingston) & Edna Nancy Hanchett (Westfield,Ma): Eva Erdene, 24 Jul 1897

Joel S & Ella F: Perley S, 07 Mar 1880

John W & Caroline W Collins: Henry, 31 May 1870; Sarah, 31 May 1870

John & Sarah Chalies: Charles, 05 Oct 1764; Wintrup, 10 Jan 1763

Jonathan & Lydia Carr: Anna, 19 Aug 1782; Elizabeth, 04 Sep 1769; Israel, 22 Jan 1780; James, 19 Aug 1784; Levi, 16 Feb 1772; Mary, 07 May 1774; Sarah, 09 Jan 1777

Jonathan & Dority: Elisebeth, 04 Jul 1769; Jacob, 27 Jan 1765; Jonathan, 26 Feb 1768; Joseph, 03 May 1763; Sarah, 23 Nov 1761; Samuel, Feb 1772; Tubathey, 30 Sep 1766

Laban & Rachel C Hunt: Caleb H, 05 Jan 1837; Hannah, 05 Oct 1841; Lucy C, 16 Feb 1844; Mary L, 12 Oct 1838

Leon P & Ellen F Winslow: Erdine M, 29 Aug 1874; George L, 08 May 1878

Leslie A & Olive Davis: Clifton E, 23 Nov 1887

L Waldo (Danville) & Elvira C: Allan (Danville), 10 Mar 1889

Norris & Emma J Stevens: Norris, 23 Jan 1880
Obediah & Lucretia: Female Child, 28 Oct 1875: Female Child, 21 May 1873;
Female Child, 26 Feb 1876
Shepherd & Julia: ---- 17 Jul 1851
COLMAN: Jabaz & Mary: Joseph, 23 Sep 1701/2
COOMS: William (Kingston) & Lettie (Scotland): Male Child, William P, 29 Jun 1887
COOPER: Benjamin & Lydia Bartlett: Abigail, 15 Mar 1785; Benjamin, 26 Feb 1783;
Lydia, 23 Nov 1778; Lydia, 2 Nov 1780; Polly, 24 Apr 1776; Priscilla, 02 Nov 1780;
William, 02 Jan 1788
COSER: John & Jean Nichels: Aleen, 24 Aug 1760; David, 27 Jan 1754; Jean, 18 Jan 1756;
John, 02 May 1751; Jonathan, 13 Oct 1747; Samuel, 03 May 1745; Thomas, 01 May
1743; William, 12 Apr 1758
COWELL: George (New York City) & Emma L Marshall (Kingston): Annie E, 18 Sep 1882;
Florence Adeline, 24 Mar 1886
CRAFT: Samuel & Hannah Hoit: John T, 13 Dec 1839; Nathan G, 04 Mar 1844;
Sarah A, 01 Apr 1842
CROWELL: Dennis E (Cassey,Me)& Luella Thompson (Newton): Ralph H, 05 Jun 1896
CURIER: Jeremiah: Haner, 01 Apr 1842; Jeremiah, 19 Dec 1738; Juda, 13 Oct 1741
CURRIER: Franklin: Male Child, 27 Apr 1870; Female Child, 28 Jan 1869
DARLING: Benjamin & Hannah Clark: Susana, 04 Jan 1759
Daniel & Suzanne Webster: Abraham, 26 Dec 1746; Benjamin, 30 Mar 1738;
Daniel, 10 Aug 1741; John, 27 Jul 1735; Mollie, 24 Oct 1748; Ruth, 19 Sep 1744
John & Mary Sawyer: Lidda, 03 Sep 1761; Mary, 14 Mar 1759
DAVICE: John Davice & Hannah Wadlah: Elener, 30 Jun 1749; John, 16 Jul 1759;
Jonathan, 20 Mar 1751; Juda, 07 Apr 1752; Phinihas, 25 Mar 1754
Philip & Meriam Webster: Marey, 20 Jul 1759; Webster, 27 Jul 1751
Zeekel & Sarah England: Davis Fellows, 28 Jan 1757; Francies, 24 Mar 1761; Sarah,
17 Mar 1763; Stephen, 26 Apr 1759
DAVIES: Jeremy & Mary Blasder: Ebenezer Blasder, 26 Sep 1768; Jeremy, 26 Dec 1765;
Moley, 12 Jul 1771; Moses, 14 Feb 1764
DAVIS: Alonzo F (Barnstead) & Eva L Gile (Candia): Ethel 24 Mar 1902; Parker Jessie,
01 Sep 1898
Hiram & Anna: Female Child, 24 Dec 1872
John Pike(Newburyport,Ma) & Mary J Severance (Kingston): Marguerite Alice,
05 Dec 1895
Levida D(Kingston) & Isella Huse (Kingston): Vera Louise, 12 May 1899; William K,
20 Mar 1890
Richard & Hattie: Alice F, 02 Aug 1880
R. W. & Hattie: Jenette Stacy, 02 Sep 1884
Ruben & Elisabeth Jonson: Morah, 22 Jun 1768: Nathaniel, 27 Aug 1765; Phebe,
25 Feb 1771; Ruben, 05 Jan 1773; Thomas, 10 Apr 1767
DAY: Charles S (Rochester) & Mary E Lyford (Kingston): Cora S, 19 Oct 1894; Grace Belle,
21 Jan 1887; Male, 23 Feb 1889
DeROCHEMONT: David & Elizabeth Gale: Ernest H, 11 Jul 1874
DIMOND: Israel & Mary Chandler: Epheram, 22 Apr 1751; Hannah, 01 Mar 1760; Isreal,

08 May 1757; John, 18 Sep 1762; Mary, 15 Aug 1749DODGE: John & Anna Heath:
Anna, 03 Sep 1766; Hannah, 23 Feb 1771; John, 11 Sep 1764; Ruth, 18 Dec 1762;
Selvenas, 29 Jan 1768
John & Hannah: John, 28 Feb 1742
DOE: Frank F (Durham) & Mary Addie Farnum (Lawrence,Ma): Female, 31 Jul 1886;
Male, 06 Dec 1888
DOW: Amasa & Lydia Robey: Amasa, 17 Jan 1729
Amasa & Hannah Buswell: Samuel, 22 Mar 1755; Sarah, 21 Mar 1752
DOWNING: Jonathan & Sarah: John, Mar 1743; Samuel, 02 Dec 1748
John & Ellen Clark: Leveret C, 25 May 1870
DUNN: S Barton & Emma D Evens: Annie P, 17 Jul 1878
EASMON: Ebenezener & Mary Sleper: Ebenezener, 14 Jul 1729; Edward, 14 Jan 1731/2;
Haner, 29 Apr 1741; Jonathan, 28 Jul 1737; Mary, 13 Aug 1734; Sammel, 26 Mar 1727
Joseph & Patiencs Smith: Elisabeth, 21 Oct 1729; Joseph, 03 Jun 1735; Mary,
18 Apr 1741; Patiencs, 14 Dec 1738; Philip, 23 Sep 1742; Shuer, 23 May 1731;
Timothy, 25 Feb 1736/7
Thomas & Abigel French: Abigel, 10 Jul 1737; Edward, 25 1732/3; Obediah,
21 Oct 1729; Phebes, 02 Jan 1740/1; Thomas, 23 Apr 1735; Sara, 27 Mar 1738
EASTMAN: Benjamin & Margaret Graves: Anne, 06 Jun 1750; Edward, 23 Feb 1734;
Elisebeth, 06 Jul 1747; John, 24 Feb 1741; Margret, 30 Sep 1736; Mary, 03 Apr
1736; Sarah, 27 Jun 1743
Benjamin & Mary Pollard: Timothey, 15 Jan 1774
Ebenezer & Sarah Fifield: Ebenezer, 25 Oct 1760; Jonathan, 18 Apr 1765;
Only Daughter, 24 Mar 1803; Peter, 30 Sep 1768
Edward & Hannah Whicher: Hannah, 12 Nov 1762; Mary, 28 Dec 1768;
Thomas, 09 Oct 1761; Thomas Sleeper, 08 Dec 1771
Edward, 3rd & Anna Judkins: Benjamin, 01 Jan 1759; Hannah, 12 Feb 1764;
Joel, 23 Nov 1760
Jacob & Sarah Wells: Jacob, 24 Apr 1775; Sarah, 26 Dec 1771
Jonathan & Mary Eastman: Calvin, 24 Nov 1818: Charles L, 12 Jul 1816; Enoch, 09 Jun
1809; John, 13 Aug 1807; Marritta, 17 Jul 1811; Oliver D, 24 Apr 1814
Joseph & Hanah Calef: Hanah, 14 Nov 1754; Sarah, 14 Jul 1751
Joseph & Jomina Smith: Hannah, 06 Nov 1757; Henery, 04 Jul 1763; Jemima,
22 May 1766
Peter & Jemima Wells: Elilsebath, 03 Aug 1774
Samuel & Sarah Clough: Ebenezer, 24 Apr 1746; Elisabeth, 26 Apr 1739; Ezekiel, 21
Oct 1736; Nehemiah, 20 Jan 1747; Shuah, 05 Dec 1731; William, 31 Jan 1734
Stephen & Miriam Quimby: Mary, 13 Jan 1770
Timothy & Mary Blasdel: Benjamin, 12 Feb 1752; Jacob, 31 Jul 1745; Samuel,
16 Oct 1749; Stephen, 17 May 1747
William & Mary Bean: Jeremiah, 15 Apr 1760; Miriam, 10 Apr 1764; Sarah,08 Feb 1762
EATON: Albert E & Carrie: Female Child, 11 Feb 1887
Albert C (Plaistow) & Annie F Lancaster (Haverhill,Ma): Dorothy L, 10 Jun 1894
George: Male Child, 05 Apr 1872
Theophilus & Abigal Fellowes: Abigal, Jul 1763; Ebenezer, 22 Aug 1756; Elisabeth,

20 Jul 1749; James, 27 Jan 1769; Jonathan, 24 Feb 1752; Judeth, 29 Feb 1742; Moses,
08 Feb 1745; Sarah, 28 Apr 1759

EDNEY: George W (Middleton,Ma)& Mary Collins (Kingston): Ernest Leon, 10 Nov 1889;
George P, 30 Dec 1886; John W, 22 Oct 1898; Willie D, 20 Jan 1883

ELKENS: Obediah Elkens & Abigaiell French: Abigail, 26 May 1736; Jacob, 08 Feb 1732/3;
Jacob, 25 May 1734; Obediah, 23 Jun 1741; Sarah, 03 Sep 1738; Sary, 31 Aug 1731

ELKINS: Charles (Kingston)& Sarah (Mass.): Male, 12 Jul 1886; Male, 11 Oct 1887

Ernest (Kingston) & Annie (Mass.): Male, 04 May 1887

Joseph & Elisabeth: Anah, 10 Oct 1726; Doretha, 17 May 1732; Elesebeth,
30 Apr 1730; Margret, 02 Dec 1725; Mary, 01Jun 1734

George E & Annie R Call: Blanch J, 09 Oct 1874; Frank E, 11 May 1879; Georgia, 28
Dec 1883

Engn. Jeremiah & Elizabeth Tole: Hannah, 15 Apr 1793

John & Laura West: Male Child, 23 Oct 1877

Moses & Annah Shaw: Caleb; Ephraim, 30 Aug 1710: Henry, 22 Mar 1720;
Joannah, 15 Jul 1715; Joseph, 01 Feb 1702/3; Mary, 05 Aug 1704; Mehetable,
13 Jun 1713; Mehetable, 20 Jul 1706; Moses, 20 Jul 1717; Obidiah, 19 Jul 1708

ESTMAN: Samuell & Shuah Fifield: Elesebeth, 31 Mar 1725; Timethy, 06 Jan 1720/1

EVANS: Edward & Nettie: Lilla P, 27 Dec 1880

FELLOWS: Insign Joseph & Sarah Green: Calob, 04 Feb 1748; Elizibeth, 10 Dec 1757;
Hannah, 24 Feb 1756; Mary, 05 Apr 1753; Mary, 14 Nov 1761;
Joseph FELLOWS: Philip, 18 Jun 1749

Joseph & Elisabeth Young: Abigal, 20 Aug 1749; Anne, 16 Oct 1756; Elisabeth,
01 Jan 1744; Joseph, 13 Jul 1740; Joseph, 26 Jul 1752; Mary, 12 Sep 1754; Nathaniel,
02 Jun 1747; Samuell, 14 Aug 1738; Sarah, 03 Nov 1742

Joseph, Jr & Margret Webster: Abel, 03 Apr 1765; Benjamin, 07 Oct 1760; John,
03 --- 1767; Joseph, 18 Oct 1756; Margret, 25 Feb 1763; Mary, 03 May 1758; Zeekel,
25 Aug 1754

Sammell, Jr & Sarah Webster: Joseph, 27 Feb 1714; Sammell,14 Jun 1712

Thomas & Sarah Muchmore: Ebenezer, 15 Sep 1768; Elizebeth, 22 Jun 1757; Hannah,
21 May 1755; Jacob, 04 Apr 1764; Rachel, 06 Dec 1759; Ruth,
14 Jul 1766; Samuel, 05 May 1753; Sarah, 20 Oct 1746; Timothy, 05 Sep 1748;
William, 07 Sep 1750

FIFIELD: Benjamin Frank (Kingston) & Etta L Martin (Sandown): Benjamin F, 15 Feb 1896;
Donald Eugene, 02 Feb 1899; Female, 26 Aug 1886; Lillian Brown, 08 Aug 1881

John, Jr & Dorretha Fifield: Abraham, 21 Aug 1752; Doratha, 09 Apr 1738; Edward,
22 Jan 1748; Edward, 06 Apr 1735; Elisabeth, 08 Jan 1742; Jonathan, 19 Mar 1746;
John, 01 Oct 1733; John, 17 Jan 1749/50; Joseph, 22 Mar 1740; Martha, 16 Jan 1744;
Mary, 16 Jan 1744; Mary, 31 Aug 1759; Sarah, 28 Aug 1736; Shuah, 17 Jan 1749/50

John & Elisabeth Grealy: Elisabeth, 01 Nov 1741; Mary, 25 Oct 1743; Nathaniel,
11 May 1739

Joseph & Sarah Sharbon: John, 17 Dec 1712; Margaret, 06 Jul 1716; Sammell,
28 Oct 1704; Shuah, 13 Mar 1702/3

Joseph, Jr & Anne Badger: Betey, 04 Dec 1762; Dorethy, 12 Feb 1762; Joseph,
06 Jan 1769; Lois, 28 Mar 1760; Sharborn, 12 Nov 1760

-10-

Samuel, Jr & Mary Eastman: Amos, 12 Jun 1770; Peter, 09 Oct 1758; Samuel, 16 Jun 1765

Samuel & Joanna Clifford: Ebenezer, 10 Dec 1751; Elisabeth, 16 Jan 1754; Hannah, 05 Oct 1737; Joanna, 17 Feb 1744; John, 07 Apr 1736; Joseph,12 Sep 1731; Joseph, 29 Jul 1743; Peter, 09 Aug 1740; Samuell, 25 Jul 1733; Sarah, 21 May 1736; Sarah, 05 Jan 1739; Shua, 20 Jan 1728; Steven, 10 Dec 1746

FITTS: Richard & Abigail: ----, 15 Sep 1851

FLANDERS: George E (So Kingston)& Lucy E Felch (Seabrook): Dora F, 03 Apr 1889; Florence C, 19 Jan 1894; Male Child, 08 Oct 1887; Minnie, 11 Apr 1898

Jacob & Mercy: Jacob, 14 Aug 1715

Jacob & Naomi Darling: Joseph, 27 Jul 1753: Mercy, 27 May 1745

FLEMMING: Martin (Ireland) & Mary Collins (Ireland): John Joseph, 14 Jun 1898

FLOOD: Richard & Mary Tande: Rachel, 17 Sep 1788

FOGG: Charles: ----, 08 Oct 1869

FONTAIN: John: John, 17 Jan 1880

FOOT: Isaac & Merriam Stevens: Dority, 13 Oct 1759

Jacob & Sarah Carr: Betty, 18 May 1784; Dorothy, 10 Oct 1789; Elias Carr, 07 Sep 1779; Jacob, 12 Mar 1787; John, 29 Mary 1775; Levi, 03 Apr 1792; Lucretia, 11 May 1797; Mary, 25 Jun 1777; Sarah, 09 Sep 1781

FOWLER: Arthur & Sarah A: Bessie E, 01 May 1880

FREEMAN: Joseph (Germany) & Rosa Leisman (Germany): Hannah, 12 Jul 1895

FRENCH: Abraham & Sarah Smith: Abigal, 01 Jan 1770; Elisse, 12 Jan 1759; Lowes, 31 Aug 1767; Robert, 23 Mar 1761; Sarah, 09 Jul 1764

Beniman & Ruth Honton: Elisabeth, 28 Mar 1742; Sarah, 24 Sep 1743

Benjamen & Judah: Judah, 16 Jan 1729/30

David & Ruhamah Choat: Abigal, 10 Oct 1758; John, 25 Jun 1751; Ruhamah, 17 Feb 1748; Sarah, 21 Aug 1754

Frank W (Kingston) & Hattie M Collins (Boston,Ma): Lillian Francis, 20 May 1898

John G (Kingston) & Addie (Davis) Avery (Kingston): Clarence I, 20 Oct 1890; Earl Leon, 05 Mar 1897; Eldred Howard, 19 Feb 1895; Erma May, 05 Jul 1899; Harvey Russell, 22 May 1892; Henry M, 03 Feb 1903; Herbert Cleveland, 11 Sep 1888; Lelia Christine, 19 Jan 1902; Lela May, 05 Mar 1887; Lillian Francis, 20 May 1898; Walter L, 26 Dec 1883

Jonathan & Johaner Elkins: Elisabeth, 11 Apr 1739; Henery, 26 Oct 1738; Henery, 25 Jan 1747; Johna, 14 Jan 1752; Johnaer, 18 Aug 1737; Jonathan, 01 Jun 1741; Jonathan, 15 Apr 1744; Mary, 18 Feb 1750; Mehetibel, 23 Nov 1754

Moses J & Aleian F Clark: George, 30 Apr 1864; Nellie F, 11 Aug 1865

Moses P & Mary E Smith: Annie L, 07 Feb 183-; Ariannae, 03 Feb 1833; Ellen, 17 Apr 18--; Hannah M, 25 Oct 1829; John P, 17 Feb 1828; Mary A, 04 Sep 1834; Moses J, 12 May 1821; Robert, 29 Oct 1826

Nathaniel, Jr & Abigel Esmon: ---, 31 Oct 1740; Abigal, 17 Jan 1744; Abigel, 04 Mar 1731; Abraham, 22 Apr 1733; Elisebeth, 04 Mar 1731; Marthay, 05 Mar 1749; Mary, 22 Nov 1746; Secombe, 31 Oct 1740; Nathaniel, 10 Feb 1735/6; William, 23 May 1738

Nathaniell & Sary Judgkin: Beniman, 25 Feb 1717; Jonathan, 19 Apr 1713; Nathaniell, 01 Apr 1709; Sammell, 24 Oct 1705; Sarah, 25 Sep 1715; Sary, 20 Feb 1710

Samuel & Abigel Godfree: Samuel, 06 Jun 1739
Simon & Sarah Heard: Abigaiell, 08 Apr 1713; Daveid, 20 Aug 1719; Jacob, 12 Aug
1715; Rachall, 12 Aug 1717; Ruth, 29 May 1711
FROST: Prescott M & Judith Colcord: Sarah R, 04 Jul 1847
William L (Rowley,Ma)& Carrie B Smith (Kingston): Delia, 20 Sep 1894; Female,
11 Sep 1901
FRYE: Aranzo D (Maine) & Etta M (Monroe): Lance Leroy, 10 Apr 1890
FURBER: John & Roxby : Bertha Bell, 28 Sep 1874; Elsie Medora, 17 Jan 1878
GALE: Dr Amos & Hannah Gilman: Amos, 15 Oct 1768; Benjamin, 25 Nov 1771; Gillman,
13 Sep 1766; Jonathan, 19 Dec 1773
Dr Amos, Jr & Sally Bartlett; Amos Gilman, 17 Feb 1807; Ezra Bartlett,13 Oct 1797;
Josiah Bartlett; Levi Bartlett, 29 Aug 1800; Mary Greeley, 21 Aug 1815; Sarah Bartlett,
05 Sep 1811; Stephen Madison, 10 Oct 1809
Eben: Male Child, 30 Jan 1870; Male Child, 21 Aug 1882
Ezra B & Ruth White: Amos L, 21 Aug 1828; Ezra White, 09 May 1824; Josiah B,
02 Jul 1838; Mary B, 20 Jan 1835; Rebecca, 16 Nov 1840; Richard, 21 Feb 1826; Sarah
R, 12 Feb 1832
Ezra B & Emily Atwood: E.F. Hemans, 07 Oct 1843; Ellen L, 09 Mar 1848; Harriet N,
17 Jul 1845
Gilman & .....: John, 22 Oct 1790
Jacob & Suzaner: Ammos, 09 Apr 1744; Amos, 22 Apr 1743; Benjamin, 05 Mar 1748;
Daniel, 02 Sep 1739; Eli, 23 Feb 1745; Elifilit, 05 Sep 1741; Henery, 02 Oct 1754; John
Colines, 26 Nov 1750; Mary, 22 Nov 1747; Stephen, 12 Oct 1752; Stephen, 05 Jan 1756;
Suzaner, 28 Nov 1737
Perley S (Kingston) & Mary E Hewitt (Nova Scotia): Ralph B, Apr 1897; ..... 11 Dec
1888
GARLAND: Daniel N Garland (Kingston) & Cora M Brackett (Brentwood): Female, 09 Sep
1889; Reba Uretta, 10 Aug 1898
Nathaniel W (Kingston) & Mary Alice (Minnie) Brown (Kingston): Florence, 26 Feb
1903; Lloyd Randolph, 10 Aug 1898; Ralph N, 31 Mar 1895; Waldo Joseph, 23 Jan 1891
GEORGE: Archie L & Lizzie E: Female Child, 21 Aug 1882; Male Child, 16 Dec 1883
Delbert O(Derry) & Martha J Hemphill (Derry): Freeland Ralph, 19 Oct 1897; Kenneth,
09 Oct 1898
Gedeon & Deborah Stevens: Doley, 02 Sep 1769; Deborah, 08 Aug 1762; Elisabeth,
12 Aug 1786; Gideon, 08 Nov 1760; Hannah, 09 May 1779; James, 21 Mar 1767;
John, 07 Nov 1764; Mary, 08 Jul 1759; Nathaniel, 06 Sep 1783; Samuel, 25 Oct 1776;
Sarah, 08 Jul 1774; Stephen, 17 Dec 1771
Ora P & Abbie Silloway; Fred Rufus, 18 Mar 1873
Stephen S (Sandown) & Edna F West (Kingston): Annie May, 25 May 1888; Mary
Abbie, 07 Apr 1886; Male, 05 Jan 1891
Wilfred W (England)& Bertha Bartlett (Newton): Male, 23 Sep 1900
William & Hannah Johnson: David Quimby, 01 Feb 1793; Ebenezer, 06 Feb 1790
William & Abigal Peasle: Jacob, 25 Oct 1786; James, 01 Dec 1771; John, 15 Feb 1784;
Jonathan, 21 Mar 1774; William, 28 Jan 1777; William, 15 Oct 1779
GILES: Henry (Lee) & Effie S (E Kingston): Leroy Lester, 20 Sep 1893

GILLMAN: William & Mary: Dolle, 01 Jul 1746
GILMAN: Eugene C (Mass.)& Mary J (Mass.): Male, 07 Sep 1886
     Jacob & Abigel Moodey: Abigal, Mar 1763; Jacob, 14 Oct 1747; John, 01 Feb 1742;
     Jonathan, 06 Aug 1754; Nathaniel, 03 Sep 1745; Peter, 25 Jan 1751; Samuel, 03 Oct
     1749; Stephen, 24 Aug 1757
     Steven & Mary French: David, 22 Nov 1747; Dorithy, 26 Oct 1749; Elisabeth, 03 Sep
     1756; Jacob, 09 Mar 1743; Mary, 18 Jun 1752
GLIDDEN: Daniel (Chester) & Anabel Green (Stoneham,Ma): Sadie M, 17 Jun 1899
GOODRICH: Moses P & Sarah: Jean, 13 Jun 1882
     Olive Ann Goodrich, 25 Oct 1831 (Parents unknown)
GOODWIN: Daniel L & Sarah F Brown: Dorothy G, 26 Jul 1885; Helen G, 20 Sep 1879;
     Inez L, 21 Jul 1882; Lydia, 23 Feb 1873; Mattie E, 28 May 1875; Susie F, 22 Jan 1878
     Hazen O & Mary: Emma Agnes, 20 Jan 1885; Female Child, 23 Mar 1875
GORDIN: Daniell & Margaret: Abner, 24 Nov 1712; Eleksander, 29 Jan 1715/6; Elisebeth,
     28 Jun 1709; Margrett, 27 Oct 1714; Mary, 20 Feb 1711
GOSS: John (Amesbury,Ma)& Grace Witham (Deerfield)): Horace Clifton, 15 Aug 1899;
     Bertha Maud, 14 Jul 1895
     Joseph & .....: Dile, 15 Aug 1744
GRAHAM: John & Love Sanborn: Elesibeth, 02 Sep 1720
GRAVES: Jacob & Abigial Sanborn: Jeremiah, 13 Mar 1774
GREALY: Jonathan & Martha French: Moses, 10 Oct 1736
     Joseph: Elisabeth, b 14 Sep 1721; Mary, 09 Apr 1723
GREELY: Joseph, Jr & Elisabeth Dudley: Elenor, 11 Oct 1752; Elisebeth, 08 Aug 1749;
     Joseph, 22 Feb 1758; Joseph, 22 May 1865; Mary, 28 Apr 1755; Mary, 31 Dec 1762;
     Noah, 29 Jul 1760; Samuel, 27 Aug 1745; Samuel, 16 Sep 1747; Sarah, 07 May 1743
GREEN: Abraham & Sarah: Anna, 01 Apr 1750; John, 03 Feb 1742/3; Martha, 24 Sep 1741;
     Martha, 13 Jul 1748; Sarah, 01 Sep 1746
GREENLEY: J William & Letitia: Female Child, 17 Nov 1879
GRIFFEN: Ebenezer Griffen & Mary Colcord: Ebenezer (Griffin), 07 Mar 1766; Ebenezer
     (Griffin), 23 Sep 1766; Elizebath (Griffin),05 Jan 1764; Mary (Griffin), 20 Oct 1767;
     Samuel (Griffin) b 03 Jul 1762
     Ephram & Mary: Jonathan, 26 Feb 1746; Mary, 14 Sep 1744
     Isaac & Susaner Clough; Elisabeth Clough, 08 Nov 1728; Isaac, 05 Aug 1731; Mary,
     23 Jun 1734; Phebe Clough, 28 Dec 1725
     John & Hannah Bean: Ane, 16 Mar 1746; Hannah, 16 Sep 1744; John, 08 Sep 1751;
     Sarai, 29 May 1749
     Theophilis & Haner: Ann, 18 Aug 1722; Benjamin, 08 Nov 1730; Eliphelet, 24 May
     1720; Joseph, 28 Jun 1728; Thomas, 04 Sep 1725
GRIFFIN: Stuart & Lizzie A : Male Child, 13 Jan 1886
HALL: Levi W & Julia: Female Child, 31 Jan 1872
HAM: George & Abbie Porter: Male Child, 14 May 1873
HANSON: John B & Mary A Wells: Female Child, 25 Jul 1870; Male Child, 28 Aug 1874
     Samuel & Dorothy Fellows; Arianna, ...; John B, 20 Oct 1842
HARRIS: Stanley Otis & Amelia Bishop; Julia Bishop, 20 Dec 1879
HARROLD: George & Nancy J Severance: Female Child, 17 Apr 1875

HARSA: John & Elisabeth Judkins: Elisabeth, 18 Mar 1744; Ica-bod, 03 Aug 1752; John, 26 Mar 1749; Peter, 16 Jul 1742; Sammel, 08 Sep 1746

HARSE: John & Elisebeth: Mary, 29 Aug 1754

HARVEY: Jonathan & Susana: Jonathan, 14 Oct 1757; Joseph, 09 Mar 1762

HASKELL: Leslie & Mary S: Harry A, 10 Mar 1878

HEATH: Weld & Eliza Winslow: A daughter, 10 Jun 1845; Harriet, 11Jul 1836; Hiram F, 11 Apr 1842; John M, 22 Jul 1839; Mary M, 19 Feb 1830; Nancy, 21 Apr 1832; William, 01 Mar 1834

HEBIRD: Daniel Hebird (Hubbard) & Ruth Huse: Ruth, 09 Jan 1744

HILLIARD: John T: Mabel E, 10 Jan 1871
Will H (Kensington) & Flora E Jewell (Stratham): John C, 22 Jul 1899; Leon W, 05 Dec 1892; Mildred, 25 Jul 1891; William Russell, 17 Mar 1897

HOIT: Thomas J & Henriette: -----, 11 Apr 1852

HOMAN: Joseph & Sarah Walton: Elihu Thayer, 28 Mar 1790

HOOK: Dyer & Hannah Brown: Abram, 17 Nov 1745; Dyer, 21 Jan 1749/50; Elisha, 18 Nov 1747; Hannah, 24 Oct 1757; Israel, 17 Jan 1754
Humphry & Hannah Philbrick: Hannah, 19 Dec 1754; Jacob, 30 Jul 1752; Jediah, 02 Mar 1756; Martha, 09 Aug 1750; Mary, 13 Jul 1748
Jacob & Elisabeth; Frances, 10 Feb 1742
Jacob & Mary Bachilder; Elisabeth, 25 Jun 1750; Mary, 16 Feb 1756; Pheneas, 01 Jun 1753; Sarah, 26 Jun 1759

HOYT: John W (Malden,Ma) & Nancy Severance (Kingston): Otis Edward, 02 Jul 1897
Leonard H & Annie May Huse: Marion Edith, 15 Feb 1898; Mildred L, 25 Nov 1896
Thomas E & Minnie Etta Carter: Maud Francis, 21 Mar 1897

HUBARD: Richard, Jr & Elisebath Webster: Abigal, 10 Jul 1762; Benjamin, 24 Oct 1766; Dorcas, 14 Feb 1772; Mary, 24 Jul 1768
John(Hubbard) & Jonna Davice: Francis, 17 Dec 1761; John, 28 Sep 1758; Margiret, 02 Apr 1755; Nane, 25 Feb 1757; Richard, 01 May 1764

HUBBARD: John & Jane: Doratha, 08 Jan 1705; Jennirah, 03 Mar 1711; John, 21 Jul 1706; John, 28 Jan 1715
Richard & Abigaill Davies: Dorety, 25 Jul 1722; Elisebeth, 25 Sep 1724; Grace, 22 Dec 1730; John, 12 Apr 1733; Martha, 06 Nov 1726
Richard & Abigel Tayler: Anne, 17 Oct 1738; Beniman, 12 Nov 1744; Grace, 08 Jan 1736/7; Jeddiah, 15 Jul 1755; Margret, 30 Aug 1740; Mary, 21 May 1735; Richard, 03 Dec 1742
Richard & Elizabeth Webster: Elizabeth, 12 Jul 1776; John Hills, 02 Nov 1773; Richard, 18 Dec 1779

HUBBURD: Jeremiah & Marcy Jousou: Jane, 05 Feb 1725/6; Joseph, 11 Mar 1723/4; Marcy, 26 Mar 1732; Richard, 11 Aug 1728

HUNT: Olando & Lucy Winslow: Nancy H, 19 Apr 1827; Paul, 18 Jun 1830; Sarah J, 13 Jul 1837
Philip & Nancy Merrill: William, 09 Nov 1808

HUNTON: Benjamin & Marey(Marcy) Quimby: Anna, 13 Aug 1766; Benjamin, 06 Apr 1765; Hanah, 13 Nov 1763; Mary, 15 Dec 1761; Nathanel, 16 Jun 1759; Samuel, 10 May 1768

Benjamin & Juett(Judith) Clough: Philip, 28 Nov 1751; Sarah, 17 Mar 1756
Charles (Huntoon) & Mariah Smith: Charles, 15 Dec 1755: Elisabeth, 03 May 1771;
John, 04 Jan 1753; John, 15 Jul 1773; Josiah, 01 May 1757; Mariah, 13 Oct 1750;
Jonathan, 04 Jan 1754; Nathaniel, 21 Jun 1764; Rebacker, 28 Nov 1770; Ruben, 07 Sep
1761; Ruben, 03 Dec 1768
HUNTOON: John & Mary: Samuel, 18 Jan 1718
John, Jr & Elisebeth Bede (Beede): Aaron, 09 Jun 1758; Calob, 01 Aug 1765; Eli, 20 Jul
1766; Elijah, 20 Nov 1768; Joshua, 15 Jun 1763; Moses, 31 Aug 1755; Stephen, 15 May
1761
Nathaniel & Anne Darbon: Sarah, 11 Jun 1745
Philip & Hannah: Sarah, 21 Apr 1703
Philip, Jr & Ann Eastman: Beriman (Honton), 12 Sep 1729; Haner, 19 Jan 1721;
Jonathan (Honton), 02 Oct 1740; Philip (Honton), 08 May 1737; Ruth (Honton),
11 Feb 1723; Scribner, 09 Jan 1725/6; Scribner (Honton), 08 May 1731
Samuell & Hannah Lad: Charles, 18 Mar 1755; Nathaniel, 06 May 1757; Peter,
10 Nov 1743; Peter, 31 Jul 1745; Peter, 04 Jan 1748; Samuell, 12 Oct 1749; Samuell,
12 Oct 1750
HUSE: Mole (Molly) Huse (No parents - no date given)
Bodwill Huse, 06 Mar 1741 (No parents given)
Isrel, Jr & Mary: Abigel, 03 Nov 1744; Haner, 23 Oct 1744; Jonathan, 19 Aug 1745;
Joseph, 04 Jan 1751; Mary, 18 Nov 1754
Nathan & Nellie (Ellen) Rogers: Charles F, 28 Aug 1870; Lois S, 05 Sep 1872
William F & Lucy A: Annie May, 01 May 1881
INGALLS: Dr. Fred W (Canterbury) & Nellie F French (Kingston): Winifred Pearl,18 Dec 1886
JENKINS: George F (Amesbury,Ma)& Mary Calkins (England): Female, 03 Apr 1892
JENNESS: Frank & Mary: Female Child, 22 Aug 1877
JOHNSON: George H: Female Child, 19 Oct 1876
JONES: John & Abby: Male Child, 17 Sep 1873; William, 15 Mar 1867
John & Hannah Dow: Jacob, 30 Dec 1749; John, 27 Apr 1753; Mehitabel, 23 Mar 1751;
Meriam, 24 Sep 1755
Joseph & Abigel Flanders: Abigail, 19 Jun 1762; James, 10 Jul 1759; Johana,16 Apr
1753; Joseph, 16 Feb 1757; Philip, 09 Oct 1745; Richard, 19 Nov 1750; Susana, 01 Apr
1748
Nathan & Allas: Jon, 21 Jan 1750; Jonathan, 01 Sep 1756
Nathan & Hannah Dow: Merreum, 09 Aug 1747; Nathan, 13 Dec 1753
JONSON: Thomas & Hannah Colbey: Enoch, 19 May 1800; Levi, 24 Oct 1801; Ruth, 17 Oct
1797; Sally, 17 Oct 1797; Sukey, 02 Apr 1798
JUDKINS: Athur R (Kingston)& Delia Page (Brentwood): Elsie Elizabeth, 04 Aug 1893; Male,
13 Feb 1890; Stanley Page, 27 Aug 1896
Caleb & Mary Huntoon: Anna, 27 Feb 1778; Caleb, 30 Mar 1783; Hilton, 23 May 1786;
Mary, 18 Jul 1780; Mehitable, 03 May 1788
Elbridge F (Kingston) & Nellie Isabelle Butler (Seabrook): George E, 05 Aug 1894;
Grace Ethel, 04 Jun 1885; Lottie Vivian, 22 Nov 1891; Male Child, 16 Dec 1883
Enoch B & Nellie: Female Child, 21 Dec 1878
Henry & Mary Barnet: Abigail, 26 Aug 1781; Abigail, 04 Aug 1787; Esther, 04 Mar 1790

Henry & Mary French: Hanah, 09 Sep 1777;Henry, 27 Mar 1783; Joel, 03 Jun 1785; Mehitabel, 24 Nov 1794; Stephen, 21 Jun 1792

Moses & Hannah Cheney: Female Child, 16 Jan 1877

Joel & Mehitabel Ealkins: Benjamin, 18 Apr 1749; Caleb, 16 Jan 1753; Henery, 05 Dec 1750; Joseph, 23 Aug 1743; Levanas, 11 Sep 1741; Mehetable, 22 May 1747; Moses, 05 Feb 1737; Sammel, 08 Jun 1736

John & Esther Sweat: Elesebeth, 14 Apr 1764; Elisha, 01 Jun 1758; John, 11 May 1753; Martha, 01 Aug 1751; Mehitebal, 07 Mar 1766; Samuel, 08 Jun 1760; Sarah, 24 Sep 1762; Stephen, 02 Mar 1756

John & Marthy Hook: William, 29 Jan 1745

John W & Nellie Rogers: Male Child, 29 Oct 1874

John H & Sarah A: Male Child, 07 Jan 1879

Joseph & Rebecca Sanborn: Betty, 02 Mar 1772; Louis, 12 Sep 1769; Moses, 28 Jun 1780; Rebecca, 07 Oct 1777

Josiah & Mary: Anne, 19 Feb 1751; Jonathan, 20 Dec 1759; Josiah, 25 Aug 1762; Judah, 17 Mar 1756; Philip, 29 Aug 1754

Lenord & Sarah Cram: Leonard, 26 Aug 1770; Obadiah, 16 Aug 1764

Ensign Moses & Ruhama French: Moses, 23 Feb 1774

Samuel & Sarah Bowhorne: Johel, 01 Mar 1757

Simon B & Catherine Hoit: John H, 01 May 1848; Mary L, 06 Mar 1845

KEEN: Willis E (Kittery,Me) & Alice E (Haverhill,Ma): Female, 13 Dec 1887; Ida Eliza, 17 May 1893

KEEZER: William J (Hampstead) & Nellie A (Kingston): Male, 03 Jan 1888

KELLEY: Alvi I (Northwood) & Belle Wilcox (Barrington): Female, 06 Sep 1895

    Daniel Kelly: Nellie May, 17 Sep 1869

    George Washington & Malina Keezer: Charles Edward, 18 Feb 1884

    David & Mary Greenfeald: Betey, 30 Oct 1771; Jeams, 29 Jan 1774; Ruhami, 17 Mar 1769

KIDDER: Ed (Manchester) & Mary E Kelley (Haverhill,Ma): Helen M, 11 May 1892

KIMBALL: Amos & Martha Spofford: Male Child, 14 Mar 1873

    Capt Benjamin & Abiah Kimball: Abiah, 25 Jan 1794; Amos, 22 Jul 1810; Benjamin, 30 Oct 1803; David, 17 Jan 1806; Elisabeth W, 06 Nov 1812; Joseph Hasin, 05 May 1808; Mary, 16 May 1801; Russel, 07 Dec 1798; Sally, 18 Apr 1796

    Elmer E & Francis L: Chester A, 18 Mar 1883

    Frank A (Middleton,Ma)& Kate S (Kingston): Male, 07 May 1889

    John P: Effie Etta, 27 Apr 1870

    Lewis H (Hampstead)& Blanch A Quimby (Kingston): Elise May Charlotte,23 Mar 1896

KING: Charles E (Attleboro,Ma) & Ada S Webster (Kingston): Herbert Stephen, 23 Nov 1895; Howard Edward, 10 Oct 1898

KINISTON: Richard & Mary Tucker: Mary , 28 Mar 1759; Rachal, 22 Dec 1756; Ruben, 02 Aug 1751; Sarah, 02 Mar 174--

LAD: Daniel & Mehetable Philbrick: Anna, 25 Jun 1718; Daniel, 25 Jan 1725/6

    Elisabeth, 11 Feb 1716/7; Hannah, 17 Apr 1720; Joanna, 27 Jul 1735; John, 21 Oct 1737; Mary, 02 Jan 1722/3; Mehetable, 30 Jun 1713; Stephen, 30 Aug 1728

LADD: John & Elesebeth Sanborn: Doratha, 02 Nov 1730; Jonathan, 25 Aug 1724; John, 07
    May 1720; Love, 25 Mar 1716; Love, 01 Feb 1728; Nathaniell, 17 Jun 1722; Trueworthy,
    01 May 1726
    Nathaniel & Sarah Cliford: Benjamin, 02 Jun 1749; Elisebeth, 06 Jan 1756; Isaae, 02 Jun
    1749; Jeramiah, 03 Oct 1742; Love, 28 Sep 1746; Nathanal, 28 Sep 1744; Sarah, 13 Dec
    1757
    Otterro (Plaistow)& Gertrude M Page (Kingston): Bertha Augusta, 25 Apr 1899; Marcia
    Evelyn, 06 Apr 1897; Orlando, 23 May 1901
    Truworthy & Lidda Harriman: Bettia, 03 Sep 1756; John, 06 Jan 1755; Jonathan, 07 Aug
    1751; Lidda, 04 Jan 1759; Lova, 29 Jan 1761; Mehitabel, 26 Jan 1753
LEAVIT: Emerson & Mary: Amma, 13 Feb 1757; Eleclevit, 23 Jun 1754;Mary, 21 Feb 1755
LOCK: Sammell & Margaret: Abigel, 12 Dec 1730; Edward, 18 Dec 1741; Hannah, 31 Jan
    1731/2; Margret, 07 Oct 1725; Sammel, 18 Feb 1744; Sammel, 22 Apr 1728; Sary,b- 15
    Aug 1736 - d 17 Oct 1745; Sary, 01 Jan 1746; Sary, 07 Apr 1750; Thomas, 01 Jan 1746;
    Ward, 09 Jun 1734
LONG: Richard & Eallases Moode: Lida, 28 Oct 1745; Ruth, 17 Jul 1747
    Richard & Ellen (Nellie): Edna D, 19 Feb 1876; Female Child, 02 Dec 1877; Male Child,
    04 Oct 1874; Male Child, 20 Oct 1879
LORD: Albert Edward & Hanah Elizabeth Kelley: Herbert Erving, 13 Nov 1885
LOTHIAN: John A (Scotland) & Catherine D Cunningham (Scotland): Male, 04 Feb 1898
LOVERING: Samuel & Mary Gooden: Abigail, 14 Dec 1757; Benjamin, 1738; Elisabeth, Nov
    1760; Hannah, 09 Sep 1762; Joseph, 01 Jan 1749; Moses, 10 Jun 1751; Samuel, 14 Mar
    1754
LOWEL: Ruben & Perseler: Persiler, 07 Jun 1764; Reasma, 17 Jul 1762; Sarah, 05 Jan 1767
LOWRY: George (Kingston)& Georgianne Morrison(Salem): George Victor, 25 Mar 1892
LUFKIN: Edward & Sarah Moodey: Bate, 05 Apr 1738; Edward, 05 Sep 1730; Hanah, 05
    May 1751; John, 03 Mar 1753
LUNT: Henery & Abigal Morrill: Elisabeth, 12 May 1745; Ezekil, 04 May 1748; Ruth, 09 Feb
    1742
LYFORD: J. S (Lawrence,Ma) & L. S. (E. Kingston): Female, 26 Sep 1888
    Joshua E & Emma: Male Child, 09 Mar 1884
MACE: George E & Mary Whittier: Charles Henry, 15 Apr 1882
MAGNUSSON: Martin (Gloucester,Ma) & Hattie E Philbrick (Springfield,Ma): John James,
    23 Sep 1899
MARCH: Charles E (E Kingston) & Annie Huse (Kingston): Lewis Irving, 31 Jul 1894
    John March & Margrit Bean: Hittie, 01 Apr 1744; John, 01 Apr 1737; Lois Ann,
    25 Dec 1830; Mary, 09 Aug 1732, Mary, 01 Dec 1736; Myiriah, 27 Apr 1746;
    Myiriah, 05 Apr 1754; Steven, 27 Jul 1741; Samuel, 15 Oct 1734; Uriah, 05 Apr 1752
MARDEN: J Dunlop & Ella Ingalls: Male, 05 Jan 1881
MARSH: Charles E (E Kingston) & Carrie B Huse (Kingston): Female, 05 Aug 1889;
    Male, b 21 Dec 1887/8; Melvin F, 22 Sep 1891
MARSHALL: Arthur H (Kingston)& Minnie Dudley (Brentwood): John Samuel, 29 Nov 1899
    Herbert W (Kingston) & Lela M (Kingston): Female, 09 Sep 1887
    John P & Sarah J Collins: Maud, 29 Aug 1874
    Samuel C: Alice N, 12 Jul 1870

Herbert Walter & Lelia M Brown: Ethel Brown, 02 Jun 1891; Maud, 29 Aug 1874

MARTIN: Fred K (Rumford,Me) & Ida (So Kingston): Charles K, 22 Apr 1888

George & Etta M Nason: Male Child, 05 Feb 1884

Isreal : Male Child, 07 Aug 1870

John : Lorinda J, 08 Aug 1870

Kate H (Kingston): Ernest Albert, 18 Feb 1893

Levi B & Ella R: Andrew J, 14 Apr 1870; Jessie M, 01 Jan 1885

Thomas H(Kingston) & Eva Frazier (Nova Scotia): Carrie, 02 May 1887; Clarence F, 04 Jul 1889; Female Child, 02 May 1887

MARTYN: George S & Amanda M: George F, 11 Oct 1872

MEEKS: Charles & Mary A Tucker: Charles B, 15 May 1884; Frank, 25 Jan 1880; Lucinda, 28 Jul 1878; Samuel, 04 Oct 188

MERRICK: Henry & Abbie W Fifield: Female, 22 Jul 1872

MARCH John March & Margrit Bean: Hittie, 01 Apr 1744; John, 01 Apr 1744; Mary, 09 Aug 1732; Mary, 01 Dec 1736; Myiriah, 05 Apr 1754; Samuel, 15 Oct 1734; Steven, 27 Jul 1741; Uriah, 05 Apr 1752

McCLINTOCK: Joseph & Sally Potter : Elizabeth, 09 Apr 1793

McCOMB: James (Calis,Me) & Sarah E (Kingston): Raymond Pierce, 22 May 1893

MEEKS: Charles (Sandown) & Mary A Tucker (Kingston): Bernice May, 12 Jul 1893; Fred Clifton, 04 Sep 1891

MERRIL: Stephen & Elisabeth: Elisabeth, 03 Dec 1737

MERRILL: Joshua & Dorcas Richardson: John, 04 Mar 1794; Polly, 07 Dec 1795

MILLS: Benjamin & Dorcas: Betsey, 31 May 1791; James, 02 Jul 1793; Polly, 10 Apr 1796; Priscilla, 19 Aug 1798

William J (Kingston) & Josephine Sprague (Kingston): Charles, 14 Apr 1892; Emeline, 18 Jul 1887; William, 02 Aug 1890

MORIEL: Jacob & Mary: Henery, 14 Aug 1717

MORKEN: John & Mary Morken: Joseph, 15 May 1740; Mary, 11 Nov 1725; Paul, 08 Jul 1727; Reoda, 31 Oct 1741

MIRRILL: Henrey & Susana Folsham: Affi, 22 Jun 1752; Henry, 22 Apr 1749; Mary, 24 May 1742; Merriam, 17 May 1755; Mirriam, 14 Jul 1746; Sarah, 28 Sep 1757; Susanah, 10 Apr 1744

Jacob & Mehitabel: Jacob, 24 Dec 1756; John, 23 Feb 1730; Mary, 09 Oct 1754; Mehitabel, 31 Oct 1751

MORSE: Ebenezer & Betsey Colcord: Nancy Colcord, 16 Mar 1800; Stephen, 23 Oct 1802

John & Hanah Muse: Benjamen, 12 May 1722; Elesebeth, 22 Apr 1716; John, 05 Nov 1714; Ruben, 28 Nov 1720

NASON: Albion (Kingston) & Annie Page (Kingston): Arrie Bell, 17 Sep 1875; Bert A, 29 Oct 1884; Eugene, 27 Dec 1886; Female Child, 29 May 1882; Harold P, 21 Mar 1889; Irving Waldo, 13 May 1891; Iva Blanche, 03 Nov 1893; Jesse R, 14 Aug 1897; Male Child, 24 Feb 1880; Philip S, 03 Oct 1899 Will, 01 Jul 1873

Freeman L (Kingston) & Lila Hunt (Somerville,Ma): Paul Clifton, 22 Mar 1896

NAYSON: Albert (Nason) & Laura D Fifield: Eldora, 22 Sep 1880; Laura Evelyn, 25 Sep 1900; Neva May, 18 Feb 1877

Nathan (Nason) & Sarah N Page: Male Child, 17 May 1813

NICHOL: Olive Nichol: ----, 18 Jan 1851
NICHOLS: Albert E: Albert E, 14 Jul 1870
    Charles W: Albert E, 14 Jul 1870; Alice M, 19 Sep 1873
    Frederick G & Sarah Williams: Sarah Williams, 18 Sep 1825; Stephen F, 21 Apr 1829
    Nicholas & Catherine: Salome, ----; Stephen William, 02 Oct 1795
    Oliver P & Dorothy Colcord: Alfred, 22 Mar 1820; Angelett, 22 Mar 1827;
    Charles E, 09 Mar 1832; Charlotte, 21 Jul 1822; Frederick, 25 Apr 1818; Oliver,
    22 Jun 1824
    Oliver P & Eliza Robinson: Gilman R, 02 Dec 1834; Joseph M, 20 Apr 1839; Sarah F,
    07 Nov 1837
    Perrin W (Sandown)& Alice G Perry (So Hampton): Frederick S, 01 May 1894
    Stephen F & Sarah E Chase: Clara, 31 Aug 1867; Perrin W, 12 Feb 1865; Stephen
    William, 08 Aug 1874
    William C : Clifton W, 25 Jan 1876
NICKLES: James & Marey: Joseph, 09 Oct 1769
NOYES: John & Diana Cockram: John Cockram, 22 Sep 1772; Lemuel, 28 Sep 1773
OAKES: Thomas H & Jennie: Jessie, 30 May 1878; Male, 28 Oct 1875
O'CONNOR: Michael & Mary: Michael J, 23 Jun 1841; William, 10 Jul 1843
ORDWAY: Jonathan & Hannah Morriel: Hanah, 06 Jul 1747; Nemiah, 25 Nov 1749
OSGOOD: Fred E (Contoocook) & Mary A (Hallowell,Me): Male, 13 Dec 1890
PAGE: Benjamin & Mary French: Mary, 20 Sep 1760
    Clarence H (Danville) & Alice J(Kingston): Marion, Orrel Allen, 08 Apr 1897; Valerin
    Augusta, 16 Jul 1898
    Ebenezenr & Haner Shepard: Benjamin, 23 Aug 1749; Bette, 24 Dec 1755; Ebenezer,
    01 Jun 1747; Israel (Paige), 17 May 1752; Mary, 05 Jul 1745
    Epharam & Hanah Currir: Betty, 05 Jan 1760; Hanah, 24 Dec 1757; Mary, 23 Dec 1755
    Ezra & Augusta Shaw: Female, 02 May 1876; Leslie, 18 Aug 1878
    Jabez & Sally Kimball: Moses, 18 Mar 1806; Thomas, 10 Jan 1800
    Jabez & Abigel: Henery (Paige), 17 Jul 1750; Thomas, 30 Apr 1743
    John & Ane Webster: Benjamin, 01 Sep 1750; Benjamin, 10 Oct 1752; Elisabeth,
    10 Oct 1752: Mary, 28 Jan 1760; Sarah, 18 Jan 1757
    Joseph & Mary: ----, 02 Jul 1852
    Thomas & Lucy Winslow: Esra, 19 Mar 1834
    Thomas & Eliza Bickford: Irene F, 28 Dec 1840; Levis, 07 Nov 1835; Levis, 07 Mar
    1839
    Ulysses G (Kingston)& Iona Currier (Danville): Carroll B, Howard Currier, 21 Apr 1898
PALMER: Samuel & Nancy Philbrick: John R, 08 Jan 1828
PARKER: Frank H (Kingston)& Alice T Holt (Epping): Sarah, 23 Mar 1895
PATTEN: Aaron & Sarah Chase: Charles, 28 Jun 1817; Louisa, 08 Oct 1807; Mary, 08 Aug
    1809; Sarah Ann, 02 Jun 1813; Susanna, 01 Apr 1811; William, 28 Jun 1815
    Colcord & Mariah R Fletcher: Clandeus B, 07 Apr 1828; Henery L, 04 Apr 1836;
    Ichabod B, 28 Apr 1825; Jabez F, 21 Jan 1821; Maria R, 02 Jul 1823; Mehetable,
    31 Jan 1833; Ora L, 16 Feb 1831; William C, 24 Jun 1819
    Ora P Lizzie: Susie Clapp, 20 Dec 1872
    William & Mehitebal Colcoard: Aaron, 01 Sep 1775; Colcord, 21 Sep 1789;

Hannah, 03 May 1785; Isaac, 18 Jun 1787; Lois, 15 Oct 1779; Mehitable, 21 Jan1782; Susana, 30 Jun 1777

PEARSON: John & Abigal: Elisebath, 28 Oct 1773; James, 25 Aug 1771; Rebeka, 04 Jan 1770

PEASLEE: Albert F (Newton) & Mary E (Kingston): Male, 30 Apr 1891

Daniel & Elizabeth Seccombe: Jacob Challis, 03 Oct 1808; Martha Challise, 24 Feb 1807; Sarah Topan, 18 Dec 1805; Simimons Seccombe, 03 Oct 1808

Jacob & Huldah; Elija, 15 Jul 1741

Luther D & Mary S; Carrie Elisabeth, 05 Nov 1869; Female, 18 Apr 1868; Female, 28 Jun 1872

PHILBRICK: J..... & Susan; John C, 13 Jun 1882

James M & Mary S Chase: William J, 30 Jan 1880

Jedidah & Mary Taylor; Benimian, 06 Mar 1734; Beninian, 04 Jul 1728; Hannah, 06 Feb 1724; Jedidiah, 17 Aug 1742; Jeremiah, 02 Jan 1722; Joseph, 04 Nov 1748; Sammell, 11 Feb 1739/40; Thomas, 11 Jan 1726; Thomas, 23 Oct 1730; Thomas, 01 Jan 1727/8

Jeremiah & Mary Stevens: Elisabeth, 15 Dec 1749; Jedidiah, 04 Feb 1744/5; John, 22 Apr 1747

Samuel & Sarah Sanborn: Abraham, 16 May 1771; Jedediah, 05 Nov 1767; Jeremiah, 13 Mar 1769; John, 13 Sep 1774; Sarah, 22 Aug 1776

Thomas & Mehetable Ayers: A daughter, 13 Jan 1681/2; A son, 30 May 1683; Ann, 14 Mar 1691; Elisebeth, 17 Oct 1686; Hannah, 26 Mar 1693; Jedediah, 13 May 1698; Mehetabel, 26 Mar 1693; Samuel, 13 May 1698; Thomas, 09 Jun 1704; Timothy, 12 May 1689

PIERCE: Charles H (Warren,Me) & Clara E Bartlett (Kingston): Floyd B, 14 Sep 1894

Frank L (Kingston) & Elsie M Furber (Kingston): Lewis Merton Angus, 18 Oct 1898

Frank & Eliza: Female, 31 Jan 1873

John W & Anna: Frank, 10 Sep 1870; Mary E , 10 Sep 1870

James A & Cynther : Walter B, 25 Jan 1878

PILON: Joseph & Elen: Mary E, 01 May 1882

POLLARD: Frances & Sarah Webster; Betty, 22 Aug 1753; Isaac, 01 Mar 1758; John, 11 Apr 1748; Jonthan, 09 Aug 1749; Marey, 11 Feb 1756; Moley, 28 Jul 1751

Jacob & Sarah Seccombs: Jonathan, 04 Dec 1808; Simmons Seccomb, 10 Aug 1807

PRESCOTT: Edgar S & Carrie F Webster: Lissie M, 17 Dec 1881

Eugene A (Kingston) & Sarah A French (Kingston): Albert R, 23 May 1892; Female, 05 Oct 1888

John & Roxcina Sanborn: Emma F, 16 May 1873

Lewis F (Newtone) & Bessie A Marden (Kingston): George F, 23 Aug 1883; Mabel, 16 Sep 1879; Florence, 27 Feb 1891

Richard & Clara J Bickford: Harry L, 07 Feb 1879

Richard B & Mary L Perver: Flora A, b 17 Oct 1824; Laure, 20 Aug 1822; Mark, 29 Mar 1827; Richard, 08 Apr 1839

PRESSY: Paul & Mary Hubard; Bata, 26 Apr 1752; Hanah, 11 Jun 1759; Molla, 27 Jun 1756

PRIMROSE: Edward & Hannah .....: Male, 22 Nov 1852

George H (SoKingston) & Blanche C Clayton (So Brookville,Me): Charles Harmon, 30 Jan 1893; George Roy, 16 Sep 1886; Rodney Bertram, 28 Jul 1895

PRINCE: Isaac & Dorothy Calef: Dorothy, 18 May 1787
  James & Mary Ladd: Benjamin Ladd, 24 Jul 1782; Henry, 03 Jun 1787; James, 28 Feb
  1781; Mary, 08 May 1784; Sarah, 12 Jul 1785
PROCTOR: James & Abigel: Easter, 13 Jun 1762; Ebenezer, 05 Mar 1757; Elisebath, 03 Sep
  1753; John, 07 Apr 1767; Juder, 02 Jan 1760; William, 08 Apr 1767
  Jonathan & Martha Graves; Amos, 16 Oct 1778; James, 13 Sep 1777
  Thomas Proctor & Fanney Kimball: Fanney, 09 Nov 1778; Lidea, 24 Oct 1776
PURINGTON: Jacob (Fremont) & Sylvia Garist (Lebanon,Me): Walter, 23 Sep 1895
QUENBE: David & Abigaiell Webster: David, 04 Dec 1731; Elisabeth, 16 May 1737; Els, 17
  Nov 1726; John, 16 May 1737; Mary, 30 Jan 1743/4; Sammell, 10 Apr 1729; Sarai, 30
  Jan 1743; Timothy, 10 Apr 1750
QUERO: Andrew & Annie Ball: Rossie Bernice, 20 Jan 1897
QUIMBEY: Eliphlet & Mary Juel; Andrew, 04 Oct 1750; Daniel, 09 Sep 1755; Jonathan, 15
  Aug 1753; Mary, 03 Dec 1747; Mary, 27 Nov 1750
  John Quimbey & Martha Sargent: Jacob, 30 May 1759; Jemimah, 06 Sep 1761; John, 29
  Apr 1757; Moses, 29 Sep 1755
  John & Jeminah: Jeremiah, 13 Dec 1748
  Trustram & Susana Blasdel: Betty, 25 Feb 1765; Daniel, 03 Nov 1755; Elifelet, 11 May
  1768; Hanah, 04 Jan 1761; Mary, 07 Dec 1754; Susana, 12 Dec 1762
QUIMBY: Aaron & Anne Bachelder: Anne, 03 Aug 1757; Hanah, 30 Mar 1754; Unes, 02 Apr
  1756
  Daniel & Abigail Hubbard: Benjamin, 15 Dec 1785; Daniel, 04 Jan 1783; Richard,
  10 Dec 1783
  Moses Eugene (E Kingston)& Etta L Morse (Kensington): Eva Lillian, 12 Aug 1888;
  Mary Edith, 20 Oct 1891
  Jeremiah & Hanah: Elisebath, 04 Jul 1757; Jean, 07 Aug 1755; Moses, 13 Apr 1725
  Moses & Susan M Conner: Charles, 18 Nov 1840; George F, 15 Dec 1837; John J, 10
  Nov 1836; Mary L, 23 Oct 1844; William H, 29 May 1843
  Philip & Mary J Swett: ----, 18 Aug 1851
  Samuel & Ann Young: Anne, 22 Sep 1760; Mary, 01 Dec 1756; Samuel, 28 Jan 1759
RANO: Elias & Mary Severance: Elisabeth, 24 Jan 1744; Hannah, 30 Mar 1749; John,
  27 Apr 1752; Mary, 28 Feb 1746; Samuel, 23 Apr 1743
REMAILLARD: Peter (Canada): Male, 06 Apr 1889
REMICK: John & Hannah Brackett: Charles, 24 Feb 1842; Sarah A, 26 Mar 1843
REYNOLDS: Alphonzo S (Boston,Ma) & Emma F(Madbury): Elmer, 22 Mar 1886; Female, 01
  Jul 1884; Female, 25 May 1889; Henry L, 04 Jun 1880
  Charles & Maria: Charles H, 25 Mar 1873; Female, 08 Feb 1878; William, 05 Apr 1880;
  Charles O, 04 Jan 1881; Female, 08 Oct 1877; Male, 28 Oct 1875; Male, 21 Jun 1870
  Dr. Thomas D & Mary Fannie Smith: Female, 05 Mar 1875
RICHARDSON: Herbert B (Tunbridge,Vt)& Ida French (Kingston): Ernes L, 24 Apr 1894;
  Male, 11 Aug 1892; Milo Robert, 18 Nov 1896
ROBEY: Ichabod & Lucy: Lidrea, 23 May 1703; Ruth, 03 Sep 1707; Susanah, 02 Aug 1713;
  William, 06 Nov 1709
  Samuel & Hanah Ordway: Jonathan, 15 Oct 1756
ROBIN: Charles: Male, 07 Sep 1869

ROBINSON: Charles W (Epping) & Louisa M (Kingston): Blanche Agnes, 14 Nov 188; Male,
12 Sep 1886

Charles Robinson: Charles, 04 Jan 1881; Female Child, 08 Oct 1877; Male Child,
28 Oct 1875; Male Child, 21 Jun 1870

ROCK: Philip: Female, 18 Feb 1876

ROGERS: Ferdinand Charles (Kingston) & Mary Thompson (Newton): Edna May, 18 Aug
1897; Helen Christina, 25 Nov 1898

Frank F (Kingston) & Sadie E Williams (Brentwood): Forest Frank, 27 Oct 1898

Moses H & Ellen Welch: Mary Lena, 09 Oct 1864

Moses W & Mary Jane (Jennie) Winslow: Celia Belle, 02 Jan 1890; Edna May,
09 Apr 1883; Frank P, 27 Jan 1876; Harry N, 04 Nov 1870; Irene Delmar, 15 Jun 1884;
Peter, 14 Apr 1880

William & Jemina L (Junia) Severance: ----, 14 Feb 1851

ROUEL: Daniel & Juda Davies: Haner, 24 Dec 1737; Jacob, 01 Oct 1735; Juda, 08 Oct 1733

ROUELL: Philep & Jeminah: Hannah, 18 Mar 1724/5

ROWE: Ichabod & Dority Juel: Hanah, 06 Aug 1765

SAEYS: William E & Mary A: Harry Colcord, 23 Nov 1893

SANBORN: Charles & Lizzie: Male, 31 Dec 1877

Abraham & Abigel Clifford: Deborah, 08 Jan 1742; Isaac, 06 Mar 1752; John,
19 Feb 1740; Joseph Cliford, 30 Nov 1737; Judith, 30 Nov 1748; Sarah, 16 Mar 1739;
Sarah, 02 Jul 1745; Sarah, 08 Feb 1746; Shuah, 11 Feb 1750

Benjamin & Dorryty Lad: Benjamin, 07 Nov 1760; Dorety, 29 Jan 1756; Elce, 20
Nov 1748; Elisabeth, 15 Nov 1746; Lida, 10 Apr 1758; Samuel, 25 Dec 1762

Benjamin & Theodate Bachelder: Dorothy, 10 Nov 1766; Hulda, 22 Jan 1769; Mary,
23 Jan 1763

Dan T & ..... Elkins: Male, 24 Apr 1885

David & Dollie Gilman; Benjamin, 10 Mar 1782; David, 03 Jul 1780; Dolie, 09 Mar
1788; John, 26 Jun 1784; John Calef, 27 Aug 1794; Sarah, 08 Sep 1797

Frank M (Buffalo,NY) & Mary S (Merrimac,Ma): Bertha Eleanora, 07 Nov 1892;
Female, 18 Jun 1888; Female, 17 Jan 1891

Israel & Patta Morgan: John Bachelder, 26 May 1797; Lydia, 26 Dec 1794; Polly,
29 Apr 1791; Sally, 16 Aug 1789; Simeon, 04 Jan 1794

John M & Clara: Blanch C, 02 Nov 1883

John Quimby & Elizabeth Kimball: Polly, 15 Feb 1791; Timothy, 04 Apr 1787

John Sanborn & Elizebath Hoock (Hook); Hannah, 12 Sep 1787; Jacob Hook,
20 Jan 1774; John, 06 Oct 1776; Molly, 21 Dec 1778; Moses, 04 May 1790;
Peter, 24 Dec 1781; Phinehas, 21 Oct 1784; Stevens, 19 Oct 1771

Jonathan Sanborn & Elizabeth: Benjamin, 02 Jan 1711; Dorethe, 30 Aug 1705;
John, 19 Dec 1710; Love, 30 Aug 1702; Mary, 08 Dec 1713; Sarah, 18 Apr 1708

Jonathan & Lydia Severance: Catran, 01 Jul 1788

Jonathan, Jr & Sarah James: Jonathan, 08 Mar 1764; Isreal, 03 Feb 1767

Jonathan Sanborn, Jr & Mary Bachelder: Jethro, 20 Nov 1738; John, 08 Sep 1736;
Jonathan, 08 Mar 1764; Joseph, 03 Aug 1770; Josiah, 17 Oct 1750; Mary, 20 Nov 1738;
Mary, 29 Dec 1754; Phinias, 17 Mar 1747; Rebacker, 10 Jun 1744

Joseph W & Levina S: Benjamin, 21 Jun 1869; Male, 04 Sep 1869

J. Warren & Eva: Female, 28 Oct 1875; Helen M, 14 Apr 1881

Manson M (E Kingston)& Grace (Boston,Ma): Grace Elizabeth, 02 Jan 1889

Lt William & Mary Sleeper: Benjamin, 03 Apr 1765; Dolla, 12 Nov 1763; Hulda, 15 Dec 1752; Jethro, 15 Nov 1755; Joseph, 03 Apr 1765; Margret, 02 Nov 1751; Moley, 13 Jan 1758; Noah,15 Oct 1761; Peter, 13 Aug 1767; Tristram, 13 Oct 1759; William, 13 Mar 1769

Paul & Bette Cirrer: Benjamin, 21 Aug 1747; Mary, 26 Oct 1748; Paul, 21 Dec 1752; Tristrum, 04 Nov 1756

Paul & ....: John, 28 Dec 1743; Jonathan, 23 Nov 1738

Peter & Mary Sanborn: Beniman, 26 Dec 1739; John, 10 Mar 1733/4; John, 20 Sep 1736; John, 22 Mar 1749/50; Mary, 10 Mar 1738; Peter, 01 Jun 1735; Peter, 27 Jan 1747/8; Sarah, 01 Mar 1743

Samuel & Elisabeth Colcord: Benjamin, 20 May 1719; Dorethy, 03 May 1721; Elisabeth, 07 Apr 172-

Samuel, Jr & Hanah Tucker: Elisabeth, 24 Apr 1755; Hanah, 07 Dec 1762; Jonathan, 07 Dec 1762; Joseph, 17 Dec 1751; Sarah, 16 Feb 1753

Timothy & Ellas Quimby: Abigal, 10 Sep 1749; Benjamin, 27 May 1747; David, 24 May 1753; Else, 23 Dec 1758: Mary, 28 Mar 1761; Quimby, 09 Jul 1766; Samuel, 08 Nov 1755; Sarah, 01 Oct 1763

Trustrum & Abigaill Blake: Deborah, 27 Jan 1733/4; Elisah, 08 Dec 1748; Hanah, 12 Aug 1740; Hanah, 15 Aug 1736; John, 25 Nov 1731; Lida, 15 Aug 1736; Moses, 17 Jul 1742; Simen, 02 Feb 1752; Simon, 20 Dec 1744

SAWYER: Benjamin, 02 Mar 1716 (Parents not listed)

Benjamin, Sr & Mary Bean: Benjamin,Jr, 27 Aug 1738; Benjamin, 29 Apr 1742; John, 27 Aug 1751; Mary, 25 Sep 1739

Joseph & Dorethy: Dorethy, 14 Dec 1740; Judeth, 06 Oct 1745; Sarah,13 Oct 1749

SAYER: Gedeon Sayer & Sarah: Gedeon, 13 Oct 1751; Hannah, 16 May 1760; James, 30 Jan 1755; Jotham, 15 May 1757; Ruben, 08 Sep 1765; Sarah, 08 Oct 1762; Tamar, 08 Oct 1762

SCHELLING: Charles R & Harriet N Shaw: Mary Susan, 13 Jan 1878

John & Lucy: Harlan P, 09 Feb 1852

SCRIBNER: Edward & Rachiel Webster: Benjamin, 14 Nov 1745; Ebenezer, 21 Jul 1748; Edward, 16 Dec 1742; Hannah, 23 Nov 1735; John, 08 Sep 1740; Thomas, 01 Jan 1738

Samuel & Hanah Webster: Ebenezer, 28 Mar 1755; Elisabeth, 14 Aug 1762; Hannah, 02 Feb 1747; Iddo, 11 Nov 1752; Joseph, 12 Feb 1746; Josiah, 11 Jul 1750; Mary, 05 Oct 1759; Samuell, 28 Dec 1743; Suzaner, 29 Oct 1741

Thomas & Hannah Welsh: ----, 18 Nov 1709; Edward, 27 Apr 1711; Elizabeth, 01 May 1709; Sammell, 07 Mar 1713; Sammell, 29 Apr 1716

Thomas & Sarah Colbey: Batte, 10 Aug 1763; Ebenezer, 02 Jul 1761

Thomas & Sarah Clifford: Deborah, 07 Sep 1705; John, 06 Dec 1703

SECCOMBE: Joseph & Ruth: Ebenezer, 19 Jun 1778; Dorothy, 09 Jul 1771; Dorothy, 15 Mar 1779; Elisabeth, 10 Mar 1773; Elisabeth, 09 Feb 1781; Joseph Toppan, 02 Mar 1786; Mary, 11 Jul 1775; Mehitable, 15 Mar 1779; Sarah, 12 Jun 1783

SEAVER: Daniel P & Dolly C George: Carrie Belle, 02 Nov 1874; Dora Estella, 02 Aug 1872; George, 05 May 1870; Georgianna, 05 May 1870; Male, 17 Aug 1867

John P (Sandown)& Florence G (So Hampton): Male, 27 Mar 1889

SEGUIN: John (Biddeford,Me) & Delia Dominick (Great Falls): Charles Edward, 29 Jan 1897

SENTER: Leslie M (Kingston) & Laura A Collins (Kingston): Ella Lena, 09 Nov 1893; Eva
    May, 30 Apr 1892; Loren M, 17 Dec 1895

SEVER: Thomas & Martha Webster: Calif, 12 Sep 1746; Eliger, 19 Dec 1762; Elisabeth, 19
    Apr 1750; Elisha, 20 Aug 1767; Martha, 24 Mar 1756; Mary ----; Thomas, 19 Nov 1752

SEVERENCE: Benjamin, Jr & Jude Nicole: Benjamin, 19 Nov 1758; Juda, 26 Sep 1756;
    Lowes, 06 Mar 1764; Moley, 19 Sep 1771; Nicals, 15 Oct 1766; Sarah,19 Nov 1758;
    Sarah, 26 Mar 1769

Benjamin Severance & ....: ....., 24 Nov 1869; Female, 07 Jun 1868

Ebenezer & Dority Elitt: Dorety, 06 Oct 1760; Ebenezer, 08 Sep 1768; Namoi, 03 Feb
    1758

Epharm Severence, Jr & Elisabeth Sweat: John, Sep -----; Judeth, 25 Mar 1756; Moses,
    19 Mar 1752; Peter, 06 Mar 1754

Jacob & Jane H Abbot: Benjamin, 10 Aug 1721; Emily J, 05 Jul 1835; George L,
    06 Nov 1841; Junia L, 13 Aug 1830; Mary T, 28 May 1819

Jacob & Mary Tucker: Jacob, b 07 Oct 1795; Jonathan,25 Nov 1800

Jacob & Sarah: Mary, 12 Aug 1755

John, Jr & Rachel Heath: Nathan 09 Sep 1808

Jonathan & Cattren: Benjamin, 22 Jan 1731

Jonathan & Hannah J Judkins: Flora, 07 Apr 1832: Hannah F, 07 Mar 1837; Jonathan A
    02 Jul 1834

Jonathan, Jr & Tryphena Neckels: Catten, 28 Aug 1755; Jonathan, 31 Jul 1757; Sarah,
    28 Mar 1769

Jonathan, Jr & Mehitabel Brown: Jonathan I, 04 Jul 1781; Lida, 26 Jul 1762; Mary,
    26 Jul 1762

Mason S (Kingston)& Ellen J (Nellie)Colford (St Johns, Nfland): Ellen B, 04 Apr 1897;
    Mary Emily, 04 Jul 1889

Mason L & Nellie: Hattie J M, 09 Feb 1880; John, 03 Apr 1881

Nason & ..... : Nancy Gertrude, 08 Aug 1876

Ora P & Ruth: ---- 09 Dec 1851

Samuel & Hannah Winsle: Elisebath, 05 Aug 1773; Jannah, 08 Jul 1769; Katharine, 09
    -- 1778; Phebea, 31 Aug 1771; Samuel, 25 Aug 1775

SHAW: Benjamin & Rebeka Follinsbee: Follinsbee, 17 Dec 1750; Mary, 13 Jan 1748
    Emer J (So Hampton) & Mattie M (Brentwood): Leroy Wilfred, 05 Sep 1893
    Ichabod & Sarah Moulton: Abigail, 14 Apr 1759; Moley, 21 May 1763; Sarah,
    21 May 1757

SHELDON: Charles P (Maine)& Fannie Knapp (Stewartstown): Alice Jeannette, 16 Jul 1894

SHEPARD: William & Mary A: Male, 11 Mar 1878

SHEYS: William E (E Haverhill,Ma) & Mary A (Kingston): Harry Colcord, 23 Nov 1893

SILLOWAY: Anginette Silloway & (David Wilson) : Alonzo Silloway, 24 Jan 1881
    Benjamin W & Mary Severance: Allice, 21 Sep 1777; Benjamin, 27 Aug 1784;
    George, 04 Mar 1787; Jacob, 07 Jul 1779; Sarah, 27 Feb 1775; Sarah, 26 Dec 1781
    Everett W (Kingston) & Ella B Hill (Kingston): Grace B, 18 Jan 1897; Isaac W, 28 Jan
    1891

George Frank (Kingston) & Mary Lucy Shaw (Worcester,Ma): Cora May, Mar 1898;
Female, 05 Aug 1890; Female, 25 Mar 1892
Isaac W & Emma J West: Frank W, 07 Nov 1883
Jacob & Allsee Webster: Benjamin, 21 Sep 1752; Greely, 11 Aug 1759; Jacob,
11 Dec 1755: John, 23 Jun 1750
Jacob (Kingston) & Annie Sleeper (Sandown): Roy Howard, 10 Aug 1898
J. W. & Emma: Alden W, 11 Dec 1876
Eliza A Silloway: (Winslow)Male, 28 Oct 1875
SIMES: John & Mary Martin: Female, 06 Jul 1897
SMITH: Frank A (Exeter) & Kate A Martin (Kingston): Irving Arthur, 25 Mar 1896; Jesse, 05
Jul 1894
Frank F (Salisbury,Ma) & Ida M Fowler (Seabrook): Fannie Louise, 13 Jan 1897;
Harriett Edna, 22 Feb 1895
John A (Dover) & Lydia Ann (Kingston): Grace, 01 Oct 1886
Lewis C (Kingston) & Christina A Stopp (Malden,Ma): Female, 24 Jan 1898; Female,
27 Dec 1900; Hettie Christina, 20 Jun 1894; Laura Alberta, 18 May 1896; Lilla Bell, 11
Aug 1888; Male, 19 Apr 1886
SLEEPER: Aaron & Ane Clough: Abigal, 27 Jul 1762; Ann, 17 Sep 1757; Hannah, 01 Nov
1767; Jonathan, 28 Feb 1754; John, 21 Mar 1749; Sarah, 09 Oct 1750
Aaron & Elizabeth: Ebenazer, 24 Apr 1702; Mary, 21 Feb 1705/6; Mehetabell,
25 Apr 1701
Aaron & Sarah: Daniell, 09 May 1715; Edward, 26 Oct 1719
Beniman & Abigel Coffien: Abigal, 14 Dec 1746; Mary, 25 Aug 1745; Thomas, 11 Feb
1747; Tristrum Coffin, 26 Jun 1744
Beniman & Hanah Lofring: Anne, 10 Oct 1765; Benjamin, 03 Dec 1767; Hanah, 21 Jan
1761; Mary, 04 May 1759; Sarah, 05 May 1762
David & Margeet Scribner: David, 08 Sep 1748; Giden, 25 Jul 1744; Peter, 23 May 1749
Hezekiah & Martha Wood: Hezekiah, Oct 1762; Heziah, 20 Mar 1766; Jonas, 11 Feb
1754; Joseph, 29 Dec 1750; Loies, 27 Aug 1763; Luse, 03 Apr 1757; Martha, 20 Mar
1766; Nehemiah, 24 Jan 1747
John B Sleeper & Mary Burbank: David, 05 Mar 1799; Hannah, 15 Dec 1794; John,Jr,
28 Apr 1791; Molly, 14 Mar 1780; Samuel, 15 Oct 1766; William, 19 Nov 1776
John & Juda Bager: Aaron, 10 Mar 1779; John, 13 Jul 1783; Jonathan, 25 Jun 1775
Jonathan & Molly: Anna, 01 Oct 1798
Richard & Martha Fifield: Doley, 25 Nov 1769; Elisebeath, 15 Feb 1763; Jonathan,
01 Jun 1767; Martha, 16 May 1772; Richard, 31 Aug 1786; Levi, 22 Apr 1777;
Meriam, 12 Dec 1764; Molly, 19 Oct 1781; Sherburn, 04 May 1784
Samuel & Sarah Davis: Elizabeth, 18 May 1817
William & Abigal Sleeper: Abigal, 11 Jun 1753: Betty, 11 Jan 1763; Heniah, 10 Oct
1741; John, 13 Jul 1759; Mary, 13 Jul 1759; William, 29 Sep 1756; William, 17 Mar
1765
William & Dorrethy Blasdel: Ane, 01 Sep 1748; Anna, 29 Jan 1755; Dorrethy, 07
Apr 1760; Elisabeth,07 Apr 1760; Elisesesbeth, 27 Jun 1757;John Blasdel, 31 Aug
1752
SLEPER: Hezekiah Sleper & Elizabeth Sleper: Abigaill, 29 Apr 1720; Elesebeth, 28 Jun 1717

Thomas & Mary Colcoard: Elizabeth, 08 Sep 1723

SMIETH: Abraham & Mary: Ann, 01 Dec 1729

William & Elesebath Seley: Richard, 03 Sep 1732; William, 29 Sep 1729

SMITH: William & Haner Fellows; Anah, 10 Oct 1726; Doretha, 17 May 1732; Elisabeth, 14 Aug 1735; Margret, 01 Dec 1725; Mary, 01 Jun 1734

Clark P & Henrietta: ----, 27 Nov 1851

George E & Harriett S (Hattie) Judkins: Female Child, 25 Aug 1881

Isaac & Meheteble Buziel: Elisabeth, 08 Mar 1756; Jonathan, 24 Nov 1748; Joseph, 02 Aug 1746; Mehetabel, 26 Feb 1750

J. SMITH & .... : Forrest, 18 Feb 1882

John A & Lydia: Male, 08 Oct 1884

Stephen R: Female, 27 Mar 1879

Nathan & Marie: ----, 11 Dec 1851

Stephen R & Annie: Male, 15 Jun 1871

William & Haner Fellows: Richard, 29 Sep 1729

SNOW: Joshua & Anna Bean: Anna, 17 Jun 1740; Elisabath, 06 Jan 1742

SONIER: Julius (Nova Scotia) & Nellie Simes (Brandon,Vt): Lillian May, 05 Nov 1898

SPEARING: Eliza V, 01 Jan 1831 (Parents not listed)

SPOFFORD: Oren & Susan C Clement: Livingston, 25 Feb 1835

ST CLAIR: James & Emma: Bertie P (James), 08 Feb 1881

STEVENS: Aaron & Mary: Mehitebal, 02 Sep 1758

Beniman & Sarah Fifield: Beniman, 03 Oct 1737; Ebenezer, 30 Sep 1747; Elisabeth, 25 Mar 1742; Samuel, 29 Jan 1740

Benjamin, Jr & Anne Colcord; Benjamin, 13 Nov 1767; Elisebath, 23 Apr 1763; Samuel, 28 Jul 1761; Sarah, 13 Nov 1765

Ebenezenr & Mary Colcoard: Ebenezenr, 18 Feb 1738; John, 03 Mar 1770; Moses, 05 Sep 1771; Paul, 01 May 1775; Peter Colcord, 27 Jun 1773

Ebenezer & Hannah Stevens: Benjamin, 18 Jun 1776; Ebenezer, 26 Jul 1772; John, 05 Mar 1771; Samuel, 25 Aug 1774; Sarah, 29 Jul 1768

Ebenezer, Jr & Sarah Emerson: Ebenezer, 10 Feb 1763; Elisabeth, 20 Aug 1768; Mary, 23 Nov 1764; Samuel, 01 Apr 1761; Sarah, 30 Mar 1766; Sarah, 16 Sep 1766

Ebenezer, Jr & Sarah Stevens: Benjamin, 08 Nov 1790; Benjamin, 21 Nov 1794; Hannah, 12 May 1792; Joanna, 17 Jan 1805; John, 15 Apr 1787; Mary C, 16 Jun 1796; Peter, 25 May 1785

Ebenezer, 3rd & Eleanor Hill: Amos, 13 May 1790; Betsey, 03 Apr 1793; Hills, 04 Feb 1798; Polly, 12 Sep 1795; Sally, 06 Feb 1792

Frank W (Kingston) & Lora M (Brentwood): Carl Stewart, 16 Sep 1895; Rosamund M, 30 Mar 1893

John & Mary Hubard: Anne; Elisebath, 25 Mar 1757; John, 17 Sep 1758; Mary,------

John Stevens & Ruhamah Fifield: Pluma, 08 Dec 1800; Ruhamah, 19 Sep 1806; Sally, 08 Oct, 1804; Samuel Hubbard, 20 Nov 1802; Sherburn, 13 Dec 1798

John, Jr & Lydia Wadleigh: Edward Greely, 11 Sep 1789; Mary Wadleigh, 13 Apr 1795; Samuel Huse, 15 Jul 1783

Joseph & Sarah E: John Bradley, 29 Sep 1872

Mary Elizabeth, 07 Jul 1877 (No parents listed)

Samuel W & Hattie N Stevens: George B, 02 Jun 1880
Samuell & Suah Fifield: Samuel, 30 Jan 1751
Samuell & Hannah Morriel: Benjamin, 10 Jan 1754; Ebenezer, 04 Dec 1753; Edward,
08 Feb 1768; John, 03 Nov 1761; Moses, 26 Apr 1756; Peter, Mar 1766; Sarah, 13
Nov 1757; Sarah, 27 Mar 1759; Shuah, 27 Nov 1759
STOCKMAN: Robard & Lidia Stockman: Mary, 27 Dec 1722; Johanah, 05 Aug 1726
STRAW: David & Mary: Jonathan, 03 Jan 1744; Judah, 10 Jan 1750
STUART: Samuel & Grace Hubard: Abigail, 26 Mar 1792
    Stephen & Sarah Pesle: Anna, 08 May 1776; Betsey, 29 Sep 1797; Ebenezer, 07 Dec
    1794; James, 05 Apr 1782; Moses, 12 Oct 1784; Sarah, 05 Jan 1787; Stephen, 25 Dec
    1779
SWEAT: John Darling & Elizabeth Clifford: John, 06 Oct 1779; Stephen, 04 Oct 1775;
    Timothy, 21 Jan 1772
    Rev Moses & Hannah Eastman; Homer, 21 Oct 1783
    Moses & Lovinia George: Female, 05 Nov 1878; Female(stillborn), 15 Oct 1877;
    Daniel, 17 Sep 1876; Female, 08 Oct 1884; Nellie Frances, 12 Feb 1881
    Samuel & Mary Jones: Mary, 09 Sep 1768; Samuel Jones, 26 Aug 1767
SWEET: Benjamin, Jr & Mary Eliot: Abigal, 16 Dec 1761; Anna, 28 May 1766; Benjamin,
    19 Jul 1768; Dorothey, 03 Sep 1770; Mary, 02 Apr 1764; Mehetibal, 03 May 1773;
    Moses, 03 Dec 1777; Nomoi, 17 May1775
    Elisha & Abigel Sanborn: Abigel, 08 Jul 1744; Elisha, 02 Dec 1751;Hannah, 13 Apr
    1747; Stephen, 21 May 1739; Sarah, 04 Jan 1741/2
    Nathan & .... : Nathan, 11 may 1739; Thomas, 11 May 1747
    Nathan & Mary Darbon: Bethiah, 27 Sep 1731; Darbon, 16 Oct 1733; Derbon, 29
    Dec 1744; Hulda, 29 Jul 1741; Mary, 26 Mar 1737; Moses, 03 May 1757
    Stephen & Sarah Garlu: Abigail, 28 Aug 1772; Elisha, 28 Jul 1780; Hannah, 27 Mar
    1776; Jane, 17 Jun 1782; John, 09 Feb 1763; Joseph, 30 Jan 1762; Nathaniel, 09 May
    1768; Noah, 08 Apr 1778; Sarah, 08 May 1766; Stephen, 20 May 1770
SWETT: Benjamen & Abigaiell Darling: Beniman, 31 Dec 1736; John, 10 Jun 1741; John
    Darling, 07 Jun 1750; Moses, 03 Dec 1729; Moses, 23 Dec 1754; Naomy, 13 Mar
    1739; Sammell, 15 Dec 1744
    Elisha & Sarah Sweet: Ester, 07 Aug 1730; Joseph, 09 Jan 1732/3; Steven, 18 Dec
    1734
    John & Bethiah: Ane, 17 Dec 1726; Beniannen, 17 Oct 1707; Elizabeth, 26 Dec ----;
    Moses, 28 Nov 1714; Nathan, 09 Jun 1711
TANDE: Richard & .... : Abigel, 30 Dec 1741; Elisabeth, 19 Dec 1736
    Richard & Rachel: William, 06 Aug 1723
    Samuel & Hannah Lovere: Richard, 18 Dec1752
    William & Mary Morgen: Abigal, 29 Dec 1750; Elisabeth, 02 Mar 1746; Mary,
    04 Nov 1749; Mary, 02 Nov 1752; Mary, 28 Apr 1762; Parker, 18 Feb 1758;
    William, 24 Dec 1754
TANDY: Abel & Rachal Smith: Anne, 05 Oct 1754; Mehetibel, 10 Apr 1757; Rachal,
    02 Sep 1752; Samuel, 12 Mar 1759
THAYER: Calvin, b 29 Jul 1800 (no parents listed)
    Calvin & Sarah: Clara Eda,01 Oct 1848; Elihu F, 25 Feb 1844; William F,13 Mar 1846

Rev Elihn & Hannah Calef: Elihn, 25 Aug 1802; Hannah, 06 Aug 1788; Hannah, 29 Jul 1787; John, 04 Apr 1795; Judeth, 26 Feb 1785; Mary, 24 Feb 1782; Patty, 14 Jun 1798; Samuel, 31 Jul 1789; Sarah, 16 May 1792

THOMPSON: George W & Mari: Triplets, 29 Mar 1881

    Nathan & Sarah Prescut: Hanah, 01 Nov 1762; Levi, 18 Nov 1767; Moley, 16 May 1765; Richard, 18 Sep 1775; Samuel, 02 May 1773; Sarah, 14 Jun 1760

    Samuel, Jr & Catrn Tucker: Barshaba, 04 Mar 1774; Ezra, 04 Jun 1771; John, 14 Mar 1758; Mehitebel, 13 Feb 1765; Moses, 20 Feb 1763; Pheba, 23 May 1760; Samuel, 05 Aug 1777

    Thomas & Judeth Blasdel: Abigail, 10 May 1782; Hannah, 10 May 1776; Miriam, 16 Jul 1784; Molly, 16 Jul 1779; Ralph, 11 Apr 1789; Sarah, 22 Sep 1786; Thomas, 22 Dec 1791

THORN: James & Hannah Brown: Betty, 24 Apr 1764; Hannah, 15 Oct 1749; Jeams(James), 09 Aug 1755; Mary, 20 Jan 1757; Nathan, 17 Jul 1759; Sarah, 15 Sep 1751

    John & Elisabeth Brown: Abraham, 20 May 1754; Abraham, 31 Jan 1757; Elisabeth, 18 May 1736; Jemina, 10 May 1737

THYNG: Clarence & ....: Charles G, 26 Sep 1870

TILTON: L Benson & .....: Henry B, 16 Oct 1870

    David & Rebeaka Green: David, 27 Jan 1755; Elisebeath, 10 Jun 1756; Jemina, 19 Jun 1753; Lois, 02 Jan 1758; Mary, 25 Oct 1750; Rachal, 17 Feb 1752

    Josiah & Sarah Flanders: David, 27 Oct 1735; Josiah, 22 Oct 1743; Mariba, 09 Mar 1738; Philip, 10 Apr 1741; Sarah, 27 Mar 1750

    Timothy & Rebeaka Green: David, 10 Sep 1765; Elisabeth, 07 May 1761; Joannah, 13 Sep 1751; Joseph, 07 Sep 1748; Nathan, 03 Feb 1757; Wilam, 13 Dec 1753

TINSLO; Margret, -- Jan 1735 (no parents listed)

TOMSON: Sammel & Mary Bartlet: Moses, 16 Oct 1734

TOPPAN: Rev Amos & Margret Sanborn: Mary, 28 Jan 1771

TOWLE: Calob & Rebaka: Anner, 28 May 1728; Caleb, 28 Dec 1737; Elisha, 12 Jan 1730; James, 31 Dec 1747; Jeremie, 19 Jun 1745; Mary, 04 Nov 1732

    John Everett (Danville) & Effie Austin (Haverhill,Ma): Effie Elva, 25 Dec 1897

TRASK: Joseph (Salem) & Lillian E Williams (Hampton): Annie Mae, 25 Feb 1884; Florence Lillian, 30 Jun 1887; William Gardner, 25 Oct 1885

TUCK: Herbert H & Nellie: Harvey Eugene, 20 May 1885

TUCKER: Benjamin & Juda Thuriel: Hanah, 04 Jan 1754; Jannah, Sep 1762; Jonathan, 29 Jul 1751; Mary, 27 Sep 1756; Thomas, 21 Aug 1749

    Charles R (Kingston) & Florence (Cornwallis, N.S.): Male, 19 Feb 1890

    Ezra, Jr & Hipsebah Prese: Maria, 01 Mar 1763

    Jere C & Clara M: Female, 26 Feb 1878

    Jeremiah & Rosetta Woodward: Female, 16 May 1876

    John & Deborah Sanborn: Elisha, 26 Oct 1772; Henry, 08 May 1775; Moses, 15 Jul 1769

    John F & Ida F Curtis: Female, 01 Aug 1880; Female, 12 Apr 1881; Female, 18 Mar 1885; Male, 27 Feb 1878; William F, 30 Oct 1873

    Joseph & Alice Sanborn: Amos, 05 Nov 1788; Jacob, 26 Jul 1791

    Joseph & Hanah Young: Joseph, 09 Jun 1757

    Joseph, Jr & Mary Foot: Joseph, 23 Aug 1800

Moses & Joanna: Elisabeth, 08 Apr 1741; Haner, 22 Sep 1743; Joseph, 22 Oct 1748; Mary, 05 Oct 1751; Rubin, 19 Jun 1747; Sarah, 05 Oct 1751

Moses & Rachel Cook: Jacob Peaslee, 08 Aug 1818; John, 22 Oct 1748; Lucy W, Jan 1808; Lydia, 31 Mar 1798; Peter Sanborn, 25 Dec 1793

Otis & Sarah Cheney: Female, 08 Mar 1877

Samell & Mary Elkens: Beniman, 25 Sep 1727; John, 05 Sep 1732; Jonathan, 02 Jan 1724/5

Wallace M (Kingston) & Lettie E Tucker (Boscawen): Female, 05 May 1886; Female, 02 Dec 1888; Maxine Estelle, 01 Sep 1899

TYLER: Frank A (Lawrence,Ma) & Jane Cortland (N. Weare): Elizabeth French, 17 Apr 1895

VARRELL: George A & Sarah: Female, 27 Dec 1888

WALTON: Calvin & Anna E: George Oliver, 27 Nov 1873

WADLEIGH: Daniel & Dolly Bartlett; Daniel, Jr, 13 Aug 1793; Hannah, 26 Jun 1797; John, 10 Jan 1789; Joseph, 20 Oct 1790

Joseph B (Kingston) & Elizabeth Gerneny (Baltimore,Md): Clarence Benjamin, 19 Aug 1895

WADLEY: John & Mary Dent: Achsah, 13 Feb 1763; Daniel, 21 Sep 1758; Martha, 05 May 1765; Mary, 24 Sep 1760

WADLY: Benimen & Jude: John, 22 Oct 1730

WALKER: John E & Ida F: Female, 12 Apr 1881

WALTON: Thomas F (England) & Mary E Stevens (Kingston): Barbara Katherine, 25 Jan 1895

WATSON: Ebenezer & Elisebath Severance: Anne, 02 Feb 1768; Betty, 11 Apr 1759; Hulda----; Thomas, Aug 1763

Hannah Watson: Ichabod, 01 Jun 1744

WEBBER: John & Hannah Tucker: Benjamin Tucker, 10 Oct 1788; Daniel, 01 Oct 1790; Judeth Thurla, 25 Sep 1791; Sally, 22 Dec 1794; Sarah, 11 Nov 1793; Thomas, 20 Nov 1800; William, Mar 1833

WEBSTER: Abraham & Martha Emons: Francis (Female), 30 Mar 1764

Albert S (Kingston) & Allice L (Danville): Herbert R, 07 Jul 1891

Albert & .....: Male, 27 May 1875

Beniman & Elisabeth Stuard: Anna, 18 Oct 1728; Beniman, 18 Dec 1732

Beniman & Mary Sawyer: Dorethy, 30 Oct 1750; Elisabeth, 15 Jun 1740; Jacob, 03 Sep 1742; Jacob, 15 Feb 1744/5; Mary, 30 Sep 1747; Sarah, 01 May 1754; William, 22 May 1738

Charles & Alice Huse: Female, 03 Mar 1896

David G & Judith Webster: David, 26 Apr 1818; Jeremiah B, 25 Dec 1824; John A, 12 Oct 1829; Jonathan, 26 Apr 1808; Jonathan, 26 Apr 1818; Joseph, 28 Dec 1811; Joseph, 03 Dec 1812; Ruth Ann, 05 Aug 1820

Ebenazer & Hannah Judgkin: Ebenezer, 10 Oct 1714; Iddo, 09 Feb 1727/8; John, 04 Aug 1719; Joseph, 15 Sep 1724; Mary, 15 Sep 1724; Rachel, 14 Mar 1710; Susanah, 09 Jul 1712; William, 26 Aug 1716

Elihu & Ruth: ----, 09 Apr 1851

Henry D & Caroline: Georgia A, 16 Jul 1878; Georgianna, 11 Apr 1874; Mattie, 20 May 1876

Iddo & Jena Goss: Benjamin, 07 Jan 1757; Jena, 12 Feb 1747; Mary, 06 Nov 1761
Isaac & Sarah Downing: Daniel, 05 Feb 1750: David, 13 Nov 1748; Enos, 10 May
1755; Epheliat, 20 Apr 1772; Gideon, 07 Jun 1758; Hope, 23 Jul 1769; John, 08 Jan
1752; Jonathan, 15 Apr 1762; Joseph, 22 Mar 1764; Love, 15 Nov 1773; Lyddea,
28 Aug 1764; Mary, 30 Oct 1760; Sarah, 23 Jul 1769
Isaac, Esq & ....: William, 30 Jan 1814
Isae Webster & Sarah Downing; Giden, Dec 1716; Samell, 26 Mar 1714; Samell,
25 Aug 1715
Capt Jacob & Elisebath George: Ane, 25 Jun 1787; Benjamin, 04 Aug 1767; Jacob, 26
Jun 1791; John, 14 Apr 1782; Luce, 22 Mar 1777; Mary, 11 Dec 1772; Sarah, 05 Jan
1770; Susana, 18 Mar 1775; William, 25 Sep 1779:
Jere B & Lydia A: Hattie M, 04 Nov 1873
Jeremiah & Elisabeth Lad: Elisabeth, 28 Oct 1738; Elisabeth, 02 Nov 1730; John,
05 Feb 1732/3; John, 30 May 1736; Nathaniel, 03 May 1735
John A & Judith (Abby) Buswell: Laura, 06 Apr 1850
John & Ruth Clough: Hanah, 28 Aug 1746; Hanah, 30 Sep 1756; Humphery, 20 Mar
1740; Humphry, 14 Apr 1764; Isrel, Jul 1753; John, 10 Sep 1744; Margret, 17 Jan
1732; Margret, 01 Dec 1735; Martha, 20 Nov 1737; Rebeacor, 10 Aug 1750; Ruth,
28 Aug 1733; Sarah, 17 Jan 1742; Stephen, 01 Jan 1754
John & Martha Carter; Hopey, 29 Apr 1774; Isaac, 24 Apr 1779;
Jacob, b 20 Jul 1781; Lydia, 03 Jul 1789; Martha, 22 May 1787; Mary, 17 Dec   1772;
Miriam, 18 Sep 1776; Sarah, 12 Mar 1784
John L (E Kingston) & Mary A Prescott (Newton): Bertha L, 01 Feb 1885; Harold
Prescott, 15 Jun 1893; Helen Lillian, 27 Sep 1895; Walter Everett, 22 Dec 1886
Jonathan & Elisezebath Sleper; Elisabeth, 07 Mar 1729; Elisebath, 22 Aug 1737;
John, 09 Mar 1740; Joseph, 07 Mar 1729
Jonathan & Nancy York; Elvira J, 28 Oct 1844; Mary Jane, 19 Mar 1847
Joseph & Sarah Long; Albert Merce, 15 Oct 1846; Emily F, 16 Oct 1842; LaForrest,
24 Jul 1858
Joshua & Abigal; Joshua, 03 May 1729
Judah Davies (Webster): Jonathan Webster, 08 Jul 1757
Levi B & .....: Fredrick N, 01 Jun 1870
Samuell & Dirrethy Staniel: Burnam, 08 May 1761; Burnnum, 18 Oct 1740; Elisabeth,
11 Jan 1745; Elisebeth, 08 Mar 1756; Joseph Staniel, 02 Apr 1754; Rachiel, 17 Feb
1747; Rachiel, 07 Dec 1751; Sammel, 01 Jun 1749; Sarah, 02 Jan 1742
Samuell & Elizabeth Burnnum: David, 30 Sep 1738; Dirrethy, 10 Sep 1738; Sarah,
20 Nov 1734
Thomas & Sarrah: Abygail, 15 Apr 1706; Benionnan, 24 Aug 1701; Elizabeth, 11 Jan
1710; Sammell, 03 Apr 1708
Thomas & Mary Greely: Alies, 10 Jan 1724; Elizabeth, 27 Mar 1718; Martha, 16 Jun
1722; Mary, 31 Mar 1719; Merian, 08 Aug 1729; Sarah, 31 Mar 1719
Thomas & Juda Noyse: Judah, 07 Jun 1741; Levi, 20 Feb 1742; Sarah, 12 Oct 1839
William & Polly Davis: Catherine, 15 Mar 1806; Jacob, 09 Jun 1799; John, 03 Mar
1801; Samuel, 13 Mar 1804; William, 08 Sep 1809
W. M. (Kingston) & Cora (Kingston): Female, 04 Sep 1888

WEED: David & Abigal Judkins: Abigal, 23 Sep 1750; Anna, 15 Aug 1762; Benjamin,
03 Nov 1767; David, 24 Jun 1748; Elihaj, 30 Jul 1744; Jonathan, 18 May 1753;
Joseph, 23 Mar 1760; Samuel, 24 Jul 1746; William, 14 Apr 1765
WELCH: George W (Wilmot)& Mary Susan Keezer (Hampstead): George Norris, 29 Dec
1895; Mary Jane, 09 Sep 1900; Walter M, 27 Dec 1888; William, 08 Jan 1899
Joseph & Debrah Scribner: Benimas, 20 Sep 1739; Samuel, 26 Jun 1742
Philep & Sarah Wolsford: Sarah, 13 Mar 1739
Samell & Mary: Abigaiell, 07 Mar 1724/5; Benjamen, 13 Jan 1706/7; David, 30 Jun
1720; Jabbatha, 10 Mar 1708/9; Martha, Feb 1712/13; Mary, 20 Jan 1717/18; Philip,
08 Jul 1715
Sammel & Elener Clough: Elenor, 30 Nov 1752; Reuben, 15 Feb 1740; Ruben, 13 Sep
1750; Samuel, 13 Dec 1748
Thomas & Elisebath Prese (Pressy): Amos, 28 Feb 1767; Arklos, 05 Jun 1764;
Deberah, 22 Jun 1762; Moses, 11 Jan 1754; Thomas, 08 Mar 1755
WELS: Philip & Mary: Dorathy, 28 Jul 1742
WELSH: Joseph & Debrah Scribner: Geniman, 20 Nov 1735; Joseph, 20 Feb 1733; Moses,
08 Jun 1731; Thomas, 13 Oct 1727; Thomas, 13 Oct 1729
WEST: Andrew J & Hattie Winslow: Female, 16 Jan 1869
Daniel A (Haverhill,Ma) & Dora E Seaver (Kingston): Fred C, 04 Mar 1896; Mary
Abbie, 26 Aug 1894; Nellie Sophronia, 31 Jan 1892; Ralph B, 09 Nov 1901
Fred F (Haverhill,Ma) & Flora Mabel Pinkham (Gloucester,Ma): Charles Henry, 12 Jun
1896; Elsie Veala, 12 Jun 1898; Owen Earl, 08 Dec 1901
Walter S (Kingston) & Ruth H Nason (Kingston): Chester, 07 Jun 1894; Nellie Mary,
08 Sep 1892; Will B, 18 May 1896
Walter & Philena: Nathan A, 19 Feb 1877
WHICHER: Wiliam & Phebe Moirel: Abigel, 30 Jul 1745: I saac, 03 Feb 1737; Ruben,
15 May 1740; Ruben, 29 Nov 1741
WHIPPLE: George E (Kingston) & Mary F Knight (Bideford,Me): Ruth E, 01 Apr 1894
Sanford & Eliabeth: Female Child, 28 Oct 1875; Female Child, 08 Feb 1882
WHITE: John (Portland,Me) & Mary (Lowell,Ma): Male, 15 Jul 1889
WHITTIER: Charles B (Wolfboro) & Susie H Robinson(Kingston): Charles Walter: 22 Nov
1896; Male, 11 Oct 1897
Charles W (Danville) & Lilla May Page (Poland,Me): Lewis Byron, 03 Dec 1889
Jacob & .....: Female (stillborn), 20 Jul 1870
WINSLEY: Sammell (Winslow) & Catern: Hannah, 28 Nov 1710
WILSON: Luther J & Mary E Williams: Amy, 27 Jan 1886
WILSON: Luther J (Kingston) & Mattie J Stevens (Kingston): Bernice Chase, 24 Mar 1896
WINSLO: Elisha (Winslow) & Mary Sleeper: Berirnais, 10 Feb 1728; Cattarn, 08 Nov 1738;
Elisabeth, 28 Aug 1747; Haner, 05 Apr 1741; Jonathan, 14 Feb 1730; Mary, 13 Dec
1732; Sammell, 18 May 1726; Zebeulen, 01 Jun 1734; Zebulan, 30 Aug 1744
WINSLOW: Benjamin & Mary Clough: Abbiah, 16 Aug 1770; Elisha, 05 Jun 1766; Mary,
29 Oct 1767
Ephraim & Hannah Colcord: Anna, 17 Sep 1759; Bartholamu, 04 Oct 1757; Hitte,
18 Apr 1755; Lida, 07 Mar 1766; Mary Calcord, 10 Jan 1771; Meriah, 14 Mar 1762
George & Mary; ----, 21 Mar 1851

Horace G (Kingston) & Eldora E Nason (Kingston): Foster William, 01 Jun 1899; Hazel L, 26 Jun 1902; Gladys Alberta, 13 Nov 1896

Jacob & Tryphena Severance; Jacob, Jr, 24 Sep 1779

John & Elisabeth French; Elisabeth, 14 Sep 1764; Hannah, 08 Jul 1768; John, 28 Oct 1774; Martha, 11 Feb 1766; Mary, 11 Feb 1766; Nathaniel, 08 Sep 1778; Sarah, 30 Dec 1776

John, Jr & Polly Webster: Eliza, 16 Feb 1808; Lucy, 13 Sep 1805; Nancy, 26 Sep 1796; Samuel Spofford, 16 Jun 1810; William, 25 Dec 1800

Samuell & Jean French: Martha, 17 May 1751

Samuell, Jr & Phaba Buswell: Hannah, 23 Jul 1764; John, 17 Oct 1769; Samuell, 08 Jan 1767

Samuel M & Julia Merrows: Anna Belle, 08 Oct 1884; Male Child, 07 Jan 1877

William & Eliza A Silloway: Female Child, 16 Aug 1870; Horace, 15 Jul 1872; Male Child, 22 Dec 1877; Male Child, 28 Oct 1875

William & Polly Severance: Caroline A, 06 Jun 1846; Edward, 09 Sep 1848; George, 13 Apr 1820; Harriet, 03 Nov 1840; James, 10 Mar 1838; John T, 15 Jul 1824; Martha, 06 Feb 1828; Mary J, 28 Oct 1831; Samuel H, 26 Mar 1834; Samuel M, 14 Apr 1844; Sarah, 08 Jun 1836; William, 22 Aug 1829

WOODMAN: Frank A (Kingston) & Edith Kendall (Fremont): Female,17 Aug 1888; Male, 02 May 1886; Marion E, 11 Jan 1896; Willard D, 28 Aug 1893

Joshua & Eunis: Benjamin, 18 Oct 1759; David, 04 Dec 1747; Elisabeth, 04 Dec 1756; Eunis, 18 May 1736; Hanah, 08 Oct 1750; Jonathan, 25 Jul 1746; Joseph, 27 Mar 1749; Joshua, 14 Dec 1736; Mary, 30 Mar 1755; Moses, 25 Mar 1743; Samuel, 19 Nov 1744; Sarah, 28 Jun 1752

Joshua, Jr & Hannah Blasdel; Hannah, 10 Feb 1789; John, 06 Apr 1784; Judeth, 10 Sep 1777; Nathan, 23 Aug 1780; Nathan, 12 Aug 1789

Left. Samuel & Juduth French: Daniel, 19 Aug 1779; Elihn, 20 Jun 1797; Joshua, 18 Aug 1777; Judeth, 16 Sep 1794; Nathan, 07 Dec 1789; Polly, 14 Mar 1792; Samuel, 21 Jan 1786; Sarah, 25 Jul 1782

WORTH: Joseph & Ane Stanyan: Lyda, 09 Mar 1753

YORK: Joseph W (E Kingston) & Ada R Chaff (Buckingham, Eng): Helen Elizabeth, 26 Jan 1897

YOUNG: Daniel & Haner Loverin: Abigal, 13 Jan 1747/8: Anna, 09 Nov 1735; Daniel, 21 Jan 1742/3; David, 13 Jul 1746; Elizabeth, 21 Jan 1744/5; Haner, 25 Dec 1740; Love, 11 Jan 1736; Samuel, 26 Nov 1738

Daniel & Mary J Page: M Etta,16 Aug 1856; John M, 06 Apr 1842; Nellie D,06 Dec 1846

John, Jr & Merriam Sawyer: John, Sep 1758

John & Sarah Curnaham: Aron, 18 Aug 1743; Aron, Feb 1733; Giddeon, 11 Oct 1734; Giddeon, 29 Apr 1738; Isriel, 15 Sep 1744; John, 18 Dec 1730; Moses, 05 Jan 1739; Moses, Feb 1733; Nathaniel, 22 Nov 1746; Sarah, 28 Feb 1732; Sarah, 01 Oct 1741; Stephen, 09 May 1736

John & Doriety Sayer: Heseciah, 03 Mar 1754; Martha, 29 May 1756; Ruth, 17 Aug 1752

John, Jr & Merriam Sawyer: Joseph, 21 Jan 1754; Sarah, Apr 1756

Jonathan & Mary Loverin: Abigal, 29 May 1749; Doraty, 27 Apr 1751; Hezekiah, 31 Oct 1736; Jonana, 30 Nov 1753; Jothern, 01 Oct 1756; Mary, 06 Jan 1748; Mary, 06 Jan 1748; Nathanal, 11 Apr 1744

Joseph & Batta Carr: Jonna, 07 Sep 1760

Joseph, Jr & Sarah Brown: Jonna, 23 Dec 1747; Joseph, 20 Jun 1749

Stephen & Dority Blaisdel: Mary, 01 Aug 1756; Sarah, 05 Mar 1754; Stephen, 09 May 1761

MARRIAGES
1694 - 1900

ABBOT: Peter (Poplin) & Miriam Smith, 11 Jun 1793
ABBOTT: Peter & Elisabath Gilmon
    Peter (Kingston) & Phoebe Sprat (Deerfield), -- Mar 1782
ABRAHAMS: William(Kingston) & Anna Severance, 19 Apr 1796
ADAMS: Henry(Newbury, Ma) & Hannah Severance (Kingston), 05 May 1799
ALEXANDER: Samuel & Dority Fifield, 04 Jul 1763
ALLEN: Samuel (Kingston) & Jemima Clough, 24 Jun 1805
APPLETON: Rev Joseph (Brookfield) & Mary Hook (Kingston), 15 Jun 1777
ARNOLD: Warren H (Danville/19)& Olla M Ladd (Danville/16), 24 Dec 1895
    (John M Arnold/ Annie A James)(Josiah Ladd/Sarah Chellis)
ASHTON: Edward G (Lynn,Ma/23) & M Josephine Senter (Amesbury/17), 22 Mar 1900
    (Arthur Ashton/M Eva Watson)(Frank Senter/Mary E Davis)
ATWOOD: Moses (Kingston) & Sukey Gale, 21 Jul 1805
AVERILL: John Francis & Mary Francis Davis, 13 Mar 1879
    (Eben Averill/Julia A Knox)(Henry Davis)
AVERY: Alfred J (Kingston/21)& Arrie Belle Nason (Kingston/24), 18 Oct 1899
    (Frank Avery/Addie M Davis)(Albion Nason/Anna Page)
    Charles H & Mary E Eastman, 11 Nov 1871
    (Joseph Avery/Elizabeth)(Nelson Eastman/ Tabatha)
AVOY: James A W & Nellie C Williams, 07 Sep 1868
AYERS: Daniel (Plastow) & Nancy Day, 22 Feb 1806
BACHELDER: Amos (East Kingston) & Sally Stocker, 11 Sep 1798
    Ebenezener & Dorety Boynton, 01 Feb 1733
    Elisha & Theodate Smith, 18 Apr 1751
    Josiah & Abigel Lampriel, 07 Feb 1728
    Nathan & Mary   ------
    Phienes & Elizabeth Gilmon, 17 Jan 1727
BACHELOR: Benjamin (Kensington) & Dorothy Sleeper (Kingston), 17 Apr 1787
BADGER: Benjamin (Kingston) & Sally Wadleigh, 04 Apr 1799
    Justin W & Nancy R Collins, 13 Jun 1871
    (Stephen Badger)   (Levi Collins)
    Stephen & Doley Webster, -- Apr 1770
    William & Elizabeth Dearborn, 07 Jun 1812
BAGLEY: Thomas W & Myra C Primrose, 22 Jul 1880
    (Thomas Bagley/Anna N....)(Edwin Primrose/Hanna P....)
BAILEY: Jeremiah (Derry) & Harriet N Magoon (Kingston), 30 Dec----
BAKIE: Daniel J & Nellie J Sanborn, 17 Feb 1887
    (James Bakie/Elizabeth Alexander)(William Sanborn/Mary A ....)
    William A (Boston,Ma/40) & Flora A Gordon (Danville/37), 25 Jan 1896 (D)
    (James Bakie/Elizabeth Alexander)(Levi G Gordon/Ann Clifford)
BALL, Albert H (Haverhill,Ma/30) & Lillian W Glover (Exeter/17), 04 Sep 1895 (N)
    (William H Ball/Mary F Sweetser) (Andrew Glover/Ida Morse)

BARBER: Robert & Penelope Hunt, 23 Mar 1743
      Robert & Abigal Bean, 09 Oct 1759
BARNARD: Steven & Mary Colins, 06 Sep 1743
BARNEY: George (Dover/22) & Nancy M Smith(Rochester/22), 23 Oct 1851
BARRY: Eben C, & Laura F Prescott, 12 Feb 1883
      James E (E. Kingston/19) & Sarah R Eaton(E Kingston/18), 02 Sep 1856
BARSTOW: Joshua(Exeter) & Hannah Webster (E Kingston), 15 Nov 1804
BARTELEE: John & Mary Quimbe, 12 Jan 1742/3
BARTLET, Dr Josiah & Maray, 15 Jan 1754
BARTLETT: Albert E (Brentwood/27) & Grace M Smith (Brentwood/28), 23 Dec 1896(B)
      (Francis C Bartlett /Mary A Rowe) (Leroy S Smith/Lizzie A Gordon)
      David (Kingston) & Polly (Dolly) Young, -- May 1804
      Dr Ezra (Warren) & Hannah Gale (Kingston), 30 Jan 1799
      Dr Levi (Kingston) & Sally Hook, 06 Nov 1791
      Ebenezer (Kingston) & Judeth Colbey (Newtown), 08 Aug 1805
      Enoch P (Kingston) & Mary E Crosbey (Kingston), 03 Sep 1852
      Isaac (Kingston)& Joanna Young, 05 Jan 1793
      Jeremiah(Kingston) & Sarah Gold (Newton), 08 Mar 1792
      Joseph B (Kingston/21) & Sarah A Philbrick(Danville/16), 08 Nov 1854
      Joshua, Jr & Sarah Badger, -- Feb 1760
      Levi S(Kingston) & Aroline E Sanborn (Kingston), 03 Dec 184
      Moses (Deerfield) & Sarah Bartlet(Kingston), 01 Mar 1779
      Nathan & Jonnah Flanders, 15 Mar 1741
      Richard B (Kingston) & Martha Medora Stevens(Kingston), 26 Jan 1879
        (Richard R Bartlett/Sarah Fellows)(Samuel W Stevens/Harriet N Collins)
      Samuell (Gilmanton) & Dorothy Clemment (Hawke), 20 Feb 1803
      William & Sylvainal (Moore) Brown, 18 Jun 1870
        (Isaac Bartlett)   (Samuel Moore/ Sylvania R Lock)
      William J & Lettie M Crane, 07 Aug 1868
        (William Bartlett/Betsey Bean)(Gilman Crane /Adalin Dresser)
      William L (Newton/21) & Emma L Fellows (Brentwood/17), 07 Apr 1861
BASSET: Jay P & Sarah A (Morrill) Tilton, 16 Jul 1860
      (Samuel Bassett/Sarah A Cram)(John Morrill/Lydia Heath)
BASSETT: Amos H & Martha (Winslow) Webster, 09 Nov 1876
        (William Winslow/Mary)
      Dr Thomas & Miranda Spofford, 30 Dec 1828
BATCHELDER: George W & Hattie D Merrill, 05 Aug 1868
        (Edmund R Batchelder /Sarah)(William W Merrill/Harriett)
      John & Nellie F Sweat, 03 Mar 1878
        (Charles Batcheldier/Nancy Purrington)(Sanborn Sweat/Lucretia Tucker)
BEALS: George E (Haverhill,Ma/26) & Alice F Davis (Kingston/21), 28 Nov 1901
        (James H Beals/Emma C Bougdon)(Richard Davis/Harriet Stacy)
      James Henry & Ernessia Bragdon, 15 Jun 1868
        (Robert Beals/Ann)(Ivory Bragdon/Sarah)
BEAN: Daniel & Abigal Clifford, 04 Mar 1745

David A (Raymond/29) & Clara H Gibson(Fremont/23),19 Jun 1859
George W & Marilla J Prescott, 10 Sep 1874
   (Enoch Bean/Anna E)(Nancy Prescott)
George H & Nellie J Prescott, 28 Aug 1869
George W & Alice M French, 12 Apr 1892
   (George R Bean/Mary M French)(Elihu T French/Laura B Carr)
Hezekiah (Hawke) & Molly Tukesbery, 03 Apr 1792
James & Sarah Brady, -- Dec 1697
John P (Kingston)& Mehitable J Bartlett(Kingston), 16 Nov 1851
Joseph & Janer Davies, 16 Mar 1725
BEEDE: Beza (Kingston) & Judith Morgan, 18 Dec 1782
Earnest S (Fremont/21) & Alice S Towle(Chester/21), 16 Nov 1895
   (Phinias Beede/Nettie) (James W Towle/Sarah)
Fred S (Amesbury,Ma/20) & Allice Merrick (Sandown/20), 09 Nov 1902
   (Oscar Beede/Hannah Webster)(Andrew J Merrick/Abbie N Pierce)
Hezekiah & Hephzibah Smith, -- Jul 1747
Hezekiah & Judeth Gove, 12 Nov 1772
Jeremiah (E Kingston) & Hannah Crayton (Exeter), 12 Aug 1800
Joseph (Kingston) & Mary Jane Seaver (Kingston), 22 Oct 1848
Oscar, (E Kingston/20) & Hannah Webster (Kingston/20), 07 Apr 1873
Phineas B (Fremont/52) & Susie B Burley (Fremont/30), 14 Jun 1884
   (Horatio Beede) (Jeremiah Burley)
BEEN: Joseph & Meriam Folsom, 13 Nov 1734
BELDEN: Zachary T & Jennie Shelden, 28 Jan 1871
   (H W Belden)   (George Shelden)
BICKFORD: Henry (Rochester) & Huldah Bunker (Dover), 13 Jan 1803
BLAIR: Robert E (Halifax,N.S/26) & Catherine C Brown (Kingston/27), 01 Feb 1869
   (Abatha C Blair/Ellen Whitten)(Nathaniel Brown/Catherine Nichols)
BLAISDEL: Timothy & Johanah Stokman, 03 Jan 1744/5
BLAISDELL: George W(Haverhill,Ma/28) & Henrietta Smith(Chatham,Ma/20), 27 Sep 1864
   Josiah T(Danville/27) & Mary C Kelley(Danville/22), 23 Jan 1855
   Ralfe 3rd & Merream Rowel, 18 Oct 1748
BLAKE: Jonathan & Lucy Robinson(Exeter),18 Feb 1777
   Stevens (Hawke) & Hannah George, 21 Apr 1800
   Thomas H(Kensington/24) & Cynthia E Bachelder(E Kingston/22), 07 Apr 1857
BLASDEL: Henry (E Kingston) & Hannah Ross(Brentwood), 20 Dec 1778
BLASDIEL: Ebenezenr & Sarah Stockman, 19 Oct 1739
BLYE: Daniel H (Haverhill,Ma/24) & Ira M Nickett (Haverhill,Ma/15), 25 Feb 1888 (N)
   (Ezra Blye/Isamiah Murphy)(Mable Nickett/Hannah Towle)
BOOTMAN: Amos & Sarah Webster, 11 Jul 1745
BORROUGHS: George (Amesbury,Ma) & Sukey Patten (Kingston), 18 May 1802
BRADLEY: B Frank & Carrie A Davis, 01 Feb 1865
   William (B-Newton/Plastow) & Judeth Challis (Kingston), 15 Jan 1798
BRAGDON: George L (B-Milton) & Caroline H Rochmont (Kingston), 03 Mar 1864

Fred L (Brentwood/21) & Emma T Prescott (Kingston/21), 08 Feb 1895
    (Augustus Bragdon/Abbie E Bartlett)(John L Prescott/Roxy Sanborn)
Fred O (Haverhill,Ma/21) & Etta L Tucker (Kingston/18), 13 Nov 1881
    (Luther M Bragdon/Azellah H ...)(Otis S Tucker/Sarah E ...)
BREWER: David (B-Beverly,Ma) & Polly S Currier (E Kingston), 18 Aug 1859
BRICKETT: Joseph W (Kingston) & Sarah E Woods (Fremont), 17 Feb 1860
BROWN: Albert (Kingston)& Flora A Prescott (Kingston), 09 Feb ---
    Benjamin (Corrinth)& Mary Quimby (Hawke), 14 Feb 1790
    Daniel & Ruth Morrel, 18 Mar 1740
    Daniel (Poplin) & Abigail Gordon, 26 Dec 1792
    Edward Everett (Kingston/22) & Bertha B Furber (Kingston/18), 01 Jan 1893
    (Nathaniel G Brown/Peace Ann Chase)(John A Furber/Roxby Ann Collins)
    Ephraim(Poplin) & Hannah Marsh, 12 Mar 1802
    Hazen B (Chester/28) & Ella B Poore (Raymond/22), 17 Jun 1896
    (Freeman M Brown/Elizabeth McDuffee/)(Rufus H Poore/Abbie E Brown)
    James (Epsom) & Hannah Smith (E Kingston), 24 Dec 1789
    John (Poplin) & Mariah Gordon, 06 Mar 1793
    John, Jr (Poplin) & Mary Davis (Kingston), 12 Nov 1846
    Joseph & Elesebeth Sayer, 29 Dec 1757
    L Norris (Fremont) & Rose A Sawyer (Danville), 24 Nov 1864
    Dr. Simen & Hannah Young, 13 Mar 1729
    William C (Sandown/23) & Annie E Judkins (Kingston/24), 24 Dec 1871
    (Isaac Brown/Asshia Batchelder)(Simon B Judkins/Catherine Hoyt)
BROWNING: Welcome (Hopkinton,RI/22) & Lizzie M Hook (Exeter/20), 17 Aug 1872
    (Samuel R Browning/Mary...)(Charles Hook/Anna E ...)
BRYANT: William (Haverhill,Ma) & Elizabeth Judkins (Kingston), 12 Jan 1791
BURBANK: Hale (Brentwood) & Elizabeth (So Hampton), 23 Apr 1782
    Jonathan(Brentwood) & Ruth Gove, -- Apr 1789
BUSH: Burt A (No Brookfield/26) & Marion Sanborn (Kingston/25), 09 Jun 1897
    (Chas A Bush/Frances M Haskell)(John H Sanborn/Eveline Hatch)
BUSIEL: William & Juda Davies   (no date given)
BUSWEL: James & Elisebath Clough, 03 Feb 1761
    Samuel & Mary Winslow, 14 Jan 1755
    Simons & Catteren Been (Bean), 21 Jan 1741
    William & Abigel Thorn, 13 Jul 1731
BUSWELL: Albey C (Manchester/Danville/24) & Florence A Morse (Atkinson/Hampstead/20),
    02 Mar 1865
    David (Kingston) & Sarah Sanborn, 29 Apr 1796
    Daniel & Hannah Runnels, 04 Jul 1776
    John W (E Kingston/22) & Isabella S Genness (Newburyport/23), 31 Aug 1862
    Joseph (Hawke) & Lucy Quimby, 09 May 1793
    Samuel & Mary Worthen, (date unknown)
    William (Kingston) & Elizabeth Clark (Plaistow), 28 Dec 1839
BUTLER: Jack (Sandown) & Mary Daniels, 11 Apr 1791
BUZZEL: William & Elesabeth Wenslow, 27 Feb 1745/6

BUZZELL: Calob & Mary Badger, -- May 1760
CALCORD: Sammel & Elizabeth Folsom, 13 Sep 1704
CALEF: John & Jude Chalies, 24 Dec 1754
     John (Kingston) & Sally Hanson (Epping), 09 Oct 1805
     Joseph (Kingston)& Susanna Bachelder (E Kingston), 18 Jul 1792
     Joseph (Kingston) & Miriam Bartlett (Kingston), 28 Jun 1781
     Joseph (Kingston) & Molly Hook (Sandown), 23 Sep 1789
     Joseph & Hannah Pettingell, 30 Oct 1765
     Robert (Kingston) & Polly Sleeper, 26 May 1802
     Samuel & Mary Ann Berry, 1842
     Samuel (Kingston) & Patty Wiggin (Newmarket), 31 Dec 1795
     William & Lowis, (date unknown)
CALLE: Darbe & Sarah Honton, 01 Jan 1729
CAMIT: Silas & Cattern Judkins, 27 Nov 1746
CARLTON: ------ (Newton) & ..... Favour, 25 Feb 1804
CARNEY:William H (Amesbury,Ma/19) & Nina M Collins (Kingston/20), 28 Dec 1873
     (Michael Carney/Malvina Palmer)(Franklin N Heath/Maria C Austin)
     William H (Amesbury,Ma/21) & Eldora M Tucker (Kingston/17). 26 Feb 1896
     (Michael Carney/Malvina Palmer)(Jeremiah C Tucker/Cora M Gilman)
CARR: Moody (Poplin) & Ruth Hudson (Kingston), 14 Feb 1791
     Sanders & Sarah Page, 26 Nov 1759
     Sanders & Elizebeth Pick, 20 Dec 1738
CARTER: Bagley (E Kingston) & Ruth Bagley(Newtown), 25 Jan 1802
     Elmer C (Kingston/21) & Adda N Davis (Kingston/19), 23 Dec 1878
     (Charles C Carter/Mary B Page)(O.H. Davis/Jenette Crane)
     Ephraim (So Hampton) & Martha Sever (Kingston), 08 Sep 1796
     Jeremiah L (Kingston/19) & Margaret Grout (Barney River/20), 19 Nov 1861
     John (Newtown) & Polly Whittier, 04 Sep 1800
     Orin D (B-Amesbury, Ma/Newton/22) & Sarah C Pierce (E Kingston/17), 01 Jan 1862
     Ralph H (E Kingston/20) & Sarah E Heath (Merrimac,Ma/16), 17 Jul 1899
     (George F Carter/Mary E Webster)(John B Heath/Mary E Currier)
     Richard W (Kingston) & Rebecca Farnum(Kingston), 05 Dec 1846
     Thomas (Kingston) & Dolly Moses, 15 Mar 1792
CASTER: Enoch (Newton) & Sarah Pierce (So Hampton), 25 Jun 1795
CHADWELL: Harris (Lynn,Ma/38) & Carrie F Marshall (Kingston/36), 06 Oct 1896
     (Cyrus Chadwell/Hannah Putnam)(Jesse P Marshall/Sarah F Nichols)
CHALIES: Timothey & Elisebeth Brown, 18 Nov 1761
CHALLIS: Christopher (E Kingston) & Lydia Blasdel, 06 Dec 1781
     Ezekiel & Elizabeth Challis, -- Dec 1784
CHAMBERLAIN: Harry (Strafford/21) & Maud B Hoyt (Peabody,Ma/26), 03 Feb 1901
     (Charles Chamberlain/Abbie Fifield)(John Hoyt/Nancy B Strout)
CHASE: Abraham (Haverhill,Ma/34) & Katie M (Hatie?)Jennings (Haverhill,Ma/19),
     28 Aug 1861
     Amos & Hannah Hook, 04 Jul 1827
     Charles (Kingston) & Mary Calef (Kingston), 19 Oct 1779

Edward (Brentwood) & Mary Sleeper, 25 Feb 1790
Green(Gilmantown) & Hannah Gove (Kensington),18 Feb 1790
James (Poplin) & Harriet Smith, 17 Mar 1804
John (Deerfield) & Hannah Sanborn (Brentwood), 15 Dec 1794
Paul (Newtown) & Polly Currier, -- Oct 1804
CHELLIS: Clark D & Mary A Curtis, 22 Mar 1876
CHENEY: Albert N (Kingston/28) & Mary L Silloway (Kingston/17), 12 Mar 1880
    (Nathaniel Cheney/Mary E Hoyt)(Benjamin Silloway)
    Edward L & Hannah M Tucker (Kingston), 01 Apr 1869
    (Nathaniel D Cheney/Mary E Hoyt)(Moses Tucker/Hannah)
    Edward L (Danville/44) & Nancy R (Strout) Hoyt(Millbridge,Me/36), Feb 1889(D)
    Edward (Kingston) & Sarah (Sally) Dearbon, m 12 Jul 1812 (Pelham)
    William A (Kingston/38) & Estella A Page (Kingston/16), 15 May 1886
    (Nathaniel D Cheney/Mary E Hoyt) (Ezra Page/Augusta Shaw)
CHOAT: Benjamin (Kingston) & Jane Bradbury (Kingston), 15 Oct 1777
    Jonathan & Elizebeth Moodey, 02 May 1738
CHOATE: Beniamen & Abigaill Burnnum, 12 Jun 1707
    Benjamin & Ruth Edwards, 22 Dec 1741
    Joseph L (Montville,Me/21) & Hattie Z Webster (E Kingston/17), 10 Jan 1876
    (John C Choate/Mary A Davis) (Augustus Webster/.... Buswell)
CILLEY: Benjamin L (B-Kingston/Andover/48) & Mrs Emily Gilman (Kingston/27),
    28 Oct 1860
    Clarence E (Haverhill,Ma/25) & Annie L Towle (Kingston/20), 25 Dec 1879
    (Andrew J Cilley & Susan Bartlett)(Alfred Towle & Susan M Gale)
    George B (Kingston/32) & Lela Bartlett (Kingston/20), 02 Jan 1897
    (Benjamin D Cilley/Emma J Severance)(Francis C Bartlett & Mary A Rowe)
    Joseph C (Hopkinton/25) & Catherine Davis (Kingston/ 21), 26 Oct 1854
CLARK: Daniel O (Kingston/20) & Mary E Webster (Kingston/19), 17 Aug 1857
    Greenleaf (Brentwood) & Bettey Stevens, 04 Sep 1794
    John T (Kingston/22) & Sarah E Titcomb (E Kingston/22), 10 Dec 1863
    Simeon & Johannah Eastman, 1825
    Simeon P (Exeter/23) & M Etta Fellows (Kingston/25), 06 Aug 1890 (E)
    (John T Clark/Sarah E Clark)(Samuel D Fellows/Lucy A Fellows)
    Walter S (Kingston/22) & Abbie A Sanborn (Lawrence,Ma/24), 17 Jan 1877
    (Amos Clark/Jerusha Judkins)(George W Sanborn/Sarah Badger)
CLARKE: Ward & Mary Frost, 21 Nov 1727
CLEMENT: Obediah & Sarah Flanders, 20 Dec 1733
CLEMMENT: Ebenezer (Hawke) & Sally Brown, 14 Nov 1805
CLIFFORD: Benjamin (Dorchester) & Nancy Currier (So Hampton), 17 Nov 1803
    Daniel (Kingston) & Clarinda Bartlett (Kingston), 29 Dec 1832 (S)
    David, Jr (Brentwood) & Elisabeth Griffing (Kingston), 13 Mar 1786
    John (Brentwood) & Hannah Gliden, 18 May 1786
    Joseph & Sarah French, 13 Apr 1710

Joseph & Lydea Perkens, 02 Jan 1715/16
William & Abigal Gove, 21 Apr 1746
William (Poplin) & Rachel Rundlett (Epping),05 Jun 1791
William & Sarah Towle, 22 Jan 1734
William (Kingston) & Elizabeth Watson (Kingston), 09 Jul 1783
CLIFORD: Isaac & Sarah Taylor (date unknown)
Joseph & Mary Healey, 28 Dec 1737
CLOUGH: Benjamin & Elisabeth Smith, 20 Mar 1747
Benjamin & Mary Sanborn, 01 May 1753
Benjamin (Kingston) & Joanna Young (Kingston), 06 May 1779
Corneilus & Ann Evens (Salisbury, Ma), 03 Sep 1718
Corneilus & Joannah Sanborn, 13 Jan 1714
Daniel & Sarah Baker, 30 Jun 1743
Elisha & Mary Welch, 02 Oct 1740
Joseph & Mary Jennes, 11 Aug 1708
Obdeiah & Sarah Wadleh, 17 Feb 1746/7
COLBEY: Daniel (Kingston) & Elizabeth Gilman (Kingston),01 Mar 1779
Rev Zacchens (Pembroke) & Mary Calef (Kingston), 11 Dec 1780
Simeon (Newton) & Polly Webster, 17 Nov 1801
Timothy (Newton) & Abigail Currier, 19 Feb 1803
COLBY: Joseph & Sarah Thuriel, 27 Mar 1760
Moody L (Kingston) & Nancy Chase (Kingston), 03 Oct 1844
COLCOARD: Ebenezener & Haner Fellows, 10 Dec 1720
COLCORD: Capt Daniel (Kingston) & (Mrs) Elizabeth Philbrick (Kingston), 03 Dec 1845
Edward & Mary Gording, 24 Nov 1714
Elihu T (Kingston) & Lucy A Frost (Andover), 12 Nov 1848
Frank E (Exeter/38) & Luella Thompson (Newton/29), 19 Aug 1891
(William H Colcord/Frances E Pike)(Dustin Thompson/Sarah Goodwin)
John (Brentwood) & Lydia Morrill (Brentwood), 10 May 1787
Monroe (Kingston) & Hannah Webster (Kingston), 30 Jun 1846
Samuell & Mehetabel Lad, 28 Dec 1732
Samuel A (Kingston/21) & Mary E Marsh (Amesbury/18),05 Aug 1871
(S W Colcord) (Noah Marsh/Roxey Marsh)
COLINGS: Ebenezener & Affier Meriel, -- Mar 1726
COLLINS: Andrew J (Kingston) & Lucindia Pollard (Raymond), 20 Mar 1859
Charles S (Plaistow/18) & Nina M Heath (So Hampton/15), 03 Jul 1888 (P)
(Andrew J Collins/Anna M Collins)(Franklin N Heath/Maria C Austin)
Elmer A (Newton, Jct/21) & Susie Anna Nason (Kingston/14),19 Aug 1891(N/J)
(Andrew J Collins/Anna M Collins)(Etta Nason)
Frank P (Danville/22) & Sarah H Winslow (Kingston/22), 27 Nov 1884
(Perley Collins/R Jane Collins)(William Winslow/Eliza Winslow)
George W (24) & Maria P Hardy (17), 05 Aug 1855
Henry P (Westfield,Ma/22) & Edna N Hanchette (Westfield,Ma/22),14 Feb 1893*
(John W Collins/Caroline W Collins)(Lewis Hanchette/Augusta Towle) *Westfield,Ma
Israel (Kingston) & Polly Pollard, -- Apr 1804

Jabez (Hampstead)& Olive R Eastman (Hawke),01 Oct 1761
John W (Hampstead/28) & Caroline W Collins (Kingston/20), 19 Dec 1868
   (Hezekiah Collins/Sarah Howe)(Laban Collins/Rachael Hunt)
Joseph & Sarah Bagley, 17 Jan 1760
Joseph (Hawke) & Polly Derburn, 14 Feb 1792
Laban & Rachel Hunt, 27 Nov 1833
Laban (Hampstead) & Dolly Jones (Hawke), 28 May 1795
Leon P (29) & Mary E Blaisdell (29), 14 Jan 1882
   (Laban Collins/Rachell Hunt)(David Blaisdell)
Leon P (Kingston/22) & Ellen Winslow (E Kingston/22), 15 Mar 1874
   (Laban Collins/Rachal Hunt)(George Winslow/Mary Hoyt)
Norris (Kingston/21) & Emma J Stevens (Boston, Ma/37), 21 Nov 1879
   (Sheppard Collins/Julia Judkins)(William J Stevens/Mary J Stevens)
Samuel (Hampstead) & Polly Blake (Hawke) , 24 Dec 1795
COOMBS: John (B/Effingham/32)& Martha C Davis (Kingston/35), 11 Mar 1860
CONNOR: John Sanborn (Cincinnati,Oh/27) & Anna Levietta Bartlett (Kingston/20), 1871
   (Phinias S Conor/Eliza A) (Levia S Bartlett/Caroline E Sanborn)
CORSER: Thomas (Boscawen) & Mary Downing (Kingston), 22 Aug 1782
COSER: John & Jean Nichels, -- Sep 1742
COULD: Isaac H (Newton) & Luella J Stevens (Kingston), 24 Mar 1845
CRAFT: Samuel & Hannah Hoit, before 1839
CRAFTS: John S (Kingston/20) & Susan J Carter (Newton/20), 28 Jun 1859
CRAM: Joseph (E Kingston) & Elizabeth Judkins (Kingston), 09 Sep 1790
CRANE: Gilman (Washington/70) & Hannah (Webster)Colcord (Kingston/64),19 Dec 1888
   (Jesse Crane/Susan Clark)(John Webster)
CREM: Frank H (Hampton Falls/22) & Carrie T Kelley (Amesbury,Ma/19), 30 Jun 1876
   (Benjamin Crem/Elisabeth Smith)(Barkinson Kelley/Annie E Barnes)
CROSBE: Thomas & Marie Colman, 09 Nov 1730
CROSBY: John F (B Haverhill,Ma/21) & Mary J Collins (B Danville/18), 29 Nov 1863
CROZIER: William J (Dublin,Ire/37) & Mary Norfolk (Kingston/36), 14 Jun 1902
   (John Crozier/May Broe)(William Norfold/Christina Galloupe)
CURRIER: Aaro (Newton) & Elizabeth Blasdel (E Kingston), 08 Nov 1786
   Charles M (E Kingston/22) & Alma F Chase (E Kingston/25), 16 Sep 1884
      (Ezra M Currier/Betsey Gale)(Amos C Chase/Hattie Draper)
   David (Newton) & Phebe Noyes, 04 Apr 1798
   Elijah R (Newton/23) & Clara Crane (Kingston/21), 05 May 1869
      (Thomas Currier) (Gilman Crane)
   Ephraim (South Hampton) & Elizabeth Flanders, 25 Jun 1795
   Capt. Ezra (E Kingston) & Mary Philbrick (Hawke), 09 Jun 1800
   John (E Kingston) & Polly Morrill, 04 Aug 1805
   John H (Amesbury,Ma) & Olive A Dow, 25 Mar 1845
   John P (E Kingston/23) & Sarah J Currier (Newton/19), 20 Dec 1851
   John W (E Kingston/27) & Sarah L Rundlett (Kingston/24),13 Jan 1861
   Moses (E Kingston) & Polly Carter, 13 Aug 1805

M.P. (Newton/18) & ....Gilmore (Newton/42) .....
  (Thomas Currier)(Thomas B Currier/Mary Putnam)
  Philip (Newton/25) & Sarah Brigham (Wayne,Me/24), 28 Nov 1851
CURTIS: Samuel N (Kingston) & Melissa A Collins (Kingston), 22 Feb 1844
DALTY: Ernest A (Heckmondwike,Eng/24) & Alice M Marshall (Kingston/26), 12 May 1897
  (Joseph Daltry/Anne Johnson)(Samuel C Marshall/Adeline Hurd)
DANIELS: Joseph & Margaret Bexor, 29 Aug 1805
DARLING: Benjamin & Hannah Clark, 08 Mar 1758
  Daniel & Suzanne Webster, 27 Dec 1733
  John & Mary Sawyer, 02 Mar 1758
DAVID: Hiram F (20) & Annie F Cheney (16), 26 Dec 1868
  (David S Davis/Sally S Frehawk)(Dearborn Cheney/Elizabeth Hoyt)
DAVIS: Albert H (Durham/29) & Addie L Jones (Nottingham/21), 17 Sep 1900 (D/O)
  (Levi Davis/Lucy A Bassett)(David Jones)
  Amos & Abigail Thompson, 25 Dec 1805
  Amos K (Kingston/21) & Mary L Severance (Kingston/23), 06 Oct 1861
  Benjamin & Alice Silloway, 30 Jan 1806
  Charles (Kingston/20) & Sarah E Hunt (Kingston/17), 07 Oct 1855
  Charles, (Kingston/29) & Caroline Gilman (Nottingham/Newton/28), 01 Sep 1864
  Daniel L (Kingston/23) & Susan H Holland (Ireland/Amesbury/16), 21 Sep 1862
  George (Kingston) & Sarah Larkin (Durham), 02 Oct 1842
  George W (Kingston/21) & Carrie A Winslow (Durham/Kingson/16), 22 Sep 1861
  Henry (Kingston/23) & Sarah E Kimball (Danville/19), 13 Nov 1856
  John P, Jr (Newburyport,Ma/36) & Mary J Severance (Kingston/25), 14 Jun 1894
    (John P Davis/Mary A Davis)(Benjamin Severance/Patience Severance)
  John & Hanah Wadlah, 07 Apr 1748
  John (Kingston) & Hannah Gooding (E Kingston), -- Mar 1803
  Leveda J (Newton/20) & Isella Huse (Kingston/17), 03 Aug 1889
    (Amos H Davis/Mary Davis)(William Huse/Lucy A Huse)
  Lewis H (Newton) & Roxena S Nason (Kingston), 14 Sep 1887
    (Amos K Davis/Mary L Collins)(Nathan Nason/Sarah W Page)
  Malachi (Gilmanton) & Anna Currier (E Kingston), 10 Feb 1793
  Nathaniel (Exeter) & Anna Falls (Kingston), 14 Dec 1797
  Nehemiah (Kingston) & Mary Clough, 29 Oct 1785
  Peter F (45) & Julia A Trass (41), 30 Mar 1880
    (Daniel Davis/Polly S Frohawk)
  Philip & Meriam Webster, 15 Feb 1749
  Rev J.E. (Gardner,Me) & Sophia S Judkins (Lawrence, Ma), 27 Jun 1849
  Samuel & Dorrethy Hadly, 19 Nov 1746
  Thomas (53) & Irene F Goodwin (27), 20 Apr 1898
    (Amos Davis/Nancy H Whittier)(Eliza Ann Goodwin)
  Thomas & Miriam Martin, 15 Nov 1804
  Zeekel & Sarah England, 09 Sep 1755
DEARBON: Joseph (Exeter) & Elizabeth L Shaw, 10 Mar 1844

DEARBORN: Andrew J (Portland,Me/40) & Mary E Dudley (Kingston/34), 21 May 1880
    (Abrah Dearborn) (Freman Dudley)
    James P (Danville/22) & Octavia S Batchelder (E Kingston/23), 08 Mar 1864
    John H (Candia/24) & Lilla B Towle (Kingston/20), 25 Dec 1879
    (John C Dearborn/Mary Griffin)(Darius Towle/Hannah M Diamond)
DENT: John & Sarah Sanborn, 27 Aug 1741
DENTT: Thomas & Achaicus ...., 10 Oct 1714
DERBORN: Henry (Hawke) & Molly Williams, 21 Mar 1791
DIAMOND: Melburn J & Emma M Davis, - 09 Sep 1880
DIMOND: Israel & Mary Chandler, 06 Dec 1748
    Israel & Mary Philbrick, 04 Mar 1756
DOAK: John (Newton/22) & Augusta L Smith (Fremont/23), 26 Jun 1864
DOHERTY: Frank (Ireland/Georgetown,Ma/23) & Mary Ann Perry (Newbury/23),12 Aug 1862
DOLIVER: Thomas H (Marblehead,Ma/60 & Elsie A Marden (Deerfield/51), 29 Nov 1877
    (Thomas Doliver)(Suel Marden/Sarah Avery)
DOMINICK: Alphonse (Great Falls/29) & Mary J Collins (Kingston/16), 31 Aug 1894
    (John B Dominick/Mary Browe)(Elbridge G Collins/Josephine Robinson)
DORONING: Leverett C (Kingston/32) & Laura B Packard (Haverhill,Ma/16), 25 Jun 1902
    (John N Dorning/Ellen Clark)(Albert E/ Orphie L Irving)
DORR: John W (Bradford,Ma/21) & Mary L Everley (Fremont/18), 21 Aug 1884
    (James W Dorr/Almira C Marble)(Eben Bouley/Sarah E McDaniels)
DOW: Amasa & Lydia Robey, 14 Aug 1729
    Amasa & Hannah Buswell, 16 May 1750
    Leslie E (Palermo,Me/25) Lucy A Hasson (Alma,Me/18), 10 Jun 1900
    (Moses Dow/Annie Evens)(Edward Hasson/Inez Thayer)
DOWNING: Levritt C (Kingston/25) & Ethel M Durgin (Kingston/16), 19 Jun 1895
    (John N Downing/Ellen R Clark)(George W Durgin/Mary J Williams)
DUBURN: Nathaniel & Sarah Webster, 29 Jun 1789
DUDLEY: John W (Brentwood/34) & Renda S Thyng (Brentwood/30), 04 Feb 1864
    Josiah (Brentwood)& Sarah Robinson(Brenwood), 19 Jul 1795
DUNN: S.Burton (Danville/23) & Emma F Evans (Amesbury,Ma/23), 30 May 1877
    (Samuel Dunn/Sally Hunt)(John D Evans/Mary J Bartlett)
    Francis A (Kingston/Danville/34) & Bethia J Spofford (Bucksport,Me/40)20 Nov 1864
    Michael (Ireland/Exeter/39) & Margaret Shey (Exeter/25), 20 May 1860
DURBORN: Josiah (Hawke) & Elizabeth Collins, 11 Apr 1796
DUTCH: George (Brentwood) & Avery Welch (Brentwood), 13 Nov 1785
EASTMAN: Benjamin & Margret Graves, 16 Aug 1733
    Charles L (E. Kingston) & Sarah A Greely, 17 Mar 1845
    Ebenezer & Sarah Fifield, 19 Jun 1758
    Ebenezer (Kingston) & Sarah Stevens, 22 Oct 1789
    Edward (Hawke)& Hepzibah Bean,16 Feb 1792
    Edward & Anna Judkins, m 05 May 1759
    George W & Emma E (Storr) Morse, 24 Nov 1887
    (Ebenezer Eastman/Mary S Greenleaf)(Frank H Storr/Elizabeth....)
    Jacob (Hawke)& Hannah Campbell, 16 Nov 1797

James D (38) & (Mrs) Harriet Mack (49), 04 Feb 1879
Joseph & Hanah Calef, 10 Mar 1751
Joseph & Jomina Smith, 30 Jan 1767
Joseph & Patiencs Smith, 09 Feb 1728/9
Obadiah (Hawke)& Jemima Williams, 21 Mar 1791
Samuel & Sarah Clough, 07 Nov 1728
Samuel (Sandown/24) & Susan E Philbrick (Kingston/28), 21 Mar 1855
Thomas & Abigel French, ... Jan 1729
Timothy & Mary Blasdel, 16 Jan 1745
Timothy (Hawke)& Eliza Fellows, 06 Mar 1802
Timothy (Newtown)& Lydia Perkins (So Hampton), ... Apr 1802
William & Mary Bean, 11 Sep 1749
EATON: George L (So Hampton) & Elisabeth A Deleware (So Hampton), 01 Jan 1860
Jabez (Hawke) & Susanna Colcord (Kingston), 24 Jun 1792
John S (Kensington/23) & Lois F Baston (Kensington/19), 21 Sep 1862
Theophilus & Abigal Fellowes, 23 Feb 1742/3
Willis C (Epping/21) & Ida M Silloway (Kingston/18), 17 Jan 1878
   (J.B. Eaton/Olive Edgerly)(Wadleigh Silloway/Ann Myrish Hoyt)
EDNEY: George W (Middletown,Ma/22) & Mary A Collins (Kingston/20), 24 Dec 1881 (E)
   (William W Edney/Evalainec Farnum/Sheppard S Collins/Julia Judkins)
John (Kingston/18)& Sarah A Ham (Kingston/Epping/17), 29 Oct 1864
John J (22) & Eva L Pratt (Reading,Ma/18), 08 Apr 1869
   (John J Edny/Hannah M...)(Henry M Pratt/Rebecca....)
ELIOT: Jonathan & Naomi Sweat, 18 Sep 1764
ELKENS: Obediah & Abigaiell French, 01 Dec 1730
ELKINS: Charles (45) & Sarah M Haickley (36), 25 Jul 1885 (Boston, Ma.)
   (Henry Elkins)
George E (22) & Annie R Call (22), 1873 (Amesbury,Ma.)
   (Thomas Elkins/Luellen....)
Ensn. Jeremiah (Kingston) & Elizabeth Tole (Hawke), 11 Jul 1792
John H (18) & Laura West (15), 17 Mar 1877
   (Charles Elkins/Elmira Towle)(Andrew J West/Mary F Davis)
Moses & Annah Shaw, 17 Nov 1701
ELLIOT: ---- (Haverhill,Ma) & Nancy Nicholls (Newtown), 16 Nov 1804
ELLIOTT: Jacob (Chester) & Marth Sleeper (Kingston), 22 Apr 1798
Richard (Concord) & Hannah French, 26 Nov 1801
ELLIS: Jeremiah B (Fremont) & Mary L Perkins (Fremont), 16 Feb 1861
EMMONS: John (E Kingston) & Sarah Woodman, 14 Oct 1783
ESTMAN: Sammell & Shuah Fifield, 17 Sep 1719
ETHRIDGE: Nathaniel & Dorithy Moodey, 28 Apr 1757
EVERETT: Daniel (Keene/68) & Sarah (Larkin)Davis (58), 10 Feb 1880
   (Ephraim Evelett/Diane Darling)(Daniel Larkin/Hannah Woodman)
FARLEY: Owen A (22) & Nellie F Webster (19), 08 Feb 1880
FAVOUR:Jonathan & Axey Wadleigh, 11 Apr 1782
Samuel (Newton) & Mary Stevens (Kingston), 28 Mar 1782

Samuel (New Chester) & Hoppe Brown, 26 Feb 1804
FELLOWES: Sammel & Sarah Webster, 14 Nov 1710
FELLOWS: Ebenezer & Elizabeth Brockes, 12 Nov 1718
    Insign Joseph & Sarah Green, 07 Mar 1756
    John (New Chester) & Louise Tilton (Hawke), -- Oct 1785
    John(Hawke) & Betsey Eastman, 21 Feb 1799
    Jonathan (Kensington) & Elizabeth Clifford, 25 Aug 1805
    Joseph & Elisabeth Young, 01 Jan 1737/8
    Joseph (Hawke) & Sarah Quimby (Hampstead), 05 Nov 1787
    Joseph & Elisabeth Young, 01 Jan 1737/8
    Joseph & Margret Webster, 02 Jan 1754
    Samuel & Mary Ring, 13 May 1761
    Simeon (Brentwood) & Dorothy Bartlett (Hawke), 12 Jun 1798
    Thomas & Sarah Muchmore, 04 Dec 1744
    Thomas (Hampstead) & Sally Quimby, -- Apr 1804
FERRIN: Aquila (Newton) & Abigail Colbey, 26 Jan 1792
    Jonathan (Concord) & Lois Hoyt (Newton), 25 Dec 1794
FIFIELD: Amos (Kingston) & Hannah Fifield, 05 Mar 1795
    Charles L (30) & Hannah F Trask (Brentwood/34), 11 May 1875
    Benjamin F (25) & Lizzie E Martin (Kingston/24), 05 Feb 1880
      (Simmon P Fifield/Mary E Brown)(John H Martin/Mary A Clark)
    John Jr & Elisabeth Grealy, 01 Feb 1739
    Joseph & Sarah Sharbon, 24 Apr 1701
    Joseph & Anne Badger, 10 May 1760
    Samuel (Kingston) & Martha Winslow, 09 Jul 1789
    Samuel & Mary Eastman, 21 Feb 1757
    Samuell & Joanna Clifford, 26 Aug 1728
    Sanborn (E Kingston)& Hannah Eastman (Kingston), 11 Jun 1799
    Sherburn (N Salisbury, Ma)& Alice Barnet (Hawke), 13 Nov 1785
    Sherburn (Salisbury, Ma) & Elizabeth Sanborn (Hawke), 20 Nov 1791
    Simon Page (Kingston) & Mary Elizabeth Brown (Kingston), 02 Aug 1846
FITTS: Abel (Sandown/27) & Emily S Fuller (Sandown/18), 01 May 1861
    Franklin (Sandown/21) & Abby Wyer (Sandown/18), 26 Nov 1807
    Joseph (Salisbury) & Ruhamah Judkins (Kingston), 11 Dec 1777
    Franklin (Sandown/33) & Sarah J Tabor (Sandown/28), 22 May 1869
      (Nathaniel Fittz) (Eben Tabor/Sally ....)
FLAGG: Charles H & Cora A Brown, 15 Mar 1884
    Joseph N (Grantham/39) & Morvina S Waite (Ipswich,Ma/35), 1871
      (Joseph Flagg/Relief ...)(Henry Waite/Rhoda ....)
FLANDERS: Jacob & Naomi Darling, 07 Jul 1741
    Carter (So Hampton) & Tirra Sawyer .....
    Christopher (Newtown) & Ruth Currier, 21 Oct 1802
    Dr ---- Flanders (So Hampton) & Priscilla Bartlett (Hawke), 12 Jan 1804
    Ephraim (Sandown) & Abigail Long (Kingston), 03 May 1787
    Jacob (Hawke) & Lois Davis, 17 Nov 1796

James (Warner) & Martha Greeley (E Kingston), 16 Sep 1789
James (Hawke) & Polly Diamond, 21 Jun 1804
John H (Chester/27) & Lizzie E Ball (So. Kingston/14), 04 Oct 1886
    (Philip Flanders)(William Ball/Mary F Sweetser)
FLATAU: Bernhard (Germany/60) & E.A. Sanborn (Hampton/55), 23 Jan 1879
FLOYD: George H (Epping/23) & Maria R Fogg (Raymond/23), 31 Dec 1857
FOGG: Charles H (Newburport,Ma/22) & Sarah Silloway (Kingston/18), 13 Dec 1868
    (J. Fogg/Eliza Wealch)(Wadleigh Silloway/Anna M Hoyt)
    Edson (Epping/18) & Georgie B Sanborn (Kingston/16), 14 Apr 1874
    (Martin Fogg/Jane Rollins)(George W Sanborn/Sarah B Badger)
    Willis L (Manchester) & Mary L Platt (Kingston), 12 Sep 1842
FOLLETT: Dr John A (Cen. Harbor/Kingston) & Martha E Goodwin (S Hampton/Amesbury)
    07 Dec 1861
FOLSOM: Edwin S (Epping/31) & Mabel Reynolds (Kingston/31), 25 Jun 1902
    (Thomas C Folsom/Mary Bickford)(Thomas O Reynolds/Fannie Smith)
FOOT: Isaac & Merriam Stevens, 13 Dec 1757
FORST: Prescott (Kingston) & Judith Colcord, 27 Sep 1846
FOWLER: Samuel L (W Newbury/22) & Mary A Hudson (W Newbury/22), 28 Nov 1878
    (Charles Fowler/Louisa Dudley)(Jonathan Hudson/Mary A Kennett)
FRENCH: Abraham & Sarah Smith, 15 Jan 1756
    Beniman & Ruth Honton, 12 Aug 1741
    Benjamin (Chester) & Esther Currier (E Kingston), 20 Apr 1788
    Benjamin N (Kingston/27) & Mary Jane Morse (E Kingston/27), 19 Sep 1853
    David & Ruhamah Choat, 15 Sep 1747
    Elihu T (Kingston) & Laura B Carr (Holderness), 30 Nov 1854
    Frank W (Kingston/43) & Hattie M Collins (Bsoton/25), 29 May 1897
    (John B French/Hannah Wadleigh)(Joel S Collins/Ella Averill)
    Henry (Kingston/54) & Florice A Merrill (Haverhill, Ma/23), 09 Oct 1899
    (John B French/Anna B Wadleigh)(Sam A Merrill/Harriet F Prescott)
    Henry (Kingston) & Anna Sleeper (Kingston), 23 Oct 1784
    George W (Chester/24) & .... Stickney (Kingston/20), 1871
    (David C French/Abigail Busher)(David Stickney/Elizabeth Heath)
    John (E Kingston) & Elizabeth Webster, 28 May 1800
    John W, (Sandown/24) & Jennie L Rowe (Raymond/19), 1871
    (Jonathan J French) (Dudly Rowe)
    Jonathan & Johaner Elkins, 07 Nov 1736
    Jonathan III (Hawke) & Mary Bachelor (Hawke), 27 Feb 1783
    Joseph (So Hampton) & Rhoda French, 26 Feb 1801
    Moses J (Kingston) & Aleina F Clark (Kingston), 19 Feb 1862
    Nathaniell & Sary Judkins, 24 Jun 1704
    Samuel & Abigel Godfree, 01 Apr 1736
    Simon & Sarah Heard, 24 Nov 1709
    William P (Sandown/27) & Christinia M George (Sandown/18), 1871
    (Joseph French/Almira....)(Ora P George/Abbie Silloway)
FROST: W Prescott (Kingston) & Judith Colcord (Kingston), 27 Sep 1846

William L (Rowley,Ma/20) & Carrie B Smith (Kingston/15),13 Jun 1894
   (Leonard S Frost/Delia Frost)(Luther Smith/Annie Smith)
GALE: Dr Amo, (Kingston) & Sally Bartlett, 24 Apr 1796
   Dr. Ezra B (Kingston) & Emily Atwood (So Hampton), 22 Nov 1842 (B)
   Ezra B (Kingston) & Ruth White (So Hampton), 31 Jul 1823
   Dr Israel (E Kingston) & Polly Greely, 05 Feb 1804
   Jacob & Suzaner ..... (date unknown)
   Perley (Kingston/19) & Mary E Hewett (Nova Scotia/24), 28 Apr 1888
   (Eben Gale/Lucinda E Peaslee)
   Stephen (Gilmanton) & Lois Pattin (Kingston), 22 Feb 1801
GARLAND: Daniel H (Kingston) & Cora M Brackett (Brentwood), 11 Sep 1887
   (Joseph S Garland/Lawerza N Mason)(Elbridge Brackett/Sarah Purrington)
   Joseph S (Kingston/32) & Laurenz A Garland (Kingston/27), 08 May 1856
   Nathaniel (Kingston/29) & Minni Brown (Kingston/23), 09 Mar 1890
   (Joseph S Garland/Laurenza Garland)(Nathaniel S Brown/Peace A Brown)
GEORGE: Albert M (Danville/29) & Hattie B Hall (Laconia/16), 11 Jul 1881
   (James M George/Salome W ....)(Charles B Hall/Harriett N .....)
   Elmer (Sandown/25) & Emma J Silloway (Kingston/38), 23 Jul 1892
   (Ora George/Abbie George)(Andrew J West/Mary F West)
   Fred R (Kingston/29) & Mabel E Spofford (Danville/19), 20 Aug 1902
   (Ora P George/Abbie W Silloway)(Charles A Spofford/Triphene Sargent)
   Gideon (Kingston) & Anna Chase (Brentwood), -- Apr 1782
   Gideon & Deabroh Stevens, m 07 Nov 1758
   Joseph O (Newburyport/King/25) & Mary Fellows (Kensington/19), 31 Oct 1858
   Joshua (Sandown) & Rhoda Eastman (Hawke), 28 Feb 1799
   Oscar R (Sandown/24) & Etta Webster (Kingston/18), 26 Feb 1876
   (Ora P George/Abbie Silloway)(Elihue T Webster/Ruth Hunt)
   Porter G (Kingston/28) & Florence B Kelley (Plaistow/17), 07 Mar 1889 (D)
   (Ora P George/Abbie Silloway)(George W Kelley/Melissa Keezer)
   Stephen (Hawke) & Sally Towle, 27 Jul 1797
   Stephen P & Edna F West, 22 Mar 1885 (D)
   William (Plymouth) & Elenor Fellows (Sandown), -- Mar 1789
   William (Hawke) & Hannah Jonson (Hawke), 15 Oct 1789
GIBBON: Dr Timothy (Bridgewater) & Jane Brown (Kingston), 01 Dec 1805
GIBSON: Samuel B (Fremont/25) & Lottie E Hoyt (Danville/25), 1874
   (Samuel Gibson/Hannah Bean)(Nathan Hoyt/Sarah Hook)
   William (Canterbury) & Sarah Smith (Kingston), 03 Jan 1788
GILLMAN: Daniel & Hannah Colcord, 22 Apr 1730
GILMAN: Frank J (Dover/21) & Harriet Severance (Kingston/22), 28 Nov 1901 (N)
   (Eusebe Gilman/Elibena Jacques)(Mason S Severance/Ellen Colford)
   Jacob & Mary Ladware, 01 Sep 1704
   Jacob & Abigel Moodey, 04 Aug 1741
   John W (Danville/24) & Meri Webster (Kingston/15), 10 May 1884
   (John L Gilman/Emily Wilkinson)(Albert P Webster/Betsey L Webster)
   Robert (Kingston) & Abigail Sanborn (Hawke), 02 Mar 1797

Samuel (Tamworth) & Hannah Thing (Brentwood), 05 Sep 1794
Steven & Mary French, 02 Jul 1742
GILMON, Daniel B (Fremont/22) & Frances H Pressy (Sandown/22), 07 Dec 1858
GODGES, William K (Hollowell,Me/23) & Clara E Jackson (Augusta, Me/33), 26 Jul 1864
GOODRICH, Edward & Mary Robbins, 22 May 1843
   James W (Kingston/22) & Mary A Dow (Salisbury,Ma/22), 16 Jun 1856
   S.B.T. (So Reading,Ma/Brentwood/19) & Mary Marshall (Brentwood/Kingston/16), 08 Sep 1857
GOODWIN: Daniel L (Kingston/29) & Sarah F Brown (Haverhill,Ma/18), 05 Jul 1868
      (John D Goodwin/Dolly Goodwin)(Thomas Brown/Martha Brown)
   Edward (Kingston/21) & Carrie P Pinkham (Manchester,Ma/34), 29 Aug 1897
      (Samuel Goodwin/Lucinda Tucker)(Hiram Wagner/Mary Bert)
   Hazen O (Kingston/42) & Susie Chester C (Littleton/38), 03 Jun 1895
      (Franklin B Goodwin/Sarah E White)(Mark Smith)
   Timothy (Newton/78) & Lois H Maloy (Sandown/67), 10 Mar 1888
      (Benjamin Goodwin/Abigail Southens)
   Samuel (Kingston/52) & Mary A Meek (Kingston/36), 04 Apr 1899
      (John D Goodwin/Dorothy S Marden)(Isiah Tucker/Adaline(Card) Seaver)
GORDING: Dudly (Epping)& Mehitable Sleeper (Poplin), 01 Apr 1789
GORDON: --- (Brentwood) & ..... Rainson , 04 Jun 1799
   Abraham (Brentwood) & Charlott York, 08 Feb 1788
   John (Exeter) & Mary Bachelder (E Kingston), 09 Aug 1790
   William (Brentwood) & Joanna Ladd (Brentwood), 27 Mar 1788
GOULD: Maj. Daniel (Lindborough) & (Mrs.) Mary Appleton (Hawke), 15 Nov 1798
GORON: Benjamin Porter (Danvers,Ma/21) & Loomora Guis Rochemont (Kingston/20)*
      (Alfred P Garon)(Charles Rochemont)   * 31 Oct 1869
GOSS: Alonzo (Londonderry/21) & Climerice A Poor (Fremont/21), 07 Jul 1870
      (Henry L Goss)(Boardman Poor)
GOULD: William (Salisbury) & Mehitabel Magoon (Kingston), -- Nov 1785
GRAGG: Col. William (Londonderry), & Elizabeth Abbott (E Kingston) 23 Nov 1779
GRAHAM: John & Love Sanborn, 08 Jan 1719/20
GRAVES: ---- (So Hampton) & Peggy Barstow (Exeter), 06 Apr 1803
   Benjamin (Exeter) & Polly Taylor (Brentwood), 07 Mar 1792
   Jacob (Brentwood) & Sally Brown (Poplin), 16 Aug 1795
GREALY: Jonathan & Martha French, 13 Mar 1736
   Jonathan (Kingston) & Mary Bartlett (Kingston), 12 Mar 1780
GREELY: Capt. Andrew (E Kingston)& Abagail Dow (Kensington), 07 Feb 1792
   Capt. Andrew(E Kingston) & Elizabeth Flanders, 22 Sep 1794
   Joseph & Elisabeth Dudley, 02 Dec 1741
   Reuben & Anna Greely, 28 Jun 1785
   Samuel (Salisbury) & Ruth Blasdel (E Kingston), 12 Feb 1783
GREEN: Nathan (Pittsfield) & Sally Wesbster, -- Jun 1802
GRIFFIN: Ebenezer & Mary Colcord, 02 Jul 1761
   Ebenezer (Brentwood) & Lucy Blake, 10 Apr 1797

John & Hannah Bean, 08 Sep 1743

Theophilis & Haner .....

GRIFIEN: Isaac & Susaner Clough

GRULY: Noah(Brentwood) & Hannah Morrill(Brentwood), 07 Jan 1783

HADLEY: Daniel (Plaistow/27) & Sarah A C Webster (Kingston/27), 29 Jun 1862

HALL: Anson E (Raymond/29) & Ida M (Wadleigh) Hardy(Kensington/21), 30 Apr 1874

    (Henry A Hall/Lucinda Hoyt)(Mark Wadleigh/Lovina Bowley)

HAM: George J (Portsmough/23) & Mary Abby Porter (Epping/15), 24 Nov 1870

    (Mark G Ham)(John L Porter)

HANSON: Forest J (Kingston/25) & Flora L Emerson (Merrimac,Ma/23), 16 Nov 1899*

    (John B Hanson/Mary A Wells)(W.H.Emerson/Hattie N Martin) * (Merrimac,Ma.)

    Samuel (Kingston) & Dorothy Fellows (Brentwood), 05 Jul 1836

HARDY: Peter (Kingston/48) & Abby S Robinson (Kingston/45), -- Sep 1861

HAROLD: George B (Kingston/27) & Nance Severance(Portsmouth/24), 1874

    (James Harold/Margarett ...)(John S Severance/Emily ....)

HARSA: John & Elisabeth Judkins, 21 May 1741

HART: Joseph (New Jersey/43) & Mary E Wells (Chester/54), 07 Nov 1877

    (William Hart/Anna L ...)

HAZEN: Nathan T(Beverly/Holliston,Ma/26) & Nellie M Dorman (Georgetown, Ma/20) 01 May 1864

HEAD: Addison (Portsmouth/Haverhill,Ma/23) & Nancy K Collins (Kingston/Danville/19) 12 Nov 1863

HEATH: Enoch (Hampstead) & Hannah Plummer (Hawke),-- May 1803

    Franklin G A (Kingston/20) & Ellen E Kimball(Danville/16), 24 Aug 1876

    (Franklin N Heath/Ellen A Austin)(John G Kimball/Charlotte P Willi--)

    George A (Haverhill, Ma/25) & Mary J Barnes (Allen,NY/18), 03 Sep 1873

    (John Heath/Elliza A .....)(Josiah Barnes/Sarah ....)

    Harry H (Danville/24) & Grace D Collins (Kingston/22), 02 Sep 1885

    (Franklin N Heath/Marie C Austin)(Eldridge Collins/Josephine Robinson)

    Henry H.H. (Danville/30) & Anne K Titcomb (Hampstead/27), 11 Nov 1892

    (Franklin N Heath/Maria Austin)(John Johnson/Maranda Leane)

    Simon L (Nashua) & Elisabeth Barrlows (Nashua), 27 Apr 1849

    Weld (Kingston) & Eliza Winslow, 27 Nov 1828

HEOLT: Newell B (Newburyport,Ma/19) & Mary A (Porter) Heam (Pembroke/18), 1873

    (Alfred Heolt/Sarah ....)(John Heam/Sarah ....)

HILLIARD: George W & Grace D Rollins, 02 Sep 1885

HODGDON: George Riley (Kingston/21) & Mary Elizabeth Currier (Belfast,Me/17) *

    (Robert Hodgdon/Sarah Welch)(John P Currier/Elizabeth Ring) * 02 Sep 1868

HOITT: Benjamin F (Newton/24) & Sarah Carlton (Newton/21), 13 Sep 1855

HOLMES: Henry M (Londonderry/35) & Hannah T Rowe (E Kingston/34), 17 May 1860

HOLT: George (Andover) & Rebecca Durant (Exeter), 16 Nov 1800

HOMANS: Joseph (Kingston) & Sarah Walton, 14 May 1789

HOOK: Dyer & Hannah Brown, 21 Nov 1744

    Humphry & Hanna Philbrick, 24 Nov 1747

    Jacob & Mary Bachilder, 15 Nov 1749

Jacob (Poplin) & Sarah Elkins, 17 Dec 1798
Jacob (Brentwood) & Mary Griffing (Kingston), 23 May 1787
Jacob (Brentwood) & Sally Morrill, 12 Dec 1800
Josiah (Brentwood) & Hannah Pike (Hampton Falls), 06 Oct 1799
Moses (Poplin) & Ruth Stuart, 15 Mar 1804
Peter (Chichester) & Abigail Sleeper (Kingston), 20 Dec 1787
Samuel (Sandown) & Judeth Williams (Hawke), 30 Aug 1798
HOYT: Benjamin (Hopkington) & Jane French (Kingston), 08 Feb 1788
John (Chester) & Miriam Hobbs (Poplin), 03 Feb 1790
John W (Malden,Ma/24) & Nancy G Severance (Kingston/18), 17 Jun 1895 (D)
   (John W Hoyt/Nancy R Strout)(Samuel M Severance/Ellen M Colford)
Joseph (Sanbornton) & Huldah Sanborn (Kingston), 29 Jan 1778
Leonard (Wayland,Ma/21) & Annie M Huse (Kingston/16), 22 Jun 1896
   (John W Hoyt/Nancy R Strout)(William F Huse/Lucy A Webster)
Louis G (Exeter/37) & Marie S Towle (Kingston/30), 30 Mar 1893
   (Gilman B Hoyt/Marianna J Hoyt)(Alfred Towle/Susan Towle)
Stephen (Hampstead) & Mary J Winslow (Kingston), 29 May 1855
Thomas E (Peabody, Ma/19) & Minnie Carter (Merrimac,Ma/16), 14 Aug 1897
   (John W Hoyt/Nancy R Strout)(George F Carter/Etta Webster)
William (Chester) & Betsey Bosford (Hawke), 07 Sep 1802
HUBARD: Richard, Jr & Elisabath Webster, 21 Dec 1762
HUBBARD (HEBIRD): Daniel & Ruth Huse, 23 Feb 1743/4
HUBBARD: Benjamin (Kingston) & Sukey Webster, 23 Feb 1801
Francis (Kingston) & Mehitable Judkins (Kingston), 29 Oct 1785
John & Jonna Davice, 30 Apr 1754
Richard & Abigail Davies, 27 --- 1722
Richard & Abigel Tayler, 16 Oct 1734
HUBBURD: Jeremiah & Marcy Jouson, 28 Feb 1722/3
HULL: Charles E & Abby A Abbott, 01 Jul 1866
John D (Kensington/21) & Margrett E Brewster (Stratham/18), 07 Jul 1869
   (Richard Hull)   (George W Brewster)
Richard (Nottingham/Kensington/46) & Mehitable Brewster (Warren/Stratham/35)
29 Sep 1864
HUNKINS: Isaac (Poplin) & Dolly Hoyt, 12 Jun 1792
HUNT: Olando & Lucy Winslow (Kingston), 25 Jun 1827
Reuben (Kingston) & Sarah Eastman (Hawke), 28 Feb 1793
Robert (Kingston) & Eliza Maloon (E Kingston), 12 Nov 1801
Stephen (Kingston) & Lois Welch, 16 Jan 1793
Stephen (Kingston) & Polly Woodman (Hawke), 11 Feb 1796
William W (Kingston/25) & Dora A Bartlett (Kingston/27), 09 Sep 1874
   (John Hunt/Abigail ...)(Richard Bartlett/Sally ....)
HUNTON: Benjamin & Juett (Judith) Clough, 07 Feb 1751
Benjamin & Abigel Page, -- Jan 1757
Benjamin & Marcy Quimby, 17 Jul 1758
Charles & Mariah Smith, 14 Nov 1749

Nathaniel & Anne Darbon, 07 Jun 1742
Philip & Ann Estman, 22 Dec 1720
HUNTOON: Aaron & Elizabeth Smith, 11 Jan 1781
Capt, Nathaniel (Unity) & Martha Judkins (Kingston), 26 Aug 1789
Elder Benjamin (Salisbury) & Hannah Derburn (Kensington), 21 Jun 1792
John & Elisebeth Bede, 07 Dec 1754
Josehua (Kingston) & Molly Winslow, -- Dec 1790
Samuel & Hanah Lad (no date listed)
HUNTRESS: Clarence A (Limington,Me/19) & Addie D Tucker (Kingston/18), 17 Mar 1900
(Temple C Huntress/Lucy A Dalyrimple)(Isaih H Tucker/Addie E Goodwin)
HUSE: Ebenezer (Newton) & Elia Peaslee, 28 Nov 1805
George R (Newton/24) & Ida F Runnills (Amesbury,Ma/18), 03 Jul 1871
(Stephen S Huse/Mary A Huse)(John S Runnills/Abba H ....)
Nathan L (Newton/19) & Ellen A Rogers (Newburyport,Ma/17), 09 Aug 1868
(Sanborn Huse/Mary A Quimby)(Moses A Rogers/Ellen M Welch)
William F (Kingston/22) & Lucy A Webster (Kingston/18), 04 May 1863
INGALLS: Fred W (Canterbury/26) & Nellie F French (Kingston/20), 26 Nov 1885
(Daniel M Ingalls/Ann C Hancock)(Moses J French/Alcena Clark)
INGALS: Samuel (Sandown) & Betsey Clough (Bickford), 25 Nov 1802
INGHAM: Amos R (Todorden,Eng/61) & Susan N Wentworth (Bridgton,Me/47)18 Sep 1899
(Rodger Ingham/Sarah Fielding)(Daniel Stevens /Ann Manchester)
JAMES: David S (Hampton/22) & Lurana F Philbrick (Kingston/25), 21 Jan 1869
(Samuel James/Martha James)(Edward Philbrick/Sarah Philbrick)
JACKSON: Rev. William (Dorsit,Vt) & Susanah Crain (Brentwood), 03 Oct 1796
JEFFERY: Thomas E (Lawrence/Bridgewater/26) & Georgiana A Calef (Hampton/
Chicago,IL/23), 06 Dec 1860
JENNESS: George A (Exeter/23) & Laura J Page (Brentwood/18), 13 Oct 1875
(D Webster Jenness/Philimina Harriman)(Joseph Page/.....Fifield)
JOHN: Augustus (Haverhill/42) & Sarah E Holand (Harvey) (39), 1872
(Daniel John/.... Plumer)(George Holland/Mary Ann ....)
JOHNSON: Allen (Alden) M (Danville/22) & Annie B Hoyt (Danville/21), 22 May 1880
(Charles K Johnson/Martha L Merrill)(Nathan Hoyt)
Charles K (Danville/21) & Martha L Merrill (Danville/17), 01 Sep 1854
Samuel (Boston/ 25) & Mary A Brown (Fremont/23), 16 Apr 1857
William Henry (Haverhill,Ma/25) & Grace Brickett Peaslee (Kingston/26)*
(Henry H Johnson/Mary A Johnson)(Luther D Peaslee/Mary Peaslee)* 01 Jun 1893
JONES: John & Hannah Dow, 13 Oct 1748
Joseph & Abigel Flanders, 11 Jan 1744
Josiah (Hawke) & Esther Fellows, -- Nov 1796
Nathan & Allas ....., before 1750
Olin V (Enfield/25) & Annie L Johnson (23),17 Sep 1884
(W.C.Jones/C Angie Chase)
William W (Boston) & Harriet Marsh (Exeter), 08 Sep 1845
JUDKENS: Samell & Abigaill Hereman, 30 Nov 1712
JUDKINS: Amos (Kingston) & Betsey Sweat, 18 Mar 1792

Andrew (Kingston) & Rebecca Judkins ,-- Apr 1804
Arthur R (Kingston/29) & Delia A Page (Brentwood/23),18 Dec 1888
    (Joseph Judkins/Hannah E Blake)(Joseph Page/Mary E Fifield)
Eldridge F (Kingston/28) & Hattie J Butler (Seabrook/18), 23 Mar 1879
    (Eldridge G Judkins/Polly Swain)(Collin Butler/Hannah ...)
Eldridge F (Kingston/22) & Emma A Gilman (Fremont/17), 01 Jun 1873
    (Eldridge G Judkins/Polly Swain)(John L Gilman/Emily Wilkinson)
Joel & Mehitabel Ealkins, 01 Jan 1734/5
Joel S (Kingston) & MaryAnn Locke (Kingston), 21 Mar 1847
John & Marthy Hook, 21 Nov 1744
John W (Kingston/23) & Nellie A (Rogers) Huse (Kingston/21), 1873
    (John Judkins/Caroline H ....)(Moses Huse/Ellen ....)
John & Esther Sweat, 07 Nov 1750
Jonathan (Hopkinton) & Mary Sleeper (Kingston), -- Dec 1784
Josiah & Hannah Hunton, 11 Jan 1738
Lenord & Sarah, 13 Jan 1763
Moses E (Kingston/23) & Hannah F Cheney (Kingston/18), 22 Oct 1876
    (Joel S Judkins/Mary A Locke)(Nath D Cheney/Mary E Hoyt)
Samuel & Sarah Bowhorner, 11 Dec 1755
Simon & Catherine Hoit, 11 Jan 1844
Stephen (Kingston) & Lize French (Kingston), 27 Mar 1783
KEEN: Willis E (Kittery,Me/24) & Alice E (Bartlett) Sargent (Haverhill/22),17 Feb 1886
    (Benjamin Keen/Eliza A ....)(Sylvanis S Bartlett/Sarah ....)
KELLEY: Daniel (New Hampton) & Polly Nichole, 09 Sep 1790
    William (Exeter) & Elisabeth Robinson, 29 Jul 1788
KEITH: Herbert B (St Johns,N.B./20) & Mae L Smith (Portland,Me/30), 29 May 1897
    (Modecai Keith/Katherin.....)(Stephen W Nason/Rachel Whittier)
KEIZER: William J (25) & Nellie R Collins (18),11 Feb 1884
    (William J Keizer/Mary J Williams)(Andrew J Collins/Anna M Smith)
    William J & Emma L Marden, 02 Jun 1888
KELLEY: Nathaniel K (Plaistow/22) & Clara Welch (21),17 Oct 1891 (D)
    (Alfred Kelley/Lizzie Welch)(Benjamin Welch)
KEMPTON: Eugene J (Haverhill/Ma/21) & Laura E Sanborn (Kingston/23),11 Nov 1890*
    (Judson Kempton/Caroline Kempton)(Joseph Sanborn/Lavinia Sanborn)* (D)
KENESTON: Joseph (Poplin) & Hannah Bodge, 05 Apr 1791
KIMBALL: Amos H (Kingston/36) & Mary Baker (Brentwood/29), 22 Jan 1894 *
    (Amos Kimball/Marth Spofford)(Charles Baker/Sarah Baker) * at Brentwood
    Benjamin B (Kingston/32) & Nettie M George (Sandown/25), 21 Sep 1896
    (Amos Kimball/Martha Spofford)(Perley George/Clara A Purington)
    David (Byfield,Ma/40) & Naomi C Collins (Brentwood/44), 26 Feb 1869
    (Benjamin Kimball) (David Collins)
    George W (Kingston) & Mary W P Heath (Kingston), 04 Jul 1852
    Isaac (Windsor,Vt) & Dorcas Hubbard (Kingston), 17 Sep 1789
    John P H(Rook Island,IL/21) & Nellie M West (Kingston/17), 05 May 1877
    (Charles W Kimball/Mary T Taylor)(Andrew J West/Mary F Davis)

Louis H (Hampstead/23) & Mary D Chellis (Kingston/28), 31 Mar 1883
    (John G Kimball/Charlotte P Williams)(George F Quimby/Laura W Lowry)
Lewis H (Hampstead/34) & Blanche Deland (Kingston/35), 25 Jan 1894
    (John G Kimball/Charlotte P Williams)(George L Quimby/Laura W Lowry)
Moses (Poplin) & Molly Page (Hawke), 01 Feb 1791
KIMBLE: Caleb (Exeter) & Keziah Beede (Kingston), 23 Dec 1778
KINISTON: Richard & Mary Tucker, 13 Dec 1750
LAD: Daniel & Mehetable Philbrick, 19 Apr 1712
    John & Elizabeth Sanborn, 14 ... 1713
    Nathaniel & Sarah Clifford, 12 Aug 1741
    Truworthy & Lidda Harriman, 01 Nov 1750
LADD: Benjamin & Mary French, 11 Feb 1741
LANE: James (Hampton) & Mary Long (Kingston), 10 Mar 1844
    Joseiah (Poplin) & Elizabeth Wheeler (Epping), 27 Nov 1792
LEAVIT: Moses (Sanborntown) & Abigail Challis (Poplin), 12 Sep 1804
LEYFORD: Augustus D (Brentwood/30) & Julia Davis (Kingston/20), 04 Jul 1862
LIFORD: Francis (Brentwood) & Deborah Judkins, 22 Dec 1789
LOCK: John (Poplin) & Elinor Tucker , 20 --- 1793
LOCKE: William (Lee) & (Mrs) Mary Judkins (Kingston), 14 Apr 1845
LONG: Richard & Eallases Moode,18 Aug 1743
    William & Ruth Estman, 01 Jan 1714
    William & Sarah Sheppard, 21 Dec 1719
    William & Debrah Young, 11 Jan 1721/22
LORD: Albert E (Exeter/28) & Hannah L Kelley (Plaistow/18), 27 Mar 1885
    (Nathaniel Lord/Betsey Pike)(Alfred Kelley/Hannah Sweetser)
LOURY: George P (Lowell/Kingston) & Abby E Handy (Kingston), 24 Oct 1861
LOVE : George (Haverhill, Ma) & Rachel J Lecoter (Haverhill,Ma), 24 Jul 1851
LOVEREIGN: Jesse (Loudin) & Polly Taylor (Poplin), 22 Aug 1796
LOVERING (LOVIREU): Samuel & Mary Gooden, 19 Oct 1748
LUCIER: Eugene (Salem,Ma/23) & Rose Vaillencourt (Lawrence,Ma/19), 13 Jun 1901
    (Tousan Lucier/Mary Bosquet)(Philip Vaillencourt/Lea Mieux)
LUCY: John (Ireland/Kingston/22) & Mary M Keezer (Hampstead/22), 28 Jul 1860
LUFKIN: Edward & Sarah Moodey, 06 Dec 1750
LUNT: Henery & Abigal Morrill, 11 Feb 1741/2
LYFORD: Francis (Brentwood) & Sarah Tuck, 11 Dec 1798
    James A (Lawrence,Ma) & Lizzie S Goodrich (E Kingston), 31 Oct 1887 (B)
    (Sauvere Lyford/Deborah W ....)(Preston Goodrich/Sarah L Pierce)
    John (Exeter) & Anna Hilton (E Kingston), 06 Oct 1799
MACE: George E (Newburyport,Ma/20) & Mary F Whittier (Kingston/15), 15 Feb 1878
    (George W Mace/Catherine Deveney)(Nathan Whittier/Almira Dudley)
MAGOON: Edward (Kingston) & Jehosheba Beede (Kingston), 14 Aug 1782
    Joseph (Kingston) & Rebecca Clough, 12 Dec 1791
MARCH: George W (Lowell/Danville /21) & Sarah J Carter (Clyde,NY/Berlin,WI/25)
    24 Jul 1864
    John & Margrit Bean, 10 Jun 1732

MARDEN: George W (Kingston/24) & Mary F Brown (Salisbury,Ma/21), 03 Apr 1869
(Moses Marden/Rebecca ...)(Amos T Brown/Rachel Pratt)
MARSH: Aaron B (Exeter/Brentwood/21) & Corinne B Symonds (Cambridge, Ma/22)
04 Oct 1864
Charles E, Jr (E Kingston) & Carrie B Huse (E Kingston), 23 Apr 1887 (N)
(Charles E Marsh/Abby E Mase)(William F Huse/Lucy Ann Webster)
John (Brentwood) & Hephsibah Marshal (Brentwood), 28 Feb 1788
John (Haverhill,Ma) & Sarah Severence, 11 Dec 1718
Nathan B (So Hampton/54) & Mary A (Locke)Judkins (Lee/42), 1872
(Henry Marsh/Nancy ....)(William Locke/Sarah Locke)
Nicholas (Brentwood) & Lucy Lock, 15 Dec 1794
Shepard & Carrie H Morse, 10 May 1876
Thomas W (Kingston/29) & Eva L Frazen, (Nova Scotia/17), 25 May 1886
(Thomas Martin/Catherine Davis)(John Frazen/Jennie ....)
MARSHALL: James W (Brentwood/Kingston/21) & Jemima Bartlett (Kingston/19),
13 Apr 1860
John P (Kingston/22) & Sarah J Collins (Kingston/22), 1874
(James F Marshall/Miranda Page)(Samuel S Collins/Julia F Judkins)
Richard L (Nova Scotia/25) & Lilla B Heath (Kingston/18), 31 May 1884(N)
(James M Marshall/Abbie Foster)(Frank N Heath/Maria C Austin)
MARTIN: --- (Amesbury) & Abigail Carter (Newtown), 25 Feb 1800
George E (Kingston/23) & Etta M Nason (Kingston/22), 07 Jul 1883
(Levi Martin/Rosanna Stuart)(Nathan Nason/Sarah Page)
John H & Nancy A Clark, 23 Dec 1852
Levi B (Kingston/18) & Rosanne Stuart (Kingston/18), 13 Jul 1859
MASON: Fransis (Porchmouth) & Mary Edmans, 26 Jan 1716/17
MAXEY: Hervey (Union,Me) & Sally Eastman (Kingston), 22 Oct 1805
MAYO: Henry A (Sandown) & Charlott Fitts (Sandown), 09 Mar 1756
McCABE: John F (Lynn,Ma/27) & Abbie Chamberlin (Kingston/45), 30 May 1902
(John F McCabe/Mary Clark)(Peter Fifield/Catherine Webster)
McCLINTOCK: Joseph (Kingstown) & Sally Potter (Kensington), 26 Sep 1792
McDANIEL: John (Springfield) & Hannah Morse (E Kingston), 21 Jan 1799
MEEK: Charlie B (Auburn,Ma/20) & Mary A Tucker (Kingston/17), 28 May 1877
(Alexander Meek/Jane Betcher)(Isaiah Tucker/Adeline Sever)
MELLISH: Rev John A (Kingston/31) & Sarah A Lane (Brookfield/27), 20 Dec 1855
MERRICK: Andrew J & Abbie A Pervese, 25 Dec 1879
Henry W (Danville/21) & Abbie W Fifield (Kingston/18), 13 Sep 1871
(Stephen Merrick/Harriet Merrick)(Peter Fifield/Catherine Fifield)
MILLS: Elwin C (Lebanon,Me/21) & Sarah M Davis (Sandown/23), 27 -- 1872
MOLOY: William (Watterford,Vt/Kingston/30) & Louise Keezer (NewLondon/ Kingston/39)
21 Nov 1859
MOODY: Ira (Kingston/25) & Mary P Goodwin (Kingston/36), 22 Dec 1855
Josiah (Brentwood) & Susanna Quimby, 12 May 1790
William PL (Kingston/19) & Nellie K Grey (Deerfield/24), 06 Jun 1875
(Ira Moody/Mary Goodwin)(Joseph Grey/Hannah Tuttle)

MORRILL: Henery & Susana Folsham, 30 Jan 1740/1
Nathan (Brentwood) & Judeth Dudley, 11 Jun 1795
Olliver E (Epping/38) & Elisabeth Carter (Effingham/45), 13 Nov 1878 (S/H)
(Olliver Morrill/Mehitable Coombs)
Oscar (Amesury,Ma/33) & Letitia Jane McGowan (Scotland/28), 05 Jun 1892
(John T Morrill/Elisabeth Persons)(James McGowan/Jane Wilson)
Parker (Candia) & Sally French (E Kingston), 27 Dec 1798
William (Brentwood) & Mary Gorden, 24 Dec 1789
MORSE: Daniel (Hampstead) & Mary Eastman (Hampstead), 13 Jan 1788
Ebenezer (Kingston) & Betsey Colcoard, 26 Dec 1799
Ezekiel (Newbury) & Mary Prescott (Kingston), 15 Sep 1789
Philip (Newbery/widower) & Hannah ....(Widow), 05 Nov 1730
Rosaloin & Mary E Brackett, 25 Dec 1882
MOULTEN: Caleb (Hampstead) & Abigail A Morse (Hampstead), 05 Sep 1845
MOULTON: Robert (Hampton) & Hannah Marston, 08 May 1791
MUZZE: John (Salisbury) & Hannah Winslow (Kingston), 25 Feb 1790
NASON: Alvin W (Brentwood/18) & Anna S Page (Brentwood/16), 27 Nov 1872
(Nathan Nason/Sarah R Page)(Ezra Page/Augusta Shaw)
Freeman L (Kingston/35) & Lila Hunt (Kingston/20), 30 Mar 1895 (D)
(Nathan Nason/Sarah R Page)(Paul Hunt/Affie Sleeper)
George W (Portland,Me/38) & Louisa A Harmon (Portland, Me/38), 14 May 1898
(Stephen W Nason/Rachel Loton)(Parents unknown-Adopted Daniel Chinery)
Seth F (Kingston/32) & Blanche Elkins (Kingston/24), 20 Sep 1899
(Nathan Nason/Sarah K Page)(George E Elkin/Annie Call)
NASSON: Albert F (Kingston/20) & Laura D Fifield (Kingston/20), 01 Oct 1876
(Nathan Nasson/Sara R Page)(Peter S Fifield/CatherineWebster)
NICHOLLS: Nicholas (Exeter) & Catherine Sanborn (Kingston), 07 Jan 1786
NICHOLS: Charles W (W Amesbury/Brentwood/27) & Hellen M Wadleigh (Boston/
Kingston/20), 11 Feb 1864
John B (Amesbury/Kingston/23) & Fannie Bartlett (Chester/Kingston/22)
11 Feb 1862
Oliver P (Kingston) & Dorothy Colcord, Nov 1816
Stephen F (Kingston/32) & Sarah E Chase (Kingston/26), 20 Feb 1862
NICKETT: Mabel (Canada/33) & Hannah J (Clayton)Towle (35), 05 Jul 1868
(Mitchel Nickett/Mary N Nickett)(William Clayton/Rosanna Ayer)
Michael (Exeter/23) & Francis M Goodwin (So Kingston/18), 22 Jun 1879
(Michael Nickett/Julia Chamberllain)(Frank Goodwin/Sarah White)
NORRIS: Jonathan (Epping) & Anne Thing (Brentwood), 25 Nov 1787
NOYES: Col. Edward F (E Haverhill/30) & Margarette Proctor (Derry/Kingston/29)
15 Feb 1863
George F (Haverhill,Ma/29) & Abbie Decatur (Newburyport,Ma/30), 16 Jul 1871
(Follansbee Noyes/Clarissa...)(Samuel Decatur/Abbie....)
O'CONNER: Michael & Mary ..... (no date listed)
ORDWAY: Jonathan & Hannah Morriel, 02 Jul 1746

OSBORN: Charles A (Cambridge,Ma/30) & Lizzie M (Webb) Browning, 21 Apr 1879
(Adolphus Osborn/Sarah L Green)(William H Webb/Annie M Daniels)
Suman (Fremont/27) & Annie E Jackman (E Kingston/21), 12 Nov 1879
(Enoch Osgood/Ivory A ....)(James M Jackman)
PAGE: Dr Abner (New Durham) & Hannah Tewksbury (Hawke), 10 Feb 1803
Benjamin (Gilmantown) & Ruth Bean (Brentwood), 26 Apr 1787
Benjamin (Hawke) & Rebeca Quimbey (Hawke), 05 Feb 1788
Clarence H (Danville/19) & Alice J Page (Kingston/34), 21 Dec 1895 (D)
(Herbert A Page/Florence A Griffin)(Ezra Page/Augusta Shaw)
Daniel (Hawke) & Polly Tole, 31 Dec 1789
Ebenezenr & Haner Shepard, 29 Dec 1743
Ephram & Hanah Currier, 25 Dec 1754
Ezra W(Kingston/19) & Augusta O Shaw (E Kingston/15), 28 Aug 1853
Herbert (21) & Florence E Griffin (19), 1872
(Aaron Page/Valine ...)(James Griffin/Abigail ....)
Herbert A (Danville/45) & Flora E Taylor (Kingston/33), 15 Feb 1897
(Aaron Page/Valeria Allen)(Andrew J West/Mary F Davis)
Jabez (Hawke) & Sally Kimball (Poplin), -- Aug 1799
John (Kingston/58) & Harriett Bartlett (Kingston/40), 08 Jun 1859
Jon & Ane Webster, 19 Sep 1749
Leslie H (Kingston/21) & Bertha M Swett (Kingston/21), 30 Jan 1900
(Ezra Page/Augusta Shaw)(Moses Swett/Lavinia George)
Simon (Hawke) & Phebe Sanborn (Brentwood), 25 Dec 1788
Thomas (Kingston) & Eliza Bickford, 14 Oct 1832
Ulysses G (Kingston/31) & Iona E Currier (Danville/18), 02 May 1896
(Ezra Page/Augusta Shaw)(Freeman D Currier/Mary S Keizer)
PALMER: Samuel & Nancy Philbrick, 04 Oct 1827
PARKER: Frank W (Kingston/30) & Abie T Holt (W Epping/19), 06 Aug 1893 (E)
(Nathaniel Parker/Sarah G Parker)(Luther J Holt/Sarah A Holt)
Hubert A (21) & Anna M Ambrose (Old Town,Me/21), 01 Sep 1868
Noah (Exeter) & Deborah Gilman, 21 Oct 1800
PATTEN: Colcord (Kingston) & Marieh R Fletcher, 08 Jul 1818
Ora Pearson (Kingston) & Elisabeth M Towle (E Kingston/Kingston), 20 Feb 1862
William C & Laura T Prescott, 29 Jun 1842
William C (Kingston/40) & Sarah Ann Ware (Kensington/33), 19 Mar 1860
PEASLEE: Daniel (Kingston) & Elizabeth Seecombe, 26 Feb 1805
Jacob & Huldah....., (no date given)
John S (Newton/29) & Mary A Kelly (Newton/24), 22 Nov 1864
Palatiah (Newton) & Betsy Pollard (Kingston), 04 Sep 1800
Simmons S (Kingston/61) & Mary Edis (Pembroke/43), 15 Dec 1869
(Daniel P Peaslee/Elisabeth Seacomb)(Jacob Edis)
William (Newtown) & Dorothy Campbel (Hawke), 04 Jul 1805
PERKINS: Joseph (Newmarket) & Elizabeth Torry, 09 Nov 1797
Joseph (Deerfield) & Hannah Merrill, -- Jan 1803
PERSONS: Levi (E Kingston) & Lois French, 02 Nov 1804

PHILBRICK: Edward S (Bradford,Ma/64) & Abbie P (Buswell)Webster (Kingston/49) *
    (John Philbrick/Sarah Stevens)(John Buswell/Lydia England) * 26 Nov 1873
    Jedidiah & Mary Tayler, 25 Aug 1721
    Jedidiah (Kingston) & Dolly Colcord, 28 Jun 1790
    Jeremiah & Mary Stevens, 20 Sep 1744
    Josiah (Hawke) & Sally Twrsbury, 27 Oct 1796
    Thomas & Mehetable Ayers, 14 Apr 1681
PHILLIPS: Aldison E (New Salem/29) & Mary E Marden (Deerfield/35), 31 Mar 1863
PIERCE: Charles H (Warren,Me/25) & Clara E Bartlett (Kingston/19), 20 Nov 1889
    (John G Pierce/Annie S Pierce)(William J Bartlett/Maria A Bartlett)
    Frank L (Kingston/26) & Elsie M Furber (Kingston/19), 15 Jun 1897
    (John Pierce/Sarah A Schelling)(John I A Furber/Roxby A Collins)
    Levi B (So Hampton/76) & Mary H Carter (76), 08 Dec 1887
    (Samuel Pierce/Nancy Blaisdell)
    Samuel (So Hampton) & Nancy Blasdel (So Hampton), 18 Aug 1805
PILSBURY: Caleb (Bridgewater) & Joanna French (E Kingston), 16 Jan 1803
    John (So Hampton) & Elisabeth Rowel (Newton), 27 Mar 1787
PINKHAM: John B (Lake Village/35) & Maria F Goodwin (Kingston/18), 20 Dec 1878
    (Enoch Pinkham/Eliza E Rich)(Frank Goodwin/Sarah E White/18)
PLUMMER: George (Sandown/19) & Emma Jane Hoyt (Hampstead/19), 01 Jun 1876
    (George Plummer/Caroline ....)(Stephen Hoyt/Mary J Winslow)
    John M (Rowley,Ma/28) & Amy J Bartlett (Kingston/19), 11 Mar 1889
    (John M Plummer/Elizabeth Edeley)(Enoch P Bartlett/Mary Crosby)
    Nathan (Hawke) & Rhoda Heath, 21 Nov 1794
POLLARD: Frances & Sarah Webster, 06 Sep 1747
    Jacob (Kingston) & Sally Seecombe, 28 Nov 1805
POOR: John S (Bradford/23) & Sarah E Vincent (Danville/20), 03 Sep 1864
PRENTICE: Rev. Mr Josiah (Northwood) & Nancy Wiggins, 23 Feb 1801
PRESCOTT: Charles (Kingston/23) & Georgia A Brown (Newburyport,Ma/29) *
    (Richard Prescott/Clara Bickford)(William R Brown/Louisa R Hoyt)* 15 Oct 1878
    Edgar S (Kingston/26) & Carrie F Webster (Kingston/23), 19 Mar 1881
    (Richard S Prescott/Clara J Bickford)(John T Webster/Abbie Buswell)
    Eugene A (23) & Sarah A French (26), 26 Nov 1885
    (Richard L Prescott/Clara J Bickford)(Nelson French/Mary Morse)
    John W (Kingston/25) & Roxcina Sanborn (Sandown/21), 20 Sep 1870
    (Lewis F Prescott)   (Luther N Sanborn)
    Lewis F (Newton/22) & Bessie A Marden (E Kingston/18), 04 Jul 1878
    (George W Prescott/Mary G Johnson)(Ebenezer K Marden/Margret W Hoyt)
    Richard B & Mary S Perver, 02 Mar 1820
    Warren J (Hampton Falls/Sailsbury/23) & Lavinia F Hoyt (Kingston/20)
    22 Jan 1864
PRESCUT: Simeon (Hampton Falls) & Sarah French (Kingston), 24 Oct 179
PRESSY: Paul & Hanah Felch, 01 Jan 1751
    Paul & Mary Hubard, 26 Mar 1758
PRIEST: Nathan (Kingston) & S.... Judkins (Kingston), 15 Mar 1846

PRIMROSE: George H (So Kingston/33) & Blanche C Claytin (Cape Rezien/18)*
    (Edward Primrose/Hannah C Perkins)(John Clayton/Adaline Cooms)* 24 Apr 1886
PRINCE: Isaac (Nottingham) & Dorothy Calef (Kingston), 30 May 1786
    Moses (So Hampton) & Anna Loverin (Exeter), (no date given)
PRINE: James (Lee) & Mary Ladd (Kingston), 06 Apr 1780
PROCTOR: Jeams & Abigel ..... (no date listed)
PROVOST: Frederick R (Bradford, Ma/22) & Viola A Brackett (Seabrook/16), 09 Apr 1895
    (Frederick Provost/Orrie Morrien)(D Geo Brackett/Eliza Eaton)
PURRINGTON: Francis (Kingston) & Soriah Webster (Kingston), 18 Jul 1858
    Jacob W (Fremont/26) & Sylvina C Garine(Lebanon,Me/21), 01 May 1895 (Hav)
    (Francis Purrington/Maria C Webster)(Hirem Garine/Emma Sergie)
QUENBE: David & Abigaiell Webster, 25 Dec 1724
QUERO: Andrew (Nova Scotia/53) & Mary A Ball (So Kingston/19), 06 Oct 1886
    (William Quero/Rhoda Wetherlake)(William H Ball/Mary F Sweetser)
QUIMBEY: Daniel (Kingston) & Abigail Hubbard (Kingston), 17 Jan 1782
    Aaron & Anne Bachelder, 08 Oct 1763 (in Hampstead)
    Aaron (Hawke) & Betsy Dymonds, 21 Jul 1805
    Abraham (Springfield) & Miriam Jones, 25 Jan 1804
    Benjamin (Hawke) & Mary Chrichet (Poplin), 18 Jul 1787
    Charles H (Kingston/20) & Fhilemina F Collins (Danville/Kingston), 22 Nov 1860
    Charles F & Josie M Durgin, 23 Nov 1885
    David (Springfield) & Polly Campbell (Hawke), 17 Nov 1796
    Eliphlet & Mary Juel, 01 May 1744
    Elisha (Hawke) & Hannah Badge (Kingston),16 Aug 1794
    Eugene M (So Kingston/20) & Jennie E Dorr (So Kingston/17), 03 Feb 1878
    (John J Quimby/Mary E Collins)(James K Dorr/Almira Marble)
    Jacob (Hampstead) & Anna Plummer (Hampstead), 16 Dec 1787
    John (Kingston) & Hanah Davis, 25 Dec 1798
    Moses & Susan M Conner, 15 Dec 1835
    Paul (Hawke) & Miriam (Kingston), 03 Feb 1789
    Philip (Kingston) & Mary Jane Swett (Kingston), 15 Jul 1847
    Samuel & Ann Young, -- May 1757
    Trustram & Susana Blasdel, 26 Nov 1753
QUINBY: David, Jr. & Mary Wadlagh, 19 Nov 1755
    John & Martha Sargent, 13 Feb 1753
    Moses & Juday Bean, 05 Jun 1754
RANO: Elias & Mary Severance, 08 Apr 1742
REMICK: John & Hannah Brackett, 05 Jul 1841
RENDAL: Daniel (Hawke) & Sally Barnet, 07 Nov 1794
REYNOLDS: Thomas O,MD (Chester/21) & Mary Fanny Smith (Raymond/22), 13 Jul 1870
    (Thomas F Reynolds)   (William Smith),
RICHARDSON: Herbert B (Turnbridge,VT/31) & Ida French (Kingston/29), 01 Aug 1891
    (Isaac Richardson/Alvira Bean)(Benjamin French/Mary J French)
RIGGS: Bertrand H (Caverndish,Vt/22) & Ida F Hubbard (Chesterfield,OH/18), 26 Nov 1900
    (Henry H Riggs/Lucy Rose)(Joseph C Hubbard/Cordellia Ames)

ROBERTS: Charles H (Epping/Haverhill,Ma/19) & Amanda G Eaton (Canada/20)
06 Apr 1864
ROBEY: Samuel & Hanah Ordway, 23 Dec 1755
ROBINSON: Charles H (Kingston/23) & Louisa M Smith (Epping/21), 14 Mar 1885
(Joseph C Robinson/Mary J Sever)(Oliver J Smith/Nancy L Patten)
J.C. (Stratham/38) & Mary Jane Beedy (Kingston/33), 27 Jul 1859
James O (Kingston) & Mary Bean, 31 Jul 1843
John W (Brentwood/W Amesbury/21) & Eliza G Neall (No Berwick/26), 11 Mar 1863
Jona (Brentwood) & Deborah A Dudley, 25 Feb 1800
Nicholas D (Mt Vernon) & Polly Smith (Brentwood), 22 Sep 1796
ROGERS: Frank P (Kingston/22) & Sadie E Williams (Brentwood/18), 05 May 1897 (B)
(Moses W Rogers/Mary J Winslow)(John E Williams/Ella P Page)
Fred C (Kingston/22) & Mary A Thompson (Kingston/23), 05 Mar 1896
(Moses W Rogers/Mary J Winslow)(Dustin Thompson/Sarah .....)
Joshua & Hannah Woodman, 1768
Moses W (Kingston/17) & Mary Jane Winslow (Kingston/17), 21 Aug 1870
(Moses H Rogers) (William Winslow)
William F (Kingston) & Junia L Severance (Kingston), 15 Nov 1849
ROLLINS: Daniel (Sanborntown) & Zipporah Bartlet (Kingston), 06 Nov 1800
George F (Epping/Sandown/27) & Matilda Leane-- (Raymond/Sandown/23)
23 Sep 1861
Henry P (Exeter) & Abba L Gilman (Exeter), 12 Sep 1855
ROUELL: Thomas & Abigaiell Stevens, 21 Apr 1725
ROWE: Horace (Lawrence) & Meriam Sleeper (Kingston), 13 Jun 1848
Joseph (E Kingston) & Mary Thayer (Kingston), 16 Nov 1802
Joseph F (E Kingston) & Betsey Bachelder, 21 Jan 1800
ROWELL: Ambrose E (Brentwood/33) & Mary A Gordon (Brentwood/24), 17 Mar 1869
(Addison S Rowell/Eliza B Rowell)(Lewis B Gordon/Mary Gordon)
Daniel (Perry) & Sarah Flood (E Kingston), 26 Jun 1800
Jesse S (SoHampton/39) & Martha E Kimball (Kingston/37), 04 Dec 1901
John (Epping) & Mehetable Thing (Brentwood), 05 Jan 1791
Jonathan (Epping) & Mary Philbrick (Brentwood), 19 Sep 1793
Matthias (Newtown) & Judeth Rowell, 12 Nov 1805
RUNDLETT: John P (E Kingston) & Hannah B Lawrence (E Kingston), 06 Feb 1847
SANBORN: Abner (Brentwood) & Susanna Tuck (Brentwood), 01 Oct 1789
Abraham & Abigel Clifford, 06 Jan 1736
Benjamin & Dorryty Lad, 03 Apr 1746
Benjamin (Hawke) & Betsey Rand, 28 Jul 1798
Benjamin (Kingston) & Rebecca Smith (Brentwood), 14 Mar 1802
Charles (Sandown/Haverhill,Ma/29) & Harriett Green (Chester/23), 12 Jun 1862
David (Kingston) & Dorothy Gilman (Kingston), 25 Mar 1779
David (Gilmanton) & Elizabeth Rowell (E Kingston), 06 Apr 1797
Ebenezer (Poplin) & Lydia Bean (Hawke), -- Apr 1799
Ebenezer (Epping) & Lydia Fifield (Brentwood), 30 Aug 1796
Elijah (Poplin) & Elizabeth Tilton (Hawke), 07 Sep 1779

Enoch (Newport) & Elizabeth Sanborn (E Kingston), 30 Apr 1786
George W (E Kingston) & Sarah Badger (Kingston), 25 Dec 1845
Isaac (Kingston) & Abigail French (Kingston), 04 Apr 1782
Jethro & Elisabeth Sanborn, 12 Sep 1745
John & Mehetabell Fifield, 01 Jan 1706/7
John (Meredith) & Sally Dow (E Kingston), 17 Nov 1796
John M (E Kingston/18) & Clara N Chase (Kingston/20), 14 Dec 1881
    (James M Sanborn/Elizebeth H Fletcher)(Amos C Chase/Hattie E Draper)
Jonathan (Kingston) & Mary Morrill (Kingston), 25 Apr 1787
Jonathan 3rd & Saveah James., 15 Dec 1761
Jonathan & Mary Bachelder, 13 Feb 1735
Jonathan & Mary Sweat, 26 Jan 1768
Jonathan & Sarah James, 15 Dec 1760
Joseph R (Kingston/26) & Nellie E Sanborn (E Kingston/25), 17 Mar 1864
Left. Samuell & Elisabeth Pettingel, 04 Aug 1757
Left. William & Mary Sleeper, 06 Oct 1750
Left. William & Elisebeth Weed, 03 Jun 1774
Levi F (Hampton Falls/27) & Sarah J Perkins (Rye/23), 29 Sep 1864
Lt. William (Kingston) & Elisabeth Chase (Sandown), -- Oct 1788
Paul & Bette Cirrrer, 09 Dec 1746
Peter (Kingston) & (Mrs) Mary Clifford (Kingston), 03 Jun 1783
Phinihas (Hawke) & Patience Murder (Kingston), 24 Nov 1796
Ruben (Hawke) & Polly Judkins (Kingston), 21 Jul 1802
Samuel & Elisabeth Colcord, 19 Aug 1718
Samuel & Hanah Tucker, 07 Feb 1751
Timothy & Ellas Quimby, 07 May 1746
Tristram (Kingston) & Patience Page (Kensington), 03 Dec 1782
Truftrum & Margaret Tayler, 25 Apr 1711
William (Brentwood) & Susanna Jackson (Brentwood),13 May 1789
SARGENT: Frank E (Kingston/34) & Ida Day (Kingston/25), 30 Mar 1895 (N)
    (Benjamin A Sargent/Rebecca F Peaslee)(Lafayette Day/Hannah L Bake)
James B (Danville/18) & Sarah E Rowe(16), 22 Sep 1864
SAWYER: Benjamin & Mary Mean, 23 Nov 1737
    Betfield (Newton) & Hannah Thompson (Kingston), 22 Jun 1793
    Gedeon & Sarah Bartlett, 25 Dec 1746   (Newbury,Ma)
    Nathaniel (Plastow) & Lydia Pierce (So Hampton), 10 Jan 1805
SCHELLING: Charles K (Kingston/39) & Harriett N Shaw (So Hampton/20),11 Sep 1880
    (John Schelling/Lucy W Tucker)Jessie W Shaw/Mary J Currier)
SCOTT: John (Scotland/23) & Mary Ewart Patterson (Scotland/23), 07 Aug 1891
    (John Scott/Mary Middleness)(John Patterson/Anna McNaughton)
SCRIBNER: Edward & Rachiel Webster, 08 May 1735
    John (Poplin) & Huldah Bachelder (Hawke), 29 Dec 1794
    Samuel & Haner Webster, 04 Nov 1740
    Thomas & Sarah Clifford, 25 Dec 1702
    Thomas & Sarah Colbey, 10 Sep 1760

SEARGENT: Moses (Almsbury) & Lydia Severance (Kingston), 22 Dec 1791
SEAVER: Daniel P (Kingston/21) & Dolly C George (Danville/21), 26 Feb 1860
    John P (Sandown) & Florence Z Hull (So Hampton), 02 Jan 1888 (N)
        (Daniel Seaver/Dolly ....)(John D Hull/Nellie M Brewster)
    Samuel M (Kingston) & Mary Jane Warren (E Kingston), 27 Jun 1852
SEAVY: Charles D (Kingston/21) & Cora B Rogers (Kingston/16), 22 -- 1872
        (Daniel Seavy/Mary....)(Moses Rogers/Ellen ....)
SECOMB: Revrant Joseph & Mary Thuriel, 16 Jan 1737
SENTER: Ed B (Haverhill,Ma/27) & Martha J Parker (Bartlett/25), 29 May 1902
        (Frank Senter/Mary E Davis)(Charles L Parker/Jennie L Brown)
    Leslie M (Derry/18) & Laura Anna Collins (Kingston/17),19 Aug 1891 (N/J)
        (Frank Senter/Mary E Senter)(Andrew J Collins/Anna M Collins)
    Walter H (Derry/28) & Gertrude F Stevens (Wakefield,Ma/24), 22 Sep 1899
        (Frank Senter/Mary E Davis)(Austin H Stevens/Eva A Fisher)
SERGENT: Samuel (Newton) & Mary Hunt (Kingston), 07 Jan 1790
SEVER: Elijah (Kingston) & Sarah Smith (E Kingston), 29 May 1891*(should be 1791)
    Elisha (Kingston) & Patience Carter, 15 Mar 1792
    Thomas & Martha Webster, 10 Dec 1745
SEVERANCE: Benjamin (Kingston) & Patience Seaver (Kingston), 03 Sep 1848
    Benjamin & Jude Nicoles, 05 Jun 1755
    Benjamin F (Kingston/22) & Lucinda L (Peaslee)Gale (Newton/25), 01 Aug 1873
        (Benjamin Severance/Patience Seaver)
    Ebenezer & Annah Peeles, 08 Jan 1716/17
    Ebenezer & Dority Eliot, 05 Apr 1757
    Epahram & Mary Burnham, 25 Nov 1714
    Epharm, Jr & Elisabeth Sweat, 25 Oct 1749
    Jacob (Kingston) & Jane H Abbott (Poplin), 07 Apr 1819
    Jacob (Kingston) & Mary Tucker, 12 Mar 1794
    Jonathan (Kingston) & Hannah J Judkins (Kingston), 23 Jul 1828
    Jonathan & Trypena Neckels, 05 Sep 1754
    Ora P (Kingston/65) & Elizabeth Stickney (Plaistow/65), 27 Nov 1894
        (Samuel Severance/Judith Towle)(Samuel Heath/Abiah Gile)
    Samuel (Kingston) & Judeth Towle (Hawke), 06 Jan 1802
    Samuel & Hannah Winsle, 01 Aug 1768
SHAW: Benjamin & Rebeka Follinsbee, 04 Aug 1747
    Ichabod & Sarah Moulton,15 Dec 1742
    Jeremiah (Haverhill,Ma) & Sophia McConnell (Haverhill, Ma), 20 Dec 1849
    Joseph (Brentwood) & Miriam Brown (Poplin), 30 Sep 1790
SHELDON: Joseph C (Stewartstown/21) & Martha Jenkins (Kingston/26), 27 Apr 1901
        (Charles A Sheldon/Fannie Knapp)(Levi B Martin/Ella Davis)
SHEPHERD: Jonathan (Exeter) & Elizabeth Severance (Kingston), 12 Jan 1793
    Moses (E Kingston) & Abigail Sweat (Kingston), 21 Nov 1793
SILLOWAY: Benjamin Webster & Mary Severance, 03 Sep 1774
    Benjamin (Kingston/45) & Adaline Pollard (Acton,Me/40), 1871
        (Joseph Silloway/Polly ....)(Joseph Pollard/Susan ....)

Elmer K (Kingston/30) & Emily Norton (Franklin/25), 25 Nov 1879
    (John Silloway/Mary Campbell)(William Norton/Maranda Blood)
Elmer R (Kingston/21) & Bella Clynton (Kingston/16), 02 Nov 1870
Ernest W (Kingston/26)& Ella B Hill (So Kingston/24), 08 Jul 1888 (N)
    (Wadleigh Silloway/Ann M Hoyt)(.... F Hill/Emma Tucker)
George F & Lucy E Shaw, 24 Mar 1888   (D)
Isaac W (Kingston/26) & Emma J West (Kingston/17), 27 Nov 1872
    (Wadleigh Silloway/Anna ....)(Andrew West/Mary ....)
Jacob & Allsee Webster, 03 Jun 1745
James W (Kingston/31) & Hannah A Vincent (Danville/18), 22 Jan 1872
James W (Kingston/24) & Anna E Lakin/Lowell/19), 27 Nov 1865
William & Abigal Sleeper,-- Sep 1740
SIMES: Andrew U (Brandon,Vt/28) & Abbie J Tucker (Kingston/20),13 Oct 1900
    (Francis Simes/Sarah E Murray)(John F Tucker/Ida F Curtis)
George E (Brandon,Vt/28) & Annie F Tucker (Kingston/17), 06 May 1902
    (Francis Simes/Sarah E Murray)(John F Tucker/Ida F Curtis)
SLEEPER: Aaron & Sarah ..... (date unknown)
Beniman & Abigel Coffien, 30 Jun 1743
Benjamin & Hanah Lofring, 11 Apr 1759
David & Margaret Scribner, 24 Nov 1743
Dudley (Brentwood) & Betty Robinson, 04 Jun 1795
Ezekiel (Corinth) & Grace Scribner (Poplin), 22 Feb 1798
Henry (Hawke)& Kesia Bean, 25 Sep 1794
Hezekiah & Martha Wood, 07 May 1747
Jacob (Kingston) & Dorothy (Brentwood), 20 Jun 1782
John & Affiah Sanborn, 11 Jan 1738
Joseph H (E Kingston) & Lois Irena Currier (E Kingston), 05 Nov 1848
Levi (Kingston) & Elizabeth Loverin (Exeter), 23 Feb 1800
Richard & Martha Fifield, 22 Apr 1762
Sanborn (Brentwood) & Lucy Row, 08 Jan 1798
Sherburne & Hannah Clough, 07 Dec 1758
William & Dirrethy Blasdel, 14 Mar 1745
William (Kingston) & Betsey Hubbard, 17 Nov 1801
SLEPER: John & Ann Philbreck, 05 Jun 1712
Joseph & Sarah Hutchens, 31 Dec 1713
Thomas & Mary Colcord, 06 Dec 1714
SMEE: Thomas E, (Ireland/25) & Mary J Tuttle (Nottingham/18), 08 Feb 1884*
    (James Smee/Ellen O'Neal)(David Tuttle/Mary Reynolds) *(Salisbury,Ma)
SMITH: Clark D (Kingston) & ..... DeRochemont (Kingston), 03 Oct 1847
Daniel (Brentwood) & Rhoda Morrill, 04 Nov 1794
Frank H (Haverhill/21) & Sylvina Winslow, (Kingston/24), 14 Jan 1882
    (Daniel F Smith/Susan M .....)(William Winslow)
George E (Burk,Vt/25) & Harriet S Judkins (Kingston/2), 24 Dec 1878
    (John A Smith/Mehatable M Way(Eldridge J Judkins/Polly.....)
Henry (Raymond) & Betty Scribner (Poplin), 20 Feb 1806

Isaac & Mehetable Buziel, 31 Oct 1745
Jacob (Brentwood) & Betsey Philbrick (Hawke), 28 Feb 1798
John (Kingston) & Nancy Chase, 05 Jan 1798
Jona (Loudon) & Hannah Sleeper (Poplin), -- Aug 1801
Joshua (Brentwood) & Rachel Wadleigh (Brentwood), 14 Feb 1788
Nathaniel (Brentwood) & Mehetable Quimby, 07 Feb 1792
Othaiel (Brentwood/48) & Anjilina Judkins (Kingston/54),16 Sep 1868
  (Gilman Smith/Betty Smith)
Reuben (Exeter) & Elisabeth Wadleigh, 15 Jun 1789
Richard (E Kingston) & Mary (Hawke), 25 Nov 1787
Robert (Gilmantown) & Lois French (Kingston), 26 Aug 1794
Robert (E Kingston) & Hannah Currier, 26 Jan 1795
Simeon P (Brentwood) & Anna C Dudley, 08 Dec 1800
Warren W (E Kingston/21) & Julia C Magoon (E Kingston/19), 16 Sep 1860
Warren R (24) & Mary A Adams (26), 1872
  (Orren Smith/Abby ....)(George W Adams/Maria E .....)
Walter S (Brentwood/22) & Emma M Marshall (Brentwood/20), 23 Nov 1881
  (J.Z. Smith)(J.W. Marshall)
William & Elizabeth Seley (date unknown)
William (E Kingston) & Hebitabel Currier, 25 Feb 1799
William (Gilmanton) & Betsy Currier (E Kingston), 15 Dec 1801
SNOW: Joshua & Anna Bean, 17 Oct 1739
SPOFFORD: Oren & Susan C Clement, 23 Jul 1829
  Samuel (Andover) & Lydia Peaslee (Kingston), 18 Jun 1979
STEVENS: Aaron & Mary Simons, about 1749 (P)
  Beniman & Sarah Fifield, 24 Dec 1736
  Benjamin & Lois Judkins, 20 Dec 1792
  Benjamin & Anne Colcord, 15 Sep 1760
  Capt. Ebenezer (Kingston) & Sarah Stevens (E Kingston), 27 Feb 1783
  Chase (Plaistow) & Sarah ....., 11 Nov 1796
  Daniel (Amesbury/31) & Susanna M Smith (Amesbury/18), 22 Mar 1857
  Ebenezener & Mary Colcoard, 21 Oct 1736
  Ebenezener & Doley Stevens, 19 Dec 1768   (2nd Mar For E. Stevens)
  Ebenezer & Sarah Emerson, 10 Jan 1760
  Ebenezer & Elizabeth Colcord, 05 Dec 1710
  Ebenezer & Hannah Stevens, 29 Dec 1767
  Edward (E Kingston) & Hannah Hoyt (Newton), 25 Dec 1792
  Frank W (Kingston/24) & Lora M Stevens (Brentwood/23), 12 Nov 1890 (B)
    (Samuel W Stevens/Harriet N .....)(Charles C Stevens/Mary A .....)
  John (Kingston) & Ruhamah Fifield, 13 Dec 1798
  John & Mary Hubard, 15 Apr 1756
  John (Kingston) & Lydia Wadleigh (Kingston),-- Feb 1782
  Peter (Kingston) & Joanna Fifield, 16 Dec 1795
  Peter (Hawke) & Hannah Williams, 25 Nov 1790
  Samuell & Suah Fifield, 15 Dec 1748

Samuell & Hannah Morrill, 29 Jan 1752
Samuell (Brentwood) & Elizabeth Sleeper (Kingston), -- Nov 1783
STEVENSON: George C, (Sandown/23) & Mary J Brown(Fremont/17), 15 Mar 1874
    (Peaslee Stevenson/Rhoda ....)(Daniel S Brown/Mary H ....)
    Moses P (Fremont/28) & Sarah T Sargent (Danville/27), 12 Nov 1868
    (Joseph P Stevenson/Rhoda Burleigh)(David A Sargent/Eliza B Fuller)
STEWART: George F (Salisury,Ma/23) & Althea Wilder (Newmarket/21), 30 Apr 1880
    (James Stewart/Sarah .....)(Melissa Evans Wilder)
STICKNEY: Frank P (Atkinson/24) & Anna Coffuvel (England//21), 29 Sep 1876
    (John P Stickney/Lucy Knight)(John Coffuvel/Mary Donald)
STONE: Otwell H (Machias,Me/27) & Luella J Locke (Alexandria/37), 25 Jul 1893
    (Francis W Stone/Sarah J Taylor)(Harry Locke/Anne E Tewksbury)
STRAW: Benjamin (Sandown) & Nancy Francis, 21 May 1802
    David & Mary ..... (date unknown)
    Gideon (Nottingham) & Polly Robinson (Brentwood), 22 Jul 1793
STUART: John (Newtown) & Abigail Dow (So Hampton), 03 Feb 1805
    Nathaniel (Kingston) & Hannah Collins, 02 Nov 1804
    Samuell & Grace Hubard, 13 Jul 1758
SWEAT: Nathaniel (E Kingston) & Sally Bartlett (Newton), 23 Nov 1801
SWEENEY: Henry L (Bridgewater,Ma/27) & Elen Towle (Danville/34), 25 Dec 1884
    (Edward M Sweeney/Lucy M ....)(Darius Towle/Hannah M ....)
SWEET: Benjamin & Mary Eliot, 13 Mar 1760
    Elisha & Sarah Tilton, 11 Nov 1729
    Nathan & Mary Darbon, 06 Jan 1731
    Stephen & Sarah Garlau, 25 Feb 1761
SWETT: Benjamen & Abigaiell Darling, 25 Feb 1728/9
    Moses T (Newton/21) & Lovinia N George (Sandown/18), 1874
    (Sanborn Swett/Lucretia P Tucker)(Ora P George/Abbie Silloway)
    John & Judah Young, 17 Sep 1724
TANDE: Samuel & Hannah Lovereu, 1750
TANDY: Abel & Rachal Smith, 05 Nov 1751
TAPPAN: Arthur T (Georgetown,Ma/34) & Ida B Tucker (Kingston/31), 04 Nov 1893
    (Edmund S Tappan/Olive A Rogers)(Otis S Tucker/Sarah A Cheney)
THING: Samuel (Brentwood) & Hannah Smith, 23 Jun 1791
    William (Brentwood) & Nancy Robinson, 10 Nov 1796
    Zebede (Gilmantown) & Elizabeth Ladd, 19 Feb 1795
THOMPSON: Arthur E (Newton/25) & Alice M Rogers (Kingston/18), 13 Oct 1900
    (Dustin Thompson/Sarah Goodwin)(Moses W Rogers/Jane Winslow)
    Jonathan (Kingston) & Phebe Thompson (Kingston), 27 Feb 1783
    Nathan & Sarah Prescut, 28 Nov 1758
    Robert (Epping/35) & Betsey N Blake (Epping/23), 10 Dec 1854
    Samuel & ..... Blasdel, -- Dec 1783
    Samuel & Catrn Tucker, 26 May 1757
THORN: James & Hannah Brown, 12 Jan 1748/9
    John & Elisabeth Brown, 20 Oct 1742 (2nd Marr For John Thorn)

THURSTON: Rev. Benjamin (Kingston) & Sarah Phillips (Kingston), 02 Dec 1777
TILTON: Aaron (E Kingston) & Polly Hoyt (Newton), 07 Mar 1798
    Benjamin (Kensington) & Hannah Rowe, 14 Jul 1791
    David & Rebeaka Green, 08 Feb 1749/50
    Josiah & Sarah Flanders, 08 Feb 1732/3
    Samuel (E Kingston) & Abigail Buswell, 18 Jan 1806
    Timothy & Martha Boynton, 25 Dec 1746
    Timothy (Sandown/Fremont/47) & Susan E Gove (Danville/Fremont/44), 23 Sep 1861
    Timothy (Fremont/41) & Elisabeth M Marden (Epping/30), 06 Feb 1856
TOLE: William (Raymond) & Elizabeth Sanborn (Hawke), 23 Oct 1780
TOWLE: Calob & Rebaka ..... (date unknown)
    James (Hawke) & Sally Nash (Kingston), 06 Jan 1799
    J Everett (W Danville/28) & Effie Foster Austin (Haverhill,Ma/21), 15 Nov 1893*
        (Frederick A Towle/Lucy A Hunt)(William T Austin/Julia A Foster)* (Boston,Ma.)
    Ludovicus (Kingston) & Judith Ryan (Kingston), 13 Feb 1845
    Melvin L (Danville/23) & Anna M Fifield (Kingston/2), 27 Dec 1868
        (Daniel Towle/Hannah M Diamond)(Simon P Fifield/Mary E Brown)
    Melvin L (Danville/26) & Katie Work (Bordenham,Me/20), 1871
        (Darius Towle/Hannah M ....)(Charles E Work/Sarah L ....)
TRUE: Charles F (Chester/27) & Sarah J Philbrick (Kingston/18), 20 -- 1871
    (William S True/Mary ....)(Edward Philbrick/Sarah ....)
    Reuben (Salisbury) & Rhoda Bartlett (Kingston), 22 Feb 1789
TUCK: Alfred H (Kingston/26) & Julia M Bishop/26), 17 Apr 1860
    Jonathan (Kensington) & Dolly Webster (E Kingston), 16 May 1792
    Son of DR TUCK & Daughter of SANBORN COFFIN, 17 Mar 1789
    Nathan (Brentwood) & Judeth Smith, 04 Nov 1790
TUCKER: Benjamin & Juda Thuriel, .. Sep 1748
    Benjamin (Poplin) & Huldah Bean (Hawke), 06 Apr 1796
    Charles R (Kingston/22) & Florence A Woodward (Bradford,Ma/18), 02 Feb 1899
        (Otis Tucker/Saray E Cheney)(Charles Woodward)
    Daniel (Poplin) & Elizabeth Huntington, 23 Jul 1789
    Ezra & Hipsebah Prese, 03 May 1759
    Isiah (Kingston/36) & Adeline Davis (Kingston/37), 01 Jun 1861
    Jeremiah C (Kingston/32) & Elizabeth M Libby (Groveland,Ma/46), 03 Apr 1902*
        (Moses Tucker/Hannah Martin)(William Banks/Catherine Davis) *(Lynn,Ma)
    Joseph (Kingston) & Alice Sanborn (Kingston), 05 Nov 1787
    Mason W (Danville/22) & Arvilla A March (Danville/18), 10 Aug 1856
    Moses (Kingston) & Rachel Cook, 29 Dec 1791
    Samell & Mary Elkens, 26 Dec 1723
    True (Poplin) & Polly Gordon, 08 Jan 1798
    Warren H (Andover,Ma/31) & Mary A Clark (Kingston/27), 26 Sep 1900
        (Jeremiah H Tucker/Rosetta B Woodward)(John T Clark/Sarah E Titcomb)
    William F (Kingston/22) & Nellie Simes (Brandon,Vt/22), 22 Sep 1900
        (John F Tucker/Ida F Curtis)(Francis E Simes/Sarah E Murray)

VERRILL: Robert W (Candia/26) & Mamie D Crosby (Newton/23), 02 Mar 1893
    (Robert W Verrill/Eliza E Verrill)(Asa W Hanson/Lucy Ann Hanson)
VEZEY: Jeremiah (Brentwood) & Abigail Clark, 02 Oct 1792
VINCENT: George (Sandown) & Abigail Eastman (Danville), 05 May 1845
WADLEIGH: Daniel (Kingston/31) & Maria E Hoyt (Dover/26), 24 Dec 1855
    John & Mary Dent, 27 Dec 1757
    Thomas & Margaret Rowen, 22 Sep 1748
    Jonathan (Kingston/Danville/38) & Louisa Woodman (Kingston/Danville/17)
    17 Dec 1855
WATSON: Ebenezer & Elisebath Severance, 25 Jul 1758
WEBB: Daniel (Canterbury) & Betsey Williams (Hawke), 16 Jul 1801
WEBSTER: Abraham & Martha Emons, 30 Mar 1763
    Albert P (Kingston/36) & Betsey L Webster (Kingston/18),02 Jul 1869
        (William Webster)(Elihu T Webster)
    Albert S (So Kingston/20) & Alice S Heath (20), 02 Nov 1877
        (William C Webster/Elizebeth Wilkinson)(Frank F Heath/Maria C Austin)
    Beniman & Mary Stanyen, 01 Dec 1727
    Beniman & Elisabeth Stuard, 17 Feb 1725
    Benjamin (Kingston) & Sarah Page (Hawke), 28 Apr 1785
    Benjamin K (E Kingston/37) & Lydia J Gile (Raymond/21), 28 Jan 1866
    Caleb (Hampstead) & Joanna Smith (E Kingston), 20 May 1777
    Caleb & Molley Tilton, 23 Oct 1783
    Charles E (E Kingston/27) & Alice M Huse (Kingston/19), 09 Mar 1893
        (John T Webster/Abbie F Buswell)(William F Huse/Lucy A Webster)
    Dana (E Kingston/28) & Louisa C Tilton (E Kingston/28), 19 Apr 1866
    David (E Kingston) & Judith Webster (E Kingston), 01 Sep 1808
    David G (Kingston) & (Mrs)Sarah M Adams (Salisbury), 01 Sep 1844
    Eastman (Kingston/20) & Martha J Elkins (Danville/18), 31 Dec 1874
    Ebenazer & Hannah Judgkin, 25 Jul 1709
    Elbridge G (E Kingston) & (Mrs)Plomy D England, 14 Mar 1847
    Eliphalet & Hannah Prescott, 27 Jan 1774
    Eliphelet (E Kingston)& Jane Tilton (Deerfield), 19 Jun 1820
    George (E Kingston/22) & Sophronia Magoon (E Kingston22), 13 Nov 1859
    George B (E Kingston) & Martha T Bowe (E Kingston), 07 Jul 1846
    Iddo & Jena Goss, 12 Mar 1746
    Ira H (Kingston/24) & Edith E Judkins (Kingston/23), 13 Oct 1886 (E)
        (Elihu Webster/Ruth S Hunt)(Eldridge Judkins/Polly Swain)
    Jacob (Kingston) & Abigail Carlton (Newton), 08 Mar 1802
    Jeremiah & Elizabeth Lad, 19 Jun 1729
    John T (E Kingston) & Abby P Buswell (E Kingston), 09 Mar 1850
    John & Ruth Clough, 17 Nov 1730
    John L (E Kingston/21) & Mary A Prescott (Newton/23), 17 Nov 1881 (F)
        (John T Webster/Abbie P Buswell)(George W Prescott/Mary G Johnson)
    Jonathan & Elisezebath Sleper (Widow), 1702
    Jonathan & Nancy York, 31 May 1843

Joseph (Kingston) & Sarah J Long (Kingston), 03 Jul 1842
Samell & Elisabeth Burnum, 25 Feb 1733
Samuel & Dirrethy Staniel, 10 May 1740 (2nd Marr For Samuel)
Stephen S (Kingston) & Diana C Fifield (Brentwood), 26 Dec 1850
Thomas & Dorothy Chase (Brentwood), 02 Feb 1801
Thomas (Haverhill,Ma) & Mary Greely, 19 Jun 1717
Thomas, Jr & Juda Noyes, 12 Oct 1738
William (Kingston) & Polly Davis, 26 Dec 1798
WEED: David & Abigel Judkins, 29 Nov 1743
WEEDEN: Frank A (Danvers,Ma/36) & Mary O Atkins (Haverhill,Ma/36), 24 Nov 1894
    (John J Weeden/Martha A ...)(Wilder W Thompson/Mary Copp)
WEEK: Charles B (Merrimac,Ma/28) & Hannah E Sweat (Kingston/17), 09 Jun 1878
    (Isaac M Weed/Sarah R Silloway)(J Sanborn Sweat/Lucretia P Tucker)
WELCH: Moses & Judah Woster, 18 Jun 1755
    Philep & Sarah Wolsford, 05 Jun 1738
    Sammel & Elenor Clough, 18 Feb 1746/7
    Thomas & Elisebath Prese, 26 Jun 1752
WELLS: ---- & Mercy Burbank, 05 Feb 1784
WELSH: Joseph & Debrah Scribner, 29 Dec 1726
WEST: Andrew J (Fremont/58) & Hattie (Winslow)Webster (Kingston/49), 18 Nov 1889
    (John West/Ann Marsh)(William Winslow/Mary P Severance)
    Daniel A (Kingston/20 & Dora E Seaver (Kingston/18), 30 Jul 1891
    (Andrew J West/Mary F Davis)(Daniel P Seaver/Dolly C Seaver)
    Edward (Kingston) & Miriam Thompson, -- May 1804
    Fred F (Haverhill,Ma/20) & Mabel Pinkham (Gloucester,Ma/18), 01 Aug 1895
    (Andrew J West/Mary F Davis)(Watson Pinkham/Carrie Pinkham)
    Horace W (Fremont/22) & Nellie Gordin (Boston,Ma/17), 13 Jul 1881
    (Josiah West/Hannah Gover)(George Gordin/Nellie Gordin)
    Jonathan (Poplin)& Polly Davis, 22 Feb 1798
    Jonathan & Mary Jacobs, 09 May 1779
    Nehemia (Brentwood) & Sally Row, 09 Jan 1793
    Walter S (Kingston/19) & Ruth F Nasson (Kingston/18), 08 Oct 1876
    (A.J.West/Mary F Davis)(Nathan Nasson/Sarah R Page)
WHITAKER: Moses (Weare) & Betsey Campbell (Hawke), 30 Oct 1787
WHITEHOUSE: Osmond (Kingston/24) & Emily Pollard (Raymond/23), 04 Jul 1860
WHITTIER: Nathan W(Kingston) & Almiree Dudley (Kingston), 18 Apr 1858
WHITTEN: Charles B (Wolfboro/33) & Susie H Robinson (Kingston/23), 02 Jan 1896
    (Martin B Whitten/Mary Jan Boston)(John H Robinson/Caroline P Deleware)
WHITTIER: Charles H (David/23) & Almira J Aldrich (Haverhill, Ma/16), 1872
    (George Whittier/Anison...)(Jonathan Aldrich)
    David A (Kingston) & Sarah C Chamberlain (Lyndenborough), 10 Apr 1847
    Horace K (W.Newbury/22) & Frances B Conner (Haverhill,Ma/18), 26 May 1877
    (Dudley H Whittier/Sarah A...)(John Conner/Ellen....)
    Horace (Raymond/24) & Mary L Robinson (Fremont/19), 27 Nov 1862

Jonathan (Kingston) & Polly Webster, 12 Dec 1805
Joshua (Raymond) & Lydia Poor, 11 Mar 1804
Peter (Newton) & Susannah Hoyt, 27 Feb 1800
Walter F (Kingston/22) & Lulu M Collins (Kingston/20), 08 Oct 1898
    (George W Whittier/Martha J Haines)(Andrew J Collins/Anna M White)
WICHER: William & Shep Moriel, 17 Feb 1736
WIGGIN: Alvin (Exeter/32) & Mary A French (Kingston/34), 08 Jun 1869
    (Joshua Wiggins)(Moses P French/Mary E ....)
WILDER: Frank D, (Lebanon/18) & Annie Judson (England/21), 30 Dec 1881
    (Jacob G Wilder/Abbie Goodwin)(William Judson/Sarah Warner)
WILLARD: Will L (22) & J....Jewell (19), 04 Jun 1884
WILLEY: Daniel G (Danville/26) & Rosannah West (Brentwood/19), 15 Apr 1857
WILLIAMS: Capt. Joseph (Hawke) & Sally Blake,-- Apr 1804
WILSON: Benjamin (Poplin) & Judith Brown, 06 Jul 1794
    Ebenezer (Johnson,Vt/30) & Elisabeth Currier (E Kingston/35), 25 Nov 1851
    Harry C (Lawrence,Ma/22) & Angalina L Thompson (Great Falls/26), 20 Feb 1870
    (William G Wilson)(William C Hyde)
    Luther J (Kingston/38) & Mattie S Tarleton (Kingston/33), 22 May 1895
    (William G Wilson/Esther Chase)(George C Stevens/Sarah A Hunt)
    Luther J (Kingston) & Mary E Williams, 05 Nov1884
    William G (Kingston) & Esther Johnson (Kingston), 13 Jan 1844
WINSLEY: Samell & Huldah Sweet, 03 Jan 1723/4
WINSLO: Elisha & Mary Sleeper, 04 Jan 1725
WINSLOW: Benjamin & Mary Clough, 07 May 1765
    Elisha (Nottingham) & Lydia Winslow (Kingston), 28 Jun 1792
    Epharam & Hannah Colcord, 27 Mar 1753
    Horace G (Kingston/23) & Eldora E Nason (Kingston/15), 12 Feb 1896 (D)
    (William Winslow/Elisa Silloway)(Albert T Nason/Laura Fifield)
    James W (Kingston/23) & Mary A Smith (Amesbuy/Fremont/17), 27 Feb 1861
    John (Kingston) & Polly Webster, 14 Apr 1796
    Samuel & Phaba Buswell, 09 Jun 1763
    Samuel M (Kensington/23) & Julia A Merrows (Great Falls/23), 02 Apr 1868
    (William Winslow)(Elisha Merrows)
    Samuell & Jean French, 15 Feb 1749/50
    William (Kingston) & Polly Severance (Kingston), 26 Feb 1824
WOOD: Abel (Westminster, Ma) & Sarah A Patten (Kingston), 26 Jul 1849
    Frederick E (Somerville/28) & Caroline E Peaslee (Kingston/25), 11 Jun 1896
    (Alexander M Wood/Margaret Cox)(Luther D Peaslee/Mary Clark)
WOODBURY: Alden (Lisbon,Me/57) & Augusta Woodman (Mechanics Falls,Me/60)*
    (James Woodbury/Elizabeth Woodbury(Greenleaf Woodman) *04 May 1889
    William H (Haverhill, Ma/Kingston/24) & Hattie L Witherall (Chesterfield/20)
    05 Jul 1864
WOODMAN: Elihu & Permelia Fitts, 24 Jan 1822
    John (E Kingston) & Nancy Bagley, 28 Jul 1805
    Jonathan (Candia) & Abigail (E Kingston), 13 Nov 1782

Joseph (Kingston) & Anna Wadleigh (Brentwood), 24 May 1779
Joshua & Eunis ..... (date unknown)
Moses (N Salisbury) & Hannah Eaton (Kingston), 08 Jul 1777
Samuel E & Olive Ann Goodrich, 27 Apr 1851
Samuel E & Eliza V Spearin, 13 Jan 1855
WORTH: Joseph & Ane Stanyan, 16 Apr 1752
WORTHEN: Ezekiel (Bridgewater,Ma) & Elizabeth Bachelder (Hawke),14 Jun 1792
   Samuel (Candia) & Sarah Brown (Poplin), 20 Sep 1805
YOUNG: Daniel & Haner Loverin, 23 Jan 1734/5
   Daniel (Maine/Kingston) & Mary J Page (Danville), 30 Sep 1839
   John & Sarah Curnham, 13 Nov 1729
   John & Merriam Sawyer, - - Apr 1752
   Jonathan (Kingston) & Sarah Clifford (Kingston), 28 Oct 1777
   Jonathan & Mary Loverin, 20 Oct 1741
   Joseph & Sarah Brown, 09 Apr 1747
   Joseph & Batta Carr, 25 Apr 1759
   Joseph & Elizabeth Sleper, 24 Dec 1705
   Stephen & Dority Blasdel,-- Nov 1752

DEATHS
1694 - 1900

ABBOTT: Edna, 12 Sep 1888 (Isaac Abbott/Nellie Tobyne) 5 months
    Lillian, 08 Apr 1897 (Isaac D Abbott/Nellie B Tobyne) 8 months
ABRAMS: Ella F, 21 Oct 1889 at Haverhill,Ma (Frank Abrams) 4 months
ADAMS: George, 08 Oct 1881 - b - 1836
ALLEN: Amos Jr, 09 Sep 1881 (Amos Davis/Nancy Davis) b - 1857
ANDREWS: Sarah A (McNeil) ,27 Aug 1896 (Dugal McNeil/Margaret) b - 1863
AVERY: Frank, 01 Feb 1882 (Joseph Avery/Mary) b - 1856
BACHELDER: Daniel , 06 Jan 1733 (Phienes Bachelder/Elisabeth Gilmon) b - 16 Oct 1733
    Mary, 12 Oct 1735 (Nathaniel Bachelder/Mary)
BADGER: Dorothy, 22 Nov 1883 (William Badger/Elizabeth) b - 1815
    Elizabeth (Dearborn), 21 Dec 188 3 (Nahs Dearborn/Sarah) b - 1790
BAILY: Harriet (Magoon), 05 Jan 1899 (w/o George E Bailey)
    (Joseph Magoon & Rebecca Clough)
BAKIE: James, 07 Jan 1899 (James Bakie/Elizabeth Alexander) b - 1856
BALL: Olive Ida, 17 Sep 1887 (Albert Ball /Ida Win)
BARBER: Lucy A (Noble), 30 Jan 1890 (Capt John Noble/Pamelia)
BARRETT: Lawrence, 01 May 1884
    Lawrence T, 13 Sep 1899 (John E Barrett/Lizzie Trafton) b - 1888
    Michael, 02 Aug 1894 - b 1845
BARTLETT: ....., 04 Feb 1881 (R B Bartlett) 42 days
    Elisabeth, -- Dec 1773 (Matthias Bartlett/Elisabeth Davis)
    Elizabeth (Davis), 08 Nov 1778 (w/o Matthias Bartlett)
    Elizabeth M, 11 Aug 1887 (Jonathan Bartlett/Hannah Peaslee) b - 1822
    Gertie, 27 Apr 1872- 8 months
    Junia S, 05 Oct 1887 (Levi S Bartlett/Aroline Sanborn) b - 1850
    Levi S, 28 Sep 1884 (Levi S Bartlett/Grace Sanborn) 6 months
    Mariah, 01 May 1883-b 1850
    Richard B, 08 Apr 1893 (Richard Bartlett/Sally Fellows) b - 1844
BASSETT: Thomas, 01 Dec 1889 - b 1797
BEALS: James Henry, 08 Mar 1898 (Robert Beals/Anna) b - 1847
BEAN: Anna E, 23 Sep 1889 - b 1889
    Enoch, 13 Jan 1875 - b 1816
    Joseph, 24 Mar 1753 (h/o Meriam (Folsom) Bean)
    O., 09 Apr 1872 - b 1786
    Obediah, 13 Nov 1888 (Obediah Bean/Nancy Cooper) b - 1807
BERRY: Eben, 30 Jun 1885 (Daniel Berry) b 1846
BLAISDELL: William, 18 Oct 1888 at St Louis, Mo - b 1834
BLASDEIL: Sarah, 28 Jul 1744 (Ebenezenr Blasdiel/Sarah Stockman) b 08 Nov 1740
BRAGDON: Betsey M (Henderson), 01 Oct 1893 (Stephen Henderson/Sarah Roberts) b 1807
    Georgie, 01 Nov 1890 (Daniel Seaver) b 1870
    Lydia, 07 Jan 1885 b - 1808

BROWN: Annie (Judkins), 04 May 1883 (L B Judkins) b 1856
  Charles R, 21 Sep 1870 (Anna Brown) b 1868
  Jacob, 19 Feb 1878 - b 1854
  Mary, 20 Mar 1883 - b 1789
  Samuel, 16 Mar 1786 (Amos T Brown/Abigail)
  Susanah, 11 Aug 1735 (Simen Brown/Hannah)
BROWNING: Welcome, 31 Mar 1874 - b 1850
BUCKLEY: Anna J, 09 Mar 1888 (Sylvester Buckley/Agnes Mullen) b 1887
BUSHWAY: Peter, .. Jun 1881
BUSIEL: Cornelos, 11 Aug 1735 (William Busiel/Juda Davies) b 17 Jul 1731
  Joseph, 14 Aug 1735 (Wiliam Busiel/Juda Davies) b 08 Jul 1725
  Sarah, 29 Sep 1735 (William Busiel /Juda Davies) b 17 Apr 1718
BUSWEL: John, 11 Feb 1747 (Willam Buswel /Abigel Thorn) b 01 May 1743
  Sarah, 06 Apr 1752 (Willam Buswel /Abigel Thorn) b 10 Mar 1752
BUSWELL: Lydia, 31 Dec 1787 (Daniel Buswell /Hannah Runnels)
CALEF: Everett G, 06 Dec 1899 at Cleveland, Oh (Samuel Calef /Mary A Berry)
  Miriam (Bartlett), Aug 1785 (w/o Joseph Calef)
  Molly (Hook), 09 Oct 1790 (w/o Joseph Calef)
  Samuel, 12 Feb 1890 at Exeter (h/o Mary A Berry) b 1810
CAMPBELL: Arthur W, 29 Dec 1878 (Alfred H Campbell /Hattie C) 3 months
  Buel C, 01 Aug 1889, (Buel Campbell /Esther)
CAPERON: Charles C, 01 Jan 1884 (Charles C Caperon/Nellie) 9 months
CARLTON: George W, 17 Apr 1881 - b 1810
CARRIER: Perlie, 09 Oct 1880 (Frank Carrier) 6 months
CARTER: Enoch C, 30 Jan 1885 (Enoch Carter/ Sarah Pierce) b 1809
  Merrill, 22 Mar 1876 - b 1812
CASS: Livingston, 28 Aug 1877
CATER: Samuel, 1878 - b 1836
CHAMBERLAIN: Jason S, 19 May 1898 (Sylvester Chamberlain/Ann M Snyder) b 1858
CHASE: Amos, 29 Dec 1873 - b 1803
  Emily A (Belden),   04 Jul 1890 - b 1846
  Hannah (Hook), 23 May 1888 (Josiah Hook/Sarah Whittier) b - 1811
CHENEY: Hannah M, 20 Aug 1885 b - 1842
  John, 14 Dec 1870 (Dearborn Cheney/Mary Cheney) b 1852
  Mary, 1883 (Isaac Hoyt) b 1821
  Nathaniel, 28 May 1880
CHOAT: Abigaill, 15 Apr 1717 (Beniamen Choate/Abigaill Burnnum)
  Abigel, 20 Mar 1736 (Beniamen Choate/Abigaill Burnnum) b 27 Mar 1723
  Abigaill (Burnham), 21 or 24 Apr 1829 at Brentwood
  Benjamin, 07 Dec 1715 (Beniamen Choate/Abigaill Burnnum) b 07 Aug 1715
  Benjamin, 26 Nov 1753 (h/o Abigaill Burnnum) b 1680
  Benjamin, 19 Jan 1749 (Benjamin Choat/Ruth Edwards)
  Jerimiah, 25 May 1722 (Beniamen Choate /Abigaill Burnnum) b 12 Aug 1721
  Jonathan, 09 Jan 1752

Jonathan, 03 Aug 1742 (Jonathan Choat/Elizabeth Moodey)

Joseph, 18 Jan ---- (Benjamin Choat/Ruth Edwards)

CHOATE: Abigail, 19 Nov 1710 (Beniamen Choate /Abigaill Burnnum) b 02 Jun 1710

Luse, 23 Dec 1717 (Beniamen Choate /Abigaill Burnnum) - Stillborn

CHOATT: Abigaiell, 15 Apr 1717 (Beniamen Choate/ Abigaill Burnnum) b 16 Sep 1711

Benjamin, 07 Dec 1714 - b 30 Dec 1713

Benjamin, 28 Jul 1758

CILLEY: Andrew J, 21 May 1889 (h/o Susan Bartlett) (Aaron Cilley/Lydia Dodge) b 1818

Benjamin D, 08 Dec 1876 (Aaron Cilley/Lydia Dodge) b 1812

Emma J (Severance) (Jacob Severance)----- (date unknown)

Susan, 16 Nov 1889 - b 1816

CLARK: ...., 11 Jul 1889 (Charles W Clark/Nellie Little)

Charles, 08 May 1881 - b 1805

Daniel O, 06 Oct 1883 (Amos Clark/Jusecha)b 1837

Johnanna E, 30 Oct 1881 - b 1807

Kate C, 27 Feb 1896 (Walter S Clark/Abbie Sanborn) b 1878

Walter Otis, 15 Jun 1886 (Walter S Clark/Abbie Sanborn) 8 months

CLARKE: Mary (Frost), 17 Jul 1735 (w/o RevWard Clarke)

Rev.Ward, 05 May 1737 (h/o Mary (Frost) Clarke)

CLIFFORD: Joseph, 07 Jan 1747 (Joseph Clifford /Mary Healey) b 21 Mar 1745

Ledea (Perkens), 08 Sep 1723 (w/o Joseph Clifford)

Levi B, 02 Nov 1890 (John Clifford /Deborah Sinclair) b 1812

CLIFORD: Isaac, 11 Sep 1745 (Isaac Clifford/Sarah Taylor) b 01 May 1721

John, 03 Nov 1735 (Joseph Cliford/Ledea Perkens) b 14 Aug 1719

Joseph, 11 Oct 1735 (Joseph Cliford/Lydea Perkens) b 09 Dec 1721

Sarah (French), 06 Dec 1714 (w/o Joseph Cliford)

Tristrum, (Isaac Clifford/Sarah Taylor)....... (date unknown)

Zacariah, 23 May 1752 (Isaac Clifford/ Sarah Taylor) b 21 May 7130

CLOUGH: Joseph, 25 Feb 1716 (Joseph Clough/Mary Jennes) b 17 May 1713

Mary, Apr 1716 (Joseph Clough /Mary Jennes) b Apr 1716

Mary, 28 Aug 1778 (Cornelos Clough/Mary Levit)

Moses, 31 Nov 1720 (Joseph Clough/Mary Jennes) b 30 Sep 1720

COLCOARD: Abigel, 20 Oct 1735 (Ebenezener Colcoard/Haner Fellows) b 18 May 1733

Ebenezer, 07 May 1766

Haner, 25 Sep 1735 (Ebenezener Colcoard/Haner Fellows) b 26 Aug 1730

Left.Sammel, 05 Oct 1736 (h/o Mary)

Mary, 29 May 1739 (w/o Sammel Colcoard)

Mary, 01 Nov 1735 (Ebenezener Colcoard/Haner Fellows) b 01 Aug 1735

Mary Ann, -- Sep 1843 (Capt Daniel Colcord)

Mary, 07 Aug 1862 (20)

Peter, 19 Mar 1727/8 (Ebenezer Colcoard/Haner Fellows)

Peter, 07 May 1732 (Ebenezener Colcoard/ Haner Fellows) b 22 Apr 1732

Peter, 07 Oct 1844 (69)

COLCONE: Samuel C, 18 Feb 1877 (Samuel W Colcone) b 1850

Samuel W, 29 Jan 1875

COLCORD: Benjamen, 30 Jan 1713 (Sammell Colcord /Elizabeth Folsom) b 10 Jan 1713

Daniel, 31 Mar 1879

Dolly, 06 Apr 1827 (Daniel Colcord/Polly Woodman)

Ebenezer, 01 May 1724 (Ebenezer Colcoard/Haner Fellows)

Elizabeth, 09 Aug 1735 (Samuell Colcord/Mehitabel Lad)

Hannah, 21 Oct 1774 (Daniel Colcord /Doley Clifford)

Hannah, 17 Apr 1751 (Samuell Colcord/Mehitable Lad)

Julia, 12 May 1845 (34) (w/o Daniel Colcord)

Louis, 29 Mar 1831 (Daniel Colcord/Polly Woodman)

Monroe, 04 Jul 1887 (Daniel Colcord/ Polly Woodman) b 1823

Peter, 05 Nov 1749 (Samuell Colcord/Mehitable Lad)

Polly, 21 Jul 1844 (ll mos) (Daniel Colcord/....)

Polly (Woodman), 28 Mar 1831

Sarah, 08 Aug 1862

Samuel, 18 Feb 1877 (27) (Samuel W Colcord/.....)

Samuel, 15 Apr ---- (Samuell Colcord/Mehitable Lad)

Samuel, 29 Jan 1875

Mrs. Samuel, 14 Dec 1844 (24)

Samuell, 26 Nov 1748 (Samuell Colcord/Mehitable Lad)

COLLIER: Adeline M, 07 Feb 1874 - b 1828

Julia, 25 Aug 1890 at Boston, Ma   2 months

COLLINS: Andrew J, 28 Apr 1885 (Elias Collins / Betsy .....) b 1836

Charles Elmer, 14 Apr 1896 (Elmer Collins / Susie A Nason) b 1895

Charles S, 26 Oct 1888 (Andrew J Collins / Anna M Smith) b 1818

David F, 12 Feb 1893 at Exeter (Samuel Collins / Julia Judkins) b 1849

Dolly, 20 May 1893 (L. Collins & Dolly Jones) b 1817

Ellen (Winslow), 18 Sep 1879 (George Winslow) b 1851

George, 28 Sep 1879 (Leon Collins / Ellen) 17 months

John Wesley, 12 Jul 1896 (Hezekiah Collins/ Sarah Mowe) b 1839

Rachel, 19 Oct 1893 (Stephen Hunt/ Polly Woodman) b 1815

COLMAN: Jabaz, 08 Sep 1724 (h/o Mary Colman)

Joseph 08 Sep 1724 (Jabaz Colman / Mary)

CONNOLLY: Laurence, 04 Dec 1889 - b 1854

COWELL: Annie E, 07 Oct 1883 (George F Cowell / Emma)14 days

CRAFTS: Hannah E, 19 Oct 1883 (John C Crafts) b 1807

CRANKE: Adaline, 25 Jul 1884 (John Dresser / Mary Dresser) b 1821

CREGAN: John B, 06 Mar 1898 (Michael Gregan /Mary Woodbury) b 1867

Mary, 01 Nov 1899 (William Woodbury / Fanny Winchell) b 1845

CROMWELL: Ralph, 02 Jul 1896 (Dennis Cormwell / Luella Thompson) 27 days

CURRIER: Charles, 28 Jul 1886 (Joseph Currier / Nancy) b 1824

Edward S, 03 Jul 1898 (Joseph D Currier / Lena)b 1881

Franklin, 12 May 1883

CUSHING: Thomas P N, 27 Sep 1893 (Philip Cushing / Isadora Rock) 1 year

DARLING: Daniel, 13 Nov 1760 (h/o Suzaner (Webster) Darling)
    David, 22 Jan 1767 (Daniel Darling / Suzaner Webster)
    Ruth, 15 Jan 1760 (Daniel Darling / Suzaner Webster) b 19 Sep 1744
DAVIS: Alfred, 16 Oct 1884 (Joshua Davis / Hannah Tuttle) b 1812
    Amos, 17 Jul 1881 - b 1814
    Amos, 09 Sep 1881 (Amos Davis / Nancy Davis)
    Harriet (French), 12 Jul 1878
    Henry, 15 Oct 1894 (Thomas Davis / Nancy) b 1833
    Mary A (Bartlett), 18 Oct 1899 (Jacob Bartlett / Polly True) b 1820
    Mary Jane, 12 May 1888 at Haverhill,Ma (Gilman Crane) b 1842
    Nathaniel, 24 Nov 1769 (Ruben Davis / Elisabeth Jonson)
    Phebe, 07 Jan 1791 (Ruben Davis / Elisabeth Jonson)
    Polly S (Tucker), 23 Mar 1890 at Brentwood (Moses Tucker /Rachael Cook) b 1806
    Ruben, 24 Feb 1877 - b 1793
    Sarah, 14 Aug 1895 (Isaac Merson/ Mary Kenney) b 1813
DAY: Charles J, 22 Feb 1896 at South Berwick, Me - b 1860
DEARBORN: Andrew J, 02 Oct 1880
DECATUR: Edwin Forrest, 28 Aug 1858 at Exeter (Clarence B Decatur/Isabelle Forrest)
    b - 26 Feb 1913
DENTT: Abraham, 24 May 1715 (Thomas Dentt / Achaicus) b 09 May 1715
DEROCHMONT: Charles H, 08 Oct 1881 (h/o Mary Payson)
    Daniel P, 19 Mar 1896 (Charles H DeRochmont / Mary Payson) b 1829
DIEVER: Sally, 12 Aug 1884 (Henry Diever & Nancy) b 1814
DOWNING: Alcina, 20 Nov 1879 - b 1873
DUNN: , Hattie Celia, 07 Jun 1879 (Charles Dunn / Mary) b 1867
EALKINS: Jacob, 28 Mar 1733 (Obediah Elkens / Abigaiell French) b 08 Feb 1732
EASMON: Jonathan, 07 Mar 1740 (Ebenezener Easmon / Mary Sleper) b 28 Jun 1737
EASTMAN: Eben, 08 Jun 1885 (Peter Eastman / Mary) b 1811
    Eliza Ann (Calef), 04 Oct 1898 at Exeter (Robert Calef / Mary) b 1814
    Mary G, 11 Aug 1893 at Lexington - b 1815
EATON: Mildred, 01 Dec 1887 (Albert Eaton / Carrie Lancaster) 9 months
EDNEY: Eseline, 26 Jan 1887 - b 1826
    Eva Maude, 28 Aug 1876 at Middleborough, Ma b -1892
ELKENS: Anah, 11 Aug 1735 (Joseph Elkens / Elisabeth) b 10 Oct 1726
    Deacon Moses, 09 May 1737 (h/o Annah Shaw)
    Doraty, 15 Aug 1735 (Joseph Elkens / Elisabeth) b 01 Jun 1734
    Elisabeth, 13 Aug 1735 (Joseph Elkens / Elisabeth) b 30 Apr 1730
    Henry, 27 Mar 1720 (Moses Elkens / Annah Shaw) b 22 Mar 1720
    Mehetebel, 09 Dec 1711 - b 20 Jul 1706
ELKINS: Henry, 17 Sep 1707
ERICKHORN: Mary, 21 Jan 1884 at Boston, Ma - b 1818
EVELETH: Sarah W (Lakin), 04 Jul 1898 (Daniel Lakin / Hannah Crockett) b 1819
FARNUM: Mary Ann (Ellison), 08 Nov 1890 (Joseph Ellison / Betsy Dor) b 1826
FELLOWS: Ebenezeur, 05 Feb 1741 (h/o Elisebeth (Brockes) Fellows)

Sammell, 12 Oct 1714 (h/oSarah (Webster) Fellows)
FIFIELD: Dority, 22 Mar 1765 (w/o John Fifield)
Joseph, 07 Jun 1761 (h/o Sarah Sharbon)
Martha, 12 May 1716 (w/o John Fifield)
Mary, 25 Feb 1744 (John Fifield / Doratha) b 16 Jan 1744
Mary E (Brown), 22 Dec 1895 (Benjamin Brown / Mary Colcord) b 1817
Sarah (Sharbon), 03 Apr 1765 (w/o Joseph Fifield)
FOGG: Edson, 06 Apr 1874 (Martin Fogg/Jane Rollins)b 1856
George S, 11 Jun 1884 - b 1826
FOLLANSBY: Nash Parker, 25 Jul 1881 - 8 months
FOYE: James H, 10 Aug 1896 - b 1836
FRENCH: Annie M, 13 Mar 1899 at Everett, Ma - b 1873
Caroline, 23 Aug 1890 (Joseph French) b 1808
Clara, 04 Apr 1872 (John B French)
Elizabeth (Kimball), 10 Aug 1883
Harvey C, 15 Nov 1886 (John G French / Abbie) 13 months
Henery, 30 Sep 1746 (Jonathan French / Johaner Elkins) b 26 Oct 1738
Izetta, 27 Jan 1870 - b 1798 (w/o John French)
Johaner, 16 Aug 1737 (Jonathan French / Johaner Elkins) b 18 Aug 1737
John B, 08 Mar 1888 (h/o Izetta French) b 1818
Jonathan, 14 Jun 1741 (Jonathan French / Johaner Elkins) b 01 Jun 1741
Jonathan, 29 May 1744 (Jonathan French / Johaner Elkins) b 15 Apr 1744
Joseph (Twin), 27 Aug 1746 (Jonathan French / Johaner Elkins) b 29 May 1745
Lela May, 18 Aug 1887 (John G French / Addie M Avery) b Mar 1887
Margarett T, 04 Jul 1886 - b 1803
Mary (Severance), 15 Apr 1883 (John Severance) b 1803
Mary (Twin), 05 Sep 1746 (Jonathan French / Johaner Elkins) b 29 May 1745
Mary J, 24 Nov 1893 at Concord - b 1826
Rachall, 28 Sep 1717 (Simon French / Sarah Heard) b 12 Apr 1717
Secombe, 21 Sep 1743 (Nathaniel French Jr / Abigel Easmon) b 31 Oct 1740
William, 23 Sep 1743 (Nathaniel French Jr / Abigel Easmon) b 23 May 1738
FROST: Susie, 23 Jan 1881 (Edward Frost / Cornelia) b 1863
FURBEN: Nancy C (Wadleigh), 08 May 1886 - b 1821
GALE: Amos, 29 Apr 1743 (Jacob Gale / Suzaner) b 21 Apr 1743
Henery, 19 Oct 1754 (Jacob Gale / Suzaner) b 02 Oct 1754
John, 12 Jun 1896 (John Gale / Mary Colby) b 1819
Susanna, 24 Oct 1754 (Jacob Gale / Suzaner) b 12 Oct 1752
GARLAND: Lloyd R, 26 Feb 1899 - 6 months
GEORGE: ....., 21 Aug 1883 (Archie L George / Lizzie E)
Abbie, 05 Oct 1896 (w/o Ora P George) (Joseph Silloway / Polly Cass) b 1832
Kenneth, 02 Dec 1898 (Delbert George / Martha Hemphill)   2 months
Mary Abbie, 07 Apr 1886 (Stephen George / Edna)
GILMAN: Joseph W, 20 Jan 1876 (Lewis Gilman) b 1849
Mary J (Farrington), 28 Oct 1895 (Daniel Farrington / Ruth Bartlett) b 1810

Ruth, 31 Jan 1880
GLIDDEN: Sadie M, 17 Sep 1899 (Daniel R Glidden / Anna B Grace) 3 months
GOODWIN: Charlotte A, 20 Apr 1898 (Timothy Goodwin) b 1837
    Daniel L, 01 Oct 1890 (John Goodwin / Dorothy Martin) b 1839
    Ines Louisa, 08 Apr 1883 (Louis Goodwin / Sarah F)
    John D, 18 Apr 1885 (Daniel Goodwin / Sarah)b 1816
    Lewis M, 03 Oct 1872 (Lewis Goodwin / Sarah) b 1871
    Lucinda P, 03 Mar 1886 (Moses Tucker / Hannah Tucker) b 1848
    Mary E (Shores), 23 Jul 1885 (Oliver Shores / Mary) b 1858
    Rufus G, 26 Jan 1893 (Gilman Goodwin / Dorothy Eliot) b 1827
GORDING: Margrett, 21 Jan 1715 (Daniell Gordin / Margret) b 27 Oct 1714
GREEN: Levi, 06 Feb 1890 at Brentwood - b 1802
GRIFFIN: Georgie Maud, 09 Mar 1893 at Haverhill, Ma - b 1889
    Nettie May, 10 Sep 1894 at Haverhill, Ma - 3 months
HALL: George, 16 Jul 1870 - b 1825
HAMMELL: John, 20 Nov 1885
HANSON: Dorothy, 16 Aug 1889 (Simon Fellows / Dorothy) b 1813
HARDY: Peter, 15 Sep 1898 (Jonathan Hardy / Hannah) b 1819
HARROLD: Nancy J, 10 May 1874 (J. S. Severance / Emily) b 1849
HEATH: Charles F, 1876 (Frank Heath) b 1862
    Flora, 11 Oct 1889 (Harry Heath / Nellie Collins) b 1888
    Nellie (Collins), 21 Nov 1889 (Eldridge Collins / Mary Robinson) b 1864
HEVEK: Nancy E (Maxcey), 23 Mar 1881 - b 1814
HIGGINS: Sarah, 09 Dec 1870 - b 1809
HILLIARD: John T, 23 Jan 1899 (Charles Hilliard / Abigail Tilton) b 1834
HOYT: Grace, 21 Jul 1885 (George H Hoyt / Isabelle)b 1873
    Lucina, 19 Jun 1886 (Ezra Hoyt) b 1834
HUBARD: Abigal (Tayler), 09 Dec 1768 (w/o Capt Richard Hubard)
HUBBARD: Abigaiell (Davies), 25 Sep 1733 (w/o Richard Hubbard)
    John, 06 Sep 1705 (John Hubbard / Jane) b 21 Jul 1706
    Joseph, 18 Mar 1756 (Jeremiah Hubard / Marcy Jouson) b 11 Mar 1723
    Left. John, 25 Sep 1723 (h/o Jane)
    Richard, 21 Apr 1755 (27) (Jeremiah Hubburd / Marcy Jouson)
    Capt. Richard, 11 Nov 1780
HULL: George, 04 Mar 1896 (Richard Hull) b 1853
HUNT: Eben W, 17 apr 1885 (Stephen Hunt / Mary Woodman) b 1816
    Orlando, 28 Apr 1890 (Stephen Hunt /Mary Woodman) b 1807
HUNTOON: Sammell, 22 Jul 1710 (Philip Huntoon / Hannah)
    Sarah, 15 May 1708 (Philip Huntoon / Hannah) b 21 Apr 1703
JENNESS: Frank W, 06 Sep 1874 (Frank H Jenness / Emma) b 1873
JOHNSON: Edgar B, 28 Apr 1896 (William Johnson / Maud L Anderson) b 1851
    Nancy (Plummer), 10 Jun 1887 (Samuel Plummer / Aua Farce) b 1805
JONES: Abbie, 03 Dec 1886 - b 1843
    John, 10 Mar 1886 (John Jones / Abigail) b 1867

JONSON: Louis, 24 Oct 1801 (Thomas Jonson / Hannah Colbey)
JUDKINS: Abigail, -- Nov 1782 (Henry Judkins / Mary Barnet)
    Charles, 04 Jun 1868 (William Judkins)
    Deacon Simeon B, 09 Jul 1877 - b 1812
    Franklin B, 30 Nov 1885 (Elbridge Judkins / Hattie J Butler) b 1883
    Mary (French), 22 Dec 1778 (Henry Judkins)
    Mehetable, 13 Jan 1749 (Joel Judkins / Mehetabel Ealkins) b - 22 May 1747
    Nellie E, 09 Aug 1895 at Haverhill, Ma
    Polly (Swain), 27 Feb 1886 (Ruben Swain) b 1825
    Sammel, 23 Feb 1741 (h/o Abigaill (Hereman) Judkins)
    Sarah C, 05 Mar 1890 at Boston, Ma - b 1816
    Stephen N, 23 Apr 1886 at Boston, Ma - b 1811
KEENE: Eliza J, 01 May 1890 - b 1870
KEEZER: Bertie A, 01 Apr 1888 (William Keezer / Nellie A) 3 months
    Nellie A (Collins), 12 Jan 1888 (Andrew Collins / Annie Smith) b 1869
KELLEY: Alfred, 30 Oct 1881 - b 1800
    Alonson, 04 May 1890 at Boston, Ma - b 1817
    Grover, 31 Aug 1887 (Daniel Kelley)
KELLY: Edna L, 20 Oct 1896 (George Kelly / Melinia Keezer) b 1892
    Katie May, 21 Nov 1849 (Charles Chamberlain / Abbie Fifield) b 02 Jan 1881
    P.F. (Bartlett), 31 May 1899 at Roxbury, Ma (David Bartlett / Dorothy Young) b 1820
KEY: Annie, 21 Jun 1886 (Orastes Key & Mary A) b 1864
KIMBALL: Fanny, 24 Mar 1884 - b 1809
    Frank, 07 May 1889 (h/o Kate Gray)
    George W, 27 Feb 1877 (John Kimball) b 1832
    James S, 13 Jun 1878 (Amos Kimball)
    Melvin, 20 Sep 1889 (Eldridge Kimball / Jane Leach) b 1856
KNIGHT: Albert N, 03 May 1874 - b 1844
KNOX: John, 08 Feb 1886 - b 1801
LAD: Love, 19 Jun 1720 (John Lad / Elesebeth Sanburn)
LADD: Mehetabel (Philbrick), 23 Jan 1779 (Capt Daniel Lad)
LEACH: Henry, 21 Dec 1895 (Henry Leach / Sarah)b 1812
LOCK: Abigel, 14 Mar 1731 (Sammell Lock / Margaret)b 12 Dec 1730
    Haner, 17 Jun 1735 (Sammell Lock / Margaret) b 31 Jan 1731
    Sammel, 28 May 1729 (Sammell Lock / Margaret)b 18 Feb 1744
    Sary, 17 Oct 1745 (Sammell Lock / Margaret)b 15 Aug 1736
LONG: Ann, 06 Apr 1718 (William Long / Ruth Estman) b 01 Oct 1716
    Joseph, 09 May 1721 (William Long / Sarah Sheppead) b 21 Feb 1721
    Mary E, 27 May 1886 at Saco, Me
    Ruth (Eastman), 06 Apr 1718 (w/o William Long)
    Sarah (Sheppard), 07 Mar 1720 (w/o William Long)
LOUTT: Elizabeth, 03 Apr 1761 (Henery Loutt)
LYFORD: Emma A (Judkins), 10 Aug 1898 (Simon Judkins) b 1847
MAGOON: Emily F, 07 Sep 1896 (Joseph Magoon / Emily Rebecca Clough) b 1810

Mary, 17 May 1879 - b 1793
MAILLET: Jules, 13 May 1899 (Thomas Maillet / Julia Fitzback) b 1857
MARDEN: Jennie A, 16 Jun 1878 at Epsom, (Charles E Marden / Rosetta L Sanborn)
MARSH: ....., 08 Jun 1877 (John Marsh) b 1876
....., 07 Aug 1889 (Charles Marsh / Carrie) 2 days
Captain Nathan, 1879 - b 1818
Charles H, 03 Dec 1873 - b 1841
Mary (Silloway), (Benjamin Silloway) (date unknown)
Mary A, 27 Nov 1889 - b 1831
MARSHALL: Clarence E, 28 May 1890 at Haverhill, Ma - b 1874
James F, 10 Jun 1887
Mary, 30 Nov 1874 - b 1792
Mary M (Belden), 01 Aug 1883 - b 1833
Sarah F (Nichols), 25 Oct 1885 (Oliver Nichols/ Eliza)
MARTIN: , ..., 04 Nov 1870 (Isreal Martin / Mary Martin)3 months
Ernest Albert, 26 May 1893 (Kate A Martin)3 months
Jesse, 28 Apr 1886 (Levi Martin / Ella) b 1885
John H, 21 Apr 1881 - b 1826
Levi B, 03 Jan 1890 (Thomas Martin / Catherine Davis) b 1846
Mary Matilda, 06 Jun 1873 (Thomas Martin / Mary) b 1847
Sophia W, 25 May 1873 (George S Martin / A.M. Martin) b 1860
McCOMB: Sarah E (Pierce), 17 Mar 1893 (Franklin Pierce / Lucy Edney) b 1873
MEEK : Jane (Belcher), 09 Jun 1885 (Elisha Belcher / Hannah)b 1826
MERRILL: William W, 21 Aug 1895 (Phillip Merrill / Nancy) b 1810
MERRITT: Wellington, 22 Mar 1889 - b 1841
MILLS: Willia, 08 Oct 1890 (William Mills / Josephie Sprague) 2 months
NASON: Ellen M (de Rochmont), 03 Oct 1890 (Charles W deRochmont/Mary Payson) b 1834
Nathan, 27 Aug 1897 (Nathan Nason / Mary Wentworth) b 1831
NICHOLS: Charles W, 26 Mar 1885 - b 1837
Eliher T, 30 Oct 1877 (Frederick Nichols) b 1832
Eliza (Robinson), 22 Oct 1889 (Gilman Robinson) b 1905
Oliver P, 27 Jun 1883 - b 1794
Capt. Nicholas, 28 Sep 1830
Sarah W, (Frederick G Nichols)
NICKETT: Joseph E, 23 Dec 1898 (Michael Nickette/Julia Champane)
Julia (Champlain), 01 Oct 1890
NICKETT: Lewis M, 02 Feb 1896 (Michael Nickette/Julia Champlains)
O'CONNELL: Thomas, 26 Jun 1889- b 1819
OAKES: Jennie, 07 Jun 1878 - b 1850
OSGOOD: ....,13 Dec 1890 (Fred Osgood/Mary Swain) b 1895
PAGE: Eliza (Bickford), 19 May 1888 - b 1804
Thomas, 10 Oct 1879 - b 1809
PALMER: James, 03 Jul 1868 - b 1810
Sarah, 10 May 1885 - b 1808

PARKER: Nathaniel, 17 Jan 1897 (Nathaniel Parker / Sarah Hardy) b 1814
        Sarah, 09 Sep 1895 (Frank W Parker / Alice T Holt) 5 months
PATTEN: Lizzie, 11 Oct 1874 (Alfred Towle) b 1838
        Maria R (Fletcher), 06 Apr 1880 - b 1796
        William G, 05 Jan 1873 (Colcord Patten)b 1820
PEASLEE: Caroline A, 16 Nov 1898 (Daniel Peaslee / Elizabeth Secomb) b 1822
        Elizabeth (Elicomb), 13 Feb 1869 (Simmonds Elicomb/Mary Appen) b 1781
        Mary C, 11 Jun 1878 (Luther D Peaslee / Mary S Peaslee)
        Mary E, 17 Sep 1877 - b 1826
PEVERE: Louisa (Fola), 01 Sep 1877 - b 1809
PHILBRICK: Beniman, 10 Sep 1730 (Jedidiah Philbrick / Mary Tayler) b 04 Jul 1728
        Beniman, 27 Jan 1735 (Jedidiah Philbrick/ Mary Tayler) b 06 Mar 1734
        Edward S, 08 Sep 1887 (John Philbrick / Sarah Stevens) b 1809
        Estella, 26 Aug 1878 (James M Philbrick / Mary S)
        Hannah, 18 Jan 1696 (Thomas Philbrick / Mehetabel Ayers) b 19 Dec 1695
        Jedidiah, 03 Dec 1743 (Jedidiah Philbrick / Mary Tayler)b 17 Aug 1742
        Jedidia, 20 Mar 1754 (h/o Mary (Tayler) Philbrick)
        Jeremiah, 09 Mar 1754 (h/o Mary (Stevens) Philbrick)
        Left.Thomas, 01 Jan 1711 (h/o Mehetabel (Ayers) Philbrick)
        Sammel, 21 Nov 1711 (Thomas Philbrick / Mehetabel Ayers) b 13 May 1698
        Thomas, 13 Jun 1704 (Thomas Philbrick / Mehetabel Ayers) b 09 Jun 1704
        Thomas, 08 Sep 1730 (Jedidiah Philbrick / Mary Tayler) b 11 Jan 1726
        Thomas, 16 Aug 1735 (Jedidiah Philbrick / Mary Tayler) b 23 Oct 1730
        Thomas, 27 Jan 1735 (Jedidiah Philbrick / Mary Tayler) b 01 Jan 1737
        Timothy, 17 Nov 1711 (Thomas Philbrick / Mehetabel Ayers) b 12 May 1689
PHILLIPS: Mary E, 25 Mar 1896 at Boston - b 1826
PLUMMER Hannah (Hunt), 10 May 1885 (Stephen Hunt) b 1800
        Jane, 10 Dec 1886 (Samuel Plummer / Ann) b 1802
PRESCOTT: Elizabeth (Webster), 29 Oct 1894 (John Webster / Hannah) b 1810
        George W, 19 Jan 1883 - b 1813
        George, 15 Dec 1877 (George W Prescott) b 1853
        Lewis F, 11 Jun 1877- b 1808
PRIMROSE: Edward, 15 Sep 1896 - b 1800
PURINGTON: Fannie M, 12 May 1896 (Francis Purington / Lorie C Webster) b 1875
        Loriah C, 30 Dec 1899 (Jacob Webster / Hannah Quimby) b 1842
        Sylvia, 14 Nov 1895 (Hiram Parish / Emma Seigler) b 1874
        Walter T, 24 Sep 1895 (Jacob Purrington / Sylvia Parish) - 1 day
QUIMBY: Arthur M, 19 Aug 1899 (Moses E Quimby / Jennie Dorr) b 1879
        Dolly, 13 Oct 1873 (Jona Pollard / Sarah Pollard) b 1789
        John J, 17 Dec 1894 (Moses Quimby / Susan M Connor) b 1836
        Mary S (Cotten), 29 May 1885 (Thomas Cotten / Aliah Fellows) b 1837
        Moses, 26 Feb 1876 (Stephen Quimby / Polly)b 1811
        Ora L, 09 Nov 1890 - b 1888
REED: John, 05 Jun 1889 - b 1831

REINBOLD: Louise, 09 Aug 1886 (Charles Reinbold / Maria)b 1882
REUNAILLARD: Peter, 08 apr 1889
REYNOLDS: ....., 25 May 1889 (Alphonzo Reynolds / Emma Wingate)
    Daniel, 22 Jul 1880
    Grace Mary, 28 Aug 1886 (Alphonzo Reynolds / Emma) b 1884
    Junia S, 28 Feb 1879 (Charles Reynolds) b 1878
    Sarah (Bassett), 18 Nov 1890 (Thomas Bassett / Susanna McGregor) b 1805
RICHARDSON: Leon Eustace, 08 May 1893 (Herbert Richardson / Ida French) 8 months
    Milo L, 29 Oct 1897 (Herbert B Richardson / Ida L French) 11 months
ROBEY: Ichabod, 15 May 1757 (h/o Lucy) b 1664
ROBINSON: Andrew W, 13 Sep 1870 (Charles O Robinson) b 1869
    Ellen E, 10 Mar 1874 - b 1844
    John Henry, 01 Feb 1888 (Iva Robinson / Nancy Korn) b 1821
    Joseph, 14 Feb 1885 - b 1821
ROGERS: John W, 28 Apr 1881 - b 1854
ROLLINS: James H, 19 Jun 1890 at Worcester - b 1836
ROWE: Laura (Bartlett), 12 Jan 1898 (David Bartlett / Dolly Young) b 23 Jan 1898
SANBORN: Benjamen, 07 Apr 1718 (Jonathan Sanborn / Elizabeth) b 22 Jan 1711
    Benjamin, 1879 (Joseph W Sanborn / Levina S) b 21 Jun 1869
    Clifton, 17 Sep 1885 (Daniel Sanborn / Abbie) 4 months
    George Washington, 30 Mar 1894 (John Sanborn / Abigail Currier) b 1817
    Harry, 20 Aug 1874 (James Sanborn / Mary)
    Helen M, 12 Oct 1881 - 4 months
    Isaiah, 13 Jul 1893 (Simon Sanborn / Roxanna Mills) b - 1821
    John, -- Feb 1710 (Jonathan Sanborn / Elizabeth) b 19 Dec 1710
    John, 11 Feb 1734 (Peter Sanborn / Mary) b 10 Mar 1733
    John, 06 May 1737 (Peter Sanborn / Mary)b 20 Sep 1736
    John W, 21 Sep 1887 (Monroe Sanborn) b 1863
    Capt Jonathan, 20 Jun 1741 (h/o Elizabeth)
    Lizzie E, 24 Aug 1890 (George Sanborn / Sarah) b 1869
    Mary (Judkins), 28 May 1885 (Eldridge Judkins &/Polly Swain)b 854
    Mary A (Rowe), 24 Jun 1889 (Joseph Rowe / Mary Mayer) b 1806
    Peter, 21 Dec 1735 (Peter Sanborn & Mary) b 01 Jun 1735
    Rebekah, 12 Jul 1746 (Jonathan Sanborn / Mary Bachelder) b 10 Jun 1744
    Sarah, 28 Dec 1743 (Abraham Sanborn / Abiegel Clifford) b 26 Mar 1739
    Sarah, 28 Jul 1746 (Abraham Sanborn /Abiegel Clifford) b 02 Jul 1745
    Sarah (Badger), 05 Apr 1888 (William Badger / Elizabeth Dearborn) b 1825
    Simeon, 09 Mar 1794 (Israel Sanborn / Patta Morgan)
    Trustrum, 04 Nov 1756 (Paul Sanborn / Bette Cirrer) b 04 Nov 1756
    William R , 30 Nov 1890 - 1806
SANBURN: Dorethe, Nov 1706 (Jonathan Sanborn / Elizabeth) b 30 Aug 1705
    Elisha, 20 Nov 1749 (Trustrum Sanburn Jr / Abigaill Blake) b 08 Dec 1748
    Hanah, 09 Oct 1743 (Trustrum Sanburn Jr / Abigaill Blake) b 12 Aug 1740
    Jethro, 30 May 1717 (Trustrum Sanburn / Margrett Tayler) b - 20 Dec 1715

Simon, 28 Nov 1749 (Trustrum Sanburn Jr / Abigaill Blake) b 20 Dec 1744
SARGENT: Grace Mary, 16 Apr 1893 (Frank Sargent / Nancy) 9 months
    Nancy E, 06 Dec 1893 (Thysey Sargent / Nancy Judkins) b1872
    Rowland P, 14 Dec 1890 - b 1873
    Sally, 17 Sep 1890 at Davenport, Iowa - b 1801
SCHELLENG: Anna, 24 Mar 1873 (Nathaniel Brown / Maria Fletcher) b 1833
    John, 11 Dec 1879 - b 1806
    Leonard, 30 Mar 1889 at Brentwood - b 1806
    Lucy W (Tucker), 26 May 1893 (Moses Tucker / Rachel Cook) b 1808
SCRIBNER: Sammell, 31 Mar 1715 (Thomas Scribner / Hannah Welsh) b 29 Mar 1713
    Sarah, 07 Sep 1705 (Thomas Scribner)
SEAVER: Dolly (George), 16 Nov 1897 (Currier George / Sophrona Spofford) b 1840
SECCOMBE: Dorothy, 19 Oct 1777 (Simmons Seccombe / Mary Toppan)
    Elisabeth, 09 Sep 1777 (Simmons Seccombe/ Mary Toppan)
    Mehitable, 28 Dec 1802 (Simmons Seccombe / Mary Toppan)
SENTER: Eva, 03 Jun 1897 (Leslie Senter / Laura Collins) b 1892
SEQUIN: Wilfred, 02 Sep 1896 (John Sequin / Delia Domnick) 6 months
SEVERANCE: , B. W., 11 Oct 1885 (Jacob Severance / Jane Abbott) b 1821
    Emily B, 21 Jun 1886 (Phillip Severance) b 1826
    Hannah (Judkins), 06 Nov 1895 (Joel Judkins / Nancy Dudley) b 1809
    Jane, 10 Jan 1876 - b 1799
    Jonathan, 22 Oct 1888 (Jacob Severance / Mary Tucker) b 1801
    M Emily, 23 Nov 1893 (Severance / Nellie Colford) 4 months
SHAW: Charles, 05 Apr 1888 (Jesse Shaw) b 1858
    Daniel D, 18 Feb 1876 - b 1817
    Jessie W, 08 Oct 1887 - b 1813
    Orin W, 21 Feb 1896 (James Shaw / Mary J) b 1854
    Warren P, 28 Sep 1893 (Jesse W Shaw / Mary J Currier) b 1841
SILLNA: John, 31 Mar 1741
SILLOWAY: Allice, 06 Oct 1778 (Benjamin W Silloway / Mary Severance)
    Alonzo, 20 Jan 1881 (D Wilson Silloway / Anginette) 7 days
    Elomer R, 04 Nov 1895 (John Silloway / Mary C Campbell) b 1849
    Frank D, 16 Nov 1880 (Wadleigh Silloway) b 1856
    George, 06 Mar 1787 (Benjamin W Silloway / Mary Severance)
    Ida May, 07 Apr 1876 (J. W. Silloway / Emma) 1 year
    Isaac W, 14 Sep 1888 (Wadleigh Silloway) b 1846
    Sarah, 28 Sep 1778 (Benjamin W Silloway / Mary Severance)
SLEEPER: Elizabeth, 27 Oct 1708 (w/o Aaron Sleeper)
    Female, 08 Aug 1704 (Aaron Sleeper / Elizabeth) b 07 Jul 1704
    Hezekiah, 30 Sep 1722 (h /o Elesebeth)
    Ithamar, 10 Nov 1708 (Aaron Sleeper / Elizabeth) b 15 Sep 1708
    Johannah, 04 Feb 1702 (Mother Of Aaron Sleeper)
SLEPER: Ann (Philbreck), 30 Aug 1716 (John Sleper)
    Thomas, 26 Dec 1746 (Thomas Sleper / Mary Colcord) b 07 Apr 1720

SLY: Frank Allen, 23 Sep 1890 (Edward Sly / Sadie Hill) 2 months
SMALL: William, 20 Jan 1890 - b 1812
SMITH: Charles H, 22 aug 1822 (Ira Smith / Hannah Maxwell) b 26 Dec 1849
    Clark P, 27 Dec 1887 (John Smith / Anna Chase) b 1809
    David C, 24 Apr 1893 (Nathaniel G Smith / Maria) b 1839
    Fanny Louise, 31 Jan 1889 (Frank Smith / Ida Fowler) b 1887
    Fred B, 16 Jul 1898 (Theodore Smith / Lorinda Bartlett) b 1823
    Irvin A, 01 Aug 1896 at Plaistow (Frank Smith / Kate Martin) 4 months
    Lucette D, 29 Nov 1890 - b 1829
    Marie A, 02 Jun 1896 at Haverhill, Ma (George Smith / Hattie Judkins) b 1880
    Mary A, 18 May 1899 at Franklin - b 1863
    Mary E, 21 Dec 1883 - b 1849
    Nathaniel C, 19 Mar 1890 (John Smith / Anna Chase) b 1808
SPOFFORD: Marsha (Johnson), 09 May 1884 (Joshua Johnson / Marsha)b 1797
STEVENS: Daniel, 02 Oct 1890 (David Bartlett / Dorothy Young)
    Edward, 09 Nov 1883 (Samuel Stevens / Abigail) b 1817
    Elisabeth, 30 Sep 1747 (Beniamen Stevens / Sarah Fifield) b 25 Mar 1745
    Elizebath (Colcord), 20 Nov 1769 (w/o Maj Ebenezer Stevens)
    Frederick C, 30 Sep 1899 at Haverhill, Ma (Samuel Stevens /Nancy Currier) b 1835
    G. S., 24 Jan 1890 at Boston, Ma.
    George Hubbard, 1787 (John Steven/Lydia Wadleigh)
    John, 25 Jan 1885 (Joseph Stevens) b 1873
    Maj.Ebenezer, 01 Nov 1749 (w/o Elizabeth (Colcord) Stevens)
    Mary (Colcoard), 16 Aug 1768 (w/o Col Ebenezer Stevens)
    Mr.Benjamin, 23 Mar 1776 (h/o Sarah (Fifield) Stevens) b 1713
    Samuel, 30 Sep 1747 Beniamen Stevens & Sarah Fifield) b 29 Jan 1740
    Sarah (Fifield), 06 Aug 1764 (w/o Benjamin Stevens)
    Sarah E., 29 Mar 1879 - b 1877
SWAIN: Ella (Philbrick), 18 Mar 1888 (James Philbrick / Mary Susan Chase) b 1869
SWEET: Derbon, 17 Mar 1736 (Nathan Sweet / Mary Darbon) b 16 Oct 1733
    Mary (Darbon), 01 May 1750 (w/o Nathan Sweet)
    Sarah (Tilton), 10 Oct 1735 (w/o Elisha Sweet)
    Steven, 08 Apr 1736 (Elisha Sweet / Sarah Tilton) b 18 Dec 1734
SWETT, Angenetta, 06 Jul 1884 - b 1840
    Joseph, 1876 (Sam Swett)
    Left. John, 03 Sep 1753 (h/o Bethiah)
    Mary, 12 Mar 1880 - b 1802
    Mary, 01 May 1750
    Moses, 28 Nov 1714 (John Swett / Bethiah)b 28 Nov 1714
    Moses, 20 Aug 1890 (Lucretia (Tucker) Swett)b 1854
TANDE: Racheel, 17 Jan 1754 (Richard Tande)
    Ricard (Richard), 1763 (h/o Rachel Tande)- b 06 Dec 1685
THAYER: Calvin, 24 Oct 1803 (Rev Elihn Thayer / Hannah Calef)
THOMPSON: Tripletts, 29 Mar 1881 (George Thompson) 1 day

THORN: Abraham, 20 Sep 1754 (John Thorn/Elisabeth Brown) b 20 May 1754
Elisabeth, 22 Nov 1741 (w/o John Thorn)
THURSTON: Betsy, 02 Feb 1879 - b 1797
TOREK: Susan F, 11 Mar 1871 (Lorenzo Torek/Susan)
TOWLE: ....., 22 Mar 1899 at Haverhill, Ma (John Towle) infant
Alfred, 27 Jan 1899 (Lydia .....) b 1818
Darius, 26 Jul 1888 - b 1825
Effie F, 17 Mar 1898 (William Austin/Julia Foster) b 1873
Kate M, 27 Feb 1894 at Concord - b 1856
Lorenzo D, 21 Apr 1884 (..... Towle /Abigail Brown) b 1813
Margaret Gale, 19 Mar 1898 at Haverhill,Ma (John Towle/Margaret Gruidell) b 1892
Susan, 12 Jan 1890 - b 1818
TOWNSEND: Sarah (Goodwin), 14 May 1899 (Ezekiel Goodwin/Irene Miles)b- 1844
Alfred H, 26 Dec 1897 - b 1833
TUCK: Charles G, 02 Apr 1894 at Manchester - b 1871
TUCKER: Edith, 13 Nov 1880
Elizabeth A, 22 Mar 1888 (John Parker / Sarah A Milio) b 1848
Hannah, 28 Oct 1888 (Thomas Martin) b 1811
Hattie, 24 Aug 1878 (Moses Tucker) b 1860
Jacob P, 03 Jan 1893 (Moses Tucker / Rachel Cook) b 1819
James W, 11 Mar 1890 (Jacob Tucker) b 1847
Maxine Estelle, 13 Oct 1899 (Wallace Tucker / Lettie Tucker)1 month
Moses, 30 Sep 1889 - b 1810
Otis Howard, 08 Apr 1890 (Charles Tucker / Florence) 1 month
William F, 13 Aug 1877 - b 1874
VARRELL: Robert W, 17 Aug 1887 - b 1824
VASSELL: Fanny, 23 Jan 1880 (Robert Vassell) b 1859
WADLEIGH: Anna (Sleeper), 15 Apr 1883 - b 1799
Daniel, 14 Nov 1896 - b 1824
Sally (Davis,) 15 Nov 1888 (w/o John Davis) b 1807
WALTON: George O, 18 Jan 1874 (Calvin Walton/ Anna Walton)2 months
WARNER: DeWitt, 03 Aug 1881 at Plaistow - b 1812
WEBBER: Daniel, Nov 1790 (John Webber / Hannah Tucker)
Sarah, 21 Dec 1793 (John Webber / Hannah Tucker)
WEBSTER: ....., 18 Sep 1888 (William Crosby / Cora Webster)4 days
Abigail D, 06 Mar 1881- b 1794
Alies, 30 Oct 1722 (Thomas Webster / Sarah Webster)
Beatrice M, 17 Sep 1874 (Jeremiah Webster) 10 Months
Burnam,08 Nov 1758 (Samuel Webster / Dorrety Staniel)
David, 12 Aug 1758 (Samuel Webster/ Elisabeth Burnnum)
Elihu P, 31 Oct 1890 (John Webster) b 1812
Elisabeth (Burnham),20 Oct 1738 (w/o Samuel Webster)
Elizabeth, 28 May 1735 (Jeremiah Webster / Elseabeth Lad) b 02 Nov 1730
Georgeanna, 03 Aug 1876 (Henry D Webster)b 1874

Hannah, (date unknown) (John Webster & Ruth Clough) b 28 Aug 1746
Harriet A, 08 Mar 1888 at Brooklyn, NY - b 1836
Humphrey, 13 Sep 1763 (John Webster / Ruth Clough) b 30 Mar 1740
Jacob, 06 Feb 1744 (Beniman Webster / Mary Sawyer) b 03 Sep 1742
Jacob, 09 Apr 1881 - b 1798
Jerry B, 22 Jul 1881
John, 27 May 1735 (Jeremiah Webster / Elseabeth Lad) b 05 Feb 1732
John, 29 Apr 1788 (h/o Ruth (Clough)Webster)
Joseph, 15 Nov 184- (David Webster / Judith)b 1812
Margret, 26 Jul 1735 (John Webster / Ruth Clough)
Marsha Elizabeth, 05 Aug 1890 at Port Chester - b 1829
Mary (Clark),20 Nov 1885 (William Clark)b 1807
Nathaniel, 26 May 1735 (Jeremiah Webster / Elseabeth Lad) b 03 May 1735
Ormond P, 06 Dec 1884 (E. J. Webster/ Ruth)b 1836
Samuel, 27 Nov 1751 (Samuel Webster / Dirrethy Staniel) b 01 Jun 1759
Samuell, 04 Mar 1714 (Isae Webster / Sarah) b 26 Mar 1714
Sarah, 15 Feb 1717 (w/o Thomas Webster)
Sarah, 28 Jan 1714 (Isae Webster / Sarah)
Sarah, 1737 (Samuel Webster / Elisabeth Burnum)
Stephen S, 22 Apr 1888 at Lynn, Ma - b 1827
Thomas, 13 May 1772 (h/o Elizabeth)
William, 11 Nov 1745 (Beniman Webster / Mary Sawyer) b 22 May 1738
WELCH: Gerinnan, Sep 1737 (Joseph Welch / Debrah Scribner) b 20 Nov 1735
    Sammel, Apr 1823 at Bow (h/o Elener Clough)
WELLS: Edson, 29 Jun 1884 - b 1810
WENTWSORTH: Dorothy, 21 Nov 1896 (C Herman Wentworth/Millicent M King) b 1893
WEST: Elsie V, 22 Jul 1899 (John E Barrett/ Lizzie Trafton)11 months
    Mary F (Bakie), 19 Dec 1890 (Daniel Bakie / Nella J Sanborn) b 1834
    Will Bragdon, 30 Jul 1896 (Walter S West) 3 months
WHIPPLE: Mary, 01 Jan 1889
WILITH: Albert, 07 Aug 1890 - 6 months
WILLIAMS: Frederic E, 24 Dec 1890 (John Williams / Ella Page) b 1870
WINSLEY: Sammel, 31 Jun 1736 (Samuell Winsley / Huldah Sweet) b 31 Jun 1736
WINSLEY (WINSLOW): Surg. Sammell, 22 Jul 1710 (h/o Catern)
WINSLO: Catern, 30 Mar 1738 (Samuell Winsley / Huldah Sweet) b 30 Mar 1738
    Huldah (Sweet), 25 Sep 1738 (w/o Samuell Winslow)
    Zebuln, 01 Jun 1734 (Elisha Winslow / Mary Sleeper) - b 01 Jun 1734
WINSLOW: Catern, 18 Apr 1737 (w/o Sammell Winslow)
    Charles, 04 Jul 1880 (Samuel Winslow) b 1878
    George, 10 Jan 1877 (William Winslow)
    Mary P, 13 Sep 1889 - b 1806
    Samuel, 03 apr 1893 (John Winslow / Polly Webster) b 1811
    Samuel M, 20 Apr 1893 (William Winslow / Polly Severance) b 1844
    William, 20 Sep 1893 (William Winslow / Polly Severance)

WOOD: Abel, 9 Aug 1890 - b 1818
    Elizabeth, 23 Aug 1876 - b 1817
    Franklin, 15 Jan 1890 (Benjamin Wood / Lucinda Merrian) b 1817
    Sara P, 27 Apr 1893 (Aaron Patten / Sarah Chase) b 1814
WOODBURY: Joanna A (Whittier), 15 Nov 1884 (Jonathan Whittier)b 1805
WOODMAN: Eliza (Spearin), 26 Apr 1885 (J. Spearin / Rosanna)b 1831
    Joshua, 04 Apr 1791(h/o Eunis)b 1708
    Nathan, 12 Aug 1789 (Joshua Woodman / Hannah Blasdel)
    Permelia, 13 Mar 1889 at Oxford, Ma - b 1802
    Samuel E, 13 Mar 1886 - b 1829
YOUNG: Aron, 17 Dec 1733 (John Young / Sarah Curnham) b 28 Feb 1732
    Giddeon, 10 Jul 1735 (John Young/ Sarah Curnham) b 11 Oct 1734
    Isriel, 30 Sep 1745 (John Young / Sarah Curnham) b 15 Sep 1744
    Joseph, 02 May 1756 (h/o Elesebeth (Sleper) Young)
    Martha, 12 Jan 1759 (John Young/ Sarah Curnham) b 29 May 1756
    Moses, 19 May 1733 (John Young / Sarah Curnham)
    Mr. John, 22 Aug 1758 (h/o Doriety (Sayer) Young)
    Nathaniel, 08 Feb 1747 (John Young / Sarah Curnham) b 11 Nov 1746
    Sarah, 28 Mar 1732 (John Young / Sarah Burnham) b 28 Feb 1732
    Sarah, 15 Oct 1745 (John Young / Sarah Curnham)
    Sarah (Curnham), 1749 (w/o John Young)

BIRTHS
1901 - 1994

ABDO: Nassif J & Clarabell Stewart: Clara, 31 Oct 1960; Pearl, 31 Oct 1960 (E);
Robert Lawrence, 11 May 1972   (Hav)
ACKERSON: Robert & Jeannette E McLane: Becky Louise, 02 Jan 1974 (Hav)
ACOX: Perry B (Elburn,Il) & Victoria P Lamb(Dundee,Scot): Eugene Albert, 11 May 1930
ADAMS: Clyde A & Wendy Hart: Scott Allen Clyde, 19 Nov 1973 (E)
Leon F & Nova A Collins: Cheryll Ann, 20 Sep 1948; Lynn Ann, 20 Feb 1968 (E)
Leon F ,Jr & Cynthia A Pool: Michael Stephen, 06 May 1987 (E)
James H & Roberta J Papas: Robert Wade, 07 Aug 1970 (Hav)
Joseph M & Lynn A Adams: Kyla Marie, b 29 Apr 1989 (E)
AHLBERG: Richard F & Joann E Herman: Sonja Erika, 11 Jun 1977 (E)
AIKEN: Allen N & Judith A Rollo: Charles Neill, 26 Feb 1965   (Hav)
Maurice S (NH) & Joanne P Butterfield (Derry): Colleen Jo, 08 Oct 1960(E); Laurie
Jane, 15 Sep 1952 (E Derry)
AIKENS: James J & Patricia E Darnsney: Dawn M, 24 Jan 1966; Laura Lee, 17 Jun 1968
(Ports); Melissa Ann, 17 Aug 1970 (E)
ALBEE: Nathan W & Jane E Kimball: Jennifer Sue, 24 Aug 1981 (Hav)
ALBERTS: Alan J & Cynthia J Wagler: Aaron Jessen, 12 Nov 1973 (E)
ALDEN: Karl M & Edna D Mitchell: George Warren, 09 Jan 1953; Karen Lea, 01Jun 1948 (E)
ALPERT: Alan E & Brenda Thompson: Matthew Robert, 11 Apr 1990; Samantha Lynn, 12
Jun 1992 (E)
AMATO: David R & Tammi M Collins: Krista Marie, 12 Jun 1989 (E)
AMAZEEN: Clarence,Jr & Ernestine C Parker: Jane E, 19 Aug 1956 ; Judith Ann, 07 Feb 1958;
Sherry Lynn, 22 May 1955 (E)
AMELIO: Paul R & Terry A Haywood: Ralph Paul, II, 11 Jul 1973 (E)
ANDERSEN: Robert H Andersen & Marjorie E Jones: Albert George, 06 Apr 1949; Carl
Robert, 06 Nov 1960; Jean Ruth, 25 Nov 1950; Joan Elinor, 25 Nov 1950; Kenneth
Norman, 22 Sep 1954: Ralph Henry, 31 Oct 1947 (E)
ANDERSON: Christopher M & Karyn E Korman: Patrick Roark, 05 Dec 1994 (E)
Harold C & Kathleen A Jeans: ...., 14 Dec 1959 (E)
ANGELUCCI: Michael Angelucci & Cynthia Tocchini: Branden Albert, 26 Jan 1993; Emily
Rose, 26 Jan 1993 (E)
ANZIVINO: David M & Denise A Costa: Jordan David, 10 Jan 1987 (E)
APPLETON: Glenn D & Lesley Hambrough: Mark Hambrough, 19 Apr 1979 (E)
ARAKELIAN: Harry S & Rebecca M Jones: Corey Daniel,16 Jan 1976;Poppy, 20 Jun 1971(Hav)
ARATA: Robert J & Christine S Vornberger: Stephen Robert, 29 Jan 1994
ARNOLD: George E , Jr & Shirley B Waitt: George, 3rd, 23 Feb 1955 (E)
Walter R & Barbara E Small: Deborah Ann, 07 Jan 1962;Donna Marie, 09 Jun 1964 (E)
ARON: John E & Margaret E Waters: Glenna, 30 Oct 1971; Heather Aron, 28 Apr 1970 (E)

ARRETT,Raymond H (SoKingston) & Florence Rollins (Lynn,Ma): Janet, 08 Apr 1929
ASHTON: Edward G (Lynn,Ma) & Josie M Senter (Amesbury,Ma): Arthur S.B.,
　　05 Oct 1900; Martha R, 28 Jul 1909
AUBE: Albert (St Chas. Bell.,Can) & Josephine Laflamme (St Geo.Windsor,Can): Evelyn
　　Ann, 25 Feb 1945 (E)
AUBRY: James L & Ernestine A Naimoli: Cindy, 17 May 1967 (E)
AUGER: David C Auger & Jane W Carroll: Bradley James, 23 Jul 1970; David J, 11 Aug 1962
　　Judi Lynn, 08 May 1960 (E)
　　David J & Jennifer A Simpson: Ryan Reid, 07 Nov 1992 (E)
AUTRY: Charles G & Tamara J Patrick: Kimberly Elizabeth, 28 Mar 1989 (Ports)
AVERY: Alfred J (Kingston) & Arrie B Nason (Kingston): Ernestine C, 17 Oct 1902;
　　Raymond E, 23 Jul 1909
　　Raymond E & Exilda C Foster: Cynthia Ann, 17 Apr 1944; Female, 21 Dec 1936;
　　Sandra Elaine, 10 Dec 1940
AYERS: Chester W, Jr & Roberta I Arnold: Randolph Earl, 13 Mar 1974; Richard
　　Eugene, 06 Nov 1963 (E)
　　Chester W,III & Diana L Rand: Rebecka Ann, 01 Aug 1977 (E)
　　Phillip E & Rhonda L Silva: Jesse Cole, 19 Jun 1993 (E)
BABCOCK: John W & Elizabeth G Black: Douglas Wesley, 28 Apr 1981 (E)
BABSON: David E & Sandra L Budd, Jeffrey David, 02 Jan 1963 (Law)
BAHAN: Scott, C & Marie A Meade: Tess Marie, 11 Oct 1994 (E)
BAILEY: Arnold W & Deborah H Reed: Shalissa Dianne, 09 Nov 1989 (Ports)
　　Joseph P & Susan L Donahue: Natash Lynne, 03 Aug 1991 (E)
　　Joseph P & Carla A Dewitt: Jennifer Elizabeth, 17 Jul 1994 (E)
BAILLY: Charles L (Haverhill Ma) & Laura Bouchard (Epping): Lucille Annie, 18 Nov 1929
BAITZ: Kurt W & Lynn M Killam: Tyler Evan, 30 Jul 1992 (E)
BAKE: Ralph H (Lawrence,Ma) & Laura E Nason (Kingston): Norma Evelyn, 22 Mar 1926
　　Ralph R & Virginia L Sevareid: Thomas Ralph, 06 Aug 1964 (Columbus,Oh)
BAKIE: Gordon J & Pamela A Lancaster: Deborah Lynn, 01 Jun 1967; Elizabeth Anne,
　　30 Dec 1965; Peter Gordon, 18 Sep 1969 (E)
　　John J Bakie & Dorothy L Thereau: Elizabeth Imogene, b 18 Jul 1939
　　Warren G (Kingston) & Marion L Allard (Peabody Ma): Gordon James, 18 May 1942
BALUKAS: Paul R & Cynthia A Cunningham; Sarah Elizabeth, 01 Jul 1986 (Hav)
BARDGETT: John W & Amy Badger: John Walter, 10 Sep 1976 (Hav)
BARNES: Paul S & Ruth H Christie: Paula Rose, 22 Dec 1949 (E)
BARON: Richard D & Linda M Ferris, Jennifer Mary, 01 Jul 1981 (Law)
BARRETT: Raymond H (Kingston) & Florence Rollins(Lynn,Ma): Janet, 07 Apr 1929; June,
　　29 Sep 1921; Norman Jean, 13 Jul 1933; Robert E, Aug 16 1925
　　John W & Ashleigh Marvin: Cebastian Joseph, 21 Jan 1992; Mercedes Leigh, 09 Sep
　　1994 (Nashua)
BARRY: Frederick J & June M Webb, ... , 28 Nov 1958 (Newburyport,Ma)
BARTECCHI: Kenneth M & Cynthia A Eaton: Allison Amelia, 09 Jan 1981 (E)
BARTLETT: Arnold W (Manchester) & Jessica Palmer (Wayland,Ma): Arnold Whitney,Jr,
　　22 Sep 1948; Jessica, 11 Jan 1952; Mary Bronwyn, 14 Sep 1953; Martha Angharad,

14 Sep 1953; Michael, 10 Jan 1950; Robert Montgomery, 02 Feb 1955 (E)

Benjamin T & Verna B Dares: Kimberly Ann, 08 Nov 1983 (E)

Gregory S & Lisa H Dondero: Gillian Lee, 16 Jun 1990: Lauren Elizabeth, 14 May 1993 (E)

William S,Jr & Marilyn Bake: Nancy Lee, 07 Dec 1957; Steven Alan, 21 Sep 1964 (E)

BARTON: George O, Jr & Margaret M Willey: Robert Otis, 28 May 1948 (E)

BASILIERE: Philip C & Debra M Smith: Alexandra Lynn, 16 Jan 1994 (E)

BASSETT: George H & Barbara Beyrent: George, 25 Jul 1962 (E)

BASTIEN: James A & Dianne M Bryant: Jennifer Lynne, 15 Apr 1975; Peter James, 15 Apr 1975 (Hav)

BATTLES: Nathan T (Amesbury,Ma) & Diane L Margeson (Cambridge,Ma): Carol Anne, 26 Oct 1953; James E, 12 Aug 1956; Robert Alann, 27 Dec 1951;Thomas Arnold, 24 Sep 1959; Virginia L, 24 Jul 1961 (E)

BEAM: Robert A & Louisa S Chabot: Dannielle, 11 Sep 1974 (Hav)

BEAN: Lawrence G & Debra A Wheeler: Victoria R, 23 Apr 1992 (E)

BEAULIEU: Russell B Beaulieu & Pamela J Kelley: Beth Ann, 30 Oct 1978 (E)

BECKFORD: Alan H (Haverhill,Ma) & Charlotte E Mack (Haverhill,Ma): Alan Howard, II, 09 Sept 1951 (Methuen,Ma)

Harold & Rebecca Stevens: Robert M, 23 Feb 1923

Harold W (Newburyport,Ma) & Barbara Stephens (Kingston): Richard S, 02 Aug 1920

BECOTTE: J Albert & Eleanor A Roberts: Katrin Lorraine, 30 Mar 1963; Valori Alice, 03 Aug 1964 (Methuen,Ma)

BELL: Lawrence E & Joline A Dion: Ryan Scott, 05 Jan 1991 (E)

BELMER: Donald (Lynn, Ma) & Marie Woodman (Haverhill,Ma): Gladys Natalie, 05 Mar 1927; Male, 23 Apr 1924

BELMONTE: Charles E & Dianne E Young: Brian William, 21 Aug 1965; Kimberly Anne, 31 Jan 1967 (E)

BELSCHENER: Richard G & Lidia E Matos: Eric Eliezer, 03 Oct 1991 (E)

BENNETT: Bruce & Joanne M McCarthy: Jeffrey Todd, 26 Aug 1975 (E)

Robert (Newark, NJ) & Eldora M Tucker (Kingston): Bruce, 14 Oct 1950; Patricia Ann, 19 Oct 1942; Shirley, 19 Sep 1946 (E)

Robert W,Sr & Joann Abdo: Robert William,Jr, 16 Apr 1967; Sharon T, 05 Feb 1966 (E)

Wendell (Leominster,Ma) & Beatrice Goldthwaite (W Kingston): June Marilyn, 17 Sep 1937; Wendell Farrar Jr, 02 Mar 1942

BERGSTROM: Jeremy M & Marnie J Cleary: Alexander Thomas, 28 Nov 1987 born in (Saratoga Spring,NY)

Richard W & April J Thomas: Sarah Elizabeth, 08 Dec 1978 (E)

BERNIER: Raymond A & Constance J Reed: Jo Ann, 05 Oct 1975; Rae Anna, 25 Dec 1978 (Ports); Randi Lee, 12 Mar 1977; Tamara Dawn, 13 May 1972 (Hav)

BERRIER: Frank,II & Jean M McMahon: Frank John, 25 Apr 1971 (Kittery,Me); Sean Daniel, 21 Jan 1974 (E)

BERRY: Richard A & Charlene N Batchelder: Gardner Richard, 31 Dec 1949 (E)

BEVERIDGE: David S & Jane L Pariseau: Joshua McKenzie, 10 Dec 1980 (Hav)

BIBBO: Christian W & Lisa K Pakkala: Christian Pekkala, 26 Sep 1992; Katriina Pekkala, 12 Apr 1991 (E)

BICKFORD: Wallace J & Ruth Thompson: ....., 01 Oct 1921
BIERY: Dennis W& Christine Dixon: Kara Catherine, 16 Mar 1974 (Law)
BIRCKHOLTZ: John C & Brenda I MacNeil: Kristen Dawn, 14 Mar 1987 (Law)
BILODEAU: Bruce A & Nancie L Kohlauff: Corey N, 29 Jun 1981 (E)
BINGEL: John A & Sandra E Avery: Shelly Jo, 09 Apr 1964 (E)
BISHOP: Charles F & Grace Collins: Charles Franklin, 27 Jan 1932
      Lloyd W Bishop & Norma M Newman: Lloyd W, Jr, 11 Apr 1970 (Derry)
BLAKE: Philip M Blake,Sr & Sandra G Huntington: Cynthia L, 22 Dec 1962; Gregory Paul, 19
      Apr 1964 (E); Philip M, 04 Feb 1962 (Hav)
      William D & Gwendolyn M Ingalls: Vicki Laura, 17 Mar 1958 (E)
BLATTENBERGER: Ronald E,Jr & Julie C Lemieux: Amy Michelle, 19 Aug 1987 (Law);
      Tina Marie, 01Dec 1989 (E)
BLAIS: Paul O & Heidi Charles: Holly Katherine, 29 Mar 1979
BLAISDALL: Herbert H & Marcia E Simes: Joyce Ann, 21 Feb 1948 (E)
BLANCHARD: Daniel G & Susan L Scatterday: Daniel Russell, 26 Oct 1990 (Ports)
BLOOD: Barry M & Susan J Sanborn: Kevin William, 18 Jan 1973
BOISSELLE: Paul M & Kim M Morse: Melinda Marie, 01 Jan 1979 (Hav)
BOISVERT: Bruce P & Maria L Salmas: Jennifer Anne, 11 Aug 1986; Michelle Rene,
      11 Aug 1986 (E)
BONCZKIEWICZ: Stanley & Pearl E Dominello: Jeremy James, 10 Aug 1979 (E)
BORGES: Michael F & Jeannette M Mills: Michael F, 13 Feb 1975 (Hav)
BORIN: Joseph P & Loraine D Kent: Joseph J, 19 May 1966 (Amesbury,Ma)
BOUCHARD: Paul E & Gloria A Turcotte: Paula Jean, b 14 Oct 1954; Rose M, b 22 Sep
      1956 (E)
BOUCHER: Homer & Anna Cilley(Georgetown,Ma): Female, 29 May 1925
BOUDREAU: David W & Jean T Costello: Mark David, 14 Feb 1988 (Hav)
BOULAY: Richard P & Judith A Vernon: Brent Paul, 27 Jan 1971 (Hav); Lara Kathryn,
      19 Jan 1973 (E)
BOULTER: Edward K & Valerie A Vinciguerra: Meredith, 25 Jul 1981 (Hav)
BOURGELAIS: Frederick N & Cynthia J Dale: Paul F, 09 Jul 1966; Phillip D, 14 Sep 1962 (E)
BOURQUE: Calvin R Bourque & Maureen P Hickey: James Michael, 19 Sep 1970; John
      Joseph, 09 Nov 1968; Robert Richard, 15 Oct 1969 (Hav)
BOVINO: Michael J, Jr & Diane M Kasner: Leaha Marie, 03 Oct 1990 (E)
BOW: David K & Eileen M Sears: Jessica Marie, 13 May 1987 (E)
BOWEN: Nelson(Saxton's River,Vt) & Muriel Dining (Stratham): Dorothy Ellen, 05 Jul 1945 (E)
BOWER: Arthur J (Methuen,Ma) & Marion Bodwell (Hollowell,Me): Shirley, 09 May 1927
      Robert P & Freida I Bunker: Franceska, 23 Mar 1953 (E)
      Cedric M & Pearl L Corey: Daniel Thomas, 13 Aug 1959 (E)
BRADBROOK: Robert A & Muriel L White: Claude Jeffrey, 19 Sep 1948 (E)
BRADING: John D & Lauren J Baldini: Kenya Rachelle, 05 May 1991 (E)
BRADLEY: Charles A, Sr & Catherine V Lipsky: Cathy Ann, 03 Sep 1957 (E)
BRADSHAW: John D & Virginia L Bourdelais: Jeremy Arthur, 12 Oct 1977; John Dee,
      24 Dec 1975; Shelley Lee, 04 Dec 1973   (Hav)
BRADY: Henry R & Gayle A Pourinki: Caitlyn Dorothy, 18 Sep 1987 (Salem,Ma)

Samuel P & Janice A McNeil: Ruth Ann, 28 Feb 1967(E)

BRAGDON: Ernest P (Kingston)& Doris L Nye (Mason): Brenda J, 25 Jul 1938

John A (Kingston) & Annie Whippen (St Albans,Vt): Jean,16 Mar 1924; Priscilla W, 22 Apr 1916

Robert I & Patricia Pierce: Charles Henry Jerome, 02 Jun 1955 (E)

BRALEY: Jack K & Barbara J. McGirr: Brooks V,17 Jul 1961; Jandara Lee, 13 May 1951 (Hav)

Richard R & Dona G Eldridge: Lillian Rose, 03 Jun 1970; Richard Ronald, Jr., 17 Jan 1972 (E)

Stephen H, Sr & Linda M Harriman: Denise Lee, 29 Dec 1978; Stephen Herbert,Jr, 30 Nov 1974 (E)

Wayne L & Brenda L Rogers, 04 Dec 1979 (E)

BRANDON: George F & Diane M Giggi:Karen Elizabeth, 04 Sep 1986 (E)

BREAULT: Ronald W & Mary E Goode: Brianna Cunningham, 31 Mar 1993 (E)

BREWITT: Thomas, 2nd & Carole Cadorette: Thomas J, 08 Nov 1966 (Law)

BRIDGHAM: Alan M & Linda L Dunne: Brittany Lee, 26 May 1991; Michelle Marie, 27 Apr 1994 (E)

BRIGGS: Donald W & Anna-Belle L Girroir: Donald W, Jr, 24 Mar 1955; Donna Lea, 13 Oct 1951 (E)

David R & Ruth M Fowler: Dawn Eleanor, 01 Jan 1973 (Hav)

Charles S & Sheila A Robinson: Samantha, 23 Jan 1976; Stacey, 25 Apr 1973 (E)

BRINDAMOUR: Robert Louis,Jr & Susan L Cole: Robert Thomas, III, 28 Mar 1978 (E); Brett Owens, 24 Jan 1987 (Ports)

BRITTON: George (Haverhill,Ma) & Lilla M George (Kingston): Florence May, 29 Jan 1940; George Britton 3rd, 25 Apr 1942

BROUGHTON: David J & Dorothea A Doucette: Jonathan David, 29 Sep 1971 (Hav)

BROUILLETTE: Bruce C & Nancy J Sanders: Allison Anne, 23 Feb 1981; Amy Alexis, 25 Feb 1977; Beth Colby, 15 Apr 1979 (Hav)

BROWN: George J & Mary S Gourdouros: David Alan, 31 Mar 1969 (Ports)

Norman R & Susan M Wentworth, Lindsay Marie, 19 Dec 1980 (Dover)

Thomas L & Kathleen A Thibault: Nicole Marie, 25 Oct 1977 (Hav)

Richard S & Marnie A Decatur: Arielle Myrinda, 20 Feb 1994 (D/O)

BRUSSO: Neil T & Linda L Nason: July L, 02 Sep 1966; Wendy Sue, 08 Apr 1965 (Man)

BUCHANAN: Francis A & Lucille Mara: Cynthia Ann, 07 Aug 1958 (Lynn,Ma)

BUCKLEY: Gregory F & Phyllis R Talacki: Kathryn Louise, 26 Jul 1981; Peter Gerald, 25 Nov 1978 (E)

BUNKER: Louis C (Tamworth) & Annie M George (Brentwood): Female, 27 Aug 1925

Stanton L & Priscilla A Tuck: Elizabeth, 09 Jun 1955; Louis Stanton, 25 Mar 1958 (E)

BURBANK: Frank A & Susan J Colby: Jennifer Ruth, 22 May 1971; Kris Dawson, 08 May 1974 (Hav)

BURKE: Albert V(Lynn,Ma) & Helen E Reynolds (Newburyport,Ma): Evelyn May, 10 May 1920

Brian A & Patricia McIntire: Chad Patrick, 16 Mar 1981 (Law)

James E & Debra A Donahue: Carl W, 07 Feb 1988 (E)

James (Lynn,Ma) & Ruth Nason (Kingston): Richard Clayton, 09 Sep 1934

Richard C & Rosemarie C LaRoche: Darline Beatrice, 14 Apr 1958; Karl Richard, 06 Sep 1955; Kevin Richard, 06 Sep 1955; Linda Lea, 08 Jun 1954; Matthew C, 04 Feb 196(E)

BURLEIGH: Kenneth D & Donna F Bowley: Joseph Kenneth, 24 Feb 1987 (E)

BURLESON: Billy H & Cynthia A Avery: Pamela Jean, 02 Nov 1964 (Kittery,Me)

BURNETTE: Gerald M & Priscilla L Dunn: Patricia Lynn, 25 May 1965 (E)

BURNS: Richard F Burns & Susan A Barthelenghi: Jason Peter, 01 May 1982 (Law)

BUSWELL: Lawrence A & Gertrude J Southwick: Lawrence Alfred,Jr, 18 Oct 1960 (E)
Leonard C & Mary J Clarke: Deborah Joan, 28 Apr 1963 (E)
Richard G & Ann C Foy: Glenn Edward, 12 Sep 1972; Heather Ann, 09 Apr 1969 (E)

BUTCHER: Homer (Pittsfield) & Anna Cilley (Georgetown,Ma): Audrey M, 01 Jun 1924

BUZZELL: Bradley E & Kathleen A Gavin: Kristen Mae, 15 Mar 1988; Theresa Marie, 10 May 1983 (E)
Frank E & Jacqueline M Smith: Bradley E, 24 Jul 1962;Heidi Belinda, 28 Nov 1964; Richard Frank, 06 Jan 1967 (E)
Maurice A & Colleen M Jordan: Hanah Zillah, 30 Sep 1994; Katharine May, 29 Mar 1991 (E)

CALDWELL: Charles E & Linda F Merrill: Charles Edward,II, 13 Feb 1983; Heidi Bolt, 06 Apr 1987 (E)

CALL: Raymond E & Judith A Madore: James Christopher, 28 Jun 1969; Richard Alan, 28 Jun 1969; Robin Ann, 08 Nov 1967 (E)

CAMERON: Peter P& Carol A Guzowski: Jonathan Leo, 26 Apr 1986; Lindsay Michelle, 05 Aug 1983; Scott Peter, 06 Feb 1981 (E)

CAMMETT: Earl V (Haverhill,Ma)& Esther P Senter(Kingston): Elaine F, 22 Feb 1921; Loren Earl, 05 Feb 1932

CAMPBELL: James P & Judith A Adams: Courtney Adams, 13 May 1973 (E)
James W & Paula B Fortier: Benjamin Richard, 26 Dec 1992

CAMPO: Robert A & Sharon A Mello: Anthony James, 03 Oct 1986(E)

CANNEY: Douglas A & Linda M Langlois, Mark Christopher, 02 Nov 1980 (Hav)

CAPELESS: John E & Janice M O'Brien: Edward Thomas, 15 Aug 1973; James Joseph, 15 Aug 1973 (Ports)

CARALUZZI: Joseph P, Sr & Jean R Anderson: Joseph Peter, Jr, 18 Jul 1973

CARD: Harry B & Sandra F Boucher: Cheri Lynn, 05 Nov 1969 (Hav) Dawn Renee, 29 Jul 1971 (E); James Andrew, 13 Aug 1972; Laurel Lee, 33 May 1974 (Hav)

CARIGNAN: Brian P & Deann M Demonico: Ashlee Patrise, 23 Sep 1982; Hilary Anne, 01 May 1979 (Winchester,Ma)

CARLBERG: Paul W & Dora J Wells, 28 Aug 1990 (E)

CARLETON: Wilbur G & Edna E Gurney: Barbara Ruth, 24 Apr 1927

CARLSON: Richard D & Diane J Lafayette: Zachary Andrew, 12 Apr 1987 (Derry)
Robert A & Marjorie D Robinson: Heidi Linnea, 15 Mar 1969; Nancy Karoline, 17 Jul 1970 (E)

CARNCROSS: Gordon C & Sally K Richardson: Scott Charles, 11 Jul 1992 (Methuen,Ma)

CARR: Harry J & Lois D Rogers: Seth Patrick, 02 Oct 1967 (Hav)
Theodore H & Rebecca L Bither: Tina Lee, 14 Feb 1979

CARRICK: William F & Helen T Mansfield: William Frank,Jr, 16 May 1959 (E)
CARRINGTON: James W & Mary E Chase: Matthew Joseph, 27 Sep 1980 (Hav)
CARROLL: Everett W (Merrimack,Ma) & Lois W Bunker (Sandown): Female, 23 Oct 1938;
    Jane Webber, 11 Mar 1942; Male, 30 Nov 1939
CARRUTHERS: Marcel M & Geraldine L Aborn: Catherine May, 04 May 1973;Ronnie Lynn,
    05 Mar 1971 (E)
CARSON: William R & Katherine T Egan: Nicholas Cameron, 10 Oct 1993 (E)
CARTER: Clayton C & Linda M Monroe: Carie Mae, 17 May 1978; Jason Monroe,
    03 Aug 1970 (E)
    Cory & Donna L Sundquist: Toni, 30 Jan 1979
    Cory & Susan E White: Keri Anne, 11 Dec 1990 (E)
    Harry G & Ida P Bicknell: Doris Frances, 14 Jul 1930
    Harry L (Kingston) & Ida Chellis (Haverhill,Ma): Earle Stanton, 05 Mar 1926; Walter
    Grantley, 27 Aug 1927
    Layne & Robin L Ready: Cara Nicole, 01 May 1992; Jessica Karin, 23 Feb 1988 (E)
    Ralph H (Kingston) & Sarah E Heath (Merrimac,Ma): Ralph H, 03 Jan 1900
    Walter G (Kingston) & Janice E Holmes (E.Kingston): Candia Ann, 19 Nov 1948; Cory,
    02 Sep 1957; Dawn, 03 Jun 1952; Jayne, 26 Jun 1956; Layne, 16 Aug 1959; Sheryl Lee,
    29 Sep 1949; Walter Grantly, Jr, 06 Apr 1954 (E)
CASEY: Michael E & Kimberly Lafayette, Rayane Beryl, 15 Dec 1979 (E)
CASKIE: David M & Patricia A Sigo: Steven David, 25 Aug 1957 (E)
CASTRICONE: David T & Patti J Hamilton: Jason David, 25 Jan 1978; Rachel Lynn, 17 Oct
    1979 (Law)
CAVARIE: Frank (Cambridge,Ma) & Mattie Dutton (Deerfield): Frank Lee, 10 Jul 1917; Rheta
    Priscilla, 07 Oct 1920
CHAISSON: Michael A & Carolyn A Snow; Michale Albert,Jr, 01 Jun 1986 (Hav)
CHAMBERS: Michael A & Denise E Erkel: Alan Todd, 23 Sep 1986; James Scott, 13 Nov
    1987 (E)
CHAMPAGNE: Robert R & Annie A Piper: Scott Robert, 18 Dec 1970 (Kittery,Me)
CHAMPION: Donald R & Dorothy C Huse: Donald Richard,Jr, 23 Apr 1959; James M, 26 Jun
    1962; Nancy Jean, 06 Sep 1960 (Salem,Ma)
    Donald R, Jr & Samantha Chamberlain: Mariposa Dorothy, 17 Jun 1994; Sara Erminia,
    25 Jan 1991 (E)
CHARLESTON: William H & Sheryl L Carter: Brett Allen, 01 Jan 1978 (E)
CHARPENTER: Robert B & Penny Lee Hett: Robert Bruce, Jr, 15 Feb 1972 (E)
CHASE: Charles(Kingston) & Anna Ferguson (Litchfield, Il): Charles Amos, 23 Sep 1901
    Frank W, Jr & Patricia E Davies: Amanda Patricia, 21 Jul 1979; Steven Anastes,
    26 Nov 1974 (E)
    Paul G (Stratham) & Bernice M Lamb(Scarboro,Me): Virginia Mary, 15 Sep 1932
    Richard I & Katherine Clark: Joanna Clark, 30 Jul 1991 (E)
CHENEY: David (Kingston) & Christine S Thurber (Nova Scotia): Glenn Lindon, 11 Apr
    1939; Male, 01 May 1928; Paul Leroy, 17 Jul 1933
    David (Kingston)& Gladys Lougee (Meredith): ----, 01 Sep 1914; ----, 20 Oct 1915;
    ....., 18 Apr 1921; Male Child, 06 Jan 1917; Marion E, 07 Sep 1918; Phyllis Elinor,
    03 May 1920

Laburton (Danville) & Hattie M Haynes (Newton): Edna J, 26 Feb 1901
Lawrence B (Kingston) & Celia A Farnsworth (Cherryfield,Me): Mary Ellen, 19 Dec
    1948 (Hav); Nancy Jane, 23 Mar 1952 (E)
Roland W (Kingston)& Ellen V Bliss (Weare): Female , 06 Feb 1916; Lawrence Bliss,
    29 Feb 1920
CHESLEY: Elmer E & Diane J Cross: Carey Lyn, 10 Jun 1977 (Hav)
CHEVALIER: Scot E & Susan D St Laurent: Cecilia J, 10 Nov 1989 (E)
CHOOLJIAN: Mark A & Michaelle J Dube: James Anthony, 17 Aug 1990; Robert Malcolm,
    07 Aug 1992 (E)
CHOUINARD: William V & Lorraine A Pettie: James Anthony, 11 Aug 1968 (Hav)
CHRISTENSEN: Lyle E & Lorraine Ticehurst: Kerri Lynne, 15 Apr 1970; Laurie Jeanne,
    05 Feb 1964; Todd Nels, 20 Oct 1967 (Hav)
CHRISTOPHER: Anastes & Donna J Chase: Daniel Paul, 30 May 1975 (E)
CHUBBUCK: Daniel H & Gertrude A Palmer: Linda May, 12 Dec 1948 (E)
CHURCHILL: Edward W,Jr & Linda L Walker: Edward Wagner,III, 24 Jun 1969 (E)
CITORIK: David P & Julie A Melvin: Kristen Elaine, 38 Mar 1986 (E)
CLAPP: James A & Diane M Sarica: David J, 25 Nov 1979 (Winchester,Ma)
    Wallace (Malden,Ma) & Rosa Doyle (Haverhill,Ma): Robert Newell, 20 May 1937
CLARK: Donald H & Priscilla Bodwell: Donald James, 31 Dec 1960; Dorothy Jo,14 May 1964;
    Lucinda J, 17 Jul 1956; Theodore John, 09 Mar 1954 (E)
    Harvey E (Derry) & Alice B Cronin (Somerville,Ma): Harvey Dale, 03 Oct 1947; Susan
    Pamela, 06 Nov 1950 (Hav)
    Walter S & Joan L Bodwell: Steven D, 06 Jun 1961 (E)
    Walter S & Donna M Hilton: Bryan Edward, 29 Jan 1977 (E)
    Wilbur J (Kingston) & Dorothy L Towne(Newburyport,Ma): Francis Etta, 20 Jul 1932
CLARKE: Ronald A & Donna M Snell: Brett Adam, 11 Aug 1972 (Hav)
CLAYTON: Philip R Clayton & Cathy M Surette: David Roy, 19 Sep 1989 (Hav)
CLEMENTS: Arlan T & Jacqueline Walsh: Geneva Sara, 12 Aug 1957; Lisa A, 22 Apr 1961(E)
    Chester H (Everett, Ma) & Catherine Morse (Exeter): Jennie Fay,10 Jul 1945; Carleton D,
    07 Sep 1938
    David R & Linda A Richards: Jill Ann, 23 May 1982; Michael Renwick, 09 Aug 1979 (E)
    George & Jean F McLaughlin: Linda Joyce, 25 Oct 1946 (E)
    Renwick G & Hildamay Cargill: David Renwick, 16 Dec 1955; Nancy, 20 Aug 1959 ;
    Pamela, 18 Feb 1954 (E)
COHEN: Daniel L & Carol M Doerr: Allison Theresa, 22 Nov 1989 (E)
COLE: Frank A & Vivian F Collins: Baby Boy, 01 Jul 1960
COLIN: Edward H & Janet M French, Lorraine Karen, 02 Jun 1964 (Amesbury,Ma)
COLLINS: Charles E, Sr (Epping) & Doris Thompson (Lowell,Ma): Charles Elmer,Jr, 29 Mar
    1952; Michael Robert, 30 May 1955 (E)
    Clarence (Kingston) & Lois Raycroft: Evelyn A, 29 Jan 1921;Norma Belle, 13 Jul 1931;
    Stewart L, 19 Jan 1925; Walter E, 05 Jul 1923
    Leon E (Kingston) & Josephine L Hutchins (Wakefield): Larry Morse, 20 Oct 1941;
    Vernon Hutchins, 19 Jan 1938; Vivian Fay, 26 Mar 1940
    Leon E (W Epping)& Joan A Guimond (Bristol): Leona Earlene, 25 Jan1952 (E)

Leon E, III & Corinne A Daniels: Christina Marie, 07 Jun 1976 (E)
Melvin R & Candy A Gould: Russell Allen, 15 Jun 1983 (Man)
Oral (Kingston) & Daisy Jasper (Kingston): Edna Arline, 15 Feb 1925
Oral W (W Epping) & Verna M Middleton (Brighton,Ma): Brian D, 26 Nov 1956;
Stanley Bruce, 26 May 1951 (E)
Quinton R & Ernestine A LeClair: David Joseph, b 07 Jan 1960 (Man); Roy Erwin,
12 Jan 1959 (E)
Raymond D,Jr & Mollie M Leitzes: Jesse Douglas, 09 Sep 1969 (Dover); Sara Jane,
27 Jun 1972 (E)
Thomas J & Jennifer A Mazzone: Coady Daniel, 18 Aug 1993 (E)
Vernon H & Grace M Desrochers: Alice Elizabeth, 18 Jun 1969; Alta Avis, 27 May 1968;
Josephine Louisebell, 22 Jan 1967 (E); Darlene M, 21 Jan 1966 (Hav)
COMEAU: Dana C & Barbara A Keefe: Michael Dana, 31 Aug 1972; Susan Barbara,
14 Apr 1971 (Hav)
Gregory J, Sr & Cynthia J Ward: Gregory J, Jr, 13 Dec 1979 (E)
Richard D & Rosemarie McCusker: Peter Richard, 14 Dec 1979 (Hav)
COMTOIS: George A & Martha B Barnes: Charles Arthur, 21 Dec 1960 (Kittery,Me)
CONANT: Charles B (Buckfield,Me) & Marion S Clark (Kingston): Gardner Hollis,17 Dec 1914
David G & Patricia Fennell: : Kevin A, 28 Jun 1961; Rebecca Jayne, 18 Jan 1967;
Ronald Alfred, 01 Jun 1959 (E)
Gardner H (Kingston) & Christine M Duston (Chester): Judith Dale, 19 Mar 1936; Sandra
Lee, 10 Feb 1939
Kevin A & Loria A Dubois: Timothy Alan, 23 Aug 1992; Zachary David, 13 Apr 1991(E)
CONKEL: Gregory C & Brenda A Jensen: Samuel Martin, 28 Feb 1994 (Derry)
CONNELLY: John J,Jr & Eloise A Pare: Katherine A, 03 Apr 1970 (Newburyport,Ma)
CONRAD: Richard E & Linda M Tyler: Frances Louise, 09 Mar 1987 (Winchester,Ma)
CONSENTINO: John (Haverhill,Ma) & Dorothy Hasper (Kingston): Nora Jean (E)
CONTE: Darryl & Brenda C Lambert: Aaron Geoffrey, 25 Mar 1971 (E)
CONTI: Donald J & Karen A Principe: Nicole, 12 Aug 1983 (E)
CONTRAROS: Ronald J & Martha L Curtis: Lori Lee, 31 Jul 1981 (Hav)
COOLEN: Barry E & Lynn R Gittings: Derek Wayne, 30 Nov 1991;Katherine Rae, 04 Apr
1987; Nicholas Emerson: 16 Apr 1990 (E)
COOMBS: Peter R & Beverly A Houhoulis: Meghan Elizabeth, 03 Jan 1983 (E)
COOPER: Robert A & Dorothy A Bezanson: Jason Edwin, 29 Nov 1983 (E)
CORDELL: Edward M & JoAnn Foster: Tina Diane, 30 Apr 1970 (E)
CORLISS: Lawrence M & Theresa H Walton: John F, 15 Feb 1966 (E)
CORNISH: Glen B (Sayre,Pa) & Elmira M Dostie (Holyoke,Ma): Glen Burdett, Jr, 26 Feb 1936;
Nancy Louise, 26 May 1940
Glen B, Jr & Joyce A Evans: Alan Burdette, 24 Jan 1955; Mark Edward,14 Feb 1957 (E)
CORNISH: Robert J & Anna M Thonis: Beth Janine, 11 Jan 1971 (E)
CORSAUT: Howard C & Karen M Gentile; Laura Jean, 05 Jun1986 (Stoneham,Ma)
CORSER: Karl W,Jr (Concord) & Janet E Kemp (Kingston): Ann Elizabeth, 09 Mar 1952
(E); Judith E, 25 Jun 1956 (Kittery,Me); Robert Austin, 26 Jun 1954 (Washington,DC)
CORSON: Charles P (Raymond) & Della Young (Sandown): Bettie, 20 Dec 1927

COSTA: Joseph V & Melanie E Frye: Elizabeth Marie, 27 Jan 1987 (E)
COTE: Alfred F (Lowell,Ma) & Patricia L Robidou(Lynnnfield Ctr,Ma):Pamela Jane, 27 Nov
    1952 (E Derry)
    Paul G & Sheree L Guerrin: Kyle Jameson, 25 Feb 1983 (E)
COTTER: Thomas E, Jr & Deidre M O'Reilly: Catherine Anne, 23 Mar 1993 (E)
COUPAL: Joseph (Allenburgh,NY) & Esther Langlois (Exeter): Joseph R, 28 Feb 1923;
    Vincent, 19 Nov 1934
COUTURE: Russell W& Patricia M Boardman: Scott Daniel, 14 Nov 1967 (Hav)
COVIELLO: James M & Sonseeray N Chaney: Ronda, 08 Mar 1975 (E)
COWDERY: James C & Amelia A Farney: James Kenneth, 24 Jul 1979 (E)
COWHIG: Dean K & Doreen A Edwards: David Anthony, 27 Jan 1988 (Salem,Ma);
    Lyndsey Marie, 27 Apr 1989 (E)
COWLES: Frederick M & Merlene J Noyes: Amy Rebecca, 30 Jan 1973; Jonathan Frederick,
    06 Mar 1971 (E)
CRAIN: Richard A & Charlotte Quinlan: Meredith Louise, 19 Jan 1953 (E)
CRAMER: Lance E & Lisa K Madland: Britney Morgan, 13 Aug 1983 (E)
CRAFT: Paul A & Dina L Clinton: Ashley Louise, 26 Nov 1991 (E)
CRANDELL: John H & Shirley F Gagnon: Kevin J, 19 Aug 1966 (Methuen,Ma)
CRAY: William R, Jr & Joan L Peterson: Rodney W Cray, 15 Jun 1966 (E)
CROSBY: Henry V,Jr & Constance S Cynewski: Henry V,III, 26 Jan 1961(Amesbury,Ma)
CROSS: Cecil L (Milford,Ma)& Ruth M Winslow(Kingston): Lawrence Russell, 05 Nov 1934
    John L & Sandra Burns: Tina A, 01 Apr 1983 (E)
    Thomas C & Barbara A Joseph: Dean R, 18 Jan 1966 (Methuen,Ma)
CROSTON: William J & Cynthia A Leavitt: Daniel Kelly, 16 Jan 1979 (Hav)
CROWELL: Albert O,Jr & Phyllis L Whitney: David M, 01 Aug 1954; (E)
    Dianne Elizabeth, 10 Jun 1953; Deborah Ann, 10 Jun 1953 (Hav)
CRUMMITT: William P (Epping) & Carrie E George (Kingston): Charles W, 03 Jan 1914
CULLEN: Charles G & Joan A Bathrick: Patricia Jo, 01 Dec 1955 (Epping)
CUNNINGHAM: Edward A & Gwendolyn A Jensen: Alexander Richard, 24 Nov 1981;
    Alicia Catherine, 06 Apr 1986 (Man)
CURETTE: Edward W & Chyral E Calloway: Elizabeth Velma, 31 Jan 1990 (E)
CURRIER: Charles A & Mary A Gatcomb: Michelle Denise, 15 Sep 1965 (E)
    Dennis N & Pamela Gould: Brian Scott, 16 Oct 1972 (E); Kristin, 19 Feb 1969 (Hav)
    Eugene (Raymond) & Flora George (Kingston): Forest Elwin, 05 Oct 1928
    Leslie W,Jr & Thelma W Merrill: Sally Merrilyn, 23 Dec 1945
    Magloire (Canada) & Mary Remillard (Canada): Alice, 07 Dec 1902; John C.E.,
    25 Sep 1901
    Richard P Currier (Concord) & Eleanor M Tozier (Concord): Dennis Niles,
    28 Dec 1946 (Waltham,Ma)
    Richard P,Jr & Doreen M Byrne: Kenneth A, 31 Jul 1962; Lisa A, 30 Dec 1966 (E)
CURTIS: George L Curtis (Monroe,Me) & Elizabeth Gough(GreenRidge,NY): .... , 26 Jun 1927
CURWEN: Christopher D & Kathleen R Dekker: Christopher Blakeslee, 27 May 1980(E)
CZERWINSKI: Frank N & Agnes C Peet: Cheryl, 10 Jan 1976 (E)
D'AMBRA: Michael M & Verna E Jones: ....., 27 Apr 1966 (E)

D'AMELIO: Paul R & Carolyn J Natale: Joseph Michael, 05 Oct 1977 (E)
DAGGETT: Wayne E & Joyce A Wright: Arin Joy, 08 Aug 1977 (Hav)
DAIGLE: Edward R & Dawn B Lefebvre: Amanda Rae, 07 Apr 1982 (Hav)
DALTON: Donald (ThornHill,TN) & Velma Collins (Naples,ME): Rojean Nezzle, 20 Mar
      1952; Zee Donald, 09 Dec 1953 (E)
DALTON: Wayne J & Joanne Koravos: Jason Joseph, 26 Sep 1977 (E)
DALY: James E (Salem, Ma) & Catherine Marney (Salisbury,Ma): Grace C, 17 Sep 1901
      Victor R & Grace M Polese: Brendan, 31 Jul 1969; Joel Victor, 23 Jul 1971 (Law)
DAME: William D & Nancy L Friend: Joel William, 07 Sep 1976 (E)
DANFORTH: Ronald L & Barbara R Carlton: Diana Lynne, 21 Jan 1965 (Ames)
DANGREMOND: Thomas H & Susan A Qualtieri: Samuel Thomas, 23 Jan 1981 (E)
DANIELS: Richard W & Julianne Pineo: Heather Nicole, 04 Jun 1983 (E)
      Peter W & Madeline M Barlow: Jedediah Emerson, 09 Dec 1978
DARCY: John J & Linda C Crummett: Jamie Michelle, 05 Jul 1971 (E); Jason Michael,
      02 May 1979; Shawn Christopher, 03 Nov 1968 (Ports)
DARNSTAEDT: Danny & Nancy E Makarchuk: Christine, 13 Jun 1982; Jason, 28 Jun 1975
DAVENPORT: David R & Patricia E Newman: David Richard,Jr, 26 Jun 1974 (E)
DAVEY: Charles & Judith A Brown: Scott Edward, 12 Feb 1965 (E)
DAVIES: Norman F & Doris J Yeany: Sue Ellen, 22 Oct 1954 (E)
DAVIS: Daniel J & Lori-Ann G Hughes: Jonathan Stephen, 20 Apr 1991 (E)
      Donald C & Elsie M Skidmore: Donald Cory,Jr, 16 Mar 1979 (E)
      Edward A & Wanda P Davis: Jennifer Rae, 18 Jan 1955 (E)
      Everett J (Durham) & Elizabeth M Goodwin (Amesbury, Ma): Martha E, 25 Jan 1909
      Hugh H & Diana C Hunicke: Alexander Hugh, 03 Dec 1993; Hope Arlene, 31 Jan 1992
      (Ports)
      John R & Patricia A Marr: Brendon Reed, 11 Jan 1973 (E)
      William K (Kingston) & Pearl Robinson (Newton,Ma): ----, 09 Jun 1914
DAVULIS: James J & Brenda J Bourdelais: Laura Beth, 13 Jul 1982 (E)
DAY: Carlton H, Sr & Joyce E Myotte: Carlton Herbert, Jr, 04 Nov 1964 : Daniel J Day,
      12 Mar 1967 ; Matthew Mark, 14 Dec 1970 (E)
      Charles T, Sr & Rosemary A Bernier: Charles Thomas,Jr, 19 Jul 1967; Kathleen
      Rosemary, 10 Mar 1969 (E)
      Daniel C & Phyllis A Miles: Daryl Charles, 27 Jan 1970 (E)
DECAREAU: Michael E & Elaine M Becotte: Michael Edward, Jr, 18 May 1975 (E)
DECATUR: Clarence B, II & Mary E Ray: Christine Beth, 10 Sep 1967 (E)
      Dr.Edwin F (Greenwood,Ma)& Estelle A Tallman (Providence,RI): Edwin Forrest, Jr,
      28 Apr 1944; Lee Tallman, 14 Aug 1941; Stephen Hazelwood, 17 Jan 1937 (E)
      Edwin F, Jr & Estelle M Bailey: Edwin Forrest, III, 20 Apr 1977; Robin Melissa,
      10 Sep 1975
DeCOITO: Richard J & Rosemarie C Palmeria: Richard James, 02 Jun 1972 (Hav)
DeGROAT: Howard L & Charlotte B Johnson: James Dean, 21 Apr 1964 (E)
DELOREY: Edward S & Jean M Eldridge: Lauren Mary, 18 Sep 1986 (E)
DeLUCA: Joseph J,Jr & Cheryl C Towne: Dean Douglas, 26 Aug 1967; Joseph John,Jr,
      11 May 1965 (Law)

DEMAINE: Stanley K & Shelley A Hughes: Jessica Lynne, 10 Mar 1980 (E)
DEMBKOSKI: John T & Julie M Rhuda: David Ryan, 07 Jan 1986 (Dover)
DEMERS: Harold G & Evelyn L Tewksbury: Mark S, 04 Jul 1961; Michael Hebert,
    24 Nov 1967; Richard G, 27 Oct 1962 (E)
DENNIS: Edward M,Jr & Debra L Bowers: Edward Montgomery, III, 22 Jul 1994 (Beverly,Ma)
DeROCHEMONT: Ernest (Kingston) & Ethel W King (Malden,Ma): Isabelle G, 12 Jul 1915;
    Male Child, 20 Jun 1918; Eleanor G, 06 Sep 1916
    Joseph R & Roberta Willey: Brian J, 17 Nov 1966; David A, 16 Apr 1961; Dawn Mary,
    07 Dec 1963 (E)
DESCOTEAUX: Ronald H & Terrance L Wells: Annmarie, 17 Jan 1979 (Hav)
DESILETS: Norman & Phyllis E Bent: Tammy Louise, 11 Dec 1963 (E)
DESMARAIS: Leo & Norma Phillips: Rusty Lee, 07 Aug 1956 (Hav)
DEVINE: Patrick J Devine & Lisa A Georgeou: Alexander Patrick, 25 Mar 1993 (E);
    Christopher Michael, 05 Feb 1989 (Ports)
DEVOST: David P & Lynda C Senter: Bronson Slade, 12 Oct 1980; Drue Rafe, 28 Aug 1982;
    Dyllon Shea, 13 Oct 1994; Elysia Andrea, 05 Jul 1977; Saunders Blake, 16 Jul 1992 (E)
DIAS: Keith A & Lisa A LaValley: Krystin Elyse, 33 Aug 1987 (Dover)
    Robert J & Miranda Bundzinski: Kelli Marie, 17 Feb 1987 (E)
Di BERNARDINIS: John D & Lisa M Violette: Miranda, 16 Aug 1991 (E)
DICK: Wayne A & Vickie A Chabot: Brian Michael, 26 Feb 1973 (Hav)
DICKE: David W & Irma M Rubeqa: Kyle J, 05 Oct 1962; William W, 21 Feb 1961 (Hav)
DIETZ: George V & Philomena F Simone: Beth Frances, 19 Feb 1963 (Methuen,Ma)
DILORENZO: Daniel S & Denise S Cartier: Guiliana Maria, 04 Mar 1993 (E)
DILTS: David A & Janet R Bevers: James Jason, 02 Feb 1975; Jeremy Andrew, 27 Nov 1977
DIMES: Douglis & Florence E Partridge: Dagne Ellen, 28 Jun 1963; Deirdre Marit, 12 Nov
    1964 (E)
DIONNE: Bruce A & Noela A Mahon: Sherry Lynn, 01 Dec 1969; William Edward, 23 May
    1971 (E)
DIORIO: Joseph P & Anne M Murray: Jarred Patrick, 23 Oct 1992 (E)
DOD: William T & Sandra L Johnson: Betsy Ann, 01 Feb 1968 (Salem,Ma); Kerry Lyn,
    17 Jun 1971 (E)
DOLLIVER: Bryan R & Joyce A Magunsson: Corey Bryan, 25 Apr 1978 (Ports)
    Gerard (Boston,Ma) & Maude Powers (Biddeford,Me) Susanne Hale, 18 Feb 1947 (E)
    Gerard R,Jr & Sandra I Pond: Bryan Roy, 15 Jun 1957; Peter Charles, 21 Jun 1960 (E)
DONAHUE: Clifford R & Adele M Amirault: Baby Boy, 18 Mar 1963; Russell Allen,
    03 Mar 1965 (Lynn)
DONAHUE: Kerry J& Linda A Luponi: Rebecca Lynn, 29 Jul 1971 (E)
    Michael J & Teresa M Aromano: Assunta Romano, 08 Jun 1979 (E)
    Jeffrey J & Janet E Burke: Eric Jeffrey, 31 Aug 1983 (E)
DOVIDIO: Bruce & Patricia Diodati: Sabrina, 03 Mar 1993 (E)
DOWNES: James R & Mary A Edwards: Catherine Mary, 20 Dec 1973 (Hav)
DOYLE: Michael, Jr & Louise E Tucker: Diane Marie, 05 Sep 1948 (E)
DRAKE: Thomas R & Linda M Blais: Sean Matthew, 30 May 1978 (E)
DRAWDY: Ronald J & Anne D Bradstreet: Rebecca Elizabeth, 15 Dec 1993 (Man)

DRISCOLL: Timothy R & Lucille L Carbonneau: Keith John, 20 Sep 1987 (Derry)

DROGIN: Marc & Martha E Adams: Robert Asher, 23 Jun 1970 (E)

DRURY: Peter J & Karen A Mercier: Kevin Noel, 07 Aug 1983 (E)

DUBE: Gerald C & Sherry J Tuck: Lacee Camille, 29 Dec 1992 (E)
   Thomas J & Janis L Condran: Megan Leigh, 09 Jun 1975 (Ports)

DUCHEMIN: Bruce L & Pamela M Underwood: Todd Leslie, 04 Feb 1967 (E)
  Bruce L & Carol M Kohlauff: Tracy, 27 Feb 1971 (Hav)
  Frederick A & Muriel E Cheney: Bruce Leslie, 20 Oct 1944

DUFOUR: Omer & Ida Brissette: Omer Wilfred, 30 Jan 1931; Robert Arthur Roland, 09 Jan
  1931

DUGGAN: Robert E & Norma C Smith: Jamie Lea, 05 Jul 1983; Jill Marie, 19 Mar 1981
  (Winchester,Ma)

DUMAIS: Jeffrey N & Karen A Gallant: Andrew James, 15 Apr 1987 (E)

DUNBUR: Richard B & Irene M Jones: David Craig, 22 Nov 1959; Peter K, 06 May 1961 (E)

DUNLOP: William S & Gwendolyn J Jeffrey: Brian Robert, 24 May 1987 (E)

DUNN: Alan M & Susan V Hill: Jennifer Susan, 21 Mar 1983 (E)
  Chester (Essex,Ma) & Ernestine Morse (Lynn,Ma): Nancy Ann, 14 Nov 1946 (E)

DUQUETTE: David N & Alma L Williams: David Norman, 06 Feb 1981 (Hav)

DURANT: John J & Carolee B White: Randall John, 30 Oct 1964 (Hav)

DURGIN: David L & Jacqueline D Brockelbank: Wade Curtis, 01 Apr 1973 (E)

DUTTON: David F& Natalie Taylor: Jennifer Susan, 30 Oct 1963 (E)
  Ralph T & Stephanie K Springer: Cassandra Lynn, 25 Aug 1979; Troy Michael,
  24 Oct 1976 (E)

EASTMAN: Charles W, Jr & Anne-Margrethe Skuggenik: Erica Anne, 26 Nov 1964 (E)
  Steven W & Donna Cail: Susan Pamela, 28 Dec 1969 (Hav)

EATON: Calvin W& Michele Priore: Calvin William, Jr, 26 Aug 1973; James Alan, 22 Mar
  1977 (Ports)

ECKEL: William S & Maureen A Dadekian; Ara William, 07 Oct 1986 (E)

EDDY: Harold R & Josephine L Adams: Sharon Lee, 29 Jun 1969 (E)

EDGECOMB: Walter W, II & Diane M Murry: Chelsea Elizabeth Rose, 12 Aug 1983 (Dover)

EIB: Robert & Dianne J Lussier: Meredith Grace, 29 Oct 1994 (E)

ELDRIDGE: Richard W & Lillian F Gallison: Helen Mae, 24 May 1969 (Hav)
  Richard W & Jane V Holland: Dorothy Vale, 08 Sep 1976; Philip Brian, 14 May 1978;
  Richard Warren, III, 16 Aug 1974 (E)

ELLIOTT: Kenneth E & Sarah J Hartford: Kevin Michael, 05 Apr 1971; Joey L, 06 Sep 1962;
  Melvin William, 07 Apr 1965 (E)
  Warren D & Carolyn J Parshley: Laura Ruth,14 May 1971; John Donald, 30 Dec 1969 (E)

ELLIS: David M & Brenda J Tonnessen: Ashley Elizabeth, 14 Jan 1990 (E)
  George S & Linda Lee Huntington: Stephen Kelly, 23 Jan 1967 (E)

EMERSON: David M & Ginette Tuxbury: Dianne Madeleine, 24 Jan 1973 (E);Jonathan David,
  05 Oct 1971; Kurt Leslie, 16 Aug 1969 (Hav)

EMILIO: Gary & Susan J Batchelder: Christopher Luis, 07 Jan 1975 (E)

EMMETT: Mark J & Beth A Rines: Robert Lewis, 29 Jun 1990 (Derry)

ESKIN: Ronald B & Alice A Kleinhans: Daniel Ashmore, 13 Jun 1986 (E)

ESTES: David A & Lorraine L Day: Christopher Matthew, 25 Sep 1973 (E)
ESTRICH: Douglas A & Joyce L Austin: Hannah Austin, 29 May 1992 (E)
EVANS: Arthur W, Jr & Madeline L Robie: Arthur Warren, 3rd, 26 Apr 1958; Kevin
    Scott, 13 Sep 1963 (E)
    Reginald (Londonderry) & Doris Frency (Royalton,Ma), Richard Lewis, 07 Aug 1928
EVERSOLE: Russell J & Diane J Brockelbank: Vincent Travis, 13 Feb 1973 (E)
EWING: Lawrence J & Alice E Clayton: Robert Lawrence, 27 Jul 1949 (Hav)
FAIRBROTHER: Harry K & Cheryl LWhittredge: Kyla Morgan, 03 Dec 1989 (E)
    Robert C & Rita E LaMotte: Karen Ann, 13 Jun 1967; Michael D, 26 Apr 1966 (Hav)
FARMER: James G & Laurie F Gadwah: Morgan Huntington, 06 Dec 1991 (E)
FARR: William M, Sr & Sandra G Huntington: William Malcolm, Jr, 31 Dec 1967 (Law)
FASCIONE: James J & Christine M Gendreau: Deanna Lyn, 28 Aug 1987 (Law)
FAUCHER: David G & Martha J Clark: Michael David, 10 Sep 1976 (Dover)
FAULCONER: Kenneth B & Ellen L Hartung: Nicholas Kent, 07 Feb 1990 (Concord,Ma)
FAULKINGHAM: Donald L, Jr & Karen F Ready: Katelyn, 01 Feb 1986 (E)
FAXON: Merle (Plaistow)& Elizabeth Gove(Haverhill,Ma): Merle Wilmont, 30 Oct 1934
    Paul T & Darlene J Hales:Kylie Elyse, 30 Mar 1994 (E)
FAY: Everett W & Dorothy L Thereau: Deborah Ann, 29 Mar 1949; Pamela, 12 Mar 1957;
    Timothy Everett, 13 Apr 1951 (E)
    Robert H (Worcester,Ma) & Ruth E Wheeler (S Lincoln,Ma): Dennis Earl, 05 Mar 1947
FEENEY: Roy R & Gladys L Hunt: Robert R, 05 Jan 1923
FELIX: David & Janet T Allain: David Joseph, 19 Oct 1977 (Methuen,Ma)
FELLOWS: Frank R Fellows (Haverhill,Ma)& Janet B Tozier (Plaistow): Glenna Louise, 28
    Feb 1947; Janet Anne,16 May 1945; Ralph Edward, 21 Aug 1945 (Hav)
FERRIN: Shirley R (Deerfield) & Jennie Boulanger (Canada): Clarence, 11 Jan 1909
FERRUOLO: John A & Gae P Iaci: John James, 15 Jul 1965 (Law)
FERULLO: Robert (Boston,Ma) & Doris I George (Kingston): Joyce Susan, 13 Feb 1947 (E)
FICHERA: Mark T & Elizabeth A Bordon: Kristin, 01 May 1983 (E)
FISHER: Michael J & Debra L McCollough: Kendall Rojean,19 Jun 1991 (E)
FISK: Robert F & Frances G Brown: Bonnie Suzanne, 19 May 1963 (Ports)
FISKE: Eric B & Nancy E Stringer: Craig Adam, 05 May 1983 (E)
    Robert F & Frances G Brown: Lynda Mae, 08 Jun 1954 (E)
FITTON: David A & Susan E Arnold: Stephanie Lynn, 11 Dec 1989 (E)
FITZMEYER: Dennis J & Nancy E Browne: Peter Mickel, 15 Feb 1977 (E)
FITZPATRICK: Richard M & Jane E Caron: Sean Richard, 11 Apr 1975 (E)
FLANDERS: Allen F & Arlene J Henry: John Allen, 07 Feb 1950 (Hav)
    Herchel A (Kingston) & Carrie Jones(NovaScotia): Allen Frederic, 15 Mar 1928
    John W & Dorothy J Littlefield: David Alan, 17 Apr 1973 (E)
    Richard A & Donna J Caverly: Amy Rebecca, 08 Dec 1978; Kimberly Ann, 28 Nov
    1977 (E)
FLUET: Mark D & Marla J Anderson: Adam Marcus, 09 May 1990 (E)
FOLDING: Daniel J & Cindy Aubry: Matthew Louis, 16 Dec 1991 (E)
FOLLANSBEE: Somerby C, Jr (Amesbury,Ma) & Geraldine Cole (Haverhill,Ma): Janice Anne,
    17 Jun 1953; Martha R, 07 May 1956; Steven Colby, 09 May 1951 (E)

FORDE: Lawrence R & Denise M Donegan: Chelsey Marie, 25 Mar 1987 (Winchester,Ma)
FORSYTHE: Douglas A & Carol J Claudio: Daryl Trent, 09 Oct 1979 (E)
FOSTER: David M & Paula S Janusz: Christopher David, 04 Aug 1978 (Law)
    Frank W (Haverhill,Ma) & Wilfred A Towle(Hampton): Doris H, 11 Aug 1924; Herman,
    08 Jun 1931
    John E & Joan M Dudley: Bonnie D, 21 Jul 1956 (E)
FOWLER: David M & Georgeanna Tidd: Christopher Charles, 25 Dec 1972 (Hav)
FOY: James M & Sandra J Pizar: Jeffrey Mark, 03 Dec 1965; Michael John, 21 Jun 1963; Scott
    James, 09 Jul 1968 (Hav)
    Michael J & Sara G Heckman: Katherine Carey, 16 Oct 1989; Lauren Colby, 20 Sep
    1991 (E)
FRANK: Thomas J & Teresa A Noyes: Thomas Constantine, 01May1989 (Hav)
FRASER: Robert W Fraser & Cynthia T Stone: Stacy Lynn, 03 Jan 1971 (E)
FREDERICK: Edward C & Pamela J Veregge: Brendan Edward, 07 Jul 1981 (E)
FRIEND: William H Friend & Florence R Townsend: David William, 04 Jul 1950 (Hav);
    Janet Lea, 20 Aug 1953 (E)
FRYBURG: George A & Jane E Baker: Daniel Phillips, 17 Dec 1990 (E)
FRYE: Leroy (Kingston) & Vera M Cilley (Kingston): Grace E, 29 Apr 1914
FUGERE: Stephen M & Kristie A Wagoner: Lacey June, 24 Dec 1981 (E)
FURLONG: Mark W & Judith Leslie: Thomas William, 14 Mar 1987 (E)
GAGE: John A & Sheila Ramey: Brian Richard, 13 Feb 1965 (Hav)
    Robert J & Gale T Martin: Matthew Robert, 16 Jul 1982 (E)
    Steven J,Sr & Betty L Garrard: Steven James,Jr, 17Apr 1970 (E)
GAGNON: Adelard J (Canada) & Bertha M Goss (Kingston): Madeline V, 28 Aug 1914
    George H & Colleen J Aiken: Michael Aiken, 09 Aug 1987 (E)
    Hal E & Cynthia L Goutier: Dawn Elizabeth, 09 Nov 1981; Stephanie Marie,
    04 Feb 1981 (Hav)
GALLAGHER: Gerald P & Phyllis M Carpenter: James Paul, 20 Dec 1970; Kevin Sean,
    02 Nov 1969 (E)
GALLANT: Kenneth R & Beverly M Jacques: Toni Lyn, 28 Jan 1977 (Law)
GALLISON: George R, Jr & Kelly J Holmes: Heather Jean, 26 Apr 1994;Jason Richard, 23
    Apr 1987 (E)
    George R & Lorraine C Mahar: Sandra Ann, 11 Feb 1967 (E)
GALLOWAY: Christopher A & Karen M Madej: Zachary Christopher, 19 Sep 1989 (E)
GANNON: Michael E & Cheryl L Matuscak: Derek Chas, 31 Jan 1988 (E)
GARDENOUR: Larry L & Diane Leslie: Lori Beth, 05 Sep 1973 (Hav)
GARLAND: Ralph (Kingston)& Mildred Hanson (Kingston): Ruth Hanson, 06 Mar 1932
GATES: Billy L & Amy Magnusson: John David, 30 Jul 1973 (Boston,Ma)
GAUDETTE: Joseph A & Peggy E Grover: Donna D, 12 Mar 1962; Roy A, 12 Mar 1962 (E)
GAUNT: Andrew W & Denise M Lawrence: Keri Ann, 07 Oct 1989 (E)
GAUTHIER: Charles E & Ellen M Bradley: Andrew John, 20 Mar 1972; Karen Elizabeth,
    22 Feb 1969 (E)
    David A & Maureen J Donovan: Lee Ann, 29 Dec 1973; William David, 22 Apr 1970 (H)
GEANEY: Paul F & Karen Z Hutchinson: Daniel Francis, 24 Dec 1983 (E)

GEIL: Mark D & Heidi L Krueger: Amy Lynn, 30 Oct 1993 (E)
GEISSER: John A & Nancy J Noyce: Cathy Ann, 14 Apr 1967; Robert Adam, 11 Apr 1969 (H)
GEORGE: Allen P & Charlotte L Anderson: Scott Michael, 12 Feb 1963 (E)
    Calvin E (Kingston) & Gladys Weatherbee (Plymouth,Ma): Carrie Eunice, 26 Oct 1936;
    Melinia Isabella, 17 Dec 1932
    Carl H & Joanne E Chase: Carl Hazen,Jr, 01 Oct 1953; Derrek Stephen, 21 Jul 1963 (E)
    Charles A & Wilma A Marple: Deborah Alaine, 02 Jan 1957; Gwyn Alma, 25 May 1963;
    Mark Allen, 05 Oct 1959 (E)
    Francis P & Adelaide Nichols: Donald Leon, 01 Jun 1959; Ricky F, 17 Jul 1961
    (Methuen,Ma)
    Grover O (Derry) & Alice G Nason (Portland,Me): Clifford M, 14 Aug 1909; Muriel V,
    25 Oct 1910
    Henry L & Marie L Lemay: Male child (stillborn), 11 Sep 1953; Marie L, 14 Mar 1956;
    Ora Porter, 17 Apr 1944 (E)
    Louis W & Deborah K Bilodeau: April Kay, 04 May 1977; Tracy Lee, 21 Feb 1973 (E)
    Michael L & Joan A Meisner: Jennifer Lynne, 09 Jul 1989 (Hav)
    Ora P (Kingston)& Ellen M Cosgrove (Salem): Henry, 24 Feb 1916; Leila May, 19 Aug
    1920; Lila May, 19 Aug 1920; William J, 18 Nov 1925
    Ora P & Mary Abdo: Christopher Paul, 23 Oct 1967; John H, 08 Aug 1963; Mary Lee,
    12 Nov 1965 (E)
    Porter (Sandown) & Florence Kelley (Plaistow): Raymond W, 03 Jun 1915
    Walter (Kingston) & Inez Tewksbury (Danville): Agnes Marion, 19 Aug 1926; Allen
    Porter, 24 Jul 1930; Carl Hazen, 13 May 1932; Female, 17 May 1934; Florence Ada, 09
    Jul 1928; Warren W, 03 Dec 1923
    Warren W (Kingston) & Marjorie A Nason (Kingston): Louis Warren, 11 Mar 1947;
    Rosalie Suzanne, 12 Oct 1954 (Hav)
    Wilfred F (Kingston) & Henrietta M Ledoux (Amesbury,Ma): Beverly Ann, 15 Nov 1939;
    Female, 30 Mar 1944; Frances Marie, 18 Aug 1936; Russell Wayne, 23 Sep 1946 (E)
    William J & Carol A Weatherbee: David James, 09 Nov 1951;Donald William, 10 May
    1949 (E)
    William J & Irene T DiFloures: William J, Jr, 24 Aug 1962 (E)
GERAKAS: Achilles & Vivian Mavroforou: Hariklia Jane, 29 May 1991 (E)
GERRISH: Richard C & Joy L Ingalls: Candace Joy, 20 Feb 1981; Erin Hope, 03 Aug 1983
    (Hav)
GERSKOWITZ: Paul R & Joanne M Gosselin: John Paul, 18 Feb 1982 (E)
GERSTMAN: Howard & Patricia M Hardy: Joseph Michael, 09 Apr 1990 (E)
GETCHELL: Paul A & Alice T Gibbons: Brian Nettle, 26 Feb 1979; Keith Alexander, 28 Nov
    1975 (E)
GIANAKAKIS: Gregory N & Debora E Dowling: Nicole Lee, 24 Feb 1992 (E)
GIBBS: Oscar E (Orleans,Vt) & Nellie M Jones (Lyndonville, Vt): Glenn C, 06 Dec 1918;
    ......, 05 Oct 1921
GIBSON: George T & Frances A Romano: Elizabeth Anne, 02 May 1977 (Methuen,Ma)
GILL: Charles E, Jr & Barbara I Caris: Charles John Matthew, 14 Jul 1993 (E)
    James J & Donna M Hayward: Elizabeth Ann, 02 Sep 1986 (E)

GILLIS: Donald W & Margaret Dyer: Female, 21 Jun 1910
GILMAN: Frank A & Harriet A Severance: Ralph W, 04 Jan 1910
    John S & Yvonne M Laplume: Lucy Ann, 31 Oct 1946
    Lyndon R & Karin E Maback: Hannah Elisabeth, 27 Apr 1989; Nathaniel Maback,
    03 Aug 1987 (Ports)
GIRARD: James K & Jane J Kettell: Dennis Joseph, 24 Feb 1960 (Ipswich,Ma)
    Kenneth L & Jo Ellen Snook: Amber Glen, 20 Apr 1989 (E)
GLIDDEN: Raymond F & Shirley E Davis: Jessica Ann, 23 Feb 1973 (Hav)
GOAD: Ralph (Lynn,Ma) & Gladys Lougee(Meredith): Laurie Clayton, 12 May 1933; Spencer
    Allen, 28 Nov 1929
GOBEIL: Guy J & Susan R LeBlanc: Rachel Rose,28 Apr 1989 (Hav); Rebecca Lorraine, 30 Jan
    1991; (Newburyport,Ma); Zachary Lucien, 04 Sep 1986 (Hav)
GODBOUT: William H& Grace E Collins: William Herbert, 28 Nov 1940
GOLDTHWAITE: Benjamin (Newton) & Thelma D Bunker (W Brentwood): Karl Stanton,
    31 Dec 1944; Wayne Sargent, b 02 Jan 1942 (E)
GONYER: Philip J & Mildred Chatelle: Dianna Jean, 03 Aug 1959 (Hav)
GOODHUE: Clayton E & Margaret M Conroy: Brian Clayton, 08 Aug 1972 (E)
GOODWIN: George D & Rita C MacDonald: Louis Donaldson, 03 Aug 1958 (E)
    John M & Edna E Saleri: Russell McKnight, 29 Mar 1959 (Ports)
    John D (Plaistow) & Myrtle B Taylor (Haverhill,Ma): John A, 19 Jan 1902
GORDON: Clyde M & Helen B Willey: Ann, 26 Feb 1949 (E)
GORMAN: James W & Maureen M Sargent: Barbara B, 22 Nov 1962; James Warren, 12 Dec
    1959; Shawn O'Brien, 12 Dec 1965;William R, 19 Jun 1961 (Hav)
GOSSELIN: Edmund & Virginia Bedard: Leo J, 28 May 1921
GOUGUEN: James M & Marie F Anderson: Mindy Louanne, 07 Jan 1979 (E)
GOULD: Daid S & Brenda Thompson: Alison, 07 Feb 1962 (Hav)
    Lawrence A & Catherine V Ducharme: Andrew Robert, 04 Feb 1987 (Hav)
    Lewis N, Jr & Colleen M Grenon: James Michael, 14 Nov 1994; Matthew Lewis, 14 Apr
    1993 (E)
GOULET: Dennis P & Susan E Underwood: Jonathan Peter, 20 Sep 1983; Melissa Susan,
    26 Oct 1979 (E)
GOURLEY: Michael R & Karen Tarbox: Jason Michael, 25 May 1977 (E)
GOVE: John F (Exeter)& Mildred M Young (Lowell,Ma): Stanley G, 10 Nov 1938
GRANT: Arne K & Patricia S Gielar: Jason Richard, 08 Dec 1979 (E)
GRAY: Thomas A & Heidi S Beaulieu: Melanie Jean, 29 Apr 1978 (Law)
    William C & Pamela L Pizar: Courtney Lynne, 24 May 1970; Stacy Lynne,
    29 Aug 1973 (Hav)
GREANEY: Daniel D & Martha A Modlick: Kevin Scott, 20 Dec 1965 (E)
GREENE: Frank G & Laurie I Arnold: Mallory Lynn, 31 Mar 1987; Morgan Mary, 01 Dec
    1989 (E)
GREENLEAF: Clayton D,Jr & Beverly M Fowler: Jeremy Allen, 19 Oct 1970; Joseph Alden,
    13 Oct 1970 (E)
GREENWOOD: Frederick W (Branford,Eng) & Esther M Neilsen (Gloucester,Ma): Frederick
    William, Jr, 26 Mar 1942

Frederick W,Jr & Jill K Wheeler: Kevin Todd, 13 Apr 1964 (E)

GREY: Peter W & Dominique C Mills: Talia Miquel, 20 Jul 1986 (Rochester)

GRIFFIN: Francis E & Robyne M Vincent: Melissa Ann, 21 Nov 1982 (E)

GROGOWSKI: Andy (Russia) & Amy Wyka (Russia): Male, 17 May 1901

GROVER: Augustine A & Marjorie E Malone: Cynthia L, 01 Oct 1961; Gary Michael,
06 Apr 1959; Gregg Sinclair, 06 Apr 1959 (E)

GUILE: Frederick C & Florence M Merrill: Randy Francis, 15 Oct 1971 (Hav)

GUIMOND: Arthur E (Lawrence,Ma)& Virginia C Palmer(No Salem): Robert Arthur,
10 Apr 1941

GUNDERSEN: Robert A & Patricia I Wolfe: Alexandra Irene, 04 Mar 1991 (Ports)

GUNTER: Brenist A & Sandra L Soucy: Julia Ann, 06 May 1964 (Hav)

GURSKY: Michael S & Linda C Irving: Krystina Michelle, 08 Jul 1981 (Hav)

GUTHRO: Gerald G & Paula J Cote: Melissa Ann, 22 Apr 1979 (Lynn,Ma);Michelle Elaine,
30 Oct 1981 (Hav)

GUYETTE: Edward J (Bolton,Vt) & Hazel L Jasper (Ossipee): Edward Joseph, Jr, 08 Jul 1939;
Ronald Edward, 30 Jul 1937

GWINN: Robert A & Nancy F Whitehead: Megan Carrington, 06 Jul 1982 (E)

HAIGHT: Eugene F & Faythe Foster: Dean Stephen,12 Mar 1954; Kendra J, 28 Jun 1962 (E);
Sally Lee, 16 Sep 1952 (Nashua); Scott Foster, 06 Dec 1967 (E)

HALE: Robert G & Nancy A Call: Daniel William, 16 Mar 1968; James Donald, 05 Mar 1965;
Jennifer Ann, 11 May 1974; Michael S, 28 Sep 1962; Robert M, 18 Mar 1961 (E)

HALEY: Thomas J & Patricia D Mosson: Christine M, 01 Aug 1966 (Hav)

HALLET: David R & Virginia C Bitzer: Kimberly Anne, 23 May 1976 (E); Kristine Elizabeth,
06 Jul 1990 (Ports)

HAMOR: Scott L & Joanne C Furlong: Katherine Grace, 11 Jun 1993 (E)

HAMPE: Robert E & Kathryn A Keeler: Jason Cody, 18 Nov 1982; Joel Scott, 23 Jun 1975 (E)

HANNAGAN: Charles F & Elizabeth A Goodwin: Ann Colleen, 05 May 1963 (E)
Michael A & Jacqueline J Turgeon: Kelly Jo, 07 Aug 1981 (Ports)

HANNON: Ray A & Lori A Lavoie: Jeremy Ray, 08 Nov 1986 (E)

HANSON: Forest J (Kingston) & Florence L Emerson (Merrimac,Ma): Mildred Doris,
18 Oct 1900

HARMS: Eric D & Karen D Ahern: Nicholas Alexander, 01 Mar 1988; Ryanne Kathleen,
23 Jan 1989 (Derry)

HARMON: George H & Mary C Holmes: Richard J, 16 Apr 1956; William Edward,
18 Nov 1953 (E)
Richard J & Patricia Sheperd: Mariah, 17 Apr 1978 (E)

HART: Robert Alan & Susan P Clark: Jeffrey Robert, 13 Aug 1973;Wendy Michele,
31 May 1971 (E)

HARTFORD: Gary A & Sharon A Berry: Gary Allen,Jr, 29 Nov 1972 (E)
Daniel,Sr & Emma E Parker: Daniel Franklin, 04 Oct 1967;Julie Kay, 01 Mar 1965 (E)
Shirley B & Jennie Vallerie: Arthur B, 22 Aug 1910

HARTREY: Daniel J & Sharon A Connelly: Max Daniel, 27 Feb 1987 (E)

HARTWELL: John H & Susan G Stevens: Nicholas Albert Stevens, 16 Jun 1994 (E)

HARVEY: Lawrence S & Cathleen A Quinlan: Jaime Paul, 28 Sept 1978; Joshua Ryan,
11 Aug 1982 (E)

HASTINGS: Aubrey E (Fitchburg, Ma) & Ruth H Rodriques (St Michael, Azores): Jon Michael, 27 Jan 1949; Patricia Ruth, 05 Dec 1946 (E)
HAUGHEY: Charles H & Marguerite E Shand: Marguerite Jane, 09 Feb 1969 (E)
HAWKES: Bruce K & Helen M Langlois: Tammy Marchelle, 26 Sep 1976 (E)
Ralph K & Marcia I Collins: Bruce Kendell, 10 Dec 1953 (E)
HAWTHORNE: James E Hawthorne & Pauline Nason: Cornelius John, 10 Apr 1948 (Kittery,Me)
HAYES: Matthew B & Pamela S Mosmann: Tanya, 18 Jun 1968 (Man)
HEAD: Lester F (Charlottown,NS) & Helen Plummer(Winchester): Judith Ann, 05 Jul 1937
HEALEY: Richard J & Martha J Driscoll: Jennifer Mary, 17 Oct 1980; Patrick Richard, 26 Apr 1982 (E)
HEATH: Charles H (Kingston) & Clara B Pervere (Sandown): Edgar E, 07 Aug 1910; Oscar L, 17 May 1909
Edgar (Kingston)& Anna M Kenney(Amsterdam,NY): Margaret Eileen, 08 Feb 1936; Mildred Frances, 28 Feb 1934
Fred (Kingston) & Lillian Palmer (Merrimac,Ma): Elizabeth E, 01 Jan 1918
Fred M & Dale E Dalzell: Jean Elizabeth, 25 Mar 1970 (Hav)
HECKEL: Paul C & Elaine D Isherwood: Laura Audrey, 08 Feb 1991 (E)
HECKMAN: Scot T & Joan T Kinney: Terri Lynn, 20 Dec 1983 (Man)
HEITZ: Mari A & Francine A Fazio: Stefanie Jaye, 13 Oct 1991 (E)
HEMINWAY: Mark L & Linda H Derry: Jeffrey Mark, 16 Feb 1988 (E)
HENSHAW: George E & Lillian A Kersis: Richard Francis, 29 Apr 1959 (Law)
Richard F & Wendy S Ingalls: Richard Ingalls, 18 Aug 1984
HERRICK: Stanely T (Haverhill, Ma) & Claire J Mattison (Haverhill,Ma): David Allen, 09 Dec 1951; Dennis Allen, 09 Dec 1951 (E)
HICKS: Stanley G & Debra S Kelley: Meredith Irene, 15 Oct 1992 (E)
HILL: Frederick E & Pattiann Picard: Shaune Edward, 28 Aug 1976 (E)
HODGSON: Richard T & Cheryl Jenkins: Kate Elizabeth, 01 Apr 1968 (Newburyport,Ma)
HODSDON: John R & Caroline M Graves: Margaret Elizabeth, 28 Oct 1980 (E)
John R,Jr & Judith N Allen: Mark John, 17 Oct 1964; Timothy James, 26 Mar 1968 (E)
Lee H & Carol A Figley: Joshua Patridge, 08 Oct 1972 (E)
HOGUE: Carleton J & June E Theriault: Matthew Carl, 01 Oct 1970 (E)
HOLLAND: David E, Jr & Kathleen M Lewis: Daniel Jacob, 14 Aug 1976 (Methuen,Ma)
Herbert F, Jr & Jennie M Eldridge: Herbert Frederick,III, 13 Oct 1971; Jason George, 26 Apr 1974 (E)
Timothy R & Barbara A Ireland: Billie-Jean, 20 Aug 1971(Methuen,Ma)
HOLMES: George E & Brenda L Colby: Chantel Lorraine, 02 May 1978 (E)
Walter B & Claudia J Osinolski: Rebecca Lucy, 24 Apr 1972 (Hav)
HOOPER: Henry (Canada) & Maggie Stone (Canada): Frank Henry, 05 Aug 1901
HOLSIPPLE: Arthur E & Tammy M Ferruolo: Michael Arthur, 07 May 1992 (E)
HOULE: John R & Carole Lacomb: John Dennis, 11 Feb 1976 (Law)
HOW: James D (Haverhill, Ma) & Marjorie Estes (Haverhill,Ma): Female Child, 15 Sep 1918
HOWCROFT: James R & Mary E Gambino: Susan Lynn, 13 Jan 1972 (Hav)

HOWARD: Frederic F (Roxbury,Ma) & Christine M MacKillop (Cape Breton):Edmund O, 18 Oct 1916
    Robert L & Evelyn E Brown: Jeremy Ian, 26 Oct 1970 (E)
HOYT: John W (Malden,Ma) & Nancy Severance (Kingston): Ethelind, 28 Sep 1901
    Kenneth C & Pauline A Kearns: Kenneth Collidge, Jr, 16 Nov 1979 (Ports)
HUBER: Dennis R Huber & Judith G Rowell: Alison Dawn, 15 Apr 1974 (E)
HUCKS: George A & Michelle M Mastracci: Erin Vanessa, 28 Dec 1982 (E)
HUCKINS: Edmund J (Newton,Ma) & Mary L Thibeault (Haverhill,Ma): James Edmund, 11 Jul 1951 (Hav)
HUGHES: Robert A & Patricia C Rousseau: Kimberly Ann, 02 Sep 1963 (E)
HUNT: John A & Nancy L Chase: David Adam, 05 Aug 1964 (Chelsea,Ma)
HUNTINGTON: Peter W & Norma L Still: Mildred Lorraine, 14 Sep 1964 (E)
HUNTRESS: Clarence (So Livingston,Me) & Addie Tucker (E Kingston): Eunice G, 16 Oct 1917
    Richard E (Haverhill, Ma) & Barbara J Currier (Haverhill,Ma): Richard Edward, Jr, 23 Jun 1948; Randy Gene, 13 Apr 1951 (E)
HUOT: Donald R & Claire R Ross: Michelle Marie, 06 Feb 1968; Troy D, 22 Jul 1966 (E)
HURLBURT: Gardner M & Kathleen A Baumgartner: Christopher Gardner, 06 Nov 1970 (E)
HURLEY: Joseph J, Jr & Lynne M Wayman: Eric Christopher, 25 May 1991 (E)
    Norman R & Cheryl A Gongas: Sarah Agnes, 22 Jan 1992 (Newburyport,Ma)
    Robert P & Margaret I Welch: Robert Philip, 02 Aug 1960 (Hav)
HUSSEY: Lawrence W,Jr & Deborah J Munns: Shawn Patrick, 19 Sep 1986 (E)
HUTCHINSON: Henry W & Beryle A Hutchins: Katherine Ann, 21 Jun 1946 (E)
HUXSTER: Clifford J & Katie L Rowe: Caleb Addison, 06 Jan 1988 (Ports)
ILLER: Keith E & Gail L Ryker: Kristen Gail, 20 Jun 1993 (E)
INGALLS: David E & Muriel D Abbott: Elizabeth Nina, 03 Jan 1974 ; Jonathan David, 04 Jun 1971 (E)
    Gary & Dianne L Chouinard: Casey Diane, 21 Sep 1992; Corey Robert, 25 Feb 1988 (Newburyport,Ma)
    John J & Linda L Wightman:Karen Ann,11 Dec 1969; Kevin Michael, 25 Feb 1972(Hav)
    Russell M & Corabell F Mitchell: Russell Mayne, Jr, 18 Jul 1939
INGERSOLL: Jonathan E, III & Nancy A Borden: Anne Elizabeth, 04 Nov 1982; Jennifer Borden, 07 Feb 1980 (E)
IPPOLITO: Frank R & Maureen B Devaney: Shannon Marie, 20 Feb 1993 (E)
IRAM: Richard D & Lois E Peters: Heather Jolene, 01 Apr 1974 (E)
IRELAND: David J & Sylvia A Deveau: 20 Sep 1991 (E)
IRVINE: Wendell J & Laura P Irwin: Linda Roberta,17 Apr 1953; Laura Rebecca, 17 Apr 1953 (E)
IRVING: Walter G & Annie Hill: Walter F, 28 Nov 1910
JACKSON: James R & Selma R Harris: Karen Lynn, 01 Nov 1958 (Melrose,Ma); James R, Jr, 26 Jun 1961 (E)
JACOBSEN: Jeffrey W & Lorna E Higney: Cody James, 09 Apr 1994; Connor Ross, 26 Aug 1990 (E)
JOHNSTON: Mark E & Lois A Edgerly: Brittany Morgan, 01 Mar 1994 (Ports)

JUKUBASZ: Robert F & Kathleen A O'Brien: Andrew Scott, 14 Jul 1983; Timothy Michael, 21 Jun 1981 (Hav)
JANDL: William K & Donna M Murphy, Zachary James, 14 Mar 1988 (Stoneham,Ma)
JANES: Robert P & Janice R Bartlett: Robin (Bartlett-Janes), 24 May 1979 (E)
JANKE: Herbert G (Winburne,Pa) & Lorna A Campbell (Bellwood,Pa): Sylvia Jean, 21 Mar 1944 (E)
JASPER: Charles N (Manchester) & Ethel Hartford (Boston,Ma): Dorothy E, 27 Aug 1923; Female, 08 Nov 1924; Female, 19 Aug 1920
JAWORSKI: Edward J & Janet L Tanguay: Jonanthan Edward, 12 Nov 1982; Keri Lynn, 05 Jun 1980 (E)
JENDRICK: Dennis S & Mary T Becker: Paul Stephen, 28 Nov 1969 (E)
Edmund J & Faith A Nolan: Edmund Joseph, 26 Jul 1964 (Hav)
JENNINGS: Dana F & Florence M Britton: Dana Andrews, 05 Oct 1957; Florence Marie, 26 Oct 1958 (E); Michael Porter, 20 Jun 1971 (Hav)
JILLSON: David H & Marilyn L Colby: Keith D, 22 Jul 1961 (Derry); Mark Stephen, 18 Mar 1960 (E) ; Scott Alan, 07 Feb 1965 (Kittery,Me)
JOHNSON: Carl E & Julia A Osborne: Michael J, 01 Oct 1962 (E)
David A, Jr & Janet L Seely: Kristianne Lilly, 20 Oct 1980;Matthew Roy, 11 Oct 1982 (E)
Douglas D & Lori D Thornton: Jodi Lynn, 09 Mar 1989; Jolene Diane, 26 Mar 1987 (E)
Kent W & Rita S Karciauskas: Elizabeth Nicole, 13 May 1987 (E)
Raymond D & Theresa M Hadley: David Raymond, 22 Nov 1978; Raymond David, Jr, 27 Nov 1977 (E)
Joel T & Sharon L Tebo: Amy Leigh, 25 Nov 1983 (E)
Alexander S (Springfield,Ma) & Patricia M Morrissey (Springfield,Ma): Thomas Scott, 11 Mar 1952 (E)
Ivan M & Charlotte B Bates: Tammy Lynne, 14 Aug 1970 (E)
JOME: Robert G & Patricia A Doyel: Gerald Robert, 28 Mar 1973 (E)
JONES: Edward F Jones & Dorothy H Spofford: Kenneth Robert, 21 Feb 1954; Michael Allen, 29 Jan 1957 (E)
Harry B (NovaScotia) & Dora Fanning (NovaScotia): Harold William, 02 Nov 1927
James M & Elizabeth I Jette: Karen E, b 04 May 1961; Kevin James, 16 Jul 1959 (E)
Jimy & Joanne M Timmins: Jacob Evan, 24 Nov 1991 (E)
Richard P & Ellen Warner: Joanna Ellen, 10 Jul 1980; Tracey Lee, 19 Oct 1981 (E)
William F & Sally A Lester: William Frederick, 09 Feb 1971 (Hav)
JORDAN: George W & Denise J Dupuis: Joshua, 01 Mar 1978 (Winchester,Ma)
Kenneth A& Betty E Leo: Patricia Sean, 11 Sep 1965 (E)
JUDKINS: Irving (Kingston) & Mildred FitzPatrick (No Billingham,Ma): ----, 15 Oct 1914
JUAREZ: Perry G & Eileen M Sebetes: Alicia Jacqueline, 16 Aug 1991, Leanne Renee, 01 Apr 1993 (E)
KABALA: Michael L & Catherine M Fuller: Andrea Lucia, 08 Apr 1994 (Man)
KEGLEY: Thomas A & Gloria Hagen: Thomas Frederick,Jr, 24 Jun 1957 (E)
KEARNEY: John P & Linda J Cabral: Lauren Elizabeth,12 Jun 1986; Erin Marie, 03 May 1989 (Hav)

KEIRAN: Alan J & Barbara A Skillings: Mary K, 29 Apr 1966; Scott R, 03 Dec 1962 (E)
KEITH: Glenn & Susan Westerberg: Christian John, 01 Jan 1989; Zachary George,
    04 Aug 1986 (E)
KELLER: John M & Cynthia J Rondeau: Travis Robert, 21 Jul 1983 (E)
KELLEY: Charles E (Kingston) & Sarah J Martin (Sandown): Charles W, 29 May 1909;
    Chester C, 26 Jul 1915
    Fred (Kingston) & Katie M Chamberlain (Northwood): Female, 02 Jul 1909; Male,
    26 Sep 1910
    George W (Kingston) & Estella L Brown(Exeter): Female, 18 Oct 1936; Male,
    29 Mar 1933; Male, 09 Jul 1934
    George W & Dorothy C Taylor: Alberta Emma, 21 Aug 1954; Albert Leroy, 21 Aug
    1954 (E)
    James M & Carolann G Martin: Rory Elizabeth, 30 Dec 1982 (E); Wyatt Everett,
    24 Jun 1981 (Hav)
    Lawrence T (Sandown) & Helen M Hamblett (Derry): Edgar Melvin, 04 Jan 1930
KELLY: Floyd M & Patricia L Stanton: Benjamin Jason, 25 Sep 1971 (E)
    James J & Donna L Towne: Bradley James, 07 Jan 1975 (E)
    Vance M & Diane L Merrick: Paige Nicole, 04 May 1990 (E)
    William R & Karen K Kerkhoff: Shalagh Susan, 23 Apr 1982 (E)
KEMP: Charles W (Fair Haven, Ma) & Winifred Ingalls (Kingston): Male, 22 Jun 1916
    Donald A & Norma L Chick: Dale Harvey, 08 Nov 1959; Linda L, 29 Jul 1956; Scott
    Rogers, 11 Dec 1960 (E)
    F.W. (Otisfield,Me) & Lillian M Boynton (Bridgeton,Me): Ruth Hancock, 05 Sep 1902
    George A (Utica,NY) & Josephine Rogers (Canaan,Vt): Donald Austin, 25 Apr 1930;
    Janet Elaine, 28 Apr 1934
KENDALL: Edward F & Marion F Smith: Gordon Edward, 24 Jun 1957; Richard Perley,
    22 Dec 1959; Rebecca Jean, 23 Aug 1965 (E)
KENNEDY: Wayne D & Denise M Demers: Amanda Denise, 14 Mar 1986 (E)
KENT: William G & Alison P Driscoll: Patricia Ann, 15 Feb 1983 (Law)
KENYON: Stephen M & Cynthia L Pavinich: Jack Robert, 07 Jul 1993;Michael Anthony,
    14 Nov 1994 (Derry)
KERKHOFF: David P & Margaret-Ann M Dickey: Jason David, 21 Jul 1987 (E)
KERRY: Randall F & Veda A Stark: Rachel Leah, 09 Dec 1993 (E)
KERVIN: Frank I & Diane M Nichols: Kristi Lee, 16 May 1982 (E)
KIDDER: Arthur E (Newton) & Gladys Johnson (Rumford,Me): Female, 11 Jun 1917;
    Edward B, 20 Jun 1918
    Roscoe R (Newton) & Flora A St Pierre (New Bedford,Ma): Lillian V, 18 Jul 1909
KILLAM: Alfred H & Carol L Evans: Lisa Ann, 07 Dec 1960; Lynn Marie, 24 Jun 1963 (E)
    Chester H & Alice M Greenwood: Gary Allen, 13 Jun 1954 (Kittery,Me)
    Harold & Patti J Leclair: Tori Lyn, 28 Oct 1978 (E)
KING: Harold J (Malden,Ma) & Letitia Ringer(Louis Head,NS): Clyde Elbridge, 04 May 1937;
    Gladys Virginia, 04 May 1938
    James R & Diane H Russell: Caitlin Azelea, 02 Jul 1987 (Malden,Ma); Lacey Jasmine
    Eileen, 03 Apr 1990 (Stoneham,Ma)

Samuel M & Patricia L Ackerson: Timothy McGuire, 16 Aug 1974 (Hav)
KINNAMON: Bryan L & Susan M Waller: Sara McKey, 09 Dec 1976 (E)
KINNEY: Wayne & Gennie G Kilburn: Terry Jean, 14 Aug 1967 (Hav)
KIRSCH: Carl D & Jayne Carter: Carl David, Jr, 17 Dec 1975 (E)
KITSAKOS: Peter J & Bonnie J Hardy: Cameron Alexander, 25 Jan 1990 (E)
KLIEGLE: Devin P & Mary I Rosales: Max Wolfgang, 16 Sep 1993 (E)
KLINE: Gary J & Anita L Fagerquist: Matthew James, 01 Apr 1983 (E)
KLUNDERUD: Vernon J & Judith C Brown: Jamie Lynn, 24 Jul 1983 (E)
KNOST: Peter N & Joan P Cole: Amanda Bliss, 08 May 1973 (Hav)
KOLIAS: David A & Susanne M Perry: David Allen,Jr, 15 Feb 1988; Rachel Anne, 02 Nov
    1986; Renae Lyn, 25 Feb 1993; Salina Nicole, 30 Mar 1994 (E)
    William C & Nancy A Farley: William Charles, Jr, 28 Jun 1974 (E)
KOLKHORST: Stephen S & Mary J Pertzborn: Christopher Nicholas, 07 Dec 1978 (E)
KOMENDA: Brian S & Lisa M Megna: Jesse Stewart, 23 Jul 1986 (Derry)
KORN: George A & Joyce A Woodward: Doris Lee, 01 Oct 1978 (Hav)
KOSSAKOSKI: Stephen A & Eileen Cole: Kristopher Cole, 19 Mar 1990 (E)
KOZLOVSKI: Albert D & Pamela D Lankhorst: Sara Anne, 06 Feb 1977 (E)
KRUGER: Hans- Joachim & Marie K Thorngren: Cecilia Anna, 22 Jun 1993; Nicklas Andreas,
    21 Mar 1990 (Ports)
KRUKLIN: David B & Debra Smith: Gregory Scott, 04 Oct 1983 (Law)
KUZIRIAN: George, Jr & Yvette R Chiasson: Jessy William, 25 Mar 1989; Kyle George,
    23 May 1993 (E)
KURTZ: Paul J & Gretchen E Renko: David Adam, 06 Jan 1971 (Hav)
KUSTRA: Gerard J & Elaine A Furtek: Kristine Lee, 05 Feb 1972(Hav)
LABELLE: Raymond E & Virginia D Bennett: Raymond Elmer, Jr, 16 May 1946 (E)
    Raymond E, Jr & Diane J Lafayette: Heidi Jean, 23 Jul 1971 (E); Robin Ann, 09 April
    1968 (Chelsea, Ma); Raymond E,3rd, 24 Sep 1969 (Kittery,Me); Scott Jesse, 24 Jan
    1974 (E)
    Samuel (Plaistow) & Viola Collins (Kingston): ----, 06 Nov 1915; Female, 11 Jan 1920;
    Male, 04 Aug 1923; Male, 11 Jan 1927
LACOMBE: Vaughn A (Winslow, Me) & Eleanor Hook (Boston,Ma): Anne, 14 Sep 1952 (E)
LAFAYETTE: Dale T & Donna M Braley: Shawn Paul, 15 Aug 1972; Tawnya Desiree,
    28 Aug 1975 (E)
LAFLEUR: Fred (Chelsea,Ma) & Aelie St Laurent (Epping): Female, 11 Nov 1934
LAJEUNESSE: Lucien M & Marilyn S Wengel: Dale L.G., 22 Jun 1966 (Ports)
LAKE: Robert T & Sally L Allen: Eric Charles Adam, 03 Jun 1965 (Hav)
LAMB: Errol B (Hampton,Va)& Helen Evans (Groton,Vt): Errol Benson, Jr, 28 Jul 1934
LAMBERT: Eric M & Laura J Mitchell: Megan Jane, 09 May 1992 (E)
    Ernest W & Ann E Graham, Cynthia A, 09 Oct 1961 (Kittery,Me)
    George J & Kathleen Nelson: Kathellen Ann, 03 May 1950 (Hav)
    Gerard F & Joanne E Dondero: Joseph Francis, 20 Apr 1980 (Hav)
LAMONT: Noel (Kingston) & Ella A Lyford (E Hiram,Me): Louis Alfred, 04 Mar 1914
LAMY: Richard N & Jennifer L Larosa: Rebecca Anne, 27 Oct 1982 (Law)
LANCEY: Lance W & Carol A Whittredge: Tara Lee, 19 May 1983 (E)

LANCIANI: Richard E & Sylvia F Senter: Angela Lee, 06 May 1970 (Hav)
LANDERS: Theodore F & Barbard Chamberlain: Kim, 10 May 1955; Katherine, 26 Oct 1959;
    Keith Edward, 09 Oct 1957 (E)
LANG: Arthur W & Dorothy E Nason: Arthur Paul, 10 May 1944
    Richard A & Wendy J Manuel: Heather Kristin, 28 Apr 1980 (E)
LANGLEY: Frederick & Joyce E Rubin: Eric, 19 Mar 1971 (E)
LANSEIGNE: Louis A & Melvinetta F Mote: Amber Alyss, 09 Mar 1994 (E)
LANZA: Peter J & Nancy J champion: Adam Peter, 22 Apr 1992 (E)
LAPTEWICZ: Walter J, Jr & Nancy E Cousins: Matthew John, 13 Oct 1983 (E)
LARKIN: George J,Jr & Pauline M McNulty: Patricia Ann, 23 Apr 1966; William A,
    03 Dec 1964 (E)
LARSEN: James L (Worcester,Ma) & Anne L Ross (Lynn,Ma): John Ross, 07 Aug 1941
LARSON: Charles F & Carolyn Sanborn: Cathy Ellen, 12 Jul 1958 (E); Craig G, 28 Dec 1956
    (Kittery, Me)
    Perry W & Doreen G Dube: Haley Grace, 21 May 1991; Shane Patrick, 10 Jun 1986 (E)
LASSOR: Richard C & Dorothy E Hartford: Brian L, 10 Mar 1966; Charlene Sue, 01 Dec 1967
    (Dover)
LATFORD: James N & Ann R Pratt: Gordon Robert, 15 Oct 1969 (E)
    James A & Karen G Wilson: Danielle Ann, 25 Jan 1988 (E)
LAURA: John A & Emily B Szulowski: Edward Paul, 28 Dec 1964: John A, 6 Oct 1962 (Hav)
LAURENCE: John J & Karen N Roberts: Heather Ruth, 28 Nov 1977 (E)
LAVALLEE: Brian P & Mary K Gill: Virginia Ann, 27 Aug 1993 (E)
LAVALLEY: John E & Deborah R Hakenson: Katie Renee, 12 Aug 1979 (Hav)
LAVOIE: Joseph W & Linda G Durgin: Samantha Jo, 01 Apr 1987 (Hav)
    Norman R & Janet A LaFontaine: Cheryl Ann, 14 Sep 1963 (E Derry); Ellen Mary,
    18 Apr 1967 (Hav); Joseph William, 29 Jul 1964; Russell N, 01 Oct 1962 (E Derry)
    Ronald V & Constance A Mitchell: Lisa Mary, 06 Feb 1960 (Methuen,Ma)
LAW: David M & Marie DiPiro: Lisa M, 17 Aug 1961 (Hav)
    Scott B & Nanceann M Villetta: Scott Jacob, 09 Oct 1986 (Law)
LAZOS: Alexander & June Barrett: Cherlyn, 17 Jun 1950 (Hav)
LEANDER: Carl R & Joan P Livesey: Heather Marie, 16 Apr 1991 (E)
LEATE: George & Nellie McNeive: Joseph E, 20 Jan 1938
    George P (Lawrencetown.NS)& Margaret McNewe (Ayres Village,Ma): Helen Catherine,
    16 Aug 1928; Mary Elizabeth, 21 Mar 1926
LEATHE: Harold (Melrose,Ma) & Mary L Mense (Reading, Ma): Mary, 06 Nov 1915
LeBARON: Charles E & Virginia N Thaxter: Rose Marie, 29 Sep 1948 (E)
LeCAIN: Ronald L & Donna J Gerhard: Nicholas William, 24 Aug 1983 (E)
LeCLAIR: Edward Z & Carolyn D Holmes: David Alan, 04 Aug 1965; Debra Ann,15 Feb
    1967 (E)
LEDESMA: Lazaro & Ana L Gorra: Jennifer Ann, 21 Jan 1987 (Law)
LEEMAN: Albert W,Jr & Janice F Roy: Shawn Allen, 29 Oct 1986 (E)
LEEPER: Durward D & Mary L Spies: Donna Kay, 04 Dec 1944 (E)
LeGAULT: Alfred (Haverhill,Ma) & Bertha Collins(Kingston): Alfred E, 06 Jul 1924; Robert
    Leslie, 01 Jun 1930

LENNON: John L Lennon & Joan F Booth: Jeremy David, 01 Oct 1971   (E)
LEONARD: Norman M & Patricia A Dobie: Jill, 23 Aug 1959 (E)
LENANE: Thomas F & Sharon E Cummings: Michael James, 18 May 1981 (E)
LENESKI: Victor J & Eleanor J Woodbury: Anthony James, 30 Jan 1989 (Hav)
LePAGE: Peter O LePage & Gail L Wilson: Mary Ann, 15 Dec 1981; Michael Corey,
   11 Aug 1978 (E)
LERMOND: Ernest S & Marilyn R Avery: Devin Mark, 26 Sep 1958; Katherine Rae,
   08 Mar 1960; Lisa Ann, 05 Apr 1963 (E)
LESSARD: Brian F & Marie E Ahearn: Danielle Marie, 26 Oct 1981 (E)
LEVEILLE: Richard F & Mary L Gibson: Steven Reginald, 28 May 1967 (Hav)
LILLY: Glenn R & Kathleen M Collins: Joshua John, 16 Mar 1979; Michelle Anne,
   09 Jun 1980 (E)
LoCASCIO: Robert J & Mary A Comeau: Tyler Robert, 24 Sep 1987 (Hav)
LOCKE: Augustus E (Newton) & Alice L Marshall (So Hampton): Ethelyn M, 26 Apr 1914
LOCY: Douglas A & Areta C Wawryszyn: Tania Christina, 05 Jul 1974 (E)
LONG: Christopher S & Cindy L Desjardins: Jennifer Marie, 15 Feb 1991 (E)
   Kenneth (Walpole,Ma) & Martha A Huntress (Kingston): Dorothy Ellen, 03 Sep 1941;
   Kenneth Walter, 15 Mar 1944 (E)
   Wheeler H (Deerfield) & Mattie Brown (Bedford,Ma): Annie F, 29 Sep 1915
LOVERING: Lloyd E & Dorothy E Daly: Jeffrey Lloyd, 26 Apr 1963 (E)
LUNDQUIST: Mark E & Martha J Dooley: Jennifer Leight, 15 Aug 1992; Kristina Ann,
   12 Jan 1994 (Derry)
LUSONA: John D & Betty J Stewart: Claudia Jean, 13 May 1949 (E)
MacDONALD: Bruce W & Beverly A Pierce: Daniel Bruce, 06 Jan 1963; Kim I,
   20 Jul 1961 (E)
   John (W Newbury,Ma) & Irene Simes(Haverhill,Ma): Female, 04 Oct 1927
   Paul R & Barbara K Demers: Holly Ann, 21 Oct 1957 (E)
MacKENZIE: Ronald T & Diane M Chouinard: Jennifer Lynn, 20 Aug 1987; Kelly Marie,
   13 Aug 1986 (E)
MacNEILL: Ronald J & Priscilla J Doncaster: Adam Michael, 31 Oct 1994 (E)
MacNEVIN: Raymond G & Doreen M Sadowski: Nicole Marie, 14 Nov 1986 (E)
MACHANDO: Gabriel, Jr & Brenda L Greenman: Michael Adam, 15 Jan 1970 (Ports)
   James H & Claudette C St Laurent: Zachary Paul, 14 May 1980 (E)
MAGNUSSON: Alan E & Mary E Penney: Hannah Mae, 09 Aug 1990; Jedediah James, 26 Feb
   1993 (E)
   Conrad L & Phyllis M Evans: Alan Evans, 18 Sep 1958 (E); Brain Keith, 08 Sep 1968
   (Hav); Kevin J, 15 Feb 1961; Robert Scott, 23 Jan 1965   (E)
   Glenn A & Lyn M Foucher: Shauna Marie, 23 Feb 1983 (E)
   Kevin J & Lisa A Lermond: Dana Rae, 17 Sep 1992; Erica Ann, 06 Apr 1989 (E)
   Martin (Gloucester,Ma) & Hattie Philbrick (Springfield): Harriet E, 15 Sep 1909
   Robert S & Kristina J Duston: Corinne Lee, 01 Apr 1991 (E)
   Theodore S & Ruth F Call: Glenn Alan, 23 Nov 1955; John W, 18 Dec 1961; Joyce Ann,
   31 Jan 1958 (E)
MAHLERT: Brian M & Shelley A Stephens: Meagan Courtney, 31 Mar 1987 (E)

MAILLOUX: Mark S & Stacey M Hamel: Emily Margaret-Elaine, 12 Oct 1994 (E)
MALLOY: Howard G & Kay M Braley: Carol Joane, 29 Nov 1954; Catherine May,
   17 Dec 1955 (Hav); Howard George,Jr, 21 Sep 1968 (E)
MALYNN: John P & Sandra L Green: Shane Patrick, 19 Dec 1973 (Hav)
MANSFIELD: Charles R & Glenda B Dingee: Charlene Elizabeth, 24 Nov 1958 (E)
   James E & Virginia F Mitchell: Luke Robert, 11 Sep 1987 (Hav)
   Robert B & Ardis L Vadeboncoeur: Kerry Lee Ardis, 19 Nov 1973 (Hav)
MANSFIELD: Thomas T & Joyce B Bradford: Jason Bradford, 07 Dec 1970; Tracy Lynn,
   14 Apr 1969 (Hav)
MARBLE: John O (Bradford,Ma) & Susie Sanborn (Lake Village): Harriet Nesbit, 03 Apr 1900
MARCOTTE: Harry G, Jr & Florence W Walch: Anne Marie, 26 Oct 1955 (E)
MARCOU: Isreal & Gloria C Gaudette: Genevia Ann, 15 Mar 1948 (Brentwood); Priscilla
   Rose, 29 May 1949 (E)
MARCOUX: Patrick J & Lucinda J Clark: Matthew Jason, 01 Mar 1974 (E)
MARDEN: Charles F & Joyce A Hume: Joshua Hames, 06 Oct 1977 (E)
MARGESTON: David E & Lori E Thomas: Jamey Man, 28 Feb 1978 (E)
MARPLE: William (Kingston) & Helen Gay (Natick,Ma): Arliner Alaine, 27 Sep 1928
MARQUIS: David R & Dianne C Maddalena: Christopher David, 06 Mar 1991 (E)
MARRONE: Alfred J & Diane M Azzarelli: Stephanie Ann, 19 Jun 1987 (Law)
MARSH: Gene L & Jacqueline G Snyder: Christopher Goddard, 19 Oct 1960 (E)
MARSHALL: Joseph E & Pauline M Ballard: Jeffrey Eric, 28 May 1964 (Newburyport,Ma)
   Larry E & Judith A Legasse: Kimberly Irene, 14 Jul 1960 (E)
   Robert W & Joann R Pierce: Heidi Joan, 23 Jan 1955 (E)
MARSTON: Charles B (Essex,Ma) & Alice Currier (Medford,Ma):Male, 10 Oct 1925
   Robert P & Virginia M Goudreault: Elizabeth L, 14 Dec 1962 (Hav)
MARTEL: Raymond G & Pearl M Scott: Deborah L, b 10 Oct 1956; George G,
   17 Sep 1961 (E)
MARTIN: Charles A & Rita E Nason: Edward Alfred, 03 Apr 1963 (E); Leisa I, 26 Apr 1961
   (Hav); Scott Arnold, 11 Jun 1965 (E)
   Charles F & Shannon L Waters: Emily Erin, 02 Aug 1994 (E)
   Clarence F (Kingston) & Mildred H Efison: Earnest Arthur, 11 Jun 1930
   Everett A (Kingston) & Annie M Brown (Sandown): Alberia, 17 Jan 1914; Eleanor P,
   08 Jul 1916; Gertrude, 19 Dec 1918; Male, 11 Sep 1910
   Everett G & Elizabeth M Bailey: Abraham M, 06 Oct 1966; Charles Fred, 27 Mar 1969
   (Hav); Christine, 27 Jan 1971; Deborah Marie, 30 Apr 1963(E Derry)
   Hollis D Martin & Suzanne C Noble: Robert Donald, 01 Jun 1953 (E)
   Hollis D (Kingston)& Vinie St John (Fremont): Roland Earl, 30 Nov 1936
   Melvin E (Kingston) & Ruth Emery (Sandown): Donald Melvin, 07 Apr 1936;
   Harry Leslie, 01 Feb 1936; Wayne Elmer, 26 Jul 1946 (E)
   Robert D & Janet T Drury: Tammy Joy, 13 Feb 1977 (E)
   Wayne E & Geneva M Hill: Julie Ann, 05 Feb 1973 (E)
MASCIO: Dennis R & Linda S Mealey: Corey Robyn, 21 Mar 1980 (Hav)
MASCIOLI: David A & Lorianne J Sebetes: Nicholas David, 15 Aug 1991 (E)
MASON: Norman & Frances H Hatch: Anne, 05 Jan 1940

MATHEWS: Richard J, Jr & Elaine M Mahon: Barbara Mae, 04 Jul 1967 (E)
MAUGHAN: Harold E & Dorothy E Long: Boyd Harold, 22 Jul 1976 (Nashua)
MAULE: Robert D & Elizabeth Singer: Patia Grace, 29 Aug 1981 (E)
MAURIER: Donald H & Isabel S Dominiquez: Yolanda, 23 Aug 1983 (Law)
    William & Michelle C Kimball: Michael Joseph, 02 Jun 1992 (E)
MAXWELL: Ralph H, Jr & Phyllis M Paradie: Judith Marie, 09 Aug 1964 (E)
    Thomas F & Judy S Kmiec: James Edwin, 23 Mar 1974; Lori Ann, 17 Jun 1976 (Hav)
MAY: George F, Jr & Martha J Dehey: Whitney Allison, 20 Nov 1983 (E)
MAYHEW: George A & Debra A Crescentini: Kevin David, 19 Dec 1978 (Ports); Paul Alden,
    27 Sep 1975 (E)
MAYO: Robert E, III & Sandra L Collins: Robert Emerson, IV, 31 Aug 1980 (Hav)
McASKILL: Edward C & Diane J Greeley: David Allen, 15 Aug 1960; Edward Charles, Jr,
    01 Mar 1959; Michael Lee, 11 Nov 1963 (EA)
    Robert F & Lorraine M Dodier: Michael James, 27 Nov 1959 (Hav)
McCURDY: Herbert J & Roberta MacMillan: Robert John, 16 Jan 1950 (E)
McDONALD: Bernard A & Donna M Simard: Jeffrey Alan, 22 Nov 1968; Jody Ann,
    22 Apr 1966; Julie Anne, 05 Dec 1969 (Hav)
    William A & Joanne W Donahue: Kyle John, 29 Aug 1969 (E)
McDOUGALL: Robert C & Jef Flanders: Kate Flanders, 04 Apr 1991 (Concord)
McGONIGLE: Steven P & Barbara J Soden: Abbie Lynn, 04 Nov 1978 (Concord)
McKEEN: Robert H & Esther L Newton: Jeremy Arthur, 15 Jan 1981
McKENNEY: Norris F,Jr & Evelyn M Thibeault: Donna Lee, 25 May 1964 (E)
McLAUGHLIN: Allan R & Sheila Butruccio: Michael Allan, 17 Jul 1964 (Hav)
    Brian J & Sheila M Murphy: Mark William, 05 Dec 1968 (Hav)
McLELLAN: Edward C,II & Anita L Hamblen: Edward Carlton, 23 Jan 1994; Nicholas Noah,
    28 Dec 1989; Samuel Austin, 11 Nov 1991; William Arthur,III, 19 Feb 1988 (E)
McNEIL: Stanley (Nova Scotia) & Edith M Hunt (So Hampton): Helen, 07 Jan 1902
McPHEE: Joseph F & Cecile H Bonin: Jeffrey K, 14 Apr 1961 (Amesbury,Ma)
    Robert M & Malinda A Cronan: Ian Cronan, 22 Nov 1971 (E)
McROBBIE: Robert T & Joyce E Grondin: Kimberly Ann, 16 Jun 1967 (Law)
MEACHAM: Lloyd R & Gretchen B Nash: Seth Cqarter, 14 Aug 1981 (E)
MEISNER: Steven A & Paula K Gray: Matthew James, 23 Mar 1986 (Ports);Mellony Ann,
    20 Dec 1983 (E)
MERCER: David W & Joyce S Ferullo: Adam Wayne, 10 Oct 1972 (E)
MERCHANT: Hugh D & Mary Ann Tedeschi: Grace Mary Ann, 11 Mar 1957 (Law)
MERCURIO: James P & Mary L Givens: Daniel James, 30 Jun 1980 (E)
MERRICK: Lester H & Ruth A Ard: Lester Herbert, 08 Sep 1968 (Hav)
    Robert L (Kingston) & Anne J Crymble (Lowell,Ma): Elizabeth Louise, 28 Oct 1958;
    Marjorie Ann, 29 May 1948; Robert Charles, 07 Aug 1953 (E)
    Walter P (Danville) & Gladys Robinson (Cambridge,Ma): ....., 22 Oct 1921; Female, 09
    Apr 1923; Walter, 10 Feb 1920
MERRIFIELD: Kenneth L & Theresa A Perrault: Russell Alan, 15 Sep 1957 (Amesbury,Ma)
MERRILL: Dana L & Paula J Morrison: Barbara Elizabeth, 26 Aug 1991; Dana Louis,Jr,
    11 Sep 1987 (E)

Reid N & Karen L Alexander: Alison Elizabeth, 10 Feb 1989; Sarah Ann, 01 Jul 1991 (E)
METCALFE: George R & Gladys V King: Deborah Marie, 04 Jul 1963; Keith Evan,
29 Mar 1959; Russell Alan, 02 Jul 1960 (E)
MEYER: Charles W, Jr & Ernestine Bonequi: Matthew, 24 Dec 1970 (E)
MILBURN: Norman (E Kingston) & Ethel Clements (Everett,Ma): Mary Stanley, 18 Mar 1936
MILLBURY: William B (Nova Scotia) & Edith Burpee (Haverhill, Ma): Female, 20 Apr
1910; Female ,05 Nov 1918; Male, 21 Mar 1927; Theodore, 22 Jul 1922
MILLER: Leo S & Doris M Miller: Linda Sue, 19 Jun 1957 (Kittery,Me)
Donald M & Madelyne U Page: Glenn Perley, 21 Apr 1950 (Hav)
Donald M & Janet C Barrett: Thomas John, 24 May 1953 (Hav)
Glenn P & Leslie C Porter: David Matthew Jordan, 28 Mar 1982 (Hav)
John H (Bellwood,Pa) & Frances VanAvery(Kalamazoo,MI): Mary Francis, 09 Aug 1927
Leroy J & Carol E Howe: William Francis, 26 Oct 1972 (Law)
Warren E & Linda M Morrill: Paul William, 27 Dec 1975; Robert Everett, 15 Feb 1975
(Hav)
MILLETTE: David E & Deborrah A Crowell: Shon David, 12 May 1971 (Hav)
MISENHEIMER: John C & Carol A Pitkerwick: Heidi Dee, 09 Feb 1965; Tara Irene,
14 Apr 1970 (E)
MITCHELL: George W & Carol L Lynch: George William, Jr, 18 Mar 1974 (Kittery,Me) ;
Robert Delaney-Tucker, 11 Apr 1977 (E)
MOLDICK: Walter (Hyde Park,Ma) & Evelyn M Thereau (Derry): Martha A, 23 Mar 1938
MOLLOY: James C, III & Charlene A Smith: Ryan James, 24 May 1977 (Arlington,Ma)
MONDOR: Francis A & Gale A Cogswell: Taylor Anthony, 20 Feb 1983 (E)
MONK: David W & Debra J McIntyre: Jason Edward, 29 Sep 1982 (Winchester,Ma)
MONTONI: Jay N & Carol A Ryerson: Jay Nicholas, Jr, 01 Dec 1980 (E)
MOODY: William L (Kingston & Annie I Simes (Kingston): Shirley June, 07 Aug 1930
MOOERS: Robert H & Susan A Arnold: Rebecca Lynn, 18 Jun 1977 (E)
MOORE: Donald J & Patricia M Ormes: Bonnie Lea, 29 Aug 1963; Lonnie Lee, 29 Aug 1963
Scott R, 28 Feb 1962 (Somerville, Ma)
Michael C & Catherine M MacKinnon: Michael Andrew, 15 Apr 1987; Samantha Ann,
10 Aug 1991 (Man)
MORAN: John C & Deborah L Boutwell: Christopher John, 12 Jun 1989; Devinne Christina,
25 Sep 1987 (E)
MOREAU: Joseph & Jean G Larson: Jo-Anne Theresa, 05 Jul 1965 (Hav); Loria Susan,
16 Oct 1963 (E)
MORGAN: Frank V & Judith A Gormley: Maureen Ann, 21 Jul 1964 (E)
MORGENSTERN: Richard E & Heidi Ouellette: Kara Maria, 29 Dec 1991; Michael Richard,
14 Jan 1989 (E)
MORIARTY: Leo J & Olive F Papineau: Paula E, 02 Sep 1966 (E)
MORIN: Vaught J & Pauline A Fontaine: Rachelle Ann, 16 Jul 1972 (E)
MORRILL: Fred A & Bessie Tucker: Fred A, 24 Aug 1910
MORRIS: Edward J & Laura A Zilch: Elizabeth Ann, 16 Feb 1986 (E)
MORRISSEY: Stephan P & Joanna Watkins: Stephan Alexander, 06 Jun 1986 (E)
MORROW: Allen M & Cynthia M Cutliffe: Justin Allen, 10 Sep 1987 (E)

MORSE: Charles H, Jr & Janice Mae Cass: Michael Douglas, 19 Jul 1957 (E)
Edward F & Judith A Farrar: Jennifer Ann, 08 Jan 1973 (Hav)
George A, Jr & Corinne A Ivas: Cody Joseph, 21 Feb 1983 (Stoneham,Ma)
Lawrence R & Florence M Jennings: Leanne Michele, 16 Oct 1983 (E)
Robert A & Marion Lewis: Brian Edward, 21 Apr 1965 (E); Robert Alfred,
13 Jul 1963 (Hav)
Robert L & Virginia D Morse: Benjamin Warren, 12 Oct 1975 (E)
MOSSE: Robert K & Jocelyn Solomon: Geoffrey Robert, 31 Mar 1980 (Weymouth,Ma)
MUDGE: David T & Priscilla J Hill: Kandi Jean, 21 Jun 1974 (E)
MURPHY: Joseph (Exeter) & Angie M Mitchell(Exeter): Charlotte Alma, 04 Feb 1927
Michael P & Deborah L Hinds: Meghann Leigh, 25 Jun 1983 (E)
Thomas J & Katherine A Goudreault: Shawn Thomas, 18 Aug 1992 (E)
MURRAY: Charles J & Rita E Saulnier: Deborah Anne, 08 May 1969 (Beverly,Ma)
Michael A & Rachel E Holt: Austin Edward, 07 Oct 1986; Matthew Albert,
02 Mar 1989 (E)
Richard R & Alice L Fowler: Debra L, 18 Dec 1962; (Hav); Donna Lee, 05 Aug 1964;
Linda Lee, 09 Apr 1966 (E)
NARY: Timothy J & Martha L Porter: Cynthia Sue, 22 May 1972 (E)
NASH: Thomas E & Lynn A Fales: Michael Thomas, 29 Dec 1980 (E)
Thomas E & Lori A Foucher: Joseph Thomas Wise, 02 Jul 1994 (E)
NASON: Alden E & Beatrice M Tucker: Alden E, Jr, 08 Apr 1955 (E)
Donald H (Kingston) & Glory M Moore (Brooklyn,NY): Rita Ellen, 16 Mar 1941
Elden C & Louise A Coffin: Kevin Michael, 08 May 1967; Lisa M, 21 Aug 1961 (Hav);
Shirley Louise, 24 Aug 1960 (Amesbury,Ma)
Elvin F (Kingston) & Marion E DeCota (Weare): Freeman Elvin, 25 Mar 1947; Suzanne
Rose, 22 Oct 1955 (E)
Eugene N (Kingston) & Etta F Brown (Sandown): Celia I, 26 Nov 1917; Eldin Clinton,
12 Oct 1932; Helen Josephine, 13 May 1920
Ernest (Kingston) & Esther O Patch (York,Me): Lillian A, 28 Sep 1909; Marjorie A ,
26 Apr 1924; Roger E, 21 Sep 1915
Freeman L (Kingston) & Mildred Marshall (Merrimac,Ma): Charlotte, 12 Feb 1918 ;
Dorothy E, 18 May 1924; Elizabeth B, 03 May 1916; Female, 01 Jun 1920; Lora L, 07
Apr 1915; Male, 03 Apr 1926; Nathan, 11 May 1909; Pauline 05 Jun 1925: ....., 01 Jun
1921
Freeman E & Regina I Verville: Kerrie Lyn, 07 Feb 1973; Mark Freeman,19 Jul 1977 (E)
Harold (Kingston) & Mary E Wilburn(Kensington): Hazel M, 02 Mar 1923; Sylvia
Myrtle, 01 Jan 1925
Herbert C (Kingston) & Dora B Marple (Lynn,Ma): Brenda Louise, 30 Jul 1941
Roger E (Kingston) & Thelma E Jasper (Kingston): Linda Lee, 24 Jan 1945; Roger
Edward, Jr, 04 Oct 1945 (E)
Seth F (Kingston) & Blanche Elkins (Kingston): ----, 11 Jun 1914; Florence, 04 Feb
1910; Lester Farnsworth, 17 Aug 1901
NEAL: Richard A & Rhea M LaFlamme: Kathy Ann, 08 May 1959 (E)
NEDEAU: Russell W & Miriam M Peko: Russell Wayne, Jr, 18 Nov 1983 (Ports)

NEVERS: Wendell P & Mary G White: Patrick James, 26 Jun 1969 (E)
NEWELL: Gerard & Gloria G Batchelder: Gerard Newell, 20 Feb 1955 (E)
NICHOLS: Carl (Woburn,Ma) & Zoey M Gonyer (Bethel,Vt): Roger Harden, 24 Sep 1951 (E)
 Frederic L (Kingston) & Therese Porter,(Merrimac,Ma): Robert Frederic, 26 Jun 1927
 Liondel J & Clarina B Roels: Diane Marie, 11 Feb 1960 (E)
 Robert F & Joan E Walter: Judith Elizabeth, 12 Mar 1950 (E)
 Stephen J & Laurie A Lamouica: Tyler James, 04 Jul 1991 (Ports)
NICHOLSON: John P & Kimberley J Nowell: Rachel Theresa, 08 May 1989 (Hav)
NILSSON: Wayne L & Karen A Lamb: Mary, 09 Apr 1968 (Derry)
NOLETTE: Jean P & Janice L Johnson: Sandra Jean, 28 Apr 1969 (E)
NOMEY: Arthur (Montreal,Can) & Jean Bethuen (Yarmouth,NS): Nancy Lee, 26 Oct 1936
NORMAND: Eugene V & Jean R Santin: Sarah Beth, 09 Jan 1980 (E)
NORRIS: Joseph J, Jr & Barbara A Cornish: Joseph James, III, 27 Feb 1949; Robert Grant, 13
 Jan 1951 (E)
 John D (Malden,Ma) & Barbara F Rock (Exeter): John Donald,Jr, 18 Sep 1952; Lynne
 Marie, 07 Dec 1948 (E)
NORTON: Frederick G & Sue J Ritter: Patrick Earl, 27 Apr 1978 (Ports)
NOURY: Gregory A& Saundra L Friend: Amanda Katrina, 20 Feb 1986; Hailey Kristin,
 28 Mar 1983 (E)
 Paul L & Katherine L Bouchard: Paul Louis, 15 Jan 1963 (Hav)
NOYES: Lawrence F & Marion E Palmer: Lawrence Walter, 22 Nov 1941
 Leon L & Beverly J Sabatino: Daniel Leon, 23 May 1977 (Hav)
 Stacy A & Linda A Joray: Heather Ann, 16 Jul 1983 (Hav)
 William C & Eunice Jones: Heidi Ann, 03 Mar 1971 (E)
NUDD: David P & Diana L Felch: Jessie Elizabeth, 20 Feb 1982 (E)
OAKMAN: Walter F (Marshfield,Ma) & Echia Joseph (Norwell,Ma): Kenneth H, 20 Feb 1920
O'BRIEN: James J & Elaine M Gilman: Mary Elizabeth, 18 Jul 1979 (Ports)
 John F & Christiane Buchal: Patrick John, 24 Nov 1970 (Hav)
O'DONNELL: James S & Marjorie J Murray: Daniel Jay, 02 Oct 1974 (Salem, Ma)
O'MARA: William E, Jr & Jeanne L Rybinski: Thomas Allen, 23 Jun 1994;William Edward,III,
 31 Jul 1990 (Man)
OKOLO: Roger V & Debra L Manuel: Heather Lena, 06 Dec 1980; Jennifer Lee, 05 Aug 1979
 (Stoneham,Ma)
OLESON: Eric J & Colette I Marcotte: Eric Jon, 14 Dec 1970 (Hav)
 Eric J & Cheryl L Ticehurst: Jared Lars, 25 Oct 1976; Jeremy Jon, 28 Feb 1975 (E)
OMALY: Mills R & Sharon Hayes: Jennifer Sims, 04 Jul 1971 (Hav)
ONUFER: Andrew B & Jessamyn P Denuzzio: Laura Elizabeth, 10 Sep 1992 (E)
ORLANDO: Robert M & Hazel L Forsmark: Lillian Kathryn, 05 Jul 1967 (Hav)
ORNELLE: John A, Jr & Kelly E Hanson: Hannah Shay, 11 Jun 1990 (Manchester)
OSGOOD: Douglas E & Diane J Edson: Michelle Marie, 18 Jun 1970 (E)
 Edward A & Eileen T Godfrey: Kathryn Ann, 27 Jan1989 (Stoneham,Ma)
 Everett R & Hazel J Kennedy: Alicia, 14 Jul 1957 (E)
OUELLETTE: Frank R & Lisa M Arsenault: Kristin Marie, 01 Dec 1986 (E)
 Roger M & Bettie Corson: Heidi, 02 Apr 1961; Holly, 09 Aug 1958; Scott H,
 12 Jun 1966 (Hav)

OWEN: Michael L & Mary I Cadorette: Christine Michelle, 14 Jan 1972 (Hav)
   William A & Elaine Lieb: Michael William, 17 Jul 1975 (Law)
PAAKKONEN: Gene H & Linda M Gunn: Christopher Alan, 26 Apr 1972 (E)
   John A & Paula J Tripp: Sabrina May, 18 Nov 1972 (E)
PAGE: Herbert L & Marjorie Poor: Donna Jean, 15 Jul 1955 (E)
   John H (Kingston) & Catherine Mason (Boston,Ma): Ida E, 25 Apr 1921; John W, 04 Feb
   1910; Mabel M, 16 Oct 1918
   Norris (Hampstead) & Mildred Parker (Chester): John Norris, 16 May 1927
   Ulysses S (Kingston) & E Iona Currier (Danville): Albertine Ione, 28 Dec 1920
   Walter R & Myra L LaFleur: Eric Joseph, 23 Jan 1969; Robert Alan, 21 Feb 1968 (Hav)
   William C & Judith C Dinsmore: Andrew Chase, 29 Mar 1964 (E)
PAGLIARULO: Charles V, Jr & Donna J Page: Tina Jean, 03 Mar 1976
PAIGE: Richard & Millicent A Woods: Thomas Edward, 25 May 1959; Linda Maire, 11 Aug
   1957; Sandra L, 17 Sep 1961 (E)
PALARDY: Richard D & Carolyn F West: Faye D, 11 Nov 1961 (E)
PALMER: Manford L (Oxford,Me) & Annette Callaghan(Solon,Me): Patricia Ellen,
   28 Sep 1936
   Richard J,Jr & Ann T Holbrook: Nicholas Steven,16 Jul 1987(Winchester,Ma)
PALMESE: Daniel & Jane L Lovisone: Marc Daniel, 29 Sep 1970 (Law)
PALUMBO: Vincent J, Jr & Carol M Higgins: Robert William, 02 May 1991; Steven Edward,
   02 May 1991 (Hanover); Vincent James III, 03 Nov 1986 (E)
PAQUET: David E, Jr & Robin E Ayers: David Michael, 21 Jul 1976; Jason Edward,
   17 Feb 1981 (E)
PARENTEAU: Wilfred A & Marion L Hall: Gary Hall, 10 Jun 1954; Jeffrey D, 28 Mar 1957 (E)
PARKER: Neil R,Sr & Norma Jean Taylor: Bonnie J, 07 Jul 1962; Neil Robert, Jr, 27 Nov
   1964 (E)
   Neil R,Sr & Brenda J Rowell: David John, 18 Jul 1974 (E)
   Robert C (Georgetown,Ma) & Robena G Swett (Kingston): Brenda Joyce, 28 Sep 1939;
   Hope Robena, 29 Feb 1938
PARSHLEY: Elmer W (Lynn,Ma)& Vivian M Shaw(Exeter): Evelyn Mae, 27 Aug 1949;
   Robert Elmer, 07 Jan 1942 (E)
PATRICK: Henry (Kentucky) & Doris M Gonyer (Stockbridge,Vt): Alan Dale, 14 Jan 1951(E)
PATTERSON: Carl N & Frances E Wiggin: Dennis Carl, 31 Jan 1953; Diane Lee, 11 May
   1955 (E)
PAUL: Robert A & Phyllis G Dinsmore: Richard Eric, 03 Nov 1969 (E)
PEARCE: David W & Darlene M MacKenzie: Dustin William, 28 May 1983 (Hav)
PEASE: John F & Sandra L Turner: Wendy Elaine, 09 Sep 1967 (Hav)
PECKER: Edwin F & Mary M Dyke: Cindy Elaine, 15 Jul 1967 (Hav)
PELLERIN: William J, Jr & Karen L Harvey: Graham Harvey, 04 Jul 1982; Robyn Lee,
   18 Oct 1977
PELLETIER: Angel R & Therese F Chouinard: Marc J, 27 May 1962 (Hav)
   Joseph A & Judith K Lyman: Daniel Russell, 17 Jul 1972; Diane Brett,
   26 Nov 1973 (Ports); Shawn David, 06 Aug 1969 (Hav)
   Robert J & Jody L Mahair: Jennifer Lyn, 16 Feb 1983 (E)

PELTIER: John R & Dawn A Parker: Julie Ann, 20 Jan 1963; Linda P, 15 Aug 1961; Scott C, 08 Aug 1966 (E)
PELTONOVICH: John W & Barbara J Cash: Tyler Albert, 03 Apr 1991 (E)
PENNEY: James D & Nancy A Arsenault: Carol Frances, 08 Mar 1969; Mary Elizabeth, 05 Sep 1963 (E)
PEREZ-ANDUJAR: Natividad & Marie L George: Elvis Mark,04 Jan 1973; Rickey Nato, 15 Feb 1972 (E)
PERKINS: Alan L & Cynthia E Pendleton: Benjamin James, 14 Sep 1987 (Hav)
    John C, Jr & Gail D Huckins: Andrea Grace, 14 Sep 1978 (E)
PERNOKAS: Arthur D & Dianne M McCormick: Christina Marie, 11 May 1994 (E)
PERRAULT: Lawrence D & Sheila A Gingras: Lawrence Donald, 26 Apr 1964 (Hav)
PERREAULT: Albert J & Mary E Lowes: Raymond Joseph, 05 Apr 1949 (E)
    Albert W & Eileen Jackson: Michael Albert, 18 Dec 1970 (E)
PERRY: David J & Sally P Kellaway: Deborah Ann, 02 Sep 1964 (E)
    Michael W &Violet M Walters: Amy Kathleen, 03 Nov 1970 (E)
    Edmund W & Frances E Bowen: Mark Edmund, 27 May 1970 (Hav)
PETERS: William,V & Kyong Ae Park: Lindsay Ann, 07 Oct 1986 (Law)
PETERSON: Edward D & Cheryl A Peck: Alyssa Nicole, 06 Apr 1994 (E)
PETTENGILL: John W & Madelyne Page: Jill Paulette, 19 Apr 1950 (E); John Francis, 27 Nov 1948 (Hav); Mark B, 21 Apr 1955; Matthew Page, 14 Aug 1958 (E)
PHELAN: Albert D & Sharon L Curtis: Bethea Alden, 14 Feb 1993 (Boston,Ma)
    Fenton A, Jr & Ruth F Sullivan: Jean Marie, 23 Sep 1964 (E)
    Robert J (Everett,Ma) & Louise A Murphy (Boston,Ma): Virginia Marie, 05 Sep 1951 (Melrose,Ma)
PHANEUF: Kevin A & Renne D Dumont: Kelsa-Lynne, 05 Mar 1989 (Hav)
PHILBRICK: Elwood E & Dorothy M Bilodeau: Russell Eugene, 22 Nov 1948 (E)
    Russell G (Plaistow) & Eunice Floberg (Everett,Ma): Russell Gordon, Jr, 01 Dec 1949; Terry Lynn, 15 Dec 1946 (E)
PHILLIPS: Charles C & Shirley E Nickerson: Shirley Ellen, 10 Oct 1958 (E)
PICANSO: Gerald L & Mary E Sullivan: Pauline Louise, 15 Apr 1979 (Derry)
PICONE: Richard A & Maria E Wheaton: Danielle Maria, 31 Jul 1982 (Hav)
PIERCE: Arthur E, Jr & Susan E Ward: Amanda Sue, 06 Oct 1980; Matthew Stanley, 01 Jul 1979 (E)
    Ernest L (Attleboro,Ma) & Carrie Pennington (Pawtucket,RI): Male, 21 May 1923
PIKE: Raymond F & Joyce A Crosby: Robert Wayne, 29 Mar 1990 (E)
    Robert & Nancy A Gordon: Joan S, 12 Jul 1966 (Hav)
PITKIN: Frederick E, Jr & Victoria C Keir: Florence Joyce, 07 Oct 1974; Stephanie Eve, 29 Apr 1972 (E)
    Gerard N & Anne C Haberski: Matthew Gerard, 19 Jun 1981 (Hav)
    Harlan L (Haverhill,Ma) & Audrey LeDoux (Kingston): Albert Harlan, 14 Mar 1951 (E)
    Newell V & Gloria G Batchelder: Richard Jenness, 09 Nov 1960 (Hav); Ronald R, 21 Jun 1956 (E)
PITTS: George (Waldoboro,Me) & Flora Arnold (Hudson, Ma): Female, 22 Apr 1916
PLANTE: David A & Linda J Wright: Amy Elizabeth, 16 Mar 1991; Jenny Lynne, 25 Apr 1987 (E)

Guy G & Constance Y Jalbert: Renee Jeanne, 16 Jun 1964 (E)
PLATT: Walter & Gloria E Plissey: Randolph Sherman, 16 Feb 1965 (E)
PLATUHAS: Sladas (Lithuania) & Eva Platukas: John, 12 Nov 1920
PLATUKYS: George (Exeter) & Bernice B Kotuli (Haverhill,Ma): Joanne Barbara,
    11 Mar 1934
PODRADCHIK: Barry & Brenda F Lamkin: Steven Todd, 12 May 1967 (Hav)
POLAND: Gary C & Cindy L Amsden: Clayton Charles, 27 Dec 1977; Lura Elizabeth,
    15 Jan 1980 (E)
POLIQUIN: Thomas G & Audrey M Sargent: Suzanne Michelle, 08 May 1978 (Boston,Ma)
POND: Henry H,Sr & Gail S Merrifield:John Fitzgerald Kennedy, 08 Aug 1964; Joseph Henry,
    08 Aug 1971 (Hav); Lorraine T, 17 May 1962; Michael S, 24 May 1966 (E)
PORTER: Richard R & Janet L Friend: Dawn Melanie, 05 Apr 1974; Troy, 28 Apr 1971 (E)
POST: Charles W & Elaine M Devereaux: Charles William, Jr, 31 Aug 1979; Phillip Alexander,
    29 Nov 1980 (Hav)
POWERS: James E & Yvette Hamel: James Edward, 15 Jun 1967 (Hav)
    John H & Valerie M Spinale: Justin James, 12 Nov 1981 (E)
PRATT: Robert P & Donna M Eicher: Paul Robert, 14 Jan 1973 (Hav)
PRENAVEAU: Leo M & Kathy L Alberts: Christopher Justin,15 Jan 1973; Lisa Bentley,
    03 Sep 1971 (E)
PRESCOTT: Fred L & Bessie E Tucker: Donald L, 07 Sep 1902
    Harry (Kingston) & Maud Emery (Waterboro,Me): Bernice E, 21 Feb 1909; Female,
    28 Apr 1901
    Russell E & Susan A Lyons: Carley Rose, 12 Sep 1991; Maggie Sue, 09 Nov 1990 (E)
    Thomas R & Linda S George: David Andrew, 29 May 1976 (Hav); Michael Paul,
    20 Nov 1974 (E)
PRICE: Alfred N & Dianne Brackett: Erik Allen, 25 May 1968 (E)
    Kevin J & Linda J Perry: Ryan Joseph, 25 Jul 1989; Stephanie Lynne, 14 Mar 1986
    (Salem,Ma)
PRIDE: James E & Barbara J Ingham: Mark Todd, 23 Apr 1974 (Malden,Ma)
PRIEST: Ronald G Priest & Debra L Hudson: Jolin Koren, 19 Dec 1976 (E)
PRIME: Ronald C Prime & Dorothy E Helm: Eric K, 17 Jan 1966 (Methuen,Ma)
PRIMROSE: Zelda F Primrose, 06 Feb 1901 (no parents listed)
PROULX: Maurice J (Epping) & Marie J Bernier (Epping): Andre Maurice, 03 Mar 1951;
    Thomas James, 03 Sep 1953 (E)
PROVENCHER: David L & Heather D Seely: Evan Seely, 02 Aug 1991; Travis Eugene, 22 Feb
    1987 (E)
PROVOST: Thomas J & Karen S Lawney: Michael Francis, 27 Nov 1975 (E)
PRUNIER: Bernard W & Katherine M Kramer: Patricia Estelle, 18 Oct 1970 (Hav)
PURCELL: William M & Donna C Provencher: Michael William, 14 Feb 1977 (E)
PURVIS: Wallace & Cecile Gablosky: Paul Douglas, 31 May 1954 (Hav)
PYNN: George W Pynn & Sandra G Long: Ronald Joseph, 26 Jan 1959 (E)
QUIMBY: Ronald L & Virginia S Kimball: Susan Lynne, 06 Feb 1954 (E)
QUINNEY: John A & Joyce Scondras: Lisa Joy, 17 Mar 1983; Steven John, 26 Jan 1978 (E)
QUINTAL: Carlos & Norma M Micheroni: Nicholas Micheroni, 05 Jun 1982 (E)

RABIDEAU: Lawrence D & Sheila D Hannan: Todd Clinton, 08 Sep 1987 (Ports)
RADIGAN: Francis J & Mary A Littlewood: Donna Maria, 11 Feb 1971 (E)
RAJOTTE: Leon F & Jeannette D Beauregard: Mark Allen, 15 Feb 1959 (Kittery,Me)
RAMEY: Fred F,Jr & Jayne E Pandelena: Dustin Robert, 20 Jan 1987 (Law)
RAMSEY: David R & Gail K Clements : Jennifer Rae, 08 Feb 1977 (Exeter)
RAND: Ronald J & Rosalie O Walsh: Ronald J, Jr, 28 Feb 1962 (Hav)
RATTA: John & Barbara Perrault: Jon Scott, 10 Oct 1957 (Hav)
RAY: Earl M (Kingston) & Dorothy Wiggin (Woodstock,Vt): Earl Melvin,Jr, 16 Mar 1931;
     Sally Ann, 16 Sep 1933
     Joseph, Jr (Auburn)& Mildred Edgar (Amesbury,Ma): Female, 23 Feb 1937
RAYMOND: Edmond R & Natalie J Bixby: Edmond Richard, 03 Feb 1963 (Hav)
     Paul B & Lenora J Blaisdell: Amanda Gail,12 May 1975; Deanna Lynne,11 Jun 1970 (E)
READY: Joseph G & Lucy A Gilman: Joseph M Ready, 03 May 1966 (Hav)
     William D & Asta R Sander: Karen F, 12 Jul 1966; Sherry Anne, 05 Feb 1963 (E)
REID: Clyde D & Velma J Haynes: Pamela Susan, 04 Mar 1968 (E)
REMINGTON: Shawn H & Jo-Ann Hall: Derek Michael, 19 Dec 1979 (E)
REYNOLDS: Albert J, Jr & Jean A Hanright: Albert Jesse,III, 21 Sep 1978 (E)
     Anthony M & Sharon T Williams: Joseph Edward,01 Sep 1965; Nancy,18 Oct 1966 (Hav)
     Arthur H & Ruth E Landry: Bruce Arthur, 24 Mar 1948 (Waltham,Ma)
     Barry K & Roxanne R Baster: Grace Laura, 18 Apr 1972 (E)
     Gary L & Barbara J Straughan: Jason William, 14 Nov 1978 (E)
     Norman R & Rita A Senter: Denine A, 03 Nov 1966 (E); Kelly Lynn, 17 Feb 1963 (Hav)
     Ralph (Exeter) & Blanche B Barton (E Boston,Ma): Elizabeth B, 03 May 1916
RHEAULT: Richard P & Deborah M Cabral: Cassandra Geraldine, 26 Mar 1989 (E)
RICH: James E & Karen M Ventimiglia: James Phillip, 09 Sep 1991 (E)
RICHARDS: David M & Claudia F Gilman: Bethany Faith, 21 Jun 1967; Mark Aaron, 25 Feb
     1964 (Hav)
RICHARDSON: Forden (Nova Scotia) & Clara Schofield (New Brunswick): Robert Allen,
     30 Jul 1945 (Hav)
RICKER: John D & Jean S Adams: James Paul, 28 Oct 1967; Janna Michele, 20 Apr 1970 (E)
RIDER: William (Providence, RI) & Alice Beaumont (Beverly,Ma): Female, 25 Aug 1916
RIDLON: Ronald L & Rena E Pollini: Ronald Lee, 07 Nov 1960 (Carroll)
RILEY: James J & Laura A Sadler: Jennifer Lee, 22 Dec 1981 (E)
     Walter E & Constance M Murphy: Nancy Jeanette, 15 Aug 1964 (Hav)
ROBB: Robert C & Sandra A Schultz: Andrea L, 27 Sep 1961 (E)
ROBERTS: Ralph E & Marcia J Bailey: Keith Ralph, 15 Mar 1960; Peter E, 14 Dec 1961 (Hav)
     Roy E & Joanne L Day: Heidi Marie, 24 Jan 1979 (Hav)
     Wayne D & Joyce Nicholson: Michael Edward, 01 Mar 1972   (E)
ROBERTSON: David K & Cheryl A Coulouras: David George, 18 Jun 1983 (E)
     Kenneth D & Rhonda L Haight: Kalene Marie, 07 Sep 1993 (E)
ROBICHAUD: Brian E & Karyn D Bowlby: Jillian Brooke, 02 Nov 19832 (Law)
ROBIE: Bernard E (Kingston) & Natalie J Braley (Brockton,Ma): Jeffrey J, 09 Sep 1956;
     Michael Bernard, 25 Sep 1952 (E)
     Forrest R (Chester) & Mabel L Page(Kingston) Russell S, 25 Apr 1924

Jeffrey J, Jr & Julie S Perkins: Jessie MacKenzie, 20 Dec 1981 (E)
Loren & Cecile A Latour: Cheryl A, 23 Apr 1961; Deneen Jane, 12 Aug 1964; Morton
Elmer, 14 May 1970 (E)
Morton E (Chester)& Helen A Page(Kingston): Baby Girl, 10 Feb 1947;Carroll G, 23 Dec
1938; Forrest Francis, 21 Mar 1936; Francis May, 01 Jan 1930; Loren, 27 Sep 1933;
Madeline Louise, 13 Jul 1927; Male, 10 Apr 1925
ROBINSON: Charles W (Kingston) & Louisa M Smith (Epping): Doris Ethel, 14 Dec 1901
George F (Manchester) & Alice E Hartford (Deerfield): Lizzie, 07 Sep 1901
Hollis J (Somerville,Ma) & Patricia L Carter (Liverpool, N.S.): Julie Anne, 07 Jul
1951 (E)
Merton S (Kingston) & Annie Goodwin (Sandown): Male, 09 Apr 1909
ROBITILLE: William E & Jean G Flower: Cynthia Ann, 03 May 1966 (E)
ROCHUSSEN: Edward L & Virginia J Senter: Edward Louis, 29 Jul 1940
ROCK: Leonard (Brentwood) & Eva M Pero (Hillsboro): Joseph L, 17 Feb 1915; Elizabeth
Frances,11 Nov 1926
Ralph (Brentwood) & Nellie Swett (Kingston): ----,30 May 1915; Female, 14 Oct 1910;
Robert D, 01 Apr 1917
Richard M & Amelia A Farney: Richard Michael,Jr, 28 Jan 1987 (E)
RODGERS: Forrest F & Mary L Meeks: Jennifer Lynn, 03 Aug 1972 (E)
ROGERS: William A, Jr & Rebecca J Kendall: William Alan, 14 Oct 1990 (E)
ROMANO: Benedetto & Susan G Boisseau: Jacqueline Elizabeth, 04 Jun 1986; Kristina
Suzanne, 04 Jan 1991 (E)
RONCO: Glen W & Marie N Martin: Emily Marie, 28 Mar 1981 (E)
ROSS: Stephen D Ross & Nancy E Santangelo: Amanda Margaret, 16 Jul 1990; Amy Anne, 07
May 1989 (E)
ROULEAU: Douglas B & Linda J Madsen: Leona Lynn, 31 Dec 1970 (Hav)
Mark S & Deborah M Klinch: Jamie Lee, 16 Sep 1979; Peter James, 11 Oct 1982 (E)
Wayne M & Diane M Therrien: Steven Wayne, 12 Jan 1976 (E)
ROWE: Charles E & Janet L Winter: Scott Edward, 08 Aug 1963 (E)
Harry & Judith A Martin: Susan Lee, 05 Apr 1965 (E)
Herbert H & Evelyn Z Gonyer: Eddie Lawrence, 25 Jun 1963 (E)
ROWELL: John R & Hope R Parker: Amy Lynn, 12 Jul 1976; Bonnie Joyce, 20 Oct 1980 (Hav)
RUCKENBROD: John A & Eleanor A McVicker: Joshua John, 18 May 1981; Neil Robert,
25 Feb 1983 (E); Leah, 29 Nov 1979 (Winchester,Ma)
RUMERY: Horace G (Lyman,Me) & Lois E Gowens (Haverhill,Ma): Mabel H, 30 Dec 1902
RURAK: Richard J & Debra C Collins: Alison Marie, 10 Apr 1982 (E)
RUSSELL: Dana S & Eleanor M Robinson: Kirsten Sydney, 19 Dec 1963 (E)
Stephen B & Ann-Susan Megas: Jonathan (Megas-Russell), 03 Oct 1982 (E)
RUSSMAN: Richard L & Adele G Albern: Brett Muir, 09 Feb 1977; Ryan Lansing, 10 Jul
1974 (E)
RUSTANI: Jonus & Gjuner Qoku: Besnik Rustani, 02 Mar 1989 (E)
RYAN: John (Ireland) & Lena Welsh (Manchester):----, 14 Sep 1915
Kenneth W & Kimberly A Denise: Daniel Stephen, 25 Sep 1992 (E)
SABLE: Gregory R & Terry L Pendleton: Troy Benjamin, 25 Aug 1986 (E)

SADLER: Joshua P & Tricia A Marshall: Tyler Lucas, 04 Nov 1993 (E)
SAGER: Thomas K & Judy L Stevenson: Allison Lindsay, 30 Aug 1979; Ashley Courtney,
03 Apr 1983 (E)
SALVATORE: Chica F & Carole L Brigham: George Richard, 07 Nov 1980 (E)
SAMOISETTE: Richard A & Brenda J Bragdon: Richard Adrian, 28 Jun 1964; Troy Prescott,
22 Sep 1968 (Hav)
Robert K & Lynda I Rose: April Rose, 06 Apr 1973; Kenneth Robert, 06 May 1974
SANBORN: Alden M & Joyce K Rhodes: David M, 06 May 1962; Terri Don, 28 Nov 1960 (E)
E Charles & Thelma J Whitehouse: Scott Charles, 12 Aug 1963 (E)
SANFORD: David E & Kathleen M Lewis: Christine Jayne, 01 Sep 1978 (Methuen,Ma); John
David, 16 Jun 1982 (E)
SARGENT: Eliot M & Constance L Colcord: Linda Jo, 10 Jun 1970 (E)
Lawrence (S BerwickMe) & Marion Gove (Haverhill,Ma): William Ray, 31 Jan 1930
SAWYER: William T & Lorna A Szalkucki: Hannah Elizabeth, 07 Sep 1990; Kimberly Angela,
11 Sep 1982 (E)
Steven D & Hazel R Thompson: Rebecca Dawn, 02 Jun 1979 (E)
SCANLON: Michael P & Patricia A Flanders: Lisa Michelle, 11 Apr 1977 (E)
Michael P Scanlon & Kathy A Malek: Michael Patrick, Jr, 02 Jul 1981 (E)
SCHMITZ: Steven J & Donna E Lindsey: Lindsey Marie, 16 Mar 1986 (E)
SCHREIBER: George S (Manchester,CT) & Doris L McGugan (Manchester Ct): James Edward,
22 Nov 1952 (E)
SCHREINER: Richard J & Beverly E Smith: Erik Arthur, 21 Oct 1973 (E)
SCHUH: Charles E & Suzanne M Brindle: Christopher Stewart, 14 Aug 1991 (E)
SCOTT: William F & Marjorie A Battles: Jeffrey D, 17 Jan 1956 (E)
SEARS: Richard A.E. & Norma J Barrett: Cynthia J, 28 Feb 1956; Richard Raymond,Jr,
28 Jun 1960 (Hav)
SEAVER: Bertram A & Darlene L Waldron: James Richard, 01 Mar 1973 (Hav)
SEAVEY: Wayne C & Patricia A Richardson: Robin Lynn, 23 Jun 1969; Ronald Wayne,
08 Aug 1964 (E)
SEILER: Gerald B & Rosanne J Howard: Jordan Elizabeth, 14 Aug 1991 (E)
SENTER: Allen S (Merrimac,Ma) & Mary L Barnard (Brocton,Ma): Ernest Raymond,
08 Oct 1903
John H,Jr & Beverly Jo Glougie: Sharise Lee, 01 Nov 1969; Stanley Forrest,17 May
1968 (E)
Leslie (Kingston) & Laura Collins (Kingston): Esther, 29 Apr 1902
Richard D & Eileen M Zaremski: Christopher Richard, 17 Sep 1987 (Hav)
Richard W (Haverhill,Ma) & Sylvia M Nason (Kingston): Lynda Carol, 22 Jun 1954;
Richard Douglas, 18 Feb 1952 (E)
Theodore F & Yvonne E Gauthier: Troy Howard, 10 Jan 1965 (Hav)
Walter (Kingston) & Gertrude Stevens (Wakefield,Ma): Male, 04 May 1910; Ruby E,
13 Mar 1909
SERSON: David L & Patricia A Robichaud: Thomas Levi, 08 Apr 1983 (Malden,Ma)
SHALLOW: James R & Pamela G George: Samantha Jo, 03 Apr 1993 (E)
SHANDA: Frank A (Bohemia) & Mabel Morrison(NovaScotia): Female, 21 Mar 1925; Male,
19 Dec 1923

SHARIO: Don C & Pamela A Streeter: David J, 20 Oct 1990 (E)
SHAUGHNESSY: Robert M & Pamela M Garipy: Geoffrey Michael, 15 Oct 1986 (E)
SHEEHAN: Edward T & Naureen F Cuff: Eric Timothy, 07 Jan 1972; Karen Cuff, 03 Apr 1970
    (E); Kathleen Cuff, 11 May 1969 (Medford,Ma)
    Paul P & Antoinette A Canty: Monique, 27 Apr 1972 (E)
SHEPARD: Karl W & Suzanne Hickey: Lisa Jean, 20 Feb 1978 (Hav)
SHIELDS: John J & Sharon L Morrissey: Kyla Lynn, 10 Aug 1989 (E)
SHIPPEY: Roderick F (So Adams,Ma)& Rose M LaFleur (Haverhill,Ma): Catherine Marie,
    05 Sep 1932; Louise, 09 Dec 1934
SHOOK: G Randall & Carmen M Kauffman: Amber Lynn, 17 Jul 1968 (E)
SHUTE: George R & Pamela A Demers: George Robert, Jr, 21 Oct 1974; Heidi Jean, 09 Apr
    1972 (E)
SILLOWAY: Frank W (Kingston) & Annie B Osgood (E Kingston): Celia, 03 Jul 1915; Myron
    W, 29 Dec 1909
    Isaac W & Ethel Gillis: Male, 02 Jun 1910
SILVA: Arthur J & Rhonda L VanKnowe: Brianna Lea, 24 Sep 1990 (Stoneham,Ma)
    Joseph J & Priscilla L Kamin: Anthony Jacob, 23 May 1994 (E)
    Joseph P & Cheryl Venner: Anthony Joseph, 11 Apr 1990 (E)
SILVERMAN: Jerome M & April J Thomas: Jereme Mark, 29 Aug 1968 (E)
SILVERS: John T & Maureen G Guilfoyle: Maegan Elizabeth, 15 Jan 1987 (Lowell,Ma)
SIMES: Andrew (Brandon,Vt) & Abbie Tucker (Kingston): William EG., 06 Nov 1901
    George (Brandon,Vt) & Annie Tucker (Kingston): George, 17 Oct 1902
    Marvin E & Faye E Hillsgrove: Dennis Alan, 27 Jul 1948; Lauri A, 25 Jun 1956 (E)
    Raymond H & Doris H Parker: David Kenneth, 28 Sep 1955; Douglas Keith, 04 Jan
    1960; Dwight Kurtis, 16 Sep 1951; Janet Lee, 02 Feb 1953 (E)
    William G (Kingston) & Ruth George(Kingston): Roland Allen, 03 Oct 1928
SIMMERING: David G & Elizabeth I Bakie: Judith Adine, 20 Aug 1957 (E)
SIMPSON: Clarence (Cambridge, Ma) & Mabel Greehan (Cambridge, Ma): Male, 21 Jan 1915
    William G & Joan E Reid: Jennifer Ann, 15 Jun 1966; Richard Reid, 03 Jun 1967 (E)
SKIDMORE: Frank W & Debra L Snyder: Christopher Daniel, 07 Mar 1982
SKINNER: Vincent P & Judith G Staggenborg: Nicolse, 27 Aug 1963 (E)
SLOAN: Bruce A Sloan & Suzanne H Dolliver: Elisha Grace, 26 Feb 1972 (E)
SMITH: Carl F, Jr & Helen D Eastman: Muriel E, 18 Aug 1956 (E)
    Dennis C & Kimberly J Martin-Lafelur: Samantha Jo, 03 Jun 1986 (E)
    Fred & .....: Abbie Jane, 12 Feb 1910
    Forrest R & Kandra M Hanson: Sean Patrick, 26 Oct 1972 (E)
    James F & Joyce L Raymond: Matthew James, 16 Aug 1973 (Hav)
    Lawrence B,Jr & Judith Cronk: Daniel Grayson, 17 Aug 1963 (E); Debra M, 03 Aug
    1966; Donna Jean, 28 Apr 1959; Jeffrey W, 21 Oct 1961 (Hav)
    Michael D & Laura K Sykes: Michael Warren, 31 May 1981 (E)
    Richard K & Bertha E Stukas: Diane Marie, 07 Sep 1953 (E)
    Warren D & Janet A Gervais: Audrey Annette, 13 Jan 1972 (E)
    Warren D & Shirley A Nason: Glenda Frances, 02 Nov 1960; Kathleen Marie,
    15 Aug 1958; Leanne Avis, 14 Jul 1955; Michael Dennis, 16 Jan 1954 (E); Sheryl Jean,
    23 Jul 1965 (Hav)

SNOW: Daniel C & Christine M Griffin: Daniel Charles, Jr, 17 Sep 1991 (E)

Harold E & Virginia L Harmon: Debra Gail, 27 Jan 1957 (E)

SOTERAKOPOULOS: Thomas D & Debra J Illsley: Stephen Thomas, 18 Aug 1994 (E)

SOUSA: Angelo M & Diane L Byrne: Erica Leigh, 09 Jan 1992 (E)

SOUTHWICK: Ralph E & Florence G Caron: Peter A, 26 Aug 1956 (E)

SPATES: George N,III & Marilyn N Wood: Kingsley Alexander, 28 Oct 1989 (Hav)

SPEARS: William A & Marilyn A St Laurent: Melissa Ann, 05 Dec 1968 (E)

SPINA: Michael & Deborah A Kelly: Alicia Michele, 11 May 1990 (E)

SPINELLA: Thomas D & Jean M Turgeon: Elaine Marie, 10 Sep 1955 (E)

SPOFFORD: Jordan F & Carolyn R Strout: Amy Grace, 26 Dec 1958; David A, 08 Sep 1961;
John Earl, 27 Jun 1957; Peter Daniel, 11 May 1963; Susan Carol, 15 Feb 1965 (E)

ST HILAIRE: Gerard L & Miriam F Trevens: Craig Keith, 03 Dec 1959; Richard David, 19 Apr
1958

ST JEAN: Russell A & Debra E Souza: Joshua Paul, 12 Feb 1991 (E)

ST LAURENT: Bruce A & Joan M Richter: Suzette Marie, 05 Apr 1964 (Hav)
Romeo R & Arlene M Webster: Donna Lee, 24 Jul 1949; Kathleen ,12 Mar 1953;
Rodney, 06 Mar 1957; Sheryl Anne, 09 May 1951 (E)

ST ONGE: James E & Elaine H Allaire: Daniel James, 26 Nov 1964; Joan Elizabeth, 02 Dec
1963 (Hav)
Paul F. & Anne P Pasquale: Christopher H, 30 Mar 1944; Matthew Raffaelle, 30 Mar

STACKPOLE: Scott K & Janet R Fraser: Jeffrey Scott, 16 Jun 1970; Timothy James, 08 Jun
1971 (E)

STANDRING: David T & Corrine M Wenmark: Mark Earle, 03 Aug 1971(Kittery,Me)

START: Frank R & Joan M Leroux: Allison Madeline, 03 Aug 1983 (E)

STATES: Franklin P,IV & Margaret A Gormley: Franklin Pierce, V, 05 Oct 1977;Roseanne
Katherine, 11 Aug 1979; Thomas Ryan, 08 Dec 1982 (E)

STEER: Harold A & Helena L Dame: Mathew James, 10 Jul 1978; Michael Patrick, 25 Oct
1976 (E)
Jonathan P & Katherine A Sykes: Margaret Parkhurst: 07 Mar 1991 (E)

STEEVES: Kenneth W & Cynthia A Robinson: John Quinn, 07 Nov 1968 (Hav)

STEHENSON: James H & Linda M Doncaster: James Jacob, 23 Jun 1980

STERN: Robert E,Jr & Donna E Paine: Heather Lyn, 23 Mar 1969; Robert Edward,III, 22 Jul
1970 (E)

STEVENS: Alan H & Linda M Barlow: Michael Robert, 24 Jun 1967; Thomas W,01 Apr
1961 (E)
Arthur G & Ann L Robbins: David G, 08 Nov 1956; Eric Arthur, 03 Oct 1960; Nancy
Anne, 13 Mar 1955; Philip Lincoln, 12 Feb 1958 (E)
Brian L & Lisa E Montoni: Jessica Lee, 22 Jun 1980; Trisha Lee, 08 May 1986 (E)
Carl S (Kingston) & Dorothy A Leggett (Idaho): Carl Stuart, 19 Feb 1926
Gary P & Michele Riopel: Janine Michele, 21 Aug 1987 (E)
J Edward (Brentwood) & Annie E Locke (Concord): Alan Harvey, 11 Jan 1933; Lois
Anne, 11 Jul 1929
James E & Laura R Irvine: Christine Sue, 24 Aug 1978; Rebecca Leigh, 19 Dec 1976 (E)
Jeffrey & Penny L Perham: Kimberly Anne, 19 Feb 1983 (E)

Lawrence & Luella M Farmer: Brian Lee, 31 Oct 1957; Christopher Andrew, 14 Mar 1965; Gail Ann, 25 Dec 1959; James Edward, 08 Apr 1953; Jeffrey, 21 Oct 1961; Mark, 24 Dec 1954; Mary Elizabeth, 07 Apr 1963 (E)

Mark & Sherry L Drake: Andrea Lynn, 10 Sep 196 (E)

Richard S, Sr & Betty A Field: Raymond John, 15 Dec 1963; Richard S, II, 22 Jan 1962 (E)

STEWART: Charles H & Jennie R Marcou: Alva James, 08 Dec 1963; Gloria Jean, 12 Nov 1964 (E)

John E (Haverhill,Ma) & Thelma D George (Brentwood): Jacqueline Marie, 31 Aug 1952 (Kittery,Me)

William A & Donna L Sturgess: Alexander Donald, 24 Oct 1972; Melanie Anne, 14 Aug 1970 (E)

STILSON: Carl E & Barbara E Hall: David M, 02 Mar 1962 (Manchester)

STRAW: Charles E & Victoria J Theoharis: Samantha Sue, 17 Jul 1978 (Hav)

STREETER: Paul J & Sherry R Lavoie: Timothy Paul, 26 Jan 1991 (E)

Philip J & Phyllis J Tidd: Pamela Ann, 30 Mar 1965; Paul Joseph, 09 Apr 1963; Philip J, 03 Aug 1966 (Hav)

STRENGTH: Edward, Jr & Judith T Ritchie: Gina Marie, 05 Jan 1972 (E)

STRICKLAND: Edward & Nina Files: Edward Sharion, 14 Oct 1933

STUBBS: Lyle H & Rita M Deminie: Kathy Ann, 19 Jul 1963 (Hav)

STUKAS: Charles & Beatrice Dankaut: Bertha E, 16 Jul 1921

Charles (Russia) & Lucy Dovken (Russia): ----, 05 Sep 1914

SUE: Frank F (Castle Shannon,Pa) & Helen M Leblanc (Sheridan,Me): Jerry Peter, 09 Dec 1955; Ronald Albert, 13 May 1951 (Kittery, Me)

SWANSON: Emil B & Faith L Salvini: Jennifer Ellen, 23 Sep 1963; Rebecca Diane, 28 Oct 1964 (Hav)

Warren E & Judith E Hill: Katrina Eileen, 24 Apr 1967; Kirsten Elaine, 26 Apr 1968 (E)

SWEENEY: Michael J& Sue Ann Morse: John Michael, 15 Jul 1978 (E)

SWEET: Wallace W & Josephine A Delorenzo: Steven Michael, 10 Aug 1950 (E)

SWEETLAND: Richard G & Joanne DiBaise: Nicole Susan, 01 Oct 1979 (E)

SWEETSER: Robert W & Nancy E Hall: Alexander Daniel, 04 Mar 1988; Branden Tyler, 04 Mar 1988; Jamie Lee, 15 Feb 1987 (E)

SWEEZEY: Scott N & Gina M Flatania: Aisha Nicole, 06 Mar 1991; Amelia Noel, 19 Oct 1993 (Derry)

SWETT: Daniel W (Kingston) & Anna B Winslow (Kingston): Bernice M, 24 Apr 1909; Irving L, 17 Aug 1914; Janice A, 30 Jul 1917; Lloyd E (Sweet), 11 Mar 1925; Robean G, 10 Mar 1916; ....., 18 Nov 1921

Franklin (Kingston)& Shirley V Tracy (Kingston): Franklin James, 30 Jun 1945; Peter Wayne, 07 Jul 1958; Tracy, 29 Jan 1951 (E)

Wallace W (Kingston) & Josephine A Delorenzo (Bronx,NY): Thomas Wayne, 26 Jan1952; Wallace Wadleigh, Jr, 06 Apr 1949 (E)

SWINERTON: Ernest A & Ruth E Crosby: Andrew E, 01 Sep 1958; David Eric, 25 Jul 1964; James E, 29 Sep 1961; Peter Ernest, 30 Apr 1960 (Amesbury,Ma); Timothy Eron, 20 Apr 1970 (E); Thomas Edward, 05 Jan 1963 (Amesbury,Ma)

SYCZ: John E & Margaret M Gaydosh: Sarah Beth, 12 May 1982 (E)
TAAJES: Gerard J (Holland) & Louise M Mangane (Malden), Eleanor May, 04 May 1926;
    Elizabeth A, 09 Jan 1930; Robert Donald, 18 Dec 1931
    Robert D & Norma F Simes: Brian Scott, 16 Oct 1958 (E)
TATRO: William E (Dover) & Hazel M Warren (Newton): Robert Arnold, 09 Jun 1941
TAYLOR: Dennis J & Carol A Greenlee: Elizabeth Helen, 11 Jul 1977 (Law); Jonathan
    Michael, 13 Aug 1976 (E)
    Felix H & Barbara M Jasper: Derwain Felix, 19 Jun 1958 (E)
TEED: John (Pembroke) & Frances Ball (Kingston): Female, 02 Feb 1909
THERIAULT: Michael & Louanne Twombly: Chad Raymond, 03 Feb 1986 (E)
THOMAS: Russell H & Edna M Garland: Janet Ann, 27 Mar 1948 (E)
THOMPSON: Paul N & Juliann Rosati: Eli Roger Rosati, 18 Mar 1993; Justine Elizabeth,
    22 Jan 1990 (E)
THORSTENSEN: Lee T & Janet M Verrier: Erik Robart, 17 Mar 1973 (Woburn,Ma)
THURLO: George A & Annette M Bonin: Christopher John, 17 Jun 1958; Denise M, 27 Nov
    1961; Jean L, 15 Dec 1956; Philip James, 04 Dec 1959; Timothy C, 21 Dec 1962 (Hav)
THURLOW: William R & Deborah A McGlew: David Mathew, 05 Jul 1974 (E)
THURSTON: David E & Marlene J Gillen: Christopher Ryan, 07 Feb 1976; Leslie Dianne,
    09 Jun 1977 (Dover)
TIDD: Daniel H & Elaine M Spinella: Trisha Maria, 16 Jul 1977 (E)
TILTON: William H & Jean G Larson: James Michael, 31 Jul 1959 (E)
TIMMONS: William A,Jr & Natalie E Marquis: George Marquis, 17 Jan 1987 (E)
TOBIN: Richard J & Tammie J Allen: Amanda Ann, 08 Jul 1987; Richard James, Jr, 07 May
    1991 (E)
TOLEMAN: Stephen J & Joyce V Paul: Benda Lee, 24 Jun 1982 (E)
TOWNSEND: Paul W(Waynsville,NC) & Agnes J Garland (Pineola,NC): Ann Garland,
    16 Aug 1932
TRACY: Clarence (Haverhill,Ma) & Lillian Thomas (Gloucester,Ma): Glenn R, 15 Jul 1924;
    Rae Cedell, 13 Sep 1925
TRAVERS: Mario & Dorothy M Lazure: Steven Mark, 07 Mar 1965 (Hav)
TREFRY: Amasa C & Ivah L Wagg: ....., 21 Jun 1921
TROMBLEY: Ronald G & Christine Lacarubba: Benjamin Michael, 20 Mar 1978; Stephen
    Maxwell, 30 Jun 1979 (Law)
TUCKER: Moses E (Kingston) & Ellen F Currie (Cambridge,Ma): George Edward, 23 Jan
    1946 (E); John Moses, 01 Nov 1952 (Amesbury,Ma); William Thomas, 22 Nov 1942
    William F (Kingston) & Nellie F Simes (Brandon, Vt): Annie F, 23 May 1914; Eldora,
    09 Mar 1916; Ida Louise, 02 Jan 1903
TURNER: Bruce R & Penny L Spainhower: Cheryl Marie, 19 Dec 1972 (E)
    David L & Cheryl A Patterson: Dean Alan, 11 Sep 1977 (E)
    Herbert W & Rose M Lesage: Herbert Willard, 14 Feb 1973 (Hav)
    Jeremiah P & Constance I Lessard: Pamela Jean, 16 Jul 1975 (Hav)
TURNQUIST: David C & Mary L Millis: David James, 13 Dec 1982 (E)
TUTTLE: Garfield L & Diana K Davis: James Adam, 24 May 1981 (E)
    Gary N & Carole A Wallace: David Edward, 26 Jan 1964 (E)

TWOMBLY: Henry (Somersworth) & Effie Page: ----, 26 Jan 1914; Elvin D, 03 Aug 1909;
Male, 21 May 1910
Ralph E,Jr & Marilyn J Woodward: Beth Ellen, 20 Feb 1964; Leanne, 07 Jan 1962;
Ralph E, Jr, 09 Mar 1963 (E)
UEBRIG: Jurgen H & Ineborg Hillmann: Sebastien, 17 Jun 1980 (E)
UERKWITZ: Donald D & Diane M Nichols: Jason Donald, 22 Jan 1979 (E)
UMPHREYS: Timothy R & Donna E Morrow: Charles Allen, 08 Dec 1992 (E)
UNDERHILL: Dexter W & Katherine C McCormick: Jay Stewart, 10 Jun 1964 (E)
Richard L & Glenda M Buswell: Dawne Marie, 20 Jun 1967 (Amesbury,Ma)
UNDERWOOD: Charles K, Jr & Janet L Mullen: Kelly Lynne, 05 Mar 1975 (E)
VADEBONCOEUR: William H, III & Donna M Mazur: Jon Luc, 06 Oct 1993 (Man)
VAN SICKLE: Quentin R & Gloria J Caswell: Michelle Jean, 09 Feb 1968 (E)
VARNEY: Richard H (Jonesboro,Me) & Merla E Fenton (Jonesboro,Me): James Wendell,
05 Feb 1942
VENUTI: Armando J, Jr & Leona L Perusse: Theresa Marie, 18 Mar 1980 (E)
VERRILL: Daniel F & Pamela Clements: Alexander Cargill, 29 Sep 1989; Joshua Clements,
04 Sep 1983 (E)
VINCENT: George F & Edrie M Verombeck: George F Vincent, Jr, 21 Apr 1954 (E)
Leo R (Cookshire,Can) & Margaret E Simes (Kingston): Donna Rae, 27 Dec 1950 (E);
Eleanor Ann, 08 Apr 1941; Raymond Edwin, 28 Jul 1944; Robert Leo, 06 Jun 1932; John
Lester, 24 Dec 1943
Robert L & Natalie L Johnson: Judy Lynn, 03 Jul 1957; Lee-Ann, 02 Aug 1956 (E)
VIRNELLI: Leo J & Jane J Szalkucki: Leo John, 30 Jun 1992 (E)
VONDERHEIDE: James A & Lisa M Dushais: Kendra Danielle, 16 Apr 1981 (Stoneham,Ma)
WAITT: Clark B & Paula J LaFleche: Michelle Ann, 28 Dec 1966 (E)
WAJDA: Michael J & Kathryn A Reardon: Kristine Frances, 01 Apr 1972 (Ports)
WAKEMAN: Ernest G & Donna M Lasch: Kathryn Aroline, 04 Apr 1983; Kristen Marie,
11 Mar 1987 (E)
WALKER: Alan J & Kathryn D Parsons: Emma Kate, 26 May 1971 (E)
Charles S, Jr & Dianne D St Jean: Craig Steven, 16 Dec 1981 (E)
Edward A & Priscila Standish: Katherine, 22 Mar 1969 (E)
Dean B & Sandra E Landers: Sabrina Ann, 09 Nov 1976 (E)
WALMSLEY: Lawrence (England) & Hellen Griffin (Lawrence,Ma): Arline Helen,
b 03 Aug 1927
WALSH: Rodger F & Mary H DeRoche: Jon David, 15 Dec 1972; Judith Mary, 03 Oct 1975 ;
Mark Rodger, 05 Feb 1970 (E); Stephen Edward, 22 Mar 1968 (Methuen,Ma)
WALTERS: Warren W & Margaret J Rankin: Katherine Leigh, 28 Jul 1982 (Concord)
WALTON: Herbert I (Watertown,Ma)& Ruth E Bessom(Swampscott,Ma): Jacqueline Ann, 30
Aug 1949; Jeffrey Lee, 19 Jan 1951; Peter Calvin, 12 Jan 1955; William Ivan, 09 Jul
1947 (E)
WARD: Stephen D & Cathy A Bradley: Crystal Lee, 02 Nov 1978 (E); Stephen David,Jr,
10 Dec 1986 (Dover)
WARREN: Philip A Warren & Eva Greene: Sally Eva, 02 Oct 1949 (E)
Wayne E & Wanda M Giard: Kevin Russell, 09 Jul 1978 (E)

WARRINGTON: Edwin G,Jr & Patricia E Lyons: Eileen Erin, 04 Jul 1964; Mark Lyons, 17 Oct 1958 (E)

Mark L & Dorothy M Morgan: Robyn Lyn, 30 May 1978 (Ports)

WASHBURN: Charles & Mary G Smith: C Andrew, 03 Apr 1972 (Salem,Ma)

WASON: Jonathan & Dianna L Matson: Mindy Hope, 12 Aug 1975 (Hav)

WATSON: John W (Greenland) & Lucinda Meek (Kingston): Ruth M, 09 Mar 1901

WATTS: Frank R & Susan K Chandler: Jennifer Lyn, 08 Feb 1988; Jeremy Scott, 23 Sep 1989 (E)

Stephen W,Jr & Lena J Beckman: Frank Robert, 06 Feb 1964; Robert Stephen, 06 Oct 1960 (E)

WEADER: Jim H & Susan E Jones: Jeremy Edward, 30 Aug 1979; Joshua Boyd, 27 May 1975 (E)

WEATHERBY: Thomas H & Marie A Savoie: Cameron Scott; 04 Jun 1992; Curtis Patrick, 20 Oct 1993 (E)

WEAVER: Robert E, Jr & Julie A Faulkner: Jeffrey Daniel, b 17 Jun 1978; Rebecca Grace, 05 Mar 1975 (E)

WEBSTER: Walter E (Kingston) & Bertha Kruger (Kingston): ----, 24 Jan 1914; Walter Everett, b 14 Jul 1916

Charles E (E Kingston) & Alice Huse (Kingston): Male, 08 Aug 1909

Isaac R, III & Susan M Collins: Jessica Marie, 22 Apr 1991 (E)

WEEDEN: John H & Florence I Potts:Michael A, 05 May 1955; Patricia Florence, 11 Mar 1954 (E)

WEEKS: David C & Linda A Gardner: Dennis Steven, 25 Jun 1969 (E)

WEESE: Donald L, Jr & Cornelia E Haynes: Dereck James, 21 Jul 1981; Donald Lee, III, 13 Jul 1978 (E)

WELCH: Paul A & Joan M Pickard: Kelly Marie, 19 Apr 1975 (Hav)

WENDELL: Richard D, III & Sandra A Tobin: Sarah Danelle, 12 Sep 1974 (E)

WENTWORTH: David E & Nellie J Geisser: David E, Jr, 10 Jul 1956 (Man)

WENTZEL: Charles S & Margaret E Willey: Megan MacLeod, 01 Mar 1979 (E)

WESPISER: Robert D & Marguerite K McAvoy: Katherine Ann, 24 May 1970; Kendra Ellen, 29 Sep 1971(Hav)

WEST: Audie L & Cheryl A Bisson: Joelene Margaret, 08 Dec 1977 (E)

Chandler B (Danville) & Edna A Collins (Kingston): Catherine Ann, 05 Nov 1947; Chandler Bruce, Jr, 14 Apr 1958; Kevin Morris, 23 Aug 1960 (E)

Charles H (Kingston) & Audrey E Yeaton(Kingman,Me): Florence Lucille, 25 Jul 1927

Henry C (Kingston) & Blanche E Brickett (Haverhill,Ma): Barbara Blanche, 13 Aug 1927; Bernard Russell, 28 Jun1939; Errol Francis, 07 Nov 1943; Elizabeth Jane, 09 Jul 1929; Male, 24 Sep 1923; Male, 04 May 1941;Walter Edwin, 24 Dec 1932; Westley S, 09 Jan 1925

Kevin M & Geneva S Clements: Charles Theodore, 28 Jun 1991 (E)

Leon & Edna M Deming: Wendal L, 25 Mar 1940

Ralph W & Karleen J Quinney: Stephanie Lauren, 17 May 1981 (Hav)

Walter S (Kingston) & Ruth H Nason (Kingston): Henry Clinton, 14 Aug 1900

..... West & Dorothy E Jasper: Myrna Joyce, 04 Mar 1944 (E)

WEYLER: Kenneth L & Carol A Wisentaner: Donald Allen, 16 Aug 1970 (E)
WHALEN: Paul & Patricia A Carlucci: Ann Marie, 20 Feb 1986 (E)
WHEELOCK: Robert C & Marilyn Sheehan, Gary Charles, 02 Jan 1968 (Hav)
WHITE: Charles R & Martha I Bird: Clifton James, 27 Mar 1973 (Hav)
    Ernest E & Patricia A Leonard: Jean Marie, 23 Sep 1964 (E)
    George J & Debra A Hutchinson: Jonathan Richard,27 Nov 1991 (E)
    Harold H & Shirley R Bishop: Clifton James, 27 Mar 1973 (E)
    Ronald H,Jr & Kathleen E Bateman: Kathryn Elizabeth, 02 Feb 1989 (E)
    Walter & Linda A Krebs: Natalie Jeanne, 08 Dec 1969 (Hav)
    William P & Natalie J Brown: Lori Ann, 01 Jul 1965 (E)
WHITING: Neil A & Linda L Larrabee: Kelly Lee, 02 Jun1977; Kimberly Marie, 22 Jan
    1975 (E)
WHITNEY: Louis B (Hyde Park,Ma)& Elizabeth B Nason (Kingston): Phyllis Louise,
    04 Dec 1932 (K); Robert Wayne, 24 Oct 1944 (E);William Donald,18 May 1934 (K)
    Robert W & Donna M Young: Jason Thomas, 28 Dec 1971; Shelly Ann, 20 Mar
    1970 (Hav)
WHITTIER: Harold W & Eleanor L Hills: Brian Richard, b 08 Sep 1950 (Hav)
    John M & Sheila J Voll: Eric John, 09 Sep 1976; Leslie Jean, 22 Apr 1974 (E)
    Walter F (Concord) & Lulu M Collins (Kingston): Harold Walter, 10 Apr 1920; Laura M,
    21 Apr 1917
    William H (Concord) & Ora E George (Derry): Auilfred K, 29 Mar 1909
WICHROSKI: John F & Mary A Freeland: Michael John, 17 Aug 1973 (E)
WIEGLEB: Walter A & Eileen S Chesney: Laura Jean, 24 Jan 1969 (Hav)
WIGGIN: Glenn P & Patricia E Holt: Aidan Chelsea, 22 Apr 1992 (E); Kiah Casey, 13 Apr
    1989 (Hav)
WIGHT: Andrew S & Paulette J Derochers: Christopher Andrew, 25 Jul 1972; Jennifer Lynn,
    16 Jun 1969 (Hav)
    Robert A & Nancy K Cooper: Heidi, 19 Jun 1964; Peter Joseph, 27 May 1954; Rebecca,
    19 Apr 1962 (Winchester,Ma)
WILBUR: Robert M & Gail J Mowry: Karen Gail, 05 Nov 1970 (Law)
WILKINS: Scott A & Karen L Ferriero: Jonathan Scott, 19 Feb 1975 (Law)
WILLARD: Robert W & Clare C Parkes: William Robert, 19 Mar 1967 (E)
WILLIAMS: George E & Florence L West: Bruce Gerald, 19 Jul 1948 (E)
WILLIAMSON: Peter F & Lisa A Guagnini: Jessica Ann, 04 Jan 1991; Joseph Bradley, 25 Feb
    1987 (E)
WILLMAN: Edward F & Constance A Neville: Mark Edward, 14 Apr 1971 (Nashua)
WILLSON: Jeffrey L & Jane H Woodbury: Steven Jeffrey, 01 Jun 1977 (E)
WILSON: Peter E & Virginia L Johnson: Jared Reid, 27 Nov 1977 (E)
WINSLOW: Dale G & Donna L Briggs: Kyle Gates, 27 Oct 1980 (ES)
    Harland A & Pauline E Whitehouse: Dale Gates, 03 Jun 1948 (E); Harland Wayne,
    29 Aug 1940
    Horace G (Kingston) & Eldora E Nason (Kingston):Harland A, 11 May 1917; Varina,
    22 May 1909
WINTER: Eugene & Mary Jan Blanchette: Leanne Jane, 07 Sep 1964 (E)

Sandy M & Debra L Felch: Jan Matthew, 23 Feb 1982 (E)
WITLICKI: Henry C & Denise A Desmarais: Edward Henry, 15 Apr 1982 (E)
WOOD: Daniel E & Maryellen Langlois: Erin Marie, 13 Oct 1994 (Hav)
    David F & Ellen M Harper: David Gene, 05 Sep 1974 (Danvers,Ma)
WOODBURN: Donald S & Marjorie J Francis: Donald J, 01 Oct 1966 (Hav)
WOODBURY: Chester C & Barbara F Harris: Chester Tenney, 21 Jun 1953; Jane Harris,
    27 Feb 1949 (E)
    Mark P & Karen Wilich: Katryn Wilich, 04 Feb 1987 (E)
WOODMAN: Clarence E (Dover) & Lillian M Jones (Weston,Ma): Female, 28 Feb 1931;
    Virginia, 02 Aug 1925
WOODWORTH: Donald H & Nancy A Shaw: Daniel Shaw, 22 Jun 1987; Michael Alan,
    02 Aug 1982 (E)
WRIGHT: Clement A & Kathleen M Chapman: Candra Jean, 24 Oct 1967; Christine Marie,
    10 Sep 1964 (E)
    Richard B & Melinda L Wood: Benjamin Frederick, 21 Aug 1991 (E)
    Robert J & Joan A Ricker: Robert James, 03 Aug 1964 (Hav)
WYDOLA: Mark J & Kathleen A Dobie-Bossi: Benjamin John, 04 Apr 1989 (Hav)
WYKA: Jan (John) & Fannie Cuscova: ....., 22 Jul 1921; Annie, 29 Sep 1910
YESKELVITCH: Joseph (Haverhill,Ma) & Amanda M Sargent (Springvale,Me): Janice M,
    08 Sep 1938
YOCHUM: Gregg E & Irene S Hardy: Jennifer Lee, 24 Nov 1975 (Law)
YORK: James E, Jr & Marion E Woodworth: Avaline Marion, 13 Jul 1959; Dale Kenneth,
    17 Jan 1957 (E)
    John H & Bertha MacRae: Marjorie A, 16 Aug 1923; Shirley Ann, 22 Mar 1925
YOUNG: Ernest D & Jacqueline L Ellis: Roni Gene, 02 Aug 1967 (E)
    Forrest S & Pearl E Gray: Scott S, 17 Mar 1961 (Hav)
    Gary K & Mary C Thompson: Audra Elizabeth, 25 Jun 1980 (Hav)
    Joseph R & Kathleen R Colby: Jason Richard, 19 Oct 1973; Jeffrey Richard, 11 Mar
    1975; Kellie Rebecca, 17 Jul 1977 (Hav)
    Paul A & Anne Allwarden: Caroline Margaux, 21 Apr 1992 (E)
YOUNGQUIST: Stanley O & Shirley P Mattsson: Robert Ethan, 26 Apr 1960 (Man)
ZAPORA: Daniel F & Katherine A Onorato: Samuel Joseph, 19 Feb 1990 (E)
ZIES: Gregory A & Lora J Voulgaris: Elizabeth Ashley, 15 Feb 1990; Michael Andrew, 19 Aug
    1987 (E)
ZIMNOWSKI: Leonard P, Jr & Linda L Glazier: Leonard Paul, III, 27 Jan 1978 (E)
ZOCCO: Philip J & Kirsten L Crosby: Rebecca Liane, 30 Jun 1994 (Man)

MARRIAGES
1901 - 1994

ABATE,: Joseph C (Andover,Ma) & Susan L Livingston (Andover,Ma), 15 Aug 1987
ABBOTT: Robert K (Kingston) & Marjolaine R Jean (Eliot,Me), 29 Mar 1979
ABORN: Merle (Belmont/18) & Georgianna Kelley (Kingston/16), 02 Aug 1930
    (James H Aborn/.....)(Charles Kelley/ Sarah J Martin)
ACHTERMAN: Ralph H (Pleasant Plains,Oh/21)&Dona J Beach (Freeport,N.S./16),*
    (C.A.Achterman/ Maude Ertel)(John Beach/ Christine Thurber)   *11 Aug 1933
ACKERSON: Robert L (Kingston) & Jeanette E Mc Lane (Atkinson), 10 Jul 1971 (P)
ACOX: Walter E (Granada,Mn/25) & Gloria E Hagen (Boston,Ma/18), 20 Apr 1946
    (Esmond Acox/ Alice Oliver)(Charles Hagen/ Ida Ringer)
ADAMS: Gary C (Somerville, Ma) & Deborah A Dearborn (Somerville,Ma), 24 Jun 1978
    James H (Reno,Nv) & Roberta J Simmons (Kingston), 06 Aug 1968
    Leon F Jr (Kingston) & Cynthia A Pool (Kingston), 03 Oct 1981
AIELLO: Frank J (Weymouth,Ma) & Ruth Hendrickson (Dedham,Ma), 18 Mar 1950
    (Pat Aiello/ Mary ....)(Carl A Hendrikson/ Ruth M Mattson)
ALBERT: Dale E, (Kingston) & Ruth S Ready (Kingston), 13 Oct 1990
    Michael M (Lynn,Ma) & Dorothy L LeJeune (Lynn,Ma), 08 Nov 1963
ALBERTS: Michael J (Durham,Ma) & Pamela J Tilton (Kingston), 04 Jun 1977 (B)
ALLARD: Steven K (Kingston) & Lu Ann M Arsenault (Kingston), 06 Jul 1991
ALLRED: James D (Newbury,Ma) & Nancy L Witham (Newbury,Ma), 20 May 1984
AMATO: David R (Kingston) & Tammi M Collins (Danville), 28 Jan 1989
AMAZEEN: Clarence (Plaistow) & Ernestine C Parker (Kingston), 11 Jul 1953
    (Clarence Amazee,Sr/Gladys Wentworth)(Allen J Parker/ Madeline E Senter)
AMBREY: Francis M (Kingston) & Deborah R Tillson (Kingston), 07 Feb 1976
AMBROSE: Benjamin P (Bradford,Ma) & Christine D Rattey (Bradford,Ma), 18 Aug 1956
    (Benjamin Ambrose/ Irene Corier)(Raymond Martel/ Edna Middleton)
AMBROISE: Yvon V (Boston,Ma) & Myreille Valmyr (Boston,Ma), 17 Nov 1994
AMES: George E (Rockland,Me/39) & Laurie P (Wiggin) French (Exeter/40), 03 Aug 1915*
    (Alonzo C Ames/Elizabeth L Swift)(Alvin Wiggin/Mary A French)   *(Hollis)
ANDERSEN: Ralph H (Kingston) & Anne M Goodell (Monticello,Ny), 02 Nov 1969
ANDERSON, Anders III, (Bradford,Ma) & Leanne A Smith (Kingston), 14 Feb 1985
    Gary A (Newburyport,Ma) & Glenna M Clarke (Kingston), 15 Sep 1974
    Robert W (Craftsbury,Vt) & Jeannette B Martin (Craftsbury,Vt), 01 Nov 1968
    Thomas L (Kingston) & Denise M Kennedy (Kingston), 03 Nov 1990
    Walter J (Somerville,Ma) & Christine M MacDonald (Somerville,Ma), 08 Apr 1951
    (Albert Anderson/Katherine Coward)(John Macdonald/Mary MacNeil)
ANDREWS, Bruce G (Kingston) & Blanche Deshais (Kingston), 18 Aug 1990
    Bruno (Lynfield,Ma) & Valencia Narkum (Lynnfield,Ma), 04 Sep 1955
    (Joseph Andrews/ Victoria Zwierzehowski)(Anthony Doda/ Sophia Krugel)
    Francis S (Kingston) & Beverly F Henderson (Kingston), 19 Feb 1965

Wayne F (E Kingston) & Joyce M Mathews (Kingston), 13 Nov 1971 (N)
ANDUJAR: Natividad P (Kingston) & Marie L George (Kingston), 26 Sep 1971
ANGELONE: William C, Jr (Lawrence,Ma) & Glenda F Smith (Kingston), 26 Jun 1982
ANNINO: James R, Jr (Brockton,Ma) & Marie P Carbonara (Brockton,Ma), 05 Mar 1955
   (James R Annino & Mabel Mederio)(Pasquale Carbonara & Josephine Spadea)
ARCHER: John N (Kingston) & Patricia M Elkins (Kingston), 29 Jun 1985
ARMSTEAD: George B, III (Derry) & Christina Hurni (Newbury, Ma), 25 Aug 1990
ARMSTRONG: Merton W,Jr(Fremont) & Francoise A Pelletier (Kingston), 24 Jun 1968 (N)
ARNOLD: Walter R (Kingston) & Clarabell Bruso (Kingston), 19 Jan 1984
ARONS: Noval E (Peabody,Ma) & Nancy L Dion (Salem,Ma), 14 Feb 1961
   (Roy Arons/ Ruby Handley)(Ernest Dion/ Helen Cannon)
ARSENAULT: David J (Raymond) & Theresa E Gray (Raymond), 21 May 1977
ASHLEY: Scott W (Kingston) & Susan J Jackson (Kingston), 07 Feb 1986
ASHTON: Edward G (Lynn, Ma/23) & M Josephine Senter (Amesbury,Ma/17), 22 Mar 1900
   (Arthur Ashton /M Eva Watson)(Frank Senter/Mary E Davis)
   Maurice E & Eula Dudley, 24 Aug 1921
   (Alonzo Bishop/Lillian Fuller)(Elmer Collins/ Susie Nason)
ASHWORTH: James R (25) & Grace A Black (25), 04 Jul 1937
   (William E Ashworth/Mabel D Holmes)(James C Black/ Grace D Doyle)
ATTARIAN: James (Tewksbury,Ma) & Donna M Fox (Tewksbury,Ma), 14 Dec 1956
   (James J Attaria,Sr/Dorothy Bigelow)(Wilbury Fox/ Dorothy Wemesfelder)
AUCLAIR: John M (Haverhill,Ma) & Marion L Murphy (Kingston), 29 Oct 1960
   (Felix A Auclair/ Georgianna Jones)(Charles N Jasper/ Ethel Hartford)
AUGE: David J (Fremont) & Jennifer A Simpson (Kingston), 10 Sep 1988
AUGER: David C (Newton) & Jane W Carroll (Kingston), 04 Oct 1959
   (William J Auger/ Mary E Denham)(Everett W Carroll/ Lois W Bunker)
AVERSANO: Joseph P, Jr (Kingston)& Karen A Burton (Hillsboro), 22 Sep 1990
AYERS: Chester W (So Hampton) & Roberta I Arnold (Kingston), 03 Jul 1957
   (Chester W Ayers/ Mildred Jordan)(George E Arnold,Sr/Edith C Arnold)
   Chester W, III Kingston) & Diana L Rand (Kingston), 08 Jan 1977
   Chester W, III (Kingston) & Debra A Wilks (Amesbury,Ma), 03 Oct 1980
   Chester W, III (Kingston) & Roberta R Como (Berwick,Me), 16 Jul 1987
   Phillip E (Kingston) & Rhonda L Silva (Kingston), 16 Feb 1991
AYLWARD: Carl D (Kingston) & Lisa A Neddy (Exeter), 30 Apr 1982
AZIZ: Roger J, Jr (Methuen,Ma) & Elaine M Gianni (Methuen,Ma), 24 Jul 1994
BABCOCK: Josiah, Jr (Milton,Ma/24) & Blanche C Sanborn (Kingston/20), 07 Sep 1904
   (Josiah Babcock/ Martha E Aldrich)(Dr. John M Sanborn/ Clara N Chase)
BACIGALUPO: John H (Haverhill,Ma/20) & Dorothy M Decosta (Haverhill,Ma/18),*
   (Fred Bacigalupo/Edith Hayes)(Wesley A Decosta/Helen Curry)   *19 Jun 1949
BAILEY: Arnold W (Kingston) & Deboara H Reed (Kingston), 28 May 1988
   Howard W (Haverhill,Ma) & Michel A McComiskie (Haverhill, Ma), 21 Sep 1985
BAIN: Warren A (Kingston) & Paula M Wood (Kingston), 06 Jun 1992
BAITZ: Kurt W (Kingston) & Lynn M Killam (Kingston), 17 Aug 1991
BAKE: David P (Kingston) & Jeanie K Kinnamon (Kingston), 08 Apr 1989

Ralph H Lawrence,Ma/27) & Laura E Nason (Kingston/24), 27 Jun 1925
 (Herbert Bake/Mary M Megson)(Albert F Nason/Laura Fifield)
 Thomas R (Kingston) & Lisa A Hilton(Newton), 09 Sep 1989
BAKER: Christopher D (Framingham,Ma) & Robin E Cohen (Framingham,Ma),
 30 Aug 1981
 Daniel A (Kingston) & Patricia M Blinn (Kingston), 13 May 1985
 Jeffrey (Stoneham, Ma) & Deborah Andrews (Stoneham, Ma), 25 Aug 1990
 Melbourne (Brockton,Ma) & Helena F Correla (Taunton,Ma), 13 Sep 1952
 (General H Baker/ Mannie Manning)(Lowden Correia/ Florence Carlisle)
BAKERTJES: Michael J (27) & Georgiana Zaharoponton (24), 14 Jun 1936
 (James Bakertjes/Maria Nichols)(Harry Zaharoponton/Lena Varvaras)
BAKIE: Gordon J (Kingston) & Lee H DeRevere (Kingston), 22 Jul 1992
BALBONI: Fred J (Boston,Ma/24) & Hilda M Keenan (Boston,Ma/19), 27 Aug 1932 (E)
 (Romano Balboni/ Emma Ardisoni)(Walter F Keenan/ Margaret Milward)
BALL: William H (Chester/57) & Mary F Runnels (Laconia/60), 08 Jun 1903 (P)
 (Aaron Ball/Sarah Brown)(Albert Sweetser/Rebecca Berry)
BALLARD: Larry M (English,IN) & Sandra L Bukowski (Kingston), 25 Jul 1968
BALUKAS: Stacy L (Kingston) & Patricia A Johnson (Kingston), 29 Jun 1991
BANDOUVERES: James S (Poland, Me) & Mary C Mitchell (Poland, Me), 28 Jul 1991
BANKS: Lawrence C (Orlando, Fl) & Betty J McRae (Hanover, Ma), 18 Nov 1990
BARBARISI: James R (Revere,Ma) & Rosemary Cardello (Revere,Ma), 03 Jul 1975
BARCLAY: George I (Kingston) & Donna M Lasater (Danville), 14 Feb 1991
BARDGETT: John W (Kingston) & Amy M Badger (Lynn,Ma), 30 Sep 1972 (Saugus,Ma)
BARKAS: Robert A (Kingston) & Joan S Lamy (Kingston), 18 Oct 1981
BARNES: Bruce A (Kingston) & Beverly J Goodhue (No Hampton), 01 Mar 1964 (H)
 Earle L (Gloucester,Ma) & Dorothy J Adams (Gloucester,Ma), 22 Sep 1950
 (Earle H E Barnes/Eleanor T Brackett)(Charles Adams/Adailade Baker)
BARNSTEIN: John A (Kingston) & Sheila L Hamblen (Kingston), 21 Jan 1977
BARNUM: Larry P (Plaistow) & Christine A Sarcione (Kingston), 23 Oct 1994
BARRETT: John W (Kingston) & Ashligh Marvin (Kingston), 18 Sep 1993
 Raymond H (Kingston/22) & Florence D Rollins (Amesbury,Ma/20), 12 May 1917
 (John Barrett/Elizabeth T ....)(Frank Rollins & Dora Dow)
BARRY: Arthur L (Kingston/37) & Margaret H Hughes (Kingston/40), 27 Mar 1947
 (William Barry/ Anna M Shields)(Charles Hughes/Winifred Mannix)
 Charles G (Manchester) & Madeleine C Barry (Kingston), 01 Aug 1970 (M)
 Joseph R (E Boston,Ma) & Irene M Del Favero (E Boston,Ma), 30 Dec 1954
 (John Barry/ Bridget Hines)(Charles Dobbins/ Theresa Rogers
 Richard A, Jr (Lowell,Ma) & Priscilla Standish (Lowell,Ma), 17 Jul 1993
BARTLETT: Clarence E (Nashua/36) & Eugenie O Larivee(Cambridge,Ma/26), 02 Feb 1917
 (Francis Bartlett/Mary A Rowe)(Frank Larivee/Octavie Veillette) (Nashua)
 Greenleaf K(Derry/60) & Nella G Whipple (Kingston/41), 09 Jun 1917
 (Greenleaf C Bartlett & Charlotte J Kelly) (Sanford Whipple /Mary E Sanborn)
 Gregory S (Kingston) & Lisa H Dondero (Kingston), 17 Sep 1988
 Michael P (Merrimac,Ma) & Janice A Nichols (Kingston), 28 Sep 1974 (N)
 Steven A (Kingston) & Vickie-Lynn Brewer (Barrington), 26 Jul 1986

Walter W (Kingston/36) & Sadie L Taylor Haverhill,Ma/23), 27 Mar 1909
(FrancisBartlett/Mary A Rowe) (Alphonso Taylor/Flora W West)
William, Jr (Kingston) & Lois Lee Stinson (Stratham), 24 Jun 1978 (Not)
William (Kingston) & Tamela J Sanborn (Kingston), 16 Sep 1978
William S, III (Kingston) & Tamela J Sanborn (Kingston), 03 Jul 1985
BASLER: Peter P (Plymouth,Ma) & Nancy Merrill (Kingston), 13 Dec 1969   (N)
BASSETT: Jon E (Kingston) & Marcia A Bennett (Newfields), 31 Aug 1974 (Newfields)
Joseph A (Fremont/22) & Shirley M Corson (Kingston/23), 08 Aug 1947
(George A Bassett/Nellie P Davis)(Charles P Corson/Delia M Young)
BASILLIERE: Philip C (Kingston) & Debra M Smith (Kingston), 19 May 1990
BASSO: Paul R (No Grafton, Ma) & Cindy E Pecker (Kingston), 27 Oct 1990
BATCHELDER: Bruce (Kingston) & Nancy R McIntosh (Kingston), 09 Jun 1978 (P)
Erwin W (Haverhill,Ma) & Dorothy R Beaudoin (W Newbury,Ma), 25 Jul 1953
(Lois Batchelder)(Eben Emery/ Eva J Demeritt)
Ralph M, Jr, (Kingston) & Frances M Altman (Greenland), 05 Dec 1992
BATEMAN: Raymond (Woodford,Vt) & Cindy M Tuttle (Kingston), 26 May 1978
(Newmarket)
BATTLES: Robert A (Kingston) & Marjorie H Bowen (Kingston), 10 Sep 1977
BEALS: Robert C (Kingston) & Naomia A Newman (Exeter), 30 Jun 1979
George E (Haverhill,Ma/26) & Alice F Davis (Kingston/21), 28 Nov 1901
(James H Beals/Emma C Bougdon)(Richard H Davis/Harriet Stacy)
BEAN: Frank J (Brentwood/31) & Annie E Morrill (Amesbury,Ma/25), 02 Jul 1910
(Charles W Bean/ Mary A Towle)(C.P.Morrill/ Hannah Martin)
BEAULIEU: Jean R (Kingston) & Suzetta L Patnaude (Kingston), 31 Dec 1993
BEAUREGARD: Ronald N (Kingston) & Judi A Alonzi (Kingston), 13 Oct 1971
BECHARD: , Ernest J, (Detroit,Mi) & Viola Mello (Detroit,Mi), 09 Jul 1960
(Alfred Bechard/ Delina Tetrault)(William J Mello/ Amelia S Souza)
BECKER: John L (Kingston) & Amy L Montebianchi (Kingston), 23 Mar 1980
BECKFORD: Alan H (Kingston) & Charlotte E Orenzo (Haverhill,Ma), 18 Jul 1951
(Harold Beckford/Barbara Stevens)(Albert LeGault/Mildred L Mack)
BECOTTE: Joseph H (Kingston) & Louise G Howarth (Kingston), 24 Aug 1985
BEEDE: Fred L (Amesbury,Ma/20) & Alice Merrick(Sandown/20), 09 Nov 1902
(Oscar Beede /Hannah Webster)(Andrew J Merrick/Abbie N Pierce)
Fred S (Amesbury,Ma/33) & Alice M Babb (Lynn,Ma/37), 19 Jul 1915
(Oscar Beede/Hannah Webster)(Henry M Babb/Sarah A Graves)
Jonathan W (Brentwood) & Elizabeth A Weyler (Kingston), 30 Jun 1990
BELANGER: Joseph H (Exeter) & Cathie L Mayo (Kingston), 30 Mar 1970   (E)
BELL: Frank D (Sea Isle City,NJ) & Christine Bond (Kingston), 24 Dec 1971
William R (Plaistow) & Rachael A Nason (Kingston), 19 Nov 1966 (S)
BELLEMORE: Walter M (23) & Martha Mitchell (24), 01 Jul 1934
(Albert Bellemore/Mary Pridel)(Louis B Mitchell/Mary Wheeler)
BELLINO: Philip J, II (Chelmsford, Ma) & Diane M Barra (Chelmsford, Ma), 08 Sep 1990
BELMONTE: Louis (Somerville,Ma) & Tina L Butner(Dorchester,Ma), 06 Sep 1968
BEMIS: Phillip R (Brighton,Ma) & Patricia A Gincauski (Brighton,Ma), 03 Feb 1962

BENNETT: Robert (23) & Eldora M Tucker (25), 26 Nov 1941 (D)
    (William Bennett/Lena I Bird)(William F Tucker/Nellie F Simes)
    Robert E (Hudson,Ma) & Patricia E Taranto (Marlboro,Ma), 07 Mar 1959
    (Robert Bennett/ Thelma Newcomb)(Joseph Taranto/Eleanor Uzilro)
    Robert W (Kingston) & Joanne Abdo (Danville), 21 Aug 1965 (M)
    Wendell F (20) & Beatrice R Goldthwaite (23), 28 Feb 1937 (Ports)
    (Albert G Bennett/ Hattie E Farrar)(Ernest Goldthwaite/ Nellie M West)
BENOIT: Joseph H (Kingston/61) & Lucy A Noyes (W Newbury,Ma/56), 04 Jan 1948 (P)
    (John B Benoit/Rosa L Chaussie)(George E Noyes/Augusta Smith)
BERGER: Andre R (Kingston) & Elisabeth A Blanchard (Kingston), 26 Oct 1991
BERGERON: Wilbert J (Kingston) & Virginia M Dube (Kingston), 01 Jul 1950
    (Mitchel Bergeron/Emma Mylot)(Deloss P Herne/Marion Downey)
BERGSTROM: Jeremy M (Kingston) & Marnie J Cleary (Plaistow), 27 Dec 1986
    Richard W (Kingston) & April J Silverman (Kingston), 11 Dec 1975 (P)
BERGQUIST: Herbert R (Concord) & Flora L Rogers (Kingston), 20 Jun 1954
    (Herbert C Bergquist/ Irma Neubert) (Ellsworth B Rogers/ Helen V Cummings)
BERKOVICH: John L (Haverhill,Ma) & Evelyn H Wildes (Haverhill,Ma), 10 Sep 1954
    (Morris N Berkovich/ Lena Alter)(Wilfred Wildes/ Mildred B Hodgdon)
BERNABY: Peter M (Kingston) & Sharon A Eldredge (Exeter), 01 Nov 1966 (E)
BERNARDINI: Norman F (Epping) & Susan J Tilton (Kingston), 17 Apr 1960
    (Lawrence Bernardini/ Renie Bailey)(Leonard Tilton/Rheta P Cavaric)
BERRY: Gardner R (Kingston) & Lois A Buckless (Salem), 08 Dec 1967 (S)
    Gardner R (Kingston) & Kathy A Gursky (Exeter), 20 Aug 1977
    Richard (Portsmouth/32) & Charlene Patterson (Kingston), 23 Feb 1947
    (Wyatt Berry/ Margaret Freeman)(Gerold Batchelder/ Alice Richardson)
BERTZOS: Robert E (Sterling,Ma) & Petronella N Wherrity (Sterling,Ma), 15 Nov 1986
BETTY: George C (Haverhill,Ma) & Jeanette L Morse (Kingston), 30 Jul 1957
    (George Betty/ Ethel Chase)(John Boulanger/ Louise Feilteau)
BILODEAU: Malcolm F (Haverhill/ 25) & Alyce Bloomfield (Haverhill/20), 22 Jun 1931
    (Arthur Bilodeau/Edith West)(Harry Bloomfield/ Fanny Kaplan)
    Roger D (Concord) & Annette E McFadyen (Concord), 29 Aug 1962
BINGEL: John A (Plaistow) & Sandra E Avery (Kingston), 07 Jun 1957
    (Arnold B Glover/ Daisy B Thompson)(Raymond E Avery/ Exilda C Foster)
BIRD: Joseph H (Brentwood) & Rosemary A Calerone (Kingston), 03 Jul 1991
BISHOP: David A (Woburn, Ma) & Sandra A Masson (Woburn, Ma), 23 May 1992
    Chester F (Fremont/24) & Grace Collins (Kingston/19), 21 Feb 1930
    Robert R (Topsfield,Ma) & Carole J Blaisdell (Boxford,Ma), 11 Feb 1967
    Ronald P (Richmond,Va) & Donna R Goodwin (Richmond,Va), 22 May 1982
    Thomas F (Kingston) & Barbara C Rose (Kingston), 07 Apr 1974 (S)
BISSON: Ranie R (Merrimac,Ma) & Joan M Hamilton (Kingston), 15 Jun 1968
BITHER: Cecil J (Salisbury,Ma) & Lenora E Estes (Salisbury,Ma), 20 Aug 1956
    (John Bither/ Rachael Shields)(Fred Williams/ Ruth Sheehan)
BITOMAKE: William L, Jr (Raymond) & Diane L Patterson (Kingston), 27 Jun 1981
BLACKBURN: Steven R (Kingston) & Dawn Carter (Kingston), 22 Jan 1971 (N)
BLAISDELL: Steven C (Kingston) & Elisha G Sloan (Kingston), 03 Oct 1994

BLANCHETTE: Thomas E (Farmington) & Sallyanne Gould (Kingston), 23 Jun 1979
BLATTENBERGER: Ronald E, Jr (Kingston) & Julie C Lemieux (Kingston), 04 Mar 1985
BLATTI: John C (Salisbury,Ma) & Kimberly L Wood (Salisbury,Ma), 02 Oct 994
BLAUVELT: Maurice W (No Attleboro,Ma) & Mae V Dill (No Attleboro,Ma), 14 Jun 1968
BLINN: John A (Kingston) & Mary Ann Mc Cluskey (Haverhill,Ma), 11 Mar 1966
BLISS: Craig T (Merrimac, Ma) & Kim A Manter (Merrimac, Ma), 18 Jan 1990
BLOOD: David A (Kingston) & Rose M Henson (Kingston), 16 Jun 1990
BLUMENTHAL: Al (24) & Sadie Stone (23), 23 May 1937
    (Isaac Blumenthal/ Molly Davis)(Jacob Stone/ Bessie Hurwick)
BODWELL: Daniel T (Kensington) & Joyce E Milbury (Kingston), 09 Sep 1960 (Ken)
    (Harold W Bodwell/ Dorothy C Turner)(Norman W Milbury/ Ethel E Clements)
BOISSELLE: Albert J (Haverhill,Ma) & Evelyn I Surrette (Haverhill,Ma), 10 May 1958
    (Joseph Boissell/ Exelda Sansoucie)(Melvin House/ Margaret Kennedy)
BOLAND: John W (Wakefield,Ma) & Charlene F Ulwick (Wakefield,Ma), 21 Oct 1961
    (Francis J Boland/ Ruth Casey)(Walter N Ulwick/ Mary Doyle)
BOLDUC: Corey A (Fremont) & Julie A McDonald (Kingston), 12 Sep 1992
    John K (Fremont) & Sheryla A St Laurent (Kingston), 20 Dec 1969 (F)
BOLOGNA: Edward (Haverhill,Ma) & Judith A Rush, 09 Aug 1958
    (Edward C Bologna/ Jennie Buccini)(Thomas Rush,Jr/Helen S Shaw)
BOND: Peter A (Kingston) & Diane T Becotte (Kingston), 13 Jun 1975 (N)
BONIN: Richard J (Kingston) & Karen A Sadler (Groveland,Ma),15 Oct 1988
BONNELL: Samuel (Georgetown,Ma) & Mary E Quirke (Haverhill,Ma), 01 Jun 1968
BOOKINGS: Frederick R (Medford,Ma/77) & Madeleine E Lesperance (Medford,Ma/43),*
    (Henry Brookings/Annie Colgan)(Harry Major/Lillian Corey)   * 17 June 1949
BOOMER: John W (Lubec,Tx) & Melissa JBoomer (Rochester), 15 Jul 1961
    (William W Boomer/ Marguerite Joy)(George L Boomer/ Grace Murray)
BOOMHOWER: Mark J (Kingston) & Tammy L Wickens (Atkinson), 04 Aug 1984
BORGHETTE: Anthony J (30) & Josephine Tobio (27), 25 Nov 1937
    (Marianna Borghette/ May Luca)(Andrew Tobio/ Jennie De Laca)
BORNSTEIN: Peter H (Brookline,Ma) & Linda L Upham (Kingston), 07 Aug 1976 (P)
BORRELLI: Ralph (Kingston) & Linda D Collins (Kingston), 17 Mar 1993
BOSS: J Harold (Kingston) & Williamina P Peacock (Scarborough,Ont), 14 Nov 1969
BOTAISH: Joseph F (Dedham,Ma) & Ann L Clark (Roslindale,Ma), 04 May 1964
BOUCHARD: Louis J (Kingston) & Elaine M Mathews (Kingston), 15 Jul 1978 (N)
BOUCHER: Roland E, Jr (Haverhill,Ma)& Dona C Weldy (Kingston), 15 Jun 1974 (P)
BOUCHICAS: Joseph M (Newton) & Lynn A Adams (Kingston), 22 Oct 1988
BOUNDS: William C (Milton,Ma) & Zane F Hamlet (Hyde Park,Ma), 09 Oct 1954
    (Emmett C Bounds/ Marie Aultman)(Archie Hamlet/ Elizabeth Johnson)
BOURBEAU: Louis O (Reeds Ferry/28) & Eunice Nichols (Kingston/30), 19 Mar 1949
    (Ovila F Bourbeau/Eva Vallee)(Frederic S Nichols/Therese N Porter)   (M)
BOURGELAS: Frederick N (Newton) & Cynthia J Dale (Kingston), 01 Apr 1961
    (Frederick M Bourgelas/ Marie Roussel)(Edward O Dale/ Dorothy Lamb)
BOURGEOIS: Leo D (Salem) & Rebecca Nicholls (Kingston), 28 Jun 1969 (Keene)
BOWERS, Jonathan J (Kingston) & Kathleen L Dias (Kingston), 11 Mar 1989
BOWLEY: Martin W (Exeter) & Sharon L Page (Kingston), 09 Sep 1972 (E)

BOWMAN: Herbert E (Arlington,Ma) & Georgia H Moreland (Somerville,Ma),19 Sep 1956
        (Sunmer E Bowman/ Ella Farnham)(Frank C Moreland/ Mary E Hartley)
BOYLE: Hugh J (Kingston) & Vivian E Casey (Bradford,Ma), 07 Apr 1974   (N)
BOYLORN: Willie (Dorchester,Ma) & Carrie Lee McKinnon (Dorchester,Ma),04 Jul 1974
BRADBROOK: Alan L (Everett,Ma) & Nancy L Bunker (Kingston), 18 May 1968
        Robert A (Kingston) & Theresa M White (Kingston), 23 Apr 1966
BRADLEY: Asa M (Brewster Ma/74)&Elizabeth B Webster (Boston,Ma/50), 06 Jul 1930 *
        (Cyrus A Bradley/ Locretia Foster)(Frederick Briggs/ Annie Briggs)   * (Newfields)
        Charles A, Jr (Kingston) & Janice E Coffey (N Hampton), 30 Sep 1972   (E)
BRAGDON: Ernest P (Kingston/28) & Doris L Nye (Brookline/26), 09 Jun1925 (Brookline)
        (Fred L Bragdon/Emma F Prescott)(Ernest W Nye/Addie H Segre)
        John A (Kingston/18) & Annie R Whippen (St Albans,Vt/22), 04 Dec 1915
        (Fred L Bragdon/Emma Prescott)(Frank W Whippen/Minerva Swan)
BRAGG: Walter E (Kingston) & Karen J Freeman (Kingston), 26 Sep 1992
BRALEY: Brooks V (Kingston) & Jane E Stanley (Fremont), 08 May 1982
        Bruce K (Kingston) & Helen V Gille (Exeter), 28 Sep 1974 (Nashua)
        Richard R (Kingston) & Dona G Eldridge (Kingston), 23 Nov 1968 (N)
        Stephen H (Newton) & Linda M Harriman (Kingston), 01 Sep 1974 (Deerfield)
BRANDT: Francis L (E Kingston) & Joann E Anderson (Kingston), 16 Apr 1977
BREDA: John E (Braintree,Ma) & Eleanor P Crispo (Tewksbury,Ma), 09 Oct 1964
BRENNAN: Thomas B (40) & Eleanor L Anderson (36), 28 Jun 1939
        (James Brennan/Mary Gunning)(Frederick Morgan/Emily Rounds)
        William N (Reading,Ma) & Veronica F McQuarrie (Marblehead,Ma)-04 Feb 1961
        (William F Brennan/Sylvia M Dooley)(Charles A McQuarrie/Katherine C O'Connor)
BREWSTER: Don A (Kingston) & Marilyn E Langlois (Kingston), 08 Sep 1984
BRIAN: John J (Brewster,NY/24)&Ellen Jones (Kingston/33), 22 Jan 1905   (S/K)
        (William Brian/Catherine Simpson)(John Jones/Abigail Burke)
BRIGGS: David R (Plaistow) & Ruth M Fowler (Kingston), 26 May 1972 (P)
        Donald W, Jr (Kingston) & Donna M Lafleche (Kingston), 06 Jun 1981
        Kenneth F, Jr (Kingston) & Carol A Spencer (Ashland), 06 Mar 1977 (Littleton)
        Kenneth F, III (Kingston) & Sharon L Holmes (Jewett City,Ct), 09 Jun 1968
        (Mansfield, Ct)
BRITT: Dennis N (Hampton) & Susan J Irvine (Kingston), 16 Apr 1988
BRITTON: Curtis (Haverhill,Ma/23) & Arline Stubbs (Haverhill,Ma/ 21), 16 Oct 1930
        (Herbert Britton/Florence Richards)(Walter Stubbs/Ina Randall)
BROCK: Frederick H (Stoneham,Ma) & Gwendolyn L Hunter (Reading,Ma), 13 Oct 1954
        (Herbert J Brock/ Edna L McCord)(William H.T. Hunter/ Mildred Robbins)
        Herbert J, Jr (23) & Margaret M Morris (20), 27 Feb 1936
        (Herbert Brock/Edna L McCord)(Humphrey Morris/Mary McGaffigan)
BROCKELBANK: Robert C, Jr (Kingston) & Susan G Perry (Haverhill,Ma),05 Feb 1972 (P)
BROOME: Carroll D (Kingston) & Concetta V De Sisto (Kingston), 30 Apr 1964
BROULETTE: Bruce C(Kingston) & Nancy J Sanders (E Hampstead), 29 Jun 1973   (P)
BROWN: Arthur F (Dover/23) & Marion E Wallace (Sanbornville/23), 03 Oct 1917 (D/O)
        (Edward E Brown/Bertha B Furber)(Edwin S Wallace/Sarah E Whitehouse)

Austin C (Haverhill,Ma/28) & Doris E Cronan (Bradford,Ma/22), 23 Dec 1948
(John E Brown/Bessie ....)(John J Cronan/Marion B Brown)
Christopher R (Kingston) & Gayle E Brown (Salem,Ma), 13 Jul 1985
Donald P (Randolph,Ma) & Theda C Petrie (Dedham,Ma), 12 Jun 1954
(Harold Brown/ Frances Del Signore) (John M Petrie/ Margaret Cleary)
Edward W(Littleton,Ma) & Nancy E Sullivan (Boston,Ma), 12 Jul 1970
George A, Sr (Kingston) & Marguerite M Hamel (Kingston), 02 Oct 1976
Harold A (No Randolph,Ma) & Rosemary E Muldoon (Milton,Ma), 13 Aug 1953
(Harold H Brown/ Frances Scimone)(Frank B Muldoon/ Margaret Qualters)
Harold R (Beverly,Ma) & Florence M Dalton (Beverly,Ma), 01 May 1964
Harold M (24) & Rachael I Bennett (28), 12 May 1934
(Walter Brown/ Isabella Phillips)(Albert G Bennett/ Hattie E Farrar)
Jay E (Edgewood, IA/49) & Effie B Quero (Kingston/44), 15 Jul 1931
(Joseph Brown/Matilda Scribner)(Andrew Quero/ Mary A Ball)
John N (Kingston) & Freda A Clark (Kingston), 09 Jul 1966
John W (Beverly,Ma) & Patricia A Troubetar (Beverly,Ma), 31 Oct 1962
Kenneth R (Kingston) & Tamera J Last (Watertown, Ma), 13 Oct 1990
Richard (Kingston)& Catherine F Clements (Kingston), 12 Oct 1968
Richard T (Newton) & Linda Fay (Kingston), 28 Apr 1962
William L.G. (30) & Alice M Kent (24), 04 Jun 1938
(John N Brown/ Annie B Tracy)(James A Kent/ Anna B Christian)
BROWNELL: John S (Lynn,Ma) & Patricia Walsh (Revere,Ma), 23 Apr 1953
(George S Brownell/ Rose Stevens)(John Walsh/ Ethel Cotter)
BROWNLIE: Thomas A (Kingston) & Sherry L Amazeen (Kingston), 17 Oct 1980
BRUCE: Donald R (Exeter) & Bertha A Carter (Kingston), 05 Sep 1959 (E)
(Joseph S Bruce/ Wileamina Waleryszak)(Harry L Carter/ Ida Bickell)
BRUSSARD: William P (Kissimmee,Fl) & Elizabeth W Wise (Lynn,Ma), 01 Jan 1989
BRUSSO: Neil T (Fremont) & Linda L Nason (Kingston), 22 Jun 1963
BRYANT: Charles (Andover,Ma) & Virginia M French (Andover,Ma), 01 Oct 1961
(Charles A Bryant/Anna Heinz)
BRYAR: Winton S (35) & Dorothy A Davidson (25), 11 Oct 1941(E)
(Fred W Bryar/Grace M Smith)(Lewis H Davidson/Agnes K McDonald)
BUCHANAN: John F (Lawrence,Ma) & Greta DeWitt (Haverhill,Ma), 21 Sep 1955
(Frank S Buchanan/ Lillian M Larkin)(Charles Hodgdon/ Myrtle Larkin)
BUCKLEY: James R (Somerville,Ma) & Louise Norton (Somerville,Ma), 20 Aug 1959
(Eugene Buckley/ Alice Forester)(Thomas P Norton/Eleanor Barry)
BUNKER: Edward A (N Billerica,Ma) & Maybelle F St.Jean (N Billerica,Ma),14 Dec 1984
Stanton L (Kingston/25) & Priscilla Tuck (Milo,Me/22), 31 Dec 1945
(Louis C Bunker/Annie M George)(John E Tuck/Harriet E Osgood)
Stanion L (Kingston) & Priscilla A Bunker (Kingston), 04 Mar 1965
BUONANNO: Anthony G (Lawrence,Ma) & Carol A Feole (Lawrence,Ma), 29 May 1965
BURBANK: Daniel W (Kingston) & Barbara E Stewart (Kingston), 22 Aug 1980
BURBINE: Benjamin A (Peabody,Ma) & Mary L Eftim (Peabody,Ma), 14 Dec 1962
BURDICK: Gregory A (Woburn, Ma) & Deborah A Flynn(Woburn, Ma), 27 Jun 1992
BURKE: Devin W (Westminster,Ma) & Cynthia M Killam (Kingston), 26 Jun 1976

Donald C (Ipswich,Ma) & Barbara K O'Brien(Ipswich,Ma), 17 Aug 1986
James E (Kingston) & Debra A Donahue (Kingston), 31 Aug 1985
John H, III (Kingston) & Mary L Sautter (Kingston), 30 Dec 1986
John W (Kingston) & Renee S Nichols (E Kingston), 17 Feb 1990
Richard C (Kingston) & Rosemarie LaRoche (Rochester),05 Dec 1953 (N)
   (James J Burke/ Ruth E Nason)(Arthur A LaRoche/ Beatrice Therrien)
Richard C (Kingston) & Malizzie S Riel (Epping), 09 Sep 1967 (N)
Walter R (Kingston) & Pauline S Gauthier (Amesbury,Ma), 06 Apr 1958 *
   (James J Burke/ Ruth E Nason)(Ernest A Gauthier/ Lina Cote) *(Amesbury,Ma)
BURLESON: Billy H (Kingston) & Cynthia A Avery (Kingston), 14 Mar 1964
BURLEY: Paul M (Pepperell, Ma) & Kathy L Davey (Wakefield, Ma), 14 Sep 1991
BURLINGAME: Walter (Wrentham,Ma) & Sandra L Plante (Plainville,Ma), 02 Jan 1960
   (Walter D Burlingame/ Dorothy F Schaefer)(Richard D Plante/ Lea R Allard)
BURNELL: Fred A (Everett,Ma/24) & Doris S Storey (Melrose,Ma/18), 12 Jul 1929
   (Fred A Burnell/Jeanette Grover)(Chester Storey/Florence Blake)
BURNETTE: Gerald M (Portsmouth) & Priscilla L Dunn (Kingston), 14 Feb 1964
BURNHAM: Maurice L (W Newbury,Ma) & Joanne Boriska (Haverhill,Ma) 11 Jul 1962
   Theodore E, III (Kingston) & Theresa J Belanger (Kingston),11 Aug 1990
BURNS: Brian W (Lawrence,Ma) & Marilyn A Clocher (Kingston), 13 Jun 1970 (S)
   Steven J (Lowell,Ma) & Linda J Vancoppenolle (Methuen,Ma),13 Nov 1969
BURY: Frederick F (23) & Grace Limerick (23), 19 Apr 1936
   (Frank Bury/Agnes Siska)(Thomas Limerick/Mary Carroll)
BUSCH: Richard J (Kingston) & Patricia A Fale (Kingston),19 Sep 1987
   Edward K (Newton) & Yvonne M Friend (Kingston), 03 Aug 1975(P)
BUSHONG: Glen D (Kingston) & Cynthia J George (Kingston), 07 Sep 1974   (N)
BUSHWAY: Donald J (Kingston) & Deborah A Ciriello (Lawrence,Ma), 14 Aug 1993
BUSSIERE: William H (Kingston) & Mary B Morrill (Kingston), 27 Mar 1970 (N/J)
BUSTON: Willis G (Kingston) & Suzanne Moran (Kingston), 27 Nov 1982
BUSWELL: Lawrence A (E Kingston) & Gertrude J Southwick (Kingston), 11 Oct 1959
   (Ralph H Buswell/ Etta M Webster)(Ralph E Southwick/ Florence G Caron)
   Lawrence A, Jr (Kingston) & Martha E Young (Kingston), 02 Sep 1991
BUTCHER: Homer (Pittsfield/38) & Annie M Downing (Georgetown,Ma/26), 31 Jan 1924
   (John Butcher/Fronie King)(Samuel Cilly/Mary S Young)
BUZWELL: Samuel G (Epping/20) & Alice S Smith (Boston,Ma/16), 23 Apr 1909
   Samuel G (Epping/20) & Alice S Smith (Boston,Ma/16), 23 Apr 1908
   (Albert C Buswell/Lillian H Wilcox)(Lovell P Smith /Viola Neal)
BUZZELL: Bradley E (Kingston) & Kathleen A Gavin (Newton), 27 Nov 1982
   David R (Haverhill,Ma) & Valerie E Spry (Haverhill,Ma), 28 Mar 1955
   (R Leon Buzzell,Jr/Victoria Kaskiewicz)(John A Spry/ Dorothy E Holden)
   Walter E (Wilton/24) & Ada F (Guillow) Stockwell (Gilsom/42), 30 Sep 1914*
   (Arthur E Buzzell/Ellen M Draper)(G.A.Guillow/Lizzie A White) *(Newmarket)
CABRAL: Paul J (Exeter) & Lori L Genovese (Kingston), 12 Jul 1992
CACCIOLA: Paul J (Medford,Ma) & Deborah A Hayes (Medford,Ma), 31 Nov 1976
CADIERO: William J, Jr (Kingston) & Deborah A McManus (Kingston), 25 Sep 1993

CALL: Charles W (Exeter) & Mary E Dolliver (Kingston), 19 Apr 1952 (E)
  (Arthur J Call/ Mabel C Lane)(Gerard R Dolliver/ Maude E Powers)
  Frank P (Brentwood) & Betty K Sprague (Kingston), 29 Nov 1959
  (Edward E Call/ Thelma I Dixon)(Walter E Sprague/ Katherine E Hislop)
CAMILIO: Joseph (Lynn,Ma) & Anna Shanahan (Lynn,Ma), 29 May 1960
  (Louis Camilio/ Lillian Curro)(William Corcoran/ Agnes Mealey)
CAMMPO: Robert A (Kingston) & Sharon A Mello (Kingston), 16 Dec 1983
CAMP: James W (Lowell,Ma) & Carol J Tryder (Lowell,Ma), 12 Aug 1988
CARDER: John J (24) & Evelyn Sevigny (25), 12 Oct 1940 (Nashua)
  (Frank Carder/May Williams)(William Sevigny/Albina Belleville)
CARIGNAN: Christopher T (Kingston) & Kathleen L Hamblin (Kingston), 21 Nov 1992
CARLEY: John G (Groveland,Ma) & Laura J Parker (Groveland,Ma), 13 Feb 1971 (N)
CARLSEN: Frank A (Kingston) & Joyce E Russo(Brighton,Ma), 05 Dec 1964
CARLSON: Carl G (Winchester,Ma/27) & Pauline Macauley (Malden,Ma/21), 23 Sep 1949
  (Werner A Carlson/Gerda K Peterson)(Malcolm A Macauley/Doris L Leisk)
CARLTON: Wilbur G (Newton/20) & Edna E Gurney (Amesbury/24), 27 Oct 1917 (N)
  (William M Carlton/Roxy J Emery)(Fred L Gurney/Susie N Stewart)
CARLUZZI: Joseph P (New York) & Jean R Andersen (Kingston), 18 Mar 1973
CARMICHAEL: Steven D (Kingston) & Laura J Carlson (Hampstead), 25 Aug 1991
CARMILIA: James (Lynn,Ma) & Catherine M Buccuzzo(Lynn,Ma), 25 Jul 1970
CARNEY: Philip E (Lawrence,Ma/42) & Loretta Bradford (Canada/37), 21 Oct 1933
  (James J Carney/Annie Sexton)(Patrick Kinsella/Mary Lee)
CARR: Ronald C (Lawrence,Ma) & Nancy J Ouellette (Lawrence,Ma), 02 May 1987
CARRICK: William F (Kingston) & Helen T Mansfield (Kingston), 27 Dec 1958 (N)
  (Harold M Carrick/ Ida P Rollock)(John A Mansfield/ Thelma R Wardell)
CARROLL: John A (Kingston) & Christine M Roy(Nashua), 17 Mar 1990
CARROW: Robert M (Kingston) & Eileen DeCoito (Atkinson), 10 May 1972
CARTER: Dana P (Waban,Ma) & Sonja B Olsen (W Newton,Ma), 08 Jan 1953
  (Lyndall F Carter/ Margaret Walker)(Godney B Brothen/ Ole H Olsen)
  Elmer C (Kingston/50) & Mary E Barker (Patten,Me/43), 30 Oct 1907 (Hudson)
  (Charles Carter/May B Page)
  Walter G, Jr (Kingston) & Donna M Gill (Kingston), 16 Nov 1973 (N)
CARUSO: Anthony L (Dorchester,Ma) & Joan Duffley (Neponset,Ma), 10 Aug 1962
CASEY: Michael E (Kingston) & Kimberly Lafayette (Kingston), 15 Sep 1978
  Francis M (Framingham,Ma) & Patricia Galvis (Framingham,Ma), 13 Mar 1965
CASHMAN: Michael J, Jr (Kingston) & Wretha P Gee (Amesbury,Ma), 20 Mar 1988
CASIELLO: Albert P(Somerville,Ma) & Mary E Stanzione (Somerville,Ma), 24 Jul 1961
  (Albert Casiello/ Angelina DeRosa)(John Stanzione/ Edna McKenna)
CASTRICONE: Joseph (Kingston) & Judith Gillis (Salem), 09 Jul 1958
  (Antonio Castricane/ Domenica DePrima)(Clayton Gillis/ Ariel Gillis)
CATES: Wayne (Salisbury,Ma) & Lenore S Keir (Kingston), 21 Nov 1971 (N)
CAVARIC: Frank L (24) & Elsie E Beckman (29), 23 Jul 1941 (E)
  (Frank Cavaric/Mattie D Dutton)(George Beckman/Ada Wilbur)
CAVARIE: Frank (Cambridge,Ma/33) & Mattie C Dutton (Deerfield/27), 12 Jul 1916
  (John Cavarie/Josephine Blaskovac)(Frank Dutton/Priscilla Mills)

CAYER: Richard (Kingston) & Carrie E Carr (Kingston), 20 Jan 1977
CECCHINI: Maurice G (Washington,D.C.) & Judith D Conant (Kingston), 17 Jan 1960
    (Nicola Cecchini/ Philomona ....)(Gardner H Conant/ Christine M Duston)
CELESTE: Salvatore A (Boston,Ma) & Marilyn E Staratt (Saugus,Ma), 16 Jul 1954
    (Rosario Celeste/ Anna Nocilla)(William Staratt/ Elsa Stockinger)
CETLIN: David (Russia/29) & Eva Goldsteine (Cambridge,Ma/23), 22 May 1932
    (Charles Cetlin/ Marie Gellerman)(Jacob Goldstein/ Ethel Shruba)
CHABOT: David A (Kingston) & Lora L Callorda (Alexandria,Va), 29 Jul 1989
CHAMBERLAIN: Alfred R, Jr (Brentwood) & Cheryl P Waitt (Kingston), 17 Jul 1962
   Beverly (Kingston/25) & Mary S Rowell (Kingston/22), 17 Mar 1928
    (Harry Chamberlain/Maud Hoyt)(E Chase Rowell/ Agnes Sargent) (D/O)
   Harry (Strafford/22) & Maud B Hoyt (Peabody,Ma/20), m 03 Feb 1901*
    (Charles Chamberlain/ Abbie Fifield)(John Hoyt/Nancy H Strout) (* Peabody,Ma)
   James E (Kingston/36) & Doris M Smith (Kingston/24), 02 Jun 1929   (R)
    (John Furlong/Abbie Fifield)(Fred A Smith/ Bessie A Kelley)
   Sterling (E Kingston) & Florence B Thomas (Kingston), 17 Sep 1961
CHAMPION: Donald R, Jr (Kingston) & Samantha Chamberlain (Kingston), 12 May 1990
   James M (Kingston) & Cathaleen A Farrar (Kingston), 22 Oct 1988
CHAMPNEY: Louis C (21) & Arlene V Sweeney (18), 26 Dec 1937
    (Amede Champney/ Mary A Hoey)(Raymond Sweeney/ Helen Haley)
CHAPMAN: Donald M (Exeter) & Debra L Roberts (Kingston), 15 Sep 1980
   Marshall R (Atkinson) & Corinne A Ivas (Kingston), 10 Nov 1973 (N)
   Stanley R (Bradford,Ma) & Carole J Verombeck (Kingston), 21 Apr 1953
    (Marshall Chapman)(Stephen Verombeck/ Shirley Parker)
CHAPUT: Charles D (Haverhill,Ma) & Marilyn W Barthelmess (Haverhill,Ma), 24 Feb 1984
CHARLESTON: William H (Hampton) & Sheryl L Short (Kingston), 07 May 1976
CHASE: David D (Kingston) & Charlotte E Smith (Kingston), 12 Sep 1959
    (David D Chase/ Jane Thompson)(Charles N Jasper/ Ethel M Hartford)
   Daniel, Jr (Kingston) & Debra L Kinney (Kingston), 06 Jun 1981
   Frank W (Haverhill,Ma/23) & Agnes George (Kingston/19), 15 Jun 1946 (D)
    (David D Chase/Jane Thompson)(Walter George/Inez Tewksbury)
   Frank W, Jr (Kingston) & Patricia E Davies (Fremont), 17 Jun 1972 (F)
   Howard (Newton/29) & Stella M Carter (Newton/26), 16 Aug 1909 (N)
    (Amos C Chase/Emily Belden)(Charles N Carter/Emma A Carter)
   Jesse W (Kingston) & Alma B Janvin (Kingston), 23 Sep 1976
   Paul G, Jr (Kingston/20) & Florence V Goodwin (Amesbury,Ma/18), 03 Jul 1949
    (Paul G Chase/Bernice L Lamb)(William L Goodwin/Della A Haley) (P)
   Richard I (Danville) & Catherine Clark (Kingston), 11 Oct 1986
   Timothy L (Kingston) & Cynthia M Bowley (Newton),14 Feb 1975
CHAU: Vi Tri (Lawrence,Ma) & Minh Que Pho (Lawrence,Ma), 26 May 1984
CHAUSSE: Donald R (Kingston) & Emma L Coffey (Kingston), 23 Dec 1967 (Ken)
CHENELLE: Ronald L (Lawrence,Ma) & Nancy A Crossen (Lawrence,Ma), 08 Sep 1984
CHENEY: Albert E (Kingston/18) & Edna MacDonald (Newton/19), 07 Aug 1932
    (David D Cheney/Gladys Lougee)(William MacDonald/Ann Judson)
   Arthur G (Concord) & Patricia A Brooks (Kingston), 26 Dec 1970 (P)

David (E Kingston/22) & Gladys E Lougee (Meredith/14), 29 Mar 1914 (EK)
  (Edward B Cheney/Nancy R Strout)(Albert E Lougee/Stella M White)
David (Kingston/36) & Christine S Beach (Nova Scotia/29), 20 May 1928 (R)
  (Edward Cheney/Nancy Strout)(Alonzo Furber/Annie ....)
George L (50) & Bertha W (Graham) Gale (43), 01 May 1938 (Pittsfield)
  (George W Cheney/ Carrie Noyes)(Angus N Wilbur/ Sarah E Sheifelt)
Lawrence (WKingston/21) & Celia A Farnsworth (Waltham,Ma/24),18 Mar 1946
  (Roland Cheney/Ellen Bliss)(Fred Farnsworth/Lydia Willey)   (D)
CHENG: Beato T (Lowell, Ma) & Radhika E Lewin (Lowell, Ma), 03 Aug 1990
CHESTNUT: Vincent P (Tisbury,Ma) & Betty-Ann Wright (Tisbury,Ma), 17 Apr 1993
CHEVALIER: Joseph O, Jr (Dracut,Ma) & Rhoda L Carney (Tewksbury,Ma), 07 Jun 1986
CHEVELIER: Scot E (Kingston) & Susan D St Laurent (Kingston), 25 Mar 1989
CHETWYND: Elton R (Portland,Me) & Dorothy I Hyson (Boston,Ma), 04 Feb 1950
  (Malcolm Chetwynd/Lottie Tarr)(Raymond E Hyson/Gladys I Washburn)
CHILDS: Kenneth (Kingston) & Georgette Panagiotopolos (Manchester), 06 Aug 1955 (M)
  (Ray H Childs/ Madeleine Stevens)(Alfred Bergeron/ Mary M Book)
CHRISTIE: Andrew, Jr (Haverhill,Ma) & Carol A Ball (Norwalk,Ct), 26 Feb 1969
  (Honolulu, HI)
CHRISTENSON: Carol J (Medford, Ma) & Marion A Severie (Woburn,Ma), 02 Sep 1962
  Thomas W (Medford,Ma) & Ann Marie Jordan (Medford,Ma), 14 Jun 1962
CHRISTOPHER: Anastes (Haverhill, Ma) & Donna J Chase (Kingston), 11 Mar 1972 (P)
CIARFELLA: Vincent (Wakefield,Ma) & Edith C Ludia (Medford,Ma), 01 Feb 1958
  (Lewis Ciarfella/ Rose Callana)
CICATELLI: Louis J (Revere,Ma) & Jean A Cicatelli (RevereMa), 16 Aug 1959
  (Lorenzo Citatelli/ Eliza Mancini)(Louis Gariety/ Alice Streeter)
CICCARRELLO: Frank X (Kingston) & Janice M Budrewicz (Atkinson), 01 Oct 1978 (A)
CICHON: Anthony (Dorchester,Ma) & Eva Paszkowskai (So Boston,Ma), 29 Apr 1963
CILLEY: Laburton G (Kingston/24) & Marcia Peterson (Columbia Falls,Me/21), 24 Jun 1905
  (Clarence E Cilley/Annie L Towle)(Benjamin Peterson/Margaret Tupper)
CLAPP: Robert E (Revere,Ma) & Laura L Lutz (Kingston), 17 Sep 1983
CLARK: Alan T (Rochester) & Juanita C Holt (Kingston), 02 Sep 1972
  Edward B (Kingston/33) & Eunice Lanagan (Salem/21), 22 Sep 1924 (S)
    (Walter S Clark/Abbie Sanborn)(Daniel A Lanagan/Ethelyn M Bailey)
  Eugene S (Kingston/27) & Louise E Marshall (Manchester/27), 02 Jun 1945 (M)
    (Henry H Clark/Emily Healey)(Harlan Marshall/Martha Eriman)
  Gerald B (22) & Elinor Wells (18), 29 Nov 1936
    (George Clark/Emily May Baxter)(John Wells/Esther Butler)
  Harry S (Kingston/33) & Emma L Druger (Exeter/35), 15 Dec 1920 (E)
    (Walter S Clark/ Abbie A Sanborn) (Herman L Kruger/ Amelia O'Raska)
  Harry S (Kingston/59) & Lucille Gove Hobbs (Hampton/50), 15 Jun 1947 (H)
    (Walter S Clark/Abbie A Sanborn)(Cyrus A Gove/Minnie D Smith)
  James P (Stoughton,Ma) & Mildred S Carbral (Stoughton,Ma), 17 Feb 1959
    (Paul Clark/ Francis Reddy)(George Fowler/ Eveline Holmes)
  John W (Kingston/23) & Dorothy S Towne (Kingston/19), 01 Nov1920
    (Simeon P Clark/ Mary E Fellows)(Evero W Towne/ Ellen F Dockam)

Peter A (Pittsfield,Ma/60) & Elizabeth Webster (Boston,Ma/36), 06 Jun 1927
　　(M.F.Clark)　　(Frederick Briggs)
Robert (Lynn,Ma) & Caroline G Alexander (Lynn,Ma), 25 Mar 1960
　　(Robert A Clark/ Mildred M Johnson)(George E Batchelder/ Thelma Alexander)
Russell J (Hampstead) & Nancy M Sammartano (Kingston), 04 Sep 1993
Walter S (Kingston) & Joan L Bodwell (Kensington), 27 May 1951 (Ken)
　　(Ernest D Clark/Evelyn Morris)(Harold W Bodwell/Dorothy C Turner)
Walter S, Jr (Kingston) & Donna M Hilton (Newton), 14 Jan 1972 (N)
CLARKE: Thomas A(Haverhill,Ma) & Emma W Sirrell (Haverhill,Ma), 19 Sep 1953
　　(James Clarke/Rose A Garmache)(Harry Wyman/ Emma C Heseltine)
CLARKSON: Thomas H (Haverhill,Ma) & Eileen A Comeau (Kingston), 01 Oct 1971 (N)
CLEARY: Curtis A (Kingston) & Sarah E Marden (Newton), 29 Oct 1980
CLEMENT: Arlan T (Kingston) & Amelia J Hudson (Andover,Ma), 22 Feb 1970
　　Cecil A (20) & Alice Milbury (18), 08 Dec 1934
　　(Walter J Clement/Emma J Dorr)(William Milbury/Edith Murdock)
David R (Kingston) & Linda A Richards (Newton), 21 May 1977
Ferris R (Revere,Ma/21) & Geneva B Goodwin (Kingston/21), 10 Oct 1925
　　(Robert R Clements/Jennie Little)(John D Goodwin/Myrtle Taylor)
Robert J (Raymond) & Carlene A Lennon (Kingston), 19 Nov 1988
Ronald T, Sr (Methuen, Ma) & Debra L Owens (Kingston), 08 Sep 1992
CLINE: Norman A (28) & Frances E Braley (23), 24 Jul 1937 (F)
　　(William F Cline/ Ethel Genet)(Gaston Braley/ Ella Whittier)
CLOUGH: Ralph H (Auburndale,Ma) & Irene A Luccardi (Auburndale,Ma), 19 Jul 1957
　　(Ralph H Clough/ Dorothy F Holt)(Frank DiBlasio/ Marguerite DiProfio)
CLOW: John G (Wolfeboro/21) & Wealthea Nason (Wolefboro/20), 25 Jun 1949(Wolfeboro)
　　(J Roscoe Clow/Ruby Farnham)(Lester F Nason/Anna Peck)
COFFEY: Thomas J, Jr (Andover,Ma) & Nancy L Gallant (Andover,Ma), 29 Aug 1987
COFFMAN: Bruce L (Kingston) & Donna L Mainville (Kingston), 02 May 1987
COHEN: Stephen E (Dorchester,Ma) & Jeanne M Zagami (Dorchester,Ma), 23 Aug 1987
COITO: John J (Newton) & Virginia Mae Fuller (Kingston), 08 Nov 1975　　(P)
COLBROTH: Preston (Ludlow,Me/24) & Helen E Dudley (Amesbury,Ma/20),02 Jul 1933(H)
　　(Charles N Colbroth/Nettie McLaughlin)(James Dudley/Nellie May Stevens)
COLCORD: Edward D (Wakefield,Ma) & Marilyn R Wilkins (Malden,Ma), 12 May 1968
　　Frank E (Exeter/38) & Luella Thompson (Newton/29), 05 Jan 1901
　　(William H Colcord/Frances E Pike)(Dustin Thompson/Sarah Goodwin)
COLE: Frank W (Raymond) & Vivian F Collins (Kingston), 22 Feb 1960 (R)
　　(Frank H Cole/ Bertha I Salo)(Leon E Collins/ Josephine L Hutchins)
Wayne A (Newburyport,Ma) & Helen M Bartley (Newburyport,Ma), 14 Jan 1966
COLLINET: Harold F, Jr (Chicago, Il & Susan E Caverly (Beverly,Ma), 05 Oct 1962
COLLINS: Brian D (Kingston) & Theresa I Duerr (Fremont), 28 May 1977　　(F)
Clarence E (Kingston/21) & Lois Abbie Roycroft (Boxford,Ma/17), 05 Jun 1918 (H)
　　(Elmer Collins/Susan Mason)(James A Roycroft/Nellie A Rokes)
Eugene F (Haverhill,Ma) & Rose Eddy (Haverhill,Ma), 10 Oct 1952
　　(Edson F Collins/ Susan F Seaver)(Anthony LaBounty/ Rose LeBlance)

James S (Salem,Ma/25) & Mildred J Hilliard (Kingston/25), 11 Jan 1917
    (James Collins & Ellen Milner)(William Hilliard/Flora E Jewell)
Larry M (Kingston) & Elizabeth A Simano (Chester), 05 May 1962 (Raymond)
Leon E, Jr (Kingston) & Joan A Guimond (Brentwood), 30 Apr 1950   (D)
    (Leon Collins/Josephine L Hutchins)(Arthur Guimond/Virginia Palmer)
Leon Earl, III (Kingston) & Corinne A Daniels (Newton), 24 Jan 1976   (N)
Merville S (Kingston) & Gloria L Herrick (Danville), 01 Dec 1956 (D)
    (Leon E Collins,Sr/Josephine L Hutchins)(Melvin R Merrick/ Gertrude Demaine)
Oral W (Kingston/24) & Daisy N Jasper (Kingston/16), 26 Jul 1924
    (Elmer A Collins/Susie Nason)(Charles N Jasper/Ethel M Hartford)
Oral W (Kingston/ 20) & Catherine M Taajes (Danville/ 20), 16 Jun 1920 (N/D)
    (Elma A Collins/ Susan Nason)(Nicholas E Taajis/ Emma Bausema)
Oral W, Jr (Kingston/20) & Verna M Middleton (Kingston/18), 14 Jun 1947
    (Oral Collins,Sr/Daisy N Jasper)(Arthur J Middleton/Laura Clements)
Perley S (56) & Leila G James (30), 21 Aug 1936   (Ports)
    (Joel S Collins/Ella F Averill)(Leslie G James/Sadie E Dudley)
Quinton R (Kingston) & Dorothy M LeClair (Epping), 07 Aug 1953   (F)
    (Leon E Collins/ Josephine L Hutchins)(Wilfred S LeClair/ Florence A Bagley)
Quinton R (Kingston) & Ernestine A Brown (Fremont), 22 Feb 1958
    (Leon E Collins,Sr/Josephine L Hutchins)(Ernest J LeClair/ Mary E Bailey)
Vernon H, (Kingston) & Grace M Hilberg (Raymond), 07 Aug 1965 (R)
William N (Kingston/28) & Minnie E Hoyt (Merrimac,Ma/26), 02 Feb 1909
    (Norris D Collins/Emma J Stevens)(George F Carter/Mary E Webster)
COMEAU: Gregory J (Plaistow) & Cynthia J Ward (Kingston), 17 Jun 1978
    Norman A (Kingston) & Patricia A Bennett (Kingston), 20 Jul 1968 (N)
    Robert N (Haverhill, Ma) & Deborah L Banks (Haverhill, Ma), 27 Oct 1990
COMTOIS: George A (Hampstead) & Martha B Barnes (Kingston), 05 Jul 1959 (H)
    (Gerard Comtois/ Pauline Ricker)(John A Barnes/ Priscilla Estes)
CONANT: Charles B (Buckfield,Me/25) & Marion S Clark (Kingston/25), 23 Jun 1909
    (Hiram A Conant/Flora A Atkins)(Walter S Clark/Abbie Sanborn)
    David G (Kingston) & Patricia Fennell (Blun,Ga), 26 Jun 1955
    (Gardner H Conant/ Christine Dustin)(James C Fennell,Sr/Elena McKenzie)
    Gardner H (19) & Christine M Dustin (19), 15 Apr 1934   (P)
    (Charles B Conant/ Marion S Clark)(John M Dustin/ Maude B Parker)
    Kevin A (Kingston) & Lori A Colter (Kingston), 03 Jun 1988
CONNELLY: Bartley (So Hampton) & Lucille Johnson (Kingston), 02 Nov 1962
CONNER: Lewis I, II (Kingston) & Christine M Webb (Kingston), 07 Apr 1989
CONSTANTINO: John, Jr (Haverhill,Ma/25) & Dorothy Jasper (Kingston/23), 16 Apr 1947 (F)
    (John Consentino/Nora Sarro)(Charles Jasper/Ethel Hartford)
    Philip V (Atkinson) & Joanne M Walsh (Kingston), 26 Jun 1965 (P)
CONTE: Darryl (Kingston) & Brenda C Lambert (Kingston), 02 May 1969 (N)
COOK: Charles A (Kingston) & Rose A Collette (Kingston), 07 Oct 1989
    Donald E (Kingston) & Donna N O'Connor (Amesbury,Ma), 10 Jul 1975 (N)
COOLEY: Rodney D(Haverhill,Ma) & Jo-Ann S Sullivan (Haverhill,Ma), 08 Aug 1987
COOMBS: Oward R (Kingston) & Sheila A Small (Kingston), 19 Sep 1986

COPPOLA: Joseph E (Kingston) & Mary A Saunders (Kingston), 17 Jul 1976
CORLISS: Lawrence M, Jr (Kingston) & Christine M Miller (Homburg,W Ger), 16 Jan 1982
    Lawrence M, Jr (Kingston) & Petra A Otte (Iveshiem,Ger), 26 Oct 1986
CORMIER: Robert R (Beverly,Ma) & Gail L McRae (Beverly,Ma), 16 Aug 1970
CORNELL: Donald E (Saugus,Ma) & Lucille A Gauthier (Salem,Ma), 18 Aug 1955
    (Edgar P Cornell/ Katherine Kishton)(Alfred Gauthier/ Rose E Houle)
CORNFORTH: Charles R (Wollaston,Ma) & Norma P Clayton (Wakefield,Ma), 25 Jun 1952
    (George Cornforth/ Mabel Luce)(Earton Goodwin/ Mary Munroe)
CORNISH Daniel W (Georgetown,Ma) & Pamela Van Buskirk (Georgetown,Ma),23 Sep 1989
    Glen B, Jr (Kingston) & Joyce A Evans (Brentwood), 31 Oct 1954
    (Glen B Cornish,Sr/Elmira Dostie)(John C Evans/ Clarice Prescott)
CORSAULT: Howard C (Kingston) & Karen M Gentile (Kingston), 29 Sep 1985
CORSER, Karl W, Jr (Concord) & Janet E Kemp (Kingston), 26 Dec 1951 (E)
    (Karl W Corser/Selma Turnquist)(George A Kemp/Josephine Rogers)
COSGROVE: Robert I (Brockton,Ma) & Beverly A Madan(Brockton,Ma), 17 May 1958
    (Francis P Cosgrove/ Lillian Johnson)(Harold Madan/ Lorraine Sharpe)
COSTA: Everett (Kingston) & Sandra R Ireland (Hampton), 31 Aug 1974
    Scott M (Kingston) & Mary P Dupont (Kingston), 14 Apr 1989
COSTELLO: Matthew T (Kingston) & Margaret J Cahill (Haverhill,Ma), 21 Aug 1993
COTE: Edward C (Haverhill,Ma) & Linda M Cote (Haverhill,Ma), 24 Jun 1968
    Paul G (Kingston) & Sheree-Lee Guerrin (Holyoke,Ma), 16 May 1981
COTTON: Keith A (Groveland,Ma) & Kimberly H Snow (Groveland,Ma), 23 Jan 1987
COUILLARD: Norman L (Methuen,Ma) & Susan J Brunette (Methuen,Ma), 29 Aug 1986
COURT: Ronald J (Kingston) & Lee R Galante (Kingston),04 Jun 1994
COVEY (Cookson): George E (Methuen,Ma/23) & Blanche A Robinson (Kingston/19),*
    (Joseph Cookson/Maria Currier)(Charles W Robinson/Louisa M Smith) *23 Oct 1907
COX: Roland O (Kingston) & Roseann Hodgdon (Kingston), 29 Jan 1977
CRAFTS: Clifford E (Kingston) & Dorothy M Sargent (Kingston), 21 May 1971 (E)
    Robert L (Kingston) & Gloria J Drury (Kingston), 19 Aug 1973 (Seabrook)
CRAMER: Lance E (Kingston) & Lisa K Madland (Kingston), 26 Jul 1983
CRESSEY: Daniel G (Westboro,Ma) & Bernice B Whalen (Westboro,Ma), 02 Aug 1962
CRETAROLO: Aldo (Haverhill,Ma) & Geraldine G Brown (Haverhill,Ma), 27 Sep 1952
    (Alexander Cretarolo/ Angelina Spero)(Edwin A Brown/ Mary Cavanaugh)
CROCKER: Bruce E (Wilmington,Ma) & Rita B Clark (Wilmington,Ma), 16 Sep 1989
CROCKETT: John D, III (Kingston) & Lisa E Wildes (Hampton Beach), 13 Dec 1991
CROSS: David A (Kingston) & Jean M Crites (Kingston), 25 Aug 1984
    Lawrence R (Kingston) & Nancy F Hancock (Concord), 18 Jun 1960 (Concord)
    (Cecil Cross/ Ruth Winslow)(William Hancock/ Florence Gaudreau)
CROVETTI: Neil (Seabrook) & Jody L Streeter (Kingston), 27 Jan 1968 (N)
CROWE: Frank L (Kingston) & Susan P Hubbell (Atkinson), 22 May 1992
CROWELL: Albert O, Jr (Raymond) & Phyllis L Whitney (Kingston), 14 Oct 1951
    (Albert O Crowell/Annie E Card)(Louis B Whitney/Elizabeth B Nason)
    Gregg D (Derry) & Phyllis P Wilder (Kingston), 19 Nov 1983
    Kenneth G (Kingston) & Angela F Philbrick (Kingston), 04 Apr 1992
    Martin E (Kingston) & Diane C Largay (Kingston), 28 Dec 1963 (W)

Robert A (Randolph, Ma) & Jean M Macy (Randolph, Ma), 17 Apr 1972
CROWLEY: Joseph P (Somerville,Ma) & Carol M Solari (Chelsea,Ma), 23 Jun 1960
(Jerome Crowley/ Helen A Long)(John P Solari/ Genevieve L Marusa)
CROZIER: William J (Dublin,Ire/37) & Mary Norfolk (Kingston/36), 13 Jun 1902
(John Crozier/Mary Broe)(William L Norfolk/Christina Galloupe)
CULLANINE: Edmond M (Haverhill,Ma) & Gloria A Bucigalupo(W Newbury,Ma), *
(Timothy Cullanine/ Greta Hudson)(Charles James/ Annie Chase) *09 Oct 1954
CUMMINGS: David J (Haverhill,Ma) & Janet A Nerney (Lawrence,Ma),18 Sep 1981
Kenneth S, Jr (Kingston) & Nancy A Torrey (Newton), 12 Sep 1981
Wilfred G (Woburn,Ma) & Ruth A Harding (So Braintree,Ma), 01 Jan 1957
(Charles A Cumings/ Rae M Mitchell)(George Lentz/ Annie M McKechnie)
Wilfred G (Hyannis,Ma)& Florence E Morrison (Yarmouth,Ma), 25 Sep 1965
CUNNINGHAM: Patrick T (Kingston) & Jeannine M Randall (Kingston), 30 Jul 1994
CURRIER: Dennis N (Kingston) & Pamela Gould (Kingston), 29 Aug 1968
Dennis B (Kingston) & Lynda A Cyr (Ontario,Can), 23 May 1982
Fred S (Haverhill,Ma) & Mary E Huntoon (Haverhill,Ma), 10 Dec 1958
(John B Currier/ Eva M Mae)(Justin C Ballou/Charlotte L Sullivan)
Richard P, Jr (Kingston) & Jane E Small (Brentwood), 18 Dec 1954 (Concord)
(Richard P Currier,Sr/Eleanor Tozier)(Stanley G Small/ Muriel E Bryant)
CURTIS: Allen A (Brockton,Ma) & Nancy K Kelleher (Holbrook,Ma), 02 May 1959
(Albert Curtis/ Alice Nittell)(Paul E Kelleher/ Laura S McLaughlin)
CUTTER: James R (Salisbury,Ma) & Mildred M Meinerth(Kingston), 31 Jan 1981
Joseph H (Quincy,Ma) & Ann R Harding (Quincy,Ma), 19 Sep 1951
(Joseph H Cutter/Jennie Gerstel)(Millard S Harding/Ruth Lentz)
DAGGETT: Wayne E (Kingston) & Joyce A Wright (Haverhill,Ma), 26 Oct 1974 (P)
D'AMELIO: Ralph P (Kingston) & Terry A Hayward (Kingston), 02 May 1986
D'AMORE: John A (Haverhill,Ma) & Linda M Tersigni (Kingston), 17 Jun 1989
D'ANGELO: Sabatino (Melrose,Ma) & Doris M Hagen (Melrose,Ma), 16 Oct 1956
(John F Spencer/ Margaret Lockland)(Samuel Meuse/ Amelia Meuse)
DAIGLE: Edward R (Kingston) & Dawn B Lefebvre (Haverhill,Ma), 13 Sep 1981
DALY: Arthur F (Malden,Ma) & Helga Tomaschko (Malden,Ma), 14 Jan 1965
DAME: Kenneth H (Kingston) & Joanne L Murley (Fremont), 10 Nov 1973   (F)
William D (Fremont) & Nancy Lee Friend (Kingston), 24 Mar 1973
DANEAU: Joseph W, Jr (Amesbury,Ma) & Lynn B Tocci (Amesbury,Ma), 25 Oct 1986
DANFORTH: Ronald L (Plaistow) & Barbara R Carlton (Kingston), 25 Aug 1962 (P)
DANIELS: Arthur R (41) & Helen M Chase (26), 12 May 1938
(Edward A Daniels/ Alice Fraser)(Thurston S Chase/ Annie Jackson)
DANIELSON: Leland G (Salisbury,Ma) & Nancy L Dobson (Salisbury,Ma), 06 Dec 1963
DAOUST: Richard G (Kingston) & Margaret E Farley (Haverhill,Ma), 24 Oct 1964 (W)
DARCY: John J (Kingston) & Linda C Crummett (Newton), 26 Aug 1967 (N)
DARLING: George S (Kingston) & Joan B Tremblay (E Kingston), 18 Dec 1965
William L (Kingston) & Susan A Burnham (Kingston), 10 Nov 1984
William L (Kingston) & Linda L Libby (Plaistow), 23 Jun 1962
DAVEY: Charles (Kingston) & Judith A Brown (Kingston), 21 Sep 1963 (E)
DAVID: Brian E (Danville) & Adrienne M Byron (Kingston), 07 Jun 1992

DAVIDSON: Wallace L (Cambridge,Ma/37) & Ivy R Turner (England/27), 01 Sep 1929
(Henry Davidson/Amelia L Banks)(Arthur Turner/Olivia Heyworth)
DAVIS: Albert H (Durham/29) & Addie L Jones (Nottingham/21), 17 Sep 1900 (D/O)
(Levi Davis/Ludy A Bassett)(David Jones)
Charles E (Salem,Ma/21) & Sadie E Mason (Boston,Ma/19), 23 Aug 1923
(Emerson Davis/Mirah Huckins)(Catherine Mason)
Edward R (E Kingston/34) & Marguerite A Tuttle (Peru,Me/21), 28 Dec 1904
(Richard H Davis/Harriet Stacy)(Luther M Tuttle /Amelia C Fiske)
Frank E (Kingston) & Mary G Hawkes (Wakefield,Ma), 27 Aug 1958
(Arthur C Davis/ Ida W Fredrickson)(Ernest C Hawkes/ Laura B Smith)
Glenn W (Haverhill,Ma) & Mary J Brodie (Lawrence,Ma), 27 Sep 1969
Paul F, II (Kingston) & Kyongson K Wilkes (Kingston), 27 Mar 1981
Robert W (No Andover,Ma) & Mary E Clohecy (Haverhill,Ma), 18 Nov 1956
(Freeman J Davis/ Gertrude Werk)(William Clohecy/ Celana St Lawrence)
Ronald B (Kingston) & Natalie H Keeley (Kingston), 18 Sep 1982
Steven E (Ft Lauderdale,Fl) &Myrna J D'Entremont (Ft Lauderdale), 04 Jan 1978
DAY: Carlton H (Kingston) & Joyce E Myotte (Kingston), 20 Jun 1964 (E)
Shawn P (Boston,Ma) & Jodi L Kenney (Boston,Ma), 02 Jan 1993
DEARBORN: Stephen C (Kingston) & Christine M Holmes (Kingston), 30 Jul 1994
DEBURRA: Harry A (Methuen,Ma) & Anna H Lessard (Haverhill,Ma), 30 Nov 1970
DECAREAU: Mark D (Kingston) & Heather A Biladeau (Brentwood), 18 Jul 1981
Michael E (Kingston) & Elaine M Becotte (Kingston), 22 Jun 1974 (N)
DECATUR: Edwin F, Jr (Kingston) & Estelle M Bailey (Hampton Falls), 15 Apr 1972 (E)
DeCELLE: Robert A (Haverhill,Ma) & Carole A Magri (Salisbury,Ma), 28 Jun 1986
DeFURIA: Dana R (Medford, Ma) & Julie A Josephson (Gloucester, Ma), 31 Dec 1991
DEGNAN: John F (Malden,Ma) & Marilyn J Fisher (Malden,Ma), 10 Oct 1952
(Joseph P Degnan/ Ramona A Cruso)(Robert F Fisher/ Pauline Harper)
DeGROAT: Clyde L (Kingston) & Linda J Sites (Kingston), 02 Oct 1971 (EK)
DELP: Ronald W (Danvers,Ma) & Betty A Ragon (Danvers,Ma), 03 Aug 1970
Ronald W (Danvers,Ma) & Betty A Ragon (Danvers,Ma), 14 Jan 1961
(Joseph W Delp/ Dorothy Clark)(Leroy W Ragon/ Mildred E Eaton)
DeLUCA: Salvatore (Danvers,Ma) & Margaret Miller (Danvers,Ma), 06 Jul 1958
(Dominick DeLuca/ Anna Pirrotta)(Carl W Miller/ Bernice Wing)
DEMAINE: Stanley K (Danville) & Shelley A Hughes (Kingston), 27 Nov 1976
DEMAND: Francis T (Newburyport,Ma) & Viola H Thomas (Newburyport,Ma),17 Apr 1959
(George Demand/ Ruth Driscoll)(Chester Thomas/ Sadie Mason)
DEMARAIS: Leo G (Kingston) & Inez M Gray (Haverhill,Ma), 15 Jun 1951 (Hav)
Leo V Demarais/Isabel Sheldon)(Daniel A Gray/Caroline A Wort)
DEMERS: Carl G (Kingston) & Sandra P Perkins (Newton), 27 Aug 1960 (N)
(Charles A Demers/ Irma Donaldson)(Philip A Perkins/ Carrie B Chase)
DEMETIE: Theodore (45) & Frances L Adams (25), 25 Sep 1938
(Govan Demetie/Catherine Stavio)(Charles W Adams/Alta E Edwards)
DEMPSKI: Dennis W (Haverhill,Ma) & Linda M Caillouette (Kingston), 27 Sep 1969 (N)
DENNIS: Richard E (Haverhill,Ma) & Dorothy E Gormley (Haverhill,Ma), 09 Sep 1952
(Charles A Dennis/ Melvina Deceau)(John H Lovering/ Emma E Coombs)

DENOMME: Robert A (Kingston) & Suzanne H Sloan (Kingston), 01 Jan 1981
DENTON: Joshua W (59) & Emma J Caldwell (31), 20 Jun 1938
    (Joshua Denton/Eliza Lowcock)(Morand H Caldwell/Emma Fernandez)
DePALMA: Antonio (Agawam,Ma) & Geneva Dansereau (Agawam,Ma), 06 Nov 1964
DePETRILLO: Paul R, Jr (Kingston) & Kathleen A Winn (Kingston), 20 May 1989
DEPROFINO: Daniel J (Kingston) & Leisa J Jillson (Plaistow), 23 Jun 1984
DeROCHMONT: Ernest (Kingston/40) & Ethel M King (Kingston/26), 19 Sep 1914
    (David De Rochmont/Elizabeth A Gale)(Charles A King/Celia I Johnson)
DERRAH: Edward H (74) & Alice S Dyson (73), 06 Sep 1941 (D)
    (Alexander Derrah/Sarah E Hadley)(Crosley Heyworth/Rachel Coupe)
DERUSHA: Craig M (Oregon City, Or) & Deborah E Brown (Oregon City,Or), 13 Nov 1993
DESCHENES: Brian J (Kingston) & Courtney L Gray (Kingston), 01 Aug 1992
DESILETS: Norman C (Raymond) & Phyllis E Atwood (Kingston),19 Apr 1963
DESMARAIS: Rusty L (Kingston) & Melodie L Emery (Fremont), 17 Jul 1976
DE SOTO: Charles J (Tyler,Tx) & Jeannette M Taylor (Lynn,Ma),13 Jan 1962
DeSTEFANO: John R (Tewksbury,Ma) & Diane M Ryan (Tewksbury,Ma), 08 Sep 1985
DESROSIERS: Robert E (Nashua) & Patricia A Griffin (Kingston), 24 Mar 1973 (Windham)
DEVINE: John K (Hampstead) & Elaine J Bucci (Kingston), 06 Jun 1987
DEVLIN: Frank E, II (Atkinson) & Donna J Durgin (Kingston), 20 Oct 1973 (N)
    Richard E,Jr (Kingston) & Christina S Lydiard (Kingston), 17 Sep 1994
DEVOST: David P (Kingston) & Lynda C Senter (Kingston), 03 Mar 1973
DURGIN: Stephen B (Kingston) & Patricia Y Field (Kingston), 21 Jan 1994
DEWHURST: Albert (43) & Emma Williams (41), 04 Mar 1941 (P)
    (Albert Dewhurst/ Jennie R Welch)(.... Williams/Alice Booker)
DIAMOND: Marvin (Kingston) & Nancy E Donahue (Kingston), 06 Dec 1981
DIAS: Anthony C, Jr (Kingston) & Karen L Dias (Kingston), 05 Jul 1983
    Keith A (Kingston) & Lisa A Lavallee (Wells,Me), 14 Mar 1987
    Robert (Kingston) & Miranda Budzinski (Kingston), 25 Oct 1986
DIBIASE: Giulio U (Everett,Ma) & Linda M Constantino (Norwood,Ma), 28 Sep 1977
DiCHIARA: Francis J, Jr (Kingston) & Michele L Brown (Laconia), 07 Oct 1972(Laconia)
DIEMAND: Daniel J (Brookline, Ma) & Lori A Buswell (Brookline, Ma), 08 Sep 1990
DIGIOSIO: Robert B (West Mifflin, Pa) & Paula J Mascioli (Kingston), 13 Oct 1990
DINGLEY: Donald L (Auburn,Ma) & Marion S (Clark) Conant, 08 Jun 1952   (D)
    (Samuel Dingley/ Mary T Layton)(Walter S Clark/ Abbie A Sanborn)
DINTRUFF: Richard P (Rochester,NY) & Margaret A Black (No Andover,Ma), 12 May 1951
    (Carl P Dintruff/Madeline LaBarr)(Henry Black/Thomasina Duncanson)
DION: Joseph G (Andover,Ma) & Sally A Webster (Andover,Ma), 23 Nov 1984
DIONNE: Bruce A (Epping) & Neola A Mahon (Kingston), 10 Feb 1968
DI NITTO: Alfred (22) & Antonetta Aurelio (18), 16 May 1942
    (Cosmo DiNitto/ Furtunato Russo)(Bonifacio Aurelio/ Christiana Damico)
DI PIETRO: John A (Beverly,Ma) & Barbara J Mason (Jamaica Plains,Ma), 05 Apr 1963
DOANE: Ernest R (Lynn,Ma) & Patricia Bland (Nahant,Ma), 24 Jul 1966
DOD: William T (Kingston) & Sandra L Johnson (Kingston), 13 Aug 1967 (P)
DOEGE: Jonathan H (Kingston) & Susan E Page (Beverly,Ma), 16 Jun 1989
DOHERTY: William R (Kingston) & Judith A Killion (Westford,Ma), 04 Sep 1977 (N)

DOIRON: Harold E, Jr (Lexington, Ma) & Kathleen A McFague (Kingston), 18 Feb 1972
DOLLIVER: Bryan R (Kingston) & Joyce A Magnusson (Kingston), 01 Nov 1977
DOMINI: Kenneth R (Haverhill,Ma) & Donna A McChesney (Kingston), 24 Jul 1968 (S)
DONAHUE: Bernard (Lawrence,Ma) & Marilyn J Cavanaugh (Lawrence,Ma), 15 Oct 1960
    (Timothy B Donahue/ Marjorie Lauzon)(William F Cuddy/ Sadie Barnett)
    Clifford R (Kingston) & Adele M Peters (Lynn,Ma), 14 Jan 1961
      (John C Donahue/ Eunice Mitchell)(Louis Amirault/ Bernice Thibodeau)
    Gary D (Kingston) & Deborah Jo Riley (Kingston), 22 Nov 1975 (N)
    Michael J (Kingston) & Theresa M Romano (Kingston), 14 Sep 1974 (N)
    Sean P (Tucson, Az) & Carol A Mauer (Tucson, Az), 18 Aug 1990
    Robert H (Tewksbury,Ma) & Mary E Cormier (W Chelmsford,Ma),04 Apr 1987
DONOVAN: Michael E (Kingston) & Carla J Kellerher (Kingston), 13 Aug 1994
DONCASTER: George F, Jr (Kingston) & Trnra C Newell (Anniston,Al), 07 Jul 1981
DOUGHERTY: Thomas H(Northwood) & Kathleen F Miller (Kingston), 24 Jan 1969 (Durham)
DOUGLAS: Kenneth F (25) & Doris Coe (21), 28 Jan 1938   (Seabrook)
    (Frank D Douglas/ Lizzie M Morse)(Harry Coe/ Florence A Pearl)
    Richard W (Epping) & Catherine B Harmon (Kingston), 04 Sep 1977
DOWNING: Mark P (Fremont) & Lynn M Boomhower (Kingston), 26 Nov 1983
DOW: Leslie E (Palermo,Me/25) & Lucy A Hasson (Alm,Me/18), 10 Jun 1900
    (Moses Dow/ Annie Evans)(Edward Hasson/Inez Thayer)
DOWLING: Michael (Kingston) & Donna M Barnard (Kingston), 31 Dec 1986
    Leverett (Kingston/32) & Laura B Packard (Haverhill,Ma/16), 25 Jun 1902
    Leverett C (Kingston/45) & Anna M Cilley (Georgetown,Ma/18), 22 Sep 1915
    (John N Downing/Ellen Clark) (Samuel L Cilley/Mary S Young)
DOWNS: James R (Kingston) & Maryanne Edwards (Kingston), 10 Oct 1970 (N)
DRAWDY: Ronald J (Kingston) & Anne D Bradstreet (Newton Jct), 13 Sep 1991
DRELICK: Anthony (Kingston) & Natalie Meyer (Hampton Falls), 25 Sep 1966 (H/F)
    Joel D (Exeter) & Karen A Fairbrother (Kingston), 05 Sep 1987
DREW: David A (Kingston) & Sandra A Gallison (Kingston), 07 Sep 1991
    Denis L (Kingston) & Christina G Frizzell (Kingston), 07 Oct 1988
    Everard (Lawrence,Ma/23) & Emma Wilkinson (Lawrence, Ma/23), 03 Sep 1910
    (Herman S Drew/ Carrie M Carr)(Charles H Wilkinson/Mary J Hancock)
DRISCOLL: John H, Jr (Lynn, Ma) & Joan D Mansfield (Lynn,Ma), 27 Aug 1988
DROHEN: Edward D (Atkinson) & Margaret R Eaton (Kingston), 27 Nov 1970 (A)
DROWNES: Richard (Haverhill,Ma/25) & Irene Grimmer (St Stephen,N.B./22), 26 Apr 1930
    (Herbert W Drownes/ Marion Maley) (Hill Grimner/ Ida Berryman)
DRURY: Alan H (Kingston) & Judy I Johnson (Fremont), 12 May 1973 (F)
    Peter J (Kingston) & Karen A Mercier (Fremont), 21 Jun 1980
DUBE: Charles A.J, Jr (Lawrence,Ma) & Rose M Scaglione (Lawrence,Ma), 11 Nov 1978
    Roland J (Kingston) & Denise R Sanborn (Kingston), 06 Jul 1990
    Thomas J (Kingston) & Janis Condran (Exeter), 19 Aug 1972   (E)
DUBOIS: Michael G (Kingston) & Winifred M Dubois (Kingston), 15 Jul 1978 (N)
DUCEY: Thomas F (39) & Ella A Lamont (43), 02 May 1937 (Boston, Ma)
    (Thomas Ducey/ Catherine Landers)(James A Lyford/ Lizzie S Goodrich)

DUCHARME: Richard E (Haverhill,Ma) & Kathleen M Wheeler (Lynn,Ma), 28 Jul 1963
DUCHEMIN: Bruce L (Kingston) & Carol M LaBarbera (Haverhill,Ma), 16 May 1970 (N)
    Michael S (Kingston) & Linda L Reilly (Kingston), 22 Jul 1978 (P)
DUDLEY: Robert M (Haverhill,Ma) & Polly Harper (Haverhill,Ma), 14 Feb 1993
DUFALT: George J (Chelsea,Ma) & Gertrude R Connelly (Chelsea, Ma), 27 May 1954
    (Alfred Dufalt/ Lena Smith)(Joseph Bennett/ Sarah Shea)
DUFFIN: Brian J (Kingston) & Lorraine A Wilder (Kingston), 24 Oct 1970 (N)
DUFOUR: David D (Kingston) & Loretta J Silvano (Medford,Ma), 03 Jul 1984
    Omar W (Haverhill,Ma/25) & Ida Brissette (Lynn,Ma/22), 21 Jun 1930 (P)
    (Wilford Dufour/ Rose Savignor)(Onesime Brissette/Monique Harvey)
DUGAN: William T (Kingston) & Frances I Faulkner (Kingston), 07 Dec 1954
    (John A Dugan/ Edna Crowley)(Frank Lemos/ Mary Walker)
DUNBAR: Charles L (Kingston) & Mary Jane L Timmons (Kingston), 24 Jul 1976 (E)
DUNDERDALE: George ,Jr (Andover, Ma) & Deborah Paone (Andover, Ma), 16 Mar 1991
DUNN: Alan M (Kingston) & Susan V Hill (Nashua), 12 Sep 1981
    Chester H (26) & Ernestine I Morse (22), 12 Sep 1940
    (William C Dunn/Mary A Cogswell)(Arthur A Morse/Bertha M Graham)
    John T (30) & Rita E Rourke (22), 29 Aug 1941
    (Thomas J Dunn/Mary McNulty)(William Rourke/Gladys Carrie)
    William R (Kingston) & Norma L MacDonald (Beverly,Ma), 26 Sep 1958
    (William L Dunn/ Ethel C Miller)(Harry L Butman/ Marjorie M White)
DURKEE: Robert A (Kingston) & Michele J Miller (New York,NY), 23 Jan 1959
    (Ralph C Durkee/ Irene Burnham)(Isador Miller/ Selma Jaffe)
DURLING: John F (Kingston) & Martha A Greaney (Kingston), 25 Jun 1977
DUQUETTE: Michael E (Haverhill,Ma) & Kathleen S Sonsava (Haverhill,Ma), 18 Nov 1968
DURGIN: David L (Kingston) & Jacqueline D Brockelbank (Kingston), 22 Feb 1973(E/K)
DUSTON: Leslie W (Hampstead/32) & Laura M Whittier (Kingston/30), 13 Jul 1947 (N/J)
    (Levi F Duston/Myrtis French)(Walter Whittier/Lulu M Collins)
DUTTON: Ralph T (Kingston) & Stephanie K Springer (Kingston), 26 Aug 1973
EASTMAN: Richard H (Kingston) & Susan L DesRoche (Atkinson), 02 Mar 1990
    Steven W (Kingston) & Donna Brandon (Haverhill,Ma), 19 Jan 1972
EATON: Alphonzo D (Kingston) & Margaret M Goodhue (Kingston), 11 Aug 1987
ECKSTEIN: Mark D (Murrells Inlet, S C) & Christine L Allfrey (Murrells Inlet, S C)
    08 May 1992
EDDY: Harold R (Kingston) & Josephine L Adams (Kingston), 07 Dec 1968   (EK)
    Milton (Attleboro,Ma) & Bette A Joubert (Attleboro,Ma), 27 Nov 1954
    (Milton C Eddy/ Anna M Stevens)(Joseph A Joubert/ Lucia M Allard)
    Stephen W (Kingston) & Donna M Cole (Kensington), 23 Oct 1976   (Ken)
EDGAR: John D (Kingston) & Shari Anne Ready (Amesbury,Ma), 08 Jun 1985
    Robert H (Kingston) & Barbara Ann Ratta (Kingston), 08 Oct 1976   (N)
EDMISTON: Ronald L (Bellwood,Pa) & Rebecca J Clark (Kingston), 06 Jun 1968
EDWARDS: James I (Kingston) & Deborah L Alberts (Kingston), 06 Sep 1969 (N)
    Michael F (Kingston) & Debra I Parent (Kingston), 15 Oct 1994
EDWINSON: John E (Kingston) & Donna M Phelan (Kingston), 19 Nov 1983
EIB: Robert L (Kingston) & Dianne J Lussier (Kingston), 15 Sep 1990

EIDAM: Carl L (Haverhill,Ma) & Sandra S Auger (Haverhill,Ma), 26 Aug 1994
EISENBERG: Harry (Kingston/64) & Julia Glynn (Mattapan,Ma/64), 05 Jul 1945
    (Benny Eisenberg/Gertie ....)(Abraham Raphael/Annie Perkas)
    Sidney A (Kingston/27) & Esther M Goldstein (Kingston/17), 25 Mar 1945
    (Harry Eisenberg/Hanna Solberg)(Samuel Goldstein/Anna Isaacson)
ELDON: George E (Seabrook) & Sandra J Finney (Kingston), 01 Sep 1990
ELDRIDGE: Arthur G (Kingston) & Sharon R Warren (Salem), 31 Jan 1981
    John (Roxbury, Ma/20) & Dorothy Dangore (Roxbury,Ma/19), 09 Nov 1930
    (Austin Eldridge/Helen Corcoran)(James Dangore/Margaret Spellman)
    Richard W, Jr (Kingston) & Jane V Holland (Kingston), 23 Mar 1974
ELLIOTT: Gerald G (Kingston) & Theresa A O'Brien (Raymond), 14 Nov 1963 (N)
    Kenneth E, Jr (Kingston) & Estelle M Howard (Haverhill,Ma), 31 Oct 1970(NJ)
    Warren D (Epping) & Carolyn P Hutchins (Kingston), 23 Mar 1968
    William A (Atkinson) & Margaret Jean Cahill (Kingston), 21 Aug 1993
    William L (Dorchester,Ma) & Ruth H Thompson (Randolph,Ma), 01 Mar 1969
ELLIS: Danna L (Hampton) & Virginia H Hennrikus (Kingston), 13 Dec 1967
    David H (Kingston) & Karen D Deserres (Kingston), 24 Aug 1983
    Harry V, Jr (Haverhill,Ma) & Leslie E Lauder (Haverhill,Ma), 04 Sep 1970
ELLSEY: Robert R (Lawrence,Ma) & Nora E Chapman (Lawrence,Ma), 15 Feb 1962
ELOTMANI: Fouad (Haverhill,Ma) & Donna L Murray (Kingston), 18 Oct 1986
ELWELL: Kevin (Kingston) & Holly J Ferrara (Kingston), 23 Oct 1988
EMERSON: Frederick G (Plaistow) & Barbara F Rouleau (Kingston), 16 Apr 1983
    George (Haverhill,Ma/73) & Alva M Sanborn (Brentwood/75), 17 May 1930
    (George W Emerson/.....) (Benjamin Veazey/ Hannah Morrill)
    John R (Kingston) & Susanne C Crosby (Kingston), 12 May 1974 (N)
EMERY: Steven C (Fremont) & Ellen M Lavoie (Kingston), 11 Apr 1987
ERAMO: Thomas P (Haverhill,Ma) & Helen Dekeon (Haverhill,Ma), 16 Jan 1953
    (Celeste Eramo/ Linda Villinucci)(Xenophon Dekeon/ Florence Kakkales)
ERICKSON: Theodore (Nantasket,Ma) & Helena G Rietzel (Jamaica Plains,Ma),02 Oct 1944
    (John A Erickson/Anna Gustafson)(John L MacLellan/Angelina Morrison) *(P)
ERICKSON: Ralph V (Kingston) & Barbara H Ramsey (Manchester), 17 Dec 1945 (M)
    (Carl Erickson/Alma Friese)(Robert Ramsey/Lucy Price)
ESKIN: Ronald B (Kingston) & Alice A Kleinhans (Kingston), 20 Aug 1983
ESTELLE: Brian S(E Kingston) & Eileen E Warrington (Kingston), 13 Aug 1983
ESTES: Nathaniel W Swampscott,Ma/36) & Grace D Lyford (Kingston/17),09 Mar 1906 *
    (James C Estes/Clara E Rich)(James A Lyford/Lizzie S Goodrich) *(Amesbury,Ma)
ESTY: Robert R (Pease AFB) & Amy F Bardgett (Kingston), 07 Apr 1984
ESDRA: Joseph C (Somerville,Ma) & Marguerite B Cormier (Lynn,Ma), 06 Feb1959
    (Earl Esdra/ Rose Croci)(Armand F Heueready/ Eva St Jean)
ESTRICH: Douglas A (Kingston) & Joyce L Austin (Kingston), 21 Jun 1986
EVANS: Arthur W, Jr (Kingston) & Madeline L Robie (Kingston), 26 Dec 1951
    (Arthur W Evans/ Bertha Rogge)(Morton Robie/Helen Page)
    Arthur W, III (Center Ossipee) & Carol A St Onge (Kingston), 10 Oct 1986
    David W (Kingston) & Allison A Lodge (Meredith), 02 Jan 1986
    Donald C (Kingston) & Elizabeth A Bergeron (Haverhill,Ma), 25 Apr 1970 (A)

James A (Newton) & Cyndy L Jordan (Kingston), 28 Jan 1989

Vernon W (Kingston) & Jane Grygorcewicz (Haverhill,Ma), 12 Jul 1976

EVERSOLE: Russell J (Haverhill,Ma) & Diane J Brockelbank (Kingston), 16 Oct 1971(E)

EWING: Douglas A (Kingston) & Leslye Cain (Plaistow), 08 Jul 1979

Robert L (Kingston) & Ester E Davis (Kingston), 23 Jul 1981

FACE: Herbert (Kingston) & Lois E Maxim (Kingston), 21 Sep 1956

    (Herbert S Face,Sr//Eliza Hoswell)(Frank E Maxim/ Alice L Comer)

FAIRBANKS: Donald R (Springfield,Ma) & Thelma J Rose (Springfield,Ma), 16 Jul 1953

    (Owen A Fairbanks/ Florence L Diehl)(Thomas U Rose/ Claudine L Webb)

Harold J (23) & Helen L O'Donnell (21), 22 Oct 1938

    (Arthur Fairbanks/Lidia Hoffman)(Edward A O'Donnell/Pauline Roche)

FAIRBROTHER: Harry K (Kingston) & Cheryl L Fitzgerald (Kingston), 08 Jul 1989

FALES: George W, III (Kingston) & Joyce A Willneff (Newton), 23 Aug 1980

FANGEALLOZ: Ernest A (W Bridgewater,Ma) & Marilyn G Lambert (Brockton,Ma), 22 Dec 1962

FANTASIA: Richard, Jr (Lowell,Ma) & Angela E Bonvino (Lowell,Ma), 29 Jan 1988

FARLEY: William J (Charlestown,Ma) & Anne H Donovan (W Roxbury,Ma), 21 Mar 1964

FARRAR: William B (Plaistow) & Diane M White (Kingston), 28 Mar 1964

FAUCHER: David G (Somersworth) & Martha J Clark (Kingston), 16 Aug 1975

FAXON: David C (Kingston) & Carol A Piva (Kingston), 29 Jun 1979

FELLOWS: Frank R (Kingston/22) & Janet B Tozier (Plaistow/21), 25 Feb 1944 (P)

    (George H Fellows/Eva J Bruyere)(Allen D Tozier/Mary E McKenzie)

Ralph E (Kingston) & Mary P Blackburn (Kingston), 13 Nov 1970 (N)

FEOLI: John R,III (Haverhill,Ma) & Coleen R Mitchell (Haverhill,Ma), 21 Nov 1986

FERGUSON: Joseph C (Kingston) & Constance E Forsythe (Kingston), 17 Jul 1982

Paul (Exeter) & Maura Jo Keeley (Kingston), 08 May 1983

FERRARA: Walter J (Kingston) & Marcella J Sweeney (Kingston), 07 Oct 1989

FERRARI: Stephen E (Kingston) & Pamela A MacArthur (Kingston), 11 Apr 1992

FERRIS: Frank A (Kingston) & Helen G Laskey (E Kingston), 04 Feb 1962

FERRISI: Adolph A (So Weymouth,Ma) & Janice A Swett (Kingston), 20 Sep 1952 (P)

    (Joseph Ferrisi/ Josephine Pecoraro)(Daniel W Swett/ Anna B Winslow)

FERRULO: John Hames, Jr (Kingston) & Tracy L Whyte (Newton), 23 May 1982

Robert (Kingston/23) & Doris George (Kingston/23), 07 Apr 1946 (D)

    (William Ferrulo/Annie Ristaino)(Walter George/Inez Tewksbury)

FERULLO: William P (Kingston/24) & Hazel M Nason (Kingston/21), 25 Feb 1945 (D)

    (William Ferullo/Annie Ristaino)(Harold Nason/Mary Wilbur)

FERRY: Richard A (Cambridge,Ma) & Marjorie Vokey (Dorchester,Ma), 11 May 1957

    (Anthony Ferry/ Alberta Papsidoro)(Ambrose Vokey/ Helen Reynolds)

FICI: John A (Haverhill,Ma) & Ramona A Soucy (Georgetown,Ma), 03 Dec 1955

    (Paul Fici/ Maria Scavotti)(Joseph Soucy/ Zelie Desrosiers)

FIELDSEND: Donald P (Exeter) & Carolee Bond (Kingston), 29 Dec 1956

    (Russell Fieldsend/ Rose A Nichols)(Raymond Bond/ Dorothy Collette)

FILES: David E (Haverhill,Ma) & Kathleen D Stewart (Haverhill,Ma), 24 Feb 1968

FILLMORE: Maurice J (Kingston) & Jo-Ann H Remington (Kingston), 13 Jul 1984

FINCH: Dean A (Kingston) & Lillian E Topoulos (Kingston), 26 Jan 1962

FINLAYSON: Robert A (Arlington,Ma) & Muriel L Cross (Kingston), 21 Oct 1961
        (Robert Finlayson/ Retha I Norris) (Cecil L Cross/ Ruth M Winslow)
FINN: Darrell J (Haverhill,Ma) & Laurie J Boucher (Kingston), 07 Oct 1989
FISET: William A (Haverhill,Ma) & Susanne R Nason (Kingston), 01 Sep 1984
FITZGERALD: Kenneth D (Haverhill,Ma/21) & Marilyn G Nilsson (Haverhill,Ma18), *
        (Laurie Fitzgerald/Helen Kimball)(Gegnar E Nilsson/Vivian Cheney) *20 Nov 1948
FLAMMIA: Michael H (Haverhill,Ma) & Natalie E Church (Haverhill,Ma), 20 Feb 1960
        (Joseph J Flammia/ Fannie Capadulop)(Oscar Fecteau/ Myrtle Wentworth)
      Peter A (Haverhill,Ma) & Karen A Chase (Haverhill,Ma), 10 Dec 1966
      Thomas A (Haverhill,Ma/27) & Irene A Dangaar(Haverhill,Ma/23), 22 Dec 1949
        (Joseph J Flammia/Fannie Capodelupo)(William A Dangaard/Elinor Welch)
FLANDERS: John H (Chester/46) & Hannah A Gale (Ipswich,Ma/50), 17 Jun 1905
        (Phillip Flanders/----) (Daniel Webster/Sarah A Durgin)
      Philip J, Jr. (46) & Miriam Scoullar (47), 27 Nov 1942
        (Philip J Flanders/Ella M Watson)(Francis Scouliar/ Una Taylor)
FLEURY: Henry R, Jr (Kingston) & Linda L Wilson (Kingston), 22 Sep 1984
FLOREA: John P (Everett, Ma) & Doreen A Rutledge (Everett, Ma), 31 Aug 1991
FLYNN: Richard T (Woburn,Ma) &Cindy A Kimes (Woburn,Ma), 15 Aug 1987
      Stephen M (Newton) & Debora M Riley (Kingston), 27 Aug 1977 (N)
FOGARTY: Alan S (Kingston) & Alice J Kearns (Newfields), 23 Jul 1983
      Edwin J (Derby,Ct) & Susan E Ahlberg (Kingston), 24 Jun 1989
FOLDING: Daniel J (Exeter) & Cindy A Aubry (Kingston), 21 May 1988
FOLEY: Dennis H (Salem,Ma) & Diane C Knowlton (Beverly,Ma) , 04 Mar 1965
      William J (Newton Jct/26) & Alice C Avery (Danville/19), 07 Dec 1905 (P)
        (William J Foley/Ellen Kennedy)(Orrin S Avery/Sarah V Darbe)
FOLLANSBEE: Thomas L (Kingston) & Linda St Laurent (Kingston), 23 Apr 1983
FOLSOM: Donald E (Salisbury,Ma/22) & Betty J Currier (Kingston/18), 11 Apr 1948 (D)
        (Eugene G Folsom/Helen Pettengill)(Lloyd M Currier/Beatrice N Cook)
      Edwin L (Epping/31) & Mabel Reynolds (Kingston/31), 25 Jun 1902
        (Thomas C Folsom/Mary Bickford)(Thomas O Reynolds/Fannie Smith)
FONTAINE: Frank (Winchester,Ma) & Lea A Kenney (Stoneham,Ma), 27 Jan 1959
        (Frank Fontaine/ Alma C Wakeham)(Henry Kenney/ Ancle Tulaba)
FOOTE: Harry (Salisbury,Ma) & Joanne Little (Salisbury,Ma), 16 Jul 1963
FORD: Wendell D (Kingston/19) & Mary Gillion (E.Boston,Ma/19), 16 Jun 1920
        (Arthur E Ford/ Mary A Chick)(Martin Gillio/Annie Dauncey)
FORESTER: Albert J (Kingston) & Rochelle Ingersoll (Kingston), 01 Nov 1977
FORSYTHE: Douglas A (Kingston) & Joanne F Brashier (Plaistow), 23 Oct 1993
FOSS: Alvin E (Somersworth/28) & Alice E Bragdon (Kingston/27), 09 Nov 1904
        (Edgar F Foss/Amanda Dolloff)(George L Bragdon/Martha A Know)
FORTIER: Jean P (Brentwood) & Julie A Lamb (Kingston), 26 Nov 1988
FOSTER: John T (Salem) & Jennifer K Barthelmess (Kingston), 04 Jun 1988
FOWLER: Walter B (Bradford,Ma) & Shirley M Dudley (Haverhill,Ma), 25 Dec 1956
        (Sidney Fowler/ Lizzie Dow)(Ralph Clough/ Dorothy Holt)
FOY: Jeffrey M (Kingston) & Melissa R Bulao (Kingston), 01 Oct 1988
      Michael J (Kingston) & Sara G Heckman (Kingston),12 Apr 1986

Peter E (Newton) & Denise L Crescentini (Kingston), 22 Sep 1979
FRADSHAM: James F (Lowell,Ma) & Maureen P O'Brien (Medford,Ma), 01 Feb 1964
FRAIZE: Malcolm L (E Taunton,Ma) & Karen L Miller (E Taunton,Ma), 23 Oct 1993
FRAME: George E (Kingston) & Marion E Frame (Exeter), 12 Jun 1960
    (Joseph A Frame/ Fannie B Bowle)(John H Elkins/ Lizzie Conner)
FRANCIS: Frank E (Liverpool,NY) & Ruth F Smith (Newmarket), 10 Jan 1959
    (Albert E Francis/ Elizabeth Whitley)(William Smith/ Annie Knight)
    Leo C (Everett,Ma) & Gwendolyn Theele (Malden,Ma), 03 Jun 1959
    (Manuel Francis/Theresa Kelsay)(Arthur Theele/ Leta Critfa)
    Steven M (Kingston) & June C Dunne (Kingston), 27 Oct 1986
    Willard A (29) & Lois W Bunker (21), 03 Mar 1934 (Somersworth)
    (Albert B Francis/ Olivia Millen)(Louis C Bunker/ Annie M George)
FRANCOEUR: Dennis N,Jr (Newton) & Lisa M Nason (Kingston), 27 Apr 1985
FRAZER: James K (Kingston) & Jane E Amazeen (E Kingston), 13 Jul 1974   (P)
    John B (Kingston) & Monica K Conley (Quincy,Ma), 17 May 1969
    Thomas H (Kingston) & Barbara J Hunter (Kingston), 23 Sep 1989
FREEDMAN: Daniel S (Dorchester,Ma) & Carol A Swanson (Roxbury,Ma), 07 Mar 1959
    (George Freeman/ Sally Freeman)(John A Swanson/ Pearl E Swanson)
FREEMAN: Charles S (Kingston) & Priscilla B Golden (Kingston),12 Dec 1981
FRENCH: Eldred H (Kingston/19) & Pearl E Woodbury (Salem/19), 25 Dec 1914
    (John G French/Addie Davis)(Louis F Woodbury/Frances Story)
    Hebert C (Kingston/26) & Linnie A Maxham (New Boston/25), 18 Jul 1914
    (John G French/Addie Davis)(Charles B Johnnott/Susan E Keith)
    Melvin W (Kingston/22) & Katherine C Bailey (Nova Scotia/25), 01 Jul 1926/27 (P)
    (John G French)(Lambert L Bailey)
FRIEND: Charles A (Kingston/23) & Pearl E Christiansen (Kingston/19), 03 Jul 1944
    (William H Friend/Della N Harriman)(Otto W Christiansen,Sr /Sarah E Willos)
    Russell C (Kingston) & Lisa D Swanson (Kingston), 22 May 1983
FRIZZELL: Arnold T (Newton) & Pamela M Wilder (Kingston), 06 May 1972 (N)
FRUZZETT: Michael J (Brockton,Ma) & Sandra M Nelson (Plymouth,Ma), 02 Mar 1963
FUGERE: Stephen M (Kingston) & Kristie A Britton (Kingston), 14 Oct 1980
FULLER: David B (Kingston) & Brenda L Ashford (Kingston), 12 May 1990
    Leon E (Haverhill,Ma) & Dorothy Gove (Kingston), 07 May 1977
FULTON: Thomas B (Kingston) & Catherine Richmond (Kingston), 17 Oct 1981
GAGE: David L (Danville) & Marie T Holland (Kingston), 14 Jun 1969
    John A (E Kingston) & Sheila Ramey (Kingston), 17 Nov 1962 (P)
GAGLIARDI: Vincent L (Haverhill,Ma) & Michelle T Plante (Bradford,Ma), 29 Sep 1984
GAGNON: Dennis A (Kingston) & Julie A Guyette (Kingston), 27 May 1978 (N)
    George H (Kingston) & Colleen J Aikens (Kingston), 25 Aug 1984
    John E (Kingston) & Josephine J Birch (Kingston), 01 Jul 1983
GAIESKI: James A (Kingston) & Gail E Garson (Kingston), 31 Dec 1985
GALLANT: Edward T (Agawam,Ma) & Martha R McKenzie (Kingston), 28 Jun 1986
GALLERANI: Ugo J (Kingston) & Antoinette R Eaton (Haverhill,Ma), 21 May 1971
GALLISON: George R,Jr (Kingston) & Kelly J Holmes (Fremont), 22 Jun 1985
GALLOWAY: Christopher (Kingston) & Karen M Madej (Plaistow), 25 May 1985

GALVIN: John J (Kingston) & Jean M Rizzo (Peabody,Ma), 10 Nov 1984
GAMELIN: Scott D (Exeter) & Deborah A Gill (Kingston), 26 Jun 1971)N)
GANLEY: John J (Kingston) & Lisa Grootenboer (Kingston), 14 Oct 1989
GANNETT: Ronald A (Kingston) & Constance Grootenboer (Newton), 26 Jan 1980
GARCIA, Carlos E (Kingston) & Dawn M Panos (Kingston), 05 Aug 1989
    Kevin J (Lowell, Ma) & Lisa M Johnson (Lowell, Ma), 12 Jun 1992
GARDNER: Robert F (Lynn,Ma) & Ann L Brown (Peabody,Ma), 19 Jun 1960
    (Andrew H Gaynor/ Mary E MacDonald)(Robert Hicks/ Pearl Brown)
GARELLO: Kenneth A (W Brookfield,Ma) & Judith A Okolo (W Brookfield,Ma),05 Jun 1993
GARFOLA: Patrick J (Brockton,Ma) & Mary A McLaughlin (Whitman,Ma), 27 Jan 1967
GARLAND: Ralph N (Kingston/34) & Mildred D Hanson (Kingston/28),05 Oct 1929 (Rye)
    (Nathaniel/Minnie Brown)(Forrest Hanson/Florence Emerson)
GARWITZ: Lawrence D (Kingston) & Dora F Cormier (Kingston), 30 Sep 1960 (Seabrook)
    (Bert Garwitz/ May Raper)(Clovis Cormier/ Henrietta Cormier)
GASKILL: Edwin L (48) & Pauline M O'Donnell (41), 29 Sep 1934
    (Nanna Gaskill/ Emma Holbrook)(John Roche/ Helen Hannon)
GASSE: ThomasA (Kingston) & Bonnie M Mathews (Kingston), 08 Oct 1988
GATES: Billy Lee (Orlando,Fl) & Amy Magnusson (Kingston), 14 Aug 1968
GAUDET: David P (Fremont) & Judith M Maxwell (Kingston), 27 Oct 1984
    Gary A (Fremont) & Betty A Dunbar (Kingston), 19 Jun 1976 (N)
    Joseph P (Fremont) & April L Maxwell (Kingston), 03 Mar 1981
GAUDETTE: Frederick G (Exeter) & Susan L Short (Kingston), 17 Jul 1992
GAUTHIER: Richard L (Coventry,RI) & Norma C Know (No Scituate,Ma), 13 Feb 1962
GAZNICK: Anthony (Kingston) & Loueva Baker (Epping), 04 Dec 1965 (EP)
GEILEAR: Edward A (Brockton,Ma) & Eleanor G Busby (Brockton,Ma), 18 Oct 1952
    (George Geilear/ Florence Houde)(Joseph W Busby/ Doris MacKenzie)
GEORGE: Calvin E (Kingston/29) & Gladys Weatherby (Plymouth/23), 05 Sep 1932 (A)
    (Porter George/Florence Kelly)(George A Weatherby/Rose B Jennings)
    Calvin E (Kingston/23) & Edna MacLeod (Exeter/17), 14 Sep 1927/28 (A)
    (Porter G George/Florence Kelley)(Herbert E Lord/Ida M Manning)
    Carl H (Kingston) & Joanne E Chase (Haverhill,Ma), 21 Feb 1953 (D)
    Carl H, Jr (Kingston) & Carolyn H Henecke (Newton),02 Mar 1973 (N)
    Derek S (Kingston) & Dawn M Fales (Kingston), 03 May 1986
    Donald L (Bradford,Ma) & Sondi J Faxon (Bradford,Ma), 16 Jun 1984
    Fred R (Kingston/29) & Mabel E Spofford (Kingston/19), 20 Aug 1902
    (Ora P George/Abbie H Silloway)(Charles A Spofford/Triphene Sargent)
    Gary M (Kingston) & Jan M Ryerson (Newton), 15 Jun 1980
    Grover O (Derry/22) & Alice G Nason (Portland,Me/24), 28 Oct 1907 *
    (Fred P George/Josephine Spollett)(George W Nason/Cora Knowles) *(Chelsea,Ma)
    Henry L (24) & Marie L Lemay (18), 16 May 1940 (P)
    (Ora P George/Ella Cosgrove)(Edward Lemay/Rose A Commier)
    Joseph D (Kingston) & Eleanor J Tozier (Plaistow), 11 Apr 1959 (P)
    (Daniel W George/ Victoria Rondeau)(Duncan Tozier/ Marguerite E Cheney)
    Joseph D (Kingston) & Barbara J Wentworth (Newton), 17 Aug 1962
    Keith A (Kingston) & Barbara A Cunningham (Kingston), 25 Sep 1982

Leon L & Esther A Bowley, 31 Jul 1921 (P)
Louis W (Kingston) & Deborah K Bilodeau (Kingston), 20 May 1972 (N)
Ora P (Kingston/26) & Ella Cosgrove (Hampstead/38), 25 Nov 1925
   (Porter George/Florence Kelley)(James Cosgrove/Edith Merrick)
Ora P (Kingston/34) & Mildred L Clow (E Hampstead/25), 24 Jan 1924
   (Porter George /Florence Kelly)(George A Clow/Priscilla Clow)
Randolph C (Amesbury,Ma) & Jane M Carney (Kingston), 14 Feb 1987
Stephen (Kingston) & Roxann Adams (Kingston), 09 Nov 1974 (N)
Walter M (Kingston/22) & Inez Tewksbury (Danville/19), 15 Jan 1915 (E/K)
   (Porter George/Florence Kelley)(Allison Tewksbury/Ada Goodwin)
Wilfred F (Kingston/20) & Henrietta Ledoux (Amesbury,Ma/17),18 Nov 1933 (A)
   (Porter G George/Florence B Kelley)(Albert Ledoux/Annie Sicard)
William J(Kingston) & Irene T DiFloures (Haverhill,Ma), 11 Sep 1960
   (Ora P George/ Ella Cosgrove)(Luigi Di Floures/ Julia J Kapello)
William J (Kingston/22) & Carol A Weatherbee (Kingston/25), 24 Dec 1947 (D)
   (Ora P George/Ella Cosgrove)(George Weatherbee/Rose A .....)
GERO: Raymond O (21) & Edith M Fernald (20), 08 May 1940
   (Marshall Gero/Jennie Crowley)(Harold L Fernald/Ruth A Smith)
GERRISH: Vernon M, Sr (Kingston) & Faye E Nutt (Kingston), 16 Jul 1983
GERSKOWITZ: Paul R (Kingston) & Joanne M Gosselin (Kingston), 26 Jun 1981
   Robert R (Kingston) & Kathleen Apar (Salem), 30 Jun 1990
GETCHELL: Paul A (Kingston) & Alice T Gibbons (Boston,Ma), 11 Jul 1970 (P)
GIALLONGO: Robert W (Kingston) & Marcelle P Fisette (Kingston), 01 Jan 1992
   Serafino (23) & Mary Siathowaska (18), 20 Sep 1936
   (Angelo Gaillongo/Beatrice Anaragis)(Walter Siathowska/Rose Surowiec)
GIBBONS: Stephen M (Lawrence,Ma) & Theresa A McGlinchey (Kingston), 26 Aug 1989
GIBBS: Edward, (Birmingham,Eng/23) & Blanche J Pitts (Worcester,Ma/23), 04 Jul 1914
   (Edward Gibb/Clara F Bromage)(Willard C Pitts/Rosanna M Elliott) (N)
GILBERT: Frederick M (Hampstead) & Susanne D Winslade (Kingston), 27 Oct 1973
GILES: William F (Lynn, Ma) & Carol A Davidian (Lynn, Ma), 29 Jun 1991
GILMAN: John S, Jr (Kingston) & Jennie F Clements (Kingston), 17 Dec 1962
   Lyndon R (Brentwood) & Lois A Stevens (Kingston), 01 Oct 1950
   (George U Gilman/Laurel Waddington)(J Edward Stevens/Annie Locke)
GILROY: James M (Lynn,Ma) & Dorothy L Jenkins (Lynn,Ma), 15 Sep 1973
GIDLEY: Albert E (36) & Helen Coppinger (23), 12 Aug 1937
   (Samuel Gidley/ Jennie Smith)(John Coppinger/ Anna O'Brien)
GILL: James J, Jr (Kingston) & Donna M Hayward(Kingston), 27 Apr 1986
GILLEN: Franklin J (Danville) & Pearl M Martel (Kingston), 25 Oct 1969
GILLINICK: Edmund N (Willimantic,Ct) & Sarah B Brace (Marblehead,Ma),02 Feb 1955
   (Joseph Gillinick/ Eva Aubin)(Edward B Porter/ Rosina E Tinker)
GILMAN: Frank J (Dover/21) & Harriet Severance (Kingston/22), 28 Dec 1901 (N)
   (Eusebe Gilman/Elisebena Jacques)(Mason S Severance/Ellen Conford)
   Frank B (Malden,Ma) & Alice M Anstey (Stoneham,Ma), 11 Nov 1957
   (Charles H Gilman/ Edith M Holmes)(Frank Anstey/ Helen C Tomlinson)

GINTAUTAS: Peter A (Champaign,Il) & Debra K Krumm (Boulder, Co),27 May 1994
GIORGI: Donald M (Kingston) & Jill M Reinhold (Epping), 18 May 1985
GLICK, Wayne E (Ottumwa,Ia) & Wilma A Marple (Kingston), 14 Jan 1951 (N/J)
    (Troy S Glick/Grace Davis)(William A Marple/Helen Gay)
GOBELLE: David R (Portsmouth) & Linda M St Hilaire (Kingston), 16 Oct 1965
GODBOUT: William H (33) & Grace E Bishop (29), 22 Jun 1940 (D)
    (Florence J Godbout/Alice Richardson)(Elmer Collins/Susan A Nason)
GOLDBAUM: Richard E (Kingston) & Evelyn R Pinder (Kingston), 26 Jan 1978 (N)
GOLDBERG: Sidney A (Lynn,Ma) & Bette A Zellen (Lynn,Ma), 22 Jun 1964
GOLDBLITH: Errol D (Melrose, Ma) & Linda A Ward (Lexington,Ma), 16 Mar 1962
GOLDEN: Brian R (Kingston) & Christine D Caron (Exeter), 30 Jul 1988
    Robert A (Boston,Ma) & Eleanor M Ford (Boston,Ma), 07 Feb 1962
GOLDIE: Richard V (W Bridgewater,Ma) & Jeanne K Shaw (Canton,Ma),07 Jan 1950
    (George W Goldie/Hattie E Young)(Walter P Shaw/Eva M Huntress)
GOLDTHWAITE: Stephen (Kingston) & Betty M Hammond (Raymond), 08 Oct 1954 (R)
    (Benjamin Goldthwaite/ Thelma Bunker)(Lyman R Hammond/ Blanche Davis)
    William E (Newton/25) & Adeline C Bonenfant (Epping/22), 13 Oct 1929
    (Everard Goldthwaite/Grace E Sargent)(Emile Bonenfant/Emelia LaBranche)
GOLDMAN: Alan D (Cambridge, Ma) & Pamela J Schreiber (Kingston), 30 Dec 1972 (E)
    Henry (Haverhill,Ma) & Denise M Gosselin (Haverhill,Ma), 30 Jul 1989
GOOD: Bryan C (Kingston) & Marie A McCann (Kingston), 01 Nov 1987
    Robert P (Milton,Ma) & Ruth M Mackin (Milton,Ma), 05 Sep 1956
    (John J Good/ Grace M Lombard)(Harold F Mackin/ Olive E Follansbee)
GOODHUE: Clayton E (Kingston) & Margaret M Conroy (Kingston), 08 Aug 1968
GOODMAN: David G (Ashland, Ma) & Deborah A Gendron (Ashland, Ma), 23 Jun 1990
GOODRICH: Daryl R (Magnolia, Ma) & Nancy J Kennedy (Magnolia, Ma), 13 Oct 1990
    Michael A (Seabrook) & Judianne Marr (Kingston), 17 May 1986
GOODWIN: Charles (Amesbury,Ma) & Irvana C Green (W Newbury,Ma), 20 Mar 1958
    (Charles E Goodwin/ Lillian Wilson)(Henry Morrill/ Hallie Hardy)
    Charles H (Bradford,Ma/31) & Isabelle Jordan (Kingston/33),09 Nov 1948 (E)
    (Hollis C Goodwin/Ann Matheson)(Ernest H Derochemont/Ethel King)
    Daniel L & Amanda E Clucher, 03 Jul 1921 (D)
    Edward (Kingston/53) & Ida Currier (Amesbury,Ma/42), 03 Oct 1921
    (Samuel Goodwin/Lucinda Tucker)(Elmer Collins/Mary Wilson)
    Michael E (Kingston) & Karen N Laurence (Kingston), 09 Jul 1983
GORDON: Arthur O (Alberton,PEI/39) & Blanche G Garceau (Haverhill,Ma),14 Nov 1905
    (William H Gordon/Christie A Owens)(William O Garceau/Amelina Catudal)
    Leonard C (Kingston) & Thelma L Bishop (Kingston), 14 Dec 1974 (S)
    Richard B (Cambridge,Ma) & Mary McDougall (Cambridge,Ma), 16 May 1952
    (Wendell B Gordon/Evelyn Bennett)(Allan K McDougall/ Myrle Gillespie)
    William J (Lawrence,Ma) & Arlene R Thomas (Lawrence,Ma), 18 Jun 1976
GORMAN: Robert E (Middleton,Ma) & Mary R Goudreau (Danvers,Ma), 05 May 1957
    (Clarence E Gorman/ Eunice Russell)(Wilfred Goudreau/Veronica Morin)
GOSS: James E (Kingston) & Patricia A Indoccio (Derry), 21 Jun 1969 (Derry)

Henry E (30) & Alma R Woods (35), 02 Sep 1939
    (Cyril E Goss/Matilda Barrett)(George Brouillard/Regina Cote)
Kenneth J (Exeter) & Cheryl A Phelan (Kingston), 19 Sep 1975 (N)
Russell P (Haverhill,Ma) & Dorothy M Churchill (Haverhill,Ma), 28 Jun 1994
GOSSMAN: Gene L (Newton) & Sharon R Cocozza (Kingston), 12 Mar 1977
GOUDREAULT: Joseph J (Amesbury,Ma)& Robin D Chapman (Amesbury,Ma),08 Sep 1979
GOULD: David S (Kingston)& Carol A Champion (Kingston), 29 May 1976
    Kenneth H (Derry) & Selma R Jackson (Kingston), 29 Nov 1981
    Lewis N, Jr (Kingston) & Colleen M Grenon (Kingston), 24 Aug 1991
GOUTHIER: Randy (Kingston) & Robin L Vail (Kingston), 14 Jun 1985
GRAHAM: Jon D (Lynn,Ma) & Barbara Winchell (Lynn,Ma), 26 Dec 1962
    Luther F (44) & Leila M George (16), 13 Oct 1936 (P)
    (John F Graham/Alma E Wood)(Ora P George/Ella May Cosgrove)
    Walter R (Lawrence,Ma) & Barbara Graham (Lawrence,Ma), 01 Mar 1950
    (Walter Graham/Ida Charoux)(Victor Kingsman/Ida Greenwood)
GRANT: Addison W (Nova Scotia/23) & Katherine McCormick (Roxbury,Ma/20),28 Jan 1928
    (Robert Grant/Ada Lewis)(Parker McCormick/Agnes B Gilroy)
    Arthur H (Poland,Me/40) & Ida B Kemp (Fairhaven,Ma/27), 23 Jan 1914
    (Charles F Grant/Emeline Berry)(Z Willis Kemp/Mary Boynton)
    Henry C (Jamaica Plain,Ma) & Barbara C Young (Dorchester,Ma), 02 Oct 1955
    (Harry C Grant/ Margaret Yeoman)(Simeon Young/ Sarah J Harris)
    Richard A (Madison,Me) & Katrin L Becotte (Kingston), 10 Aug 1985
GRASSI: Esio J (Roxbury,Ma) & Norma G Bridges (Roxbury,Ma), 12 Sep 1963
GRAY: Arthur (Kingston) & Gertrude H Amiss (Melrose,Ma), 25 Jun 1955 (Seabrook)
    (Arthur F Gray/ Anna Campbell)(Tazewell Amiss/ Anna Broderick)
    Winifield R (Topsfield,Ma) & Carol E Giles (Topsfield,Ma), 13 Nov 1959
    (Daniel R Gray/ Elizabeth Holden)(Harris Giles/ Marjorie Linnekin)
GREANEY: Daniel D (Newton) & Martha A Modlich (Kingston), 18 Jul 1959
    (Thomas Greaney/ Irene Allard)(Walter R Modlich/ Evelyn Thereau)
    Kevin S (Kingston) & Heidi L Misenheimer (Kingston), 18 Aug 1990
GREEKE: Richard P (Middleton,Ma) & Joan F Rizya (Lynn,Ma), 08 Mar 1961
    (Dell M Greeke/ Clare M St Laurent)(John C Rizya/ Mary Muzichuk)
GREELEY: Arthur B (Haverhill,Ma/22) & Ida M McGarigle (Charlottetown,PEI/17), *
    (Erastus P Greeley/Louisa ----)(William McGarigle/Jane McNeil)   *20 Sep 1905
    Robert T (Beverly,Ma) &Albertina R Speliotis (Beverly,Ma), 13 Oct 1988
GREENE: Frank G (Newton,Jct) & Clarabell Bruso (Kingston), 19 Jan 1984
    Robert F (Reading,Ma) & Hannah L Lord (Melrose,Ma), 04 May 1960
    (Harold Greene/ Lillian Hayes)(Norman D Lord/ Cecile Bishop)
GREENLEAF: Joseph H,(Brockton/21) & Ellen B Severance (Kingston/19), 31 May 1916
    (Clarence Greenleaf/Grace Nickerson)(Mason Severance/Ellen Colford)
GREENWAY: Steven D (Manasses,Va) & Brenda L Hamel (Kingston), 18 Oct 1986
GREENWOOD: Frederick W (Kingston) & Jill K Wheeler (Kingston), 01 Sep 1962
GREGG: Eric J (E Kingston) & Michelle D Currier (Kingston), 28 Sep 1985
GREGOIRE, Clinton A (Haverhill, Ma) & Shirley A Cheney (Kingston), 27 May 1954
    (Lewis Gregoire/ Josephine Bezier) (Paul E Hamel/ Dorothy E Ross)

Robert J (Kingston) & Teresa A Decareau (Plaistow), 07 Aug 1976
GREY: Peter W (Kingston) & Dominique C Mills (Exeter), 21 Oct 1978 (E)
GRIFFIN: Anderson S (Raymond) & Susan A Wentworth (Kingston), 07 Feb 1987
Donald J (Needham, Ma) & Jessica S Morse (Wareham, Ma), 21 Aug 1972
Francis E, Jr (Kingston) & Robyne M Vincent (Kingston), 26 Sep 1981
G David,Jr (Kingston) & Linda J Summartano (Kingston), 24 Jan 1992
Kenneth M (Harmony,Me) & Lisa D Melby (Larimore,ND), 18 May 1993
John J (Danvers,Ma) & Laverna G Brown (Danvers,Ma), 11 Apr 1966
Robert C (No Hampton) & Nancy J Cheney (Kingston),11 Aug 1973 (N/Danville)
GRONDIN: Alfred T (Exeter) & Judith A Marshall (Kingston), 23 Mar 1968   (E)
GROVER: George E (Kingston) & Mary O Desroches (Epping), 04 Apr 1964 (E)
John S (Kingston) & Nina L Matson (Kingston), 23 Jul 1983
William E (N Reading,Ma) & Grace L Martin (Reading,Ma), 22 Nov 1958
      (Augustine Grover/ Flora Nickerson)(Everett H Martin/ Lucy A Martin)
GUILDERSON: Joseph L (Somerville,Ma) & Marilyn M Muller (Somerville,Ma),29 Jul 1962
GUISTO: Joseph R (Boston,Ma) & Josephine Guisto (Everett,Ma), 31 Mar 1950
      (Rocco Guisto/Fellippa Palascina)(Joseph Mainone/Lena Cravotte)
GUNTHER: William G (Kingston) & Charlotte A Raymond (Dracut,Ma), 05 Jul 1953*
      (Fredrick H Gunther/ Gladys Shanks)(Roswell M Raymond/ Hazel Wiggin)*(Lowell)
GUPTIL: Roger S (Berwick,Me/25) & Constance M Sanborn (Northfield/21)02 Mar 1914
      (Frank S Guptill/Hila M Pinkham)(Oscar P Sanborn/Anna C Morrill)
GURSKY: Michael (Kingston) & Linda C Irving (Kingston), 15 Jun 1981
GUTIERREZ: Alex(Elisio) (Kingston) & Christine P Rondeau (Kingston), 24 Nov 1987
HAAS: Allen J (San Diego,Ca) & Debra L Jahnel (Kingsport,Tn), 19 Aug 1988
HADFIELD: David J (Kingston) & Doris T Snow (Kingston), 25 Jul 1987
HADLEY: Richard B (Arlington,Ma) & Sharon J Hubbard (Brookline,Ma), 11 Jul 1964
HAFFNER: Donald L & Jean P Richards, 06 May 1955
      (Harrison F Haffner/Anna Cullouis)(Clarence Richards/Medina O Celli)
HAGAN: Michael J (Kingston) & Theresa M Love (Kingston), 20 Jul 1991
HAGEN: Frederick G (Merrimac,Ma) & Mildred F Nolan (Merrimac,Ma), 22 Nov 1973
George E (Haverhill,Ma) & Marguerite R Munday(Smithtown,Ma), 01 Dec 1957
      (Lester G Hagen/ Grace Bascom)(Ernest Perreault/ Marion Legasse)
HAGGETT: Lorenzo (Hampstead) & Bette M Merrifield (Kingston), 16 Aug 1957 (Strat)
      (Lorenzo W Haggett/ Frances Carr)(Kenneth Merrifield/ Theresa A Perrault)
HAGGERTY: Rex S (Kingston) & Luann M Willey (Kingston), 31 Dec 1984
HALL: Charles A (Plymouth,Ma) & Ann M Kelly (Plymouth,Ma), 18 Sep 1987
Charles A (Plymouth,Ma) & Diana R Price (Kingston), 16 Mar 1985
Chester A (Kingston) & Della N Harriman (Kingston), 28 Jun 1957
      (Anderson Hall/ Florence A Stevens)(Walter Harriman/ Josephine Simes)
Marcus A (Branford,Ct) & Marjorie Wight (Guilford,Ct), 25 Jun 1955
      (Robert B Hall/ Rena Smith)(Ralph M Wight/ Florence Callaway)
William K, Jr (Leicester,Ma) & Susan E Estey (Leicester,Ma), 30 Oct 1969
HALLWORTH: Thomas M (Newburyport, Ma)& Susan K Paradis (Haverhill, Ma)29 Aug1992
HAMEL: Michael P (Kingston) & Brenda L Hogue (Kingston), 16 Apr 1977
HAMMER: Thomas E (Bradford, Ma) & Leah I Comeau (Bradford, Ma), 14 Feb 1991

HAMMOND: Charles R (Bridgewater/55) & Elizabeth A Lawrence(England/49),16 Mar 1909
  (Rodney Hammond/Abigail Frost)(James Robinson/Elizabeth Waldron)
  Robert T (Kingston) & Gloria L Hutchins (Kingston), 30 Mar 1991
HAMILTON: Frank A (Kingston) & Mary M Colson (Newton), 27 Jun 1970 (N)
  Robert M (Kingston) & Sharon L Swanton (Kingston), 10 Oct 1987
HANLEY: Peter R, Jr (Kingston) & Judy A Daigle (Kingston), 21 Feb 1981
HANNAGAN: Charles F (Plaistow) & Elizabeth A Lacerte (Brentwood), 09 Dec 1961
  (Wilbur Hannagan/ Francis Cullen)(D Lewis Goodwin/ Amanda Clutcher)
  Michael A (Kingston) & Jacqueline J Durso, 01 May 1976
HANNAN: David D (Haverhill,Ma) & Marion L Nolan (Kingston), 24 May 1974
HANNON: Charles T (Burlington,Ma) & Leslie A Pascoe (Billerica,Ma), 17 Aug 1986
HANSFORD: Leonard F (Lynfield,Ma) & Judy A Johnson (Kingston), 09 Sep 1987
HANSHAW: Lawrence (Nova Scotia/36) & Stella R White (Brentwood/38),18 Jun 1927/28 (B)
  (Simeon Hanshaw/Sarah ....)(Joseph Rock/Helen Dudley)
HANSON: Harry E, Jr (Kingston) & Ruth E McDonough (E Hampstead), 01 May 1982
HARMON: Kenneth D (Kingston) & Carolyn E Elkerton (Kingston), 08 Oct 1955
  (Victor H Harmon/ Ida B Brown)(William Elkerton,Jr/Elida G Barker)
  Paul W (Barrington) & Dorothy C Champion (Kingston), 26 Jun 1994
  Richard J (Kingston) & Patricia Shepherd (Kingston), 03 Sep 1977 (Not)
HARGRAVES: Todd D(Merrimac,Ma) & Elena F Messner (Merrimac,Ma) 20 Nov 1993
HARMON: Alfred F (28) & Virginia H Bryant (16), 16 Sep 1942
  (Asbra Harmon/Lena Elvin)(Robert I Bryant/Helen B Euletia)
  Asbra (Madison/44) & Erma Hutchins (Kingston/33), 05 Dec 1931 (Seabrook)
  (Arthur Harmon/Henrietta Anderson)(John French/Addie Davis)
HARMS: Craig J (Andover,Ma) & Carolyn A Arena (Andover,Ma), 05 Jun 1987
HARPER: Joseph H (Kingston) & Mary E Tobin (Kingston), 28 Oct 1978 (N)
HARRIMAN: Dennis L (Kingston) & Doreen A Caillouette (Kingston), 09 Dec 1972 (N)
HARRINGTON: Paul J (Everett,Ma) & Carol M Beauregard (Kingston), 18 Aug 1962
HARRIS: John W (Kingston/35) & Lillian Gardiner (Kingston/36), 19 Oct 1946
  (Leslie Acker/Effie Morse)(James Gardiner/Georgia White)
  Robert S (34) & Josie S Edwards (52), 04 Jul 1936
  (Robert G Harris/Ella F Brooks)(Joseph A Horton/Ida J Goodrich)
  Sam E (Terrell,Tx) & Shirley R Valanti (Bristol, RI), 23 Jun 1962
HARRISON: Gary B (Epping) & Susanne K Brockelbank (Kingston), 23 Apr 1966
HART: Robert A (Saugus,Ma) & Susan P Clark (Kingston), 29 Aug 1969
HARTFORD: Gary A (Kingston) & Sharon A Berry (Kingston), 25 Sep 1971
  Shirley B (Deerfield/29) & Jennie Auger (Canada/33), 17 May 1908
  (William H Hartford/Ella F Stewart)(Joseph Vallier/Genase St Peter)
  William H, Jr (Kingston) & Marcia A McFarland (Plaistow), 06 Aug 1970(P)
HARTMAN: Charles J (Arlington,Ma) & Janet C Gilman (Kingston), 16 Feb 1964
HARTSELL: James E (Kingston) & Vicky A White (Hampton), 08 Dec 1979
HARTWELL: John H (Kingston) & Susan G Stevens (Kingston), 25 Sep 1993
HARVEY: Thomas L,Jr (Portsmouth) & Marjorie F Childs (Kingston), 15 Apr 1967 (E)

HASELTINE: Francis D (Andover,Ma) & Phyllis A Pecci (Haverhill,Ma),29 Mar 1958
    (Caroll E Haseltine/ Mary Anderson)(Frank P Pecci/ Lena Mazzotta)
    William F (Plaistow) & Joyce L Greenlee (Kingston), 21 Jun 1975 (P)
HATCH: Alfred B (Haverhill,Ma) & Nina M Pullen (Haverhill,Ma), 01 Aug 1964
    Roger H (Kingston) & Louise A Castonguay (Kingston), 04 Jul 1952 (M)
    (Harold R Hatch/ Hazel Moore)(Joseph H Gastonguay/ Louise Benoit)
HATCHELL: Calvin W (Kittery,Me) & Sylvia A Greenwood (Kittery,Me), 12 Feb 1962
HATEM: Ronald (Methuen) & Joan M Breen (Andover,Ma), 07 Aug 1963
    Ronald F (Methuen,Ma) & Marie A Young (Lawrence,Ma), 23 Dec 1957
    (Ferris Hatem/ Louise Bolous)(Joseph Young/ Bertha Saulervicz)
HAWKES: Bruce K (Kingston)& Helen M Lattime (Kingston), 18 Oct 1975
    Ralph K, Jr (Merrimac,Ma) & Marcia I Collins (Kingston), 02 Sep 1950 (D)
    (Ralph K Hawkes/Ada Fowler)(Oral W Collins/ Daisy Jasper)
HAWKINS: Leonard R (Kingston) & Meredith D Wysocki (Kingston), 29 Jan 1983
HAYES: William F (Norwood,Ma/36) & Dorothy Heffernan (Kingston/25), 05 Apr 1947
    (Michael Hayes/Mary Barry)(Paul Heffernan/Marie O'Toole)
HAYNES: Richard A (Kingston) & Eileen J Duffy (Manchester), 15 Aug 1981
    William H, III (Kingston) & Pamela L Nickerson (Plaistow), 29 Feb 1980
HAYWARD: Charles L (Salisbury,Ma) & Jean H Goodwin (Salisbury,Ma), 09 Jun 1989
HAYWOOD: Frederick W, Jr (Davie,Fl) & June M Reichert (Davie,Fl), 25 Jun 1988
HEAD: Lester F (22) & Helen B Plummer (18), 14 May 1936   (Ken)
    (Arnold Head/Sadie M Wyand)(Fletcher Plummer/Hannah B Smith)
HEATH: Charles H (Kingston/26) & Belle Pervere (Sandown/23), 09 Sep 1905 (D)
    (Andrew F Heath/Ellen Kimball)(Edwin Pervere/Emma F Simond)
    Edgar N (Kingston/22) & Annamai Kenny (Amsterdam,NY/19), 22 Jul 1933 (E)
    (Charles H Heath/Belle Pevere)(John Kenny/Margaret Rimmer)
    Fred A (Kingston/23) & Grace E Avery Kingston/25), 01 May 1906
    (Franklin G A Heath /Ellen E Kimball)(Frank S Avery/Mary Addie Davis)
    Fred A (Kingston/31) & Lillian P.Dundas (Merrimac,Ma/35), 20 Sep 1914
    (F.G.A. Heath/Ellen E Kimball)(Charles H Palmer/Elizabeth Baker)
    Howard C (Danville/26) & Jeannette S Davis (Kingston/25), 15 Aug 1910
    (John F Heath/ Emma Collins)(Richard H Davis/ Harriet Stacy)
HECK: James J (Wilmington,Ma) & Pamela A Schaier (Wilmington,Ma), 10 Jul 1988
HECKEL: Paul C (Kingston) & Elaine D Isherwood (Kingston), 26 Apr 1986
HECKMAN: Scot T (Kingston) & Joan T Kinney (Atkinson), 30 Jun 1983
HEFFERMAN: Paul I (Kingston/49) & Hazel C Williams (Kingston/44), 07 Feb 1948 (E)
    (Patrick Hefferman/Ellen Cooney)(Melvin York/Lucinda Smith)
HEFFNER: Donald L (Tipp City,Oh) & Jean P Richards (Mattapan,Ma), 06 May 1955
    (Harrison F Heffner/ Anna Cullouis)(Clarence Richards/ Medina O Celli)
HEIKKLIA: Leonard A (S Carver,Ma) & Angelina M Gregory (Brockton,Ma/),08 Dec 1962
HEMEON: David D, III (Exeter) & Patricia L Horning (Kingston), 22 Oct 1977
HENDERSON: Brian K (Melrose,Ma) & Constance Collins (Melrose,Ma), 22 Oct 1989
    Lloyd L (Kingston) & Linda L Johnson (Exeter), 21 Nov 1964 (N)
HENDRIGAN: Gary W (Tewksbury,Ma) & Dianne L Spinale (Tewksbury,Ma),26 Jun 1993
HENNESSEY: Joseph D (Kingston) & Tammie L Bolton (Kingston), 17 Sep 1994

HERMAN: Bruce R (Fremont) & Patricia S Cyr (Kingston), 27 Dec 1967 (Littleton)
HERRICK: Lawrence K (Plaistow) & Sandra L Conant (Kingston), 09 Sep 1961 (P)
    (Lawrence K Herrick/Katherine P Wilbur)(Gardner H Conant/ Christine M Dustin)
HEY: Neil A (Topsfield,Ma) & Jeannette B Durgin (Kingston), 14 May 1969
HICKS: Phillip W (Exeter) & Mary A Rowe (Kingston), 05 Dec 1975 (E)
HIGGINS: Richard M (Boston,Ma) & Barbara J Shay (Milton,Ma),18 Jun 1954
    (James E Higgins/ Mary Coughlin) (Harold N Shay/ Josephine Griffin)
HILEMAN: Raymond F (Kingston) & Rita M Overka (Kingston), 22 Jul 1992
HILL: Frederick E (Kingston) & Pattiann Picard (Kingston), 25 Nov 1975 (P)
    Richard F (Kingston) & Helen F Hill (Kingston), 23 Jan 1974
HILLERY: John B (Andoer,Ma) & Maria S Colton (Haverhill,Ma), 17 May 1964)
HILLIARD: John C (Kingston/21) & Hazel R Goldthwaite (Kingston/20), 29 Sep 1920
    (William Hilliard/Flora E Jewell)(Everard Goldthwaite/Grace Sargent)
HILLIDGE: Benjamin F (Haverhill,Ma) & Mavis M Vosburgh (Haverhill,Ma), 05 Mar 1955
    (Michael Hillidge/ Christine Ayer)(George A Vosburgh/ Ina Hilliker)
HILLNER: Charles, IV (Kingston) & Cherylyn L Carleton (Kingston), 28 May 1983
HILTON: Randy T (Newton) & Kimberly A McDonald (Kingston), 03 Sep 1977
    Randy T (Kingston) & Kathryn J O'Leary (Kingston), 10 Sep 1988
HIRL: James C,Jr (Milton,Ma) & Alicia M Devlin (Quincy,Ma), 06 Dec 1962
HISCOMBE: Edward S (Kingston/25) & Dorothy C Currier (Kingston/24), 22 Nov 1941(S)
HITAJ: Skendo F (Lynn,Ma) & Marion M Kehoe (Lynn,Ma), 07 Aug 1961
    (Fazio Hitaj/ Marion Hsubij)(Michael Kehoe/ Erna L Locke)
HODGDON: Larry D (Pembroke) & Katherine E Moore (Kingston), 22 Aug 1970 (E)
    Richard T (Kingston) & Cheryl A Cook (Kingston), 03 Jul 1982
HOLBROOK: Walter A(Holbrook,Ma/54) & Stella A Clarkson (Biddeford,Me/39),16 Jul 1924
    (Abram C Holbrook/Olive M Wales)(Nathan Chadwick/Ellen A Stackpole) (M)
HOLDEN: John E (Lynn,Ma/28) & Clara H Browning (Worceser,Ma/28), 01 Oct 1920
    (John C Holden/Elizabeth Comeo)(Frank W Browning/Grace Heath)
HOLT: John E (Kingston) & Rachel F Stanley (Nashua), 17 Jan 1975   (Nashua)
HOLLAND: Charles P (Lawrence,Ma) & Rita Sullivan (Methuen,Ma), 01 Sep 1963
    Herbert F (Kingston) & Jenne M Eldridge (Kingston), 04 Sep 1971
    Richard F (Kingston) & Delores Hall (Fremont), 20 Sep 1969 (F)
HOLLENBECK: John R (Haverhill,Ma) & Irene J Weeks (Haverhill,Ma), 19 Sep 1969
HOLLINRAKE: Michael V (Newton) & Patricia A Mantone (Kingston), 21 Oct 1990
HOOPER: David J (Portsmouth) & Elfriede Dolph (Kingston), 03 Jul 1981
HOPKINS: Tommy (Beverly,Ma) & Carol L Harris (Beverly,Ma), 10 Sep 1960
    (Laurie Hopkins/ Bessie Lause)(Ralph C Harris/ Betty Moore)
HORNE: Steve N (Malden,Ma) & Margaret L Marchese (Malden,Ma),14 Feb 1989
    Daniel D (Kingston) & Sylvie M Houle (Kingston), 23 Jun 1984
    James (Boston,Ma & Joyce Pristas (Cambridge,Ma), 07 Aug 1962
    Michael D (Kingston) & Valerie M Romano (Kingston), 03 Aug 1974 (P)
    Norman T (Kingston) & Laura A Isaksen (Londonderry), 14 Sep 1985
HOSKER: John D (Kingston) & Patricia C Casey (Bradford), 19 Aug 1984
HOULE: Thomas G (Kingston) & Laura A Girard (Kingston), 08 May 1993

HOUNSHELL: William R (Lynn,Ma) & Marjorie E Lewis (Lynn,Ma), 01 Apr 1955
    (T.H. Hounshell/ Estelle Taylor)(George L Lewis/ Laura N Bishop)
HOWARD: Christopher J (Lee) & Ellen M Hume (Kingston), 22 Sep 1985
    Edward J, Jr (Exeter) & Carol J Malloy (Kingston), 15 Feb 1975
    Kenneth P (Amesbury,Ma) & Lisa M Lancey (Amesbury,Ma), 19 Nov 1983
    Robert L (Kingston) & Evelyn E Brown (Woburn,Ma), 02 Jul 1966
HOYT: Frank C (Merrimac,Ma) & Celeste C Cosgrove (Haverhill,Ma), 23 Dec 1969
    Walter (N Andover,Ma) & Raymah H Riley (Lawrence,Ma), 19 Dec 1960
    (Walter P Hoyt/ Lillian M Munroe)(Albert E Riley/ Helen R Estey)
    William J, III (Kingston) & Nancy A Beauchesne (Kingston), 07 Mar 1993
HUBBARD: John M (E Wakefield,Ma) & Tammie E Stevens (Kingston), 28 Oct 1983
HUBER: William B (Kingston) & Suzanne M Deschamps (Kingston), 30 Jun 1990
HUFF: Randy C (Kingston) & Donna L Brander (Kingston), 12 Dec 1982
HUGHES: Walter P, Jr (No Andover,Ma)& Kathleen M O'Neill (No Andover,Ma),20 Aug1988
HULL: John D (Kensington/21) & Margrett E Brewster (Stratham/18) (date unknown)
    (Richard Hull)   (George W Brewster)
HUNT: Bert C (Groveland,Ma/24) & Alice Marshall (So Hampton/16), 26 May 1906   (N)
    (Paul Hunt/Affia Sleeper)(Richmond Marshall/Lila Heath)
    Bert (Groveland/27) & Augusta B. Parker(Canning,N.S.), 18 Nov 1916 (P)
    (Paul Hunt/Afpha Sleeper)(Lemuel M Blois/Rebecca S Blois)
    Glen R (Peabody,Ma) & Deidre F Brunelle (Peabody,Ma), 26 Nov 1988
    Herbert W (Boston,Ma/21) & Agnes K Stasio (Boston,Ma/19), 04 Jul 1926
    (Frank W Hunt)   (Martin J Stasio)
    James D (Kingston) & Louisa S Beam (Kingston), 11 Aug 1984
    John A (Kingston) & Carolyn L Plante (Haverhill,Ma), 08 Jun 1968 (P)
    Kevin J (Redondo Beach, Ca) & Donna J Rowen (Redondo Beach, Ca), 10 Feb 1990
    Robert E (Kingston) & Rita T Gonyer (Kingston), 24 Nov 1962
    Willard (Reading,Ma) & Renzel R Hurd (Reading,Ma), 13 Jan 1963
HUNTOON: George P (Dedham,Ma/61) & Clara M Horgan (Newton Ctr/45), 24 Aug 1945
    (George Huntoon/Emma Tefft)(Daniel Horgan/Ellen Mahoney)
HUNTRESS: Clarence A (Limington,Me/19) & Addie D Tucker(Kingston/18), 17 Mar 1900
    (Temple C Huntress/Lucy A Dalyrimple)(Assiah H Tucker/Addie E Goodwin)
HUOT: Donald R (Kingston) & Patricia A Nadeau (Hudson), 02 Jul 1976 (Hudson)
HURLBERT: Ernest E (Kingston) & Gladys M Marche (Kingston), 04 May 1972
HURLEY: Daniel F (Billerica, Ma) & Tonnie A McFarland (Billerica, Ma), 13 Jun 1992
HUTCHINSON: Walter J (Somerville,Ma) & Celia M Williamson (Everett,Ma), 22 Apr 1962
HUXSTER: Clifford J (Blairstown,--) & Catherine L Rowe (Kingston), 18 Sep 1982
IBBOTSON: Joseph W C (Toledo,Oh/32) & Mattie M Webster (Kingston/20), 03 Sep 1906
    (William Ibbotson/Harriet Truton)(Henry D Webster/Carrie Winslow)
IMBRESCIA: Nunzio (Revere,Ma) & Jeanne M Carozza (Revere,Ma), 14 Sep 1958
    (Philip Imbrescia/ Carmella Cataldo)(Joseph R Carozza/ Margaret F McEachern)
INGALLS: Robert S (Kingston) & Beverly Robinson (Pembroke), 03 Sep 1955 (Pembroke)
    (Edmond E Ingalls/ Lita E Snall)(Joseph H Robinson/ Flossie Lewis)
INMAN: Alfred C (Harmony,RI) & Judith A Morse (Greenville,RI), 14 Feb 1959
    (Alfred H Inman/ Bertha Grachien)(Walter J Morse/ June Cyr)

IODICE: Bernard F (Fall River,Ma) & Laurence L Trainor (Winthrop,Ma), 22 Jul 1961
(John Iodice/ Mary McGovern)(Joseph Lezotte/ Adele St Laurent)
IRISH: Charles R (Exeter) & Gail A Stevens (Kingston), 16 Aug 1969
IRVINE: William J (Ashland)& Jean A Kane (Ashland), 08 Jul 1982
ISAACS Kenneth A (Kingston) & Janice E Elwell (Kingston), 22 Jul 1982
JACINTO: Urban (Methuen,Ma) & Gloria M Enus (Lawrence,Ma),14 Jul 1960
(Arbelino Jacinto/ Mary Fraitus)(Anthony Ventura/ Mary Veanni)
Zabu (Methuen,Ma) & Gertrude B St Amand (Lawrence,Ma), 16 Jul 1964
JACKMAN: A William (Manchester,Ma) & Grace B Herlihy (Waltham,Ma), 20 Jul 1969
JACKSON: Russell A (Hartford,Ct) & Eva P Girard (Haverhill,Ma), 10 Mar 1951
(Arthur Jackson/Dorothy I Fuller)(Israel Hamel/Eva Bernard)
Steven H (Kingston) & Sheila A Peacher (Kingston), 25 Apr 1981
JACOBSEN: Jeffrey W (Kingston) & Lorna E Higney (Kingston), 10 May 1986
JACOBSON: Richard D (Kingston) & Darcie A St Onge (Kingston), 14 Apr 1978 (N)
JACOTT: John E (Revere,Ma) & Carolyn G Lamonde (Lynn,Ma), 07 Mar 1971
JACQUES: William (Winthrop,Ma) & Christine A Sepe (Revere,Ma), 18 Oct 1953
(William E Jacques/ Mary A Brennan)(Anthony Sepe/ Beatrice Barton)
JAEGER: Herman L, Jr (Hooksett) & Nancy A Dunn (Kingston), 10 Aug 1972 (Hooksett)
JAKUBENS: John H (Rochester) & Elisabeth A Deguio (Kingston), 26 Aug 1975 (Roch)
JALBERT: Andrew P (Dover) & Jean M Bower (Kingston), 08 Apr 1989
JAMES: Donald E (Attleboro,Ma) & Mildred M Jordan (Plainville,Ma), 24 Oct 1964
JASKOWICK: Frank (21) & Lawdislava Bohoczyk (18), 12 Oct 1934
(Stanley Jaskowick/Margaret Gumena)(Edward Bohoczyk/Adeja Marrick)
JASPER: Charlie N (Candia/21) & Ethel M Hartford (Deerfield/21), 18 Feb 1907
(Frank Jasper/Katie Bundy) (Rufus Hartford/Hattie L Waite)
Mervin R (24) & Edith A George (19), 17 Sep 1938 (F)
(Charles Jasper/Ethel M Hartford)(Walter M George/Inez W Tewksbury)
Spencer D (Kingston) & Linda J Clements (Plaistow), 22 Jul 1967 (P)
JEAN: Robert G (Lawrence,Ma) & Dale M Bubar (Lawrence,Ma), 05 Jul 1986
JEFFREYS: Richard W (Brentwood) & Patricia A Chapdelaine (Kingston), 07 Aug 1993
JELLEY: Arnold L (Newburyport,Ma) & Esther A Holmes (Newburyport,Ma), 30 May 1957
(Alton L Jelley/ Dorothy A Hill)(George E Holmes/ Ruth Pollard)
JENKINS: Earl D (E Weymouth,Ma) & Catherine V Lutz (Weymouth,Ma), 18 Feb 1961
(John V Jenkins/ Mildred MacCaushans)(Frank Berbelcaster/ Virginia Adne)
JENNINGS: Dana F (Kingston) & Florence M Britton (Kingston), 27 Sep 1957
(Floyd Jennings/ Laura Sargent)(George Britton/ Lila George)
Dana A (Kingston) & Deborah L Krieger (Exeter), 07 Jun 1981
JENNINGS: Timothy W (Kingston) & Leigh A Mitchell (Kingston), 25 Feb 1984
JERVIS: Edward W, Jr (Kingston/28) & Norma E Bake (Kingston/23), 22 May 1949
(Edward W Jervis/Isabelle L Day)(Ralph H Bake/l Evelyn Nason)
JESTINGS: George J (22) & Ruth O Stacey (18), 31 Jul 1940 (E)
(Bernard Jestings/Mary Richards)(Lyndon J Stacey/Olive M Burbank)
JEWELL: Kevin D (Kingston) & Kristy A Mitchell (Kingston), 10 Jun 1993
Lance P (Allston,Ma) & Lesley A Query (Allston,Ma),02 Sep 1984

JEWETT: Kenneth E (Sharon/44) & Charlotte Wood (Kingston/45), 03 Aug 1949
    (Charles B Jewett/Abbie S White)(Frederic E Wood/Caroline E Peaslee)
    Richard H (Kingston) & Susan Thibault (Kingston), 18 Apr 1980
JILLSON: David H (Kingston) & Marilyn L Colby (Plaistow),19 Apr 1959 (P)
    (Harold H Jillson/ Frances B Moon)(John W Colby/ Louise W Philbrick)
    David H (Kingston) & Karen A Torrisi (Kingston), 06 Oct 1990
JIMENEZ: Alexis (Kingston) & Karen Schultz (Kingston),19 Oct1985
JOHNSON: Carl E (Pembroke) & Julia A Osborne (Kingston), 19 Oct 1968
    Dalton R (Kingston) & Barbara L Parker (Kingston), 02 Dec 1993
    Daniel J (Sarasota,Fl) & Lucy E Lake (Sarasota, F.), 31 Dec 1981
    Donald E (Kingston) & Lois M Wentworth (Milton,Ma), 22 Jun 1963 (Milton)
    Gardner A, Jr (Kingston) & Pamela A Mayoe (Kingston), 11 Jun 1983
    Joel T & Sharon L Tebo, 28 May 1983 (N)
    Peter A (Walpole,Ma) & Cathy R Coe (Carlisle,Ma), 26 Dec 1976
    Richard P (Kingston) & Patricia A Beauregard (Kingston), 06 Jun 1964
    Scott E (Chelmsford,Ma) & Victoria J McKenna (Lowell,Ma), 16 Aug 1986
    Thomas S (Plaistow) & Rosemarie McCusker (Kingston), 28 Sep 1975 (P)
    Mark E (Kingston) & Lois A St.Laurent (Kingston), 26 Jun 1993
JONES: Bobby G (Attleboro, Ma) & Bette A Eddy (Attleboro, Ma), 16 May 1972
    Carol R (35) & Grace L Teehan (26), 28 Dec 1936
    (Fred C Jones/Alvonia Dyer)(John W Teehan/Bertha M Dildine)
    George W (Somerville,Ma) & Rosamond M Stevens (Kingston), 24 Dec 1950
    (Francis A Jones/Alice M Dew)(Frank W Stevens/Lora M Stevens)
    James M (Kingston) & Elizabeth L Jette (Exeter), 02 Jul 1958 (E)
    (Samuel L Jones/ Irene A Peters)(Irenee M Jette/ Lillian B Lary)
    Leon F (Old Orchard,Me/34) & Ruth E Hall (Old Orchard,Me/30), 14 May 1949
    (Arthur L Jones/Cora L Milliken)(John Dodge/Effie Bailey)
    Thomas M (Exeter, Me) & Donna M Cole (Georgetown, Ma), 06 Sep 1990
    William T, III (Irving, Tx) & Susan D Nelson (Chagrin Falls, Oh), 05 Jul 1991
JOUVELAKAS: George J (Somerville,Ma) & Lorraine M Rufo (Somerville,Ma),22 Dec 1962
JOY: David W (Kingston) & Marjorie Walker (Kingston), 19 Feb 1988
JUAREZ: Perry G (Kingston) & Eileen M Sebetes (Kingston), 28 Apr 1991
JUDSON: Charles F (Plaistow) & Doris A Dorman (Kingston), 25 Nov 1970 (P)
    Mark A (Haverhill,Ma) & Laurie E Stultz (Haverhill,Ma), 28 Jun 1986
KANALY: Paul J (Belmont,Ma) & Mary V Morse (Kingston), 05 May 1973
KAPLAN: Irwin (New York,NY) & Charlene P Smith (Kingston), 31 May 1970
KEATING: Robert T (Lynn,Ma) & Barbara M Reickhardt (Saugus,Ma), 14 Jan 1962
KEAY: Gary C (Kingston) & Nancy J Walker (Kingston), 26 Jun 1982
KEIRAN: Michael J (Kingston) & Claire A Custeau (Hampstead),12 Aug 1972 (Ham)
    Michael J (Kingston) & Brenda A Paquet (Kingston), 06 May 1978 (P)
KEITH: Robert P (Kingston)& Marilynn S Larkin (Kingston), 26 Sep 1980
KELLEY: Charles (50) & Alma E Graham (30), 27 Jan 1935
    (George W Kelley/Malina Keezer)(John F Graham/Alma E Wood)
    Charles E (Kingston/22) & Josephine Kelley (Kingston/17), 24 Feb 1906 (Hav)
    (George W Kelley/Malina Keezer)(Levi Martin/Ella Davis)

Edward (Kingston/23) & Charlotte Martin (So Hampton/29), 25 Jan 1932 (D/O)
(Charles E Kelley/Sarah J Martin)(Albert Dewhurst/Jennie R Welsh)
Frederic (Kingston/16) & Josephine Martin (Sandown/19), 13 Jun 1903
(Daniel Kelley/Harriet Place)(Levi Martin/Ella Davis)
Frederick (Kingston/21) & Katie M Chamberlain (Northwood/25), 03 Aug 1906
(Daniel Kelley/Hattie Place)(Charles N Chamberlain/Abbie Fifield)
George W (Kingston/24) & Estella L Brown (Exeter/21), 23 Feb 1932
(Charles E Kelley/Sadie J Martin)(Clyde L Brown/Dasy Bryant)
George W (Kingston) & Dorothy C Taylor (Kingston), 02 May 1953
(Charles E Kelley/ Sadie J Martin)(Tom Taylor/ Bessie Vines)
John (Milton,Ma) & Helen G Farley (Charlestown,Ma), 16 Feb 1963
Lester C (26) & Margaret A Wallace (24), 16 Jun 1938
(John F Kelley/Mary L Donovan)(William Wallace/Anna I Feldman)
Michael W (Medford,Ma) & Kathleen M Flynn (Kingston), 17 Oct 1987
Thomas F (Methuen,Ma) & Naomi L Rockey (Methuen,Ma), 10 Jul 1987
KELLY: Frank D (78) & Edna F George (71), 02 Jul 1940
(George L Kelly/Kate M Ducey)(Andrew J West/Mary F Davis)
William R (Salem) & Karen K Kerkhoff (Kingston), 09 Aug 1980
KEMP: Dale H (Kingston) & Valene A Thebeault (Newton), 14 Jul 1979
Donald A (Kingston) & Norma L Chick (Portsmouth), 31 Jan 1953 (Ports)
(George A Kemp/ Josephine Rogers)(Norman H Chick/ Lottie N Bailey)
Edward A (Kingston) & Kimberley M McDermott (Kingston), 23 Jul 1977
George A (Utica,NY/28) & Josephine Rogers (Canaan,Vt/23),12 Oct 1928 (Reeds Ferry)
(George Kemp/Hattie B Inkpin)(Joseph A Rogers/.....)
John R (Haverhill,Ma) & Alice C Comeau (Haverhill,Ma), 04 Sep 1959
(Charles Kemp,Jr/Doris Simard)(Eli Comeau/ Arlene Timmins)
KENDALL: Richard P (Kingston) & Maylene S Emerson (Kingston), 02 Aug 1980
KERKHOFF: David P (Kingston) & MargaretAnn M Dickey (Salem), 24 Aug 1986
KERR: Randall F (Kingston) & Veda A Stark (Kingston), 01 Jun 1991
KERSHAW: William C (Newton/21) & Florence A George (Kingston/10),03 Apr 1948 (D)
(Walter B Kershaw/Elizabeth Standing)(Walter M George/Inez Tewksbury)
KERVIN: Frank L, Jr (Kingston) & Diane M Uerkwitz (Kingston), 29 Mar 1981
KESSARIS: Kenneth J (Beverly,Ma) & Nancy M Scott (Beverly,Ma), 12 Jul 1952
(James G Kessaris/ Mary Kirios)(Kingley E Scott/ Muriel E Hazell)
KETTLEWOOD: Clayton L (Dover) & Deanne L Cross (Kingston), 25 Feb 1990
KILLAM: Chester H (Kingston) & Alice M Greenwood (Kingston), 12 Sep 1953
(Dwight L Killam,Sr/Dorothy D Perley)(Frederick Greenwood/ Esther M Nielsen)
Dwight (Kingston) & Patricia A Patten (Kingston), 19 Jan 1952
(Dwight L Killam/ Dorothy D Perley)(Harold E Patten/ Hester C Winslow)
Harold D (Kingston) & Patti J Leclair (Kingston), 05 Jul 1975
Harold D (Kingston) & Cynthia L Garlington (Plaistow), 23 Apr 1988
KIMBALL: David E (Kingston/64) & Alice J Mahoney (Candia/53), 28 Jun 1947 (Epping)
(Daniel Kimball/Mary Patch)(James Mahoney/Margaret Cunningham)
Edward & Minnie C Cooke, 01 Oct 1921
(Stephen Kimball/Mary E Giddings)(Alfred McKusick/Fannie Abbott)

Eugene C (Methuen/72) & Helen A Stanyan (Manchester/62), 04 Apr 1927
   (Moses E Kimball)   (Aaron E Frye)
Spencer S (Kingston) & Pamela S Parevoliotes (Kingston), 07 Jul 1984
KIMMEL: James F (Lowell, Ma) & Gabrielle B Jackson (Kingston), 29 Feb 1992
KING: Clyde E (Kingston) & Elaine M Luddy (Plaistow), 26 Jul 1958
   (Harold J King/ Letitia J King)(Thomas L Luddy/ Stella M Lougee)
   Harold J & Catherine Cole, 14 May 1921 (E)
   John T (Texarkana,Tx) & Jessie B MacRae (Stellarton,N.S.), 01 Dec 1951
      (Andrew D King/Doris Hunt)(Clarence MacRae/Jessie Hamblen)
   Samuel M (Kingston) & Patricia L Ackerson (Plaistow), 25 Jun 1967   (P)
   William R (Chelsea,Ma) & Lorraine J Boynton (Lynn,Ma),11 Jun 1954
      (Henry W King/ Mary J Snow) (Roland I Boynton/ Dorothy E .....)
KINNEY: Wayne E (Kingston) & June B Rondeau (Kingston), 25 Dec 1984
KINSTEAD: Robert A (Haverhill,Ma/22) & Elizabeth B Bedard (Kingston/22),14 Jun 1920 (W)
   (Robert R Kinstead/Mary R Withie)(Alphonzo Bedard/Clarisa Gemier)
KIPPS: Mark R (Kingston) & Lory Sue Beck (Kingston), 16 Jan 1977
KIRK: Peter R (Stoneham, Ma) & Lauri Pappas (Stoneham, Ma), 21 Jul 1990
KIRSCH: Carl D (Kingston) & Susan P Reed (Plaistow), 19 Jun 1981
KITTREDGE: William J (Kingston) & Judith L Savage (Kingston), 18 Mar 1988
KLINE: Gary J (Kingston) & Anita A Carbone (Epping), 23 May 1981
KNAPP: Charles J (28) & Elizabeth Hall (21), 10 May 1934
   (Joseph C Knapp/Florence Jones)(Roscoe V Hall/Ella Crocker)
KNEELAND: George S (Kingston) & Sandra L Allen (Kingston), 10 Aug 1984
KNIGHTS: Charles C (Melrose/Ma/24) & Elsie E Judkins (Kingston/22), 25 Sep 1915
   (Charles H Knights/Myra L Kendall)(Arthur R Judkins/Delia A Page)
KNOWLES: John F, III (Kensington) & JoAnne Gillis (Kingston), 19 Feb 1994
KOREL: Michael E (Fairport,NY) & Sheila A Langley (Kingston), 21 Jul 1957
   (Michael H Korel/ Pauline Dererick)(Bennie B Langley/ Margaret A Lange)
KOTHE: Gary W (Amherst) & Kathryn I Gurtt (Kingston), 04 Aug 1973
KOWALCZYK: Brian S (Kingston) & Leeanne F Alux (Kingston), 22 Oct 1983
KRAMER: Stanley R (Haverhill,Ma) & Linda M Letarte (Haverhill,Ma), 27 Jun 1986
KRAUSS: Alan J (Kingston) & Joan M Dacey (Kingston), 31 Oct 1980
KRAYNAK: George (W Middlesex,Pa) & Catherine G Rowe (Kingston), 26 Dec 1987
KREGER: Alfred H (Exeter/22) & Amelia E Platukys (Maynard,Ma/20), 14 Feb 1931 (E)
   (William Kreger/Emma Schmel)(Waldos Platukys/Eva Palazewic)
KUDART: M Scott (Kingston) & Paulette Ling (Medford Lakes,NJ), 29 May 1988
KUKENE: Jeffrey W (Amesbury,Ma) & Lisa J Fales (Kingston), 11 May 1985
KUZIRIAN: George, Jr (Kingston) & Yvette R Chaisson (Kingston), 17 Oct 1987
LABELLE: Raymond E (21) & Virginia D Bennett (19), 20 Mar 1941 (D)
   (Samuel J Labelle/Viola E Collins)(William A Bennett/Lena J Bird)
   Raymond E, Jr (Kingston) & Diane G Lafayette (Kingston), 15 Oct 1966
LaBONTE: Albert A (Webster,Ma) & Bette J Jewell (Webster,Ma), 23 Nov 1963
LABRIE: John M (Salem) & Marsha K Castetter (Tampa,Fl), 13 Jun 1977
LACERTE: Gary L (Kingston) & Linda L Kemp (Kingston), 29 Jun 1974   (E/K)
LaCOMBE: William E (Taunton,Ma) & Nancy A Gosson (Taunton,Ma), 12 Mar 1966

William E (Norton,Ma) & Candee G Braley (Norton,Ma), 16 Nov 1967
LACROIX: Gerard A (Kingston) & Christine J Hart (Kingston), 24 Apr 1982
LAFAYETTE: Dale T (Kingston) & Donna M Braley (Kingston), 11 Mar 1972
LAFONTAINE: Robert A (Pelham) & Rochelle Ingersoll (Kingston), 23 Sep 1983
LaFLECHE: Ricky S (Kingston) & Kristin L Aylward (Kingston), 23 Jan 1988
LAMB: James H, IV (Kingston) & Tanya P Law (Kingston), 19 Jun 1990
    Kenneth E (Kingston) & Linda-Gaye LaProva (Haverhill, Ma), 21 Oct 1972 (N)
    Patrick M (Kingston) & Cheryl A Paradis (Lawrence,Ma), 13 Apr 1986
LAMBERT: Dennis R (Haverhill,Ma) & Aimee M Pelletier (Kingston), 10 Apr 1965 (P)
    Forrest M (Kingston) & Elizabeth M Marsh (Fremont), 07 Jun 1969 (N)
    Greg A (Brentwood) & Christine A Bean (Kingston), 21 Nov 1992
    Paul G (Haverhill,Ma) & Jarda L Belmonte (Haverhill,Ma), 21 Mar 1981
LAMONT: Louis A (22) & Ruth S Young (21), 21 Jun 1936 (P)
    (Noel Lamont/Ella A Lyford)(John A Young/Lena Middleman)
LAMONTAGUE: Charles A (21) & Esther Labell (19), 09 Nov 1934
    (Joseph Lamontague/Marie Poulin)(Samuel Labell/Viola Collins)
LAMPREY: Richard I (Kingston) & Penelope J Cheever (Kingston), 28 Jun 1986
LAMY: Richard N (Kingston) & Jennifer L Larosa (Kingston), 16 Jan 1981
LANCASTER: Kenneth G (Kingston) & Lisa M Proal (Kingston), 20 Oct 1985
LANCIANI: David A (Kingston) & Nancy L Alcorn (Salem), 08 Apr 1970
    Richard E (Kingston) & Sylvia F Senter (Plaistow), 12 Oct 1968 (P)
LANDERS: Daniel E, Jr(Epping) & Daren V Sims (Kingston), 29 Jul 1955
    (Daniel E Landers,Sr/Jennie D Harvey)(Alfred D Sims/ Ernavale Mashburn)
    Theodore F (Epping) & Barbara Chamberlain (Kingston), 31 Jul 1953
    (Daniel E Landers/ Jennie Harvey)(Beverly S Chamberlain/ Mary Rowell)
LANDRY: James J (Kingston) & Tracy A Hamlin (Kingston), 09 Sep 1989
LANE: Robert D (So Essex,Ma/24) & Nadine L Foster (Indianapolis,In/23), 02 Feb 1946
    (Ralph Lane/Marie Memple)(Frederick A Foster/Helen F Liehr)
LANG: Wheeler H (Deerfield/33) & Mattie O Brown (Kingston/32), 14 Sep 1910
    (William H Lang/ Helen M Hilton)(Nathaniel Brown/ Peace Ann Chase)
LANGAN: Stephen F (Kingston) & Kelly J O'Brien (Kingston), 22 Aug 1992
LANGDON: Paul D (Epping) & Antoinette Marotte (Kingston), 02 May 1969 (EP)
LANGEVIN: Harold A (Kingston) & Stella G Bryant (Kingston), 25 Nov 1981
LANGLOIS: Norman W (Kingston) & Danielle Y Mahar (Kingston), 24 Dec 1989
LANKHORST: Jacobus J (Arlington,Ma) & Sarah E Cohen (Boston,Ma), 17 Sep 1954
    (Abraham L Lankhorst/ Jacoba Gesina)(Meher M Cohen/ Ella M McGregor)
LANSEIGNE: Albert L (Kingston) & Kathryn J Ames (Kingston), 04 Aug 1973 (N)
LANZA: Peter J (Amesbury,Ma) & Nancy J Champion (Kingston), 06 Jun 1981
LaPRELL: Ronald S (Haverhill,Ma) & Shirley L Clark (Kingston), 07 Nov 1959 (N)
    (Arthur J LaPrell/ Mildred I Brindle)(Maurice A Clark/ Angie Bean)
LARENSEN: Michael E (Kingston) & Cindy K Wheelock (Kingston), 21 Jul 1984
LaROCHELLE: Steven C (Atkinson) & Kathleen M Noury (Kingston), 22 Jun 1985
LAROCQUE: Thomas G (Beverly,Ma) & Margaret L Klinos (Beverly,Ma), 14 Nov 1960
    (Eugene Larocque/Margaret E Minicello)(William Phinney/Margaret I Ireland)

LARSON: Charles E (Kingston) & Carolyn Sanborn (Fremont), 24 Dec 1955 (F)
(Elmer J Larson/ Gladys M Gibbons)(Curtice S Sanborn/ Dorothy C True)
LATFORD: Donald J (Kingston) & Evelyn C Chandler (Exeter), 29 Aug 1980
LATULIPPE: Gedeon, Jr (Kingston) & Kathleen A Bartlett (Kingston), 31 Dec 1976 (P)
LAURENCE: John J (Plaistow) & Karen N Roberts (Kingston), 04 Sep 1976
LAVOIE: Joseph W (Kingston) & Linda G Durgin (Kingston), 26 Jun 1983
Marc R (Kingston) & Joyce Applegarth (Kingston), 18 Sep 1987
Michael P (Hampton) & Kimberley A Geisendorfer (Kingston), 20 Oct 1990
LAZOS: Alexander (Haverhill,Ma/30) & June Lamb (Kingston/27), 01 Jul 1949 (Hamp)
(Costa Lazos/Effie Kasadimous)(Raymond H Barrett/Florence Rollins)
LAZURE: Peter B (Kingston) & Linda M Eveleth (Kingston), 28 Nov 1981
LAY: Charles D (Haverhill,Ma) & Crystal L Adams (Kingston), 22 May 1971 (N)
LAZAZZERA: Arthur N (Bradford,Ma) & Carol E Clark (Clinton,Ma), 13 May 1967
LEAMAN: Robert S (Miami, Fl) & Constance L Smith (Kingston), 04 Jun 1971 (P)
LEATHE: Norman E (Kingston) & Edith M Hill (Kingston), 13 May 1967
LEAVITT: Michael J (Methuen,Ma) & Christie D Young (Methuen,Ma), 11 Jun 1989
William H (Kingston) & Linda L Girard (Haverhill,Ma), 10 Jul 1982
LEAVY: George (Waltham,Ma/42) & Beatrice Smith (Nashua/20), 02 Nov 1916
(Thomas Leavy/Maria Lynch)(James A Smith/Emma J Smith)
LEBLANC: Edward Y (Ayer,Ma) & Shari E Frulla (Methuen,Ma), 28 May 1993
John M (Haverhill, Ma) & Marcy R Odess (Haverhill, Ma), 12 Aug 1992
Norman P (Kingston) & Lisa Vonhassel (Atkinson), 15 Sep 1984
LEDUC: George A (Sandwich,Ma) & Lucetta J Lane (SandwichMa), 28 Apr 1955
(Jeffrey F Leduc/ Orise Lavallee)(William H Lane/ Zelma J Robinson)
LEE: Quintin D (New Boston) & Sabrina G Kujat (Andover, Ma), 16 Mar 1991
LEGAULT: Alfred (Haverhill,Ma/28) & Bertha Collins (Kingston/19), 12 Dec 1923
(Leonard Leault/Adwilda Departie)(Elmer A Collins/Susan Nason)
LEGERE: William R (Danville) & Judith A Amazeen (Kingston), 05 Feb 1983
LEKAS: James M (Haverhill,Ma) & Elaine A DeBrosky (Haverhill,Ma), 04 Mar 1955
(John Lekas/ Anna Goudas)(Blessler De Brosky/ Louise Bachon)
LEITH: Robert W (Epping) & Marjorie N George (Kingston), 16 May 1980
LEMIEUX: Charles E (Kingston) & Ghislaine R Houle (Kingston), 07 Apr 1984
LENNON: James H (Kingston) & Donna L Bake (Kingston), 15 Oct 1988
Jeremy D (Kingston) & Amanda L Melvin (Brentwood), 28 May 1994
Joel B (Kingston) & Lisa G Lacombe (Victoriaville, Que), 15 Jul 1980
John M (Hooksett) & Linda G Gilbert (Hooksett), 17 Feb 1979
LESLIE: William (Manchester/39) & Helen G Bragg (Newburyport,Ma/29), 08 Mar 1928
(William Leslie/Sarah Scroggins)(Evero Towne/Ellen Gurney)
LeVANGIE: Richard B (Braintree,Ma) & Svea Lindberg (Kingston), 21 Dec 1957
(Richard LeVangie/ Ada LeVangie)(Daniel Elliott/ Olive Eldridge)
LERMOND: Ernest S (Brentwood) & Marilyn R Avery (Kingston), 14 Feb 1958
(Ernest Lermond/ Muriel E Bryant)(Raymond E Avery/ Exilda C Foster)
LeROY: Robert K (E Kingston) & Robin L Pressey (Kingston), 22 Aug 1987
LeSAGE: Jeffrey S (Salisbury,Ma) & Dawn M Deschenes (Kingston), 18 May 1985
LEVEILLE: Richard F, Jr (Seabrook) & Cynthia L Butt (Kingston), 19 Aug 1988

LEVESQUE: Lucien P, Jr (Kingston) & Cynthia A Brocklebank (Kingston), 22 Sep 1962 (P)
LEVIS: Bruce N (Belmont,Ma) & Judith S Sanborn (Kingston), 27 Jun 1953
    (Charles E Levis/ Ruth N McPhee)(Leonard G Sanborn/ Dorothy Rae)
LEWANDOWSKI: Henry F, Jr (Kingston) & Lucinda A Bakie (Kingston), 06 Nov 1964
LEWIS: Joseph R (Kingston) & Sandra E Wallace (Kingston), 11 Apr 1989
    Vernon, Jr (Kingston/28) & Mary P Bailey (Hooksett/27), 21 Aug 1948 (Pembroke)
    (Vernon Lewis,Sr/Marion B Bartlett)(Charles P Bailey/Bertha Proud)
LIGHT: Robert J (Exeter) & Doris F Carter (Kingston), 05 Sep 1953 (E)
    (Fred J Light/ Maud Gaudette)(Harry L Carter/ Ida P Challis)
LINDELL: James (Staten Island,NY) & Alberta E Lind (Staten Island,NY), 01 May 1954
    (Stedman Lindell/ Vivian Boone)(William A Lind/ Minnie Beckerich)
LINDSEY: David A (Woburn,Ma) & Jacqueline H Lemerise (Woburn,Ma), 01 May 1964
    Robert S (Fremont) & Gloria J Ritchie (Kingston), 12 Sep 1976
LISKOW: Wolfgang (Elmwood,NJ) & Deborah J Clark (Kingston), 27 Dec 1975
LISLE: Frank W (Denier,Co) & Karen L Meeks (Kingston), 22 Apr 1967
LITTLEFIELD: Harmond C (Kingston) & Marianne H Witham (Raymond), 04 Mar 1972 (R)
    Harry C (Kingston) & Katheryn A Spelios (Newton), 19 Nov 1966 (P)
    Richard H (Kingston) & Gail S Maillet (Stratham), 13 Jul 1968 (E)
LLOYD: Harold E (Merrmiac,Ma) & Fern Chase (Merrimac,Ma), 31 Jul 1993
LOCKE: Stanley E (Kingston) & Roseann JDionne (Kingston), 02 Feb 1961   (N)
    (Stanley A Locke/ Isabelle Chesley)(Forrest E Hicks/ Annie Prescott)
LOCKHART: Gary L (Bloomington,In) & Ellen A Salach (Bloomington,In),01 Mar 1982
    Richard W (Danvers,Ma) & Linda M Roberts (Danvers,Ma), 02 Dec 1959
    (Charles Lockhart/ Ruth V Thibodeau)(Paul E Roberts/ Mary G Trahan)
LOCKWOOD: James (Kingston) & Christie L Rollins (Kingston), 21 Jun 1958
    (James Lockwood/ Alice Mosley)(Thomas Rollins/ Rosie Cates)
LOIK: James B (Kingston) & Molly Tufts Wheeler (Kingston), 20 Apr 1978
LONDON: Charles D (Newfields) & Anna M Poydar (Kingston), 13 Sep 1981
LONDRIGAN: Stephen P (Haverhill,Ma) & Sabrina Simmers (Billerica,Ma), 08 Oct 1988
LORD: Melvin H (Salem) & Betty B Drouin (Kingston), 20 Apr 1985
    Robert (Danvers,Ma) & Susan Carter (Tospfield,Ma), 25 Jul 1958
    (Charles Lord/ Norma Durkee)(Francis Carter/ Mary Vicary)
    William T (Kingston) & Mary E Scheffler (Kingston), 09 Aug 1981
LOWE: Terrance W (Haverhill,Ma) & Sharon Lee Dickinson (Amesbury,Ma), 10 Oct 1975
LUCIER: Eugene (Salem,Ma/23) & RoseVaillencourt(Lawrence,Ma/19), 13 Jun 1901
    (Tonsan Lucier/Mary Bosquet)(Philip Vaillencourt/Lea Meiux)
    John T (Haverhill,Ma) & Patricia A Files (Haverhill,Ma), 07 Jun 1968
LUDVIGSEN: Ronald P (Roxbury,Ma) & Carol A Dufour (Somerville,Ma), 26 Jan 1963
LUDWIG: Kenneth E (Lawrence,Ma) & Shirley C Donovan (Lawrence,Ma), 23 Feb 1983
LUMB: Douglas S (Methuen,Ma) & Elizabeth L Bolster (Methuen,Ma), 30 Mar 1984
LUND: Theodore R (Watertown,Ct/23) & Grace H Bradley (Delmar,NY/23), 06 Sep 1929
    (Peter M Lund/Mathilde Feldthaus)(Theodore J Bradley/Anna Peck)
LUNDIN: Carl (Brockton,Ma) & Linda A Ford (Brockton,Ma), 20 Oct 1963
LUNDQUIST: Mark E (Kingston) & Martha J Dooley (Kingston), 02 Nov 1991

LUPIEN: Bernard J (Sudbury,Ma) & Linda L Chicoine (Marlboro,Ma), 28 Aug 1961
    (George A Lupien/ Mary E Wilson)(Frederick Chicoine/ Louise K Carey)
LUSCOMB: Dean G (Middleton,Ma) & Linda O Denno (Middleton,Ma), 16 Dec 1960
    (Henry F Luscomb/ Louise Gage)(Raymond M Denno/ Goldie P Ogden)
    Edwin D (Middleton,Ma) & Janice R Lilly (Lynnfield,Ma), 15 Sep 1962
LUSONA: John D, Jr (Kingston) & Sandra J Cote (Kingston), 16 Jul 1983
LYDICK: George (Kingston) & Dorothy King (Kingston), 20 Jul 1952 (D)
    (Turner J Lydick/ Anna Albertson)(James S King/ Anna E Young)
LYDON: Thomas E (S Weymouth,Ma) & Gail E Bartlett (Hyde Park,Ma), 24 Jul 1962
LYMAN: James S (Everett,Ma) & Cynthia D Irving (Medford,Ma), 24 Apr 1982
MacBRIDE: William A (21) & Marion L Toatjes (18), 19 Dec 1937 (E)
    (James MacBride/ Edith Watterson)(Gerard J Toatjes/ Louise M Mangene)
MacDONALD: Edward S (Dorchester,Ma/24) & Mary I MacLeod (Quincy,Ma/23),15 Nov
    (Malcom MacDonald/Alice Sylvester)(Laughlin MacLeod/Katherine..)   1924
    Herbert Al (Allston,Ma) & Rebecca G Mackillop (Arlington,Ma), 10 May 1975
    Kenneth G (28) & Kathleen M Goodwin (26), 04 Apr 1942 (E)
    (Malcom T MacDonald/Vivian G Cooke)(Clinton B Goodwin/Bertha Thompson)
    Paul R (Kingston) & Barbara K Demers (Manchester), 01 Sep 1956 (M)
    (John MacDonald/ Irene Simes)(Henry J Demers/ Katherine Bryan)
    Richard W (Manchester) & Sally J Vogel (Kingston), 02 Sep 1972 (Durham)
    Rodney A (Kingston) & Selena E Russell (Kingston), 12 Jun 1993
MacKENNA: Charles H (Haverhill,Ma) & Meredith D Martin (Merrimac,Ma), 10 May 1964
MacKENZIE: Ronald T (Kingston)& Diane M Chouinard (Plaistow), 14 Feb 1986
MacLAUGHLIN: George S (Kingston) & Carol S Scott (Kingston), 12 Sep 1981
MacLEOD: William D (Kingston) & Wendy A Gallant (Kingston), 10 Aug 1973
MACOMBER: Chester E (Exeter) & Marjorie E (Wesley)Stevens (Kingston), 06 Mar 1954
    (Walter W Macomber/ Margaret Tracey)(James W Wesley/ Charlotte Sweet)
    Walter W (Kingston/39) & Clara H Fenno (Kingston/50), 14 Jul 1920
    (Charles F Macomber/Emma White)(Daniel Higgins/Marilla Frisbee)
MADDOX: Richard J (Andover,Ma) & Dianne E Crowell (Kingston), 29 Nov 1985
MAGNUSSON: Alan E (Kingston) & Mary E Penney (Kingston), 09 Aug 1986
    Carl E (Kingston) & Linda L Healey (Chester), 18 Jul 1970(Chester)
    Glenn A (Kingston) & Lyn M Foucher (Newton), 07 Jun 1980
    John J & Hope Stevens, 21 Jul 1921 (Brentwood)
    Kevin J (Kingston) & Lisa A Lermond (Kingston), 07 Jun 1986
    Robert S (Kingston) & Kristina J Duston (Hampstead), 18 Aug 1990
    Waldo M (Kingston/26) & Isabelle M Grace (Kittery,Me/24), 12 Aug 1932
    (Martin Magnusson/Hattie Philbrick)(Ernest B Grace/Luella Bowdoin) (P)
MAHANY: Philip L (Medford) & Phyllis M Emmons (Medford), 14 Nov 1969
MAHER: Philip L (Kingston) & Donna P White (Seabrook), 10 Jan 1987
    Robert (Lynn,Ma) & Marilyn Priore (Kingston), 09 Aug 1980
MAHON: Edward P (Kingston) & Christine LaBranche (Plaistow), 03 Dec 1966 (P)
    Thomas (Kingston) & Virginia L Treantafel (Manchester), 24 Mar 1970 (M)
    William E (25) & Concetta Morgano (25), 09 Oct 1940
    (Joseph Mahon/Mary Sankey)(Corrado Morgano/Gaetana Coppolo)

MAHONEY: Daniel P (Kingston) & Beth E Twombly (Kingston), 01 Jun 1991
    James L (Lowell,Ma) & Kathleen L Brown (Lowell,Ma), 30 Aug 1986
MAILLOUS: Mark S (Kingston) & Stacey M Hamel (Kingston), 04 Dec 1993
MALIK: Richard T, Jr (Kingston) & Nancy J Baldwin, 08 Jul 1993
MALLARD: Robert H (Peabody,Ma) & Alice R Carrigan (Peabody,Ma), 10 Jul 1959
    (Arthur Mallard/ Marie B Gagnon)(Thomas Carrigan/ Marion R McHugh)
MALLIAROS: George M (Dracut,Ma) & Coleen M Martin (Dracut,Ma), 04 Mar 1985
MALONEY: Keith J (Haverhill,Ma) & Sandy Lemieux (Kingston), 20 Aug 1994
MANIX: William E, III (Kingston) & Debra L Murray (Kingston), 07 Nov 1981
MANN: Robert W (Alton Bay) & Kathleen A Wilson (Kingston), 13 Dec 1969 (Rochester)
MANNHEIMER: Marc E (Bradford, Ma) & Catherine J Ferrara (Kingston), 04 Jul 1990
MANSFIELD: Charles R (Kingston) & Glenda B Dingee (Fremont), 05 Jul 1958
    (John A Mansfield/ Thelma Wardell)(Ralph G Dingee/ Ellen E Shah)
    Robert T (Plaistow) & Janice A Cooper (Kingston), 08 Aug 1952 (P)
    (Louis S Mansfield/ Claudia E Chard)(Francis D Cooper/ Lillian M Scott)
    Robert R (Kingston) & Ardis L Vadeboncoeur (Kingston), 05 Aug 1972 (N)
    Thomas G (Kingston) & Lorraine R Drapeau (Plaistow), 04 Jan 1964 (W)
    William C (Kingston) & Sandra J Young (E Kingston), 30 Nov 1957   (N)
    (John Mansfield/ Thelma Wordell)(Harold R Young/ Minerva Warwick)
MANSON: Gordon H (Kingston) & Nicole A Bergeron (Kingston), 08 Aug 1992
MARCHE: Louis P (Kingston) & Gladys M Merrick (Kingston), 12 Aug 1962
MARCOTTE: Earl C (Kingston) & Elizabeth S Ethridge (Lawrence,Ma), 25 Jul 1970 (B)
MARCOUX: Patrick J (Newton) & Lucinda J Clark (Kingston), 10 Aug 1973
MARDEN: Ralph W & Helen M Smith, 01 Oct 1921
MARKEY: Paul J (Kingston) & Kimberly Casey (Kingston), 07 Apr 1984
MARLING: James F (Shadyside,OH) & Rose M Culleton (Medford,Ma), 03 Aug 1952
    (James A Marling/ Leona Snyder)(Edward M Cullerton/ Alice Godsell)
MARRIOTT: Percy (Tuscon, Az) & Lillian H Hook (Tuscon,Az), 20 Jun 1980
MARSDEN: Robert B (Newton) & Faith L Travis (Kingston), 30 May 1981
MARSHALL: Byron (S Berwick,Me/43) & Evelyn Leavitt (S Berwick,Me/38), 29 Mar 1947
    (Richmond Marshall/ Lilla Belle Heath)(Hayes W Lang/Bertha M Brown)
    Clarence R (So Kingston/18) & Sadie I Tufts (Limington,Me/25),18 Mar 1905
    (Richmond R Marshall/Lilla B Heath)(James Tufts /Emily Stern)
    Herbert W (Kingston/52) & Rose Murray (Berwick,Me/38), 30 Oct 1907
    (James F Marshall/Mary M George)(George W Murray/Harriet Chick)
MARTEL: Alfred J (Kingston) & Patricia J Rogers (Kingston), 04 Jul 1976 (N)
    Raymond G (Haverhill,Ma) & Lillian M James (Haverhill,Ma), 11 Mar 1950
    (George H Martel/Henriette Dagort)(John Scott/Minnie H Shirley)
    Raymond G (Kingston) & Pearl M Peltier (Haverhill,Ma), 27 Feb 1954
    (George H Martel/ Henriette Dagart) (Roger Scott/ Mildred Jenkins)
MARTIN: Albert (Lexington,Ma) & Jean A Bernier (Beverly,Ma), 05 Oct 1958
    (Albert J Martin/ Margaret Moriarty)(Philip Bernier/ Mary Goss)
    Charles A (Plaistow) & Rita E Nason (Kingston), 14 Aug 1959
    (David A Martin/ Irene E White)(Donald Nason/ Glory M Moore)
    Charles F (Kingston) & Shannon L Waters (Kingston), 12 Jun 1993

Donald H (Kingston/44) & Frances T Ripley (Davidsonville,Md/37),12 Nov 1949
   (Charles W Martin/Ethel G Hughes)(Charles B Townsend/Rosa W Townsend)   (B)
Donald M (Kingston) & Carol A Collins (Danville), 05 Oct 1957   (E)
   (Melvin Martin/ Ruth Smith)(Howard Collins/ Grace Goldthwaite)
Everett A (Kingston/24) & Annie M Brown (Sandown/20), 10 Nov 1908 (W/K)
   (George E Martin/Etta Nason)(George J Brown/Elvira Baker)
Everett G (Kingston) & Elizabeth M Bailey (Hampstead), 04 Jul 1959 (H)
   (Melvin E Martin/ Ruth Emery)(Fred O Bailey/ Bernice M Foss)
Everett G (Kingston) & Juanita E Montoya (Hampton), 24 Aug 1983
Everett G, Sr (Kingston) & Phyllis A Thompson(Kingston), 03 Sep 1987
Herman (Middleton,Ma) & Phyllis B McKenney (Danvers,Ma), 01 Jun 1957
   (Herman Martin/ Tara Linstrom) (Raymond O McKenney/ Doris M Nickerson)
James W (Revere,Ma) & Azelma M Robertson (Lynn,Ma), 14 Aug 1953
   (Henry J Martin/ Lillian Ege)(Howard E Robertson/ Azelma M Boynton)
Jamie M (Kingston) & Patricia L Dezendorf (Hampton), 06 Jan 1984
Jeffrey F (Kingston) & Sandra D Howard (Plaistow), 28 Jun 1969 (P)
Melvin E (Kingston/24) & Ruth Emery (Sandown/21), 01 Jul 1933 (D)
   (Everett Martin/Annie M Brown)(..... Emery/Sarah Heywood)
Paul (Kingston) & Brigitte Morin (Kingston), 13 Aug 1987
Perley C & Charlotte Dewhurst, 03 Jan 1921   (B)
Robert D (Kingston) & Janet Thayer Drury (Kingston), 26 Jan 1973
Scott A (Kingston) & Gail A Birch (Kingston), 08 Jul 1989
Wayne E (Kingston) & Geneva M Hill (Exeter), 15 Aug 1970 (D)
William (Kingston) & Carol L Fontaine (Derry), 18 May 1963   (Derry)
William L (Boston,Ma) & Kazemira C Fallon (Boston,Ma), 06 Aug 1960
   (William R Martin/ Etta Borough)(Andrew Gurski/ Cecelia Dropinski)
MARTINE: John H (Kingston) & Carol M Torp (Gilford), 01 Jul 1967 (Laconia)
MARTINSON: Carl (26) & Edna M Walsh (25), 19 Apr 1936
   (Oren Martinson/ Sigrid Pearson)(Percy Walsh/ Alvonia Dyer)
MARVIN: Bradley D (Kingston) & Carol H Broadhurst (Kingston), 30 Mar 1984
MASANZ: Timothy J (Arlington,Ma) & Patricia N Locke (Arlington,Ma), 28 Aug 1993
MASCIOLI: David A (Kingston) & Lorianne J Sebetes (Kingston), 17 Mar 1991
MASLOWSKI: John E (Exeter) & Candace C Caton (Kingston), 01 Aug 1970 (E)
MASON: Robert F (Lowell, Ma) & Patricia A Muller (Lowell, Ma), 30 Oct 1990
Ronald C (Lynn,Ma) & Gertrude T Haner (Lynn,Ma), 07 Feb 1960
   (Lemuel Mason/ Marie Gardner)(Thomas J Malone/ Elizabeth O'Leary)
MASSIOS,: Christy C (Peabody,Ma) & Dianne C White (Cambridge,Ma), 15 Mar 1963
MATHEWS: Richard J, Jr (Brentwood) & Elaine M Mahon (Kingston), 20 Feb 1965   (W)
MATHURIN: Joseph E (Foxboro,Ma) & Annie B McGuigan (Plainville,Ma), 25 Sep 1954
   (Gedian Mathurin/ Margaret Simard)(Orrin G Eastman/ Rhoda E Austin)
MATSON: Wayne R (Boston,Ma) & Cynthia Fielding (E Hampton), 23 Nov 1963
MATSUBARA: T Paul (Danvers,Ma) & Rosolyn A Papamechail (Danvers,Ma), 09 Apr 1959
   (Takeki Matsubaro/ Francis White)(George Papamechail/ Alice Jones)
MATVICHUK: Robert J (Salem,Ma) & Ann F Pigulski (Salem,Ma), 01 Oct 1988
MAURIER: William J (Kingston) & Michelle C Kimball (Kingston), 29 Oct 1994

MAXFIELD: Samuel H (Portland,Me) & Faith F Parma (Portland,Me), 23 Jun 1951
    (Samuel H Maxfield/Edith McGovern)(Daniel G Parma/Alma Cartwright)
MAXWELL: Gregory A (Exeter) & Ruth C Rankin (Kingston), 04 Feb 1978
    Kenneth (Sudbury,Ma) & Donna C Coppleman (Sudbury,Ma), 24 Aug 1986
MAWHINNEY: Harold (Waltham,Ma) & Ann Elizabeth Fuccilio(Somerville,Ma),30 Jan 1959
    (John Mawhinney/Margaret Williamson)(Anthony Fuccilio/Mary Desmond)
MAYER: Charles R (Newton Ctr,Ma) & Margery E Gale (Newton Ctr,Ma), 21 Mar 1950
    (Charles G Mayer/Marion Sawyer)(Eiffel B Gale/Bertha Kessler)
MAYHEW: George A (Kingston) & Debra A Crescentini (Kingston), 04 May 1974   (N)
MAYTUN: George H (Middleton,Ma) & Patricia A Sullivan (Middleton,Ma), 16 Jan 1963
MAZZOTTA: Arthur E (Haverhill,Ma) & Deanna R Kinson (Georgetown,Ma), 12 Jul 1986
McASKILL: Edward C, Jr & Christine M Reynolds, 05 Jan 1980
McAVOY: William E (Kingston) & Eva M Sawyer(Newton), 09 Oct 1982
McCABE: John F (Lynn,Ma/27) & Abbie F Chamberlin (Kingston/45) 30 May 1902
    (John F McCabe/Mary Clark)(Peter Fifield/Catherine Webster)
McCARRON: William L (Boston,Ma/31)& Katherine N Brown (Haverhill,Ma/28),21 Sep 1904
    (James McCarron/Ellen Reidy)(Nathaniel C Brown/Annie P Chase)
McCARTHY: Albert W (Lynn,Ma) & Marie R Friars (Lynn,Ma), 10 Nov 1956
    (Gorden McCarthy/ Lillian Cashman)(Edmund Demule/ Mary Trembley)
    Charles M (Peabody,Ma) & Olivia E Fallon (Malden,Ma), 01 Jul 1967
    James F (26) & Dorothy Sehaufus (23), 04 Sep 1936
    (Robert McCarthy/ Mary Donahue)(Emil Sehaufus/ Louise Dick)
    John J, Jr (Haverhill, Ma) & Sheila M Grenon (Kingston), 17 Mar 1990
    Joseph D (Haverhill,Ma) & Joan C Rand (Haverhill,Ma), 31 Jan 1953
    (Daniel J McCarthy/ Catherine McKinnon)(Sheldon B Rand/ Cecilia B O'Flaherty)
McCLELLAN: William C (Kingston) & Martha L Eichel (Kington), 05 May 1969
McCLURE: Roger A (35) & Mary A Wicker (35), 24 Sep 1939   (W)
    (Joseph F McClure/Martha Goudy)(John Wicker/Francis Gusehlora)
McCOMB: James & Hannah F Judkins, 28 Jun 1921
    Raymond M (Kingston/32) & Ruth A Desmond (Exeter/34), 20 Jun 1948 (E)
    (Raymond P McComb/Alice M Morris)(Julius A Desmond/Mary S Moore)
McCUSKER: James P (Kingston) & Jull Ann Paquet (Kingston), 16 Aug 1980
McDERMOTT: Darren F (Kingston) & Deborah L Carignan (Brentwood), 19 Jun 1982
    Darren F (Kingston) & Sharon A Cronin (Newton), 15 Jul 1972 (N)
McDONALD: Clarence E (Central City,Ky) & Julia P Johnson (Andover,Ma), 05 Jan 1955
    (Edgar W McDonald/ Flora Allen)(Arthur L Johnson/ Julia Buckley)
    William A (Kingston) & Joanne W O'Brien (Danville), 09 Nov 1968 (D)
McDONNELL: Richard R (Lowell,Ma) & Amy Lybold (Lowell,Ma), 17 Dec 1994
McDEVITT: Edward J, III (Kingston) & Robin M Pierce (Kingston), 22 Mar 1987
McELKENNY: John F (Boston,Ma/23) & Elizabeth Truax (Nova Scotia/27), 08 Aug 1931
    (John F McElkenney/Sarah M Holloran)(Gordon Hamilton/Dorcas Nickerson)
McENNIS: George F (Kingston) & Katherine E Sprague (Kingston), 10 Dec 1964 (F)
McFADDEN: Richard J (Rochester) & Elizabeth A Bakie (Kingston), 14 Jun 1986
McFARLANE: Edward L (Salem) & Joanne M Pellegrino (Danvers,Ma), 15 Dec 1962
McGARIGLE: James J (Acton, Ma) & Carol J Hutchings (Peabody, Ma), 21 Jul 1972

McGEE: Daniel P (Kingston) & Catherine L Scott (Kingston), 27 Aug 1977   (S)
McGINCHEY: Clarence E (Columbus,Oh) & Eurith M Lloyd (Columbus,Oh),10 Jan 1983
McGLEW: Samuel B, Jr (Plaistow) & Elizabeth Villacaro (Kingston), 30 Jun 1962 (P)
McINTOSH: Robert A (Dhahra,Saudi Arabia)&Theresa A Gregoire (Kingston),26 Aug 1977
McKENNA: John D (Kingston) & Cynthia M Mahoney (Kingston), 29 Sep 1984
McKENZIE: Christopher A (Epping) & Tia M Kent (Kingston), 11 May 1991
McKINNEY: Victor C, Jr (Kingston) & Frances J Pappalardo (Kingston), 23 Sep 1978 (P)
McKINNON: Lessley (Everett,Ma) & Anna F Griffin (Malden,Ma), 28 Dec 1963
McLAREN: Robert H (Waltham, Ma) & Denise L Campo (Somerville, Ma), 06 Oct 1990
McLAUGHLIN: John J (Charlestown,Ma/29) & Florence M Curran (Danvers,Ma/36),07 Oct
          (Owen McLaughlin/Rose McGonagle)(Henry E Williams/Mary Arnold)   1928
     John L (Randolph,Me) & Kari L Mullen (Randolph, Me), 12 Oct 1991
McMANUS: Robert J (Revere,Ma) & Delores Mancinelli (Lynn,Ma), 17 Sep 1958
          (William J McManus/ Madelyn Jackson)(Albert Mancinelli/ Louise Galante)
McMINOWAY: Albert C, III (Saugus, Ma) & Susan Ciaburri (Saugus, Ma), 20 Jul 1991
McNAMARA: Dennis J (Haverhill,Ma) & Amy C Siudut (West Newbury,Ma),28 Mar 1993
     Edward J (Kingston) & Julie A Donovan (Kingston), 10 Sep 1988
McPARTLIN: Hugh F (Tewksbury,Ma) & Joanne N Reynolds (Tewksbury,Ma), 14 Oct 1989
McPHEE: Michael J (Newmarket) & Marjorie A Merrick (Kingston), 02 Sep 1967
     Robert M (Kingston) & Malinda A LaRoche (Newton Jct), 07 Nov 1970
McPHERSON: Alan B (Hampstead) & Calloway C Wight (Kingston), 29 Jun 1968
McTIERNAN: James H (Auburndale,Ma) & Mildred B Horn (Auburndale,Ma),01 Sep 1966
MEDROS: Robert G (Lynn,Ma) & Barbara E Gulezian (Lynn,Ma), 23 Sep 1963
MEEHAN: James H, III (Kingston) & Lynne A Nolin (Haverhill,Ma), 20 Oct 1989
MEEKS: Ira A (Kingston/58) & Harriett M Rodgers (Kingston/43), 29 Sep 1945   (E)
          (Charles B Meeks/Adeline Card)(William Laing/Nellie Richardson)
MEISNER: Steven A (Kingston) & Paula K Gray (Kingston), 06 Nov 1983
MELCHIONNO: William H (Revere,Ma) & Heather J Glidden (Revere,Ma),27 Feb 1982
MELKONIAN: Randall A (Kingston) & Brenda M Segeberg (Haverhill, Ma), 18 Jun 1994
MERCER: Walter (Marlboro,Ma) & Irene JBroderick (Marlboro,Ma), 05 Jul 1960
          (Jordon Mercer/ Winifred Tuttle)(Alexander Broderick/ Jennie Kubiak)
MERCHANT: Michael (Burlington,Vt) & Lovina M Melanson (Boston,Ma), 20 Dec 1971
MERCIER: James J (Kingston) & Florence M Morse (Kingston), 05 Aug 1989
MERRICK: Robert L (Kingston/23) & Anna J Crymble (Newton/22), 31 Dec 1944 (N)
          (Walter Merrick/Gladys Robinson)(Milo C Crymble/Marion H Sanborn)
     Walter P (Danville/28) & Gladys M.Robinson(Cambridge,Ma/20) 25 Dec 1918
          (Merrill B Merrick/Mary deRochemont)(William Robinson/Mary Wilson)
MERRILL: John A(Kingston) & Lynn Bartlett (Kingston), 01 Jun 1974
     Marshall E, III (Kingston) & Patricia A Tuttle (Exeter), 24 Sep 1983
MESSINA: Alfred L.P. (20) & Eileen McClary (18), 20 Jun 1938
          (Mario Messina/ Amelia Volpe)(Robert Mc Clary/ Laura Whelan)
METCALF: Ralph L (20) & Anna M Oxton (19), 17 Jun 1938
          (Charles L Metcalf/Florence E Comeau)(Charles A Oxton/Anna M Dawson)
METCALFE: George R (Exeter) & Gladys V King (Kingston), 07 Sep 1957   (E)
          (..... Metcalfe/ Ethel L Call)(Harold King/ Letitia Ringer)

MEURANT: Alfred E (Kingston) & Georgianna A Fuller (Kingston), 24 Jun 1951 (D)
(Lewis V Meurant/Barbara DeGaust)(George W Power/Mary E Dodge)
MEYER: Edward R, Jr (Ipswich,Ma) & Grace L Cloyd (Beverly,Ma), 16 Jul 1962
MICELI: Fortunata (Boston,Ma) & Arlene M Barone (Kingston), 25 Apr 1964
MICHAUD: Claude (Kingston) & Alice S Logan (Kingston), 29 Nov 1968
James A (Merrimac,Ma) & Mattie L Alexander (Merrimac,Ma),15 May 1959
(James Michaud/ Adalaide Gousse)(Walter Alexander/ Elizabeth Wood)
MIDDLETON: Bruce G, Sr (Wilmington, Ma) & Karen M O'Brien (Somerville, Ma),
01 Sep 1991
Edward F (Bradford,Ma/40)&Theresa I Pitula (Bradford,Ma/25), 21 Jan 1949
(Edward F Middleton/Julia Sampson)
Robert E (Haverhill,Ma) & Joyce A Lebaron (Kingston), 17 May 1975
MIHALIS: Stephen (Ohio) & Jean Titcomb (Boston,Ma), 21 Sep 1955
(Sam Mihalis/ Wilma Keramidas)(Albert Titcomb/ Jennie Juba)
MILBURY: Gary S (Kingston) & Dorothy Buxton (Kensington), 05 Jul 1959   (Ken)
(Norman Milbury/ Ethel Clements)(Horace Buxton/ Frances McNeill)
Gary S (Kingston) & Sylvia S Mays (Exeter), 03 Sep 1970
Norman N (Kingston/24) & Ethel E Clements (Everett,Ma/18), 07 Dec 1931
(Owen McLaughlin/Rose McGonagle)(Henry E Williams/Mary Arnold)
MILLER: Charles J, IV (Atkinson) & Leanne A Smith (Kingston), 08 Aug 1988
Donald M (Kingston/24) & Janet C Barrett (Kingston/18), 02 Nov 1947
(Perley E Miller/Mary E Ledger)(Raymond H Barrett/Florence D Rollins)
Glenn P (Kingston) & Pamela J Hamilton (Bradford,Ma), 26 May 1973
Glenn P (Kingston) & Leslie C Porter (Plaistow), 09 Apr 1976 (P)
Karl F (Wilmington,Ma) & Anne M Powers (Wilmington,Ma), 15 Aug 1993
Weldon A (Austin,Tx) & Sally A Wildman (Kingston), 12 Oct 1968 (D)
MILLETTE: David E (Kensington) & Deborah A Crowell (Kingston), 12 Dec 1970
Henry M, Jr (Haverhill,Ma) & Carol A Boulay (Haverhill,Ma), 01 Oct 1962
MILLS: David A (Melrose,Ma) & Judith W Willson (Kingston), 04 Sep 1966
Gerald (Somerville,Ma) & Mildred L Crowther (Somerville,Ma), 26 Aug 1960
(John Mills/ Caroline Mills)(Cecil F Crowther/ Rena Leard)
William J (Lawrence,Ma) & Margaret P Purcell (Kingston), 08 Aug 1969 (N)
William J (Merrimac,Ma/59) & Alma G Shaw (Merrimac,Ma/41), 01 Oct 1920
(John Mills/Sarah E Carver)(Joseph Shaw/Lizzie E Philips)
MIMOUNI: Abdelkrim (Boston,Ma) & Linda L Murray (Kingston), 31 Jul 1993
MINER: Frederic I (Kingston) & Susan A Bell (Kingston), 28 Jun 1980
MIRIBITO: Paul J (Bradford,Ma) & Alice R Mirabito (Bradford,Ma), 11 Dec 1965
MISENHEIMER: John C (Kingston) & Carol A Pitkerwick (Kingston), 05 Sep 1964 (P)
John C (Kingston) & Carol A Misenheimer (Kingston), 13 Sep 1969 (N)
MITCHELL: George W (Kingston) & Carol L Lynch (Allston,Ma), 29 Dec 1971
John A (Kingston) & Nancy M Skeffington (Quincy,Ma), 29 Nov 1969
MIXTER: Charles G, III (Kingston) & Dale A Atkins (Kingston), 28 Jul 1984
MODLICH: Walter R (Hyde Park,Ma/26) & Evelyn M Thereau (Derry/23), 27 Jun 1929 (D/Y)
(William F Modlich/Freida M .....)(Albert M Thereau/Jennie S Willson)
MOLAN: Lewis J (Weston,Ma) & Virginia A Stevens (Bronx,NY), 21 Apr 1966

MONDOR: Francis A (Kingston) & Gale A Cogswell (Plaistow), 03 Apr 1982
MONTAGUE: Thomas F (Lynn,Ma) & Mildred F Miller (Philadelphia,Pa), 19 Oct 1954
    (Patrick J Montague/ Nora Sullivan)(Harry C Ball/ Violet Allen)
MOODY: William L(S Kingston/42) & Annie I Simes (Kingston/22), 10 May 1928   (P)
    (William J Moody/Isabella Rice)(George E Simes/Annie F Tucker)
MOOERS: Gerald H (Newton) & Joan A Paquet (Kingston), 12 Jul 1975 (P)
    Robert H (Plaistow) & Susan A Arnold (Kingston), 28 Jan 1977
MOORE: Alfred L (Plaistow) & Christine M Conant (Kingston), 01 Jan 1950   (P)
    (Arthur Moore/Edith Sevestre)(John M Duston/Maude D Parker)
    David A (Plaistow) & Jean E Beals (Kingston), 08 Apr 1967
    Donald J (Kingston) & Lorraine A Glynn (Kingston), 31 Jul 1969 (Seabrook)
    Florian H (Plymouth,Ma) & Dorothy E Morse (Revere,Ma), 19 Dec 1950
    (Carl L Moore/Mona Dearth)(Clarence A Morse/Mary C James)
    Floyd (Brookline,Ma) & G Mae Sholan (Allston,Ma), 02 Jul 1960
    (Joseph T Moore/ Alice M Baldwin)(James Skerry/ Eliza Crossman)
    Joseph T (Kingston) & Donna L Carter (Kingston), 18 Jul 1993
    Raymond S, Jr (Wrentham,Ma) & Lisa C Blake (Wrentham,Ma), 09 Feb 1980
    Walter H (Newton/20) & Minnie E Burbeck (Beachmont,Ma/22), 21 Apr 1928
    (Carl G Moore/...Mac Donald)(Chas M Burbeck/Annie ....)
    William R (Kingston) & Mary K Gill (Kingston), 04 Jun 1989
MOQUIN: Joseph H (Buffalo,NY/42) & Mary A Goodwin(Kingston/53), 02 Jul 1916 (D/F)
    (Joseph H Moquin/Rosalie Martin)(Isaiah Tucker/..... Davis)
MORAN: Scott E (Newton) & Darlene M Gould (Kingston), 18 Jun 1983
    William J (Kingston) & Mildred M Wendell (Kingston), 21 Aug 1965 (Nor)
MOREAU: John E (E Kingston) & Eileen F Peltier (Kingston), 15 Jul 1962
MORESCHI: Albert F (Everett,Ma/26) & Eleanor E Keene (Boston,Ma/21), 05 May 1947
    (Frank Moreschi/Anna Bennedetto)(John W Keene/Esther Lynch)
MOREY: Steven A (Kingston) & Sharon E Landry (Kingston), 31 May 1986
MORGENSTERN: Richard E (Kingston) & Heidi Ouellette (Kingston), 07 Dec 1985
MORGAN: Frank V (Kingston) & Judith A Gormley (Hampton), 07 Dec 1963 (P)
MORIN: Ernest J (E Hampstead) & Florence M Kramer (Kingston), 07 Jul 1979
    Stephen C (Kingston) & Susan J Merrill (Kingston), 15 Sep 1989
    William A (Amesbury,Ma) & Betsy L Hoyt (Amesbury,Ma), 11 Mar 1960
    (Aloysius Morin/ Celia Pollard)(Lawrence Hoyt/ Francis Clark)
MORRILL: Fred A (Amesbury,Ma/38) & Bessie T Prescott (Kingston/21), 12 Oct 1907
    (Charles P Tucker/Susie L Lewis)(Wallace M Tucker/Lettie E Tucker)(Ports)
MORRIS: Brian Lee (Kingston) & Denise M Masse (Atkinson),07 Jun 1986
    John E, Jr (Kingston) & Karen M Costa (Windham), 05 Oct 1985
MORRISON: Gerald G (Dorchester,Ma) & Carol Morrill (Dorchester,Ma), 08 Nov 1964
MORROW: Allen M (Kingston) & Cynthia M Cutliffe (Kingston), 14 Jun 1986
MORSE: Earl G (Kingston) & Rosemary A Smith (Keene), 12 Dec 1970 (Keene)
    George A, Jr (Salem) & Corinne A Chapman (Kingston), 23 May 1981
    Lawrence R (Newton) & Florence M Jennings (Kingston), 16 Apr 1977 (Holderness)
    Lawrence E (Bath) & Lois F Gifford (Kingston), 17 Jun 1972

Merton M (Newton) & Mary A Rudd (Kingston), 11 Feb 1954
  (Earl E MorseSr/Margaret R Guiver)(Louis S Rudd/ Helen A Austin)
Paul H (Plaistow) & Rhonda Lee Ely (Kingston), 04 Sep 1976
MOSELEY: Charles D (Kingston) & Linda R Thibeault (Hampstead), 21 May 1977 (Ham)
MOSES: Donald E (Haverhill,Ma/23) & Martha C Carlisle (Haverhill,Ma/18), 14 Feb 1949
  (Earl Moses/Arlene Brown)(James T Carlisle/Evangeline Robillard)
MOSKO: Jacob J (Revere,Ma) & Gloria M Tranfaglia (Revere,Ma), 19 Oct 1950
  (Mihran Mosko/Virginia Prizio)(John P Tranfaglio/Helen Williamson)
MOSS: Walter W,Jr (Lee) & Tina M Jalbert (Kingston), 13 Oct 1990
MOUSETTE: Arthur L (Worcester,Ma) & Sheila P Linehan (Worcester,Ma), 01 Nov 1951
  (Arthur Mousette/Doris Baron)(Michael Linehan/Catherine Moran)
MOTTRAM: David B (Kingston) & Priscilla German (Kingston), 11 Aug 1984
MOWER: Todd M (Kingston) & Alice S Wyman (Kingston), 03 Sep 1988
MOXHAM: George M (Dracut,Ma) & Linda L LaFoe (Dracut,Ma), 18 Oct 1986
MUISE: Vincent S (Milton,Ma) & Barbara L Muldoon (Milton,Ma), 09 Oct 1954
  (Francis S Muise/ Alice V Colcord)(Frank B Muldoon/ Margaret E Qualters)
MUNGO: Dennis J (Lawrence,Ma) & Lynne M O'Flavan (Lowell,Ma), 21 Oct 1984
MULDOWNEY, John J (Kingston) & Wendy J Squibb (Kingston), 01 Apr 1972
  Joseph W (Haverhill,Ma) & Cheryl A Goss (Kingston), 17 Aug 1985
MULLALEY: John F (Roslindale,Ma) & Patricia A Barnett (Roslindale,Ma), 02 Aug 1964
MULLEN: Lester E (Stonington,Me/30)& Dorothy Cross (Ward Hill,Ma/31), 21 Nov 1925 (P)
  (Frank Mullen/Florence Sellers)(George Dinswine/Flora Stevens)
MURPHY: Daniel X (Somerville,Ma) & Jacqueline M Solari (Chelsea,Ma), 05 Jul 1960
  (Joseph Murphy/ Mary Cashman)(John Solari/ Genevieve Marusa)
  Richard J (Haverhill,Ma) & Marion L Jasper (Kingston), 20 May 1950   (P)
  (Robert A Murphy/Regina Foster)(Charles N Jasper/Ethel M Hartford)
MURRAY: Michael A (Belmont,Ma) & Rachel E Holt (Kingston), 16 Jun 1984
MUSE: John M (Bridgeport,Ct) & Arlene L Anderson (Bridgeport,Ct), 13 Jun 1954
  (Howard Muse/ Elizabeth Sullivan)(Harry Anderson/ Mildred Jarvis)
MYATT: John E (Andover,Ma) & Grace S Oliver (Andover,Ma), 14 Dec 1954
  (Norman F Myatt/ Mary E Gerard)(William T Sellers/ Mabel E Josselyn)
NARKJEWICZ: Paul H (Charlestown) & Beverly A Simes (Kingston), 23 Jun 1962
NASON: Alden E (Kingston/31) & Beatrice M Tucker (Kingston/26), 15 Dec 1945   (D)
  (Seth Nason/Blanche Elkins)(William Tucker,Sr/Nellie Simes)
  Elden C (Kingston) & Louise A Coffin (Amesbury,Ma), 01 Jun 1958 (Amesbury)
  (Eugene Nason/ Etta Brown)(Charles Coffin/ May Dow)
  Elvin F (25) & Annie B Ayotte (22), 26 Jul 1936   (R)
  (Freeman L Nason/Mildred Marshall)(Edward Ayotte/Anna Champagne)
  Elvin F (Kingston/34) & Marion E Decota (Exeter/25), 08 Jun 1946   (E)
  (Freeman L Nason/Mildred Marshall)(George F Decota/Estella Colburn)
  Ernest (Kingston/27) & Esther O Patch (York,Me/19), 30 Oct 1907 (York,Me)
  (Albion W Nason/Hannah S Page)(John W Patch/Patience S Tobey)
  Freeman (Kingston/38) & Mildred Marshall (Merrimac,Ma/20), 24 Nov 1907 (D)
  (Nathan Nason/Sarah K Page)(Richmond Marshall/Lilla Bill Heath)
  Freeman E (Kingston) & Regina I Verville (Newmarket), 10 Oct 1970 (Newmarket)

Herbert C (36) & Dora B Marple (21), 19 Oct 1939 (N/J)
        (Seth Nason/Blanche Elkins)(Frank Ellis/Dora Trick)
    Irving W, (Kingston/26) & Eva B Emery (Shapleigh,Me/25), 08 Nov 1917
        (Albion N Nason/Anna Page)(George H Emery/Ella M Patten)
    Lawrence W (Kingston) & Lorraine Y Marcotte (Dover), 07 Jun 1962 (Dover)
        (Irving W Nason/ Eva B Emery)(Albert P Marcotte/ Elbea H Turmelle)
    Lester F (Kingston/24) & Anna C Peck (Marshfield,Ma/23), 21 Nov 1925 (P)
        (Seth F Nason/Blanche I Elkins)(Elias Peck/Mary E Murry)
    Lester F, Jr (Kingston) & Belle L Schwartz (Portsmouth), 17 Nov 1950
        (Lester F Nason/Anna C Peck)(Samuel Schwartz/Rose Wiseman)
    Paul L (Kingston) & Karen A Blackden (N Hampton), 21 Jan 1972(N/H)
    Roger E (21) & Thelma F Jasper (16), 10 Oct 1936
        (Ernest Nason/Esther Patch)(Charles Jasper/Ethel Hartford)
    Roger E, Jr (Kingston) & Kathleen Storey (Kingston), 08 Jan 1966
    Roger E, Sr (Kingston) & Lillian V Crummett (Kingston), 29 Jun 1974 (P)
NEDEAU: Richard A, Jr (Kingston) & Kathleen M Hensiak (Milwaukee,Wi), 15 Jul 1978
NEENAN: James J (Lynn,Ma) & Doris M Nicholson (Melrose,Ma), 23 Sep 1958
        (Jerimiah Neenan/ Elizabeth Moriarty)(William Nicholson/ Marion Kierstead)
NEIL: Lawrence S (Kingston) & Mary J Caruso (Kingston), 29 Jul 1988
NELSON: Joseph E (Avon,Ma) & Donna H Anthony (Brockton), 22 Mar 1962
NETSCH: Donald A, Jr (Kingston & Jill K Pergamo (Kingston), 06 May 1994
NEVES: Louis (Lynn,Ma) & Joyce J Shepherd (Lynn,Ma), 17 Nov 1961
        (Louis L Neves/ Ann Fratus)(James Shepherd/ Marilyn Close)
NEWCOMB: Paul S (Dover, Ma) & Sandra L Braley (Kingston), 30 Apr 1972
NEWMAN: Donald E (W Bridgewater,Ma)& Christine Buker (WBridgewater,Ma),24 Dec 1962
NICHOLS: Frederic S (Kingston/22) & Therese Nye Porter(Merrimac,Ma/26), 01 Jun 1915
        (Perrin W Nichols/Alice S Perry)(Joseph W Porter/Eunice B Nichols)
    Leonard R (Kingston) & Deborah G Snow, 04 Dec 1977
    Perrin W (Kingston/58) & Ella Ainsworth (England/42), 08 Oct 1923 (Law)
        (Stephen W Nichols/Sarah Chase)(Witham Ainsworth/Lucy Lee)
    Robert F (Kingston/19) & Joan E Walters (Kingston/16), 03 Sep 1946
        (Frederic Nichols/Therese Porter)(George Walters/Ruth Chequer)
    Stephen W (Kingston/45) & Agnes S Perkins (Northwood/26), 30 Jun 1920
        (Stephen F Nichols/Sarah E Chase)(Charles S Tuttle/Lama A Dame)
    Walter W (Kingston) & Susan Bunnell (Raymond), 22 Jul 1992
NICOLOSI: Joseph J, Jr (Kingston) & Rita M Pannellatore (Kingston), 13 Apr 1986
NICOLS: David N (Lowell,Ma) & Sharon A Lloyd (Lowell,Ma), 09 Nov 1985
NIGHTINGALE: Herbert (Lawrence,Ma/32) & Flora S Langer (Germany/27), 16 Jul 1932
        (Fred Nightingale/Clara Bulock)(William Shultz/Marie Freitag)
NIGRO: Gene A (Kingston) & Martha L Walker (Fremont), 09 Sep 1978 (E)
NIEMI: Mark (Lowell,Ma) & Sharon M Jacobson (Lowell,Ma), 20 Oct 1988
NIXON: Wendell D (Washington,DC) & Marjorie M Long (Kingston), 18 Mar 1951
        (Alvin L Nixon/Mary T Weeks)(Kenneth Long/Mary E Bertrand)
NOEL: Robert J (Kingston) & Nancy A Lesczinski (Kingston), 10 Sep 1982
    Robert J (Kingston) & Nancy A Noel (Foxboro,Ma), 10 Jun 1989

Robert J (Kingston) & Rita A Senter (Kingston), 11 Jul 1980
NORMAN: Thomas C (Lawrence,Ma) & Betty K Call (Kingston), 09 Aug 1964
NORRIS: John D (Kingston/23) & Barbara F Rock (Fremont/23), 22 Feb 1947 (Brent)
    (James D Norris/Mary Gagnon)(Fred Rock/Minnie A York)
    Joseph H, Jr (Kingston) & Marilee Rohr (Eliot,Me), 08 Nov 1984
    Joseph J (Kingston/26) & Barbara A Cornish (Kingston/19), 03 Apr 1948 (E)
    (James D Norris/Mary Gagnon)(Glen B Cornish/Elmira M Dostie)
    Joseph J, Jr (Kingston) & Susanne M Michaud (Brentwood), 06 Apr 1973 (Ports)
NORTHEY: David (Topsfield,Ma) & Joan E Hopping (Ipsich,Ma), 29 Jul 1966
NORTHRUP: Arthur S (E Greenwich,Ct)& Marilyn J Reynolds (E Greenwich),03 May 1963
NORTON: Dana A (Amesbury,Ma) & Dale E Heath (Kingston), 15 Nov 1975 (P)
NOURY: Gregory A (Kingston) & Saundra L Friend (Kingston), 13 Mar 1982
    James E (Exeter) & Bonie L Carruthers (Kingston), 23 Dec 1994
NOYES: Charles D (Ipswich,Ma) & Ruth M Pickul (Ipswich,Ma), 14 Sep 1973 (P)
    Malcolm C (Newburyport,Ma) & Sylvia Little (Newbury,Ma), 26 Aug 1950
    (Rupert C Noyes/Marion Currier)(George Little/Grace E DeVeber)
NUGENT: Patrick R (Boston,Ma) & Lois A Rosene (Newtonville,Ma), 03 Jul 1957
    (Patrick R Nugent/ Sonora De LaRosa)(Albert F Rosene/ Wilfred K Young)
NUNEZ: Pedro Juan (Lawrence,Ma) & Isabel Maria Pena (Lawrence,Ma), 25 Jul 1977
NUTT: Christopher M (Salisbury, Ma) & Regina A Fassio (Salisbury, Ma), 26 Sep 1992
NUTTING: Thomas (Wakefield,Ma) & Kristen MacAllister (Plymouth, Ma), 23 Mar 1992
NYBERG: Bruce W (Newton) & Marion L Sprague (Kingston), 13 Feb 1965 (N)
    Kenneth W(Newton) & Judy L Vincent (Kingston), 15 Mar 1975 (N)
    Per (Sweden) & Eleanor M Grudberg (Stoneham,Ma), 28 Sep 1951
    (Johan Nyberg/Johanna Peterson)(Niles Grudberg/Hilda Nestor)
OBER: Milan R (Peabody,Ma) & Getrude F Porter (Randolph,Ma), 07 Sep 1957
    (Aram Ober/ Abbie Nutter)(William H Proul/ Mary Powell)
O'BRIEN: James J (Manchester) & Elaine M Gilman (Kingston), 04 Jul 1970 (N)
    Mark E (Malden, Ma) & Cara M Cassino (Malden, Ma), 22 Sep 1990
    Robert P (Hull, M) & Robin M Fucci (Stoneham, Ma), 31 May 1992
O'CLAIR: Ronald J (Kingston) & Linda S Anderson (Kingston), 12 Aug 1989
O'CONNELL: George E,Jr (Hull,Ma) & Claire C Simmons (Braintree,Ma), 02 Oct 1964
O'PACKI: Peter F, Jr (Worcester,Ma) & Donna M Brunelle (Worcester,Ma), 29 Jul 1962
O'SULLIVAN: Daniel J (Lowell,Ma) & Linda B Parent (Lowell,Ma), 02 May 1987
OLDFIELD: Howard P (Methuen,Ma/24)& Gladys M Howorth (Lawrence,Ma/21),23 Sep 1933
    (Ben Oldfield/Sarah L Palmer)(Richard Howorth/Martha Cullen)
OLENIO: Anthony (Methuen,Ma/45) & Ann Gilmartin (Lawrence,Ma/40), 26 Jun 1948
    (Ernest Olenio/Jennie Jerundo)(Edward Riley/Ann Gorman)
OLESON: Eric J (Kingston) & Cheryl L Ticehurst (Kingston), 31 Aug 1974
OLOFSON: Theodore L (Kingston) & Dianne R Magnusson (Kingston), 13 Aug 1966
OLSEN: George M (Valley Stream,LI,NY) & Maureen O'Connor (Woodmere,NY),03 Jun 1962
    Karl R (Somerville,Ma) & Maureen E Hines (Kingston), 05 Aug 1983
OLSON: Allen L (Everett,Ma) & Cornelia T Sabolewski (Chelsea,Ma), 01 Jul 1960
    (Allen T Olsen/ Elaine K Willett)(Victor Sabolewski/ Thelma A Scharegge)
OPILA: Lucien (Boston,Ma) & Leokadia Kaplon (Dorchester,Ma), 19 Jul 1962

ORDWAY: Ralph E (Kingston) &D Barbara Nason (Kingston), 20 Jan 1951 (D)
          (Harry M Ordway/Minnie Tibbetts)(William A Marple/Helen Gay)
ORLANDO: Robert M (Kingston) & Hazel L Forsmark (Augusta,Ga), 25 Feb 1967
ORNELL: John A, Jr (N Swanzey) & Kelly E.M.Hanson (Kingston), 26 Sep 1981
OSBORNE: Michael P (So Berwick,Me) & Kristy L Clark (So Berwick,Me),14 May 1994
          Roger V (Kingston) & Evelyn I Cronin (Plaistow), 15 Sep 1968 (N)
OSBURN: Doyle A (Rye Beach) &Kimberly A Finch (Kingston), 01 Jun 1984
OSGOOD: Herbert W (Salem,Ma) & Karen T Stankiewicz (Danvers,Ma), 06 Mar 1963
OUELLET: Eugene (Amesbury,Ma/25) & Julia Raymond (Merrimac,Ma/21), 01 Nov 1945
          (Oveide Ouellet/Albina Belanger)(Carol Raymond/Edna Davis)
OUELLETTE: Allen V (Kingston) & Gemma C Manalo (Kingston), 01 Oct 1994
          Frank R, Jr (Kingston) & Lisa M Arsenault (Kingston), 15 Sep 1984
          Michael J (Peabody, Ma) & Laura D LeBlanc (Kingston), 23 Mar 1991
          Richard J (Lawrence,Ma) & Lynda L Lontine (Lawrence,Ma), 14 Aug 1964
          Roger M (Raymond) & Bettie Corson (Kingston), 11 Aug 1956
             (Charles E Ouellette/ Albertha Bourgeois)(Charles P Corson/ Della M Young)
          Scott H (Kingston) & Madelynn A Reed (Kingston), 22 May 1993
PAGE: Brian R (Kingston) & Jane A Teaze (Merrimac, Ma), 01 Sep 1990
          Clarence H (59) & Delma A Lewis(55), 14 May 1936   (B)
             (Herbert Page/Florence Griffin)(Justice Gall/Anna Canderlin)
          Douglas H (Fremont) & Pamela E Merrick (Kingston), 23 Oct 1971
          Edward H (Kingston) & Nancy M Leclair (Kingston), 05 Oct 1974
          Glenn D (Kingston) & Martha A Parshley (Kingston), 14 Jun 1962
          John H (Kingston/55) & Catherine M Mason (Boston,Ma/27), 08 May 1909
             (Joseph Page/Mary E Fifield)(George W Mason/Sarah H Gale)
          John N (Plaistow/20) & Jeanne A Stanley (Kingston/16), 20 Mar 1948 (P)
             (Norris L Page/R Mildred Parker)(Arthur P Stanley/Elizabeth Richards)
          Leslie H (Kingston/21) & Bertha M Swett (Kingston/21), 30 Jan 1900
             (Ezra Page/Augusta Shaw) (Moses Swett/Lavinia George)
          Lewis H, Sr (Kingston) & Nettie M Kemp (Kingston), 05 May 1984
          Oral A & Esther Thompson, 12 Aug 1921 (Colebrook)
PAGLIARULO: Charles V, Jr (Kingston) & Donna J Page (Kingston), 31 Aug 1974
PAGNOTTARO: Alexander A(Kingston) & Dianna L Baker (Kingston), 22 Oct 1994
PAINE: Michael K (Kingston) & Ellen A Ferrell (Kingston), 01 Dec 1989
          William L (Kingston) & Lisa M Beede (Kingston), 28 Jan 1984
PALARDY: Richard D (Exeter) & Carolyn F West (Kingston) , 07 Nov 1959 (E)
             (Willow A Palardy/ Gertrude L McKenna)(Chandler B West/ Dorothy Jasper)
          Richard, Jr (Kingston) & Linda A Scott (Exeter), 29 Oct 1980
PALIS: Matthew W, Jr (Salisbury,Ma) & Lee A Fowler (Salisbury,Ma), 30 Jun 1984
PALMER: Fred E (Plaistow) & Linda G Mayo (Kingston), 10 May 1969
          Robert C (Merrimac,Ma) & Donna L Winter (Kingston), 02 Jun 1979
PAONE: Jerry V (Medford,Ma) & Josephine Negron (New York,NY), 06 Aug 1965
PAPPAS: Charles J, Jr (Revere,Ma) & Nancy P Marton (Revere,Ma), 04 Jun 1988
PAQUET: David E, Jr (Kingston) & Robin E Ayers (Kingston), 21 Feb 1976

PAQUETTE: E Arthur (Haverhill,Ma) & Iona M Parker (Haverhill,Ma), 27 Oct 1951
        (Ovide E Paquette/Georgianna Gilbert)(Charles F Harriman/Susan I Bailey)
PARE, Walter R (Haverhill,Ma) & Pamela V Woitonik (Danvers,Ma), 28 Mar 1971
PARFITT: George R (Rochester,NY) & Ann W Skinner (Rochester,NY), 01 Nov 1964
PARENTEAU: Patrick M (Epping) & Melodie J Adams (Kingston), 19 Jul 1975 (N)
PARIS: Arthur F (Haverhill,Ma) & Stella Wedgewood (Haverhill,Ma),09 Jul 1963
PARK: William M, Jr (Kingston) & Susan L Pelletier (Plaistow), 17 Oct 1992
PARKER: George H (56) & Mary W Woods (38), 03 Jul 1936
        (Charles E Parker/ Lidia Batchelder)(Joseph Welch/ Mary R Waterman)
    Henry G (Kingston) & Carol W Richards (Kingston), 20 Nov 1988
    Neil R, Sr (Kingston) & Patricia E Hubbard (Kingston),11 Dec 1982
    Neil R, Sr (Kingston) & Brenda J Pruitt (Kingston), 20 May 1973
    Ronald R (Andover, Ma) & Barbara R Eggers (Andover, Ma), 21 Apr 1990
PARSHLEY: John H (Kingston) & Barbara F Mohan (Kingston), 12 Dec 1981
    Thomas C (Kingston) & Yvonne N Carro (Brentwood), 04 Oct 1963
PARSONS: Nicholas F (Kingston) & Laverne Ward (Derry), 17 Aug 1979
PARZIALE: Anthony (Boston,Ma) & June M McCarthy (Boston,Ma), 27 Jul 1961
        (John Parziale/ Mary Barone)(Joseph Mc Carthy/ Alice Matson)
PASSANISI: Angelo C (Hyde Park,Ma) & Constance M Firth (Revere,Ma), 01 May 1967
PASSIER: Alan D (Methuen,Ma) & Susan J Aughtigan (Lawrence,Ma), 02 Jun 1986
PATTEN: James W (Amesbury,Ma) & Catherine R Chaples (Amesbury,Ma), 29 Oct 1989
PATTERSON: Del A (Kingston) & Patrica E Race (Kingston), 16 Dec 1984
    Frank V (Kingston) & Karen S Coltin (Kingston), 31 Dec 1983
PAULHUS: William C (Haverhill,Ma) & Veronique Brown (Haverhill,Ma), 27 Jul 1958
        (Ovid M Paulhus/ Cora M Shepherd)(Joseph Rondeau/ Mary Morin)
PEABODY: Mark E (Lynnfield,Ma) & Kathryn L Rodham (Lynnfield,Ma), 04 Jun 1988
    Mark (Tyngsboro, Ma) & Audry A Smith (Kingston), 29 Nov 1991
PEARCE: David W (Kingston) & Sheila A Scott (Kingston), 22 Jun 1990
    David W (Kingston) & Darlene M MacKenzie (Kingston), 23 Aug 1980
PECK: Stanley N (21) & Marjorie L Fleming (18), 15 Dec 1937 (E)
        (Arnold Peck/ Sarah Healey)(Arthur Fleming/ Bertha M Harris)
PEIRCE: James B (Stratham) & Margaret E Power (Kingston), 17 Jan 1954
PELCZAR: Bernard A (Newmarket/29) & Madeleine Nason (Kingston/22), 03 Apr 1945
        (John Pelczar/Stephania Bajorek)(Freeman L Nason/Mildred Marshall) (Epping)
PELLETIER: Adrian J (Kingston) & Judith L Brooks (Eliot,Me), 13 Mar 1964   (Ports)
    Lucien A (Kingston) & Cynthia J Huntress (Westville), 13 Aug 1970 (P)
PELLICELLI: John A (Middleton,Ma) & Dorothy M Trask (Lynnfield,Ma), 17 Mar 1961
        (Dominic F Pellicelli/ Dorothy M White)(Ernest Trask/ Eva Anderson)
PELOSI: Anthony (Everett,Ma) & Margaret Scibelli (Malden,Ma), 16 Aug 1952
        (James Pelosi/ Grace DeMartino)(Louis Scibelli/ Louise Santonelli)
PELTIER: John R (Kingston) & Dawn A Parker (Kingston), 18 Mar 1961
        (Charles J Peltier/ Pearl M Scott)(Robert C Parker/Robena G Swett)
PENZA: Dominic F, Jr (Walpole,Ma) & Arlene L Mitchell (Milton,Ma), 09 May 1964
PEPPARD: Roland A (Kingston) & Pearl M Martel (Kingston), 31 Jul 1975
    Victor J (Brentwood) & Joan M January (Fremont), 13 Jul 1974   (F)

PERKINS: Arthur (Brockton,Ma/21) & Gertrude Nash (Brockton,Ma/19), 28 Jun 1946
    (Herbert Perkins/Lena Driscoll)(Francis Nash/Agnes Tully)
    Kevin S (Kingston) & Paula J Moran (Newton), 22 Nov 1975 (Ports)
PERREAULT: Francis E, Jr (So.Hampton) & Patricia A Barrett (Kingston), 29 May 1970
    John O (Haverhill,Ma) & Cynthia L Woods (Bradford,Ma), 02 May 1969
    Michael L (Amesbury, Ma) & Laura J Evans (Amesbury, Ma), 05 Oct 1991
PERRONNE: Albert A (Worcester,Ma) & Donna L Wile (Newburyport,Ma), 17 Jun 1989
PERRY: John F (Medford,Ma) & Ruth M Brown (Medford,Ma),02 Aug 1952
    (John F Perry/ Helen Butare)(Royal G Brown/ Gertrude F Jenkins)
    Joseph A (Lawrence,Ma) & Gretchen A Seeton (Lawrence,Ma), 09 Oct 1976
    Raymond G, Jr (Kingston) & Tracy E Cook (Kingston), 09 Sep 1989
PETERS: Leslie H (Groveland,Ma/29) & Alecina Dockham (Haverhill,Ma/23), 04 Dec 1933
    (Elbridge Peters/Inez Hardy)(Leon J Dockham/Emmeline Rakotte)
    Richard F (Haverhill,Ma) & Nancy L Jennings (Haverhill,Ma), 04 Jul 1955
    (Joseph M Peters/ Isabell R Mascaro)(Edward O Jennings/ Dorothy LaValle)
    Richard F (Burlington,Vt) & Gail E Morse (Burlington,Vt), 11 Jul 1966
PETERSON: Robert L (Alexandria) & Catherine A West (Kingston), 22 Feb 1968
PETTENGILL: John W (Atkinson/25) & Madelyne P Kimball (Kingston/24), 14 Mar 1948
    (Burton C Pettengill/Anna A Chrigstrom)(Ulysses G Page/Iona E Currier)
PHELAN: Albert D (Kingston) & Sharon L Curtis (Kingston), 19 Aug 1990
PHILBRICK: Elwood E (Kingston/29)& Dorothy M Bilodeau (Haverhill,Ma/21),22 May 1948*
    (Eugene A Philbrick/Lizzie E Pickard)(Leo G Martin/Helen M Hannan)   *(P)
    John C (Kingston/24) & Mary P Wentworth (Plaistow/23), 17 Sep 1907 (P)
    (James M Philbrick/Mary S Chase)(Nathaniel A Wentworth/Isabel Hayes)
    William J (Kingston/28) & Carmon F Frost (Townsend,Ma/26), 25 Jun 1908
    (James M Philbrick/Mary S Chase)(Charles W Frost/Florence L Cooke) (R)
PHILLIPS: Barry R (Kingston) & Gail M Lindsay (Kingston), 14 Mar 1992
PICKETT: Donald D (Kingston) & Norma D Perrine (Haverhill,Ma), 21 Aug 1965
PIERCE: James B (Stratham) & Margaret E Power (Kingston), 17 Jan 1954
    (Thomas W Peirce/ Gabrielle M Dexter)(John A Power/ Margaret E Malone)
    Philip W (Haverhill,Ma) & Patricia A Houde (Kingston), 18 Jan 1987
PIKE: Bion H(Harrison,Me) & Sheila Colbath (Exeter), 18 Sep 1961
    (Louis B Pike/ Marjorie Burnham)(Floyd E Colbath/ Barbara L Eaton)
    Raymond F (Kingston) & Joyce A Crosby (Kingston), 22 Mar 1990
PILLSBURY: Dean T (Stoughton,Ma) & Alice E Smart (Boston,Ma), 23 Aug 1953
    (Roland D Pillsbury/ Evelyn F Talbot)(Francis N Smart/ Olive F Stevens)
PIMENTEL: James (E Hampstead) & Doris T Snow (Kingston), 07 Aug 1982
PITKIN: Frederick E, Jr (Kingston) & Victoria C Keir (Kingston), 30 Jan 1971
    Gerard N (Kingston) & Anne C Haberski (Amesbury,Ma), 26 Aug 1978 (N)
    Newell V (Kingston) & Gloria Barrett (Kingston), 03 Apr 1954
    (Merton L Pitkin/ Viola M Jenness) (John S Batchelder/ Eleanor M Riley)
    Ronald R (Kingston) & Cheryl-Ann Borin (Kingston),05 Sep 1984
PITMAN: Elmer T (Kingston) & Claire A Martino (Lawrence,Ma), 16 May 1969
PITTS: George F (Waterboro,Me/67) & Florence Arnold (Hudson,Ma/24),03 Jul 1915 (E/K)
    (Isaac S Pitts/Amelia Chitham)(John L Arnold/Emma Wallace)

PLAMONDON: Edgar A (Kingston) & Marion L Batchelder (Kingston), 30 Dec 1993
PLANTE: Marc H (Lewiston,Me) & Janice Smith (Lewiston,Me), 03 Sep 1960
        (Albert Plante/ Martha Dumais)(Philip K Smith/ Ada A Jordon)
PLASTERER: John B (Baltimore,Md) & Catherine A Scheffler (Kingston), 04 Nov 1984
PLATUKYS: Walter (48) & Antanie Patlanowie (48), 24 Sep 1938
        (Gabriel Platukys/Mary Linkewie)(Alec Capukaities/Pauline Marcelinte)
PLOYER: John H, Jr (Kingston) & Lillian T Girard (Kingston), 18 Jan 1966
POLEATEWICH: Steven J (Kingston) & Laurette E Harrison (Kingston), 31 Dec 1986
POLGAR: Robert S (Kingston) & Janet D Moulaison (Newton), 26 Aug 1984
POLLOCK: Richard C (Kingston) & Ellin M Hiller (Kingston), 31 Jul 1991
        Ronald E (Middleton,Ma) & Sandra A LeColst (Middleton,Ma), 14 May 1960
        (Milton R Pollock/ Josie Sheldon)(Frank T LeColst/ Priscilla Foss)
POND: Henry H (Danville) & Gail S Merrifield (Kingston), 16 Aug 1957 (Strat)
        (George Pond/ Violet Wentworth)(Kenneth Merrifield/ Theresa A Perrault)
POOLE: Robert H (Plaistwow) & Karen L Alden (Kingston), 24 Aug 1968
POPE: Lyman B (Haverhill,Ma/46) & Jean F Haselton (Haverhill,Ma/23), 05 Apr 1947
        (Edward B Pope/Anne F Roberts)(Harry H Haselton/Lillian Beattie)
        Richard A (Kingston) & Priscilla L Thibeault (Danville), 30 Jan 1961   (D)
        (William R Pope/ Hazel Bishop)(Wilfred J Thibeault/ Bertha L Hartford)
PORRO: Victor B (Kingston) & Nancy A Durkee (Kingston), 26 Jul 1961 (Newport)
        (Archie L Porro/ Agnes Pagnattoro)(Ralph C Durkee/ Irene M Burnham)
PORTER: Charles T, Jr (Pepperell,Ma) & Karen M McDonald (Kingston), 08 May 1971(N)
        Leslie L (Quincy,Ma) & Ethel L Collin (Quincy,Ma), 10 Aug 1959
        (Henry Porter/ Edna Bump)(George Lentz/ Annie Mc Kechnie)
        Richard R (Fremont) & Janet L Friend (Kingston), 23 Jan 1971
        Trent W (Raymond) & Cynthia D Collins (Kingston), 29 Dec 1974 (N)
POSKUS: Charles (24) & Myra Ward (24), 12 Jul 1934
        (Charles Poskus/Bessie Pescikus)(Marshall Ward/Stella Burnell)
POST: Charles W (Kingston) & Elaine M Devereaux (Kingston), 29 Mar 1979
        Richard J (Kingston) & Katherine M Hamblen (Kingston), 19 Dec 1987
        Scott D (Kingston) & Linda M Straw (Kingston), 01 Oct 1994
POTHIER: Robert L, Jr (Kingston) & Paula E Moriarty (Kingston), 26 Oct 1991
POWELL: Lawrence R (Salisbury,Ma) & Carol L Moulton (Haverhill,Ma), 22 Nov 1967
PRATT: John (Topsfield,Ma) & Joanne E Perkins (Georgetown,Ma), 21 Oct 1961
        (John W Pratt/ Mildred Osborne)(Roger L Perkins/ Lillian Hallock)
        Ralph W, Jr (Brockton,Ma) & Nancy E Newman (W Bridgewater,Ma), 20 Dec 1962
        Randy J (Kingston) & Joy E Webber (Kingston), 25 May 1985
        Thomas A (Kingston) & Catherine A Presutti (Salem), 26 Apr 1971 (A)
PRENAVEAU: James G (Plaistow) & Mary A Owen (Kingston), 25 Jun 1988
        Leo M (Kingston) & Kathy L Alberts (Kingston), 11 Apr 1969 (N)
PRESCOTT: Albert R, (Danville/22) & Florence W Merrick (Kingston/20), 06 Aug 1914(D)
        (Eugene A Prescott/Sarah French)(Merrill Merrick/Mary deRochmont)
        Roy E (Kingston) & Arline E Beane (E Rochester), 30 Oct 1954
        (Harry L Prescott/ Maude Emery)(Willis L Hayes/ Ora Marchand)
PRESTIPINO: Joseph E (Kingston) & Elaine J Netti (Kingston), 12 May 1979

PRESTON: William F (Franklin) & Phyllis J Palumbo (Franklin), 17 Oct 1956
        (John C Preston/ Grace Stafford)(Michael Palumbo/ Isabel Petrone)
PRIEST: Ronald G, Jr (Kingston) & Debra L Hudson (Kingston), 10 Jul 1976
PRITCHARD: John R (Kingston) & Rita I Cell (Amesbury,Ma), 26 Apr 1957 (E)
        (John R Pritchard/ Grace Hulett)(Arthur E MacDonald/ Agnes B Butler)
PROTO: Louis (E Boston,Ma) & Judith J Marr (Conway), 22 Jun 1973
PROUDE: William R (Quincy,Ma) & Ella M Conway (Quincy,Ma), 23 Feb 1963
PROULX: Armond N (20) & Ernestine Pike (18), 12 May 1937
        (John Proulx/ Eveline Fournier)(James Pike/ Esther Dow)
PROVENCHER: David L (Kingston) & Heather D Seely, 21 Aug 1986
PRUETT: Richard E (Kittery,Me/21) & Lela E Dame (Eliot, Me/18), 23 Mar 1933
        (Elmer R Pruett/Ruth C Philbrick)(William E Dame/Ethel L Dixon)
PRY: Bill J (Kingston)& Carolann M Gallagher (Kingston), 04 Sep 1993
PUGLISE: Paul F (Lawrence,Ma) & Gloria Mikolis (Methuen,Ma), 20 Mar 1965
PULTINAVICH: William C & Mary E Coffaro, 05 Oct 1960
        (William Paltinavich/ Victoria Adamovich)(Sam Coffaro/ Josephine LeBlanc)
PURCELL: Thomas F,Jr (Lawrence,Ma) & Rita A Reynolds (Kingston), 13 Jul 1969
PURINGTON: George M (Fremont/29) & Alexina James (Montreal,Can/28), 03 Jan 1908/9
        (Francis Purington/Loriah C Webster)(Moses Dow/Delima Luscia)
PURSLOW: Richard (Kingston/39) & Arivilla Labree (Kingston/32), 08 Dec 1945 (R)
        (Richard Purslow/Caroline Broadhurst)(Charles Labree/Marion Lane)
PUTNAM: Ford L, 3rd (Webster,Ma) & Margaret G Govina (Worcester,Ma), 08 Feb 1964
PYNN: George W (Newton) & Sandra G Lang (Kingston), 06 Sep 1958
        (Willis Pynn/ .... Spinney)(Arthur W Lang/ Dorothy E Nason)
QUEENAN: James J, Jr (Haverhill,Ma) & Joanne M Cumming (Haverhill,Ma), 01 Oct 1988
QUIGLEY: David F (Kingston) & Diane M Schmidt (Kingston), 25 Mar 1978
QUINN: Patrick (Lawrence,Ma) & Pamela J Bubar (Lawrence,Ma), 04 Jun 1989
QUINTAL: Dennis G (Kingston) & Karen M Porter (Kingston), 23 Feb 1980
QYERS: Chester W, III (Kingston) & Carlene M Collins (Kingston), 09 Dec 1983
RADIGAN: Frank D (Kingston) & Debra A Buller (Kingston), 20 May 1989
RADINA: David A (Kingston) & Sally A Novell (Kingston), 06 Nov 1989
RAFFERTY: Anthony P (Billerica,Ma) & Karen L Cormier (No Billerica,Ma), 13 Jul 1987
RAMSDEN: Brian E (Derry) & Catherine D Fee (Kingston), 18 Aug 1984
        Michael A (Kingston) & Marsha J Dallon (Kingston), 24 Feb 1990
RAMSEY: David R (No Andover,Ma) & Gail K Clements (Kingston), 28 Aug 1971   (N)
RAND: William (Fremont) & Brenda L Nason (Kingston), 24 Nov 1961 (N/J)
        (Forest E Rand/ Flora A Brown)(Herbert Nason/ D Barbara Marple)
RANDALL: Walter E (Ft Riley,Ka) & Dawn F Pecker (Kingston), 25 Apr 1986
RANIA: Peter P, Jr (Wilmington,Ma) & Tracy C Gagnon (Wilmington,Ma), 06 Mar 1993
RANSDELL: Cory M (Kingston) & Angel M Caldwell (Kingston), 09 May 1992
RAY: Alvin F (20) & Annabel Milbury (18), 14 Nov 1936 (Sandown)
        (Frank H Ray/Sarah L McGaren)(William B Milbury/Edith A Burpee)
RAYE: Bruce A (Lynn,Ma) & Laurie J Gaskill (Lynn,Ma), 16 Oct 1971
        David A (Lynn,Ma) & Cherrie A Partson (Lynn,Ma), 16 Oct 1962
        Dale K (Kingston) & Lesley A Clarke (Derry), 24 Aug 1990

Duane D (Kingston) & Michele R Nelson (Reading,Ma), 23 Mar 1989
READY: Joseph G (Epping) & Lucy A Gilman (Kingston), 12 Dec 1964
Joseph G (Kingston) & Ruth B Semple (Kingston), 17 Jul 1977
William D (Newton) & Asta R Sander (Kingston), 14 Oct 1960
(Warren J Ready/ Ida Gamlin)(Nils M Sander/ Ruth E Seabury)
REARDON: Michael P (Lynn,Ma) & Lorraine M Cunningham (Kingston), 05 Oct 1985
REED: Edward J (Hanson,Ma) & Phyllis J Hobson (Bryantville,Ma), 20 Feb 1965
Ephraim F (Westboro,Ma) & Lillian A Dow (Hopkinton,Ma), 11 Jul 1950
(Ephraim F Reed/Martha Brown)(Winthrop F Adams/Alpha Staples)
REES: Harry R (Kingston) & Corinne J Kimball (Danville), 30 Jun 1968 (D)
REIL: James R (Merrimac,Ma) & Barbara J Bertram (Kingston), 18 Aug 1962
REILLY: Edward J (Kingston) & Deborah A Foye (Kingston), 05 Jun 1982
REINFUSS: Thomas L (Kingston) & Margaret F Hogan (Kingston), 13 Jan 1968 (E)
REMINGTON: Shawn H (Kingston) & Jo-Ann Hall (Kingston), 13 Jan 1979
RENZONI: Joseph M (Berlin, Ma) & Virginia E Preston (Danvers, M), 05 Oct 1990
REYNOLDS: Barry K (Kingston) & Diane M Giacobbi (Worcester,Ma), 01 Jul 1989
Gary L (Kingston) & Irene M Dibease (Kingston), 23 Oct 1984
Thomas L (Lawrence,Ma) & Dayna L Kouns (Lawrence,Ma), 08 Jun 1985
RICCI: Joseph D (Lawrence,Ma) & Susan K Buse (Lawrence,Ma), 25 Jan 1971
RICCIARDONE: Bernard M (Everett, Ma) & Anna C Sheppard (Everett,Ma), 04 Jul 1954
(Antonio Ricciardone/ Pasqualine Novelli) (Dennis D Sullivan/ Minnie A Sullivan)
Bernard M (Malden,Ma/32) & Anna C Sheppard (Malden,Ma/30), 08 May 1948
(Antonio Ricciardone/Pasqualina Novelli)(Dennis D Sullivan/Minnie A Sullivan)
RICH: Lawrence H, Jr (Kingston) & Christine I Dyas (Wilmington,Ma), 16 Sep 1977
Todd C (Kingston) & Deborah J Tessier (Kingston), 21 Jun 1986
RICHARD: David J (Kingston) & Katherine R Keddy (Brentwood), 20 Apr 1991
Joseph A (Bar Hill,Me) & Virginia J Rochussen (Kingston), 08 Oct 1955
(Delphis Richard/ Mary Boule)(Charles W Senter/ Lillian Dunn)
RICHARDS: Dean (Amesbury, Ma) & Nancy E Rubino (Amesbury, Ma), 29 Aug 1992
Howard F, Jr (McGuire AFB,NJ) & Catherine D Buswell (McGuire AFB), 25 Aug 1973
RICHARDSON: Neil M (Kingston) & Constance H Raymond (Raymond), 01 Aug 1957 (H)
(Frank Richardson/ Bessie Urguhart)(William Raymond/ Gertrude Eaton)
RICKER: Scott D (Rowley,Ma) & Melody A L'Italien (Amesbury,Ma), 10 Oct 1981
RICKWALL: Frank E (Kingston) & Constance M Lord (Kingston), 25 Jun 1983
RIDDLE: James H (Kingston) & Karen L Jackson (Kingston), 05 Jul 1981
RIDER: Jonathan R (Dallas,Tx) & Julia K Heuss (Dallas,Tx), 20 Jan 1977
RIEK: Roderick V (Kingston) & Ellen G Kaplan (Neburyport,Ma), 10 Jul 1982
RIGGS: Bertrand H, (Caverndish,Vt/30) & Ida F Hubbard (Chesterfield/38), 26 Nov 1900
(Henry H Riggs/Lucy Ross)(Joseph C Hubbard/Cordelia Ames)
RIGHINI: Paul A (Kingston) &Maria A MacLeod (Haverhill,Ma), 17 Nov 1994
RILEY: Daniel R (Kingston) & Gail A Aucoin (Exeter), 12 Apr 1980
John B (Haverhill,Ma) & Clara S Dabrowski (Haverhill,Ma), 20 Aug 1954
(Melbourne Riley/ Phyllis Edwards)(Joseph E Dabrowski/ Sofie Wiecerzak)
RIVARD: Norman G (Derry) & Sylvia C Stouppe (Kingston), 04 Feb 1987

Robert H (Lawrence,Ma) & Paula L Coates (Lawrence,Ma), 31 Oct 1958
    (Alfred A Rivard/ Juliet Denault)(Albert G Coates/ Ruth Scannel)
ROBBINS: Arthur E (70) & Katherine F Slayton (51), 05 Dec 1936
    (Jacob Robbins/Clarissa Timpany)(William J Stephenson/Sarah A Shepard)
ROBERTO: Nicholas A (Wakefield,Ma) & Loretta E Lebel (Lynn,Ma), 13 Jan 1962
ROBERTS: Dennis L (Chester) & Judith A Peterson (Kingston), 19 Aug 1977 (R)
    George (Raymond/35) & Rose Kelley (Kingston/28), 29 Aug 1931
    (Frank G Roberts/Emma Currier)(Daniel Kelley/Hattie Place)
    Peter E (Kingston) & Ellen M Boden (Fremont), 03 Oct 1981
ROBERTSON: David K (Kingston) & Cheryl A Repucci (Kingston), 27 May 1983
    Scott K (Kingston) & Joellyn M Crockett (Kingston), 05 Jun 1993
ROBIE: Carroll G (Kingston) & Cinda L Wesser (Raymond), 28 Jun 1974
    Gregory E (Londonderry) & Annette L Russell (Kingston), 20 Dec 1986
    Jeffrey J (Kingston) & Julie S Perkins (Newton), 25 Aug 1979
    Lloyd A (Chester/19) & Bernice E Clarkson (Manchester/18), 26 Nov 1925 *
    (Elmer A Robie/Maude Devine)(Lutha A Clarkson/Stella Chadwick)*(Londonderry)
    Loren (Kingston) & Cecile A Record (Kingston), 09 Jul 1960
    Michael B (Kingston) & Nancy J Hall (Exeter), 14 Jul 1973   (E)
    (Morton E Robie/ Helen A Page)(Wilfred A Latour/ Eva B Forbes)
ROBINSON: Beverly E (Kingston) & Ruth A Foley (Malden,Ma, 08 Sep 1956 (N/J)
    (Malcolm Obinson/ Leona Baker)(Henry F Pope/ Amy A Berry)
    Hollis J (Somerville,Ma) & Patricia L Carter (Kingston), 01 Nov 1950   (P)
    (Hollis E Robinson/Helen E Donnelin)(Everett B Carter/Elsie Stoddard)
    Robert M (Tea,SD) & Virginia C Lanigan (Boston,Ma), 05 Sep 1953
    (Eldon W Robinson/ Alice Wheelhouse)(Dennis Lannigan/ Helen D Bean)
ROCK: Daniel H (Brockton,Ma) & Phyllis H Smith (Stoughton,Ma), 22 Jun 1952
    (Richard B Rock/ Ruth E Nelson)(Clyde B Smith/ Mazie W Harding)
    Elmer C (Kingston/22) & Jeannette E Champagne (Haverhill,Ma/18),22 Aug 1929
    (Ralph F Rock/Nellie S Swett)(Edward Champagne/Corinne Marsolais)
    Mahlon R (27) & Lucille Taylor (19), 25 Apr 1936 (B)
    (Ralph Rock/Nellie Swett)(Joseph Taylor/Gertrude Wormick)
    Richard M (Kingston) & Amelia A Cowdery (Kingston), 01 Mar 1985
    Robert D (Kingston) & Pauline R LeJeune (Haverhill,Ma), 03 Aug 1952
    (Ralph Rock/ Nellie F Swett)(Raymond Linton/ Alma Burpee)
ROCKOVITS: (Kingston) & Partricia H Moyer (Kingston), 14 Mar 1968
RODGERS: Forrest (Kingston) & Mary L Meeks (Kingston), 26 Jun 1959
    (Forrest F Rodgers/ Harriet M Laing)(Samuel Meeks/ Edna E Lane)
ROGERS: Edwin W (Kingston/33) & Marion Board Deenehy (Haverhill,Ma/43), 29 Aug 1947
                  (James M Board/Mattie G Gildart)
    John H (26) & Josephine Bialowanska (30), 19 Oct 1942
    (John Rogers/Marion McCaron)(Joseph Bialowanska/Rosalie Brezinski)
    John L (Amesbury,Ma) & Cindy M Goad (Amesbury,Ma), 09 Sep 1989
    Richard J (Lynn,Ma) & Rose M Neves (Lynn,Ma), 08 Apr 1961
    (John J Rogers/ Mary Blodgett)(Louis B Neves/ Ann Fratus)

Richard B (29) & Eleanor G Derochemont (23), 06 Jul 1940 (E)
  (Hughy B Rogers/Nancy A Dow)(Ernest H Derochemont/Ethel W King)
  Richard R (Kingston) & Natalie A Dumas (Newburyport,Ma),11 May 1974
  William A (Epping) & Rebecca J Kendall (Kingston), 18 Jul 1987
ROHDENBURG: Herman D, Jr (Kingston) & Florence I Weeden (Newton), 06 Feb 1965
ROLSER: John F (Kingston) & Laura L Hertling(Kingston), 08 Oct 1994
ROMANO: Michael A (Kingston) & Erica A Mele (Haverhill,Ma), 19 Jun 1993
ROOT: James H (Salisbury,Ma) & Judy A Davis (Salisbury,Ma), 19 Jun 1987
ROSSETTI: Michael J (Haverhill,Ma) & Lorraine T Nichols (Kingston), 17 Mar 1973 (N)
ROUBAUD: Robert B (Portsmouth) & Gail E Hankin (Kingston), 01 Feb 1980
ROUELL: Jesse L, (So Hampton/39) & Martha E Kimball (Kingston/37), 04 Dec 1901
  (George L Rouell/Mary E Colby)(Amos Kimball/Martha E Spofford)
ROUILLARD: Henley G (Salem) & Patricia A Bragdon (Kingston), 24 May 1975
ROULEAU: Mark S (Kingston) & Deborah M Klinch (Kingston), 27 May 1979
  Wayne M (Kingston) & Catherine G Colantoni (Kingston), 20 Jul 1985
ROUTHIER: Kenneth R (Kingston) & Dorothy A Gioia (Kingston), 23 Feb 1990
ROWBOTHAM: Steven J (Kingston) & Rachelle M Fyfe (Kingston), 22 Jul 1992
ROWE: Charles E (Kingston) & Kathleen A Butler (Haverhill,Ma), 19 Jun 1970 (N)
  Charles E (Kingston) & Janet L Winter (newton), 12 Aug 1962
  George M(Kingston) & Jeanne M Spencer (Kingston), 21 Jun 1988
  Harry R, Jr (Kingston) & Judith A Martin (Kingston), 26 Jan 1962 (Meredith)
  Herbert H (Kingston) & Evelyn Z Gonyer(Kingston), 30 Sep 1965
  Nicholas B (Kingston) & Lisa J Dearborn (Kensington), 08 Sep 1978 (Ken)
ROWELL: John R (Kingston) & Hope R Deziel (Kingston), 29 Mar 1975
  Weber M (Tunbridge,Vt/40) & M Elizabeth French (Kingston/48), 04 Sep 1907
  (Moses D Rowell/Susan E Wight)(John B French/Hannah B Wadleigh)
ROY: John A (Beverly,Ma) & Lee C Wells (Middleton,Ma), 30 Jan 1964
  Michael J (Amesbury,Ma) & Louise M Rickwall (Amesbury), 31 Jan 1987
  Robert E, Jr (Kingston) & Victoria D MacLean (Haverhill,Ma), 02 Jul 1994
  Ronald F (Woburn, Ma) & Barbara A Panunzio (Woburn, Ma), 12 Sep 1992
ROYCE: John B (Haverhil,Ma) & Jacqueline J Foley (Haverhill,Ma), 20 Apr 1968
  John B (Kingston) & Phyllis L St Cyr (Haverhill,Ma), 11 May 1964
ROYCROFT: Allen T (Dallas,Tx) & Dolores A Conti (Somerville,Ma), 14 Mar 1964
RUACCO: Anthony R (Lynn,Ma) & Deloris L Hilmer (Marblehead,Ma), 19 Aug 1962
RUBIN: Peter E (Peabody,Ma) & Judy S Sager (Kingston), 01 Aug 1987
RUBY: Michael J (Brighton,Ma) & Claire J Steward (Lawrence,Ma), 01 Aug 1982
RUBYCK: Frank P,Jr (Plainville,Ma) & Mae L Allison (Attleboro,Ma), 05 Jun 1964
RUDOLPH: Emerich C, III (Kingston) & Mary R Corrao (Kingston), 20 Aug 1983
RUFFEN: Christopher G (Methuen,Ma) & Cynthia J Chartier (Kingston), 28 Jun 1986
RUGGERI: Edward F, Sr (Kingston) & Betty A Woodsum(Kingston), 13 Oct 1981
  Michael S (Fremont) & Catherine A Gerskowitz (Kingston), 22 Sep 1984
RULE: Frank A (Groton,Ct) & Jo-Anne Pacheco (No Smithfield,RI), 10 Feb 1985
RUNION: Kenneth A (Lowell,Ma) & Linda J Moffie (Acton,Ma), 01 Oct 1994
RUOCCO: Anthony R (Lynn,Ma) & Christine C Babscott (Lynn,Ma), 25 Mar 1969
RUSH: Thomas, 3rd (Haverhill,Ma) & Mary D Ingalls (Portland,Me), 25 Apr 1964

RUSSELL: Brian L (Fitchburg,Ma) & Janice A Lancey (Fitchburg, Ma), 22 Jun 1990
 Eugene W (Saugus,Ma) & Doris W Allen (Saugus,Ma), 19 Apr 1952
 (William Russell/ Sarah Bates)(Charles D Whittredge/ Ida L Davenport)
 Kenneth (Kingston) & Blanche D Martin (Kingston), 18 Oct 1958
 (Philip A Russell/ Linda L Whipple)(Adolph J Martin/ Mary A Rollins)
RUSSMAN: Jeremy D (Kingston) & Dianna J Taylor (Kingston), 06 May 1991
 Richard L (Kingston) & Sheryl A Kamman (Hampton), 10 Aug 1985
RUSSO: Frank J (Boston,Ma) & Edna C DePrizio (Everett,Ma), 27 Feb 1955
 (Thomas L Russo/ Anna DeLucia)(George A DePrizio/ Alice Streeter)
RYAN: Daniel P (Malden,Ma) & Marianne K Shaughnessy (Lynnfield,Ma), 29 Jul 1960
 (John J Ryan,Sr/Gertrude McDugall)(John P Shaughnessy/ Anna G Kennedy)
 Frank M (Kingston/40) & Lillian E Biglow (Haverhill,Ma/39), 20 Oct 1920 (Westville)
 (Matthew J Ryan/Margarett E Curran)(James H Hibbard/Emma E Myers)
 Frank N (Kingston) & Brenda P Davidson (Kingston), 23 Sep 1979
 John E (Wakefield,Ma) & Louise Ann Cooper(Tewksbury,Ma), 07 Aug 1967
 Kenneth W (Cambridge,Ma) & Alice E Levine (Cambridge,Ma), 05 Oct 1968
RYPMA: Henry B (Danvers,Ma) & Emily V Carlman (Danvers,Ma), 22 May 1970
SABEN: Charles H (Bradford,Ma) & Barbara A Murray (Bradford,Ma), 24 Aug 1986
SADLER: Joshua P (Kingston) & Tricia A Marshall (Kingston), 17 Apr 1993
SALDI: Giacomo C (Kingston) & Mildred R Berube (Plaistow), 14 Jul 1972 (P)
SALEM: Edward M (Peabody,Ma) & Susan J DiLorenzo (Beverly,Ma), 30 0ct 1960
 (Alexander M Salem/ Martha R Farrah)(Anthony Di Lorenzo/ Dorothy Comeau)
SALERNO: Angelo J (Haverhill,Ma) & Betty Cadorett (Haverhill,Ma), 17 Jan 1958
 (Rosario Salerno/Nancy Aurricco)(Arthur B Cadorette/Pearl Choate)
 Joseph (Haverhill,Ma) & Shirley M Riley (Haverhill,Ma), 19 Mar 1954
 (Rosario Salerno/ Nancy Ricaurricco)(Melbourne Riley/ Phyllis Edwards)
SALOIS: William J (Lawrence,Ma) & Sonya J Sheehan (Lawrence,Ma), 25 Mar 1977
SAMOISETTE: Richard A (Haverhill,Ma) & Brenda Jo Bragdon (Kingston), 23 Dec 1961(P)
 (Arthur J Samoisette/ Juliette B Lajuenesse)(Ernest P Bragdon/ Doris Nye)
SANBORN: Alden M (Kingston) & Barbara A Lipka (Danville), 22 Jun 1991
 David M (Kingston) & Linda S Bird (Kingston), 28 Sep 1991
 Lowell E (Quincy,Il) & Amanda C Goodwin (Kingston), 20 Nov 1966
SANGER: James D.M. (N Hampton) & Nancy F Sawyer (Kingston), 11 Nov 1976 (N/H)
SARGENT: Eliot M (Kingston & Constance L Bouchard (Fremont), 134 Sep 1962
 Robert H (N Reading) & Sheila M Lambert (Kingston), 13 Jul 1974
 Ronald F (Kingston) & Dorothy M Peltier (Kingston), 27 Nov 1965
SARRETTE: David A (Kingston) & Kathleen F Devoe (Haverhill,Ma), 03 Apr 1976 (S)
SAULENAS: Larry (Tombal,Tx) & Chiquila M Palumbo (Tombal,Tx), 25 Oct 1979
SAUNDERS: Richard C (Ipswich,Ma) & Susan H Roberts (No Andover,Ma), 02 May 1959
 (Blaine Saunders/ Betty Campbell)(William Roberts/ Eleanor Jaksta)
SAVOCA: Richard A (Salem,Ma) & Lois J Duff (Salem,Ma), 08 Mar 1963
SAWYER: George M (Exeter) & Nancy F Nigro (Kingston), 21 Sep 1973 (H/F)
SCALA: Donald E (Boston,Ma) & Mildred Feole (Lawrence,Ma), 22 Nov 1967
SCANLON: Michael P (Kingston) & Patricia A Flanders (Kingston), 04 Dec 1976
 Michael P (Kingston) & Kathy A Hardy (Kingston), 04 Oct 1980

SCHEFFLER: Max R (Kingston) & Beth-Ann Zahler (Kingston), 17 Jul 1988
SCHMOOCK: Uwe (Kingston) & Jody A Fraize (Plaistow), 25 Jun 1980
SCHNEIDER: James L (Framingham,Ma) & Ann Marie Fogarty (Framingham,Ma),
    23 May 1964
SCHREMPF: Dennis A (Exeter) & Brenda L Farrow (Kingston), 04 Mar 1985
SCIBELLI: John J (Malden,Ma/29) & Clara G Kopoulos (Everett,Ma/29), 16 May 1949
    (Louis Scibelli/Louise Santonelli)(James Kopoulos /Mary G Demartino)
SCHULZ: Bernhard J (Kingston) & Charlene M Nordmann (Kingston), 13 Aug 1994
SCHUR: Richard H (Exeter) & Betty J Simes (Kingston), 17 Jun 1958
    (Hugo Schur/ Alice V Cole)(Willian G.E. Simes/ Ruth George)
SCHWARZ: Walter J (Kingston) & Ellen M Veazie (Allston,Ma), 13 Dec 1958
    (Wenzil Schwarz/ Marie Tremi)(Carl J Ward/ Elizabeth A Flaherty)
SCOTT: Emery (Marlboro,Ma/30) & Rosie Belanger (Gorham/26), 30 Nov 1907
    (Newell Scott/Arietta Foster)(JosephBelanger /Direa Desenne)
    Thomas A (Kingston) & Myrtle E Clark (Kingston), 09 Dec 1955
    (Walter D Scott/ Elizabeth Card)(Harry Miller/ Alma Burpee)
SEARLES: Leslie O (Kingston) & Roseann Mahon (Kingston), 24 Apr 1971   (N)
SEARS: Richard A (Nassau,Bahamas) & Norma J Barrett (Kingston), 15 Jun 1952 (D)
    (Richard J Sears/ Jean Rae)(Raymond H Barrett/ Florence Rollins)
    Robert A (Kingston/29) & Virginia Hatch (Brentwood/22), 08 Sep 1946 (D)
    (Alton E Sears/Grace L Trafton)(Rufus Hatch/Nelie Prescott)
SEAVEY: Warren C (Lee) & Linda E Bisson (Kingston), 15 Nov 1985
SEBETES: John P, Jr (Kingston) & Jeanne H Page (Fremont), 23 May 1970
SEETON: George E (Lawrence,Ma) & Claire M Deroche (Lawrence,Ma), 07 Jul 1987
SENTER: Charles A (Kingston) & Viola L Clarke (Kingston), 09 Nov 1974   (N)
    Ed B, (Haverhill,Ma/27) & Martha J Parker (Bartlett/25), 29 May 1902 (D)
    (Frank Senter/Mary E Davis)(Charles L Parker/Jennie L Brown)
    Harry C (Plaistow) & Beverly K Senter (Kingston), 11 Oct 1968 (P)
    John H, Jr (Kingston) & Beverly J Lehmann (Kingston), 21 May 1972
    Richard D (Kingston) & Virginia J Austin (Nashua), 25 Sep 1971 (Hollis)
    Richard D (Kingston) & Rachel Stokes (Kingston), 20 Dec 1992
    Richard D (Kingston) & Eileen M Zaremski (Kingston), 15 Sep 1979
SERAFINO: Giallongo (23) & Mary Siathowaska (18), 20 Sep 1936
SERINO: James,Jr (Saugus,Ma) & Vann Vitotilo (Malden,Ma), 26 Apr 1952
    (James Serino/ Anna Ciampa)(Carlo Totilo/ Sadie Sabastiana)
SEROUNIAN: Harry M, Jr (Everett,Ma) & Donna M Stevens (Everett,Ma), 28 Mar 1970
SESTITO: William (Sudbury,Ma) & Shirley W Mercer (Marlboro,Ma), 20 Sep 1958   (N)
    (Pasquale Sestito/Margaret Adair)(Jordan Mercer/ Winifred Tuttle)
SEVERANCE: George E (Kingston/34) & Sarah Hoyt (Brentwood/37), 30 Oct 1907
    (Benjamin Severance/Patience Seaver)(Josiah West/Hannah Glover)
SEWELL: Christian G (Amesbury,Ma) & Ashleigh Marvin (Kingston),12 Jun 1987
SHABOO: Alfred A (Kingston) & Judith A Jones (No Andover,Ma), 30 Jan 1987
SHADFAR: Jamshid (Brookline,Ma) & Heather A Herrick (Kingston),02 Jan 1982
SHAKTMAN: Lewis B (Kingston) & April L Maxwell-Gaudet (Kingston), 27 Jul 1992
SHALLOW: James R (E Hampstead) & Pamela G George (Kingston), 16 Mar 1984

SHANAHAN: Joseph R (Lynn,Ma) & Carol F Fawcett (Lynn,Ma), 28 Feb 1959
(Joseph Shanahan/Anna Corcoron)(William D Fawcett/ Eleanor Kelley)
SHARP: Robbie T (Abingdon,Il) & Jean C Pawlendzio (Kingston), 16 Jan 1988
SHARPE: Joseph G (Sylmar,Ca) & Nancy M Tkachuk (Sylmar,Ca), 06 Sep 1986
SHARRON: Fred J (Kingston) & Nancy S Brown (Kingston), 23 Dec 1989
SHAW: Bruce W (Kingston) & Mary E Clerico (Kingston), 01 Dec 1989
Ernest R (Haverhill,Ma) & Ruth C Roberts (Haverhill,Ma), 30 Apr 1951
(Leon Shaw/Bertha Beal) (Walter Roberts/Rose M Charland)
Ernest R (32) & Edna Strongman (21), 23 Jun 1934
(Leon A Shaw/ Bertha Beal)(Robert Strongman/ Mary ....)
Lacy (Boston,Ma) & Mary Elliot (Boston,Ma), 27 May 1950
(John Shaw/Mary Cagle)(William Elliott/Clara Harris)
SHEA: Richard D (Hampton) & Cynthia J Chartier (Kingston), 28 Jun 1986
Walter (Saugus,Ma) & Elsa F.B. Parsons (Revere,Ma), 10 May 1953
(Walter T Shea/ Madeline Smith)(Herbert Parsons/ Mina Bartlett)
SHELDON: Joseph C (Stewartstown/21)& Martha Jenkins (Kingston/26), 27 Apr 1901
(Chas A Sheldon/Fannie Knapp)(Levi B Martin/Ella Davis)
Mitchell J (Salisbury,Ma) & Marsha L York (Salisbury,Ma), 11 Oct 1980
SHENINGER: Eugene L (Rockaway,NJ) & Lynne M Lacandia (Rockaway,NJ),03 Jan 1981
SHEPHERD: Kenneth A (Billerica,Ma) & Lisa J Doran (Billerica,Ma), 19 Sep 1987
SHEPLEY: Peter G (New Bedford,Ma) & Marjory Gonsalves (Kingston), 26 Dec 1964
SHERMAN: Howard E (69) & Rebecca A Knowles (37), 20 Jun 1936
(Andrew J Sherman/Mary A Swett)(Edward E Knowles/Alice L Wareham)
Ulysses C (Isleboro,Me/62) & Celia MacDonald (Oxford,N.S./27), 20 Dec 1930
(Hudson Sherman/Jane Berry)(Alexander MacDonald/Annie Terhune)
SHORT: Albert G, 3rd (Newton) & Sheryl L Carter (Kingston), 16 May 1969 (EK)
Leo V (Melrose,Ma) & Elizabeth M Roode (Melrose,Ma), 04 Oct 1976
SHUTE: Edward G (Kingston) & Virginia D Spring (Kingston), 19 May 1980
George R, Sr (Kingston) & Sandra M Powell (Exeter), 01 Aug 1980
SIBLEY: Wayne A (Newton,Jct) & Bonnie F Pynn (Kingston), 05 Nov 1964
SIDERI: Mario L (Malden,Ma/29) & Lillian J Moreschi (Everett,Ma/25), 27 Nov 1947
(Joseph Sideri/Ida .....)(Frank Moreschi/Anna Beneditto)
SIDERWITCH: Kent A (Kingston) & Alice L Itz (Kingston), 31 Aug 1991
SIECZKOWSKI: James C (Haverhill,Ma) & April L Senter (Kingston),13 Jun 1981
SILLOWAY: Alden W (Kingston/30) & Sadie Rogers (Brentwood/30), 20 Mar 1908
(Woodbury Silloway/Emma J West)(John Williams/Ella Paye)
Frank W (Kingston/22) & Annie B Osgood (E Kingston/16), 30 Mar 1906
(I. W. Silloway/Emma J West)(Luman S Osgood/Annie L Jackman)
SILVA: Barry M (Kingston) & Jennifer A Russon (Kingston), 14 Feb 1987
Ellery L (Bangor,Me) & Patricia M Weimert (Pembroke,Me),07 Mar 1953
(John Silva/ Agnes Bartlett)(Lester Welmert/ Leola Lambert)
Jay J (Winthrop,Ma) & Cathy L Collins (Winthrop,Ma), 01 Dec 1984
Joseph P (Kingston) & Cheryl L Venner (Kingston), 05 Sep 1987
Paul F (Milford) & Brenda J Parker (Kingston), 30 Jun 1962 (Milford)
SILVIA: Richard L (Kingston) & Marcy J Provencher (Kingston), 27 Feb 1993

SILVIO: Joseph D (Hoboken,N.J.) & Joan G Moynihan (Malden,Ma), 03 Nov 1954
    (Anthony P Silvio/ Florence Miller)(John V Moynihan/ Gertrude Welch)
SIMS: Alfred D, Jr (Kingston) & Marcia A Woron (Newburyport,Ma), 11 Dec 1970
SIMES: Andrew V (Brandon,Vt/28) & Abbie J Tucker (Kingston/20), 13 Oct 1900
    (Francis Simes/Sarah E Murray)(John F Tucker/Ida F Curtis)
  Andrew F (25) & Mary E Perkins (21), 17 Oct 1934 (E)
    (Andrew V Simes/Abbie J Tucker)(Edward J Perkins/Mary M Hamblen)
  Dwight K (Kingston) & Linda M Letourneau (Portsmouth), 06 Oct 1979
  Edward D (Brandon,Vt/32) & Ethel Somers (Haverhill,Ma/26), 14 Nov 1915
    (Francis E Simes/Sarah Murray)(Edward H Foster)
  George (Brandon,Vt/28) & Annie F Tucker (Kingston/17), 06 May 1902
    (Francis Simes/Sarah E Murray)(John F Tucker/Ida F Curtis)
  John F (Kingston/29) & Alice M Tobey (Lynn,Ma/31), 29 Apr 1933
    (Andrew V Simes/Abbie J Tucker)(Edward J Ashton/Josephine Senter)
  Marvin E (Kingston/31) & Fay E Hillsgrove (Exeter/18), 23 Nov 1947 (E)
    Edward D Simes/Ethel H Foster)(Chester F HIllsgrove/Bertha L Pierce)
  Raymond (Kingston) & Doris H Parker (Epping), 24 Jun 1950
    (George E Simes/Annie F Tucker)(Albert C Parker/Annie E Purrington)
SIMONDS: Maurice G (Kingston) & Eleanor Waitt (Kingston), 13 Oct 1973
  Maurice G (Kingston) & Ruth E Borgkvist (Kingston), 07 Jun 1991
SIMPSON: Clarence L (Cambridge,Ma/34) & Anna M Greeham (Cambridge,Ma/33)* 28 Aug
    (George H Simpson/Caroline F Simmons)John Greeham/Ellen Colman)   *1915
  Clayton (Salem/22) & Delma H Kimball (Brushton,NY/22), 28 Sep 1928 (S)
    (Benjamin Simpson/Ada L Wood)(S Webster/Harrie O Shirley)
  Donald C (Kingston) & Amy C Taylor (Exeter), 17 Jun 1955 (E)
    (Clayton W Simpson/ Delma H Kimball)(John L Taylor/ Lucy M Burlingame)
  William G (Kingston) & Joan E Reid (Kingston), 17 Jul 1965 (P)
SIROIS: Roger J (Kingston) & Charlotte A Powers (Kingston), 22 Aug 1987
SJOSTROM: George A (Michigan/21) & Greta I Nyberg (Brockton,Ma/18), 29 Jun 1930
    (John Sjostrom/Victoria Lindquist)(Theodore Nyberg/Emily Erickson)
  John W (Michigan/20) & Francis E Heath (Kingston/20), 29 Oct 1928   (P)
    (John Sjostrom/Victoria Lindquist)(Charles E Heath/Claribel Pervere)
SLAPIK: Michael A (Austin,Tx) & Karen R Gordon (Austin,Tx), 06 Jun 1987
SLAYTON: John F (Wayland,Ma) & Marsha T Willson (Kingston), 30 Sep 1963 (Reading)
SLEEPER: William J (Kingston) & Muriel F Cleary (Haverhill,Ma), 05 Sep 1964 (N)
SLOAN: Bruce A (Kingston) & Kathleen Emery (Candia), 13 Jun 1981
  Howard D (Lynn,Ma) & Roseline M Dobie (Nahant,Ma), 10 Dec 1966
  James S (Kingston) & Wendy E Pickance (Exeter), 14 Feb 1987
SLYE: Carroll G (Amesbury,Ma/26) & Murial L Lewis (Haverhill,Ma/20), 02 Nov 1949
    (Harley Slye/Gladys Ladd)(James Lewis/Phyllis Case)
SMALL: Cecil (Roxbury,Ma/29) & Mabel G Ladd (Haverhill,Ma/25), 04 Aug 1932
    (Thomas R Small/ Emma F Bond)(Truman Ladd/ Grace M Bond)
  Danny R (Turner,Me) & Cindy M Coutermarsh (Kingston), 23 May 1985
SMART: Dennis C (Kingston) & Hannah E Brierley (Exeter), 15 Apr 1972 (N/H)

SMITH: Alfred M (Manchester/28) & Emma M Mitchell (Brentwood/18), 19 Jun 1906
(Charles Smith/Sarah Piper)(George Mitchell/Emma Rock)
Burgess C (Haverhill,Ma) & Dorothy A Nolin (Bradford,Ma), 11 Sep 1959
(Robert E Smith/ Barbara Burgess)(Albert V Nolin/ Dorothy M Rogers)
David C (Waukesha,WI), & Jane H Christie (Kingston), 29 Aug 1964
Dennis C (Kingston) & Kimberly J Martin-La Fleur (Kingston), 21 Apr 1985
Forrest V, III (Kingston) & Kathleen A Murphy (Kingston), 31 Dec 1987
Francis L.M.(E Kingston) & Bernice E Prescott (Kingston), 28 Dec 1960
(Frank Q Smith/ A Elizabeth Rennie)(Harry L Prescott/ Maude E Emery)
Frank W (Danville) & Gertrude E Martin (Kingston), 05 Mar 1961 (N)
(Charles L Smith/ Gertrude E Wood)(Everett G Martin/ Annie M Brown)
Fred A (York,Me/32) & Bessie I Kelley (Kingston/18), 26 Sep 1903
(Joseph H Smith/Susanne Perkins)(Daniel Kelley/Harriet Place)
Henry E (Kingston/55) & Katherine Doyle (Brookline,Ma/35), 30 Aug 1945
(Henry E Smith/Elizabeth Foster)(Patrick Doyle/Sarah McFee)
James C (Kingston) & Jeannie M Cunningham (Danville), 13 Apr 1963 (B)
Kenneth E (Kingston) & Evelyn T Pinder (Kingston), 30 Aug 1969 (Milton,Vt.)
Kenneth W (Haverhill, Ma) & Luann E Ferry (Haverhill, Ma), 28 Dec 1991
Leon B (Merrimac,Ma) & Sandra L Marshall (Kingston), 02 Jul 1965
Louis A (Kingston/27) & Doris H Foster (Kingston/20), 30 Jan 1945 (D)
(Louis H Smith/Mae R Bolster)(Frank W Foster/Winifred G Towle)
Michael D (Kingston) & Laura K Sykes (Kingston), 14 Oct 1978
Peter A (Exeter) & Heather England (Kingston), 19 Dec 1987
Richard C (Kingston) & Dorothy L Crafts (Kingston), 17 Aug 1963 (N/J)
Robert A (Fremont) & Barbara S Lindsey (Kingston), 06 Nov 1969 (E)
Steven P, Sr (Kingston) & Neilya A Dowling (Hampton), 23 Apr 1993
Steven P, Jr (Kingston) & Michelle A Ruest (Brentwood), 12 Jun 1987
Warren D (Kingston) & Shirley A Nason (Kingston), 22 Apr 1953 (W)
(John E Smith/ Frances Milligan)(Donald H Nason/ Glory M Nason)
Warren D (Kingston) & Janet A Gervais (Kingston), 20 Feb 1971
William (Kingston) & Robin E Latford (Newton), 07 Nov 1981
SNOW: George A (Blue Hill,Me/39) & Nellie M Leonard (25/Sutton,Vt/25),26 Nov 1936
(Arthur J Snow/Eunice A Dingley)(Arthur F Leonard/Ila B Sellon)
George (Salem,Ma) & Claudia Carey (Middleton,Ma), 16 May 1959
(George H Snow/ Elizabeth Dexter)(Howard A Carey/ F Louise Courtney)
Harry T (23) & Dena S Nason (26), 17 Feb 1940
(John H Snow/Nellie M Lynch)(Freeman L Nason/Mildred L Marshall)
Raymond F (Kingston) & Florence V Lamb (Newton), 18 Jan 1972 (N)
Terrence W (Brintree,Ma) & Michelle J Derbes (Braintree,Ma), 06 May 1987
SODAITIS: James W (Kingston) & Sheila M Landrigan (Kingston), 28 Oct 1989
SOIETT: Bruce A (Kingston) & Suzan Chouinard (Verdun,Can), 27 Jan 1986
SOUCIE: Richard P (Kingston) & Judith Anderson (Boston,Ma), 15 Dec 1963
SOUCY: Wilfred L, Jr (Merrimac,Ma) & Sharon E Tobin (Merrimac,Ma), 10 Nov 1967
SOUSA: Angelo M (Kingston) & Diane Goldsmith (Kingston), 31 Dec 1989
SOWERBY: Dwight D (York,Me)& Kathy D Wendell (Kingston), m - 15 Nov 1969

SPARKES: William J (Brighton,Ma/41) & Margaretta M Pollock (Brighton,Ma/43),12 Feb 1949
 (Ephraim Sparkes/Josephine Morris)
SPARKS: Darin S (Leeton, Mo) & Amber L Burnham (Kingston), 07 Aug 1990
SPINELLA: Thomas D (Kingston) & Jean M Turgeon (Malden,Ma), 21 Nov 1953 (W)
 (Cyrus Spinella/ Anna Mc Intyre)(Ezra A Turgeon/ Ann Cody)
SPIRITO: Michael A (Haverhill,Ma) & Darlene G Nestor (Haverhill,Ma), 22 Jul 1989
SPOFFORD: David A (Kingston) & Melody A Corliss (Kingston), 01 Dec 1984
SPRAGUE: Brian J (Tewksbury,Ma) & Carolyn Davey (Reading,Ma), 27 Jun 1987
 Charles R (W Nottingham) & Michelle L Lessard (Kingston), 22 Oct 1988
 George H (Brentwood) & Annette E Gilbert (Kingston), 07 May 1964 (B)
 George H (Kingston) & Larue J Pope (Kittery,Me), 06 Jan 1962
SPRINA: Santo R (Kingston) & Bonnie E Crockett(Kingston), 21 Apr 1972
SPRING: Theodore H (E Kingston) & Virginia D LaBelle(Kingston),15 Jul1967 (N)
SPRINGER: Charles F (New Hyde Park,Ma) & Halcyon C Hobbs (Kingston), 23 Mar 1952
 (Peter H Springer/ Dorothea M Mahler)(Edwin H Hobbs/ Lucille Agove)
SPURLING: Richard (Amesbury,Ma/20)& Delores Gaumont (Amesbury,Ma/18),18 Aug 1947
SPURR: Calvin L (Peabody,Ma) & Doris A Drew (Haverhill,Ma), 02 Nov 1963
ST DENIS: Robert G (Portsmouth,RI) & Joan A Larsen (Norwell,Ma), 27 Mar 1970
ST HILAIRE: Craig K (Kingston) & Amy E Hess (Barrington), 09 Dec 1989
 Richard D (Kingston) & Vivian A Thomas (Kingston), 05 Jul 1984
 Wayne L (Kingston) & Kathy L O'Brien (Brentwood), 27 Aug 1971 (F)
ST PIERRE: Daniel A (Kingston) & Linda M Letourneau (Kingston), 20 Aug 1994
STAPLES: Arthur J (Lawrence,Ma) & Theresa M Roberts (Lawrence,Ma), 24 Aug 1955
 (Henry Steples/ Mary Emma)(William Roberts/ Mary Charest)
STACKPOLE: Scott K (Kingston) & Janet R Fraser (Kingston), 28 Nov 1969
STANJUNAS: Philip E (Marlboro,Ma) & Linda E Buckley (Natick,Ma), 05 Oct 1965
STANLEY: George C (27) & Amanda Ouellette (22), 17 Jan 1937 (E)
 (James C Stanley/Flora Bell Dunn)(John Baptiste Ouellette/Melina Plourde)
STANWOOD: Allan L (Methuen,Ma) & Pamela Savoy (Methuen,Ma), 07 May 1988
 Russell M (Kingston) & Cynthia A Gregory (Kingston), 09 Nov 1991
STAPLES: Arthur J, & Theresa M Roberts, 24 Aug 1955
 (Henry Staples/Mary Emma)(William Roberts/Mary Charest)
 Charles D (21) & Myrtle Reynolds (20), 28 Nov 1936
 (Everett Staples/Mildred Dame)(Homer Reynolds/Margaret Daley)
 Kenneth H (E Weymouth,Ma) & Irene L Nisbet (Rockland,Ma), 20 Mar 1953
 (Ralph H Staples/ Molly S French)(Charles Littlefield/ Ida Libbey)
 Robert J (Haverhill,Ma) & Donna J Woodbury (Haverhill,Ma), 14 Mar 1970
STAPLETON: Richard E (Kingston) & Susan Rundle (Kingston), 17 May 1976
STARNES: John W (Oceanside,Ca) & Eleanor V Armstrong (Oceanside,Ca), 23 May 1986
STEAD: Charles D (Lynn,Ma) & Ann Devarenne (Danvers,Ma), 23 Jul 1955
 (Frederick Stead,Sr/Charlotte Dunn)(Charles Devarenne/ Mary Powers)
STEER: Harold A (Kingston) & Carol A O'Brien (Kingston), 13 Jun 1970 (N)
 Harold A (Kingston) & Helena L Fortier (Kingston), 14 Feb 1976
 Roger E (Kingston) & Carolyn A Sargent (Plaistow), 16 May 1970 (P)
STERN: Robert E, Jr (No Conway) & Donna E Paine (Kingston), 03 Sep 1966 (B)

STEVENS: Alan H (Kingston) & Mary L Barlow (Exeter), 02 Mar 1957   (E)
   (J Edward Stevens/ Annie Locke)(Paul F Barlow/ Thelma M Cote
   Brian L (Kingston) & Lisa E Montoni (Newton), 14 Jul 1979
   Carl S (Kingston/28) & Dorothy A Leggett (Spokane,Wa/25), 16 Sep 1924(Spokane,Wa)
      (Frank W Stevens//Lora M Stevens)
   Charles D (Epsom/32) & Elizabeth R Sweeney (Manchester/31), 06 May 1933
      (Charlie Stevens/Alma W Worth)(Jeremiah Sweeney/Catherine O'Dowd)
   David G (Kingston) & Laura A Turcotte (Kingston), 01 Jul 1983
   Eric A (Kingston) & Barbara J Mosandel (Rochester), 07 Sep 1985
   Gary P (Kingston) & Michele Riopel (Brentwood), 12 Oct 1984
   George B (Kingston/25) & Helen A Clark (Kingston/25), 17 Jan 1906
      (Samuel W Stevens/Harriet N Collins)(Walter S Clark/Abbie A Sanborn)
   George F (Haverhill,Ma/31) & Alice M Nichols (Kingston/31), 19 Sep 1904
      (Frederick C Stevens/Anna J Emerson)(Charles W Nichols/Helen M Wadleigh)
   James E (Kingston) & Laura R Irvine (Newton), 15 Sep 1973   (N)
   Jeffrey (Kingston) & Penny L Perham (Lebanon), 20 Mar 1982
   Lawrence E (Kingston/21) & Luella M Farmer (Brentwood/19), 06 Nov 1949
      (J Edward Stevens/Annie L Locke)(Lancelot Farmer/Rose L Pettis)
   Russell H (Haverhill,Ma/33) & Karlene E Banks (Haverhill,Ma/22), 17 Jan 1948
      (Howard C Stevens/Elizabeth M Foss)(Frank M Banks/Alice Ordway)
STEWART: Charles H (Kingston) & Jennie R Marcou (Kingston), 03 Jul 1963 (Seabrook)
STILLITER: John S (Rock Island,Il) & Dorothy E Powe (Rock Island,Il), 09 Aug 1986
STOSSEL: John E (21) & Helen King (19), 13 Aug 1934
      (George Stossel/Rose Gillogily)(Martin King/Ruth Fellows)
STRANGMAN: Calvin L (Kingston) & Gloria M Basso (Kingston), 30 Jul 1988
STREETER: Philip J, Jr (Kingston) & Nancy J Baldwin (Kingston), 16 Jun 1990
STRILECKIS: Gregory A (Melrose,Ma) & Maureen A Devaney (Bradford,Ma), 24 Sep 1994
STRUFFOLINO: Carmen F (21) & Rose M Dolce (18), 18 Sep 1938
      (Michael Struffolino/Millie Candilora)(Frank Dolce/Louis Ligouri)
STURGIS: Richard T (Kingston) & Linda L Rouleau (Kingston), 27 Nov 1976 (B)
   Stanley P (Lynnfield,Ma) & Anna M Morelli (Chelsea,Ma), 14 Sep 1958
      (Peter Sturgis/ Catherine Chicola)(Albert Morelli/ Genevieve Macjewski)
SULLIVAN: Cornelius T (Kingston) & Suzanne Sweeney (Kingston), 29 Sep 1990
   John T (Kingston) & Heather L Osgood (Kingston), 10 Oct 1993
   Joseph J (Lynn,Ma) & Sandra J Legere (Lynn,Ma), 22 Sep 1962
SULLY: Cledanor (Dorchester,Ma) & Marie M St Pierre (Dorchester,Ma), 07 Jul 1980
SULTAIRE: Harold L (Brentwood) & Doris E Sprague (Kingston), 18 Aug 1953 (F)
      (Julius Sultaire/ Ida L Tucker)(Walter E Sprague/ Katherine E Hislop)
   Julius C (Pittsfield,Ma/24) & Ida L Tucker (Kingston/22), 03 Feb 1925
      (Augustus Sultaire/Mary C Laine)(William F Tucker/Nellie F Simes)
SUTTON: Steven E (Manchester) & Valerie L Cline (Kingston), 15 May 1983
SWAIN: Earl E (Danville) & Gail MacDonald (Kingston), 30 Nov 1957
      (Alfred E Swain/ Mabel Frotton)(John W MacDonald/ Irene S Simes)
SWANBURG: Lloyd G (Reading,Ma) & Judith A Bennett (Kingston), 22 Feb 1974
SWASEY: Charlton J (Kingston) & Jean M Dempsey (Kingston), 14 Jul 1991

SWEENEY: Daniel (Revere,Ma) & Josephine A Mastrangelo (Everett,Ma), 08 Aug 1952
(Daniel Sweeney/ Alice Coburn)(Felix Mastrangelo/ Adeline Ditullio)
Harold L (Revere,Ma) & Lois S Frederick (Revere,Ma), 28 May 1953
(Daniel T Sweeney/ Alice Coburn)(Clarence O Frederick/ Winifred Ellison)
Richard F (Revere,Ma) & Barbara A Martin (Winthrop,Ma), 25 Oct 1953
(Daniel T Sweeney/ Alice Coburn)(Robert W Martin/ Lawrence Lizart)
SWEETLAND: Glenn C (Kingston) & Geneva S Clements (Kingston), 01 Aug 1981
SWEETSER: Robert W (Kingston) & Nancy E Hall (Kingston), 20 Sep 1986
SWETT: Daniel W (Kingston/30) & Anna B Winslow (Kingston/21), 11 Oct 1905 (Hav)
(Moses Swett /Levina George)(Samuel Winslow/Julia Merrill)
Wilbert M (Kingston/41) & Jennie A Tucker (Kingston/36), 26 Mar 1948
(Daniel W Swett/Anna B Winslow)(William F Tucker/Nellie F Simes)
SWIDERSKI: Raymond W (Peabody,Ma) & Nellie F Chabra (Saugus,Ma), 12 Jul 1952
(William Swiderski/ Stella Grusheski)(John Chabra/ Anna Solatruck)
SWINERTON: , Ernest A (Kingston) & Ruth E Crosby (E Kingston), 26 Oct 1957 (Derry)
(Elsworth Swinerton/ Virginia Warren)(Henry Crosby/ Grace Jordan)
James E (Kingston) & Cheryl A Linehan (Kingston), 14 Feb 1992
SYKES: James W.S. (Kingston) & Joanne Halitsky (Newton), 27 May 1978 (P)
Roy S (Kingston) & Kathy J Pool (Kingston), 03 Jun 1973 (P)
SYLVESTER: Gilbert A (Haverhill,Ma) & Barbara E White (Raymond), 07 May 1977 (R)
SZPAK: Matthew S (Salem) & Anna D Rizzo (Beverly,Ma), 17 Nov 1962
TAATJES: John (Holand/22) & Mary Cox (Ireland/21), 20 Sep 1924
(Nicholas Taatjes/Emma Boersema)(Thomas Cox/Bridget Galvary)
TAFT: John F (23) & Nellie A Plucinski (23), 03 Jul 1936
(Thomas Taft/Marie .....)(Joseph Plucinski/Bridget Owaniski)
TAIT: Bradford M (Hampstead) & Carol J Patterson (Kingston), 14 Jun 1955
(John H Tait/ Gladys M Angus)(John E Patterson/ Charlene N Batchelder)
TALBOT: Robert J (Providence,Ma) & Roberta M Hassett, 07 Jul 1960
(Lorenzo E Talbot/ Adele Mercier)(Robert V Hassett/ Dorothy M Chartier)
TARMY: Michael S (Seabrook) & Roberta A Carney (Kingston), 03 May 1986
TARVER: William H (Lawrence,Ma) & Sharon L Lowe (Amesbury,Ma), 30 Sep 1983
TATONE: Emil R (Methuen,Ma) & Dorothy O'Dell (Haverhill,Ma), 19 Aug 1951
(John Tatone/Mary Tatondo)(Francis B O'Dell/Catherine M Irish)
TAYLOR: Dennis J (Atkinson) & Carol A Greenlee (Kingston), 28 Apr 1973   (P)
Harry E, Jr (Kingston) & Janice Bryant (Kingston), 25 Jun 1994
TEBO: Gerald R (Newton) & Katherine J Tebo (Kingston), 25 Feb 1983
TEERI: Robert S (Northfield,Vt) & Gale C Swanson (Kingston), 30 Mar 1974 (E)
TEMPLE: Clarence B (Plaistow) & Natalie A Smith (Kingston), 01 Jun 1962 (Newton)
Darrell E (Kingston) & Martha J Clark (Kingston), 08 Sep 1977   (P)
TEWKSBURY: Fred H, Jr (Kingston) & Carole A Cleary (Portland,Me), 19 Dec 1970(EK)
THAYER: Harold (Hanson,Ma) & Kathleen D Johnson (Whitman,Ma), 19 Aug 1961
(Harold L Thayer/ Ann McCloud)(Charles S Johnson/ Helen L Warren)
THEODORE: James F (Wakefield,Ma) & Irene T Labbe (Malden,Ma), 29 Sep 1961
(James J Theodore/Catherine McVey)(Joseph Gingras/ Marie Hamel)

THERBERGE: John J (Medford,Ma) & Anne Parisi (Lawrence,Ma), 06 Dec 1953
        (Frank Therberge/ Ellen Coleman)(Joseph J Parisi/ Catherine Torrisi)
THERIAULT: Philippe A (Salem,Ma) &Jo Ann Carberry (Danvers,Ma), 20 Feb 1962
THERRIAN: Arthur R (Haverhill,Ma) & Elaine T DiChiara (Chelsea,Ma), 26 Apr 1963
THIBAUD: Todd R (Haverhill,Ma) & Susan L Klang (Haverhill,Ma), 21 May 1988
THIBEAULT: Edward T (Kingston) & Edith M Thibeault (Kingston), 14 Feb 1981
THOMAS: Charles D (Kingston) & Karen L McIntire (Hampstead), 02 Jul 1994
        Dale R (Danvers,Ma) & Joanne Chase (Salem,Ma), 23 Jul 1955
        (Arthur Thomas/ Mary C Hartman)(Raymond Chase/ Ruth Horne)
        Gary J (Denvers,Ma) & Elizabeth K Malnquist (Boston,Ma), 28 Nov 1957
        (William Thomas/Ethel Kelley)(Carl E Mainquist/ Doris E MacGarvey)
        Stanley W (Gorham,Me/26) & Dorothy L Stevens (Kingston/24), 02 Jul 1949
        (Hayward S Thomas/Marion Whitaker)(J Edward Stevens/Annie L Locke)
THOMPSON: Andrew R (Exeter) & Kerry E Rowe (Kingston), 05 May 1973   (E)
        Arthur E (Newton/25) & Alice M Rogers(Kingston/18), 14 Oct 1900
        (Duston Thompson/Sarah Goodwin)(Moses W Rogers/Jane Winslow)
        Eldon H (Haverhill,Ma) & Blanche F Crooker (Kingston), 19 Feb 1955 (W)
        (Charles Thompson/ Sarah Tarron)(Oscar Levoie/ Anna Gagnon)
        Joseph W (Kingston) & Patricia M Blinn (Kingston), 14 Jul 1982
        Thomas M (Lynn,Ma) & Linda A Rooney (Lynn,Ma), 14 Feb 1976
        Richard G (Kingston) & Carmen J Anderson (E Kingston), 12 Jul 1982
THORNER: Stewart H (Kingston) & Cindy L Phillips (Sandown), 28 Jul 1973   (E/K)
THORNTON: Paul L (Salisbury,Ma) & Joyce M Pucci (Salisbury,Ma), 09 Oct 1983
THURLOW: William R (Kingston) & Deborah A McGlew (Kingston), 15 Dec 1973
TIBBETTS: Benjamin R (Georgetown,Ma) & Kathryn M Abrams (Bradford,Ma), 09 Oct 1954
        (Benjamin S Tibbetts/ Catherine Waugh)(Leonard Johnson/ Catherine Locks)
        Richard H (Everett,Ma) & Janet V Edwards (Haverhill,Ma), 10 Jul 1973
TIDD: Daniel H (Kingston) & Elaine M Spinella (Epping), 16 Feb 1974 (N)
TILLEY: Robert K (Alton Bay) & Estelle T Decaturr (Kingston), 22 Jul 1965 (Wolfeboro)
TILTON: Paul R (Kingston) & Nancy J Devost (Kingston), 09 Oct 1982
        William H (Kingston) & Jean G Larson (Kingston), 22 Feb 1953
        (William E Tilton/ Shirley Fulsom)(Elmer J Larson/ Gladys M Gibbons)
TIMMONS: William A, Jr (Kingston) & Natalie E Marquis (Kingston), 23 Jun 1984
TISSARI: Eino W (Cummaquid,Ma) & Marian L Hallat (Cummaquid,Ma), 05 Jul 1966
TITUS: Gerald A (Topsfield,Ma/25) & Lillian C Peart (Middleton,Ma/22), 24 Jul 1948
        (Henry U Titus/Edna M Hicks)(James W Peart/Lilia M Hurst)
TOBIN: Richard J (Kingston) & Tammie J Allen (Kingston), 30 Jul 1983
TOBYNE: William L (Kingston) & Althea W Flanders (Haverhill,Ma), 20 Jan 1950
        (Lewis Tobyne/Lillian Morgan)(Charles A Thomas/Lizzie Haven)
TOLEOS: Steven (Kingston) & Betty L Scribner (Kingston), 15 Sep 1985
TOMANEK: Raymond S (Brooklyn,NY) & Jane R Willhite (Brighton,Ma), 17 Apr 1954
        (Felix Tomanek/ Honore Danek)(Edward S Noonan/ Iva Allen)
TOOMEY: Francis B (Lynn,Ma) & Gwendoline Hanson (Lynn,Ma), 16 Jul 1966
TORPEY: Dennis G (Randolph,Ma) & Sally E Irwin (Wilmington,Ma),11 Mar 1979
TORRES: Robert C (N Dighton,Ma) & Tobi A Mann (Taunton,Ma), 29 Nov 1965

TOWERS: Everett (47) & Clara Harpell (41), 05 Apr 1942
    (Jesse Towers/Zilpha Phillips)(Parmenas Morshead/Maude Ellis)
TOWLE: Stanley L (Kingston) & Judy L Nyberg (Kingston), 18 Sep 1982
TOWNSEND: Allan T (Fremont) & Cheryl A Lacerte (Kingston), 20 Sep 1974
    Gary L (Kingston) & Judith A Amazeen (Kingston), 22 Apr 1994
TRACY: Thomas (Lawrence,Ma/39) & Vesia M Cheney (Kingston/24), 23 Nov 1914
    (Thomas Tracy)   (William Cheney/Stella A Page)
TRAINOR: Brendan P (Haverhill,Ma) & Barbara A Fanaras (Haverhill,Ma), 31 Jul 1954
    (Peter E Trainor/ L Marie Donovan)(Louis Fanaras/ Rose Pappas)
TRANFAGLIA: John T (Lynn,Ma) & Eleanor A Amero (Lynn,Ma), 29 Mar 1968
TREBINO: Robert (Lexington,Ma/38) & Virginia A Betemps (Cambridge,Ma/25),03 Sep 1949
    (Stephen Trebino/Jennie Casagrandi)(Frank Jay/Frances C Gibbs)
TRIEDMAN: Max B (Haverhill,Ma/25) & Gertrude Schwartz (Philadelphia,Pa/20),07 Jan 1934
    (Samuel Tried,Man/Goldie Twabe)(Morris Schwartz/Rebecca Botzman)
TROLA: John M (Kingston) & Gayle L Newman (Northwood), 14 Aug 1993
TROY: James T (Derry) & Katherine Landers (Kingston), 26 Sep 1992
    Patrick T (Kingston) & Julie A Kinney (Hampstead), 05 Oct 1985
TRUDEAU: Raymond F (Haverhill,Ma) & Patricia A Mazza (Haverhill,Ma),13 Oct 1962
TUCK: William G (Brentwood) & Linda G Clarke (Kingston), 03 Feb 1974
TUCKER: Clayton (Gloucester,Ma/30) & Harriet F Gering (Gloucester,Ma/25),01 Nov 1931
    (B Frank Tucker/Nellie M Lane)(Herbert Gering/Sadie McLean)
    George E (Kingston) & Carol E Shepard(Hopkinton), 13 Jun 1970 (Hopkinton)
    (Walter W George/ Inez Tewksbury)(Edward Chase/ Esther Bonnell)
    Jeremiah C (Kingston/52) & Elizabet (Banks)Libby (Groveland,Ma/46),03 Apr 1902
    (Moses Tucker/Hannah Martin)(William Banks/Catherine Davis)
    John V (Kingston) & Marion L Gratton (Exeter), 30 Aug 1950 (Dover)
    (William F Tucker/Nellie Simes)(Samuel McLane/Edith Batchelder)
    John V (Kingston/26) & Blanche M Smith (Westboro,Ma/35), 13 Aug 1932
    (William Tucker/ Nellie Simes)(Ralph H Barnard/ Alice E Powers)
    William F (Kingston/22) & Nellie Simes (Brandon,Vt/22), 22 Sep 1900
    (John F Tucker/Ida F Curtis)(Francis E Simes/Sarah E Murray)
    Warren H (Andover/31) & Mary A Clark (Kingston/27), 26 Sep 1900
    (Jeremiah H Tucker/Rosetta B Woodward)(John T Clark/ Sara E Titcomb)
TULLERCASH: Victor (24) & Helen Thibodeau (22),12 Oct 1934
    (Michael Tullercash/Alice Romanofski)(Archie Thibodeau/Rose Cormeau)
TUNIS: Jean S (Dorchester,Ma) & Patricia A Little (Dorchester,Ma), 05 Apr 1984
TURCOTTE: Robert D (Kingston) & Sandra L Wheeler (Kingston), 04 Jan 1964
    (Richard L Turner/Molly Emery)(Fred Walton/Lottie Walton)
TURNER: David L (Plaistow) & Cheryl A Patterson (Kingston), 25 Oct 1968   (NJ)
    Erik W (Brockton,Ma) & Beatrice H Badger (Bridgwater,Ma), 22 Oct 1960
    (Elgin A Turner/ Ethel Peterson)(Fredericka Badger/ Edna M Wise)
    Richard L (21) & Doris Walton (18), 21 May 1934
    (Richard L Turner/Molly Emery)(Fred Walton/Lottie Walton)
TUTTLE: Charles P (Concord,Ma) & Wilkie L Ladd (Kingston),19 Nov 1964

TWOMBLY: Henry W (Somersworth/30) & Effie B Page (Kingston/30), 15 Oct 1906 (D)
(John Twombly/Laura Osgood)(Ezra Page/Augusta Shaw)
Ralph E, Jr (Kingston) & Elizabeth Thomas (Exeter), 17 Jun 1989
TYLUS: Paul (Lawrence,Ma) & Susan M Mansell (Georgetown,Ma), 07 Nov 1989
UERKWITZ: Donald D, Jr (Kingston) & Diane M Nichols (Kingston), 25 Jun 1978
UNDERHILL: Dexter W (Brentwood) & Katherine C McCormack (Kingston), 27 Aug 1960 *
(Dexter Underhill/Bessie Shays)(Stewart McCormack/Marjorie Carlisle) *Milford
Richard L (Brentwood) & Glenda M Buswell (Kingston), 27 Aug 1966
VACCA: Joseph (Brockton,Ma) & Mary M Gannon (Brockton,Ma), 21 Apr 1962
VADEBONCOUER: William (Haverhill,Ma) & Wanda L Collins (Kingston),25 Nov 1955
(William H Vadeboncoeur/ Rosilda Brisson)(Leon E Collins/ Josephine E Hutchins)
VALCANAS: Charles C (Haverhill,Ma) & Grace T Urzi (Lawrence,Ma), 20 Jul 1956
(Nicholas Valcanas/ Konstantina Lampropulas)(Sebastiano De Marco/ Agnes Fillipon)
VALLIERIE: John P (Gorham/24) & Georginni Moran(Fall River,Ma/22),10 Apr 1908/09
(Joseph Vallierie/Diena Belanger)(Peter Moran/Arbina .....)
VANCOPPENOLLE: Daniel J (Newton) & Linda M Romano (Kingston), 12 Jul 1980
VAN SICLE: Quentin R (Kingston) & Gloria J Caswell (Epping), 02 Sep 1967 (N)
VAN TWUYVER: Robert W (Ipswich,Ma) & Pamela J McGee (Ipswich,Ma),12 Oct 1963
VARNEY: Ross E (Kingston) & Anne E Kreamer (Newburyport,Ma), 14 Oct 1989
VARNEY: William R, Jr (Kingston) & Lisa M Cloyd (Kingston), 06 Dec 1986
VENO: Joseph R (No Reading) & Sandra J Zahar (No Reading,Ma), 17 Mar 1967
VERRILL: Daniel F (Kingston) & Pamela Clements (Kingston), 15 Jun 1974
VESSELS: Michael W (Birmingham,Al) & Brenda J Young (Kingston), 18 Dec 1976   (N)
VIEWEG: Gordon L (Waltham,Ma) & Helen O Belmer (Haverhill,Ma), 31 Jul 1983
VIGNEAULT: Richard A (Kingston) & Cynthia L Clements (Kingston), 04 Sep 1993
Ronald W (Methuen,Ma) & Anna G Deltwas (Methuen,Ma), 17 Jan 1962
VILLENEUVE: Nils J (Kingston) & Janice V King (Salem), 21 Oct 1983
VILLIERS: Wallace H (Kingston) & Kimberly A Griffin (Kingston), 24 Dec 1986
VINCENT: Leo R (30) & Margaret E Simes (23), 19 Jul 1934   (A)
(Frank Vincent/Elsie Brooks)(George E Simes/Annie F Tucker)
Robert L (Kingston) & Natalie L Johnson (Kingston), 28 Aug 1955
(Leo R Vincent/ Margaret E Simes)(Irving E Johnson/ Velma L Hart)
VITALE: Daniel J (E Providence,RI) & Tobi A Torres (Taunton,Ma), 01 Nov 1969
WAITT: Clark B (Kingston) & Paula J LaFleche (Plaistow), 25 Jun 1965
WALL: John S (E Kingston) & Patricia A Gifford (Kingston), 27 Dec 1958
(Ernest F Wall/ Elizabeth G Brown)(Clarence H Gifford/ Cecil M Fletcher)
WALKER: John (Kingston) & Sandra L Morton (Kingston) 25 Feb 1984
WALLACE: Edward M (Lynn,Ma) & Mary V Roy(Lynn,Ma), 03 Aug 1963
George H (Merrimac,Ma) & Florence L Basso (Haverhill,Ma), 15 Mar 1980
George W (So Kingston/50) & Florence T Austin (Newton Jct/36), 24 Jan 1907
(Samuel W Wallace/Hannah Hoyt)(Benjamin Gemeny/Mary E Roberts)
Scott G (W Newbury,Ma) & Sandra A Theofilopoulos (Haverhill,Ma),16 May 1980
WALSH: Rodger F (Kingston) & Carolyn D Gianetta (Salem), 14 Aug 1981
William F (Kingston) & Bonnie L Merrill (Stratham), 01 Dec 1959   (B)
(William N Wheat/ Mary McGall)(Leroy Merrill/ Lillian Campbell)

WARD: Stephen D (Kingston) & Cathy A Bradley (Kingston), 10 Jun 1978
WARREN: Edward R, Jr (Kingston) & Dorothy E Arnold (Kingston), 01 Jul 1977
WARRINGTON: Edwin (Kingston) & Patricia E Lyons (Putney,Ma), 20 Jun 1953
    (Edwin Warrington,Sr/Ethel L Marren)(John J Lyons/ Ethel A Aiken)
    Mark L (Kingston) & Dorothy M Morgan (Portsmouth), 21 Dec 1977   (Port)
WASZ: R James (Cincinnati,Oh) & Joanne Kerkhoff (Kingston), 27 May 1984
WATSON: Herbert B (Rome,Me/65) & Harriet A Reynolds (Hartford,Ct/55), 06 Mar 1932*
    (Albion Watson /Abbie Brooks)(William Arthur)   *(Chester)
    John T (Topsfield,Ma) & Carol J Bishop (Topsfield,Ma), 24 Jul 1960
    (Ernest W Watson/ Hazel L Armstrong)(Robert C Bishop/ Mary Swiniarski)
WATTS: Frank R (Kingston) & Susan K Chandler (Kingston), 18 Apr 1986
    Stephen W, Jr (Kingston) & Lena J Beckman (Haverhill,Ma), 31 Oct 1959
    (Stephen W Watts,Sr/Georgia Eaton)(George Beckman/ Ada Wilbur)
WEBB: Warren C (Chelsea,Ma) & Barbara A Fields (Kingston), 07 Nov 1957
    (Stephen Webb/ Florence Frazier)(Kenneth A Fields/ Pauline Arnold)
WEBSTER: Charles E (E Kingston/52) & Olivie H Francis (Windsor,N.S/42), 01 Jun 1918
    (John T Webster/Abbie P Buswell)(Jacob Milne/Ann Mosher)
    John L (E Kingston/48) & Clara Nichols (Kingston/41), 21 Apr 1909
    (John T Webster /Abbie P Buswell)(Steven F Nichols/Sarah E Chase) (Peabody,Ma)
    Robert E (E Kingston) & Sally A Linscott (Kingston), 30 Dec 1953
    (A Warren Webster/ Abbie M Evans)(Mellen C Linscott/ Constance Lamont)
    Walter E (Kingston/22) & Bertha H Kruger (Exeter/20), 31 Mar 1909
    (John L Webster/Mary Prescott)(Herman F Kruger/Amelia Raska)
    Walter N (Lawrence,Ma/25) & Florence E Bake (Lawrence,Ma/24),06 Aug 1928
    (Dean K Webster/Clarabel Hatch)(Herbert Bake/Mary M Megson)
    William H (E Kingston/39) & Elizebeth Briggs (Boston,Ma/27), 03 Apr 1907
    (John T Webster/Abbie P Buswell)
WEISBERG: Gerald (Bradford,Ma) & Kathleen S Nason (Kingston), 04 Mar 1994
WELCH: David A (Kingston) & Carol A Chandler (Exeter), 09 Oct 1982
    David (Newburyport,Ma) & Bernice Smith (Amesburg,Ma), 03 Mar 1954
    (David B Welch,Sr/ Evelyn Cote)(Raymond S Smith/ Arvilla Haskell)
    Frank H (Dorchester,Ma/37) & Grace C Sanborn (Boston,Ma/41), 25 Dec 1907
    (Samuel M Welch/Dorothy O Guay)(William J Stevens/Cecilia Loring)
    Patrick J (Kingston) & Bonnie J Richardson (Haverhill,Ma), 26 Aug 1989
    Paul A (Kingston) & Joan M Pickard (Atkinson), 29 Mar 1975
    Thomas J (Kingston) & Patricia J Venturi (Kingston), 24 Sep 1983
    William N (Lynn,Ma/37) & Eileen D Lucey (Lynn,Ma/37), 02 Mar 1946
    (William Welch/Mabel L Noble)(Michael Lucey/Ellie Lynch)
WELDY: Norman E, Jr (Kingston) & Linda D Clay (Raymond), 17 Jan 1976   (A)
WELLS: Henry G (Kingston) & Jean M Gray (Allenstown), 26 Jan 1975
WENDELL: Richard D III (Kingston) & Sandra A Tobin (Kingston), 21 Oct 1972 (N)
WENGEL: Charles H (31) & Muriel E Willey (23), 16 Aug 1942 (P)
    (August C Wengel/Mabel C Warren) & David D Cheney/Gladys Lougee)
WENTWORTH: David M (Skowhegan,Me)&Brenda L Hanson (Kingston),29 May 1976(Ports)

Fred A III (Exeter) & Marian L Phelan (Kingston), 21 Apr 1972 (N)
WEST: Allen R (Kingston/24) & Helen R George (Kingston/17), 30 May 1947 (D)
    Charles W West/Lucinda Smith)(Charles Davis/Mabel Clark)
    Andrew H (Kingston) & Lois A France (Lawrence,Ma), 17 Sep 1960
    (Henry C West/ Blanche E Brickett)(Albert France/ Jessie Walker)
    Chandler B (Danville/24) & Edna A Collins (Kingston/21), 08 Jun 1946
    (Chester W West/Alice A Lyford)(Oral W Collins/Daisy May Jasper)
    Chester W, (Kingston/21) & Alice A Lyford (Brentwood/19), 11 Nov 1915
    (Walter West/Ruth P Nason)(Francis Lyford/Carrie Holbrook)
    David A (Kingston) & Barbara E Towle (Exeter), 21 May 1971
    Errol F (Danville,Ma) & Cheryll A Adams (Kingston), 25 Jun 1966
    Fred (Haverhill,Ma/47) & Josephine Harriman (Quincy,Ma/47), 12 Apr 1923
    (Andrew J West/Mary Davis)(David Sims/Esther Archable)
    Kevin M (Kingston) & Geneva S Sweetland (Dover), 31 Dec 1988
    Owen E (Kingston/23) & Ethel L Davis (Kingston/22), 28 Mar 1925   (P)
    (Fred F West/Flora N Pinkham)(Alonzo Davis/Eva A Gile)
WESTON: Thomas R (Boston,Ma/21) & Joan Beaumont (Kingston/18), 06 Nov 1949 (E)
    (William J Weston/Sophia Hansen)(Harold B Beaumont/Irene Thornhill)
WHEELER: David G (Kingston) & Alexandra B Quarles (Portsmouth), 20 Mar 1971
    Gerald L (Amesbury,Ma) & Elaine A Moreau (Haverhill,Ma), 05 Nov 1962
    Harold A (Lawrence,Ma) & Ann Harty (Haverhill,Ma), 16 Dec 1984
    Robert B (Kingston) & Donna M Wheeler (Kingston), 09 Aug 1963
    Victor H (Kingston) & Melodie J Parenteau (Kingston), 07 Jul 1984
    Wayne R (Haverhill,Ma) & Diane Linscott (Bradford,Ma), 02 Apr 1960
    (Claude A Wheeler/ Florence Stuart)(Ernest Linscott/ Charlotte Dow)
WHEELOCK: Frederic M (34) & Dorithy E Rathbone (27), 14 Aug 1937 (H/F)
    (Franklin M Wheelock/ Etta R Goldthwaite)(James C Rathbone/ Lillian Reynolds)
WHITCOMB: Victor L (Everett,Ma/30) & Doris M Nichols (Malden,Ma/20), 08 Jul 1945
    (Victor Whitcomb/Lillian M Dodge)(Charles Nichols/Elizabeth Ford)
WHITE: Bernard H, III (Lynn,Ma) & Irene R Malo (Lynn,Ma), 26 Jan 1973
    Charles R (Kingston) & Martha L Bird (Kingston), 23 Sep 1972 (N)
    David M (Baltimore,Md) & Paula A Hanson (Kingston), 28 May 1983
    Donald A, Jr (Kingston) & Carol A Swiezynski (Exeter), 08 Jun 1974 (E)
    Ernest E (Wilmington,Ma) & Patricia A Little (Kingston), 02 May 1964 (Concord)
    Robert D (Kingston) & Barbara R Allen (Kingston), 23 May 1959
    (Samuel White/ Louise Comand)(John R Allen/ Elsie E Loubier)
    Theodore J (Mansfield,Ma) & Kathy A Vassar (Mansfield,Ma), 14 Jul 1974   (E/K)
    William P (Exeter) & Natalie J Brown (Kingston), 27 Mar 1965 (E)
WHITEMAN: Harold C (Melrose,Ma) & Marjorie B Leahy (Melrose,Ma), 04 Nov 1968
WHITENECK: Gary A (Kingston) & Barbara A Banville (Kingston), 18 Jan 1986
WHITFORD: David B (Plaistow) & Susan V Griffin (Kingston), 05 Oct 1973 (P)
WHITNEY: Louis B (Hyde Park,Ma/24) & Elizabeth B Nason (Kingston/16), 30 Aug 1932
    (William Whitney/Lena J Bird)(Freeman Nason/Mildred Marshall) (R)
    Robert W (Kingston) & Donna M Young (Lowell,Ma), 04 Oct 1969 (N)
    Stephen R (Billerica,Ma) & Judith E Veglas (Billerica,Ma), 02 Apr 1994

WHITTEN: Edward R (Kittery,Me) & Judith A Simmering (Kingston), 01 Jan 1984
WHITTIER: William H (W Concord/27) & Ora E George (Derry/20), 03 Sep 1906
    (George Whittier/Martha J Haynes)(Fred P George/Josephine Spollett) (E Hamp)
WHOOLEY: Steven R (Haverhill,Ma) & Debra L Mancini(Haverhill,Ma), 14 Jun 1987
WICKER: Joseph (Kingston) & Blanche E Hall (St Stephen,NB), 23 Feb 1974 (P)
WICOX: Richard C (Kingston) & Wendy L Page (Kingston), 02 May 1987
WICKER: Roger B (Kingston) & Vivian L Sanborn (Danville), 18 Feb 1961   (P)
    (Michael J Wicker/ Clara M Madden)(Robert E Sanborn/ Marion C Demaine)
WILBUR: Mark R (Kingston) & Janna M Ricker (Kingston), 11 Jun 1994
WILDER: Robert F (Methuen,Ma) & Renate L Beard (Methuen,Ma), 06 Jun 1981
WIGGIN: Arthur W (Exeter) & Anne P Willson (Kingston), 02 Apr 1966
WIGHT: Andrew S (Kingston) & Paulette J Derochers (Plaistow), 31 Aug 1968 (N)
WILKIE: Thomas W (Lexington,Ma) & Leslie F Parker (Woburn,Ma), 17 Mar 1962
WILKINS: Richard M (Topsfield,Ma) & Marilyn G Clark (Danvers,Ma), 25 Feb 1965
WILLEY: Charles R, Jr (Kingston/25) & Ruth E Goodsell (Manchester/26), 26 Apr 1947 (Man)
    (C Rexford Willey/Laura Skofield)(Frank Goodell/Josephine Kean)
   Rexford C (45) & Pearl M Sanderson (43), 23 Dec 1941   (P)
    (Edward F Willey/Georgie Cross)(William H Phillips/Mabel A Wormwood)
WILLIAMS: George E (Kingston/16) & Florence L West (Kingston/17), 26 Jun 1945 (Ports)
    (George Willams/Hazel C West)(Charles H West/Audrey E Yeaton)
   James E (22) & Evelyn A Brent (20), 11 Jul 1942
    (Albert H Williams/ Mary Young)(Clifford G Brent/Annie Goller)
   John G (Haverhill,Ma) & Phyllis A Ball (Haverhill,Ma), 03 Jun 1950
    (Andrew J Williams/Edna McGinnis)(Wilbur F Ball/Beatrice E George)
   Joseph F (Kingston) & Grace G Crowe (Kingston), 24 May 1986
   Nela G (Georgetown,Ma) & Lindasue Tanner (Rowley,Ma), 25 Nov 1961
    (Russell Williams/ Virginia Vidito)(Herbert Tanner/ Mildred Hoberg)
WILLS: Gene I (Kingston) & Jeanne Arthur (Kingston), 29 Dec 1988
WILLSON: Jeffrey L (Kingston) & Jane H Woodbury (Kingston), 07 Jan 1973
WILMOT: Robert ,III (Kingston) & Shirley A Rand (Kingston), 10 Oct 1981
WILSON: David E (Johnson,Vt/52) & Leonora Crossman (Cambridge,Ma/35), 02 Jun 1908/9
    (Ebenezer Wilson/Elizabeth Currier)(Oliver Dempsey/Nancy Osborn)
   Joseph V (Kingston) & Cheryl A Grenon (Kingston), 10 May 1987
   Ronald J, Sr (Kingston) & Geraldine Stevens (Kingston), 09 Sep 1989
WINSLOW: Dale, G (Kingston) & Donna L Briggs (Kingston), 21 Aug 1971
   Norman H (29) & Flora Sanborn (27), 23 Dec 1941
    (Horace G Winslow/ Eldora E Nason)(Ernest F Sanborn/ May A Tuck)
   W Wayne (Kingston) & Joan D Salo (Goffstown,Ma), 08 Jun 1963(Goffstown)
WINTER: David W (Newton) & Janet A Fellows (Kingston), 04 Aug 1962
WISWELL: Leroy A (Haverhill,Ma/20) & Mary C Rose (Middleboro,Ma/26), 26 Nov 1925
    (Alva L Wiswell/Anna L Gilford)(Joseph C Rose/Martina Damorta)
WITHAM: Mark D (Kingston) & Pamela J Scates (Kingston), 20 Jul 1990
WOOD: Daniel E (Kingston) & Maryellen Langlois (Kingston), 06 Aug 1994
   Frederic E (Somerville,Ma/39) & Charlotte F Peaslee (Kingston/38),19 Jun 1906
    (Alexander M Wood/Margaret C Cox)(Luther D Peaslee/Mary S Clark) (Hav)

Randall S (Kingston) & Angela P George (Kingston), 29 May 1994
Willie D (Guatemala City,Gaut.) & Erlinda J Martinez (Boston,Ma) 14 Jun 1962
WOODBURY: Henry L (Salem/28) & Beatrice C Chorley (Lawrence,Ma/21), 31 Dec 1931
   (Lewis F Woodbury/France Storey)(James Chorley/Eva Youney)
   Paul J (Lynn,Ma) & Barbara C Holmes (Lynn,Ma), 18 Oct 1964
WRIGHT: Albert J (Kingston) & Carol H Taylor (Exeter), 11 Oct 1987
   Robert S (Kingston) & Mary A Feitor (Kingston), 24 Dec 1988
WRIGHLEY: Richard J (Kingston) & Barbara R Howley (Kingston), 15 Jun 1980
WUNDERLICH: Robert H (Kingston) & Elizabeth A Garczynski (Kingston), 10 Nov 1984
WYATT: Harry H (Plaistow/38) & Minnie F True (Lawrence,Ma/41), 18 Jan 1915
   (Jefferson Wyatt/Laura Kimball)(Henry O True/Fannie S True) (Claremont)
WYMAN: Albert (Melrose,Ma) & Bonnie D Winchell (Malden,Ma), 14 Feb 1959
   (Albert Wyman/ Myrtle Bickford)(Richard A Winchell/ Bertha C Kibby)
WYSOCKI: Steven J (Haverhill,Ma) & Meredith D MacKenna (Haverhill,Ma), 24 Oct 1971
YANNAKOUREAS: Peter (Kingston) & Lurieann Souza (Haverhill,Ma), 25 Mar 1986
YANUS: Richard P (Kingston) & Maji-Jo Dietz (Kingston), 28 Mar 1987
YACUBACCI: Aldo J (Haverhill,Ma/29) & Helene C Doucette (Haverhill,Ma/24),15 Oct 1949
   (John Yacubacci/Mary A Simboli)(Adelard A Doucette/Yvonne M Pruneau)
YEATON: Leon G (Exeter) & Joan S Langton (Kingston), 02 Aug 1986
YORK: Scott D (Kingston) & Karen L Fish (Kingston), 01 Aug 1991
YOUNG: Albert G (Kingston) & Rhonda L Morse (Kingston), 24 Mar 1983
   Edward (Haverhill,Ma) & Rose M Sotirakipoulos (Haverhill,Ma), 09 Feb 1952
   (Edward J Young/ Milena Paris)(Arthur C Sotirakopoulos/ Angela Paptola)
   Gary K (Kingston) & Mary C Thompson (Kingston), 22 Dec 1979
   Richard J (Cambridge,Ma) & Linda J Najarian (Somerville,Ma), 03 May 1960
   (Simeon Young/ Sarah Harris)(John Najarian/ Mary Cocoran)
ZADROZNY: FrancisJ, Jr (E Braintree,Ma) & Frances D Cole (Harrisville,RI), 30 Jul 1966
ZALENSKI: Robert P (Methuen,Ma) & Glenna L Fellows (Kingston), 08 Aug 1970 (N)
ZALEWSKI: Alan E (Salem) & Andrea R Nicosia (Kingston),18 Aug 1991
ZAPORA: Daniel F (Kingston) & Katherine A Onorato (Kingston), 06 Jun 1987
ZAREMBA: Wayne M (Kingston) & Patricia E Mahoney (Kingston), 03 Sep 1988
ZARYCKI: Francis R (Brockton,Ma) & Firesia G Morgan (Brockton,Ma), 06 Sep 1963
ZELLER: Richard J, III (Kingston) & Barbara A Burbrink (Kingston), 03 Jul 1983

DEATHS
1901 - 1994

ABBOTT: Kendall P, 01 Sep 1982 at Exeter (William O Abbott/Georgia L Fitts)
ADAMS: Donald, 11 Sep 1982 (Carleton Adams/Florence Foss)
ADAMS: Leon F, Sr, 04 Dec 1990 at Amesbury, Ma (George S Adams/ Sarah Smart)
ADAMOPOULOS: Lewis, 02 Sep 1978 at Haverhill,Ma) (54)
   (Peter Adamopoulos/Vasilike Barla)
AHLMAN: Christopher, 19 Aug 1988 at Exeter (Edward Ahlman/Rosemarie Milton)
ALDEN: Karl Myron, 18 Apr 1954 (44) (George W Alden/Nellie Smith)b - Plaistow
ALDRED: William, 28 May 1992 at Brentwood
ALEXANDER: John H, 07 Jun 1951 (81) at Kingston - (Thomas B Alexander/Mary F
   Maxfield), b - Grantham
ALH: David Berger, 19 Sep 1980 at Exeter
ALLEN: Albert M, 14 May 1966 at Brentwood (83) (George Allen/Mary Foster)
   Clara Williams, 25 Dec 1932 (Edson C Blake/Almira Cushman) b 27 Sep 1864
   Woodbury,Vt (V/C)
ALLESIO: Constino P, 27 Aug 1991 at Kingston (Paul Alessio/ Elvira Goldberg)
ALTON: Elizabeth, 19 Jan 1953 at Malden, Ma (69) b - Hartlepool, England (Thornton
   Bulmer/Mary Jane Stothart)
AMES: Warren F, Sr, 24 Jan 1986 (Herbert Ames/Beatrice Rogers)
ANDERSON: ......, 14 Dec 1959 at Exeter (Harold Anderson/Kathleen Jeans)
   Leonard R, 10 Mar 1983 at Exeter (David Anderson/Tilda Nelson)
ANDREWS: Benjamin, 08 May 1936 (79) b - Hunter River,PEI (Michael Andrews/Jane Day)
   Jane W, 16 May 1931 (79) at Kingston (Noah Waris/.....)b - Charlottetown, P.E.I.
   Savilla M, 23 Sep 1910 (52) at Chelsea, Ma.
ARANGO: Leopold, Jr, 03 Nov 1984 (Leopold Arango,Sr/Raquel Garcia)
ARCHIBALD: Marie (Ann Marie),08 Dec 1993 (Ambroise Archibald/ Ambroise Goren)
ARNFIELD: Herbert G (68), 27 Aug 1972 (Alfred Arnfield/Caroline Phillips)
ARNOLD: Edith C, 03 Apr 1990 at Kingston (Walter Goodwin/ Sarah Currier)
   George E, Jr, 23 Jan 1980 at Exeter (George E Arnold, Sr/Edith C Goodwin)
   George E, Sr, 02 Jan 1983 at Exeter (George L Arnold/Maude Hartford)
   George L, 20 Mar 1967 at Brentwood (Charles W Arnold/E.M.York) (85 yrs)
   Pearl J, 12 Jan 1918 (Newburyport, Ma) - b1837 (M/S)
ARSENAULT: Natalie G, 09 Feb 1982 at Exeter (Clinton Herbert/Lillian Ames)
ARSENEAULT: Henry J, 20 Sep 1970 at Haverhill,Ma (Alfred Arseneault/Lena Gallant),
   b 1921 (V/C)
ARTHUR: Fannie E, 07 Dec 1925 (54) at Kingston (William Arthur/Jennett Wiggin)b -
   Norwalk, Ct.
ASQUITH: Max H, 28 Sep 1957 at Lowell,Ma (64) - b Allentown,Pa.

ATHERTON: Eva M, 19 Dec 1938 (67) b - Boston,Ma (Michael Sawyer)
AULICH: Maude M, 18 Feb 1980 at Hampton (Wiley Tarr/Jennie Adams)
AVERILL: Hannah A, 20 Jun 1914 (Even Averill/Julia Knox) b 12 Feb 1845 at Charlestown, Ma (P/C)
 John F, 04 Nov 1927 at East Kingston (Eben Averill/Julia Knox) b 1854 (P/C)
 Mary F, 05 May 1939 (Henry Davis/Sarah Kimball) b 15 Jun 1861 (V/C)
AVERY: ....., 28 Mar 1913 (H J Avery/Eva Nason) b 1854 (P/C)
 Alfred J, 08 Mar 1954 at Burlington, Vt (Frank Avery/Addie M Davis) b 1879 Kingston
 Arrie B, 01 Jan 1962 at Brentwood (Albion Nason/Anna Page) b 17 Sep 1875 (P/G)
 Exilda Clara,17 Mar 1967 at Exeter (Frank Foster/Winifred Towle) b 26 May 1916 (P/G)
 Raymond E, 19 Aug 1965 at Haverhill, Ma (Joseph Avery/ Arribelle Nason) (P/G)
 Sarah V, 23 Sep 1914 (James Darbe/Dorothy A Chellis) b 1862 at Danville
AYER: Delia C, 28 Oct 1901 at Plaistow - b 1858 (P/C)
AYERS: Roberta I, 06 Jan 1984 at Exeter (George E Arnold, Sr/Edith Goodwin)
AYOTTE: Joseph, 25 Sep 1925 at Kingston (69 yrs) b - Canada
BAGLEY: Alberta, 12 Aug 1938 (68) (Simon Bishop/Margaret Blackney)
BAGNULLO: Jennie, 02 May 1950 (Rosario Spinella/Anna Arnone) b 1857
BAILEY: George E, 27 Feb 1914 (Jeremiah Bailey/Harriet Magroon)b 1850 at Derry (P/C)
 Roy W, 27 Oct 1975 at Kingston (77) (Oscar L Bailey/Christie Naddeau)
 Ruth E, 23 Feb 1978 at Exeter (76) (William Eastman/Sarah Herded)
 Sarah Elizabeth, 08 Apr 1942 at Nashua (Benjamin F Cram/Elizabeth Smith) b 21 Apr 1856 (P/C)
BAKE: Herbert, 21 Feb 1951 (Frank Bake/Sarah A Butler) b 29 Feb 1872 (G/C)
 Laura E, 24 Apr 1979 at Exeter (Albert F Nason/ Laura Fifield)
 Mary Maria, 19 Feb 1959 (Robert Megson/Sarah A Fernley) b 30 Aug 1873 Bradford, England (G/C)
BAKER: Laura E, 07 Feb 1933 (81) at Boston, Ma
BAKIE: Daniel James, 22 Feb 1940 (James Bakie/Elizabeth) b 16 Jan 1851 (V/C)
 Ethelyn, 02 Jun 1973 at Exeter (James Swain/Evelyn Swain) b 21 Oct 1880 (V/P)
 Flora, 16 Nov 1926 at Haverhill, Ma (Levi S Gordon/Dorothy A Clifford) b 1858 (P/C)
 George M, 17 Aug 1935 at Exeter - b 1862 (P/C)
 James, 18 Jul 1901 at Concord (Daniel J Bakie/..... Runnelle) b 1825 (P/C)
 Marion, 08 Jul 1993 (Ernest Allard / Annie McClellan)
 Nella F, 12 May 1932 at Manchester(William Sanborn/Mary Ann Howe) b 19 Jan 1851
 Warren G, 15 Apr 1990 at Exeter (William Bakie/ Flora Gordan)
 William Alexander, 12 Jun 1941 (Alexander Bakie) b 16 Oct 1853 (V/C)
 William Alexander, 17 Oct 1941 (William Bakie /Flora A Gordon)b 20 Oct 1899 (P/C)
BALL: Albert, 26 Dec 1943 at Brentwood b - 08 Mar 1865 (H/H)
 Mary F, 01 Aug 1924 at W Kingston (Albert Sweetser/Rebecca Berry)b 28 Oct 1843
BALLARD: Miner Ellsworth, 30 Jul 1973 at Exeter (89) (Frank E Ballard/Frances Curry)
 Ruby, 14 Jul 1981 at Exeter (Fred A Jackson/Laura C Carr)
BALUKAS: Marc A, 20 May 1989 at Kingston (Robert A Balukas/Sandra Grandmont)
 Michael A, 13 Jun 1971(Konstanta Balukas/Caroline Bingel) b 15 Aug 1906 (P/G)
 Rae B, 03 Dec 1970 at Haverhill, Ma - b 1917 (P/G)

BANCROFT: Sophie, 30 Jun 1967 at Brentwood (Ernest Gall/Caroline Timme)b 18 May 1887
BANKS: Joseph L, 01 Aug 1932 (30) (Patrick W/Mary A Murray)
    Sidney F, 12 May 1950 at Exeter (Parker Banks/Ellen L Freeman) b-1867
BANNAIAN: Sarkis, 27 Jan 1975 (Margo Bannaina) b 05 Oct 1905 (P/G)
BARANOFSKY: Marie J, 18 Jan1985 at Boston,Ma (James Feeney/Helen O'Brien)
BARCLAY: Gladys, 12 Jun 1967- b 1905 (G/C)
    John M, 18 Dec 1968 at Haverhill, Ma (William Barclay/Jane McCannechie) b 17
    Dec 1907 (G/C)
    Margaret A, 26 Nov 1990 at Exeter (Eric Peterson/ Alma Ruckman)
    Phyllis, 15 Jan 1990 at Exeter (Lloyd B Chapman/ Mary Brennan)
    William, 16 Apr 1974 at Boston, Ma - b 1904 (P/G)
BARNES: Charles, 07 Mar 1976 at Kingston (99) (Silas Barnes/Lizzie Upton)
    Dora, 08 Apr 1950 (Alfred Archer/Lois Marco) b 1873
    Mabel, 11 Oct 1970 at Brentwood (88) (John Burditt/Lizzie Weston)
    Paul Sidney, 16 Sep 1976 at Exeter (Sidney C Barnes/Dora Archer) b 01 Sep 1914
BARRETT: Alberta B, 22 Aug 1992 at Manchester (Carroll B Hardy/ Bertha W Howe)
    Christie B, 02 Dec 1979 at Haverhill, Ma (William A Cheney/ Estella Page)
    Ellen, 02 Jan 1927 at Kingston (74) (William McNamara/Martha Emmons) b -Ireland
    Florence D, 09 Oct 1992 at Exeter (Frank J Rollins/ Dora L Dow)
    James, 06 Jan 1902 (John Barrett) b 1806
    John E, 19 May 1936 (Florence Barrett) b 14 Sep 1860 (M/S)
    John H, 15 Apr 1961 at Kingston (74) (Thomas Barrett/Ellen McNamara)
    John James, 15 Apr 1961 (ThomasBarrett/Ellen McNamara) b 27 Apr 1886 (P/G)
    Katherine F, 22 Oct 1959 at Exeter (78) (Thomas Barrett/Ellen McNamara) b Kingston
    Lizzie, 25 Jan 1925 at SoKingston (Benjamin Trafton/Julia A Young) b 03 Jul 1862
    Raymond Hollway, 29 Apr 1968 at Exeter (John E Barrett/Lizzie Trafton) b 11 Dec
    1894 (G/C)
    Thomas, 30 Aug 1914 (James Barrett/Mary Landregon), b - 1836 in Ireland
    Walter W, 18 Jun 1952 at St.Petersburg,Fl (79) (Franics Bartlett/Mary A Rowe) b King.
    William N, 04 Nov 1989 at Hampton (William H Barrett/Goldie F Colbroth)
BARRY: Louise D, 14 Mar 1977 at Dover (M/S)
BARSTOW: Julia F, 09 Mar 1901 (Horation Farnsworth/Ruth Woodruff) b 1818
BARTHWICK: Charles B, 15 Aug 1964 at Manchester (68) (Daniel Barthwick/Martha Bentley)
BARTLETT: Ada F, 01 Jan 1901 at Lynn, Ma (Hosea B Bartlett/Parmelia Hooke) (P/C)
    Aroline E, 10 Jul 1900 (Moses Sanborn/Elizabeth Stevens) b 1825 (P/C)
    Enoch 28 Jul 1914 (Daniel Bartlett) b 1829 at Deerfield (M/S)
    Frank B, 01 Sep 1936 at Hampton Beach - b 1888 (P/C)
    George W, 21 Mar 1940 at Haverhill, Ma - b 1865 (S/K)
    John H, 05 Nov 1923 (69) Haverhill Ma.
    Levi Stevens, 05 Jul 1940 (Levis S Bartlett/ Aroline E Sanborn)b 28 Mar 1857 (V/C)
    Lizzie E, 03 May 1962 at Epping (Madison Bartlett/Mary Sanborn)b 17 Mar 1870 (M/S)
    Luella A, 25 Jun 1971 at Methuen, Ma - b 1887 (K/V)
    Martha, 29 Jun 1929 at Exeter - b 1856
    Mary E, 21 Mar 1916 (John Crosby/Abigal S Pevear) b 1846 in Haverhill, Ma

Mary F, 26 Feb 1909 (Jacob H Sanborn/Rebecca Gale) b 1836 (E /K)
Perley, 18 Dec 1929 (48) at Haverhill Ma.
Phyllis Ardelle, 16 May 1919 at Haverhill, Ma (Bailey Bartlett/Bertha Webster) 9 days
Ruth Grace, 08 Nov 1948 (John C Sanborn/Mary A Hooke) b 30 Mar 1865
Walter Sanborn, 18 Jan 1942 (James M Bartlett/Mary F Sanborn)b 24 Jul 1858 (S/K)
William J, 12 Dec 1913 (P/C)
BARTON: Charles W, 14 Jan 1909 (Marton A Barton/Elizabeth A Hook)b-1849 in Croydon
BASCOM: Linda A, 03 Sep 1975 at Nottingham- b 1954 (P/G)
BASSETT: Miranda, 28 Mar 1900 (Samuel Spofford/Lydia Peaslee) b-1809 (P/C)
BASTIAN: Mary J, 25 Jun 1974 at Brentwood (94) (John Swant/Mary Butler)
BASTIEN: Baby Boy, 16 Apr 1975 at Boston, Ma - b 14 Apr 1975 (P/G)
BATCHELDER: Elizabeth McLean, 24 Nov 1965 at Kingston (80)
BATTLES: Wendell G, 21 Mar 1974 at Exeter (72) (William G Battles/Ethel Currier)
BATTYE: Joseph, 04 Mar 1929 at Kingston (68), b - England
BEALS: Alice Frances, 22 Jul 1939 at Exeter (Richard Davis/Harriet Stacey) b - 02 Aug
    1880 (G/C)
    George Emery, 01 Mar 1963 at Epping (Henry Beals/Emma Bragdon)b 02 Aug 1875
BEAN: Elvira A, 08 Apr 1915 at Newton, b 1830
    William K, 21Jun 1929 (59) (Nicholas Bean/... Quinn) b - Haverhill,Ma
BEAUDOIN: Joseph A, 24 Nov 1980 at Exeter (Andrew Beaudoin/Mildred Obey)
BEAULIEU: Marion C, 12 Mar 1990 at Exeter (Edwin S Williams/ Tillie Drake)
BECK: Ruth, 18 Sep 1981 at Kingston (Edward Wander/Gertrude Tavis)
BECKFORD: Baby Girl, 24 May 1956 at Haverhill, Ma, b 24 May 1956 (M/S)
BEDAL: Mary, 08 Feb 1985 at Exeter (Frank W Taylor/Elizabeth Chesley)
    Peter V, 20 Oct 1981 at Manchester (George Bedul/Rosalia Avens)
    William S, II, 29 Jan 1992 at Exeter (William S Bedal/ Susan Dreas)
BEEDE: Clarence Herbert, 25 Jul 1918 at Saugus, Ma.,(Oscar Beede/Hannah Webster) b 1877
    Fred S, 22 May 1938 (56) at Newton
    Hannah, 06 Jan 1937 at Kingston (John T Webster/Abbie P Buswell) b 06 Jan 1853
BELDEN: George, 17 Apr 1921 at Haverhill, Ma, b 1881 (P/C)
    Jennie E, 18 Jun 1913 at Haverhill,Ma, b 1837 (P/C)
    Lizzie May, 31 Mar 1901 at Haverhill,Ma, (Zachary Belden)b 1873
BELL: Lilla (Smith), 22 Nov 1939 at Quincy,Ma, b 1888 (G/C)
BELMER: Porter Donald, 11 Dec 1925 at Kingston (10) (Donald P Belmer/Maria Woodman)
BENNETT: Albert G, 15 Apr 1937 (53) (Thomas J Bennett/Julia Mosley)
    Lena Ida, 19 Jun 1960 at Kingston (Arthur Byrd/Delphine Daggle) b 16 Sep 1889,
    Natick, Ma
    Louise, 11 Aug 1984 at Kingston (Panquale Peruto)
    William A, 20 Jun 1965 at Brentwood (John Bennett/Eudora Sneed) b 08 Jul 1886 (P/G)
BENOIT: Joseph Henry, 03 Apr 1973 at Exeter (John Baptiste Benoit/Rose Chausse) b 29 Nov
    1886 (G/C)
BERGERON: Alfred J, Jr, 18 Jul 1986 at Kingston (Alfred Bergeron, Sr/Gertrude Osgood)
BERRY: Laura Frances, 22 Apr 1947 (87) at Kingston (Richard L Prescott/Clara J Bickford)
    b 24 Aug 1859 (P/C)

Edward C, 15 Dec 1979 at Manchester (Charles Berry/ Louise Ross)
Richard A, 10 Oct 1983 at Exeter (Wyatt Berry/Margaret Freeman)
BESSEY: Allen R, 05 Jun 1923 (42) (Calvin J Bessey/Phoebe Tarrall), b - Thorald, Ontario
BEVACQUA: Helen, 22 Jul 1986 at Exeter (Frank Norvish/Elizabeth Yanunites)
BINGEL: Bradley James, 01 Jul 1961 at Exeter (John A Bingel/Sandra Avery)b 29 Jun 1961
Deborah Lee, 27 Apr 1958 at Exeter (John Bingel/Sandra Avery)b 02 Jan 1958 (P/G)
BIRD: Charles H, -- Mar 1901 at Boston, Ma (....../Mary Dudley) b 1843 (P/C)
Clara M, 20 Nov 1923 at Revere,Ma (Charles Bird/Clara Chase) b 1889 (P/C)
Mabel, 14 Nov 1988 at Kingston (Charles T Cunningham/Alice Fletcher)
BISHOP: Caroline R 11 Feb 1924 at Boston, Ma, b 07 Dec 1852 (P/C)
George Steven, Jr, 14 Jul 1973 at Brentwood (George S Bishop/Helen E Crawford)
b 10 May 1921 (G/C)
BIXBY: Doris E, 04 Nov 1932 at Haverhill, Ma, b 1902 (G/C)
Barbara B, 26 Jun 1990 at Kingston (George Brooks/ Fannie Noyes)
BLAIS: Roland W, 04 Dec 1992 at Exeter (William Blais/ Anna Morin)
BLAISDELL: Herbert Henry, 06 Dec 1969 at Exeter (Edgar H Blaisdell/Gertrude Batchelder)
b 27 Sep 1897 (P/G)
Marcia Ellen, 28 Apr 1974 at Exeter (George Simes/Annie Tucker) b 14 Mar 1911 (P/G)
Newman Linwood, 02 Nov 1982 at Exeter (Alpheus Blaisdell/Gertrude Hutchins)
BLAKE: Gregory P, 07 Jan 1967 at Kingston (2) (Philip Blake/Sandra Huntington)
Lottie, 01 Nov 1927 (44) at Haverhill, Ma.
Philip M, Sr, 07 Jan 1967 at Kingston (28) (Raymond Blake/Elizabeth Merrill)
Philip M, Jr, 07 Jan 1967 at Kingston (4) (Philip Blake/Sandra Huntington)
BLANCHARD: Mary P, 05 Feb 1980 at Brentwood (Sowa Perry/Catherine Koza)
Wilfred, 05 Apr 1980 at Exeter (Joseph Blanchard/Stephanie Beauregard)
BLETHEN: Carlton Ernest, 23 Jan 1978 at Exeter (77) (Walter H Blethen/Gertrude A Craig)
BLIZZARD: Emma O (Gilman), 08 Sep 1950 at Lowell,Ma - b 15 Mar 1865
BLOIS: Henrietta, 21 Apr 1973 at Kingston (90) (George Wood/Henrietta Sawyer)
BONIN: Alfred J, 18 Aug 1961 at Kingston (70) (Moise Bonin/Allina Jette)
BOOTH: Henry T, 20 Nov 1956 at Kingston (90)
BORAH: Gladys S, 28 Oct 1925 at Kingston (4) (Delmer F Borah/Marie Merling)b-Boston,Ma
BOUCHER: Edward M, 17 Aug 1974 at Kingston (6) (Ernest R Boucher)
George W, 05 Sep 1974 at Kingston (70) (Peter Boucher/Lucy ....)
BOURASSA: Charles W, 14 Aug 1989 at Littleton (Wilfred Bourassa/Marie DeMut)
BOYINGTON: Ralph C, 13 Nov 1985 at Kingston (Harrison T Boyington/Mary Baker)
BOYLE: Alice, 11 Feb 1973 at Haverhill, Ma (59) (Edward Walling/Alice Burke)
BRADLEY: Asa M, 19 Jan 1937 at Kingston (Cyrus A Bradley/Lucretia Foster)b 09 Mar 1856
Charles A, 06 Jun 1978 at Kingston (67) (Frank Bradley/Lena Ellis)
Elizabeth B, 26 Dec 1975 at Exeter (Frederick Briggs/Annie .....)b 04 Apr 1880 (V/C)
James C, 02 Feb 1969 at Kingston (70) (James Bradley/Elizabeth Douglas)
Mary H, 15 Nov 1927 at Kingston (Charles C Emery/Hannah G Clark)b 17 Jul 1854
BRADFORD: Eleanor M, 20 Oct 1959 at Kingston (86) (Martin J Hunting/Sophia J Chase),
b - Plymouth, Ma.
BRADSHAW: Gladys R, 03 Sep 1956 at Haverhill, Ma, b 1898 (K/C)

BRAGDON: Alice E, 27 Jun 1924 at Haverhill, Ma (George Bartlett/.....)b 03 May 1855 (P/C)
Carrie, 23 Mar 1977 at Haverhill, Ma, b - 1895 (G/C)
Emma F, 15 Aug 1965 Haverhill, Ma, (John W Prescott/Roxie S Sanborn) b 1873 (G/C)
Ernest Prescott, 02 Nov 1973 at Exeter (Fred Bragdon/Emma Prescott) b 08 Jul 1896
Fred Leslie, 23 Jun 1939 at Kingston (Augustus I Bragdon/Alice Bartlett), b 01 May 1873 (G/C)
George L, 21 Jul 1901 at Kingston (George Bragdon/Betsey Henderson) b 1839
Lillian Mabel, 26 Nov 1969 at Melrose, Ma, b 1874 (P/C)
Robert I (54), 03 Sep 1972 at Exeter (George R Bragdon/Marion E Burtt)
Wesley A, 20 Jan 1924 at Everett,Ma (Augustus Bragdon/Alice E Bartlett) b 21 Apr 1877 (P/C)
BRIAN: Nellie J, 02 Oct 1909 at Kingston (John Jones/Abbie Burke) b-1872 (K/C)
BRICK: Glenna K, 16 Jun 1989 at Hanover (Glenn Mostoller/Mary K Bennett)
BRINDLE: Richard H, 07 Nov 1992 at Kingston (George O Brindle/ Florence Girrior)
BRINTON: Walter D, 06 May 1979 at Kingston (Walter W Brinton/Ethel....) b - Epping
BRITTON: ....., 02 May 1943 at Haverhill, Ma (George M Britton/Lilla M George)
b 02 May 1943 (V/C)
Baby Boy, 25 Apr 1942 at Exeter (George M Britton/Lilea May George) b 25 Apr 1942
BROUILLETTE: Bruce C, 24 Mar 1992 at Exeter (Mark A Brouillette/ Carolyn L Colby)
BROWN: Abraham S, 23 Apr 1915 at Candia (Abraham Brown/Lois Smith)b 19 Dec 1827
Nottingham (So/K)
Annie P, 27 Dec 1926 at Kingston (Samuel Chase/Mary Judkins)b 03 Mar 1840
Bertha Bell, 25 Apr 1966 at Hampton Falls (John Furber/Roxie Collins), b 28 Sep 1874
Carrie, 25 May 1967 at Brentwood (Thomas Martin/Eva Frazier)b 02 May 1887
Clara F, 08 Mar 1930 at Kingston (70) (William Day) b Georgetown
Clara L, 17 Feb 1984 at Exeter (Frederick M Hahner/Olivia Colbath)
Clyde L, 25 Dec 1968 at Haverhill, Ma, b 1887 (P/G)
Edward Everett, 10 Apr 1958 at Kingston (Cornelius Brown/Annie Brown) b 14 Jan 1871- Bradford,Ma. (G/C)
Edward Lincoln, 8 Jun 1954 at Portsmouth (Arthur F Brow/Ruth J Hersey) b - 07 Jun 1954 (New Cem)
Effie Belle, 10 Apr 1973 at Exeter (Andrew Quero/Mary .....)b 20 Nov 1886 (V/C)
Marion E, 14 Ma 1948 at Portsmouth (Edwin S Wallace/Sarah Elizabeth Whitehouse) b 24 Sep 1894 (G/C)
Martha, 01 Mar 1902 at Kingston (William McKinley/Elizabeth Williams) b 1817
Mary M, 11 Apr 1900 at Kingston, b 1832 (P/C)
BRYANT: Rita J, 08 Feb 1983 at Kingston (Ludger Ouellet/Bridget Proulx)
BRYAR: Harriet F, 10 Sep 1909 at Kingston (Parker Stevens/Mary D Willey) b 1837
BUCKLEY: Edith Violet, 26 Aug 1962 at Sandown (Samuel LeBelle/Viola Collins) b 10 Nov 1915 (P/G)
BUNKER: ...., 28 Aug 1925 at Kingston (Louis C Bunker/Annie M George)b 27 Aug 1925
Annie M, 06 Oct 1964 at Exeter (76) (Stephen George/Edna West)
David E, 13 Nov 1967 at Dakmat Lat Vietnam (21)(Stanton Bunker/Patricia Tuck)
Priscilla A, 18 Jun 1981at Exeter (John E Tucker/Harriett Osgood)

BURGER: Roy G, 04 Apr 1958 at Kingston (52) (Nicholas Burger/Edith M MacQueen) b -
Concord
BURKE: Infant, 07 Jun 1920 (birth) at Haverhill, Ma.
John J, 22 Apr 1989 at Exeter (William Burke/Catherine Callahan)
Malizzia Susan, 10 Jun 1968 at Kingston (Harry Lord/Mary ....)b 10 Aug 1934 (P/G)
Richard C, 03 Jun 1969 at Haverhill, Ma (James J Burke/Ruth Nason)b 1935 (P/G)
Ruth E, 14 Nov 1992 at Kingston (Freeman L Nason/ Mildred Marshall)
BURNHAM: Mary H, 11 Dec 1958 at Kingston (85) (George F Weed/Lucretia P Harrat), b -
Newport,Me.
Nancy A, 09 Nov 1925 at Kingston (76) (David A Gilchrist) b - Londonderry
Samuel F, 06 Aug 1959 at Kingston (82) (John G Burnham/Alice Morton), b -
Gloucester,Ma.
BURNO: Frank I, 22 Mar 1979 at Manchester (Charles C Burn/Ada Blake)
BURRILL: Nelson, 11 Mar 1966 at Exeter (74) (Frank Burrill/Hannah Mann)
BURTNER: Mary Ellen, 27 Mar 1976 at Kingston (78) (J Frank Dubois/Eva M Blaisdell)
BUSWELL: Beatrice M, 29 Oct 1966 at Exeter (42) (Richard Robinson/Laura Hillicker)
Glenn H, 14 Oct 1967 at Randolph, Vt (42) (George Buswell/Rita Johnson)
BUTCHER: Rodney E, 27 Jan 1927 at Groveland, Ma (Homer Butcher/Annie ....)
b 19 Jan 1927 (P/C)
BUTLER: Florence A, 24 Apr 1930 (76) (John Lawphy/Flora A Murphy),b-Charlottetown,PEI
Georgianna P, 28 Apr 1900 at Kingston (Thomas Butler/Rebecca Payson)
Helen E, 09 Oct 1990 at Exeter (Job S Cartlidge/ Estella Redmond)
Harvey Sherman, 11 Oct 1964 at Manchester (Luther Butler/Hattie Smith)
b 09 May 1896 (M/S)
BUTRICK: Jennie E, 08 Dec 1935 at East Kingston, b - 1857 (P/C)
BUZZELL: Arthur E, 04 Dec 1914 at Kingston (Wells S Flanders/Mary A Reynolds)
b 1856   (Chelsea, Ma)
Heidi B, 10 Dec 1964 at Exeter (12 days) (Frank Buzzell/Jacqueline Smith)
BYRON: Charles E, 23 Feb 1991 at Kingston (Charles E Byron/ Theresa Noronha)
CAHILL: Joshua Adam, 11 Sep 1982 at Exeter (Robert A Cahill)
CAHOON: Amos O, 04 Dec 1915 at Kingston (Joel S Cahoon/Rhoda Nickerson)
b 1856 (Harwich, Ma)
CALEF: Horace B, 23 Jul 1902 at Denver, Co (Samuel Calef/ Mary A Berry), b- 1852 (P/C)
CAMERON: Brenton C, 14 Sep 1951 (75) at Arlington, Ma.
CAMMETT: Earl V, 01 Oct 1979 at Exeter (John Cammett/Bertha Merrick)
Esther F, 12 Feb 1987 at Concord
CARD: Walton O, 22 Feb 1985 at Kingston (Walton O Card, Sr/Blanche E Hutchinson)
CARLETON: Alfred M, 24 Aug 1980 at Concord
Hattie M, 17 Aug 1932 at South Kingstom (William Emery)b 1865 (P/C)
Irving E, 08 Dec 1935 at South Kingston (George Carlton/Hattie Emery)b 19 May 1888
Roxie J, 02 Jun 1926 at South Kingston (70) (John M Emery/Roxanna Slack)
Wilbur G, 13 Jan 1940 (42)(William M Carlton/Roxie J Emery)
William M, 04 May 1937 (83) b - So Kingston (Jacob Carleton/Malesca Bartlett)

CARMICHAEL: Roland Stewart, 30 Dec 1983 at Kingston (Glendon S Carmichael/Doris L White)
CARREIRO: Marion L, 27 Feb 1985 at Brentwood (George Morris/Sarah Graham)
CARRICK: Harold M, 10 Oct 1963 at Exeter (57) (Matthew Carrick/Florence Ross)
    Ida P, 16 Aug 1973 at Exeter (63)(Frank Kollack/Mary Murphy)
CARROLL: Lois W, 07 Mar 1985 at Bradenton, Fl (Louis Bunker/Annie George)
CARROW: Richard H, 12 Aug 1989 at Exeter (Edward F Carrow/Abbie A Parson)
CARTER: Charles C, 01 Dec 1900 at Kingston - (P/G)
    Elmer C, 03 Jan 1926 (69) at Exeter
    Emma F, 07 Mar 1900 at Kingston (Jeremiah Carter/Elizabeth Coombs)b 1852
    George F, 23 Apr 1922 at Kingston (George F Carter/Mary E Carter)b 21 Apr 1883
    George F, 06 Nov 1915 (William F Carter/Sarah Smith)b 1856 in E Kingston (P/C)
    Harry A, 09 Apr 1975 at Brentwood (George F Carter/Mary Webster)b 07 Jun 1886
    Harry Barton, 12 Jun 1951 at Epping (Elmer Carter/Addie Davis) b 04 Mar 1880
    Ida Pauline, 12 May 1963 at Exeter (69) (Grantley W Bickell/Ida M Grantley)
    b 29 Mar 1894 (G/C)
    Mary B, 02 Apr 1901 at Kingston (Moses Page/Ruth Lane) b 1830
    Mary E, 28 Aug 1920 at Kingston (James Wescott/Elvira Giles) b 01 Jan 1869,
    b - Patten,Me (P/G)
    Sarah, 17 Mar 1917 at Brentwood, b 1839 - Somersworth
CASSIDY: Robert E, 31 Aug 1993 (James Cassidy/Agnes Smith)
CASTALDI: Vincent, 03 Jan 1994 at Exeter (John Castaldi/Maria Gioioso)
CATALDO: James, 23 Mar 1970 at Kingston (67) (James Cataldo/Madeline Charlone)
CAVARIC: Mattie Dutton, 31 Dec 1975 at Deerfield, b 1888 (V/C)
CHADWELL: Carrie W, 31 Mar 1947 (80) at Hampton
    Harris, 29 Jun 1929 at Amesbury, b 1858 (P/C)
CHAMBERLAIN: Beverly S, 22 Mar 1987 at Fremont (Harry Chamberlain/Maude .....)
    Cheryl Anne, 10 Sep 1967 at Methuen (Edward Chamberlain/Charlotte Mailos)
    James E, 26 Mar 1959 at Amesbury, b 1889 (P/C)
    James E, 08 Apr 1959 at Haverhill,Ma (70) (Charles Chamberlain/Abigail Fifield), b - Kingston
    Mabel J, 18 Feb 1910 (5 mos) (James E Chamberlain/Kate L McCabe)
    Marjorie A, 19 Mar 1937 at Exeter (Beverly Chamberlain/Mary Rowell) b 22 Jan 1930
CHAMPAGNE: Edward, 17 Feb 1975 at Exeter (65) (Louis Champagne/Merelise ....)
CHAMPION: Donald R, 13 Jun 1986 at Exeter (Frederick Champion/Margaret LaForce)
CHAPMAN: Ellen F, 27 Mar 1983 at Exeter (William Milne/Lydia Newman)
CHARTIER: Lord Paul, 03 Dec 1987 at Ayer,Ma (Victor Chartier/Jeannette Poirier)
CHASE: Amos C (76) 11 Jan 1910 (Amos Chase/ Hannah P Hooke) b - Kingston
    Charles A, 25 May 1901at Kingston (Amos C Chase/Emily Belden)b 1870 (P/C)
    Clara E, 08 Apr 1928 (75) at Boston, Ma.
    David D, 16 Jan 1973 at Exeter (Frank W Chase/ ..... Poore)b 03 Nov 1899 (P/G)
    Harry Belden, 07 Jan 1903 at Kingston (Amos C Chase/Emily A Belden) b 1877
    Jane B, 19 Jul 1957 at Haverhill, Ma (Alexander Thompson/Jessie C Finley)
    b 18 Sep 1900 - Scotland (P/G)

Jesse Winfield, 14 Dec 1977 at Kingston (72) (Willard W Chase/Clara Pearl)
Mary E, 06 Oct 1916 (67) at Boston, Ma. (Samuel Chase/ Mary A Judkins)
Samuel G, 25 Jan 1910 (76) at Boston, Ma. (Samuel Chase/ Peace Ann Chase)
CHECQUER: Henry, 16 Nov 1956 at Exeter (83) (Daniel Checquer/Eleanor Fry)
Sophia E, 20 Mar 1948 at Kingston (74)(Thomas W Bibbey/Emma J Cameron)
CHENEY: ....., 15 Aug 1922 at Newton, Ma (Hayden Cheney/Freda Osborn)b 15 Aug 1922
....., 21 Oct 1915 at Kingston (David Cheney/Gladys Longee) 21 Oct 1915 (P/G)
....., 29 Nov 1947 at Haverhill, Ma (Lawrence B Cheney/Celia Farnsworth)
b - 29 Nov 1947 (P/G)
....., 30 Jan 1935 at Haverhill, Ma (Roland W Cheney/Ellen Bliss)b 30 Jan 1935
Albert F, 22 Oct 1930 at Haverhill, Ma, b 1851 (P/G)
David Dearborn, 03 Dec 1949 at Kingston (Edward Cheney/Nancy Strout)
b 04 Apr 1891 (P/G)
Edward L, 21 Jun 1936 at Kingston (Nathaniel D Cheney/Elizabeth ....)b 01 Apr 1844
Ellen Viola, 30 Aug 1986 at Kingston (Irving Bliss/Rosella Jones)
Harold M, 05 Aug 1918 at Kingston (David Cheney/Gladys Lougee)b 06 Jan 1917
Lenora B, 21 May 1972 at Haverhill, Ma, b 1887 (P/G)
Mary Ellen, 20 Dec 1948 at Haverhill,Ma (Lawrence B Cheney/Celia Farnsworth)
b 20 Nov 1948 (P/G)
Nancy R, 21 Jun 1915 at Kingston (David Strout)b 1852 at Millbridge
Roland W, 28 May 1987 at Kingston (William Cheney/Stella Page)
Stella Augusta, 20 Aug 1960 at South Kingston (Ezra Page/Augusta Shaw),b 06 Aug
1871 - Kingston   (P/G)
William A, 19 Jan 1917 at Kingston (Nathaniel D Cheney/Mary E Hoyt)b 09 Apr 1847
Winifield S, 25 Mar 1932 at Brentwood (Nathaniel Cheney/Mary Harte)b 02 Feb 1850
CHICK: Henry Herbert, 19 May 1960 at Exeter (Lendall Chick/Sarah Webster)b 22 Jan 1881,
b - E Boston,Ma
Lendall A, 27 Feb 1926 at Exeter (h/o Sarah Webster) b 1853
CHILDS: Madeline Stevens, 18 Dec 1968 at Exeter (Walter R Stevens/Jane Pope)
b 09 Sep 1902   (G/C)
Ray H, 28 Dec 1944 at Kittery,Me (Russell Childs/Alice Colby)b - 26 Mar 1897 (G/C)
CHILSON: Harriet Ella, 12 May 1918 at Cambridge, Ma , b 1854 (P/C)
CHIPMAN: Washington, Jr, 04 Nov 1925 at Kingston (76) (Washington Chipman/Hannah B ...)
b - Barnstable, Ma
CHRISTIE: Andrew, 12 Nov 1964 at Exeter (Andrew Christie/Sophia Visna)b 15 Apr 1888
CHRISTOPHER: Louis M, 20 Jun 1925 at Kingston (23) (Joseph Christopher/Bridget Malone)
b - Boston, Ma
CHUBBUCK: Horace Bolton, 13 Feb 1938 at Kingston (Daniel Chubbuck/Emma Stackpole)
b 21 Aug 1878 - Scituate,Ma (P/G)
CILLEY: Annie Laurie, 14 Mar 1934 at Kingston (Alfred Towle/Mary S Gale) b 08 Aug 1859
Clarence E, 05 Feb 1902 at Kingston (Andrew J Cilley/Susan Bartlett) b 1854
Elizabeth, 01 Apr 1963 at Brentwood (George McLane/Jeannette Cairus) b 1884
George B, 30 Jul 1921 at East Kingston, b 1864   (P/C)
Lela May, 24 Oct 1958 at Exeter (Francis C Bartlett/Mary Ann Rowe)b 13 Sep 1876,
Kingston

CLAIR: Mary E, 10 Jan 1916 at Kingston (Joseph Clair) b 1883
CLARK: Abbie A, 25 May 1926 at Kingston (w/o Walter S Clark) (George W Sanborn/
    Sarah Badger) b 28 Mar 1852   (P/C)
    Alice Mae, 06 Dec 1970 at Exeter (William H Clark/Rose H Oldham)b 03 May 1890
    Angie L, 30 Sep 1992 at Exeter (Alfred Bean/ Mahitible Hersey)
    Dorothy S, 11 Jun 1984 at Brentwood (Evero W Towne/Ellen Dockum)
    Edward Bird, 04 Feb 1965 at Exeter (Walter S Clark/Abbie A Sanborn)
    b 02 Dec 1890   (V/C)
    Emily, 20 Apr 1968 at Brentwood (Eugene W Healey/Emma Bailey) b Jul 1891
    Emma Lena, 02 Apr 1943 at Exeter (Herman Kruger/Amelia Raska) b 15 Apr 1885
    Ernest Dudley, 01 Sep 1974 at Exeter (Walter S Clark// Abbie Sanborn)
    b 23 Jul 1894 (V/C)
    Eunice, 18 Oct 1989 at Exeter (Daniel Lanagna/Ethelyn Bailey)
    Evelyn F, 12 Feb 1977 at Exeter (George Morris/Sarah Graham)b 26 Jan 1901   (V/C)
    Wilbur J, 02 Jan 1985 at Kingston (Simeon P Clark/Mary E Fellows)
    Harry Stuart, 21 Mar 1950 at Kingston(Daniel O Clark/Mary Webster)b 01 Mar 1870
    Harry Sumner, 01 Sep 1974 at Exeter (Walter S Clark/Abbie Sanborn)b 15 Dec 1887
    Henry H, 30 Mar 1981 at Exeter (Simeon P Clark/Mary Etta Fellows)
    John T, 22 Jan 1923 at Kingston (Simeon Clark/Johanna Eastman)b 24 Jul 1841(P/C)
    Martha A, 15 Feb 1916 at Kingston (Jacob Green/Phoebe Wilson)b 30 Jun 1830 in
    Chester (P/C)
    Mary E, 06 Aug 1919 at Kingston (John Webster/Lois Colcord)b 25 Mar 1838 (P/C)
    Mary Etta, 14 Jun 1933 at Kingston (Samuel D Fellows/Lucy A Hoyt) b 16 Jun 1865
    Rodney Walter, 23 Oct 1986 at Exeter (Walter Clark/Ella Locke)
    Rose Hanna, 20 Apr 1950 at Kingston(Robert Oldham/Margaret Woodward)
    b 01 Oct 1883
    Sarah E, 18 May 1914 at Kingston (Charles Titcomb/Sarah Smith) b 15 Sep 1841 -
    E Kingston   (P/C)
    Simeon Peaslee, 13 Jun 1962 at Kingston (John J Clark/Elizabeth Titcomb)
    b 26 Dec 1866 (V/C)
    Simeon O, 25 Jan 1962 (71) at Manchester (RobertClark/Emma M Dodge)
    Theodore John, 06 Jan 1938 at Exeter (17) (Henry Howard Clark/Emily Healy) (P/C)
    Walter S, 25 Nov 1923 at Kingston (h/o Abbie Sanborn) (Amos Clark/Jerusha Judkins)
    b 01 Apr 1854 (P/C)
    Warren, 25 Mar 1940 (78) (Calvin Clark/Martha Leavey)
    Wilbur J, 02 Jan 1985 (Simeon P Clark/Mary E Fellows)
CLEARY: Curtis A, 02 Oct 1994 at Exeter (Joseph E Cleary/Rose Lucier)
CLEMENT: Catherine F,10 Aug 1985 at Exeter (Walter Morse/Catherine Fitzgerald)
CLEMENTS: Ferris Renwick, 01 Jun 1973 at Exeter (Robert Clements/Jennie Little)
    b 07 Feb 1904   (P/G)
    Geneva, 08 Mar 1940 at Exeter (John D Goodwin/ Myrtle B Taylor)b 21 Dec 1903
    Laura A, 18 Aug 1970 at Falmouth, Ma, b 1885   (P/G)
    Robert Renwick, 26 Jul 1947 at Brentwood (Robert G Clements/Emma Appleby)
    b 28 Jul 1877 (P/G)

Sarah Jean, 17 Dec 1926 at Kingston (Robert G Little/Janet Young) b 16 Aug 1873(P/G)
CLOUGH: George W, 20 Feb 1927 at Kingston (79) (Obed Clough)
    Ida A, 01 May 1932 (74) b - Coventry, RI (Eason Matteson/Marry A Potter)
    Mary, 28 Aug 1778 at Kingston (Cornelos Clough/Mary Levit)
CLOYD: John A, 19 Jul 1988 at Kingston (Frank Cloyd/Natalie .....)
COIN: Harry B, 28 May 1973 at Lawrence, Ma, b 1915 (P/G)
COLBURN: Michael, -- June 1927 (64) at Haverhill, Ma.
COLBY: Carrie M, 19 Mar 1950 at Kingston (Obediah Collins/Lucretia Tucker) b 28 Sep 1874
COLCOARD: Mary, 01 Nov 1735 at Kingston (Ebenezener Colcoard/Haner Fellows)
    b 01 Aug 1735
COLCORD: Baby Boy, 01 Jul 1960 at Manchester (Frank Cole/Vivian F Collins) b 01 Jul 1960
    Baby Boy, 29 Nov 1961 at Exeter (Frank Cole/Vivian F Collins)b 29 Nov 1961
    Baby Girl, 07 Mar 1964 at Exeter (Frank Cole/Vivian F Collins)b 07 Mar 1964
COLE: Arthur C, 06 Apr 1977 at Kingston (66) (Arthur C Cole)
    Baby Boy, 01 Jul 1960 at Exeter (Frank W Cole/Vivian F Collins)
    Baby Boy, 29 Nov 1961 at Exeter (5 hrs) (Frank W Cole/Vivian Collins)
    Baby Girl, 07 Mar 1964 at Exeter (2 hrs) (Frank W Cole/Vivian Collins)
    Marion L, 21 Apr 1979 at Exeter (Charles N Jasper/Ethel M Hartford)
COLEMAN: Ralph K, 08 Sep 1948 at Exeter (46)
COLINS: Clarence E, 31 Jan 1970 at Franklin (73) (Elmer Collins)
COLLINS: ...., 13 Jan 1925 at Kingston (Clarence Collins/Lois Raycroft)b 13 Jan 1925 (P/G)
    Alice, 29 Jul 1978 at Exeter (85) (George E Barnard/Carrie E Johnson)
    Allen G, 09 Jul 1963 at Portsmouth (L Waldo Collins/Elvira Grogan)b 10 Mar 1889
    Anna N, 18 Mar 1909 at Kingston(....Stoddard/....Smith)b 1840
    Caroline W, 12 Dec 1930 at Haverhill,Ma, b 1849 (M/S)
    Carrie Belle, 15 May 1967 at Hampton (Daniel P Seaver/Dolly George) b 02 Nov 1874
    Charles E, 23 Apr 1968 at Haverhill, Ma, b 1928 (P/G)
    Charles P, 16 Mar 1971 at Exeter (84) (Oren Collins/Flora Webster)
    Charlotte C, 03 Sep 1931 at Kingston (Charles C Reinhold/Marie Davis) b 10 Nov 1876
    Clarence Edward, 31 Jan 1970 at Franklin (Elmer Collins)b 17 Jan 1897 (P/G)
    Daisy May, 12 Feb 1952 at Kingston (44) (Charles Jasper/Ethel Hartford), b - Kingston
    Elizabeth A, 04 Oct 1984 at Exeter (Wilbur B Sweet/Lillian E Smith)
    Ella F, 10 Jan 1925 at Kingston (Eben Averill/Julia Knox) b 11 Jul 1848 (P/C)
    Elmer Andrew, 10 Mar 1938 at Kingston (Andrew J Collins/Anna M Smith)
    b 13 Sep 1870 at Kingston (M/S)
    Infant, 13 Jan 1925 at Kingston (Birth) (Clarence Collins/Lois Raycroft) b-Kingston
    James C, 27 Jun 1988 at Exeter (Arthur Collins/Florence Tickard)
    Joel S, 11 Apr 1920 at Kingston (Samuel S Collins/Julia Judkins) b 22 Feb 1844
    Leila, 04 Dec 1985 at Kingston (Leslie James/Sadie Dudley)
    Leon, 10 Jan 1971 at Exeter (Elmer Collins/Susie Anna Nason)b 28 Jan 1902 (P/G)
    Lois Abbie, 21 Oct 1972 at Allenstown, b 1901 (P/G)
    L Waldo, 08 Dec 1921 at Haverhill, Ma, b 17 Dec 1852 (P/C)
    Mary A, 02 Aug 1900 at Kingston (Michael J Collins/Margaret M ..)b 1835
    Michael Robert, 06 Jan 1956 at Exeter (Charles Collins/Doris Thompson)b 30 May
        1955, b - Exeter

Norris Dow, 21 Sep 1931 at Brentwood (Sheperd Collins/Julia Judkins)b 16 Apr 1851
Obediah, 20 Apr 1915 at Exeter, b 1848 (P/G)
Olive F, 25 Feb 1930 at Plaistow, b 1862 (P/C)
Oral W, 18 Dec 1959 at Franklin (Elmer A Collins/Susie Nason)b 28 Aug 1899, b King.
Perley S, 03 Jul 1966 at Concord (Joel S Collins/Ella F Averill)b - 07 Mar 1880   (V/C)
Ralph Lincoln, 16 Mar 1953 at Danville (Lorenzo Collins/Mary Griffin) b 28 Aug
1875 at Danville   (P/G)
Robert E, 30 Mar 1976 at Boston, Ma, b 18 Mar 1954   (P/G)
Stanley Bruce, 09 Jun 1951 at Kingston (Oral Collin/Verna Middleton)b 26 May 1951
Susie A, 02 Jul 1932 at West Kingston (Walter West/Etta Nason) b 24 Jul 1878
Waldo, 17 Dec 1921 (69) at Haverhill, Ma.
William Norris, 01 Jan 1937 at Revere, Ma, b 1881 (G/C)
COLSON: Frederick, 12 Oct 1973 at Amesbury, Ma, b 1920 (G/C)
COMEAU: Albert H, 28 Mar 1960 at Kingston (55) (Joseph Comeau/Clara Patanaude), b -
Haverhill,Ma.
Denis J, 22 May 1966 at Haverhill, Ma (59) (William Comeau/Edith Babin)
Joseph Harold, 20 Jul 1982 at Haverhill,Ma (Benjamin Comeau/Marguerite White)
Richard A, 04 Mar 1953 (16) at Haverhill, Ma (Ivan Comeau/Loretta StOnge)
CONARY: Melva E, 19 Jun 1994 (Howard F Brown/Florence Caterer)
Walter J ,Jr, 05 Jun 1991 at Exeter (Walter J Conary/ Julia Sheldon)
CONANT: Charles B, 13 Aug 1927 at So. Paris,Me (Hiram Conant/Clara Adkins)
b 09 Sep 1883   (P/C)
Gardner Hollis, 09 Aug 1947 at Kingston (Charles B Conant/Marion S Clark)
b 17 Dec 1914 (G/C)
CONNOR: Robert, 27 May 1971 at Manchester (82) (James Connor/Sarah Hermisten)
COOMBS: Richard W, 08 Apr 1992 at Exeter (Howard R Coombs/ Sylvia Bragg)
COOPER: Clarence E, 23 Dec 1938, b 1874 (G/C)
Esther, 11 Feb 1970 at Hampton (72) (Joseph T Sayward/Alice M Otis)
Ida B, 09 May 1939 at Amesbury, Ma, b 1864   (K/C)
James, 05 Dec 1957 (William Cooper/Mary A Gilman)b 16 Dec 1868 - E Kingston (G/C)
Lucy Emma, 06 Mar 1950 at Kingston (Newell Hill/Emma Tucker)b 01 Jan 1867
Susan Jeannette, 04 May 1938 at Kingston (William Fellows), b 18 Apr 1857,
b - Newton (G/C)
CORKUM: Fred N, 22 Aug 1938 at Worcester, Ma, b 1880 (G/C)
Mitchem, -- Dec 1934 at Worcester, Ma. (G/C)
CORMIER: Jean G, 06 Jan 1979 at Newton (Aquilla Cormier/ Regina Maillett)
CORNISH: Clare T, 18 Oct 1990 at Exeter (William Begley/ Marie Quelle)
Glen Burdett, 14 May 1967 at Exeter (William D Cornish/Lydia Snow) b 14 Jun 1903
William D, 24 Nov 1949 at Kingston (68) (James T Cornish/Flora Hager)
CORSON: Charles P (72) , 09 Nov 1972 at Kingston (George L Corson/Nellie B Batchelder)
Della M, 25 Apr 1991 at Exeter (Charles H Young/ Myrtie Sleeper)
CORTON: Dorothy M, 02 Nov 1992 at Kingston (Alden D Pickens/ Myrtle M Jenkins)
COTTRELL: Lila J, 03 Jan 1968 at Kingston (97) (Charles Dearborn/Rhoda A Marden)
COVEY: Merle R, 07 Oct 1914 at Haverhill, Ma (George Covey/Blanche Robinson) 4 mos

COWELL: Emma (50) 09 Dec 1910 (Samuel Marshall/ Adeline Hurd) b - Kingston
　　　Ola Mae, 15 Nov 1977 at Exeter (George Geilear/Ella Mae Wright) b 21 Jun 1893
　　　Sidney Arthur, 17 Jul 1965 at Exeter (John H Cowell/Mary Tansley) b 23 Apr 1893
CRAFTS: Louis E, 03 Apr 1963 at Exeter (50) (Enclas W Crafts/Sadie Marsh)
CRANE: Elizabeth S, 21 Feb 1910 (85) Danville/Brentwood (Caleb Smith/ Sarah Smith)
　　　Gilman, 09 Jun 1901 at Kingston (Jess Crane/Susan Clark) b 1817
　　　Hannah, 28 Jan 1902 at Seabrook (John Webster/Hannah Gale) b 1825
　　　Sabrina, 29 Aug 1902 at Kingston (Gilman Crane/Clara A Dresser) b 1844
CRESCENTINI: Guerino, 24 Jan 1981 at Kingston (Thomas Nazerino/Zelinda Uguccioni)
CRISPO: Mary T, 03 Aug 1953 (6) b- Wilmington,Ma (George Crispo/Florence Lariviere)
CROCKER: Herbert L, 18 Nov 1953 at Haverhill,Ma (66) b-Greenwood,Me (James W
　　　Crocker/ Ida Young)
CROFT: Warland, 02 Apr 1974 at Lynn, Ma (78) (Thomas Croft/Ada Eisner)
CRONK: Arthur G, 23 Sep 1965 at Exeter (Grayson Cronk/Helen Parker) b 05 Feb 1897 (G/C)
　　　Mabel L, 08 Feb 1973 at Brentwood (Thomas H Williams/Louisa Follet)b 20 Apr 1896
CROSBY: Jonathan D, 03 Apr 1980 at Kingston (John Crosby/Jane E Adams)
CROSS: Arthur R, 19 Aug 1991 at Manchester (Robert J Cross/ Mary McGonigle)
　　　Cecil L, 16 Sep 1983 at Kingston (Arthur P Cross/Sarah Howe)
　　　Ruth M, 16 Jul 1991 at Exeter (Horace G Winslow/ Eldora Nason)
　　　Walter E, 31 May 1975 at Hanover (50) (Guy Cross/ Edna Nicholson)
CROWELL: Annie E, 13 Nov 1972 at Lynn, Ma, b 1891 (P/G)
CRUMMETT: Carie E , 20 Mar 1916 at Kingston (w/o William P Crummett)(Porter George/
　　　Florence Kelley) b 28 Mar 1897 - Kingston   (P/G)
　　　Charles W, 09 Jul 1969 at Lawrence, Ma b 1914   (P/C)
　　　James, 21 Apr 1916 at Kingston (William P Crummett/Carrie E George)
　　　b 02 Mar 1916 - Kingston
　　　William Lerle, 14 Feb 1959 at Brentwood (Perley Crummett/Ramsey Damsell)
　　　b 19 Sep 1890 - Epping (P/G)
CRYMBLE: Marion H, 14 Jul 1969 at Kingston (70) (William H Sanborn/Mary J Limrock)
CUNNINGHAM: Catherine E , 19 Sep 1981 at Kingston (William Kirwain/Mary McCarthy)
CURRIE: Clara M, 28 Sep 1949 at Kingston (John F Devery/Martha White) b 03 Jul 1884 (G/C)
　　　Thomas F, 17 May 1954 at Kingston (Michael Currie/Ellen Mahaney)b - Dorchester,
　　　Ma (G/C)
CURRIER: Eva Mae, 05 May 1963 at Exeter (78) (Fred Bemis/Emiline Bryant)
　　　John C, 01 Nov 1901 at Kingston (M Currier/Mary Reuillard) 5 months
　　　Martha M, 04 Sep 1918 at Kingston (Samuel W Shepard/Jennie Brown)b 1839
　　　Mary W, 07 Jun 1913 at Danville (Neld Heath/Eliza Winslow)b19 Feb 1830
CUTHBERT: Sandra L, 24 Jan 1975 at Boston,Ma, b 1965   (G/C)
CUTTER: ...., 03 Aug 1965 at Manchester (Gerard M Cutter/Dorothy I Lord)b 03 Aug 1965
　　　Baby Boy, 27 Jan 1960 at Exeter (Gerard M Cutter/Dorothy I Lord)
　　　Baby Boy, 28 May 1957 at Exeter, b 28 May 1957 (G/C)
DADMUN: Nellie, 09 Oct 1964 at Brentwood (89) (Isaac Richardson/Abbie Kelly)
DAIGLE: George J, 04 Jan 1987 at Kingston (Arthur Daigle/Cecile Marsolais)
DALE: Edward O, 29 Jan 1958 at Exeter (71) (Jessie Dale/Emily Pomeroy) - London,England

DALEY: Catherine, 01 Feb 1936 at Exeter, b 1871 (P/C)
Grace, 29 Sep 1970 at Boston, Ma, b 12 Sep 1901 (P/C)
James Edward, 01 Apr 1939 at Exeter (Henry J Daley) b 14 Apr 1866 (K/C)
DAMPHOUSSE: Ward V, 10 Mar 1990 at Exeter (Gerald Damphousse/ Pauline Fiset)
DANSEREAU: Felix X, 22 Jun 1971 at Exeter (86)
Rosea A (82), 22 Oct 1972 at Brentwood (Onezine Brazeau/Delvina Ferron)
DARES: Harry S, 27 Jun 1994 at Kingston (Harry W Dares/Clara J ....)
Emma S, 13 Oct 1915 at Kingston (Moses Tucker/Hannah Martin) b 10 Jun 1846 - King.
DARLING: Chester R, 01 Aug 1983 at Exeter (Laurio D Darling/Hattie ....)
DAVIDSON: Andrew S, 15 Sep 1982 at Exeter (John S Davidson/Catherine McAuley)
DAVIS: Andrew J, 09 Nov 1925 at Kingston (Amos Davis) b 15 Dec 1832 (P/G)
Charles A, 06 Apr 1902 at Kingston (Alfred Davis/Lois .....)
Edward R, 14 Nov 1925 at Saugus, Ma (Richard Davis/Harriet Staples) b 1870 (G/C)
Isella, 26 Nov 1954, b 1872
John E, 16 Nov 1940 at Brentwood (Jonathan Davis/Adeline Seva) b 26 Feb 1857
Julia F, 09 Apr 1914 at Kingston (Jessie Shaw/Mary J Currier)b 1834 E/K
Lavada J, 23 Feb 1932 at Kingston (Amos K Davis/Mary Collins)b 05 Feb 1869
Lewis W, 19 Mar 1930 at South Kingston (Amos K Davis/Mary K Collins)
b 15 Jun 1867(P/G)
Lizzie May, 19 Feb 1909 at Kingston (Charles E Goodwin/Lizzie Beaumont) b 1891-
Amesbury, Ma
Luther A, 29 Oct 1950 at Kingston (Frank Davis/Elbra Osgood) b 10 Jun 1862
Mary J, 02 Apr 1947 (76) at Haverhill, Ma.
Nancy, 23 Aug 1901at Kingston, b 1818
Peter F, 02 Jun 1909 at Kingston (Daniel Davis/Polly Frowhawk) b 1836 (K/C)
Richard H, 16 Jan 1921 at Saugus,Ma - b 1842 (P/C)
Roxcena Sarah, 25 Oct 1939 at Kingston (Nathan Nason/ Sarah K Page)b 29 Aug 1862
Rufus, 22 Jan 1925 at Brentwood, b 1835 (P/C)
Sarah M, 11 Jul 1900 at Kingston (Daniel Mann/Sarah .....) b 1839
Therese Rose, 11 Jan 1947 (5) at Kingston (Albert W Davis/Nellie Platukys)
DAWSON: Ada P, 01 Aug 1955 (72) b - New Brunswick (Frederick Morgan/Susan Staples)
DAY: Clarence Sumner, 16 Dec 1957 at Exeter (Charles S Day/Mary I Lyford) b 16 Nov 1884,
Berwick,Me.
Donald E, 15 Jul 1992 at Exeter (Leon Day/ Florence Chick)
Elsie Mosette, 13 Aug 1978 at Exeter (72) (Leon E Day/Florence V Chick)
Frank B, 04 Jan 1940 at Amesbury, Ma, b 1880 (P/G)
Mary Isabelle, 08 Apr 1951 at Exeter (Augustus D Lyford/Julia A Davis)b 25 Dec 1862
Mary L, 16 Dec 1954 at Newburyport, Ma, b 1864
DEARDON: Arthur, 07 Dec 1935 at Exeter, b 1866 (G/C)
Ida,14 Aug 1947 at Brentwood (Richard Hepworth/Flora McCarthy)b 02 Aug 1869
DEFAZIO: Anthony J, 29 Jul 1978 at Kingston (73) (Giuseppe Defazio/Antoinette Defazio)
DeMANCHE: Felix W, 20 Nov 1992 at Kingston (Felix W DeManche/ Mary A Allen)
DeROCHEMONT: Daniel K, 02 Apr 1986 at Pinellas Park, Fl.
Elizabeth A, 02 Nov 1922 at Kingston (John Gale/ Mary R Gale) b - 05 Dec 1832

Ernest Howard, 28 Feb 1962 at Kingston (Daniel P DeRochemont/Elizabeth A Gale)
b 11 Jul 1874 (G/C)

Ethel, 02 Jan 1978 at Brentwood (Charles A King/Celia I Johnson) b 15 Mar 1888 (G/C)

Gladys Mae, 19 Jun 1978 at Pinellas Park, Fl. (58)

DERRAH: Alice D, 01 Jan 1955 at Brentwood, b 04 Aug 1868 in England (G/C)

Edward H, 23 Jan 1952 at Concord (84) (Alexandra Derrah/Sarah Hadley)- b Nova Scotia

Hattie J, 12 Oct 1940 (68) (Daniel A Allen/---- Proctor)

DESIMONE: Natalie E, 30 Dec 1992 at Nashua (Walter L Moore/Ethel Young)

DICKEY: James E, 01 Oct 1958 at Exeter (76) (William J Dickey/Martha J Petts), b - Peterborough

DINGLEY: Marion Sanborn, 07 Mar 1963 at Epping (Walter S Clark/Abbie Sanborn)b 1884

DOHERTY: Margaret A, 25 Sep 1955 at Kingston (Patrick Doyle/Johanna Sullivan) b 1874 - Boston, Ma

DOLLIVER: Annie M, 05 Oct 1955 at Kingston, b 1877 - England

Gerard R, Sr, 01 Feb 1993 (Charles P Dolliver/Anna Maloney)

Gerard R, Jr, 01 Sep 1990 at Exeter (Gerard R Dolliver, Sr/ Maude E Powers)

Maude E, 24 Oct 1991 at Exeter (George Powers/ Mary Dodge)

DOLLOF: Charles F, 28 Apr 1978 at Exeter (Louis W Dolloff/Rose A MacNichols)

DOMINICK: Alphonse, 13 Feb 1939 at Kingston, b 17 Mar 1865 (K/C)

Mary Julia, 18 Jun 1920 at Kingston (Elbridge Collins/Josephine Robinson) b 28 Feb 1862 (P/C)

DONAHUE: Charles Henry, 16 Apr 1981 at Exeter (Daniel Donahue/Mary McGrath)

Pearl Arlene, 11 Jul 1944 at Kingston (54) (Christopher Grant/Ida Wentworth)

Timothy E, 01 Apr 1964 at Kingston (76) (John Donahue/Mary Sullivan)

Helen A, 13 Jul 1944 at Brentwood (86) (Cyrus Pinkham/Sarah Rines)

Samuel H, 05 Feb 1918 at Kingston (James Donovan/Lucretia Bancroft) b 1835 - Thompson, Ct

DORMAN: Walter L, 28 Sep 1951 (55) at Exeter (Charles Dorman/Mina S Moore) b - St.Johnsbury,Vt.

DOW: Alfred Nason, Jr, 25 Dec 1967, (Alfred Nason,Sr) b 25 Dec 1967 (P/G)

DOWE: John H, 05 May 1915 at Kingston (William Dowe)b 1827 - Devonshire, England

DOWNES: John, 12 Sep 1944 at Kingston (74) (William Downes/Margaret Burchell)

DOWNEY: Andrew W, 17 Nov 1986 at Kingston (Walter L Downey/Anne V Jurczak)

DOWNING: Ellen R, 25 Oct 1916 at Kingston (w/o John N Downing)(Simon P Clark/ Johannah Eastman) b-27 Jan 1843 - Kingston (P/C)

Leverett C, 25 Aug 1929 at Kingston (h/o Annie Cilley) (John N Downing/Ellen R Clark) b 25 May 1870   (K/C)

Rose, 07 May 1989 at Exeter (Angelo Piantedosi/Filomena Perella)

Walter L, 18 Feb 1919 in Bradford (Leverett Downing/Annie Cilley)b 18 Feb 1919

DRAPER: Mary C, 31 May 1923 (88) (Nathaniel Kingsbury/.....)

DREW: Charles John, 29 Jan 1993 (Ernest Drew/Ruth Wilkins)

DRISCOLE: Marion L (Streib), 14 Jun 1957 at Boston, Ma (P/G)

DRISCOLL: Edward, 08 Sep 1973 at Haverhill, Ma, b 1896 (P/G)

DUBE: Leopold F, 09 Mar 1978 at Kingston (67) (Francois Dube/Zerila Rouleau)
DUBOIS: Jean Paul, 15 Apr 1977 at Exeter (41) (Leopold Dubois/Leopoldine Lusignan)
DUCEY: Thomas, 13 Jun 1967, b 1898   (K/C)
DUFFY: Catherine (55) 27 Aug 1910 (Daniel Cronin/ Mary Conners) b - Kingston
DUFOUR: Robert A, 15 Apr 1992 at Epping (Wilfred E Dufour/ Ida Harvey)
DUNN: Michael, 17 Apr 1902 at Kingston (Daniel Dunn)b 1812
     William J (50) 24 Sep 1910   (Michael Dunn/ Margaret Shea) b - Kingston
DURGIN: Irma Dorothy, 14 Aug 1975 at Exeter (Maurice F Clapp/Ethel Brackett)b 05 Feb
     1919 (G/C)
     Lydia F, 15 Dec 1913 at Kingston (Elbridge Sears/Lydia H Vaughn)b 1854
     Stephen, 15 Dec 1902 at Kingston (Zebular Durgin/..... Tandy) b 1821
DURKEE: Ralph, 05 Mar 1973 at Exeter (66) (Arthur Durkee/Cassie Stoddard)
DUSTON: Alyce A,01 Jul 1989 at Kingston (Everett Delorey/Adeline Finch)
     Charles R, 30 Sep 1969 at Kingston (79) (Charles R.H.Duston/Carrie E Somerby)
     David Douglas, 08 Sep 1961 at Kingston (David F Dutton/Natalie Taylor) b 04 Jul 1957
     David F, 17 May 1981 at Kingston (Ralph F Dutton/Harriett Parker)
DUTTON: David D, 08 Sep 1961 at Kingston (3) (DavidFDutton/Natalie Taylor), b- Kingston
DYER: Mary E, 25 Aug 1937 (82) (Alexander Fernald/Reumah Debeck)
     Orville T, 18 Nov 1928 at Kingston (80) (William Dyer/Sallie Silver) b-Sanbornton
DYSON: John, 18 May 1936 at Kingston, b 02 Oct 1859 (G/C)
EARLEY: Owen A, 17 Jan 1935 (77) at Lynn, Ma
EASTMAN: Charles B, 17 Sep 1921 at Haverhill, Ma, b 1845   (P/C)
     Charles B, 24 Aug 1918 at Kingston (A. Eastman/Maria Winch) b 1841 - Littleton
     Ira A, 04 Nov 1925 at Kingston (74) (Azra Eastman/Maria Winch) - Littleton
     Mary, 20 Apr 1940 at Concord (Henry Sturgies/....) (V/C)
     Sarah A, 18 Sep 1910 (50) at Jamaica Plains, Ma. (John N Humphrey/ Kate Goodell)
     Sarah, 18 Sep 1910 (95) Malden,Ma. (Josiah Greely/ Sally Currier)
EATON: John C (84) 17 Mar 1910 b - East Kingston
     Roland A, 18 Jan 1973 at Dover, b 1937   (G/C)
EDMANDS: Rowena S, 10 Oct 1992 at Exeter (Joseph Stead/ Emily Procter)
EDMONDS: Corinne A, 01 Aug 1990 at Brentwood (William Cormiar/ Rosanna Milot)
     Howard, 20 Jul 1985 at Brentwood (Fred Edmonds/Ella Rollins)
EDNEY: George P, 16 Dec 1982 at Kingston (George W Edney/Mary Abbie Collins)
     George W, 04 Jun 1947 (89) at Haverhill, Ma.
     Iva M, 02 Nov 1940 at Haverhill, Ma, b 1886 (G/C)
     Mary A, 24 Apr 1930 at Haverhill, Ma, b 1862
     William W, 26 Aug 1909 at Kingston (John W Edney) b 1823 in Portsmouth
EGAN: Marion Elizabeth, 28 Nov 1982 at Haverhill,Ma (Frank H Ochee/Amilda Robillard)
ELKINS: Annie R, 08 Mar 1924 at Kingston (James M Call/Martha B Houston)b 12 Sep 1851
     Bradford,Me (G/C)
     Charles, 07 Feb 1918 at Brentwood (Henry Elkins) b 07 Feb 1836 (P/C)
     Charles H, 19 Jan 1951 (73) at Haverhill,Ma.
     Frank Everett, 16 Jun 1949 at Epping (George E Elkins/Annie Call)b 11 May 1879
     George E, 12 Mar 1939 at Brentwood (Thomas Elkins/Elizabeth Prescott)b 1851(G/C)

Luella L, 24 Apr 1913 at Kingston (Lewis F Prescott/Elizabeth Webster) b 11 Sep 1827
    Thomas, 07 May 1900 at Kingston (Henry Elkins/Susanna Clough) b 1828
ELLIOT: William, 09 Jun 1945 at Exeter, b 27 Jun 1892 (K/C)
ELLIOTT: William, 09 Jun 1945 at Exeter, b 12 Dec 1862 (K/C)
ELLIS: Dana L, 16 Feb 1987 at Kingston (Morgan L Ellis/Blanche A Spencer)
    Edward A, 21 Apr 1988 at Exeter (Roys A Ellis/Ruth Ashley)
    Virginia (Hatchell), 28 Oct 1984 at Exeter
    Willard G, 17 Nov 1970 at Exeter (83) (Nathan Ellis/Jessie Giddings)
ELMER: Willmont Samuel, 19 Aug 1950 at Exeter (J P Elmer) b 29 Mar 1888 (G/C)
ELWOOD: Arthur, 14 Feb 1965 at Concord (Allison Elwood/Georgie Hall)b 10 Aug 1874
    Ina, 17 Jan 1978 at Brentwood (Almond Smith/Altie Nelson) (G/C)
EMERSON: Harriet N, 26 Mar 1934 (79) (Robert Martin/Lucy Clark)b - Rowley, Ma.
EMERY: George H, 03 Mar 1925 (70) (Monroe Emery/Temperance Goodrich),b - Boston,Ma.
ERICKSON: Carl V, 10 Jul 1945 at So Kingston (Herman Erickson/Olene Anderson)
    b .. May 1866
ERKEL: Deana Rae, 03 Mar 1985 at Hampston (Dennis E Erkel/Jananlee R Woodhurst)
ERNE: Grace L, 11 Nov 1977 at Portsmouth (Roy P Holmes) b 23 Oct 1892 (M/S)
    Halton M, 21 Sep 1979 at Brentwood (Peter M Erne/Lulu Hogal)
ESTABROOK: Elmer W, 04 May 1964 at Exeter (70) (Edward T Estabrook/Genie Edney)
EVANS Baby Girl, 13 Jul 1956, b 13 Jul 1956   P/G)
    Chester C, 16 Sep 1964 at Kingston (69) (Samuel Evans/Hatie Tyler)
    Clarice H, 20 Jul 1979 at Exeter (Walter Prescott/Helen Kidder)
    John Chellis, 31 Jul 1978 at Exeter (72) (Charles S Evans/Lois Mortimer)
    Mary N, 03 Feb 1934 at Exeter, b 1864   (M/S)
EVELETH: Louise E, 11 Apr 1992 at Brentwood (Capon Leonard/ Lillian ....)
FAILEY: Nellie Frances, 10 Apr 1936 at Lynn, Ma, b 1861 (P/G)
FALLETT: Marion A, 08 Sep 1963 at Haverhill, Ma, b 1880   (G/C)
FARLEY: Nellie Frances, 10 Apr at (75)at Lynn, Ma
    Owen Augustus, 18 Jan 1935 at Lynn, Ma, b 1858   (P/G)
FARMER: Rose Louise, 07 Mar 1989 at Brentwood (Frederick Pettis/Florence Rock)
FAULKNER: William P, 01 Mar 1914
FAXON: Elizabeth G, 12 Dec 1991 at Brentwood (Roy E Gove/ Inez Covey)
FEDERHEN: Herbert M, 26 Apr 1975 at Exeter (Herbert M Federhen/Laura Merrill Foster)
    b 21 Jul 1898 (G/C)
FELLOWS: Lucy A, 06 Nov 1921 at Kingston (William Hoyt/Harriet Hooke)b 1837
FERNEKEES: James B, 17 Jun 1984 at Exeter (Isadore B Fernekees/Melissa Cross)
FERRUOLO: Amelia, 01 Dec 1991 at Kingston (Andrew Lippo/ Giovaninna Valenti)
    John J, 30 Nov 1974 at Kingston (72) (Enrico Ferruolo/Josephine DeFonzo)
FERULLO: Angelo M, 08 Jan 1985 at Kingston (Michael A Ferullo/Adelina Bagnulo)
    Louis Nicholas, 01 Jan 1942 (39) b - Boston,Ma (Michael A Ferullo/Adelaide ....)
    Robert Michael, 05 Nov 1970 at Exeter (William Ferullo/Annie Ristaino)
    b 25 Aug 1922   (P/G)
FIFIELD: Benjamin, 21 Jun 1900 at Kingston (Simon P Fifield/Mary E Brown) b 1855
    Donald E, 24 Feb 1903 at Kingston (Benjamin Fifield/L Etta Martin) b 1899

Etta M, 15 Aug 1924 at Beverly, Ma (John Mardin/Mary Clark)b 15 Sep 1855
FINKLESTEIN: Ethel, 13 Dec 1974 at Haverhill, Ma, b 1896   (P/G)
FISHER: Laura A, 30 Dec 1947 (63) at Kingston (Elmer Towne/Isabel Towne) b -
   Newburyport,Ma
FITZGERALD: Hannah E, 17 Aug 1951 at Kingston (95) (Edward Fitzgerald/Nora Collins)
   b - Ireland
FLANDERS: Elizabeth A, 03 Nov 1931 at Haverhill, Ma, b 1884 (P/C)
   Herschel A, 31 Jul 1934 at Kingston (George F Flanders/Lucy E Felch)b 08 Oct 1887,
   Kingston   (P/C)
   Lucy E, 07 Apr 1951 at Manchester (George E Flanders/Mary Frances Knowles) b 09 Jul
   1863   (K/C)
   Perley H, 29 Apr 1958 at St.Petersburg,Fl (74)
   Philip J, 22 Nov 1941 (79) (Levi Flanders/Hannah Campbell) b - Wakefield,Ma
   Weldon, 08 Mar 1913 at Kingston (Lee E Flanders/Lucy E Felch)b 1884 (P/C)
FLETCHER: Adelbert W, 16 Sep 1960 at Kingston (86) (George F Fletcher/Annie Bisbee), b -
   Townsend,Ma.
   Florence H, 12 Dec 1956 at Lawrence,Ma (64) (Frank Titus/Ada A Porter)
   Harry T.D., 02 Jan 1961 at Topsfield,Ma. (71) (True D Fletcher/Lizzie Dustin)
FLOBERG: Carl L, 06 Jun 1955 at Kingston (Carl Floberg) b 1883 - Sweden
FLYNN: Blanche Esther, 06 Jun 1969 at Exeter (Edgar E Ormes/Mary Robinson)b 05 Mar
   1897 (G/C)
   John T, 05 Oct 1978 at Manchester (58) (Harry J Flynn/Frances McCarthy)
FOGARTY: Wayne Patrick, 02 Dec 1984 at Mayfield/Bingham, Me (Paul L Fogarty,Sr/
   Charlotte M Bragg)
FOHTER: Alfarata E, 12 Aug 1929 (79) (Gorham R Hardy/Mary Hardy), b - Rowley,Ma.
FOLLENSBEE: Martha R, 07 May 1956 at Exeter (Somerby Follansbee/Geraldine Cole), b -
   Exeter
FOLLET: Marion A, 08 Sep 1963 at Waterville,Me. (67)
FORD: ....., 22 Feb 1922 at Kingston (Wendell Ford/Mary Gilles) b 22 Feb 1922
   Mary J, 07 Nov 1925 at Kingston (66) (A.C. Chick/... Hanscom)b - Winthrop, Ma
FORSYTHE: Carol J, 09 Oct 1991 at Exeter (Jose Claudio/ Delores Echeveria)
FORTIER: Thomas Edward, 28 Sep 1930 (25) (Charles Fortier/Madeline Fortier),b-Brentwood
   Walter W, 28 May 1972 in Norway (Albert Fortier/Gladys Lord)b 18 Oct 1945
FOSTER: Frank Whittaker, 04 Apr 1972 at Exeter (Edward Foster/Alfaretta Hardy)
   b 23 Jul 1891 (G/C)
   Madeline F, 10 Mar 1921 (2) (Frank Foster/Winefred Towle)
   Winifred, 26 Aug 1976 at Brentwood (Warren Towle/Clara Emery)b 13 Aug 1893(G/C)
FOWLER: Abner J, 28 May 1990 at Exeter (Abner G Fowler/ Bernice Guerl)
   John Kenneth, 19 Nov 1976 at Exeter (75) (John W Fowler/Mary F Roach)
   Josephine, 19 Aug 1976 at Bartow, Fl., b 1883   (P/G)
   Priscilla P, 17 Dec 1986 at Kingston (Charles Austin/Alice M Plumer)
FRAIM: Everett G, 05 Aug 1980 at Exeter (John Fraim/Viola Bernard)
FRAZER: George W, 10 Aug 1959 at Concord (83) (Olive Green), b- New Brunswick
   Isabelle A, 08 Sep 1965 at Brentwood (82) (William Grieve/Janet Anderson)

Janet H, 09 Apr 1988 at Exeter (Hersey F Fraser/Isabelle Grieve)
FRENCH: Alcina F, 06 Jun 1923 at Walpole, Ma (Simeon Clark/Johnanna Eastman)b 1839
Annie, 26 Dec 1921 at Kingston (Moses P French/Mary E Smith) b 1838 (P/C)
Frank W, 16 Feb 1917 at Kingston (John B French/Hannah B Wadleigh) (P/C)
Hattie, 22 Nov 1935 at Brentwood (Joseph Collins/Ella Averill)b 1871
Herbert C, 15 Jul 1958 at Haverhill, Ma (69) (John French/Addie M Davis), b 1889 -
Kingston (P/G)
Horace John, 07 Dec 1947 at East Kingston (John French/Hannah Wadleigh)
b 21 Jul 1859 (P/C)
Jonathan, 29 May 1744 at Kingston (Jonathan French/Johaner Elkins)b 15 Apr 1744
Lillian, 10 May 1902 at Kingston (Frank French/Katie M Collins) b 1899
Mary Addie, 14 Jun 1937 at Newton, b 1860(P/G)
Maud E, 10 Aug 1927 at Haverhill, Ma, b 1883 (P/G)
Moses J, 09 Nov 1921 at Kingston (90) (Moses P French/Mary E Smith) (P/C)
Rosanna M (Gelinas), 23 Oct 1973 at Lynn, Ma, b 1902 (P/G)
Walter L, 16 Feb 1970 at Saugus, Ma, b 1883 (P/G)
Warren S (5) 30 Jun 1910 (Frank W French/ Hattie M Collins) b - Kingston
FRIEND: William H, 02 Nov 1928 at Kingston (46) (Lemuel Friend/Mary C Rowe)
b- Gloucester
FROST: Carrie Bell, 31 Jul 1929 at Haverhill, Ma, b 1879   (P/C)
Joseph R, 13 Jul 1921 at Haverhill, Ma. (P/C)
William L, 04 Nov 1937 at Haverhill, Ma, b 1874 (K/C)
FRYE: Alice Bertha, 26 Oct 1952 at Melrose, Ma (76)
John, 08 Oct 1901 at Kingston (John Frye/Bessie Deborah) b 1829
FUGLESTAD: John A, 14 Jan 1975 at Brentwood (92)   (Tollef Guistav/Dorothea Soelberg)
FULLER: Carl, 17 Sep 1968 at Portsmouth (77) (Herbert Fuller/Carrie Marsh)
Chester L, 07 Mar 1951 at Exeter (69) (Frank Fuller/Annie Littlefield) b Boston,Ma
Stephen F, 22 Apr 1984 at New Castle (Howard M Fuller/Jane Sweet)
Howard M, 04 May 1978 at Exeter (George H Fuller/Louise Adam) b 23 Feb 1906
FURBER: John J A, 24 Aug 1923 at Kingston (John H Furber/Nancy C Wadleigh)
b 27 Dec 1850 at Portsmouth   (P/C)
Roxie Anna, 17 Sep 1927 at Kingston (Samuel S Collins/Julia F Judkins)b 14 Apr 1854
FURBUSH: Minnie, 31 Jan 1965 at Somersworth (George Carter/Etta Webster)b 04 Jul 1881
FURTEK: Edward P, 09 May 1990 at Kingston (Peter Furtek/ Katherine Kupiec)
FURZE: William A, 04 Oct 197 at Hanover (....Furze/Bessie Roe)
GAGNE: Arthur A, 04 Aug 1970 at Exeter (65) (Jean Gagne/Dianna Lessard)
GAGNON: Frank J, Jr, 27 Dec 1993 (Frank J Gagnon, Sr/Helen Hughes)
GALE: Augustus, 17 Apr 1928 at Brentwood, b 1854   (P/C)
Franklin, 25 Mar 1901 at Kingston (Israel Gale/Polly Greely) b 1818
GALLAGHER: Bruce M, 01 Sep 1974 Kingston (19) (Edward F Gallagher/Florence L
Wallace)
GALLERANI: Ugo J, 07 Aug 1983 at Lawrence,Ma (Albert Gallerani/Mary Gardella)
GANNON: Ellen A, 21 Feb 1930 at Claremont (Moses Rogers) b 02 Aug 1850 (K/C)
John H, 11 Jan 1923 at Haverhill, Ma, b 1857

GARAVANTA: John, 31 Jan 1937 (51) b - Fitchburg,Ma (John Garavanta/Louise Garavanta
GARLAND: Cora M, 27 Feb 1950 at Haverhill, Ma (Elbridge Brackett/Sarah Purrington) b 02
Nov 1871 (V/C)
Joseph S, 29 Aug 1909 at Kingston (Joseph Garland/Sarah Sanborn)b 1828
Lawrence U, 16 Jul 1913 at Newburyport, Ma, b 1829 (P/C)
Nathaniel W, 11 Sep 1953 at East Derry (Joseph Garland/Lorenza Mason) b 20 Mar
1860 (V/C)
GARRITY: Edward H, 09 Dec 1966 at Chelsea, Ma (59) (Duncan Garrity/Ethel Hubbard)
GARVEY: John P, 07 Jun 1986 at Haverhill, Ma (Patrick J Garvey/Marie Walsh)
GATES: Jessie , 04 Feb 1986 at Brentwood (Gardner Owens/Bernice Brown)
GAUDETTE: Donna D, 13 Mar 1962 at Exeter (1day) (Joseph A Gaudette/Peggy E Grover)
Florence L, 22 Apr 1993 (Irenne Bergeron/Marion Vaillandry)
Roy A, 13 Mar 1962 at Exeter (1day) (Joseph A Gaudette/Peggy E Grover)
GAVEL: Gilman B, 07 Oct 1994 at Kingston (Gilman B Gavel,Sr/Minnie Baggs)
GAYTON: Carrie A, 19 Mar 1971 at Kingston (84) (Elijah Seaman/Clementine VanBuskirk)
GAZNICK: Anthony, 31 Aug 1994 at Exeter (Anthony Gaznick/Micholina Poly)
Evelyn M, 10 Apr 1975 at Haverhill, Ma (61) (Fred D Richardson/Hattie M Reardon)
GELINEAU: Hervey A, 09 May 1990 at Brentwood (Arthur Gelineau /Elma ....)
GEORGE: ...., 01 Feb 1936 at Exeter, b 01 Feb 1935 (P/G)
Archie S, 15 Aug 1934 (81) b - Danville (Harrison George/Harriett Pratt)
Arthur L, 15 Jan 1923 at Kingston (Ora P George/Abbie Silloway)b 1865 (S/K)
Baby Girl, 30 Mar 1944 at Exeter (Wilfred F George/Henrietta Ledoux)b 30 Mar 1944
Baby Girl, 28 Jan 1967 at Exeter (William George/Irene Di-Floururses)b 28 Jan 1967
Calvin E.S., 18 Aug 1939 at Brentwood (Porter George/Florence B Kelley)b 1904
Carl Hazen, 21 Jul 1973 at Manchester (Walter George/Inex Tewksbury)b 13 May 1932
Charles, 26 Jan 1902 at Haverhill, Ma, b 1843
Daniel W (81), 10 Jun 1972 at Brentwood (Stephen George/Edna West)b 28 May 1900
Devin W, 03 Sep 1976 at E Kingston (16) (Allen P George/Charlotte L Anderson)
Edna M, 23 Sep 1931 at Exeter, b 1910
Edward W, 01 Oct 1930 at South Kingston (Porter George/Florence Kelley)b 1905(P/G)
Elmer R, 25 Jan 1932 at Danville
Emma J, 29 Jan 1918 at W Kingston (Andrew J West/Mary Davis)b 04 Mar 1854
Florence, 05 Aug 1959 at Brentwood (87) (George Kelly/Melinda Keezer), b - Plaistow
Fred P, 26 Oct 1932 at Haverhill, Ma, b 1862
Harriet C, 31 Dec 1925 at Kingston (85) (Harrison George/Harriet M Pratt) b-Danville
Inez , 03 Aug 1974 at Brentwood (Alliston Tewksbury/Ada Goodwin)
b 04 Oct 1895 (P/G)
Josephine May, 29 May 1934 at Middleton, b 1867 (M/S)
Kevin W, 03 Sep 1976 at East Kingston (Allen P George/Charlotte L Anderson)
b 27 Oct 1959 (P/G)
Lizzie, 12 Feb 1940 at Kingston (Thomas Elkins/Elizabeth Prescott) b 09 Jun 1860(P/C)
Marie L, 05 Sep 1986 at Kingston
Mary Ella, 12 Jan 1961 at Exeter (James Cosgrove/Edith Merrick) b 10 Oct 1887 (P/G)
Ora P, 13 Nov 1970 at Brentwood (Porter George/Florence Kelley) b 12 Jan 1890

Percy V, 26 Jun 1910 (9 Mos) (Porter G George/ Florence B Kelley) b - Kingston

Raymond W, 27 Oct 1915 at Kingston (Porter George) b - 03 Jan 1915 King)P/G)

Walter Merrill, 22 Jul 1948 at Exeter (Porter George/Florence Kelley)b 06 Mar 1892

GERSKOWITZ: Anne E, 20 Jan 1985 at Exeter (Albert J Hanscom/Natalie Kimball)

Muriel H, 17 Mar 1984 at Exeter (Leonard Stanley/Esther Picquette)

GIARRUSSO: Angelo A, 06 Oct 1992 at Exeter (Erminio Giarrusso/ Consiglia Ragosta)

GIBSON: Effie Prentiss, 06 Jan 1973 at Exeter (Frank H Gowell/Elvie E .....)b 28 Jul 1879

Orren Kendall, 21 May 1958 at Kingston (David Gibson/Nancy Gibson)b 07 Dec 1868, b - Deering

Walter E, 19 Mar 1992 at Exeter (Orrin Gibson/ Effie Gowell)

GIDDINGS: Almira C, 28 Aug 1947 at Haverhill,Ma (84)(James Patterson/Nancy Brackett) b Nova Scotia

GIFFORD: Clarence H, 16 Dec 1990 at Exeter (Warren Gifford/ Ella Howland)

GILL: Virginia A, 28 Jun 1989 at Exeter (Clarence Trahan/ Anna Murphy)

GILMAN: John Shannon, Sr, 20 Jul 1980 at Kingston (John S Gilman/Grace C Walker)

GILMORE: Arianna, 05 Jan 1914 at Kingston (Joseph Hoyt/Mary French)b .. Aug 1832 - Hampstead   (P/C)

Mary A, 27 Sep 1968 at Kingston (93) (George G Precott/Nellie E Edgerly)

William M , 26 Feb 1920 at Kingston, b 1832 in Medfield,Ma.   (P/C)

GIRKOWITZ, Ralph, 01 May 1982 at Exeter (Harry Girskowitz/Riba Bolta)

GOLDTHWAITE: Grace E, 15 Jun 1952 at Exeter (82) (Benjamin Sargent/Rebecca Peasley), b 02 Sep 1869 - Haverhill,Ma. (G/C)

William Everard, 30 Jun 1969 at Exeter (Everard Goldthwaite/Grace E Sargent) b 12 Jan 1904 (G/C)

GOLDWAITE: Lee, 10 Jun 1967 - b 15 Jun 1967 (P/G)

GOLDWAITHE: Everard, 17 Jun 1939 at Kingston (William Goldwaithe/Sumira Brown) b 15 Aug 1857   (G/C)

GONYER: Teddy Arthur, 18 Jun 1949 at Exeter (Harold Gonyer/Theresa Gaudette) b 07 Apr 1949   (G/C)

GOODRICH: Carrie P, 02 Feb 1931 at Haverhill, Ma.

Elizabeth Emma, 23 Sep 1945 at East Derry (William H Adams/Abagail Noyes) b 05 Dec 1860   (K/C)

Florence Etta, 19 Sep 1947 at Georgetown, Ma (.... Hutchins/Eliza E Pecker)b 1861

Frank P, 15 Oct 1955 at Manchester (Moses Goodrich/Sarah Pierce)b 1882 in Kingston

Grace Marshall, 15 Nov 1933 at Derry (Samuel Goodrich/Mary S Marshall) b 21 May 1868

Laura, 16 Feb 1957 at East Hampstead (Albert Packard/Orpliece Irvin)b 08 Mar 1887 - Haverhill, NH   (New Cemetery)

Mary S, 25 Jun 1917 at Derry (Moses F Marshall/Susan Bartlett)b 1842 in Brentwood

Preston M, 13 May 1927 at Derry (Alexander Goodrich/Emily Cotton)b 21 Sep 1849

Samuel B.T., 28 Jul 1917 at Derry (Joseph L Goodrich/M.N. Sherburne)b 1839 in Reading, Ma.

GOODWIN: Albert T, 18 May 1964 at Haverhill, Ma (64) (Frank B Goodwin/Hattie Merrow)

Carrie P, 31 Jan 1931 (P/G)

Charles M, 05 Mr 1934 at Brentwood, b 1847 (P/G)
Florence, 03 Mar 1923 at Kingston (70) (Henry Goodwin/Rebecca Marden)(P/C)
John A, 04 Sep 1929 at Kingston (John A Goodwin/Myrtle B Taylor)b - 05 May 1902 Kingston (P/G)
John D, 18 Jan 1952 at Exeter (Daniel Lewis Goodwin/Sarah F Brown)b 12 Oct 1869, Plaistow (P/G)
John H, 31 Jan 1920 (78) at Haverhill, Ma.
Myrtle Belle, 02 Dec 1935 at St Peterburg, Fl., b 1882 (P/G)
Reginald, 06 Oct 1973 at Exeter (Daniel L Goodwin/Amanda Clucher)b 19 Jun 1922
Sarah F, 23 Aug 1919 at Exeter, b 1851 (P/G)
Susie F, 25 Dec 1940 at Kingston (Henry Goodwin/Rebecca .....)b 13 Feb 1851 (V/C)
Thomas F, 02 Aug 1916 at Kingston (Daniel Goodwin/Sarah F Heath) b 28 Dec 1831
GOSS: Alonzo,09 Sep 1918 at Kingston (Henry S Goss/Martha Center)b 1849 in Londonderry
Climena A, 15 Dec 1923 at Kingston (Beardman Poor/Susanna Gillam)b 29 May 1849 Fremont
William R S, 02 Feb 1971 at Exeter (Saul Goss/Jennie Brown)b 13 Aug 1903 (P/G)
GOTTWALD: Freda, 12 Mar 1957 at Arlington, Ma, b 1894 (G/C)
GOULD: Jeffrey M, 20 Aug 1985 at Concord (Lewis N Gould/Joyce L Conte)
GOVE: Inez (Connor), 10 Nov 1967 at Exeter, b 1883 (G/C)
Roy C, 16 Feb 1992 at Exeter (Roy E Gove/ Inez Connor)
Roy Edward, 08 Jan 1965 at Kingston (John E Gove /Frances Wilkins) b 08 Oct 1885
GRADY: George J, Sr, 17 Feb 1985 at Exeter (Barthlolmew Grady/Eola Sossie)
GRAHAM: Edgar Wentworth, 03 Jul 1965 at Exeter (John A Graham/Etta Wood) b 09 Jul 1895 (P/G)
Ella, 10 May 1958 at Kingston (91) (Millage Marshall/Emma Morse), b - Nova Scotia
Ellen Belle, 14 Feb 1962 at Exeter (Mason S Severance/Mary Ellen Colcord) b 04 Apr 1897 (P/G)
Luther Freeman, 14 Jul 1967 at Manchester (John Graham/Alma Etta Woods) b 04 May 1888 (P/G)
Robert T, Sr, 23 Sep 1991 at Kingston (James Graham/ Anna Thompson)
GRANT: Cora, 08 Aug 1973 at Kingston (81) (Wesley Bishop/Laura Peasley)
GRASER: George W, 10 Aug 1959 at Concord, b 23 Feb 1876 (P/G)
GRAY: Anna, 16 Nov 1990 at Brentwood (Colin Campbell/ Mary Casey)
Arthur F, 28 Jan 1986 at Brentwood (Fayette B Gray/Zana Bishop)
GREELEY: Arthur B, 23 Aug 1939 at Kingston (Erastus P Greeley)b 04 Jun 1883 (G/C)*
*Death Certificate shows Haverhill, Ma. burial site.
Arthur T, 28 Mar 1985 at Lawrence,Ma (James H Greeley/Rose Mc Kenna)
Louise M , 23 Oct 1934 (89) (Henry Achelport)b - Germany
GREEN: Prentice S, 04 Jan 1967 at Exeter (52) (Harold L Green/Edith Smith)
GREENE: Anna, 11 May 1982 at Salem
John A, 05 Sep 1967 at Brentwood (90) (Charles A Greene/Jessie F Dearborn)
GREENWOOD: Frederick W,Jr, 10 Jan 1985 at Hanover (Frederick Greenwood/ Esther Neilson)

Mary Alice, 02 Jun 1967 at Exeter (Richard Purslow/Carolina Broadhurst) b 09 Fe 1890

William, 03 Feb 1978 at Providence, RI, b 1891   (G/C)

GREGSON: John T, 31 Dec 1961 at Kingston (83) (Frederick Gregson/Martha Chester)

Julia, 08 Nov 1962 at Brentwood (83) (Guyet ..../Mary Anderson)

GRIBBIN: Leslie K, 11 Jan 1976 at Exeter (81) (Jonathan Gribbin/Nettie Knight)

GRIFFEN: Annie, 10 Sep 1932 at (65) (Woodbridge Lyford/Annie Brown)b-Lawrence,Ma

GRIFFIN: George J, 13 Nov 1981 at Kingston (John J Griffin/Alma J Dufour)

Lizzie, 09 Apr 1924 at Haverhill, Ma, b 21 Mar 1860 (P/C)

Stewart C, 28 Aug 1917 at Haverhill, Ma, b 1839

GROVES: Annie E, 11 Dec 1932 (80) (William Groves/Alice Fowler) b - Nova Scotia

GUIBOARD: George W, 16 Oct 1958 at Kingston (69) (Warren Guibord/Jeannette Mead), b - Plattsburg, N.Y.

GUYETTE: Edward Joseph, 08 Jul 1939 at Brentwood (Edward J Guyette/Hazel Jasper) b 08 Jul 1939

Hazel L, 12 Apr 1986 at Exeter (Charles Jasper/Ethel Hartford)

HABERLAND: Veronica M, 03 May 1965 at Exeter (66) (Nellie Sargent)

HACLETT: Christina B, 21 Jul 1966 at Exeter (96) (William Douglas/Marion Camberon)

HADLEY: Gertrude S, 28 Jan 1986 at Amesbury,Ma (Frank Savage/Jennie Roden)

Gordon M, 07 Feb 1986 at Kingston (James G Hadley/Sara J Horne)

HAENDLER: Frieda A, 06 Jun 1959 at Kingston (77) (Max A Haendler/Anna Englemann), b - Germany

HALITSKY: Joseph A, 30 Jan 1984 at Kingston (Joseph Halitsky/Katherine Valis)

HALL: Alexander, 10 Jun 1980 Kingston (Alexander Hall/Susan Brideau)

Della N, 31 Oct 1974 at Exeter (74) (William Harriman/Josephine Simes)

Lydia M, 17 Aug 1974 at Kingston (69) (Andrew Lebreton/Melina Arseneault)

Reta M, 01 May 1990 at Fremont (John H Longmire/ Anzie Guest)

Rodney Llewlyn, 15 Mar 1946 at Kingston, b 05 Oct 1874 (E/C)

HAM: Ralph B, 12 Sep 1951 at St Petersburg,Fl (76)

HAMBLEM: Frederick, 17 Nov 1965 at Boston, Ma, b 1929   (G/C)

HAMBLEN: Arthur Isiah Baker, 28 Jul 1952 at Kingston (Norton Hamblen/Mary Cameron) b 18 Dec 1902   (G/C)

Mary Agnes, 07 May 1976 at Haverhill, Ma., b 1911 (G/C)

HAMMOND: George C, 09 Aug 1941 (76) b - West Windsor,Ct (Stephen F Hammond/ Ellen C Perkins)

Jean L, 18 Jun 1946 at Haverhill, Ma (63) (James Wentworth/Lettie A Westover)

HAMPEL: Olive G, 28 Nov 1988 at Exeter (Charles V Browne/Josephine Leroy)

HAMPTON: Roy, 12 Aug 1982 at Exeter

HANNAGAN: Ann, 30 Nov 1976 at Kingston (Charles F Hannagan/Elizabeth Goodwin) b 05 May 1963   (P/G)

HANSEN: Alma Helene, 10 Jun 1956 at Boston, Ma, b 1880 (M/S)

Ingeborg Marie, 10 Nov 1966 at Kingston (John H Hansen/Ingeborg M Christansen) b 20 May 1892 (M/S)

HANSON: Elmira, 12 Feb 1970 at Franklin (65) (Frank Dostie/Alice Cote)

Eric D, 01 Apr 1985 at Exeter (Jan-Michael J Hanson/Elizabeth Carter)

Florence L, 06 Feb 1948 (71) (F William Emerson/Harriett Martin)
Forest John, 08 Nov 1946 at Kingston (72) (John B Hanson/Mary Wells)
Hazel M, 22 Dec 1976 at Exeter (73) (Forrest John Hanson/Florence Emerson)
John B, 22 Aug 1918 at Kingston(Samuel Hanson/Dorothy Fellows)b 1843-Brentwood
Michael E, 14 Apr 1984 at Kingston (Robert E Hanson/Carlene E Wallace)
HARDING: Marion L, 28 Feb 1980 at Kingston (Robert Abbott/Mary Jane Hayden)
HARDY: Abigail , 15 Jul 1902 at Kingston (John Perue/Elizabeth Ingalls)b 1817
    Nina, 18 Dec 1972 (73) at Brentwood (George Clough/Ida Matteson)
HARMON: Asbra, 03 Nov 1955 at Newburyport, Ma, b 1887 (P/G)
    Charles K, 21 Sep 1979 at Portsmouth (George H Harmon/Mary C Holmes)
    Erme M, 18 Dec 1974 at Haverhill, Ma, b 1899 (P/G)
HARRIAMAN: Fred A, 13 Jan 1957 at Exeter (71) (Frank Harriman/Susan Bailey), b -
    Gloucester,Ma.
HARRIS: Almira F, 06 Feb 1959 at Amesbury, Ma, (Ralph Rock/Nellie Swett) b 1906 (P/G)
    Amelia, 09 Jan 1927 at Boston, Ma (Hardy Bishop/Julis Epzoss)b 1846
HARROP: Frank J, 26 Apr 1981 at Kingston (William E Harrop/Jennie E .....)
HARTFORD: Alida M (38) 28 Mar 1910 (John C Quimby/ Ada Head) b - Haverhill, Ma
    Artie B (2 mo)10 Nov 1910 (Shirley B Hartford/ Jennie Vallarie)b -Kingston
    Clarence, 24 Jul 1909 at Kingston (Shirley Hartford/Jennie Palloire)
HARTMAN: Charles J, 28 Sep 1930 (20) (Joseph Hartman/Ruth Austin)b- Dundee,Michigan
    William C,Jr, 19 Feb 1983 at Kingston (William Hartman,Sr/Mary Edwards)
HARTSHORN: Frederick W, 16 Mar 1900 at Kingston, b 1850
HATCH: Charles E, 21 Jul 1942 (77), b - Haverhill,Ma.
    Martha Ann, 01 Apr 1926 at Kingston (79) (Reuben Hatch/Sarah Tibbetts)
    b- Malden,Ma, Aug 1842 Malden,Ma.
    Mary Bertis, 12 Mar 1920 at Kingston (..... Hutchins)b 08 Sep 1871 Cumberland
    County, Ky.
    Nellie Frances, 04 Dec 1972 at Exeter (Edgar Prescott/Carrie Webster)b 06 Jan 1892
    Rufus Clarence, 03 Jul 1968 at Exeter (Clarence Hatch/Maud Geyer)b 29 Aug 1894
HATCHELL: Katherine C,07 May 1974 at Kingston (84) (Gregory Burns/Ellen Cullerton)
HAULE : Donald L, 19 Nov 1975 at Atkinston, b 1937 (G/C)
HAWKES: Ada, 24 May 1984 at Brentwood (John L Fowler/Gertrude Pierce)
    Ralph K,Sr, 08 Dec 1959 at Amesbury,Ma (61) (Frank W Hawkes/Carrie E Sampson),
    b - Newburyport,Ma.
HAWTHORNE: Baby Girl, 02 Jun 1956 at Yokosuka, Japan (James E Hawthorne/Pauline
    Nason), b - Yokosauka, Japan
HEALEY: Margaret G (94), 11 Oct 1972 (Gregory Burns/Ellen Culleton)
    Ruth S, 03 Nov 1969 at Haverhill, Ma (93) (James M Healey/Laura Underhill)
HEAR: Lenora, 31 Aug 1940 at Plymouth (John Bartlett/.... Quimby) b May 1892
HEATH: Charles Henry, 21 Sep 1947 at Exeter (Frank A Heath/Ella E Kimball)b 19 Mar 1879
    Ellen Etta, 28 Jun 1934 at S Kingston (Gardner G Kimball/Charlotte Williams)
    b 13 Dec 1860, Danville (M/S)
    Franklin, 15 Feb 1930 (97) at Rockingham County Hospital
    Female (2 days) 19 Jul 1910 (Grace Avery) b-Kingston

Franklin Gilbert Andrew, 26 Mar 1941 at Kingston (Franklin N Heath/Myra Austin)
    b 21 Jan 1856, S Kingston (K/C)
Fred A, 23 May 1958 at Exeter (75) (Andrew Heath/Ellen Kimball), b - Kingston
Howard C, 14 Jan 1974 at Saugus, Ma. (G/C)
Jeannette S, 07 Jul 1970 at Saugus, Ma, b 1885   (G/C)
Oscar L, 23 Jun 1902 at Kingston (Andrew Heath/Ellen Kimball) b 1881
William H, 22 Feb 1919 at Newton   (M/S)
HEMMINGWAY: Eliza, 09 Apr 1929 at Kingston (71) (Thomas Scholey) b - Fall River, Ma
HENDERSON: Louise, 05 Sep 1947 (68) at Hartford, Ct.
HENSHAW: Richard I, 24 Feb 1985 at Exeter (Richard F Henshaw/Wendy Ingalls)
HERBERT: Clinton Thorndike, 30 Jul 1962 at Exeter (George C Herbert/Lucy Gove)
    b 25 Nov 1882 (V/C)
    Lillian, 15 Aug 1973 at Exeter (Arthur Ames/Natalie Virgin)b 26 Nov 1884
HERMAN: Theresa M, 11 Nov 1990 at Exeter (Patrick Northcott/ Ann Hayes)
HERNE: Infant, 02 Jul 1924 at Haverhill, Ma.
HERSEY: Jennie M, 20 Oct 1956 at Kingston (74) (George Beattie/....)
HESELTON: Mary E, 21 Aug 1987 at Brentwood (John Crosby/Alice Eaton)
    Robert M, 31 Jul 1979 at Haverhill, Ma (Hebert R Heselton/Lettie E Hayes)
HESSELTINE: Lovine (69) 03 Jul 1910 (Jula Corey/ Caroline Griswold) b - Londerry, Vt
    Winslow W, 11 Jun 1923 (82) (Ephraim Hesseltine/Betsey Putnam), b - Vermont
HICKS: Elsie M, 12 Jul 1956 at Haverhill, Ma, b 1878   (K/C)
HIGGINS: George, at Haverhill, Ma - b 03 Apr 1938   (V/C)
    George F, 05 Jul 1992 at Kingston (Frank Higgins/ Helen Houley)
HILBERG: Herbert J, 05 Jul 1965 at Brentwood (69) (Julius Hilberg/.... Stemple)
HILL: Barney, 25 Feb 1969 at Portsmouth (Barney Hill/Grace Sills) b 20 Jul 1922   (G/C)
    Dorothy L, 08 Apr 1994 at Brentwood (Arthur Libbey/Mary Sargent)
    Harry Gilbert, 17 Apr 1913 at Haverhill, Ma, b 1895   (P/C)
HILLER: Berta, 06 Sep 1991 at Kingston (Albert N Perry/ Marietta C Rishel)
HILLIARD: Flora E, 05 Dec 1916 at Kingston (Dewitt Jewell/Maria Locke)b 1864 - Stratham
    Frank, 25 Dec 1936 at Tuftonboro (Rufus K Hilliard/Nancy Poore)b 03 Nov 1850
    Hazel. 22 Mar 1981 at Littleton (Everard Coldthaite/Grace Sargent)
    John Clinton, 03 Aug 1967 at Exeter (William Hilliard/Flora Jewell)b 22 Jul 1899
    Laura Jane, 12 Sep 1932 at Tuftonboro, b 1848 (G/C)
    Louis E, 16 Mar 1970 at Hartford, Vt, b 1912 (G/C)
    Louis E, 12 Jan 1961 at Wolfeboro (82) (Frank Hilliard/Laura J Smith)
    Margaret E, 28 Oct 1974 at Ossipee, b 1884(G/C)
    William, 14 Aug 1948 at Concord (88) (John T Hilliard/Elizabeth Hobbs)
HOAR: Lenora, 31 Aug 1940 (48) at Plymouth
HOBAN: Gunhild M (Johnson), 29 Nov 1977 at Exeter (71)
HOBSON: Susie, 04 Nov 1919 at Montreal, P.Q. (Ora P Patten/Elizabeth Towle)b 20Dec 1872
HODGSON: John E, 17 Jul 1994 at Kingston George T Hodgson/Emma Earley)
HOGAN: Donna Ruth, 03 Oct 1963 at Boston, Ma, (Roland B Hogan/....) b 01 Oct 1963 (G/C)
    Mary, 09 Mar 1980 at Exeter (James McCarthy/Margaret Quinn)
HOLDEN: Charles M, 18 Jul 1927 at Kingston (48) (Orin A Holden/Emma L Merrill)
    b-Cambridge, Ma

HOLLAND: Timothy R, 25 Jun 1988 at Exeter (Herbert F Holland, Sr/Marie Kane)
  Raymond, 12 Dec 1971 at Gloucester,Ma (54) (John Holland/Annie Parker)
HOLLENBECK: Franklin Wesley, 10 Jun 1962 at Kingston (Daniel H Hollenbeck/
  Ella E Eckert) b 18 Mar 1893 (G/C)
  Grace Emma, 22 Aug 1974 at Exeter (Charles P Doliver/Anna Blackmore)b 11 Sep 1904
HOLLINRAKE: Joyce C (35), 01 May 1972 (William A Colpitts/Frances Comeau)
HOOPER: Donald J, 06 May 1983 at Kingston (Floyd B Hooper/Eula Kraft)
  Elfriede D, 06 May 1983 at Kingston (Paula Schmidt)
HORSFALL: Mary A, 19 Jun 1955 at Kingston (Frank Butterworth/Hannah Bentley)
  b 1884 in England
HOUDE: Irene E, 28 May 1990 at Exeter (G Edward Castellucci/ Esther Fecchia)
HOUSE: Sophonia W, 12 Oct 1948 at Haverhill, Ma, b 1865 (P/C)
HOWEY: ....., 25 Nov 1966 at Haverhill, Ma, b 12 Oct 1966 (G/C)
HOYT: Charles W, 06 Feb 1927 at Haverhill, Ma, b 1848 (P/G)
  Gladys F, 07 Jan 1981 at Exeter (Ferdinand C Hutchings/Alice Long)
  Kenneth, 11 Aug 1970 at Newburyport (70) (Charles Hoyt/Diantha Welch)
  Louis G, 07 Oct 1933 at Kingston (Gilman B Hoyt/Marianna Jewel)b 23 Feb 1856
  John P, 24 Feb 1900 at Kingston (Isaac Hoyt/Lydia Williams) b 24 Feb 1900
  Marianna, 02 Jul 1913 at Exeter (Asar Jewell/Theodote Page)b 21 Mar 1837
  Mary A, 20 Mar 1928 at Kingston (82) (Jonathan Osgood/Hannah Page)b - Danville
  Mary J, 22 May 1933 at Kingston (Alfred Towle/Mary S Gale)b - 06 Aug 1861
  Maurice L, 16 Jun 1984 at Exeter (Irving Hoyt/Mildred Saunders)
  Myrtle L, 12 Aug 1902 at Exeter (James Hoyt) 21 days
  Noel D, 12 Nov 1988 at Kingston (Randolph Hoyt/Whilhemina Balmfort)
HUBBS: Rose May, 31 May 1961 at Exeter (William Clifford/Elizabeth Trask)b 23 Oct 1890
HULL: Eliza Emma, 16 Dec 1971 at Franklin (Charles Hull/Lydia Cilley) b 14 Mar 1900
  Apphia, 02 May 1900 at Kingston (Samuel Sleeper/Sarah Quimby) b 1828
  Ella F, 12 Apr 1930 at South Kingston (John Hunt/Abigail Sleeper) b 1848 (S/K)
  Ora Ann, 01 Jan 1918 at Melrose, Ma (Richard Bartlett/Sally Fellows)b 1848(P/CTomb)
HUME: James Oliver Wendell, 15 Jan 1980 at Exeter (William D Hume/Mary Boutillier)
HUNT: Ella F, 12 Apr 1930 (82) (John Hunt/Abigail Sleeper) b - Kingston
HUNTRES: Addie D, 30 Oct 1973 at Kingston (91) (William Cooper/Ann Gilman)
HUNTRESS: Gordon C, 31 Jan 1970 at Boston, Ma (42) (Royal Huntress/Flossie Crosby)
  John A, 17 Mar 1920 (3) (Clarence A Huntress/Addie Tucker) b - Kingston
HURLBERT: Gladys M, 23 Sep 1981 at Exeter (William Robinson/Mae Woodward)
  Minnie D, 08 Jan 1970 at Exeter (73) (Jacob Ellis/Gertrude Smith)
HUSE: Dorothy H, 15 Sep 1989 at Exeter (William J Lynch/Ellen Quirk)
  Elizabeth F, 15 May 1937 at Haverhill, Ma, b 1855 (P/C)
  Lucy Ann, 13 Oct 1900 at Kingston(Jacob Webster/Hannah Quimby) b 1845
HUSE: Stephen S, 10 Jan 1926 (82) at Orange, Ma.
HUTCH: Charles H , 21 Jul 1957, Concord, b 05 Mar 1876 - Portsmouth (V/C)
HUTCHINS: Alice E, 25 Nov 1960 at Kingston (84) (Charles A Long/....), b - Nova Scotia
HUTCHINSON: John A, 27 Jan 1923 (73) (John Hutchinson/Elisabeth Rois) b - Paris, France
IBBOTSON: Joseph W, 29 Oct 1925 at Haverhill,Ma, b 1874 (P/C)

Mattie M, 31 Aug 1925 at Haverhill, Ma (Henry Webster/Carrie Winslow)b 1876 (P/C)
INGALLS: Lita, 11 Feb 1990 at Kingston (Burton Snell/ Armenia Marsh)
Nellie F, 16 Nar 1832 (66) at Norwood, Ma.
INGHAM: Susan M, 18 Nov 1910 (58) at New York City
IZAGUIRRE: Antonio, 12 Dec 1987 at Portsmouth
JACKSON: Annie R, 18 Oct 1967 at Kingston (86) (Alexander Henderson/Elizabeth Piggott)
George R, 20 Dec 1971 at Exeter (69) (William T Jackson/Annie T Buckley)
Dinah J, 08 Oct 1955 at Kingston, b 1883 in England
Grace E, 21 Mar 1969 at Chelsea, Ma, b 1911   (M/S)
Harry A, 23 Sep 1957 at Newmarket (77) (Hezikah Jackson/Minnie Sanborn), b -
Dorchester,Ma.
Nancy J, 25 Mar 1955 at Tarrytown, NY, b 1870 in Mooseland, N.S   (G/C)
Nelson, 29 Jun 1950 at Kingston (Alexander Jackson/Isabelle Jackson) b 11 Sep 1867
Rosilla W, 21 Jul 1914 at Kingston (Amos Jackson/Sarah Burns)b 1849 in Hamden, Me
JACQUITH: Rosanna C, 19 Apr 1929 at Kingston (85)(Nahun Raymond/Hannah Guillour)
b - Georgia, Vt
JAMES: Carrie B, 13 Jun 1909 at Kingston (William F Austin/Julia A Foster)b 1863 -
Haverhill, Ma.
Earl David, 16 Jan 1974 at Exeter (75) (Thomas James/Addy Carter)
Leslie G, 04 Apr 1956 at Kingston (88) (Frederick J James/Laura Elizabeth), b -
Hamilton, Bermuda
JANNSON: May Frances, 08 Jul 1965 at Epping (76)(William L Savoy/Mary F Higgins)
JASPER: Charles Nelson, 03 Oct 1957 at West Kingston (Frank Jasper/Katie Burke)
b 13 Feb 1888 - Manchester (P/G)
Edith A, 26 Oct 1994 at Exeter (Walter George/Inez Tewksbury)
Ethel May, 01 Mar 1965 at Exeter (Rufus Hartford/Harriet Waitte)b 06 Feb 1886 (P/G)
John Jeffrey, 27 Apr 1948 at Exeter (Marion Jasper) (P/G)
Mervin R, 23 Dec 1992 at Exeter (Charles Jasper/ Ethel Hartford)
JENKIN: Lewis S, 20 Dec 1979 at Kingston (George C Jenkins/Theresa Beaulieu)
JENNESS: George, 08 Mar 1926 at North Andover, Ma, b 1853
Nellie I, 09 Nov 1953 (69) b - Greenland (George Wentworth/Lilla Norton)
Newell C, 23 Oct 1966 at Brentwood (86) (Alonzo Jenness/Martha Brown)
JENNINGS: Shirlie, 04 May 1963 at Kingston (80) (Loren E Bailey/Helen Simpson)
JERVIS: Isabelle Lee, 12 Apr 1973 at Exeter (Frederick M Day/Ruth Magoon) b 31 Jul 1901
JEWELL Ella, 10 Dec 1934 (79) b - Boston,Ma (John Wetherby)
JILLSON: Frances E, 24 Oct 1987 at Exeter (David W Moon/Ina Dwyer)
JILLISON: Harold H, 09 Feb 1977 at Exeter (George Jillson/Clara Gardner)b 12 Dec 1896
JOHNSON: Arthur A, 10 Jan 1915 at Kingston (William Johnson/..... Alexander) b 1836 in
Haverhill, Ma.
Etta C, 11 Apr 1926 at Haverhill, Ma, b 1856   (P/C)
Fannie A, 19 Dec 1918 at Kingston (William Woodbury/Francis Winchell) b 1860 -
Calais, Me.
George H, 20 Dec 1923 at Haverhill, Ma, b 1865   (So King)
Mary Jane, 30 Apr 1919 at South Danville, b 24 May 1832 (So King)

JONES: Baby, 02 Apr 1938 at Epping, b 02 Apr 1938 (P/G)
David W (87) 19 Mar 1910 (David Jones/....) b - Andover, Ma
George W, 08 Nov 1979 at Fremont (Francis A Jones/Alice....)
Rosamond, 26 Nov 1989 at Exeter (Frank W Stevens/Lora M ....)
JUDKINS: Abbie S, 02 Apr 1916 at Kingston (James Thying/Mehitable Judkins) b 05 Aug
1820- Brentwood (P/C)
Arthur Roswell, 06 Oct 1939 at Kingston (Joseph Judkins/Hannah E Blake)
b 30 Mar 1859   (V/C)
Delia, 03 Aug 1946 at North Hampton (Herbert Page)b 13 Aug 1865   (V/C)
Eldredge, 12 Jul 1945 at Grafton, b 1894
Eldridge G, 18 Sep 1900 at Kingston (Joel Judkins/Nancy Dudley)b 1813
Enoch B, 13 Feb 1928 (77) at Haverhill, Ma.
William, 18 Nov 1969 at Haverhill, Ma (76) (Arthur W Ingalls/Betsy Bradford)
Hattie I, 24 Nov 1916 at Kingston (Colin Butler/Hannah Walton)b 1861- Seabrook(P/C)
Joseph, 22 Jun 1900 at Kingston (Henry Judkins/Lydia Brown) b 1817
Leo B, 03 Jul 1934 at York, Me, b 1892   (G/C)
Lydia Brown, 28 Mar 1939 at Kingston (Simon Judkins/Catherine Hoyt)
b 01 Apr 1853   (V/C)
Mary E, 16 Oct 1929 at Kingston (Arrow D Webster/Sarah F Kinson)b 11 Jul 1867
E Andover, NH (K/C)
Nellie A, 16 Sep 1918 at Haverhill, Ma, b 1855 (P/C)
Olivia A, 01 Jan 1902 at Kingston (William Judkins) b 1825
JULIEN: Joseph, 01 Oct 1992 at Manchester (Noel Julien/ Alice Nadeau)
Lucille J, 12 Feb 1980 at Exeter (Louis Amero/Cereta Ducette)
KAVENEY: Nellie, 06 Jan 1956 at Kingston (75) (Randolph Wells/Josephine Pritchard), b -
Pitcher, N.Y.
KEAY: Warren S, 31 Jul 1948 at Melrose, Ma (80) (Orestes H Keay/Mary A Page)
KEELEY: John Bodman,Sr, 07 May 1976 at Kingston (47) (James T Keeley/Sylvania
Canterbury)
KEELING: Maud, 10 Sep 1952 at Kingston (68) (Thomas Phipps/Annie ....), b- Leister,
England
KEIR: Kenneth D, 02 May 1988 at Bedford,Ma
KEITH: John P, 16 Dec 1937 (51) at New York
KELLEY: ....., 29 Mar 1933 at Kingston (George W Kelley/Estella Brown)b 29 Mar 1933
....., 09 Jul 1934 at Kingston (George W Kelley/Estella Brown)b 09 Jul 1934   (P/G)
....., 18 Oct 1936 at Exeter (George Kelley/Estella Brown)b 18 Oct 1936 (P/G)
....., 02 Jul 1909 at Kingston (Fred Kelley/Katie M Chamberlain)b 02 Jul 1909
Charles Edward, 26 May 1958 at Exeter (George W Kelley/Melina Keezer), b 18 Feb
1884 - Kingston   (P/G)
Charles W, 28 Aug 1909 at Kingston (Charles E Kelley/Sarah J Martin) 3 mos   (K/C)
Charlotte M, 24 May 1969 at Concord (Albert N Dewhurst/Jennie Welch) b 15 Nov
1903 (West Kingston Cem)
Chester C, 23 Dec 1915 at Kingston (Charles E Kelley/Sarah L Martin)b 26 Jul 1915
Daniel, 25 Apr 1909 at Kingston (Alfred Kelley/Eliza Davis)

Dorothy, 03 Nov 1973 at Haverhill, Ma, b 1918 (H/H)
Ernest, 14 Apr 1974 at Brentwood (Fred Kelley/Katie Chamberlain) b 02 Jun 1907
Everett W, 13 Oct 1913 at Kingston (Fred E Kelley/Katie Chamberlain)
  b 26 Sep 1910 (P/G)
Frederick Eward, 15 Nov 1942 at Kingston (Daniel Kelley/Hattie Place)b 28 Dec 1885
  Kingston (P/C)
George W, 13 Jul 1977 at Haverhill, Ma, b 14 May 1907 (H/H)
George W, 10 Oct 1921 at Kingston (Alfred Kelley/Eliza Davis) b 1843
Mary, 02 Mar 1991 at Brentwood (Frank Smith/ Elizabeth Hubbard)
Melina I, 16 Sep 1916 at Kingston (Charles E Kelley/Sadie E Martin)b 20 Sep 1912
  Kingston (P/G)
Melina I, 12 Oct 1932 at W Kingston (Jonathan Keezer/Lois Williams)b - 08 Oct 1853,
  Kingston (P/G)
Walter J, 27 Nov 1992 at Brentwood (John Kelley/ Mary Bryden)
KELLY: Katie M, 21 Nov 1949 at Kingston (68) (Charles Chamberlain/Abbie Fifield)
  Rena May, 24 Mar 1900 at Kingston (William Kelly/Lizzie Virtue) 2 months
  George W, 10 Oct 1921 (78) (Alfred Kelley/Eliza Davis)
KELSO: Jane, 03 Oct 1909 at Kingston (John Kelso/Margaret Granger) b - 1842 in Ireland
KEMP: Charles W, 16 May 1966 at Norwood, Ma, b 1888 (K/C)
  G Austin, 14 May 1977 at Exeter (George Kemp/Harriette Inkmen)b 05 Feb 1900
  Josephine Alberta (Rogers), 20 Feb 1947 at Kingston (Joseph A Rogers/Emma Gay)
    b 23 Dec 1905 in Canaan, Vt (G/C)
  Winifred Ingalls, 13 Jul 1953 at Walpole, Ma (Fred J Ingalls/ Nellie French)b 1887
KEN: Edward, 22 May 1919 at Kingston (Arthur P Ken/Hester Morris) b 12 May 1919 (G/C)
KENDALL: Edward E, 21 May 1984 at Exeter (Edward Kendall/Beatrice Lang)
KENISON: Curtis William, 17 Oct 1949 at Kingston (Stephen Kenison/Sarah Kenison)
    b 14 Apr 1859 (G/C)
  Edith M, 19 Jun 1963 (Robert Megson/Sarah A Fernley)b 30 Dec 1876
KENNEY, John, 16 Apr 1936 at South Kingston (John Kenney/Maria Mejor)b 21 May 1888
    Hungary (G/C)
KERMICK: Mildred, 28 Aug 1987 at Exeter (Carl Swanstrom/Alma Johnson)
KERR: Evelyn, 04 Jul 1920 at Milton, Ma, b 12 May 1919 (G/C)
KERSIS: Helen F, 01 Jul 1975 at Exeter (84) (William Zelinski/Mary Valeskas)
KIDDER: ....., 12 Jun 1917 at Kingston (Arthur Kidder/Gladys Johnson) b 11 Jun 1917
    (Private Burial)
  Edward H, 13 Nov 1914 at Kingston (Hiram I Kidder/Ellen F Mason)b 1862
    in Raymond
KILLAM: Dorothy P, 26 Jul 1994 at Brentwood (Eugene Perley/Elsie Howe)
  Dwight Lewis, Sr, 26 Oct 1981 at Exeter (Chester Killam/Minnie Tidd)
KIMBALL: Benjamin, 27 May 1933 at Middleton, Ma, b 1862
  Blanche A, 29 Feb 1940 at Kingston (George F Quimby/Laura Lavory) b 23 Mar 1858
  Charlotte P, 22 Oct 1918 at Kingston (Benjamin Williams/Hannah Rowell) b 1842 -
    Plaistow
  Edward, 01 Aug 1960 at Brentwood (Stephen Kimball/Mary Giddings),b 07 Jan 1876,
    Kensington (V/C)

Elizabeth J, 18 Nov 1993 (Spencer Langley/Mahaleth Latham)
Elmer H, 14 Dec 1926 at Haverhill, Ma, b 1852 (P/G)
Ernest L, 09 Aug 1909 at Kingston (Arthur P Kimball /Ellen E Williams)b 09 Aug 1881 Haverhill, Ma.
Eugene C, 08 Nov 1936 at Kingston (Moses Kimball/Marie E Gross)b 30 Jan 1854, Methuen,Ma (G/C)
Florence H, 07 Oct 1928 at Worcester, Ma (Edward Kimball) b - 1805 (P/C)
Francis V, 29 Mar 1994 at Exeter (David Kimball/Marie Lachappelle)
Gertrude, 10 Jul 1966 at Exeter (84) (Walter Tuttle/Jennie Spaulding)
Grace, 29 Dec 1914 at Kingston (John H S Sanborn/Evelyn Hatch)b 30 May 1869 Kingston (P/C)
Hannah S, 01 May 1916 at Danville (Gilman Harris/Susan Kimball)b 1861 Plaistow
Hattie F, 08 Dec 1921 (70) at Haverhill, Ma.
John G, 29 Jun 1921 at Kingston (John C Kimball /Lucy S Kimball) b 1841
John P, 27 Mar 1922 at Kingston (John Kimball /Fornier Page) b 01 Jul 1836
Julia H, 03 Mar 1925 at West Kingston (Laban Collins/Rachel Hunt)b 06 Oct 1841 Kingston (P/G)
Lewis H, 27 May 1929 at Kingston (69)
Mary E, 30 Apr 1926 at Exeter, b 1869
Mary Jane, 10 Mar 1915 at Kingston (Thomas Burchard/Jane McKinnon) b - P.E.I.
Mildred D, 20 Aug 1961 at Haverhill, Ma (John Kimball/Julia Collins) b 1873(P/G))
Minnie C, 19 May 1937 (64) b - Dracut, Ma (Alfred McKuish/Frances E Choate)
Robert B, 01 Jun 1976 at Kingston (75) (Amos M Kimball/Bernice Huckins)
Thomas Hubbard, 15 Oct 1938 at Groton, Ma, b 1868
KING: Charles A, 06 Nov 1947 at Kingston (Albert King/Angeline S .....)b 07 Oct 1865 Castine,Me. (G/C)
Charles E, 06 Oct 1920 at Peabody, Ma, b 03 May 1863 (P/C)
Harold, 29 Apr 1978 at Exeter (Charles A King/Celia I Johnson)b 05 Feb 1890 (G/C)
Helen E, 23 Jul 1988 at Laconia (William H Tibbetts/Mary McLean)
Isabel, 05 Oct 1937 at Kingston (Joseph H Johnson/Harriet Gamonell)b 27 Nov 1865
Mary Ann, 02 Jan 1987 at Kingston (James Manus/Jennie Sampson)
Samuel M, 21 Mar 1961 at Haverhill,Ma (64) (Samuel M King/Anna O'Brien)
KINNEY: Barbara Jean, 05 Mar 1980 at Kingston (William Kinney/Mary Mills)
KINSMAN: Benjamin, 14 Dec 1944 at Brentwood (70) (Walter Kinsman/Katherine Jordan)
Laura Medera, 15 Jun 1932 at Andover, Ma, b 1891 (P/C)
Richard Bartlett, 02 Jun 1932 at Andover, Ma, b 02 Jun 1932 (P/C)
KNEELAND: Ephraim (59) 24 May 1910 (Aaron Kneeland/.... Pierce) b- Georgetown,Ma
Nancy E, 04 Aug 1912 at Haverhill, Ma (William Winslow/Eliza H Silloway)b 1851
KNIGHTS: Elsie, 07 Jul 1934 at Chatham, Ma (Arthur R Judkins/ Adelia.....)b 20 Aug 1893
KOHL: John, 20 Aug 1955 (William Kohl & Dorothy Miller) b 1882 in Austria
KRAMER: Harold Joseph, 11 Mar 1976 at Kingston (George Kramer & Mae ....)b 09 Apr 1911
LABELLE: Raymond Elmer, 13 Sep 1958 at Kingston (Samuela A Labelle/Viola Collins)
        b 14 Jan 1920 - Kingston   (G/C)

Viola Edith, 08 Apr 1959 at Sandown (w/o Samuel A LaBelle)(Elmer E Collins/Susie Nason) b 04 Jan 1892 - Kingston (P/G)
LABRANCHE: Victor P, 03 Jan 1984 at Exeter (Victor P Labranche/Mary M Blaisdell)
LADD: John E, 13 Apr 1962 at Kingston (71) (Abraham G Ladd/Ruth Messer)
Gertrude, 04 Jan 1930 (62) at Danville
Olande P, 29 Oct 1901 at Kingston (Ottro A Ladd/ Gertrude Page) 1 month
Ottero A, 19 Apr 1947 (75) at Danville
LAFAYETTE: Harvey J, 30 Jun 1985 at Exeter (Jesse C Lafayette/Nellie Gustin)
LAMBERT: John, 30 May 1977 at Kingston (Gustave Lambert/Lillie Peteeaw)b 30 Aug 1908
Mildred, 11 Mar 1974 at Exeter (Alfred Bowden/Helen Vogt)b 28 May 1908   (G/C)
LANDRY: Arthur J, 04 May 1969 at Hampton (81) (Augustus Landry/Mary Guerra)
LANE: Anna M, 03 Dec 1959 at Kingston (94) (Oliver Lane/Anna Flint), b - Exeter
Alyce C, 03 Mar 1968 at Brentwood (68) (Arthur Turner/Ida .....)
Fannie, 24 Aug 1940 at Epping - b 1877   (P/G)
LANG: Cora B, 26 Jan 1939 (79) (Raymond Fletcher)
Herbert L, 17 Dec 1942 (79) (Francis Lang/Mary E Fletcher) b- Bradford,Ma.
Jennie L, 09 Jul 1959 at E Kingston (93) (Osmond P Webster/Emily Pollard), b-Kingston
Nellie W, 05 Nov 1945 at Candia (John M Parker/Addie C Underhill)b 01 Aug 1850
LANGE: Peter W, 28 Jan 1989 at Haverhill, Ma
LANGLEY: Daniel B, 17 Jun 1918 at Kingston (Edward Langley/Sally Brewer) b 1835
Candia
LANGLOIS: Barbara M, 17 Feb 1982 at Exeter (Harry A Smith/Dorothy E Twiss)
David Albion, 07 Apr 1977 at Manchester (63) (Ernest D Langlois/Frances Colcord)
LAPHAM: Leland C, Sr, 22 Apr 1984 at Kingston (Chester J Lapham/Myrtle Willis)
LAPORTE: Gertrude, 13 Feb 1975 at Worcester, Ma, b 13 Feb 1975 (G/C)
Harry E, 25 Jul 1969 at Sanford, Me, b 1898   (G/C)
LARKIN: Mabel Frances, 04 Jun 1937 at Haverhill, Ma, b 1890 (P/G)
LARSON: Elmer John, 21 May 1973 at Exeter (Charles O Larson/ Anna Johnson)
b 19 Oct 1904 (G/C)
George Ray, 11 Nov 1957 at Exeter (Elmer J Larson/Gladys Gibbons)b 08 Nov 1939,
b - Stoneham,Ma.
LAURENSON: John J, II, 17 Jun 1962 at Kingston (13) (John J Laurenson/Ruth Sicard)
LAWLESS: Alfred R, 30 Jul 1977 at Boston, Ma (Stanley Lawless/Mary Fournier) b 1907
LAWRENCE: Harry, 08 Dec 1952, Exeter (83) (Henry Lawrence/Elizabeth Schues), b -
Wakefield,Ma.
LAZURE: Norman Joseph, 01 Sep 1993 (Hector Lazure)
LEACH: Charles P, 11 Aug 1939 at Haverhill, Ma, b 1852 (G/C)
Sally A (Harvey) at Danver, Co., b 1829 - Nottingham
LEATE: George P, 23 Feb 1970 at Haverhill, Ma. (88) (Hiram Leate/....)
Joseph E, 22 Feb 1955 at Exeter (George P Leate/Nellie McNieve)b 1938 Kingston
Mary E, 17 May 1927 at Kingston (1Mo) (George Leate/Margaret McNewe)
b - So Kingston
LEAVITT: Emma (Labonte), 14 Jan 1968 at Kingston (97)
LEBLANC: Eugenie M, 21 Dec 1970 at Exeter (Joseph Gaudreault/Conanie Lauzier) b 23 Aug
1890 (G/C)

Henry Moses, 03 Apr 1967 at Kingston (Moses LeBlanc) b 14 Jul 1891 (G/C)
LEFFRAY: Henry, 14 Jul 1934 at Brentwood, b 1864 (G/C)
LEMAY: Alma Etta, 08 Jun 1947 at Kingston (86) (Wertwood Lemay/ Eliza Tupper)
LEONARD: Robert Charles, 04 Oct 1981 at Kingston (Clarence Leonard/Marjorie Armstrong)
LEVESQUE: Lucien P, 17 Nov 1978 at Exeter (64) (Pascal Levesque/Arthemise Madore)
LEWIS: Arion B, 05 Jun 1958 at Haverhill,Ma (67) (John Barrett/Elizabeth Trafton), b -
    Haverhill,Ma.
    Mario B, 05 Jun 1958 at Haverhill, Ma (John Barrett/Elizabeth Trafton)b 1891 (G/C)
    Vernon, 24 Feb 1952 at Kingston (57) (William B Lewis/Elizabeth M Coburn), b -
    Haverhill,Ma.
LEYFORD: Arthur H, 27 Sep 1918 at Kingston (Lauren Leyford/Deborah H Estes)
    b 29 Apr 1869 (P/C)
LIBERTY: George, 11 Nov 1924 at Kingston (84) (Anthony Liberty/Margarite Cassan)
    b - Canada
LIGHTOWLER: Martha S, 24 Dec 1990 at Kingston (John Schnetzer/ Martha Heil)
LINTON: Raymond, 07 Mar 1971 at Manchester (Robert Linton/Jennie Johnson)
    b 02 Dec 1885 (P/G)
LITCHFIELD: Ethel M, 18 Dec 1992 at Brentwood (Edward Pierce/ Martha Slocomb)
LITTLE: William David, 15 May 1939 at Kingston (Robert George Little/Jeanette Young)
    b 02 Jun 1883 (P/G)
LITTLEFIELD: Dorothy Sarah, 04 Jul 1947 at Exeter (Daniel L Goodwin/Sarah Brown) b 26
    Jul 1885 - Kingston (P/G)
LLOYD: Charles Robert, 27 Aug 1982 at Kingston (Fred Lloyd/Beatrice Rufus)
LOCKE: Harvey, 23 Jul 1909 at Kingston (Reuben Locke/Jane .....)b 1826 in Alexandria
    Lizzie A, 04 Aug 1927 at Danver, Co., b 1863 (M/S)
    Olive A, 14 Dec 1971 at Kingston (101) (Albert C Locke/Eliza J Varrell)
    Warren, 07 Jan 1962 at Kingston (93) (Harvey Locke/ Ann Tewksbury)
LOCKWOOD: Alice M, 10 Apr 1956 at Kingston (90) (Horation Mosley/Ann Booth), b -
    Holmfirth, England
    James, 21 Mar 1962 at Exeter (73) (James Lockwood/Alice Mosley)
LONG: Ellen, 05 Nov 1920 at South Kingston (Robert W Verrell/Eliza Foss)b 15 Jul 1854 Rye
    Fannie Eliza, 03 Oct 1966 at Exeter (Richard F Long/Ellen A Varrill)b 21 Dec 1884
    Jennie Loretta, 09 Jul 1959 at East Kingston (Osmond P Webster/Emily Pollard) b 16
    May 1866 (P/G)
    Kenneth, 22 May 1974 at Exeter (71) (George Boyes/ Ella Marna Long)
    Richard F, 01 May 1922 at South Kingston (John Long) b - 20 Aug 1849 (M/S)
LONGBOTTOM: Albert, 28 Aug 1932 (16)(Charles Longbottom/Laura Burgess) b-Methuen,Ma
LONGSTREET: George H, 23 Aug 1938 (58) at Worcester, Ma.
LONGMIRE: Doris H, 09 Feb 1989 at Exeter (John H Longmire/Anzie Guest)
LOPAUS: Annie L, 14 Jun 1946 at Kingston (76) (John Marks/Adelaide Hamilton)
LOVE: Alice , 14 Sep 1939 at Concord (Joseph A Robbins/Sarah J Bubie)b 16 Apr 1883 (K/C)
LOVEJOY: Emery W, 04 Apr 1921 at Kingston (Hubbard Lovejoy/Louise Burgess)
    b 09 Apr 1833
LOVELY: John F, 25 Aug 1951 at Kingston (23) (Earl Lovely/Katheryn M Carney)

LOWERY: Abbie Elvira, 02 Jul 1918 at Newton, b 1843 (M/S)
George P, 09 May 1915 at Newton, b 1839
Robert E, 07 May 1974 at Kensington, b 1917 (M/S)
LUND: Arthur P, 03 Feb 1959 at Kingston (57) (William Lund/Sarah J Parkinson), b -
Keighley, England
LURVEY: Franklin P, 01 Jul 1929 at Kingston (Enoch Lurvey/Rebekah Higgins)b 31 Jul 1852
LUSK: Sarah Adelaide, at Boston, Ma (Stephen P Judkins/ Sarah C Brainard), b 1842
LUTZ: Dorothy R, 11 Aug 1992 at Kingston (Linol Snyder/ Laura Jacobs)
LUWEY: Franklin P, 01 Jul 1929 (76) (Hubbard Lovejoy/Louise Burgess)
LYFORD: Angie, 27 Jun 1976 at Brentwod (Charles Tenny/Lizzy Johnson)b 01 Nov 1889
Arthur H, 27 Sep 1918 at Kingston (Lauren D Lyford/ .....Estes)b 1869 in Brentwood
Carrie Etta, 22 Aug 1945 at Exeter (Francis Cross/Alice West)b -- Aug 1872
Elden, 06 Aug 1930 at Exeter (Preston Lyford/Angie Terry)b 27 Mar 1916 (P/G)
Francis Stuart, 18 Jan 1949 at Brentwood (Augustus Lyford) b 08 Sep 1867 (G/C)
George A, 02 Dec 1935 at Brentwood, b 1864 (P/G)
Henry M, 21 Sep 1963 at Concord (79) (Joshua E.G. Lyford/Emma Judkins)
J Alfred, 18 May 1942 (77) at Somerville, Ma.
Lauren D, 14 Feb 1900 at Kingston (Lauren Lyford/Deborah Estes)b 1863
Lauren D (75) 10 Jun 1910 (Joseph S Lyford/ Lydia Lovering) b- Brentwood
Lizzie Sarah, 24 Jan 1938 at Kingston (Preston M Goodrich/Sarah L Pierce)
b 10 Sep 1868, E Kingston (P/C)
Lydia Ann, 13 Sep 1959 at Hampstead, b 1875 (P/G)
Martha Elizabeth, 07 Sep 1951 at Portsmouth (Daniel L Goodwin/Sarah F Brown)
b 28 May 1875 in Kingston (P/G)
Preston, 20 Dec 1963 at Brentwood (James Lyford/Elizabeth Goodrich)b 08 Feb 1890
LYNN: James H, 23 Aug 1927 at Kingston (39) (James H Lynn/Elizabeth A English)
b - Boston,Ma
LYONS: Myra P, 21 May 1954 at Niagara Fall,NY, b 1889 in Kingston
MacCARRON: Katherine, 28 Aug 1950 at Waltham (74) b 10 Sep 1874
William L, 28 Feb 1916 at Melrose, Ma, b 1874 (P/C)
MacDONALD: ....., 04 Oct 1927 at Kingston (John MacDonald/Irene Simes)b 04 Oct 1927
Janet, 02 Jul 1934 (88) b -Antigonish, N.S. (Archie Chrisholm/Katherine MacDonald)
MACE: Charles Henry, 06 Sep 1932 at Middleton, Ma, b 1882 (P/C)
MACK: Mabel B, 13 Nov 1988 at Exeter (Samuel E Pierce/Martha Slocumb)
MACKIE: Doris M 11 Jan 1992 at Kingston (Archibald Makie/ Mary York)
MacNEILL: Douglas B, 02 Sep 1969 at Beverly, Ma. (William MacNeill/Glenice Perkins)
b 01 Jun 1944(G/C)
MacWHINNIE: Melvin (64), 07 Nov 1972 at Exeter (Joseph MacWhinnie/Mary Annis)
MACOMBER: Clara F, 27 Jan 1953 at Stratham (Daniel Higgins/Marella Higgins)
b 04 Apr 1869, Charlestown,Ma (G/C)
Walter, 29 Jun 1921 at Kingston (Walter Macomber/Magarett Tracy) b 1910
Walter W, 12 Aug 1957 at Portsmouth, b 16 Jul 1882 - Brimfield,Ma. (G/C)
MAGNUSSON: Harriet, 01 Oct 1925 at Kingston (James M Philbrick/Mary D Chase)
b 27 Apr 1874 Springfield (P/C)

Isabelle, 12 Jan 1984 at Exeter (Ernest B Grace/Luella Bowdoin)
John J, 10 Jul 1985 at Exeter (Martin Magnusson/Hattie Philbrick)
Martin C, 07 Jun 1961 at Kingston (John Magnusson/....) b 17 Oct 1870   (V/C)
Ruth, 14 Jul 1988 at Fremont (James Stevens/Amy Whitmore)
MAGOON: Mary F, 18 Feb 1930 (79) at Portland, Me.
MAGUIRE: Edith, 06 Oct 1973 at Kingston (77) (William H Locke/Louise E Pierce)
MAHONEY: Filomena P, 02 Feb 1981 at Salem, Ma (Manuel Mattos/Mary Fertando)
MAILET: Maurice, 11 Jun 1944 at Brentwood (Thomas Mailet/Julia Fitchbury)
      b 26 Jun 1863 (V/C)
MALLOY: May (77), 26 May 1972 at Exeter   (G/C)
MANGANARO: Charles J, Jr, 03 Sep 1967 at Kingston (34) (Charles J, Manganaro,Sr/
      Anna McDonald)
MANNING: Lester G, 07 Feb 1934 (66) b - Haverhill,Ma (Eric Manning/Emma F Stevens)
MANSFIELD: Charles E, 10 Jan 1923 (60) (Charles G Mansfield/Jane C Nutting)b - Boston,Ma
      David Eric, 18 Feb 1968 at Derry, b 28 Feb 1968   (P/G)
      John A, 31 Jul 1971 at Kingston (John G Mansfield/Grace Ricker)b 22 Mar 1910 (P/G)
      Peter Allan, 30 May 1971 at Exeter, b 30 May 1971 (P/G)
      Thelma R, 22 Nov 1990 at Exeter (William Wordell/ Lottie E ...)
MANSFIELD: Virginia F, 25 Sep 1980 at Exeter (John Climo,Jr/Louise Defferro)
MARCH: Alcina A, 28 Mar 1917 at Kingston (John Webster/Lois Colcord)b 04 May 1834
      Alonzo B, 14 May 1915 at Brentwood (George March)b 1837 in Danville (P/C)
MARCHE: Jessie I, 30 Jun 1960 at Exeter (68) (Philip Morrison/Isabel Cook)b - Dorchester,Ma
      Louise Peter, 02 Feb 1967 at Exeter (77) (Peter Marche/Lydia Boggs)
MARDEN: Mary, 03 Feb 1924 at Kingston (Leonard Schelling/...) b 28 Apr 1832 Kingston
MARGESON: Charles Enos, 11 Mar 1977 at Manchester (76) (Herbert Downs/Josephine
      Phelps)
MARPLE: William Allan, 07 Feb 1973 at Epping (81) (William Marple/Harriet E Rounds)
MARSH: ....., 07 Aug 1889 at Kingston (Charles Marsh/Carrie .....) 2 days
MARSHALL: Arthur Hurd, 11 Sep 1938 at Exeter (Samuel C Marshall/Adeline Hurd)
      b 11 Aug 1864, Kingston   (V/C)
      Florence, 10 Nov 1942 at Brentwood (Charles Hatch/Ora Woodward)b 19 Aug 1864
      Harold D, 24 May 1969 at Hampton Falls (Melburn Marshall/Lydia Weston)
      b 20 Nov 1869   (K/C)
      Herbert W, 04 Dec 1910 (57)(James F Marshall/ Mary M George) b-Kingston
      James W, 01 Apr 1915 at Brentwood (Moses Marshall/Susan Bartlett)b 30 Dec 1838
      in Brentwood (P/C)
      Jennie A, 07 Mar 1928 at Brentwood, b 1841   (P/C)
      Jesse P (80) 28 Jan 1910 - b Kingston
      John P, 05 Feb 1901 at Somerville, Ma (James Marshall) b 1824
      Joseph Edward, 01 Sep 1993 (Joseph Marshall/Edith Clough)
      Lottie, 16 Apr 1967 at Hampton (Abner Buckman/Henrietta Everett)b 07 Jul 1871(G/C)
      M Lela, 28 Sep 1901 at Kingston (Elizah Brown/....) b 1858
      Mary G, 17 Oct 1948 at Boston, Ma (83)
      Minnie B. D., 25 Apr 1940 at Medford, Ma , b 1866

Nellie P, 20 Nov 1937 at Kingston, b 1861 (Kingston)
Nettie H, 10 Mar 1963 at Kingston (75) (Leverett Howe/Emily Robinson)
Samuel C, 28 Feb 1903 at Kingston (James Marshall/Mary Dudley) b 1819
MARSTERS: George S, 24 Jan 1931 at Haverhill, Ma, b 1873 (P/G)
MARSTON: Alice, 01 Feb 1981 at Haverhill, Ma (Louis N Currier/Marie-Christianna Plante)
MARTIN: Andrew, 19 Feb 1937 at Brentwood (Levi Martin/Ella .....) b 20 Apr 1872 (P/G)
Annie May, 08 Feb 1969 at Exeter (George J Brown/Elvira Baker) b 17 Oct 1888
Charles E, 25 Nov 1954 at Newton Jct, b 1876
Charles, 11 Dec 1994 at Brentwood
Clara Bell, 10 Jun 1972 at Manchester (Frank St John/Esther Currier)b 19 Sep 1898
Edward C, 08 Sep 1938 (86) b - Ipswich, Ma (Robert Martin/Lucy S Clark)
Etta M, 09 Feb 1921 at Kingston (Nathan Nason) b 30 Jun 1861 Portland,Me. (P/G)
Everett A, 02 Jan 1919 at Kingston (George Martin/Etta M Nason)b 27 Jan 1884
George Everett, 21 Aug 1940 at Kingston (Levi Martin/Rosanna Stuart)
    b 22 Oct 1857(P/G)
Hollis D, 22 Aug 1976 at Exeter (Everett Martin/Annie Brown)b 09 Jan 1912 (P/G)
Leisa Irene, 18 Jun 1964 at Methuen, Ma, b 1961 (P/G)
Mart E, 20 Dec 1916 at Kingston (James Barrett) b 1837 in Ireland
Mary H, 12 Jul 1913 at Kingston (Charles Clark/Lucy M Brown)b 04 Jun 1828 (P/C)
Melvin Elmer, 30 Dec 1978 at Exeter (69) (Everett E Martin/Annie M Brown)
Norris G, 20 Aug 1971 at Manchester (Everett A Martin/Annie M Brown)
    b 11 Sep 1910 (P/G)
Perley C, 30 Apr 1932 (43) b - Kingston (Levi B Martin/Ella R Davis)
Wayne Elmer, 24 Jun 1983 at Exeter (Melvin E Martin/Ruth Emery)
MARTINE: Dorothy E, 17 Jun 1975 at Exeter (60) (Louis P Baker/Edna Debaun) b-Epping
Lawrence B, 04 Aug 1988 at Exeter (S Wesley Martine/Laura Brooks)
MARTINO: Nancy A, 09 apr 1994 at Kingston (John Mansfield/Thelma Wordell)
MARYEA: Shirley M, 11 Jan 1994 at Kingston (Gordon Garrow/Lucille Pudvah)
MASLOWSKI: Josephine, 19 Apr 1974 at Kingston (59) (Frank Szeliga/Albina Sklarski)
MASON: Mabel D, 24 Jan 1959, at Los Angeles,Ca (80) (Frank Barnes/Mary Ann Boardman),
    b - Massachusetts
MATHIS: Wallace F, 03 Jan 1975 at Manchester (50) (Julius J Mathis/Cecila H Mullavey)
MATSON: Uno A, 11 Mar 1984 at Exeter (August Matson/Hilda Kaytto)
MATTHEWS: Richard J, Sr, 17 Aug 1974 at Kingston (60) (Nelson Matthews/Clara
    Whitehouse)
MAULE: Grace A, 03 Feb 1994 at Yarmouth,Me (Douglas H Pragnell/Clara Pluck)
Robert D, 25 Jul 1984 at Kingston (Arthur Maule/Grace Prangnell)
MAYO: Ethel V, 15 Sep 1973 at Kingston (83) (Herbert Tahyer/Gertrude .....)
McALLISTER: Henry B, 29 Feb 1968 at Lawrence,Ma (56) (Joseph McAllister/Ellen Wayne)
McAVOY: William J, 26 Sep 1985 at Kingston (Daniel J McAvoy/Sally Jurkvich)
McCABE: Abigail W, 09 Feb 1934 at W Kingston (Peter S Fifield/Catherine Webster)
    b 27 Jan 1853, Kingston (P/G)
Bernard, 15 Apr 1902 at Boston, Ma (Edward McCabe/Rose Gallagher)b 1878
John F, 30 Apr 1943 at Pembroke (John McCabe/Sarah .....)b 17 Jun 1871 (P/G)

Lawrence R, 26 Aug 1909 at Kingston (Charles Gaffan/Katie McCabe)b - 1909
Amesbury, Ma.
McCARTHY: Julia A, 20 Nov 1991 at Brentwood (Charles Clarke/ Maurya Corcoran)
Marie Agnes, 26 Jan 1986 at Exeter (George E McCarthy/Julia A Clark)
McCOLLIM: Ellen E, 09 Dec 1982 at Lawrence, Ma (E Phillip McCollim/Abbie Gordon)
Ralph L, 07 Jul1984 at Exeter (Charles McCollim/Millie Klopp)
McCOMB: ....., 27 Sep 1913 at Kingston (Raymond P McComb/Alice Morris)b 27 Sep 1913
Alice May, 25 Feb 1969 at Exeter (George Morris/Sarah Graham)
Hannah P, 04 Feb 1941 at East Kingston (Nathaniel Cheney/Mary E Hoyt)b 1859
James N, 10 May 1951 at Exeter, b 11 Mar 1866 in Calais, Me. (V/ C)
Raymond P, 13 Mar 1959 at Kingston (65) (James McComb/Evelyn Pierce), b-
Kingston
McCOY: George A, 21 Nov 1932 b - Chatgney,N.S. (Archibald McCoy/Sarah Peek)
McDONALD: William, 21 Nov 1978 at Haverhill, Ma (60) (Thomas McDonald/Delia Flaherty)
McENNIS: George F, 13 Dec 1967 at Methuen, Ma, b 14 Mar 1910 (G/C)
Katherine Eleanor, 14 Jun 1970 at Exeter (Miford Hislop/Susie .....)b 03 Aug 1915
McGLYNN: Franklin J, 23 Nov 1981 at Exeter (Franklin J McGlynn/Cecile Manning)
Leslie O, 02 Nov 1975 at Exeter (80) (George D Swallow/Kate F Morrissey)
McKEE: Thomas, 28 Oct 1909 at Kingston, b 1889 in Ireland
McLAREN: Dorothy M (1 mo) 16 Apr 1910 (Allen McLaren/ Emma Ball) b - Haverhill, Ma
McNEIL: Helen, 05 Feb 1902 at Kingston (Stanley McNeil/Edith M Hunt) 28 days
McNEILL: Beatrice Mildred, 26 Jan 1978 at Rochester, b 1891 (G/C)
Charles M, 09 Feb 1958 at Exeter (72) (George H McNeill/Harriet Hazel), b - Boston,Ma
MEANS: James P, 30 May 1994 at Exeter (John F Means/Mildred E Cavanaugh)
MEDOR: Percival C, 18 Nov 1985 at Exeter (William Medor/Bertha.....)
MEEHAN: Alice P, 17 Mar 1989 at Brentwood (Andrew F Huston/Alice M Brackett)
Gertrude C, 17 Mar 1990 at Kingston (Woodbury Hatch/ Isabel Foss)
James H, 04 Mar 1992 at Exeter (Edward J Meehan/ Harriett Spiller)
MEEKS: Charles, 16 Dec 1972 at Kingston (Charles B Meeks/Mary Abbie Tucker)b 15 May
1884 (P/G)
Fred (89), 23 Ju 1954 at Brentwood (Charles B Meeks/Mary Abbie Tucker)
b 05 Sep 1891 (P/G)
Ira Alonzo, Sr, 26 Oct 1966 at Manchester (Charles B Meeks) b 05 Feb 1887 (P/G)
Josephine, 10 Jan 1937 at West Epping (Isaac .../Josephine LeMarsh) b 04 Sep 1871
Mary, 21 Jan 1957 at Brentwood (64) (George Trafton/Mary Bell), b-S Berwick,Me
Mary A, 08 Nov 1959 at Brentwood (82) (Charles Gove/Emma Fellows), b -
Kensington (P/G)
Samuel G, 25 Feb 1949 at Brentwood (Charles B Meeks) b 04 Oct 1884 (P/G)
Fred, 23 Jun 1954 at Brentwood (Charles B Meeks/Mary A Tucker)b 1891
MEINERTH: Earl Wesley, 29 Jun 1977 at Exeter (George Meinerth/Carrie Norton)
b 16 Mar 1907 (P/G)
MELANSON: Francis J, 19 Aug 1979 at Exeter (Edgar Prescott/Carrie Webster)
MELVIN: George, 15 Feb 1924 at Kingston (83) (Robert Melvin)b-Portland,Me
MERENSKI: Alice A, 26 Sep 1991 at Kingston (Albert La Bombard/ Alma Thibideau)

Peter A, 13 Feb 1987 at Exeter (Adolph Mierzenjewski/Anna Bepnarczyk)
MERINO: Anthony J, 26 Oct 1989 at Brentwood (Domenic DiGiammarino/Mary Miraglia)
　　Bibiana, 06 Nov 1992 at Brentwood (Modesto Colasanti/ Marianina Colocici)
MERRICK: James P, 24 Oct 1953 at Boston,Ma (2) b - Corpus Chrisi,Tx (Walter F Merrick/
　　Josephine E Glisson)
　　Walter Payson, 25 Sep 1961 at Manchester (Merril Merrick/Mary DeRochemont),
　　b 07 Jan 1890　(G/C)
MERRIFIELD: Theresa, 13 Jun 1994 at Salem (Hyloite Perreault/Bessie Smith)
MERRILL: Annie B, 02 Jan 1946 at Dover (66) (James A Locke/Susan Hamilton)
　　Edward, 11 Feb 1938 at Brentwood (Beatty Merrill/Eliza Young)b 10 Jun 1864　(P/G)
　　Etta, 17 Jun 1949 at Kingston (79) (John P Kimball/Julia H Collins)b 07 Apr 1870　(P/G)
　　Harriet A, 25 Jun 1918 at Kingston(William Whittier/Charlot Carleton)b 1856- Plaistow
　　Richard D, 05 Nov 1987 at Manchester (Frank M Merrill/Marie Mathews)
　　Roy, 06 Sep 1966 at Exeter (82) (Brewer Merrill/Mary E Welsh)
MERRILLE: Harriet F, 25 Dec 1932 at West Bridgewater, Ma, b 1842　(P/C)
MERRITHEW: Earle H, 01 Feb 1952 at Portsmouth (58) (Isaac Merrithew/Lydia F Blaisdell),
　　b - Massachusetts
METCALFE: Russell Alan, 04 Jul 1960 at Exeter (George R Metcalfe/Gladys King), b 02 Jul
　　1960　(G/C)
MEYERS: Robert F, 10 Aug 1994 at Kingston (Frank Meyers/Margaret Cullen)
MIDDLETON: Robert W, 28 Feb 1949 at Kington (78) (Richard Middleton/Ann Lannin)
　　Ruben R, 28 Dec 1953 (56) b - Royalton,Vt (Robert Middleton/Susan A Williams)
　　Wilfred A, 08 Jun 1968 at Kingston (Robert Middleton/Susan Williams)
　　b 27 Jan 1899　(G/C)
MILBURY: ....., 21 Mar 1927 at Kingston (William B Milbury/Edith Burpee)b 21 Mar 1927
MILLAR: Henry Thompson,05 Jan 1968 at Exeter (John H H T Millar /Matilda Kinnon)
　　b 26 May 1881　(G/C)
MILLER: Aaron James, 10 Jul 1973 at Manchester (75) (Anthony Miller/Mary Nadeau)
　　Elizabeth, 18 Nov 1961 at Brentwood (John Burns/Margaret Black), 23 Jun 1880 (G/C)
　　Ernest E, 22 Aug 1974 at Kingston (54) (Warren J Miller/Lucy Hover)
　　Milton Denerly, 19 Feb 1949 at Brentwood, b 01 Oct 1884
　　Rosetta Hutchins, 21 Jan 1964 at Exeter (Edwin Babb/Elizabeth Brown)b 01 Aug 1886
MILLS: Edward Francis Sr, 18 Apr 1983 at Amesbury,Ma (Warren Mills/Ella .....)
　　Marion G, 13 Jan 1986 at Lawrence, Ma (Charles F Baltzer/Gladys J Apt)
MINARD: Nathaniel,24 Oct 1932 at Newton, b 1864　(P/C)
MISENHEIMER: Adele N, 14 Jan 1989 at Brentwood (Joseph Kratochivil/Josephine Mucha)
　　Madelyn, 09 Jun 1994 at Exeter (John Currier/Eva Bemis)
MITCHELL: Frank Astor, 15 Aug 1946 at Kingston (George Mitchell) b 20 Jul 1879 (G/C)
　　Lillian E.B., 19 Jan 1917 at Kingston (Robert Durkee/Abigail A Healey) b 1879
　　Rosanna, 23 Aug 1955 at Concord (William G St Hilaire/Mary Mier)b 30 Apr 1880
　　in Lynn, Ma.
MODLICH: Walter R, 15 Feb 1981 at Exeter (William Modlick/Freida Zapf)
　　Frieda Martha, 23 Jan 1977 at Exeter, b - 05 Dec 1881　(G/C)

William Frank Augustus, 25 Jan 1957 at Kingston (Joseph Modlich/Augusta Ellinger) b 17 Apr 1878 - Roslindale,Ma. (G/C)
MOELLER: Albert J, 21 May 1970 at Manchester (80) (George J Moeller/Louisa Hoeffer)
MOHAN: Meta H, 16 Apr 1986 at Kingston (Herman E Dick/Anna Kaufman)
    Thomas E, 19 Aug 1987 at Exeter (Thomas Mohan/Alice Marran)
MOLINA: Francisco,Jr, 04 Jul 1985 at Kingston (Francisco Molina/Lydia Moreno)
MONAHAN: William F, 11 Jun1963 at Kingston (80) (Josseph W Monahan/Celia Harkins)
MOODY: Ira W, 20 Jan 1931 at Haverhill, Ma, b 1860 (M/S)
    Lizzie L (Runnelles), 31 Aug 1901 at Haverhill, Ma, b 1863
    Sylvia, 28 Feb 1920 at Kingston (Edward H Evans/Nettie Moody)b 27 Dec 1884 (S/K)
MOORE: Alfred L, 07 Jan 1986 at Concord (Arthur L Moore/Edith Sevestre)
    Edith P, 15 Aug 1993 (Harry Card/ Marion Mitchell)
    Marie, 18 Aug 1976 at Brunswick, Me (73)(Joseph Frazer/Josephine Powers)
MOQUIN: Joseph, 03 Aug 1928 at West Kingston, b 04 Jun 1873 Buffalo,NY (W/K)
    Mary A, 03 Mar 1947 in Fitchburg, Ma (Isair Tucker/Adelaid Seaver)b 1863 in Kingston
MORETON: Edith M, 10 Jan 1974 at Kingston (90) (William I Moreton/Julia Blanchard)
MORIN: Gloria, 16 Aug 1976 at Exeter (George L Durgin/Natalie Wright)b 23 Jun 1926 (G/C)
MORONI: Michael F, 16 Dec 1973 at Kingston (17) (Faust Moroni/Irene Underwood)
MORRELL: Lorenzo J H, 28 Sep 1937 at Wolfeboro, b 1868 (P/G)
    Nellie P, 28 Apr 1956, Kingston (79) (Robert K Brown/Jane Symonds),- Marblehead,Ma
MORRIS: Beatrice , 22 Feb 1979 at Brentwood (George Morris/Sarah Graham)
    Edward J, 03 Jul 1966 at Kingston (33) (Lester Morris/Edna Perry)
MORRISON: Angus, 06 Oct 1935 at Brentwood, b 1852 (V/C)
    Dale W, 03 Dec 1959 (24) (Walter Morrison/Theresa Garrity), b - Mapleton,Me
    Peter N (30), 26 Apr 1972 (James P Morrison/Frances Nelson)
MORSE: Arthur Alan, 24 Apr 1968 at Kingston (John E Morse/Ida Russell)b 28 Sep 1889
    Barbara F, 07 Sep 1994 at Amesbury,Ma (Robert P Lee/Lottie M Dow)
    Bertha May, 26 Jul 1963 at Exeter (Richard Graham/Ellie Marshall)b 23 Oct 1888
    Catherine, 23 Feb 1941 (73) (Thomas Fitzgerald/Catherine Courtney) b - Ireland
    Charles E, 06 Jul 1964 at Exeter (70) (George E Morse/Celia B Sullivan)
    Frances M, 18 Jul 1969 at Exeter (53) (Charles Collins/Ethel Savage)
    George F, 29 Jun 1925 at Kingston (62) (Silas J Morse/Ellen Pitts)b- Danville
    Jennie M, 24 Nov 1969 at Concord (68) (Joseph Batchum/Julia Degreenia),Halifax,NS
    Ralph E, 21 Sep 1965 (74) (Julia Buchman)
MOSELEY: Alice, 27 May 1975 at Haverhill, Ma (60) (George W Walsh/Olive Eaton)
MOSSE: Frederick A, 08 Dec 1994 at Brentwood (Jacob Mosse/Martha Webster)
MOULAISON: Theresa M, 04 Nov 1988 at Kingston (Maurice Daley/Josephine ....)
MOURAO: Antonia D, 07 Sep 1986 at Manchester (Manuel Mourao/Rose Correia)
    June, 10 Sep 1985 at Kingston (Milton Bidwell/Hazel Grant)
MULLEN: David, 26 Apr 1972 (60)(Davis Mullen/Blanche Hamilton)
MULREY: Frederick J, 22 Feb 1975 at Haverhill, Ma (87) (Patrick Mulrey/Annie McHugh)
MUNCE: Aldana, 10 Oct 1991 at Kingston (Rupid Vail/ Grace Paschal)
MUNRO: Frank, 13 Nov 1929 (67) at Hopkinton

Sarah Sibyl, 11 May 1927 at Kingston (Hugh Smythe/..... Hazelton)b 1865 Ireland
MUNROE: Adelaid M, 22 Sep 1934 (64) b - London,England (W Cottish/.... Cockly)
MURPHY: Frank E, 25 Jan 1986 at Kingston (Dennis Murphy/.... Connors)
MURRAY: Byron J, 17 Jun 1927 at Kingston (65) (William Murray/Sophia Littlefield)
     b - Shapleigh, Me
NADEAU: Joseph P, 29 Nov 1989 at Exeter (Joseph Nadeau/Lena ....)
NANIAN: Oscar, 21 Jul 1957 at Kingston (36) (Hazset Nanian/Zabel Bedrosian),- Hartford,Ct
     Robert A, 21 Jul 1957 at Kingston (17) (Leo Nanian/Irene Haytaian),b - Malden,Ma
NASH: Leanne , 11 Sep 1988 at Exeter (Thomas E Nash/Lynn A Fales)
NASON: ....., 03 Apr 1926 at Kingston (Freeman Nason/Mildred Marshall)b 03 Apr 1926
     ....., 01 Jun 1920 at Kingston (Freeman Nason/Mildred Marshall) b 01 Jun 1920
     Albert F, 08 Jun 1927 at Kingston (Nathan Nason/Sarah K Page)b 17 Sep 1856   (P/G)
     Albion, 24 Jan 1922 at Kingston (Nathan Nason/Sarah K Page)b 4 Jun 1984   (P/G)
     Alden, 09 Jun 1977 at Exeter (Seth Nason/Blanche Ines Elkins)b 11 Jun 1914   (P/G)
     Anna, 18 Oct 1939 at Haverhill, Ma (Ezra Page/Augusta Shaw)b 1856   (P/G)
     Blanche I, 05 May 1955 at Exeter (George E Elkins/Rachal A Call) b 09 Oct 1875,
     Kingston (P/G)
     Caroline Augusta, 30 May 1937 at Methuen, Ma, b 1883   (P/G)
     Kingston
     Celia Irene, 16 Apr 1918 at Kingston (Eugene N Nason/Etta F Brown)b 6 Nov 1917
     Clarence Edmund, 27 Sep 1945 at Kingston (Albion Nason/Anna Page)b 15 Oct 1867
     Donald H, 25 Nov 1994 at Exeter (Ernest Nason/Esther Patch)
     Elvin F, 17 Jan 1992 at Exeter (Freeman E Nason/ Mildred Marshall)
     Elizabeth Smiley, 10 Feb 1959 at Kingston (Robert Little/Jeannette Young),b 23 Feb
     1878 - Halifax, N.S.   (P/G)
     Ernest, 31 May 1963 at Exeter (Albion Nason/Anna Page) b 24 Feb 1880 (P/G)
     Esther, 16 Jun 1957 at Kingston (John H Patch/Patience Tobey),16 Jun 1888 -York, Me.
     Etta F, 14 Oct 1957 at Haverhill, Ma (George Brown/Elvira Baker)b 1893 - Sandown
     Eugene Nathan, 20 Jan 1965 at Kingston (Albion Nason/ Anna Page)b 27 Dec 1886
     Eva, 19 Mar 1981at Exeter (George Emery/Ella Patten)
     Florence E, 06 Apr 1910 (Seth F Nason/ Blanche Elkins) 2 Mos b - Kingston
     Freeman Lane, 28 Apr 1959 at Kingston (Nathan Nason/Sarah K Lane)b 02 Oct 1869
     Gilbert W, 30 Jun 1966 at Haverhill, Ma (Eugene Nason/ Etta S Brown)b 1913(P/G)
     Harold Page, 30 Aug 1971 at Dover (Albion Nason/Anna Page)b 22 Mar 1889(P/G)
     Herbert Call, 07 Mar 1946 at Kingston (Seth F Nason/Blanche Elkins)b 12 May 1903
     Infant, 03 Apr 1927 at Kingston (Birth) (Freeman Nason/ Mildred Marshall)
     b Kingston
     Irving Waldo, 28 Sep 1973 at Exeter (Albion Nason/Anna Page)b 13 May 1891(P/G)
     Jesse K, 04 Dec 1909 at Kingston (Albion Nason/Anna S Page) b 1898
     Laura D, 05 Apr 1926 at Kingston (Peter Fifield/Catherine Webster)b 23 Oct 1856
     Kingston   (P/G)
     Lester Farnsworth, 16 Jun 1970 at Exeter (Seth Nason/Blanche Elkins)b 17 Aug 1901
     Lloyd Emery, 10 Jul 1950 at Exeter (Irving Nason/Eva Emery)b 06 Nov 1931   (P/G)
     Mary Ella, 25 May 1942 at Kingston (Moses Wilbur/Nellie Shufelt)b 14 Jun 1886
     Kensington (P/G)

Mildred G, 12 May 1973 at Cortlandville, b 1901 (P/G)
Mildred Lilla, 07 Apr 1926 at Kingston (Richmond Marshall/Lilla Heath)b 29 Mar 1887 Merrimac,Ma.
Nathan, 17 Aug 1937 at Concord (Freeman L Nason/Mildred Marshall)b 11 May 1908, Kingston (S/K)
Philip S, 06 May 1978 at Cortland, NY (Albion Nason/Anna Page)
Rachel S, 06 Sep 1909 at Kingston (Seth F Nason/Blanche I Elkins) 8 mos
Ralph Harold, 17 May 1974 at Manchester (Harold Nason/MaryWilbur)b 13 Apr 1926
Roger E, Jr, 23 Jan 1984 at Danvers, Ma (Roger E Nason,Sr/Thelma Jasper)
Seth Farnsworth, 29 Dec 1938 at Kingston (Nathan Nason/Sarah K Page)b 11 Jun 1867, Kingston (P/G)
Shirley L, 24 Aug 1960 at Amesbury,Ma (Elden Nason/Louise Coffin), b-Amesbury,Ma.
Thelma, 23 Oct 1972 at Boston, Ma (Charles Jasper/Ethel Hartford)b 1920
Willie N, 01 Apr 1955 at Kingston (Albion Nason/Anna S Page)b 1874 in Kingston
NASS: William Austin, 28 Apr 1950 at Kingston (Alfred C Nass/Anna Nass)b 1882
NEAL: Mary L, 23 Feb 1937 at Somerville, Ma, b 1865 (P/G)
NEALE: George C, 07 Oct 1939 (77) (Nathan Nason/Sarah K Page)
NEVANS: Cora E, 29 Nov 1925 at Kingston (72) (Wm M Randall/Martha Spofford)- Bath, Me
NEVILLE: James F, 20 Feb 1985 at Exeter (Patrick Neville/Catherine Lynch)
NEWCOMB: Lida J, 23 Jul 1941 (70) b - San Raphel, Ca
NEWGENT: Edna L (81), 18 Apr 1972 at Exeter (William T Moore/Mary E .....)b 24 Apr 1890
Herbert H, 16 Aug 1974 at Carlisle, Ma, b 1887 (G/C)
NEWMAN: Henry I, Sr, 28 Nov 1985 at Exeter (Charles H Newman/Maude Randall)
John Francis, 27 Aug 1975 at Kingston (John F Newman/Ellen ....)b 05 Jul 1892
NICHOLS: Albert E, 28 Sep 1932 at Kingston (Charles W Nichols/Helen Wadleigh)
b 15 Jul 1870, Kingston (P/C
Albert E, 28 Sep 1932 (62) b - Kingston (Charles W Nichols/Helen Wadleigh)
Alice S, 31 Mar 1922 at Kingston (Henry S Perry/Mary A Cofran) b 16 Sep 1859
Clifton, 24 Oct 1946 at Exeter (William Nichols/Helen Wadleigh)b 21 Jan 1876
Fred Alson, 08 Dec 1948 at Kingston, b 21 Sep 1894 (Kingston)
Frederick G, 10 May 1980 at Kingston
Frederick S, 20 Feb 1977 at Exeter (H W Nichols/Alice S Perry)b 01 May 1894
Helen M, 28 Nov 1920 at Kingston (Oliver D Wadleigh/Maria M Holbrook)b 19 Sep 1843 Boston,Ma. (P/C)
Perrin William, 27 Sep 1944 at Kingston (Stephen F Nichols/Sarah Chase)
b 12 Feb 1865 (V/C)
Sarah E, 20 Mar 1919 at Kingston (Anus Chase/Hannah P Hook)b 06 Oct 1835
Stanley, 17 Feb 1986 at Exeter (John Nichols/Elizabeth Daniels)
Stephen F, 30 Jul 1902 at Kingston (Frederick Nichols/Sarah Williams)
Stephen W, 21 Jan 1933 (58) at Exeter
Therese N (Porter), 01 Aug 1980 at Exeter
NICKERSON: Albert M, 21 May 1934 R Brentwood, b 21 May 1870 (G/C)
Harry E, 12 May 1975 at Exeter (Harry Nickerson/Carrie Murch)b 16 Mar 1910
Lloyd Albert, 19 May 1975 at Portsmouth, b - 1922 (G/C)

Winnie, 09 Jan 1967 at Exeter (76) (George F Carter/Mary E Webster)
NICKETT: Hanna J, 13 Jan 1909 at Kingston (William Clayton/Rosanna Ayer) b - Vermont
NICKETTE: Ella Rose, 20 Jan 1942 at Antrim (Jonathan Davis/Adeline Seaver)
NICKOLS: Fred A, 08 Dec 1948 at Kingston
NIELSEN: Niels Berthelsen,12 Jun 1953 at Exeter (Jens Nielsen/Anna Jensen)b 06 Mar 1872,
    b Denmark   (G/C)
NIGRO: Albert C, 27 Sep 1978 at Kingston (72) (Francis Nigro/Anna Monks)
NILSSON: Baby Boy, 21 Nov 1969 at Haverhill, Ma,, b 21 Nov 1969 (P/G)
    Mary, 11 Apr 1968 at Derry (Wayne Allen Nilsson/Karen Anne Lamb)b 09 Apr 1968
    Regina, 07 Nov 1970 at Boston, Ma, b 1902(P/G)
    Vivian E, 12 Jan 1979 at Haverhill, Ma (William Cheney/Stella Page)
NOLIN: Paul L, 11 Dec 1978 at Haverhill, Ma (72) (John Nolin/Julia Bassett)
NOLL: Albert J, 17 Mar 1989 at Brentwood (James Noll/Margaret Reinhardt)
NORRIS: Barbara A, 01 Feb 1994 at Exeter (Glen B Cornish,Sr/Elmira Dostie)
    Joseph James, 30 Nov 1980 at Exeter (James D Norris/Mary Gagnon)
NORTON: James Edward, 17 Feb 1974 at Exeter (21) (James J Norton/Mary E Willis)
O'BRIEN: Patrick J, 04 Jan 1971 at Kingston (1 mo) (John F O'Brien, Jr/Christiane Buchal)
O'CONNELL: Dennis W, 05 Jun 1921 at Kingston (Jeffrey O'Connell/Mary Ford)b 1848
OLESON: Cheryl J, 13 Jul 1987 at Exeter (Laurence E Ticehurst/Marie B McGrath)
OLJEY: Edward J, Sr, 16 Apr 1988 at Kingston (Joseph Oljey/Emelia Glinska)
OLMSTEAD: Bessie, 05 Aug 1974 at Revere, Ma, b 1883(G/C)
O'MALLEY: Florida, 07 May 1967 at Exeter (73) (Edward Cote/Felicite Moreau)
ORDWAY: Donnizetti A, 21 May 1950 at Kingston (Edward E Demeritt/Mertie Prescott)
    b 10 Jun 1848
ORLANDO: Joseph, 31 Mar 1967 at Boston,Ma (64) (Nicholas Orlando/Maria ....)
    Lillian C, 13 Oct 1992 at Kingston (Michael Rossetti/ Celia LaVita)
ORMERS: Edgar E, 23 Dec 1950 at Kingston, b 1881
ORMES: Edgar Ellsworth, 23 Dec 1950 at Kingston, b 16 Oct 1869 (G/C)
    Isabelle Margaret, 06 Aug 1943 at Kingston (William McQueen/....)b 12 Jul 1873 (V/C)
    Ralph, 07 Feb 1975 at Brockton, Ma, b 1905   (G/C)
OSBORNE: Herbert Sherwood, 30 Oct 1971 at Largo, Fl, b 1895 (P/G)
    Roland V, 27 Aug 1992 at Exeter (Henry L Osborne/ Frances Varney)
OSCHWALD: Eleanor F, 29 Mar 1964 at Concord (57) (Charles Barnes/Mabel Burditt)
OSGOOD: Annie L, 23 Mar 1932 (73) (James Jackman/Adrienree Flander)b - E Kingston
    Annie P, 16 Nov 1923 at Brentwood, b 16 Jul 1856
    Charles E, 01 apr 1916 at Kingston (Luman S Osgood/Annie L Jackson)b 1884
    East Kingston
OSGOOD: Everett R, 23 Jul 1959 at Concord (30) (Charles Osgood/Isabeele McAllister)
OTTEN: Kenneth D, 22 Jun 1976 at Exeter (George Otten/Marie Keller)b 12 May 1930 (G/C)
PAGE: Alice J, 08 Oct 1931 at West Kingston (Ezra Page/Augusta Shaw)b 20 Feb 1961
    Kingston (P/G)
    Bertha May, 02 Feb 1970 at Exeter (Moses Swett/Lavinia George) b 05 Nov 1878 (P/G)
    Carroll , 12 Aug 1918 at Kingston (Ulysses S Page/Etona P Currier)b 02 Dec 1902(P/G)
    Clarence, 18 Sep 1972 at Brentwood (95)(Herbert Page/Florence Griffin)b 22 Sep 1876

Effie Blanche, 01 Mar 1964 at Epping, b 1877   (P/G)
Elvira Ione, 23 Jan 1957 at Exeter (Freeman Currier/Susan Keezer)b 17 Mar 1878 -
Danville (P/G)
Esther Thompson, 18 Jun 1974 at Farmingdale, Me, b 1901 (P/G)
Flora V, 22 Jun 1928 at Haverhill, Ma (Andrew J West/Mary Davis)b 1864
Herbert A, 12 Sep 1927 at Kingston (Aaron Page/Valeria Allen) b 03 Jul 1851 Danville
Herbert L, 26 Sep 1987 at Kingston (Oscar E Page/Geneva Severance)
Howard Currier, 21 Aug 1952 at Exeter (Ulysses G Page/Etona P Currier)b 21 Apr 1898
Kingston
John H, 14 Apr 1922 at Kingston (Joseph Page/Mary Fifield) b 13 Sep 1853 (P/C)
Leslie Howard, 22 Jul 1945 at Exeter (Ezra Page/Augusta Shaw)b 18 Aug 1878 (P/G)
Minnie Estelle, 25 Aug 1951 at Exeter (Albert P Webster/Betsy L Webster)b 10 Oct
1869 - Kingston (P/G)
Sarah A, 05 Feb 1929 at Kingston (Moses Marden/Rebecca Young)b 15 Aug 1837 -
Kingston
Ulysses G, 10 Jan 1938 at Kingston (Ezra Page/ Augusta Shaw)b 21 Jan 1865- Kingston
PAINTER: Philip, 16 Dec 1983 at Exeter (Henry A Painter/Frances Weber)
PAIVA: Manuel B, 15 May 1988 at Kingston (Manuel Piava/Rosalina Vieria)
PALMER: Stephen R, 22 Nov 1950 at Kingston (Granville E Palmer/Cecile Smith)b 1942
PAPTOLA: Anna, 22 Sep 1985 at Dover (Walter Romancewicz/Annie Koahk)
PARIS: Alice Thompson, 27 May 1952 at Exeter (Luther Holt /Alice Thompson)b 28 Jul 1874
Emma Eliza, 17 Dec 1939 at Amesbury, Ma, b 1856
PARKER: Allen J, 23 Jun 1982 at Hampton (John Parker/Addie Underhill)
Alice T, 27 May 1952 at Exeter (77) (Luther Holt/Alice Thompson), b- Epping
Annabel, 08 Oct 1925 at Exeter (Nathaniel Parker/Sarah Gadd)b 1855 (P/C)
Clara E, 31 Aug 1968 at Kingston (83) Edward W Parker/Charlotte McAully)
Madeline, 21 Aug 1968 at Exeter (Charles W Senter/Lillian Dunn)b 31 May 1906 (G/C)
Robert C, 21 Oct 1977 at Exeter (Francis Parker/Esther Sargent)b 19 Aug 1912
Sarah, 01 May 1900 at Kingston (George Gadd/Jane Aldrich)b 1815
PARKINS: Bessie L, 16 Jun 1961 at Kingston (68) (John Bright/Lizica Beardsley)
Cecil F, 31 Dec 1977 at Exeter (Frederick Parkins/Marjorie Biggar)b 23 Mar 1908
PARKS, Charles 31, Mar 1921 (63)
PATRICK: Floyd S, 23 Dec 1968 at Methuen (20) (Henry Patrick/Doris Gonyer)
PATTEN: Ernest J, 02 Dec 1958 at Exeter (75) (Samuel Patten/Clara Abbott), b- Candia
Harold E, 17 Mar 1985 at Exeter (Ernest Patten/Grace Brock)
Ora P, 05 Feb 1910 (78) at Kingston/ born Verdon, Can (Colcord Patten/ Mariah
Fletcher)
PATTERSON: Lincoln B, 21 May 1936 (69) b-Norristown,Pa (George Patterson/Lydia Adams)
PEARD: Eleanor Alice, 09 Aug 1986 at Exeter (Charles Peard/Ellen Mary Cathcart)
Jennie, 28 Nov 1994 at Exeter (Charles L Peard/Ellen Cathcart)
PEASLEE: Albert F, 19 Feb 1933 at West Kingston (William Peaslee/Drucilla Locke)
b 15 Aug 1856   (P/G)
George W, 24 Dec 1955 at Brentwood (Albert Peaslee/Mary Fifield)b 1882 in Newton
Mary E, 30 Jul 1962 at Brentwood (Peter Fifield/Catherine Webster)b 1863 (P/G)

PECKER: Mary M, 24 Sep 1985 at Brentwood (James Dyke/Mary Callahan)
PELKEY: Stella, 05 Aug 1967 at Kingston (73) (Gilbert Ratte/Delina Bacon)
PELLETIER: Dennis M, 08 Jun 1991 at E Kingston (Wallace Pelletier/ Paula Goudreault)
    Hermangilde C, 15 Dec 1976 at Derry (82) (Delesphore Pelletier/Desneige Dion)
PELS: Klazina, 22 Feb 1981 at Brentwood (Jacobus Deruiter/Anna Kortebien)
PENDERGAD: William, 24 Jun 1901 at Kingston (Isaac I Pendergad/Lydia Kennistow)
    b 1853
PENNEY: Alfred E, 16 Sep 1994 at Exeter (William Penney/Annie Koerner)
    Ann Evelyn, 08 Nov 1962 at Exeter (Alfred Pettit/Annie Richardson)   b 01 Feb 1898
    Fern, 31 Aug 1987 at Brentwood (Everett Decker/Arletta Birch)
PERKINS: William F, 07 Jul 1988 at Exeter (William Perkins/Christine Walker)
    William J, 23 Jul 1985 at Exeter (Edwin R Perkins/Mary M Hamblen)
PERLEY: Fred S, 13 Nov 1944 at Brentwood, b 1887   (G/C)
PERRAULT: Blanche C, 19 Jan 1989 at Exeter (Harry W Dare/Clara J ....)
PERREAULT: Albert J, 08 Apr 1989 at Port Jervis, NY
    Mary Ellen, 11 Dec 1969 at Exeter (William F Lowes/Mary F Noon)b 30 Oct 1912
PERRY: Lottie F, 07 May 1963 Hanover (Arthur E Abbott/Georgia Pendergrace)05 Aug 1889
    Mary A, 27 Jun 1918 at Worcester, Ma, b 1838   (P/C)
    Roland L, 27 Dec 1963 at Brentwood (George Perry/..... Strain)b 11 May 1885   (P/G)
PERSAL: William Ivan, 09 Oct 1971 at Exeter (William Persal/Susie Woodbury)
    b 01 Nov 1898(P/G)
PETERS: James, 07 Oct 1969 at Haverhill, Ma (27) (Ora J Peters/Mary Burko)
PETTENGILL: Alvra V, 05 Aug 1978 at Walkefield, Ma (53)
PETTIS: Florence, 01 Oct 1950 at Brentwood (George Rock/Emma Bagley)
PEVEAR: William H, Sr, 29 Jan 1990 at Kingston(Elwin Pevear/ Florence I Hickford)
PHILBRICK: Beniman, 27 Jan 1735 at Kingston (Jedidiah Philbrick/Mary Tayler)
    b 06 Mar 1734
    Elwood E, 1986 at Kingston (Eugene Philbrick/Lizzie Pickard)
    Eunice F, 02 Aug 1958 at Kingston (38) (Carl Floberg/Ida ...)b - Everett,Ma
    James W, 04 Apr 1916 at Brentwood (Jeremiah Philbrick/Jane Sanborn)b 20 Dec 1841
    in Springfield (P/C)
    Mary S, 13 Apr 1925 at Fremont (Amos Chase/Hannah Hooke)b 26 Sep 1846
    Thomas, 16 Aug 1935 (Jedidiah Philbrick/Mary Tayler)
    Virginia C, 01 Oct 1986 at Kingston (Walter Palmer,Sr/Rose Eldroid)
PHILLIPS: Frederick Franklin, 21 Jun 1959 at Exeter (Alexander Phillips/Johan Hanlon)
    b 25 Apr 1884 - Haverhill,Ma.   (P/G)
    E Ruth, 15 Nov 1965 at Hampton (66) (....Maria Nelson)
    Shirley E, 31 Jan 1994 at Exeter (Earl F Nickerson/Elizabeth Motran)
PIANTADOSI: Phyllis P, 26 Mar 1989 at Exeter (Liberto Piantadosi/Rose .....)
PICHETTE: Marie E , 09 Aug 1988 at Exeter (Gabriel Saulnier/Oidle Belliveau)
PICARDO: Dominic, 13 Oct 1957 at Kingston (45) (Angelo Picardo/Fenezia Dimattia)-Italy
PIERCE: Cynthia B, 22 Jul 1917 at Henniker (Shepard S Collins/Julia A Judkins) b 1846 -
    Kingston
    Frank L, 04 Oct 1913 at Kingston (John Pierce/Annie Schellberg)b -- Sep 1870 (P/C)

Joseph F, 12 Jun 1934 at Kingston (Sylvester F Pierce/Sarah B Champman)
b 05 Mar 1853 - Raymond   (V/C)
Joseph V, 24 May 1957 at Kingston (75) (Easton Y Pierce/Mary Scribner)
Lucy E, 12 Jan 1933 at Kingston (William Edney/ Evelyn Farmham)b 05 Sep 1855 -
Middleton,Ma (V/C)
PITKERWICK: Alexander P, 05 May 1994 at Kingston(Charles Pitkerwick/Malvina Matechun)
Irene L, 02 Oct 1961 at Kingston (54) (Charles P Dolliver/Annie Blackmore)
PITKIN: Hazel I, 07 Dec 1976 at Exeter (69) (Newell C Jenness/Nellie I Wentworth)
PLATUKYS: Eva, 16 Aug 1938 (48) b - Lithuania (Michael Palasky/Mary Skripkiunas)
PLOYER: Winifred M (Sonia),08 Apr 1969 at Exeter (79) (William H Sonia/Martha Greenlaw)
POLEATEWICH: Arlita, 27 Jan 1990 at Exeter (William Brizzee/ Gladys Ward)
POLGAR: Robert S, 03 Oct 1992 at Kingston (Stephen Polgar/ Edna Frankenfield)
POLLARD: Earl J, 01 Oct 1963 at Haverhill,Ma (54) (Sherman Pollard/Mildred Irish)
Jewell M, 31 Jan 1964 at Haverhill, Ma (45) (George M Builbord/Edner I Kester)
POMEROY: Doris L, 20 Nov 1939 at Monson, Me   (G/C)
POMROY: Olive Lurvey, 25 May 1945 at Hartford, Ct., b 24 Feb 1852
POPE: Hazel, B, 27 Nov 1994 at Exeter (Charles bishop/Sara L Sargeant)
PORTER: George, 17 Jan 1922 at Kingston, b 1861   (P/G)
POWERS: James M, 23 Jun 1957 at Kingston (53) (Joseph P Powers/Georgia Miller)
PRAY: Helen, 11 Oct 1973 at Exeter (81) (Fred Niles/Ella B Peaslee)
PRATT: Walter L (77), 07 Dec 1972 (Walter Pratt/Minnie Perry)
PRENAVEAU: Bertin L, 04 Apr 1991 at Titusville, Fl (Joseph Prenaveau/ Rose ....)
PRESCOTT: ....., 28 Apr 1901 at Kingston (Harry Prescott/Maud Emery) 1 day
Albert R, 20 Apr 1953 at Dover (Eugene Albert Prescott/Sarah French)
b 23 May 1892, Kingston   (Sanborn Cemetery)
Carrie F, 02 Mar 1935 at Brentwood (John W Webster/Abby Buzzell)b 10 Feb 1858
Clara J, 29 Jan 1917 at Kingston (David Bickford/Elizabeth Jenness)b 07 May 1836
Edgar Sumner, 25 Oct 1934 at Brentwood (Richard Prescott)b 16 Oct 1854   (V/C)
Ernest C, 15 Jun 1934 (64) (Alden J Prescott/Lydia A Cloff)b - Salem
Eugene Albert, 01 Nov 1948 at Hampton Falls (Richard L Prescott/Clara J Bickford)
b 27 Apr 1862   (V/C)
Florence Merrick, 21 Jan 1972 at Dover, b 1894   (P/C)
Harry Leon, 09 Feb 1966 at Exeter (Richard L Prescott/Clara J Bickford)b 07 Feb 1879
Helen M, 01 Apr 1958 at Exeter (65) (Edward H Kidder/Mary E Hall) b - Kingston
Ida F, 30 Jun 1931 at Exeter, b 1861 (V/C)
John W, 12 Oct 1923 at Kingston (Lewis F Prescott/Elizabeth Webster)b 17 Dec 1844
Lauretta A, 27 May 1918 at Auburndale, Ma. (Lewis F Prescott/Elizabeth G Webster)b
08 Oct 1831   (P/C)
Mary Elizabeth, 18 Oct 1954 at Kingston (Richard J Prescott/Clara J Bickford) b 14 Apr
1865   (V/C)
Maude E, 22 Jun 1960 at Exeter (George Emery/Ella Patten)23 Jan 1880 - Waterboro,Me
Roxcena (Sanborn), 29 Jan 1940 at Kingston (Luther M Sanborn/Nancy Sanborn)
b 07 Jan 1849   (V/C)
Roy E, 30 Sep 1992 at Exeter (Harry Prescott/ Maude Emery)

Walter A, 29 Aug 1979 at Exeter (Edgar Prescott/ Carrie Webster)
PRIORE: Rita M, 29 Apr 1993 (John Newman/Elizabeth Firmingham)
PROUTY: Alvin Earl, 14 May 1984 at Exeter (William F Prouty/Ella P Nims)
    Arline M, 14 Mar 1979 at Brentwood (Albert Deroche/Susan Cheney)
PUBLICOVER: Ella Sarah, 18 Jan 1950 at Somerville, Ma (John Lowe/Isabelle Gray)
    b 28 Aug 1874
    James E, 22 Feb 1951 at Haverhill,Ma (Daniel Publicover/ ......)
PURCELL: Horation B, 31 Aug 1916 at Kingston (Horatio N Purcellia/Johannah Power)
    b 1891 in Halifax, Nova Scotia
QUERO: Andrew, 02 Apr 1909 at Kingston, b 1824 in Nova Scotia
QUIMBY: Ella May, 05 Jul 1951 at Kingston (Lorenzo Quimby/Elizabeth Marden)
    b 16 Oct 1863 in Kingston (M/S)
    Lorenzo B, 04 Jul 1900 at Kingston (Samuel Quimby/Nancy Dearborn)b 1829
QUINN: Henry J, 26 May 1929 at Kingston (85) (James Quinn/Elizabeth Driscol)b-Boston,Ma
RAE: Dorothy V, 30 Mar 1991 at Exeter (Thomas M Thornburn/ Susan W Quinlan)
RALPH: Thomas S, 16 Jun 1991 at Exeter (Frank E Ralph / Jean M Calantonio)
RAMEY: Austin E, 25 Aug 1989 at Colebrook (Perley D Ramey/Eva M Hitchcock)
RANDALL: Hazel, 10 Dec 1918 at Brooklyn, NY
RANKIN: Jessie K, 26 Jul 1975 at Exeter (John Rankin/Mary Kemp)b 24 Mar 1894 (G/C)
    John R, 29 Nov 1990 at Exeter (John Rankin/ Mary Kemp)
    Mary, 20 Sep 1975 at Exeter (John Rankin/Sarah Brown) b 25 Apr 1885 (G/C)
RAY: Mildred E, 10 Mar 1937 (24) at Exeter
RAYCROFT: James Alexander, 07 Feb 1933 at West Kingston, b 13 Oct 186- (P/G)
RECER: Alice, 22 Sep 1990 at Concord (Evert Recer/ Elizabeth Powell)
REED: Carolyn R, 04 Oct 1955 at Weymouth, Ma, b 1862 (G/C)
    Clarence A (54) 20 Nov 1910 (Alonzo Reed/ Adelia White) b - Watertown, Ma
    Frank, 04 Feb 1923 (67) (David Reed/Jane Bates) b - Whitman, Ma
    Mary, 21 Feb 1934 at Kingston (Nathaniel D Cheney/Mary E Hoyt)b 27 Sep 1845
    Kingston (P/G)
REIDY: Mildred, 17 Feb 1993 (Myron Merrifield/Cora Stein)
REINBOLD: Charles, 01 Sep 1913 at Southwick, Ma (Charles F Reinbold)b 05 May 1846
    Marcia, 06 Oct 1938 at Kingston (Henry Davis/Sarah Kimball)b 08 Aug 1857,
    - Kingston (V/C)
    William E, 29 Mar 1940 at Kingston (h/o Marcia Davis) b 06 Apr 1880 (V/C)
RENT: Nancy T, 09 Dec 1994 at Exeter (George E Taylor/Marion Full)
    William Stuart,II, 03 Sep 1993 (William Stuart Rent,I/Edith Drinkwater)
REYNOLDS: Alphonse S, 22 Apr 1913 at Haverhill, Ma, b 1847 (P/C)
    Diane M, 25 Dec 1995 at Kingston (Edgar R Benson/Anna V McGuinness)
    Henry L, 09 Nov 1900 at Kingston (Alphnso Reynolds)b 1880
    Henry W, 28 Jul 1966 at Kingston (80) (William W Reynolds/Sarah Heritage)
    Jennie S, 12 Aug 1923 (74) b - Amity, Me.
    Norman, 08 Jul 1973 at Lawrence, Ma, b 1944 (G/C)
    Thomas O, 12 Dec 1913 at Kingston (Thomas F Reynolds/Marry Currier) b 1843 (P/C)
RHOADES: Alice L, 26 Sep 1971at Kingston (96) (Leonard B Nichols/Anna Severance)

RICH: Michael Alan, 31 Dec 1977 at Kingston (18) (Lawrence H Rich/Carol Westerback)
RICHARD: Ida Lillian, 15 Oct 1934 (72) at Melrose, Ma.
RICKER: Harold E, 16 Dec 1974 at Exeter (76) (John Ricker/Minnie Chello)
RIEDY: Elymas A, 09 May 1969 at Somerville, Ma, b 1899   (G/C)
RILEY: Alfred R, 15 Dec 1978 at Exeter (46) (Irving S Riley/Esther M Nichols)
    George L, 21 Mar 1964 at Haverhill, Ma (51)
RIVARD: Alfred Joseph, 23 Jun 1970 at Boston, Ma, b 1898   (P/G)
ROBBINS: Arthur E, 16 Oct 1953 at Exeter(88)b-Rossway,N.S. (Jacob C Robbins/
    Clarissa Timpany)
    Katherine F, 28 Feb 1966 at Exeter (81) (William Stephenson/Sara Shepherd)
ROBERTS: Francis E, 13 Jun 1967 at Haverhill, Ma (56) (Henry Roberts/Lunnena Rock)
    George Gardner, 23 Dec 1971 at Kingston (Annie A Peavey)b 18 Jan 1900 (P/G)
    Herbert L, 17 Oct 1980 at Exeter (John W Roberts/Beulah Smart)
    John, 12 Jan 1968 at Brentwood (75) (John W Roberts/Beulah Smart)
    Merton E, 13 Jun 1938 (birth) at Georgetown,Ma.
ROBIE: Baby Girl, 19 Feb 1947 at Kingston (Morton E Robie/Helen A Page)b 19 Feb 1947
    Chauncey A, 07 Dec 1945 at Kingston, b 22 May 1874
    Forrest R, 22 Nov 1934 at Exeter, b 1902 (P/G)
    Frances May, -5 Mar 1931 at Kingston (Morton E Robie/Helen A Page)b 01 Jan 1929
    Mabel L, 10 Nov 1930 at Kingston (Leslie W Page/Bertha M Swett)b 01 Feb 1905
    Kingston (P/G)
    Morton Elmer, 30 Jan 1970 at Concord (Elmer Morton Robie/Caroline Maude Devino)
    b 20 Nov 1899   (P/G)
ROBINS: Joseph H, 29 Mar 1936 at Nashua (Joseph Robins/Sarah Rudier)b--- Jan 1874
ROBINSON: ....., 09 Apr 1909 at Kingston (Merton S Robinson/Annie Goodwin)
    Anna J, 27 Jan 1964 at Brentwood (64)
    Annie, 30 Dec 1972 at Dover, b 1886   (P/G)
    Charles W, 27 Apr 1931 at Haverhill, Ma, b 1863
    George E, 25 Apr 1927 at Kingston (78) b - Brentwood
    Henry Willard, 23 Feb 1947 at Kingston (77) (Henry Robinson/Anne Beauchamp)
    b in Lynn, Ma
    James O, 21 Apr 1901 at Haverhill, Ma (Judith Webster) b 1820
    Lloyd Wilbert, 23 Jul 1976 at Manchester (52) (Dwight Robinson/Gladys Warren)
    Louise M, 11 May 1949 at Amesbury, Ma (85)
    Martha J, 25 May 1970 at Exeter (101) (John Morrill/May A Osgood)
    Mary J, 16 Oct 1921 (89) at Haverhill, Ma.
    May M, 02 May 1930 (86) (Samuel Tripp/Olive Seeley) b - Argyle, NY
    Merton S, 11 Aug 1954 at Haverhill, Ma (Charles W Robinson/Louise Smith)
    b 1887 in Danville   (P/G)
    Willie E, 13 Oct 1930 at Kingston (Harriett .....) b 12 Jul 1856 Reading, Ma. (V/C)
ROCHOWIAK: John, 08 Jul 1980 at Portsmouth (Michael Rochowiak/Frances Gvet)
    Kathleen L, 02 Mar 1975 at Portsmouth (64) (Jeremiah Sullivan/Nora Murphy) (M/S)
ROCK: ....., 30 May 1915 at Kingston (Ralph Rock/Nellie Swett) b 30 May 1915 in Kingston
    Elmer C, 12 Aug 1980 at Exeter (Ralph Rock/Nellie Sweat)

Nellie Frances, 14 Nov 1946 at Exeter (Moses Swett/Lavinia George)b 22 Feb 1881(P/G)
Ralph, 17 Mar 1962 at Brentwood (Joseph Rock/ ....) b 21 Mar 1886   (P/G)
Robert D, 08 May 1994 at Haverhill,Ma. (Ralph Rock/Nellie Swett)
RODDEN: Adrien F, 10 Aug 1968 at Exeter (64) (William J Rodden/Annie B Minehane)
Cecile M, 25 Apr 1962 at Exeter (43) (Joseph Tremblay/Bridget Boudeau)
RODGERS: Forrest Frank, Jr, 29 Sep 1993 (Forest F Rodges,Sr/Harriett Laing)
ROGERS: Annie L, 08 Oct 1938 at Winthrop, Ma.
Brian S, 03 Sep 1967 at Kingston (12) (Charles Rogers/Dorothy A Sullivan)
Charles C, 03 Sep 1930 (71) at Rockingham County Hospital, Brentwood
Ellen M, 10 Dec 1901at Lynn, Ma, b 1831
Ferdinand, 29 Mar 1951 at Brentwood (Moses Rogers/Mary Jane Winslow)
b 15 May 1872 in Kingston, Ma. (M/S)
Frank P, 09 Aug 1918 at Newton, b 1874 (P/G)
Harriet A, 08 Nov 1936 at Danver, Co, b 1861 (P/G)
Hazel M, 24 Dec 1972 at Haverhill, Ma, b 1914 (P/G)
Junia L, 28 Dec 1901 at Kingston (Jacob Severance/Jane Abbott)b 13 Aug 1830
Moses, 28 Oct 1921 (63) at Haverhill, Ma,
Olpho, 25 Dec 1935 at Haverhill, Ma, b 1861 (P/G)
Richmond Basil, 18 Mar 1969 at Portsmouth (Hughey B Rogers/Nancy Dow)
b 16 Dec 1911 (G/C)
Ruth C (75), 04 Jan 1972 at Exeter (Walter B Sproule/Georgianna Meady)
ROHDENBURG: Herman D, 11 May 1965 at Brentwood (86) (Dietrich Rohdenburg/
Meta Schumacher)
ROLLINS: Gladys Fitch, 05 Oct 1977 at Exeter (William James Snow/Alice F Kelley)
b 26 Aug 1889   (P/G)
Martha E, 09 Nov 1921 (76) at Worcester, Ma.
ROTHETERS: Josephine D, 13 Oct 1966 at Exeter (81) (Thomas Madore/Delphina Devoe)
Stelianos, 28 Sep 1957 (69) (Daniel Rotheters/.....) - Zonte, Greece
ROULEAU: Clarence O, 16 Oct 1981at Kingston (Oscar N Rouleau/Emma Ryell)
ROULSTON: Robert E, 04 Jun 1954 at Kingston, b 1884 in Nova Scotia
ROUSSEAU: Mary Ann, 07 Jun 1987 at Kingston (Etienne Gagne/Philomena Pageotte)
Oliver J, 23 Mar 1981 at Brentwood
ROWE: Benjamin F, 24 Oct 1901 at Kingston (Joseph Rowe/Mary Thayer)b 1822
Amelia A, 22 Nov 1967 at Kingston (104) (George Priest/Jane Hounsell)
Edward, 02 Nov 1984 at Exeter (Edward Rowe/Edna Shay)
Jeanne M, 24 May 1992 at Exeter (William J Kilroy/ Mary Arsenault)
Nicholas B, Jr, Nov1984 at Kingston (Nicholas B Rowe,Sr/Catherine Hill)
Ralph W, 19 Aug 1984 at Kingston (Sidney E Rowe/Grace Schiller)
ROWELL: E Chase, 11 Jun 1948 at Gardner,Ma (86)
Erastus Chase, 11 Mar 1945 at Kingston (John Rowell/Mary Rice)b 14 Mar 1879
Martha E, 28 Aug 1952 at Pepperell, Ma (88)
ROY: Herve J, 03 May 1978 at Amesbury, Ma (64) (Emilien B Roy/Marie A Geoffroy)
Mary, 05 Jul 1980 at Exeter (Clarence True/Bertha Rudd)
RUBERT: Moses I, 11 Dec 1929 at Kingston (89) (Christopher Rubert) b - Passadunkeag,Me

RUBIN: Harold M, About 5 Nov 1992 at Kingston (Louis D Rubin/ Edna Marvin)
RUSSELL: Frances M, 12 Feb 1985 at Exeter (Peter Smith/Frances Mc Andrew)
    Robert, 24 Apr 1967 at Kingston (Edward Russell/Rachael Dwyer)b 01 Aug 1881
RYAN: Paul Daniel, 03 Dec 1986 at Exeter (Martin B Ryan/Catherine Brennar)
    Theresa M, 30 Jul 1937 (8) b - Boston,Ma (John W Ryan/Sarah E Delory)
SALANAS: Julius, 11 Feb 1954 at Brentwood, b 1888 in Lithuania
SANBORN: Amanda, 13 May 1971 at Quincy, Ma, b 1900   (P/G)
    Dorothy R, 05 Jun 1990 at Kingston (Algernon Rae/ Harriett Moseley)
    Edward S, 27 Aug 1945 at Kingston (John W Sanborn/Rebecca Fogg)b 08 Apr 1879
    Elizabeth Sarah, 04 Aug 1943 at Exeter (John Sanborn/Lavina Smith)b 08 Mar 1858
    John, 11 Feb 1734 at Kingston (Peter Sanborn/Mary Sanborn)b 10 Mar 1733
    John, 06 May 1737 at Kingston (Peter Sanborn/Mary Sanborn)b 20 Sep 1736
    John H S, 22 Apr 1916 at Kingston (Isaac Sanborn/Ploomy Stevens)b 07 Feb 1839
    Kingston   (P/C)
    Mabel W, 27 Mar 1956 at Exeter (80) (John W Sanborn/Rebecca Fogg) - Kingston
    Martha A, 25 Mar 1928 at Kingston (William F Sanborn/Mary A Rowe)b 24 Oct 1847
    Kingston (P/C)
    Mary A, 25 Apr 1923 (92) (Moses Hooke,Jr/Mary Brown) b - Fremont
    Sarah, 28 Jul 1746 at Kingston (Abraham Sanborn/Abiegel Clifford)b 02 Jul 1745
    Sarah C, 22 Dec 1937 at Exeter, b 1849   (V/C)
SANDS: Francis H, 15 Oct 1994 at Kingston (Elmer Sands/Marion Yell)
SARCIONE: Catherine A, 05 Apr 1992 at Exeter (John Carlstrom/ Frances Hart)
SARGENT: Ellwood P, 06 Mar 1994 at Kingston (Frank Sargent/Helen Bell)
    Joseph C, 01 Jul 1992 at Kingston (Ernest D Sargent/ Katherine A McClellan)
    Lawrence A, 30 Nov 1976 at Exeter (William Sargent/Elsie Hines)b 21 Jun 1902
SAUER: Frederic, 05 Dec 1929 (53) (Adolph Sauer/Carrol LeBean) b - Germany
SAULNIER: Richard, 21 Jan 1970 at Haverhill, Ma, b Dec 1969   (P/G)
SAVAGE: Florence L, 08 Dec 1926 at Salem, Ma, b 1872
SAVORY: Mary F, 01 Apr 1917 at Newburyport, Ma, b 1859
SAVOY: George Paul, 27 Aug 1963 at Waterville, Me, b 1896   (K/C)
SAWERBY: Baby Boy, 29 Oct 1977 at Haverhill, Ma, b   29 Oct 1977 (P/G)
SCALETSKY: Theodore, 23 Aug 1987 at Kingston (Joseph Scaletsky/Helen ....)
SCHELLENG: Harlan, 16 Nov 1919 (John Schelleng/Leney Tucker)b 07 Mar 1896 (P/C)
SCHILLER: Grace M, 16 Dec 1988 at Exeter (James McKeon/Grace Freeman)
SCHMITZ: Steven J, 29 Sep 1992 at Manchester (Stanley E Schmitz/ Dorothy M Garvey)
SCHOFIELD: Edward M, 08 Apr 1909 at Kingston(Everett Schofield) b 1852 in Milton
SCHUARTH: Julia H, 23 Nov 1969 at Boston, Ma, b 1880   (K/C)
SCHUR: Baby Boy, 06 May 1959 at Exeter (Richard H Schur/Betty J Simes)b 06 May 1959
    Betty Jane, 08 Feb 1978 at Exeter (William Simes/Ruth George)b 18 Jul 1931
SCOTT: Roger, 16 Dec 1954 at Brentwood (John Scott/Grace Brackett)1883 in Cambridge, Ma
SEAVER: Daniel R (14) 11 Nov 1910 (John P Seaver/ Florence Hull) b - Kingston
    John P, 16 Apr 1923 at Kingston (Daniel P Seaver/Dolly C George)b 05 Dec 1864
SEAVEY: Alice M, 19 Jun 1915 at Kingston (Melancton Haynes/Clara F Stratton)b 1848 -
    Rouse's Point, NY

SEBETES: John P, 15 Oct 1992 at Kingston (John Sebetes/ Margaret Banaitis)
SEMPLE: Gertrude, 27 Feb 1989 at Kingston (Rodney Wilson/Gertrude Bartlett)
Russell Bowman, 02 Mar 1963 at Exeter (George W Semple/Lorena Mingo)
b 10 Mar 1907 (V/C)
SENTER: Allen L, 06 Feb 1978 at Framingham, Ma, b 1920 (P/C)
Allen S, 22 Nov 1933 at Haverhill, Ma, b 1865 (P/G)
Arthur W, 01 May 1955 at Haverhill, Ma (Charles A Senter/Mary L Barnard)b 1895
Kingston
Charles A, 04 Dec 1989 at Exeter (Samuel A Senter/Mary L Barnard)
Ella L, 27 Sep 1909 at Kingston (Leslie M Senter/Laura A Collins)b 1895 Kingston
Helen G, 27 Jul 1917 at Haverhill, Ma. b 14 Jul 1917
John H, Sr, 21 Feb 1979 (Walter H Senter /Gertrude F Stevens)
Laura A, 18 Dec 1935 at Haverhill, Ma (Charles Collins/Anna Smith)b 1874 (P/G)
Leslie Morton, 14 Apr 1962 at Concord (Frank Senter/Mary .....)b 05 Feb 1873(P/G)
Marion E, 21 Jan 1970 at Haverhill, Ma, (P/G)
Mary Elizabeth, 02 Apr 1930 at Plaistow, b 1843 (P/G)
Mary L, 24 Jun 1913 at Haverhill, Ma, b 1872 (P/G)
Nellie Ray, 11 Oct 1934 (39) b - Millville, N.S. (Charles Hoyt/Ada Good)
Walter, 30 Mar 1938 at Dover (Frank Senter/Mary E Davis)b 15 Nov 1870 in Derry
SEVERANCE: Anthony, 21 Dec 1944 at Brentwood (Benjamin Severance)b 08 Sep 1866
Daniel, 14 Jun 1913 at Haverhill, Ma, b 1863 (P/G)
Elizabeth H, 08 Oct 1912 at Kingston, b 1829 (P/G)
Ellen M, 26 Nov 1924 (74) (William Colfax/Elizabeth Quigley)-b St Johns, Nfnld
John, 16 Jul 1945 at Brentwood, b 13 May 1864
John S, 17 May 1900 at Kingston (Samuel Severance/Judith Towle) b 1817
Ora P, 12 Feb 1914 at Kingston (Samuel Severance/Judith Towle)b 08 Dec 1829
Kingston (P/G)
Patience (86) 01 Apr 1910 (Stephen Seaver) b - Kingston
Samuel M, 21 Jan 1936 at West Kingston (John S Severance/Emily B Hunt)
b 17 Nov 1846 (P/G)
SHANDA: Charles E, 19 Apr 1920 at Kingston (Frank A Shanda/Mabel Morrison)
b 07 Jan 1916 New York City (P/C)
SHAW: Blanche, 19 May 1955 at Kingston (Theodore Kennedy/Bessie Shaw) b 1894 -
Danvers, Ma.
Earl B, 20 Dec 1955 at Kingston (George Shaw/Hulda Rand) b 1879 - Augusta, Me.
Eldridge L, 15 Jun 1959 at White Plains, NY(James E Shaw/Jennie Danforth), b 1896 -
Danvers, Ma. (P/G)
George Edmund, 05 Dec 1969 at Laconia (James E Shaw/Jennie E Danforth)
b 20 Nov 1899 (P/G)
James Edmund, 16 Apr 1936 at Kingston (Jesse Shaw/Jane Durkee)b 16 Apr 1936,
Yarmouth,N.S. (P/G)
Jennie Herrick, 16 Apr 1951 at Kingston (Aaron Danforth/Susan Brown)b 10 Feb 1867
Danvers, Ma. (P/G)
Jesse Danforth, 19 Sep 1969 at Exeter (James E Shaw/Jennie H Danforth)b 25 Mar 1898

Jessie Elmer, 16 Aug 1940 at Raymond, b 1864   (V/C)

Mary J, 19 May 1902 at Kingston (David Currier/Hannah Hooke)b 1818

Mattie M, 01 Jun 1918 at Kingston (Parker Stevens/Marinda G Rowell)b 25 Mar 1870

Ora Dearborn, 02 Jul 1947 at Lancaster, Pa (Van Buren Shaw/Elizabeth Hutchins)
b 1867   (P/G)

Paterick J, 14 Aug 1945 at Kingston, b 13 Apr 1865 in Kingston

SHEPARD: Anthony (68), 07 Feb 1972 at Exeter (John Shepard/Katherine Bunther)

William T, 28 Oct 1932 (74) b - Epping (William Shepard/Demarius Tilton)

SHERMAN: Julie W, 15 Nov 1927 (59) (George W Rich/Francis Wight) b - Portland,Me.

Lucinda M, 13 Aug 1927 (91) (Abraham Thomas/Elizabeth LeBaron) b - Fall River,Ma.

SICARD: Patricia, 20 Jun 1991 at Exeter

SILLOWAY: Allen Wadleigh, 03 Nov 1959 at Exeter, b 1876   (P/G)

Annie B, 13 Mar 1959 at Hampstead (..... Osgood/Annie Jackman)b 01 Sep 1889 -
E Kingston

Earl, 15 Feb 1910 Turner, Me/Kingston (Frank Silloway)

Ella B, 11 Aug 1951 at Newton (86)

Emily, 29 Oct 1938 at Brentwood, b 1855

Eva I, 05 Dec 1932 at Brentwood, b 1913

Everett W, 28 Mar 1941 at Newton Jct (Wadleigh Silloway/Ann M Hoyt)b 1870

Frank, 03 Nov 1931 at Haverhill, Ma, b 1884

Gerald W (4) 09 Dec 1910 (Frank W Silloway/ Annie M Osgood) b-Kingston

Joseph, 18 Nov 1919 at Concord (Joseph Silloway) b 1840   (P/G)

Myron W, 10 Jan 1977 at Hampstead, b 1809   (W/K)

Sadie E, 30 Apr 1969 at Haverhill, Ma, b 1877   (P/G)

William N, 12 Feb 1902 at Deerfield (Ehuer Silloway) b 1883

SILVA: George F (43), 11 Apr 1972 at Chester (Fernando Silva/Helen Machado)

SIMES: Abbie Jane, 10 Oct 1966 at Exeter (John F Tucker/Ida M Curtis) b 01 Aug 1880(P/G)

Alice Mae, 09 Dec 1968 at Exeter (Edward Ashton/Josephine Senter)b 20 Feb 1902

Andrew F, 21 Sep 1979 at Rochester (Andrew V Simes/ Abbie Tucker)

Andrew Vernon, 22 Mar 1955 at Exeter (Francis X Simes/Sarah Murray)b 11 Jan 1872
Brandon, Vt   (P/G)

Annie F, 17 Sep 1976 at Brentwood (John F Tucker/Ida Hill)b 18 Mar 1885

Edward Dennis, 21 Apr 1964 at Exeter (Frank Simes/Sarah Murray)b 03 Oct 1882

Ethel H, 22 Dec 1955 at Concord (66) at Haverhill, Ma (Edward Foster/Elfriede Hardy)

Francis E, 17 Jul 1924 at Kingston (Andrew Simes/Margaret Duran)b 04 Oct 1840
Canada

Frank N, 09 Oct 1955 at Exeter (Frank Simes/Sarah Murray)b 10 Jan 1870
Brandon,Vt.   (V/C)

George E, 04 May 1958 at Kingston (82) (Frank Simes/Sarah Murray),b - Brandon, Vt.

George V, 02 Sep 1925 at Racine, WI (George Simes/Annie Tucker)b 1903   (P/G)

Jean, 24 Jan 1972 at Exeter (37) (Henry Pries) b 27 Jan 1934   (G/C)

Jennie Josephine, 20 Sep 1941 at Exeter (Adolphus Jutrus/Louise Touchette)
b 25 Jun 1879(V/C)

Marvin E, 12 Feb 1985 at St James City,Fl (Edward D Simes/Ethel H Foster)

Merle K, 07 Oct 1990 at Exeter (Edward Simes/ Ethel Foster)
Pauline Gertrude, 20 Feb 1975 at Exeter (Dana Lessard/Isa Collins)b 26 Mar 1924(G/C)
Raymond H, 03 Sep 1977 at Epping (George F Simes/Annie Tucker)b 24 Jun 1921
Roland A, 01 Feb 1929 at Kingston (William Simes/Ruth George)b 03 Oct 1928(P/G)
Sarah, 19 Mar 1900 at Kingston (John Murray/Louise Mitot)b 1844   (P/G)
William Arthur, 19 Mar 1948 at Exeter (Frank E Simes/Sarah Murray)b 04 Oct 1876
William George Elmer, 20 Jun 1963 at West Lebanon (Andrew Simes/Abbie Tucker)
   b 1902   (P/G)
SIMMONS: -------, 02 Feb 1927 at Haverhill, Ma.
   Barbara M, 03 Nov 1933 at Haverhill, Ma, b -- Apr 1933
   Doris Hilda, 28 Jan 1973 at Exeter (George I Rand/Hilda Foisy)b 13 Jun 1913
SIMPSON: ....., 21 Jul 1916 at Kingston (Clarence L Simpson/Mabel Greehan)b 21 Jan 1916 in
   Kingston (Private Burial)
   Joseph Ormand, 29 May 1947 at Kingston (73) (Joseph P Simpson/Sarah L Frink)
SJOSTROM: Alina V (Johnson), 27 Mar 1924 at Hampstead b 14 Jun 1872
   Frances E, 24 Apr 1971 at Haverhill, Ma, b 1907 (G/C)
   John, 07 Jun 1929 at Haverhill, Ma, b -1876 (G/C)
SKERRY: Frederick James, 08 Aug 1965 at Exeter (Walter R Skerry/Elizabeth Morrison)
   b 31 Jan 1906 (G/C)
SKINNER: Richard A, 08 May 1990 at Exeter (David W Skinner/ Blanche M Wilson)
SLATTERY: Melvina M, 02 May 1991 at Kingston (Amidee La Blane/ Lena O'Dette)
SLEEPER: George H, 27 Apr 1947 at Kingston (82) (Charles S Sleeper/Adeline Thurston)
   b in Gilmanton
SMITH: Abbie Jane, 22 Sep 1912 at Kingston (Fred Smith/Bessie Kelley)b 14 Jan 1910 (P/G)
   Albert E, 23 Sep 1934 (73) at Boston,Ma.
   Beatrice Ellen, 21 Jun 1967 at Exeter (Frank J O'Brien/Mabel Tappan)b 06 Jul 1905
   Bessie, 26 Jul 1953 at Concord (63) b -New Hampshire (Daniel ..../Harriet Place)
   Betsey B, 31 Mar 1900 at Kingston (Robert Smith/Lois French)b 1815
   Charles, 29 Jun 1927 at Boston,Ma.
   Christina Amelia, 25 Aug 1948 at Kingston (Louis C Stepp/Mary Huddleston) b 17 Sep
   1861 (V/C)
   Ellen L, 02 Dec 1957 at Lawrence,Ma (61) (Harry Lidstone/Eva Buker)- b Weld,Me
   Emma A, 23 Oct 1979 at Brentwood (Raymond Hutchins/ Harriet E Crosby)
   Forrest, 24 Dec 1963 at Haverhill, Ma (Frank Smith/Sylvania Winslow)b 14 Feb 1882
   George E, 19 Oct 1925 at Haverhill, Ma, b 1853   (P/C)
   Gladys, 30 Oct 1930 at Elmira, NY, b 1907 (H/H)
   Ida, 31 Jul 1967 at Manchester (True W Crombie/Emma York)b 27 May 1882   (G/C)
   Jeffrey William, 11 Jan 1962 at Kingston (Lawrence B Smith,Jr/Judith Cronk)
   b 21 Oct 1961
   Lester Eldridge, 22 Dec 1968 at Kingston,b 21 Apr 1912   (G/C)
   Louis C, 28 Oct 1922 at Kingston (Clark O Smith/Henrietta DeRochemont)
   b 27 Nov 1852   (P/C)
   Mabel B, 12 Mar 1937 at Haverhil, Ma, b 1887 (P/G)
   Marie L, 09 Feb 1933 at Boston, Ma, b 1857(P/C)

Shirley A, 18 Oct 1970 at Amesbury, Ma (Donald H Nason/Glory Moore)b 1935(P/G)
William Henry, 01 Jul 1942 at Whitefield (Clark Payson Smith/Henrietta A
DeRochemont) b 07 Mar 1858 (Kingston)
SMYTHE: Harold, 27 feb 1976 at Methuen, Ma, b 08 Nov 1912 (P/G)
Harry W, 10 May 1954 at Plaistow, b 1883
SOUTHWICK: Florence T, 17 Jun 1985 at Kingston (Albert Caron/Gertrude Hill)
SPAULDING: Charles H, 27 Jul 1950 at Kingston (Elisha Spaulding/Susan Colby)b 24 -- 1880
SPELIOTIS: Peter, 31 Jul 1989 at Exeter (Nicholas Speliotis/Lamo Leontiris)
SPILLANE: Elsie M, 18 Oct 1989 at Exeter (John Saari/Lizzie Hackler)
SPINA: Santo R, 04 Jul 1985 at Kingston (John Spina/Catherine Talarico)
SPINELLA: Anna M (McIntyre), 24 Jul 1992 at Brentwood
Cyrus, 07 Jan 1970 at Kingston (Rosario Spinella/Anna Arnone)b 27 Aug 1901
SPOFFORD: Eliza J, 27 Mar 1913 at Kingston (James Spofford/Martha Johnson)
b 24 Mar 1837 (P/C)
Francis A, 07 Nov 1909 at Kingston (James Spofford/Martha Johnson)b 1828
Kingston
Samuel Johnson, 22 Feb 1926 at Groton, Ma, (P/C)
SPRAGUE: Baby Boy, 20 Oct 1971 at Haverhill, Ma, b 20 Oct 1971 (G/C)
Baby Girl, 17 Jun 1965 at Exeter (George H Sprague/Annette E Ottati)b 17 Jun 1965
Lena, 12 Mar 1958 at Exeter (70) (Charles Davis/Sarah Bean) b - Lakeport
Walter Everett, 18 Nov 1958 at Kingston (Edward Sprague/Lena Davis)b 17 Aug 1912
Everett, Ma. (G/C)
STEVENS: Andrea Lynn, 12 Oct 1976 at Boston, Ma (Mark Stevens/Sherry Lynn Drake)
b 1975 (G/C)
Carl Stuart, 20 Sep 1969 at Exeter (Frank W Stevens/Lora M Stevens)b 16 Sep 1895
Cecilia, 31 May 1900 at Kingston (John Loring/Harriet Leuch)b 1834
Elizabeth S, 24 Sep 1919 at Boston, Ma (Samuel H Stevens/Sera Johena Sanborn)
b 1844 (P/C)
Frank W, 24 Feb 1902 at Haverhill, Ma (Samuel Stevens/Harriet N Collins)b 1867
George Benair, 28 Nov 1949 at Kingston (Samuel Stevens/Harriet Collins)b 02 Jun 1880
George F, 30 Jan 1931 at Kingston (Frederick Stevens/Anna Emerson)b 17 Jan 1873
Harriet N, 28 May 1920 at Kingston (Samuel S Collins/Julia Judkins)b 21 Oct 1839
Helen, 01 Jun 1956 at Kingston (Walter S Clark/Abbie Sanborn)b 07 Jul 1880 - Kingston
John E, 08 Jun 1954 at Kingston (Parker Stevens/Lorenda Rowell)b 1865 Durham
Joseph (74) 25 Mar 1910 - b-Lawrence, Ma
Lora Mae, 26 Jan 1942 at Kingston (Charles C S Stevens/Mary Anna Hanson)
b 28 Mar 1867, Brentwood (K/C)
Mary A, 06 Jan 1913 at Kingston (Amos Hanson/Betsy Fellows)b 01 Jan 1845
Mirenda G, 14 Nov 1915 at Kingston (Ansel Rowell/Eliza B Shute)b 10 Dec 1837 -
Brentwood (P/C)
Sarah E, 21 Aug 1923 at Kingston (Edward Primrose/Hannah C Perkins)b 15 Jan 1844
Salem, Ma (S/K)
William M, 18 Jun 1941 (63) b - Newton (Oscar T Stevens/Belle L Hoyt)
STEWARD: Arthur E, 30 Jul 1959, Kingston (58) (George Steward/Cora Holmes) Manchester

STICKNEY: Henry W, 23 Jul 1932 (59) b - Compton (Samuel Stickney/Addie Smith)
STOCK: Elvira, 03 Novl 1994 at Exeter (William C Ayles/Bessie Lynk)
STRAW: Joseph L, 23 Dec 1953 (82) b - East Boston,Ma
STROUT: Flora (94),22 Apr 1972 at Exeter (George Storer/Phebe Mason)
    Leroy J, 23 Sep 1974 at Haverhill, Ma, b 1905   (P/G)
STUKAS: Kazimar Anton, 09 Dec 1965 at Exeter, b 24 Apr 1879   (G/C)
    Lillian Olga, 11 Sep 1949 at Kingston (Charles Stukas/Patricia Daukaut)
    b 05 Sep 1914   (G/C)
    Patricia D, 29 Dec 1979 at Exeter (w/o Charles Stukas)
SULLIVAN: Nellie A, 16 Sep 1918 at Haverhill, Ma, b 1855
SULTAIRE Clarence, 20 Jul 1974 at Concord (Julius Clement Sultaire/Ida Louise Tucker)
    b 08 Mar 1926(P/G)
    Julius Clement, 07 May 1971 at Brentwood (Augustus Sultaire/Mary Lane)
    b 21 Jun 1901 (P/G)
SURVEY: Prudence, 17 Dec 1930 at Chelsea, b 1858   (P/C)
SWALLOW: Josephine, 12 Dec 1970 at Kingston (Bernard J Gibbons/Anna E Webber) b 17
    May 1899   (P/G)
    Leslie Otis, 02 Nov 1975 at Exeter (George D Swallow/Kate F Morrissey) b 26 Dec
    1894   (P/G)
SWEENEY: Ellen T, 19 Mr 1900 at Kingston (Darine Towle/Hannah M Diamond)b 1851
    Henry L, 11 Mar 1921 at Kingston (Edward M Sweeney/Lucy M Thaxter)
    b 03 Apr 1858   (P/C)
SWEETLAND: Genevieve B, 19 Nov 1975 at Kingston (James Scanlon/Emma Lucier) b 27
    Feb 1894   (P/G)
SWEETSER: Gary H, 11 May 1990 at Kingston (Herbert E Sweetser/ Elaine G Breault)
SWETT: Anna Belle, 16 Jul 1973 at Exeter (Samuel Winslow/Julia Merrow) b 11 Oct 1884
    Bernice, 16 May 1930 at Kingston (Daniel Swett/Anna Winslow)b 24 Apr 1907(P/G)
    Daniel Wadleigh, 06 Dec 1960 at Exeter (Moses Swett/Levinia George)b 26 Sep 1876
    Emma Frances, 23 May 1931 at Kingston (Moses Swett/Elvira George)b 08 Oct 1884
    Franklin James, 18 Feb 1946 at Exeter (Franklin Swett/ Shirley V Tracey)b 30 Jun 1945
    Lloyd Elwin, 29 May 1953 at Kingston (Daniel W Swett/Anna B Winslow)b 10 Mar
    1925, Kingston (P/G)
SWINERTON: Emma J, 25 Jul 1910 (51) at Exeter/Charlestown(Walter Bryant/ Elizabeth
    Rankin)
    Moses, 20 Aug 1890 at Kingston (Tucker Swett)b 1854
    Rosetta F, 25 Feb 1900 at Kingston (Jacob Tucker/Mehitable Bean) b 1844
    Steven Michael, 10 Aug 1950 at Exeter (Wallace Swett/Josephine DeLorenzo)
    b 10 Aug 1950   (P/G)
SYLVAIN: Mary M, 30 Jan 1990 at Portsmouth (Martin McCarthy/ Catherine Leonard)
SYLVESTER: Gilbert A, 21 May 1991 at Kingston (Romolus Sylvester/ Marie Bacon)
TARBOX: Chester O, 04 May 1989 at Manchester (Chester A Tarbox/Alice J Lorenzen)
TAYLOR: James S, 25 Feb 1929 at Beachmonth, Ma (P.W. Taylor/Emerline C Stibbins)
    b 1869   (Kingston)
    Marion, 03 Mar 1988 at Exeter (George W Full/Delia Caisse)

TEED: ....., 02 Feb 1909 at Kingston (Frances Ball) b 02 Feb 1909 in Kingston
TEWKSBURY: Carl Henry, 20 May 1970 at Exeter, b 31 Mar 1894   (P/G)
    Mildred Inez, 07 Apr 1967 at Kingston (Seth Nason/Blanche Elkins)b 09 Sep 1905(P/G)
THEREAU: Albert, 08 Dec 1939 at Boston, Ma, b 1875   (Kingston)
    Jennie S, 19 Feb 1975 at Brentwood (Moses Wilson/Ida Ordway) b 24 Jun 1883 (G/C)
THERIAULT: Larry L, 02 Nov 1988 at Kingston (Raymond Theriault/Molly Tucker)
THERRIEN: Arthur R, 18 Sep 1991 at Dover (Frederick Therrien / Florence Geddes)
THIBEAULT: Patrick W, 17 Feb 1994 at Exeter (Henry Thibeault/Bethel L Porter)
THOMAS: Walter R, 19 Sep 1949 at Haverhill, Ma, b 1876   (P/G)
THOMPSON: Alexander G, 03 Jul 1963 at Haverhill, Ma, b 1879   (P/G)
    Arthur, 12 Aug 1958 at Kingston (Dustin Thompson/Sarah Gooding)b 15 Apr 1874 -
    Newton (S/K)
    Dustin, 12 Nov 1902 at Amesbury, Ma (Samuel Thompson/Mary A B Heath)b 1846
    Jessie C, 02 Apr 1969 at Haverhill, Ma, b 1879   (P/G)
    Maurice H, 20 Mar 1975 at Haverhill, Ma, b 12 Feb 1900 (P/G)
THORNE: Wilson H, 19 Jan 1954 at Hampton Falls (..... Thorne/..... Jones)b 1869 in Vermont
TILTON: Kate M, 25 Nov 1960 at Kingston (97) (Frank B Tilton/Susan Wadleigh)-Kensington
TITCOMB: Lendell N, 08 Jun 1950 at Exeter (Joseph J Titcomb/Frances M Bernell)
    b 21 Aug 1866   (G/C)
    Margaret V, 30 Apr 1965, b 14 Jan 1874   (G/C)
TOMESELLI: M Frances, 14 May 1992 at Kingston (John Carlstrom/ Frances H Hart)
TORRENCE: Albion G, 06 Jun 1937 (70) b - Holden,Me (Sanford Torrence/Nancy Parsons)
    Elizabeth Ann, 13 Feb 1951 at Brentwood (Ira Porter/Hannah Crosby)b 14 Jul 1872
    - Bradford, England (G/C)
TOWLE: Mary F, -- Sep 1947 at Kingston (78)(Joseph Simpson/Sarah O Frink)b - Greenland
    Melvin L, 27 Sep 1924 at Concord (Darin Towle/Hannah Diamond)b 29 Jul 1845
TOWNE: Grace F, 26 Feb 1958 at E Hampstead (87) (William R Towne/....)- Providence, R.I.
    Herbert R, 24 Feb 1963 at Exeter (64) (Herbert Towne/Grace Spink)
TOWNSEND: Redman L, 25 Feb 1966 at Amesbury, Ma, b 1894   (P/G)
    Sophronia S, 28 Nov 1915 at Kingston (Samuel S Townsend/Lydia Townsend)
    b 28 May 1833 at Barre, Vt   (P/C)
TOZIER: William M, 13 Aug 1959 at Haverhill,Ma (68) (Albert Tozier/Bessie Perley), b -
    Plaistow
TRACEY: Thomas, 17 Oct 1936 (Thomas Tracey/Mary Hayes) b 17 Oct 1876   (P/G)
TRACY: Clarence P, 06 Mar 1956 at Boston, Ma, b 24 Jul 1894 - Haverhill, Ma. (P/G)
    Lillian G, 14 Jan 1969 at Haverhill, Ma, b 1901   (P/G)
    Vesta M,22 Oct 1972 at Brentwood (William Cheney/Stella Page)b 22 Sep 1890 (P/G)
TRETT: Kenneth Elmer, 18 Jun 1974 at Shelton, Ct, b 11 Sep 1917   (P/G)
TRUE: Clark D, 12 Mar 1988 at Kingston (Clark G True/Leila A Edwards)
TUCKER: Annie F, 09 Jun 1991at Exeter (William F Tucker Sr/ Nellie Simes)
    Arthur Prescott, 24 Nov 1954 at Exeter (William P Tucker/Ella J Buttrick)
    b 18 Dec 1876   (G/C)
    Charles Roland, 28 Apr 1936 at Haverhill, Ma, b 1866 (P/G)
    Eldora M, 27 Jun 1957 at Boston,Ma. (79)

Frank G, 02 Nov 1918 at North Reading (J Peaslee Tucker/..... Bean) b 1860   (P/C)
Hattie G, 26 Dec 1918 at Kingston (Otis Tucker/Sarah E Cheney)b 03 Mar 1878
Jerry C, 25 Dec 1928 at Kingston (Moses Tucker/Hannah Martin) b 20 Feb 1850
John Franklin, 15 Sep 1938 at Kingston (Moses Tucker/Hannah Marden)
   b 02 Jun 1852, Kingston   (P/G)
Lettie E, 14 Sep 1938 at Wolfeboro, b 1862 (P/C)
Mary, 05 Feb 1967 at Kingston (John Clark/Elizabeth Titcomb)b 26 Sep 1874
Mildred, 31 Dec 1950 at Kingston (George E Follett/Ambrosene Hasey)b 16 Sep 1877
Nellie Florence, 09 Jul 1967 at Kingston (Francis Simes/Sarah Murray)b 20 Aug 1878
Otis, 25 Dec 1915 at Kingston (Moses Tucker/Hannah Martin)b 14 apr 1837
   Kingston   (P/G)
Sarah E, 26 Apr 1918 at Kingston (Nathaniel D Cheney/Mary E Hoyt) b 24 Aug 1842
Wallace M, 25 Feb 1936 at Ossipee
Warren Harvey, 27 Oct 1950 at Kingston (Jerimiah Tucker/Rosetta Woodward)
   b 03 Sep 1869 (P/C)
William Franklin, 11 Jun 1955 at Kingston (John F Tucker/Ida Curtis)
   b 27 Feb 1878 in Kingston   (P/G)
William P, 24 Sep 1921 at Kingston (Moses Tucker/Hannah Tucker) b 1845
Woodrow W, 05 Apr 1913 at Kingston (William Tucker/Nellie Simes)
   b 21 Mar 1913
Spurgeon D, 18 Dec 1985 at Kingston (Charles H Turner/Alma Cogswell)
TURNER: Spurgeon D, 18 Dec 1985 (Charles H Turner/Alma Cogswell)
TUTTLE: Ella May, 17 Mar 1927 at Plaistow, b 1853
TWOMBLY: ....., 26 Jun 1914 at Kingston (Henry Twombly/Effie Page)b 26 Jun 1914
   Kingston   (P/G)
   Loren P, 23 Jun 1914 at W Kingston (Henry Twombly/Effie B Page)b 1910 at Kingston
VALLIMONT: Chester E, 27 Jan 1987 at Kingston (Earl C Vallimont/Mary Catherine Crate)
VAN OUNSEN: Louis, 22 Jul 1954 at Kingston (August Van Ounsen) b 1897 in Boston
VICKERY: Herbert, 04 Nov 1957 at Lynn, Ma, b 1867   (New Cemetery)
VICTOR: Katie, 04 Sep 1920 (2) (John Victor/Fannie Guscora) b - Kingston
VOISINE: Renald D, 26 Jun 1992 at Kingston (David Voisine/ Jeannette Lauzon)
WADLEIGH: Clarence Benjamin, 04 Jun 1965 at Dover, b 1896   (M/S)
   Elizabeth Edith, 17 Nov 1950 at Durham (Benjamin Gemeny/Mary Roberts) b 10 Aug
   1863   (So K)
   Ella F, 23 Aug 1931 at Brentwood (Lemuel Bartlett/Sarah Page)b 15 May 1850   (P/C)
   Maria M, 09 Feb 1902 at Brentwood (Solomon Holbrook/Abbie Nason) b 1819
   Percy, 07 Nov 1968 at Concord (Elwell Wadleigh/Sarah ....) b 1900   (V/C)
WAHLEN: Paul, 21 Jul 1992 at Exeter (Paul Wahlen Sr/ Elizabeth Lutie)
WALDRON: Mattie, 23 Nov 1965 at Waltham, Ma, b 1873   (K/C)
   Ralph D, 21 Mar 1974 at Sebring, Fl, b 1880   (P/C)
   Sadie B, 15 Oct 1942 (61) (Thomas Lounder/Mary ....) b - St John's, N.B.
WALKER: Jane, 02 Feb1920 (80) (Charles Titcomb/Sarah Smith) b - E. Kingston
WALMSLEY: Arline H, 07 Aug 1927 (Lawrence Walmsley/Helen Griffin) b - Kingston
WALSH: Doris, 20 Aug 1987 at Brentwood (John Smith)

William T, 11 May 1962 at Haverhill,Ma (51) (Peter Walsh/Marie Bowers)
WANKE: James E (26), 26 Apr 1972 (Edward Wanke/Leola Jensen)
WARD: Kerry E, 13 Feb 1979, Boston, Ma (Roger A Ward, Jr/ Joyce Eusko)
WARREN: Henry J, 16 Nov 1924 (73) (William Warren/Mary Frost) b - Brownfield,Me.
WARRINGTON: Allen R, 06 Oct 1960 at New Yor, N.Y. (33)
    Edwin Glen, Sr, 06 May 1958 at Manchester (Joseph C Warrington/Sally Hastings)
    b 08 Jul 1892 - Laurel, Del. (G/C)
    Ethel Louise, 14 Feb 1965 at Concord (John Mareau/.....) b 15 Dec 1899 (G/C)
WASHBURN: Joseph H, 18 Aug 1990 at Hampton (Harold Washburn/ Sylvia M Hobbs)
WATSON: Arthur V, 24 Jan 1968 at Manchester (Edwin M Watson/Agnes C ....)
    b 09 Apr 1895 (G/C)
    Charles B, 27 Jun 1957 at Boston, Ma, b 1878 (New Kingston)
    Harriet, 30 Jun 1966 at Brentwood (George Arthur/Janet Wiggins)b 07 Nov 1873(G/C)
    Herbert B, 30 May 1954 at Kingston, b 1867 - Rome, Me.
    Maria B, 04 Jan 1930 (88) (George Seward/Lucy A Derby) b - Milton,Ma.
WATTS: Robert S, 09 Oct 1960 at Exeter (Stephen W Watts/Lena J Beckman) b - Exeter
    Stephen W, Jr, 21 May 1989 at Kingston (Stephen W Watt/Georgia Eaton)
WEBSTER: ....., 08 Aug 1909 at Kingston (Charles E Webster/Alice Huse)b 08 Aug 1909
    ....., 24 Jan 1914 at Kingston (Walter E Webster/Bertha Kruger) b 1914 - Kingston
    Alice M, 03 Jan 1917 at Kingston (William Huse/Lucy A Webster)b 21 Jan 1874
    Kingston (P/C)
    Ben R, 23 Dec 1938 (64) at Amesbury,Ma.
    Betsey L, 22 May 1914 at East Kingston (Elihu J Webster/Ruth Hunt)b 09 Apr 185- -
    Kingston (P/G)
    Carrie A, 19 Jun 1925 at Plaistow, b 1846 (P/G)
    Charles E, 08 Feb 1933 at Kingston (John T Webster/Abby Buzzell)b 08 Jul 1865 (P/C)
    Clara N, 28 Jan 1933 at Haverhill, Ma, b 1868 (P/C)
    David, 01 Apr 1901 at Kensington (David Webster) b 1819
    Emily, 04 Apr 1927 at Concord (John Pollard/Sarah Lock) b 1843
    Everett H, 24 Mar 1937 at Kingston (John T Webster/Abbie P Buswell)b 29 Oct 1855
    George A, 17 Apr 1935 at Acton,Ma (Augustus Webster/Judith Buswell)b 29 Oct 1955
    Everett H, 24 Mar 1937 (81) at Kingston(John T Webster/Abbie P Buswell)b - Kingston
    Georgianna, 03 Aug 1874 at Kingston (H.D. Webster/Caroline .....)b 11 Apr 1874
    Kingston
    Gladys May, 31 Jul 1965 at Exeter (Ererard Goldwaithe/Grace Sargent)b 23 Dec 1895
    Hannah W (Quimby), 24 Nov 1913 at Plaistow, b 1822 (P/G)
    Harold Prescott, 08 Apr 1974 at Manchester (John Webster/Mary Anvilla)
    b 15 Jun 1893 (G/C)
    Jacob, 09 Apr 1881 at Kingston, b - 1798
    John, 29 Apr 1788 at Kingston (h/o Ruth Clough)
    John F,19 Apr 1932 at Haverhill, Ma, b 1852 (P/ C)
    John H, 27 Jul 1937 (59) b - Kingston (Albert Webster/Betsy Webster)
    John L, 26 Jul 1923 at Kingston (John T Webster/Abbie Buswell)b 07 Sep 1860
    E. Kingston (P/C)

Joseph, 17 Mar 1884 at Kingston (David Webster/Judith Webster) b 1813 - Kingston
Joseph, 26 Nov 1812 at Kingston (David G Webster/Judith Webster)
Julia F, 04 Jun 1917 at Kingston (Rueben Davis/Harriet Seaver) b 19 Sep 1823
Sarah, 28 Jan 1714 at Kingston (Isae Webster/Sarah .....)
Sarah, 1737 at Kingston (Samuel Webster/Elisabeth Burnum)
William, 07 Jul 1924 at Kingston (John T Webster/Abbie Bussell) b 05 Mar 1868
WEED: Alice L, 17 Aug 1910 (31) at West Chester, Pa. (Charles L Weed/ Lizzie L Swett)
WEESE: Donald L, 20 Nov 1988 at Brentwood (Bruce Weese/Naoma England)
WELCH: Arthur C, 11 Feb 1989 at Kingston (John Welch/Elizabeth Godfrey)
    Charles W, 15 Dec 1947 at Kingston (70) (George A Welch/Harriet Davis) b in Sandown
    Frank N, 13 May 1937 at Dover (Samuel Welch/Dorothy Gray) b 10 Dec 1871   (G/C)
    Grace Cecilia, 11 Dec 1956 at Dover (William J Stevens/Cecelia Loring)b 07 Jun 1866
    John, 12 Jul 1901 at Danville, b 1817
    Mary Jane, 20 Sep 1900 at Kingston (George Welch/Susan Keezer) 11 days
    Mary Susan, 09 Mar 1938 at Brentwood, b 1856 (M/S)
    William James, 08 Dec 1963 at Danville, b 1899 (M/S)
WELLS: Frederick E, 25 Jan 1927 at Kingston (Enos Wells/Annette Morse)b 16 Aug 1857
    Stoneham, Ma. (P/G)
WENDELL: Richard Dixon, 22 Oct 1963 at Exeter (Leon G Wendell/Edna Cate)b 02 Dec
    1921   (P/G)
WEST: ....., 25 Dec 1936 at Georgetown, Ma, b 05 Sep 1936   (P/G)
    ....., 04 May 1941 (birth) b - Kingston (Henry C West/Blanche Brickett)
    Alan Walter, 08 Jun 1957 at Exeter (Walter Edwin West/Martha Clemons)b 10 Apr
    1953 (P/G)
    Allen Raymond, 07 Dec 1977 at Kingston (Charles W West/Lucinda Smith)b 19 Nov
    1922 (P/G)
    Audrey E, 10 Aug 1979 at Exeter (Bert Yeaton/ Lucille Richardson)
    Calvin C, 27 May 1965 at Newburyport, Ma (Ralph W West/Edna Seaver)b 1924(P/G)
    Carroll A, 09 Jan 1971 at Haverhill, Ma, b 1902   (P/G)
    Chandler Bruce, 01 May 1965 at Exeter (Chester W West/Alice Lyford)b 03 May 1922
    Charles, 10 Aug 1987 at Brentwood (Fred West/Flora Pinkham)
    Charles Willis, 15 Dec 1947 at Kingston (George A West/Harriett Davis) (P/G)
    Chester W, 15 Nov 1953 at Danville (59) b - Kingston (Walter West/Ruth Nason)
    Edna, 22 Sep 1970 at Portsmouth (William Deming/Ellen LaTulip)b 16 Feb 1917 (P/G)
    Ethel , 10 Mar 1961 at Danvers, Ma (Alonzo Davis/Eva .....) b 1903 (G/C)
    Florence G, 06 Jun 1950 at Haverhill, Ma (John Hull) b 11 Sep 1878 (P/G)
    Harriett Ann, 13 Aug 1925 at Lynn, Ma, b 1841   (P/G)
    Henry Clifton, 26 Jun 1973 at Danville (Walter West/Ruth Nason)b 14 Aug 1973 (P/G)
    Herbert C, 21 Mar 1964- b 11 Dec 1912 (P /G)
    Horace H, 06 Feb 1924 at Haverhill, Ma. b 1856   (P/G)
    Leon J, 21 Jan 1969 at Portsmouth (Charles W West/Lucinda Smith)b 25 Aug 1899
    Lucinda Smith, 18 Sep 1956 at Exeter (Horace West/Minnie Goodwin)b 20 Oct 1882 -
    b Kingston
    Nathan H, 22 Jan 1936 at Kingston (Henry C West/Blanche E Brichett)b 19 Aug 1936

Nellie W, 06 Mar 1917 at Kingston (Charles W West/Lucinda P York)b 22 Apr 1916
Owen Earl, 28 Sep 1966 at Exeter (Fred F West/Mabel Pinkham)b 08 Dec 1901 (G/C)
Ralph W, 16 Nov 1934 at Haverhill, Ma (George A West/Harriet Davis)b 1880 (P/G)
Richard Willis, 30 Dec 1957 at Fremont, b 1920 (P/G)
Ruth Filena, 18 Oct 1938 at Kingston (Nathan Nason/Sarah K Page)b -- Jan 1859,
Kingston (P/G)
Walter S, 02 Jul 1937 at Newburyport, Ma, b 1857 (P/G)
William Joseph, 15 Dec 1971 at Derry (Harold West/Joyce Barton)b 07 Dec 1971(P/G)
WHEELER: Theodore M, 26 Jul 1992 at Exeter (Hubert W Wheeler/ Elizabeth C Valerio)
WHEELOCK: Etta R, 31 Jul 1938 (64)b-Bryant Pond,Me (William G Golthwaite/Etta R
Lawrence)
WHIPPEN: Elise S, 15 Nov 1965 at Concord (Frank Whippen/Minerva Swan)b 02 Sep 1888
Frank W, 26 Apr 1927 at Kingston (Henry Cass Whippen/Lydia Richards)
b 20 Jun 1856(P/C)
Minerva, 08 Sep 1930 at Kingston (Henry Swan/Sophia Wilder)b 20 Apr 1859
Buckland,Ma.
WHIPPLE: Sanford, 08 Apr 1923 at Kingston (Sanford Whipple/....)b -- Mar 1844 Goffstown
WHITE: Donald Austin, 20 Jun 1971at Exeter (Charles White/Vera Sweeney)b 20 Apr 1914
Ernest L, 30 Apr 1920 in Pennsylvania (G/C)
Ernest M, 06 Jul 1973 in Newburport, Ma, b 1899 (G/C)
Hugh Stanley, 22 Apr 1933 at Amesbury, Ma, b 1897 (P/C)
Loretta O, 03 Dec 1919 at Kingston (Danie Short/Diana P Blaisdell)b 01 Dec 1864
(P/C)* Removed to G/C on 30 Apr 1920
WHITNEY: Caroline, 19 Dec 1977 at Haverhill, Ma , b 1939 (P/G)
Louis B, 07 Nov 1973 (William O Whitney/Lena I Bird)b 1908(P/G)
WHITTIER: Almira S, 26 Apr 1926 at Haverhill, Ma, b 1839 (P/C)
Annie E, 20 Apr 1963 at East Hampstead (Jacob Whittier/Rosanna Stuart)b 28 Dec 1874
Charles L, 15 Aug 1919 at South Kingston (W. Wicks) b 25 May 1868 (P/G)
Fannie, 10 Feb 1960 at Amesbury, Ma, b 1875 (M/S)
George W, 22 Feb 1917 at Kingston (George W Whittier/Eunice Locke)
b 19 Jun 1840
Jacob, 02 Oct 1912 at South Kingston (George W Whittier/Eunice Locke)
b 09 Sep 1843 (P/G)
Lulu M, 03 Apr 1950 at Haverhill, Ma (Andrew J Collins) b 24 Jun 1871
Martha J, 22 Jun 1915 at West Kingston (John Haines)b 16 Nov 1846 - Penacook (P/G)
Morris, 08 Feb 1922 at Kingston (Nathaniel Whittier/Almira Dudley)b 01 Feb 1859
Ora E, 13 Jan 1915 at Haverhill, Ma, b 13 Jan 1915 (S/K)
Rosanna, 04 Jan 1927 at South Kingston (Eben Stuart/Betsy Ferrin)b 31 Jul 1841 (M/S)
Walter Fred, 20 Jul 1944 at Kingston (George W Whittier/Martha Haynes)b 08 Jul 1876
WICKER: Franciska, 03 Jul 1938 (54) (Wojciech Guschiora/ AntoninaWicker Sudol)b - Poland
Joseph, 23 Mar 1994 at Exeter (John Wyka/Franciska Guscima)
WIGGLESWORTH: Elizabeth M, 19 Feb 1900 at Kingston (Calvin W Smith/Maryann J Shaw)
b 1868
WILLIAMS: Amanda R, 10 Aug 1928 at South Kingston (Emery Paige/Elizabeth Dow) b 04
May 1841 Hampton (S/K)

WILLSON: Anne M, 03 Oct 1992 at Manchester (George Perham/ Emily ....)
  Horace P, 24 Sep 1991 at Exeter (March P Willson/ Gertrude Jacobs)
WILSON: David, 12 Apr 1919 at Kingston (Ebenezer Wilson/Elizabeth Currier)b 13 Oct 1855
  Georgianna, 31 Nov 1926 at Kittery, Me. b - 1855 (P/G)
  Nora, 20 Feb 1943 at Concord (Jack Dempsey/Kathe Fitzgerald)b -- Sep 1866   (V/C)
WING: Harold M, 18 May 1974 (Frank Wing/Clara Mason) b 10 Mar 1905 (G/C)
WINSHIP: George W, 21 Aug 1928 (89) (George W Winship/Lucia Fifield) b - Enfield
WINSLOW: Anna M, 13 Feb 1900 at Kingston (Isaac Hoyt/Lydia Willard) b 1824
  Cora B, 03 Jan 1932 at Haverhill, Ma, b 1867 (P/G)
  Edward, 27 Oct 1902 at Lawrence,Ma (William Winslow)b 1848
  Eldora E, 26 Mar 1926 at Kingston (Albert F Nason/ LauraFifield)b 22 Sep 1880 (P/G)
  Foster W, 14 Sep 1977 at Clearwater, Fl.   (P/G)
  Julia E, 12 Feb 1903 at Kingston (E.M. Merrill/Maria Merrow)b 1846
  Laura, 01 Oct 1913 at Kingston (Horace Winslow/Eldora Nason)b 13 May 1911
  William Webster, 02 Dec 1938 at Exeter (William Winslow/Eliza Silloway)b 03 Mar
  1868, Kingston   (P/G)
WINTERS: Asa Joseph, 23 May 1952 at Concord (George Winters/Charlotte Goodspeed)
  b 01 May 1870 - Burke, N.Y.   (K/C)
  Grace B, 21 Jun 1966 at Brentwood (Charles S Day/Mary E Lyford)b 21 Jan 1887
  Infant, 26 Nov 1921 at Exeter
WISE: Lillian A, 13 Dec 1932 (71) b - Quebec (Thomas Arnold)
WRIGHT: Peter J, 28 Apr 1955 (ll mos) b - Winchester,Ma(Robert A Wight/Nancy Cooper)
WOOD: Frederic Edward, 23 Nov 1952 at Kingston (Alexander M Wood/Margaret Cox)
  b 28 Jun 1867 - Somerville,Ma.   (V/C)
WOODBURY: Chester C, 19 Sep 1992 at Exeter (Chester T Woodbury/ Blanche Webster)
  Clara A, 17 Feb 1916 at Kingston (Samuel E Woodman/Eliza V Spearinn)
  b 13 Dec 1855 in Lawrence, Ma (P/C)
  Frank Alfonso, 25 Mar 1928 in Medford, Ma, b 1860   (P/C)
  Laura B, 21 Sep 1928 at Everett, Ma, b 1885   (P/C)
WOODMAN: ....., 28 Feb 1931 (Clarence H Woodman/Lillian Jones) b - Kingston
  Laura B, 12 Oct 1928 (43) at Everett, Ma.
  Leslie S, 19 Mar 1959 at Cambridge, Ma, b 1886   (K/C)
  Lucius H, 12 Nov 1938 (69) at Saugas, Ma.
  Willard S, 06 May 1937 (48) at Boston, Ma.
WOODS: Elizabeth Y, 30 Dec 1915 at Somerville, Ma (John Schellberg) b 1845 - Kingston
WRIGHT: Elenor, 08 Feb 1920 at Brentwood   (P/C)* Moved to G/C on 30 Apr 1920
  Peter J, 28 Apr 1955 at Kingston (Robert A Wright/Nancy Cooper)
  b Mar 1954 in Winchester, Ma
WYMAN: Hazen W, 08 Jul 1976 at Exeter (William H Wyman) b 18 Feb 1904 (P/G)
YAVAROW: Josephine K, 27 Jun 1994 at Kingston (Anthony Kosekevitch/.....)
YOUNG: Eliza, 16 Apr 1910 (20) at Danville/Kingston (George W Welch/ Mary S Keezer)
  Sarah, 15 Oct 1745 at Kingston (John Young/Sarah Curnham)
  Shepard O, 03 May 1937 at Raymond - South Kingston

Female Index

Bragg, Sylvia 214
Brainard, Sarah C 235
Braley, Donna M 108,167
Braley, Frances E 142
Braley, Kay M 111
Braley, Natalie J 119
Braley, Sandra L 178
Brander, Donna L 162
Brandon, Donna 149
Brashier, Joanne F 152
Breault, Elaine G 255
Breen, Joan M 160
Brennan, Mary 163,205
Brennar, Catherine 250
Brent, Evelyn A 201
Brewer, Sally 233
Brewer, Vickie-Lynn 132
Brewster, Margrett E 162
Brezinski, Rosalie 186
Brickell, Ida 137
Brickett, Blanche 127,200,259
Brideau, Susan 225
Bridges, Norma G 157
Brierley, Hannah E 191
Briggs, Annie 136
Briggs, Donna L 128, 201
Briggs, Elizibeth 199
Brigham, Carole L 121
Brindle, Suzanne 121
Brinkle, Mildred I 167
Brissette, Ida 98, 149
Brisson, Rosilda 198
Britton, Florence 106,163
Britton, Kristie A 153
Broadhurst, Carol H 172
Broadhurst, Carolina 184, 225
Brock, Grace 244
Brockelbank, Jacqueline 98, 149
Brockelbank, Cynthia A 169
Brockelbank, Diane 99,151
Brockelbank, Susanne K 159
Broderick, Anna 157
Broderick, Irene J 174
Brodie, Mary J 146

Broe, Mary 145
Bromage, Clara F 155
Brooks, Abbie 199
Brooks, Ella F 159
Brooks, Elsie 198
Brooks, Judith L 181
Brooks, Laura 237
Brooks, Patricia A 141
Brown, Ann L 154
Brown, Annie 111,172,192, 208, 225, 237
Brown, Arlene 177
Brown, Bernice 222
Brown, Bertha M 171
Brown, Deborah E 147
Brown, Elizabeth 198,239
Brown, Elizah 237
Brown, Ernestine A 143
Brown, Estella 107,165,230
Brown, Etta 114,177,241
Brown, Evelyn E 162,105
Brown, Flora A 184
Brown, Frances G 99
Brown, Gayle E 137
Brown, Geraldine G 144
Brown, Ida B 159
Brown, Jennie 189,215,224
Brown, Judith A 96,108,145
Brown, Katherine N 173
Brown, Kathleen 171
Brown, Laverna G 158
Brown, Lucy M 237
Brown, Lydia 230
Brown, Marion B 137
Brown, Martha 185,229
Brown, Mary 219,250
Brown, Mattie 110
Brown, Michele L 147
Brown, Minnie 154
Brown, Nancy S 190
Brown, Natalie J 128,200
Brown, Pearl 154
Brown, Ruth M 182
Brown, Sarah 132, 224, 234, 235, 247
Brown, Sumira 223

Brown, Susan 252
Brown, Veronique 181
Browne, Nancy E 99
Browning, Clara H 161
Brunelle, Deidre F 162
Brunelle, Donna M 179
Brunette, Susan J 144
Bruso, Clarabell 131,157
Bruyere, Eva J 151
Bryan, Katherine 170
Bryant, Dasy 165
Bryant, Dianne M 88
Bryant, Emiline 215
Bryant, Muriel E 145,168
Bryant, Stella G 167
Bryant, Virginia H 159
Bryden, Mary 231
Bubar, Dale M 163
Bubar, Pamela J 184
Bubie, Sarah J 234
Bucci, Elaine J 147
Buccini, Jennie 135
Buccuzzo, Catherine M 139
Buchal, Christiane 243
Buchman Julia 240
Buckless, Lois A 134
Buckley, Annie T 229
Buckley, Julia 173
Buckley, Linda E 193
Budd, Sandra L 87
Budrewicz, Janice M 141
Budzinski, Miranda 147
Buker, Christine 178
Buker, Eva 253
Bukowski, Sandra L 132
Buller, Debra A 184
Bulock, Clara 178
Bump, Edna 183
Bundy, Katie 163
Bundzinski, Miranda 97
Bunker, Freida I 89
Bunker, Lois W 92,1131,153
Bunker, Nancy L 136
Bunker, Priscilla A 137
Bunker, Thelma 102,156
Bunnell, Susan 178

George, Florence A	165	Gilbert, Linda C	168	Girard, Linda L	168
George, Hannah	36	Gildart, Mattie G	186	Girrior, Florence	208
George, Lavinia 56, 180, 190,		Gile, Abiah	61	Girroir, Anna-Belle L	90
243, 249, 255		Gile, Eva	8, 200	Gittings, Lynn R	94
George, Leila M	157	Gile, Lydia J	66	Givens, Mary L	112
George, Lilla	90,163,208	Giles, Carol E	157	Glazier, Linda L	129
George, Linda S	118	Giles, Elvira	210	Glidden, Heather J	174
George, Lovinia	27, 64	Gilford, Anna L	201	Gliden, Hannah	39
George, Marie L	117	Gill, Deborah A	154	Glinska, Emelia	243
George, Marjoire N	168	Gill, Donna M	139	Glisson, Josephine	239
George, Mary	131,171,236	Gill, Mary K	109, 176	Glougie, Beverly Jo	121
George, Nettie M	52	Gill, Mary K	109	Glover, Hannah	189
George, Ora E	128,201	Gillam, Susanna	224	Glover, Lillian W	34
George, Pamela G	121,189	Gille, Helen V	136	Glynn, Julia	150
George, Ruth	122,189,	Gillen, Marlene J	125	Glynn, Lorraine A	176
250, 253		Gilles, Mary	220	Goad, Cindy M	186
George, Thelma D	124	Gillespie, Myrle	156	Godfree, Abigel	12, 46
Georgeou, Lisa A	97	Gillion, Mary	152	Godfrey, Eileen T	115
Gerard, Mary E	177	Gillis, Ethel	122	Godfrey, Elizabeth	259
Gerhard, Donna J	109	Gillis, Judith	139	Godsell, Alice	171
Gering, Harriet F	197	Gillogily, Rose	194	Gold, Pamela	95
German, Priscilla	177	Gilman, Abba L	59	Gold, Sarah	35
Gerneny, Elizabeth	29	Gilman, Ann	228	Goldberg, Elvira	203
Gerskowitz, Catherine A	187	Gilman, Caroline	42	Golden, Priscilla B	153
Gerstel, Jennie	145	Gilman, Claudia F	119	Goldsmith, Diane	192
Gervais, Janet A	122,192	Gilman, Cora M	38	Goldstein, Esther M	150
Gesina, Jacoba	167	Gilman, Deborah	56	Goldsteine, Eva	140
Geyer, Maud	226	Gilman, Dollie	22	Goldthwaite, Beatrice	88,134
Giacobbi, Diane M	185	Gilman, Dorothy	59	Goldthwaite, Etta R	200
Gianetta, Carolyn D	198	Gilman, Elaine M	115,179	Goldthwaite, Grace	172
Giard, Wanda M	126	Gilman, Elizabeth	40	Goldthwaite, Hazel R	161
Gibbons, Alice T	101,155	Gilman, Emily	39	Goller, Annie	201
Gibbons, Alice T	101	Gilman, Emma A	52	Gongas, Cheryl A	105
Gibbons, Gladys	168,196,233	Gilman, Hannah	12	Gonsalves, Marjory	190
Gibbs, Frances C	197	Gilman, Janet A	159	Gonyer, Doris M	116,244
Gibson, Clara H	36	Gilman, Lucy A	119,185	Gonyer, Evelyn Z	120,187
Gibson, Mary L	110	Gilman, Mary A	214	Gonyer, Rita T	162
Gibson, Nancy	223	Gilmartin, Ann	179	Gonyer, Zoey M	115
Giddings, Jessie	219	Gilmon, Elizabeth	1, 34, 70	Good, Ada	251
Giddings, Mary	165,231	Gilroy, Agnes B	157	Goode, Mary E	90
Gielar, Patricia S	102	Gincauski, Patricia A	133	Goodell, Anne M	130
Gifford, Lois F	176	Gingras, Sheila A	117	Gooden, Mary	17, 53
Gifford, Patricia A	198	Gioia, Dorothy A	187	Goodhue, Beverly J	132
Giggi, Diane M	90	Girard, Eva P	163	Goodhue, Margaret M	149
Gilbert, Annette E	193	Girard, Laura A	161	Gooding, Hannah	42
Gilbert, Georgianna	181	Girard, Lillian T	183	Gooding, Sarah	256

Hoyt, Hannah	63,198	Hulett, Grace	184	Hutchins, Beryle A	105
Hoyt, Lavinia F	57	Hull, Florence	61, 250	Hutchins, Carolyn P	150
Hoyt, Lois	45	Hume, Ellen M	162	Hutchins, Elizabeth	252
Hoyt, Lottie E	47	Hume, Joyce A	111	Hutchins, Erma	159
Hoyt, Louisa R	57	Hunicke, Diana C	96	Hutchins, Gertrude	207
Hoyt, Lucinda	49	Hunress, Cynthia J	181	Hutchins, Gloria L	159
Hoyt, Lucy A	212	Hunt, Doris	166	Hutchins, Josephine	93,142,
Hoyt, Lucy A	212	Hunt, Edith M	112,238	143, 198
Hoyt, Margret W	57	Hunt, Emily B	251	Hutchinson, Blanche E	209
Hoyt, Maria E	66	Hunt, Gladys L	99	Hutchinson, Debra A	128
Hoyt, Marianna J	50	Hunt, Lila	18, 55	Hutchinson, Karen Z	100
Hoyt, Mary	39 41, 52	Hunt, Lucy A	65	Hyson, Dorothy I	141
Hoyt, Mary E	211,238, 247,	Hunt, Mary	61	Iaci, Gae P	99
257		Hunt, Penelope	1, 35	Indoccio, Patricia A	156
Hoyt, Maud B	4,38	Hunt, Rachel	7, 41,232	Ingalls, Elizabeth	226
Hoyt, Maude B	140	Hunt, Ruth	47,66,258,261	Ingalls, Gwendolyn M	89
Hoyt, Minnie E	143	Hunt, Sally	43	Ingalls, Joy L	101
Hoyt, Nancy R	39	Hunt, Sarah E	42, 68	Ingalls, Mary D	187
Hoyt, Polly	65	Hunter, Barbara J	153	Ingalls, Wendy	227
Hoyt, Sarah	189	Hunter, Gwendolyn L	136	Ingalls, Wendy S	104,227
Hoyt, Susannah	68	Huntington, Elizabeth	65	Ingalls, Winifred	107
Hsubij, Marion	161	Huntington, Linda Lee	98	Ingersoll, Rochelle	152,167
Hubard, Grace	7,64	Huntington, Sandra	89,99,	Ingham, Barbara J	118
Hubard, Mary	20, 26, 57, 63	207		Inkmen, Harriett	231
Hubbard, Abigail	21, 58	Hunton, Hannah	52	Inkpin, Hattie B	165
Hubbard, Betsey	62	Huntoon, Mary	15, 145	Ireland, Barbara A	104
Hubbard, Dorcas	52	Huntress, Eva M	156	Ireland, Margaret I	167
Hubbard, Elizabeth	231	Huntress, Martha A	110	Ireland, Sandra R	144
Hubbard, Ethel	222	Hurd, Adeline	42, 236	Irish, Catherine M	195
Hubbard, Ida F	58, 185	Hurd, Renzel R	162	Irish, Mildred	246
Hubbard, Patricia E	181	Hurni, Christina	131	Irvin, Orpliece	223
Hubbard, Sharon J	158	Hurst, Lilia M	196	Irvine, Laura R	123,194
Hubbell, Susan P	144	Hurwick, Bessie	135	Irvine, Susan J	136
Huckins, Bernice	232	Huse, Alice	29,66,127, 258,	Irving, Cynthia D	170
Huckins, Gail D	117	261		Irving, Linda C	103,158
Huckins, Mirah	146	Huse, Annie	14, 17, 50	Irwin, Laura P	105
Huddleston, Mary	253	Huse, Carrie B	17, 54	Irwin, Sally E	196
Hudson, Amelia J	142	Huse, Dorothy C	92	Isaacson, Anna	150
Hudson, Debra L	118,184	Huse, Isella	8, 42	Isabelle Gray	247
Hudson, Greta	145	Huse, Lucy A	42	Isaksen, Laura A	161
Hudson, Mary A	46	Huse, Mary A	51	Isherwood, Elaine D	104,160
Hudson, Ruth	38	Huse, Molly	15	Itz, Alice L	190
Hughes, Ethel G	172	Huse, Nellie A	52	Ivas, Corinne A	114,140
Hughes, Helen	221	Huse, Ruth	14, 50	Jackman, Annie	56,145,
Hughes, Margaret H	132	Hutchens, Sarah	62	190, 243, 252
Hughes, Shelley A	97,146	Hutchings, Carol J	173	Jackson, Clara E	48

King, Ethel W	97	Krieger, Deborah L	163	LaFontaine, Janet A	109
King, Fronie	138	Krueger, Bertha H	199	LaForce, Margaret	210
King, Gladys	239	Krueger, Heidi L	101	Laine, Mary C	194
King, Gladys V	113,174	Kruger, Bertha	127,258,261	Laing, Harriett	249
King, Helen	194	Krumm, Debra K	156	Lajuenesse, Juliette B	188
King, Janice V	198	Kubiak, Jennie	174	Lake, Lucy E	164
King, Letitia J	166	Kujat, Sabrina G	168	Lakin, Anna E	62
Kinnamon, Jeanie K	131	Kupiec, Katherine	221	Lamb, Bernice	92,140
Kinney, Debra L	140	L'Italien, A Melody	185	Lamb, Dorothy	135
Kinney, Joan T	104,160	LaBarbera, Carol M	149	Lamb, Florence V	192
Kinney, Julie A	197	LaBarr, Madeline	147	Lamb, Julie A	152
Kinnon, Matilda	239	Labbe, Irene T	195	Lamb, June	168
Kinson, Deanna R	173	Labell, Esther	167	Lamb, Karen A	115,243
Kinson, Sarah	230	LaBelle, Virginia D	193	Lamb, Victoria P	86
Kirios, Mary	165	LaBranche, Christine	170	Lambert, Brenda C	94,143
Kishton, Katherine	144	LaBranche, Emelia	156	Lambert, Marilyn G	151
Klang, Susan L	196	Labree, Arivilla	184	Lambert, Sheila M	188
Kleinhans, Alice A	98,150	Lacandia, Lynne M	190	Lamkin, Brenda F	118
Klinch, Deborah M	120,187	Lacarubba, Christine	125	Lamonde, Carolyn G	163
Klinos, Margaret	167	Lacerte, Cheryl A	197	Lamont, Constance	199
Klopp, Millie	238	Lacerte, Elizabeth A	159	Lamont, Ella A	148
Kmiec, Judy S	112	Lacomb, Carole	104	LaMotte, Rita E	99
Knapp, Fannie	190	Lacombe, Lisa G	168	Lamouica, Laurie A	115
Knight, Annie	153	Lad, Dorryty	22	Lampriel, Abigel	1, 34
Knight, Nettie	225	Lad, Elizabeth	30, 66, 83, 84	Lampropulas,Konstantina	198
Know, Martha A	152	Lad, Hannah	15, 51	Lamy, Joan S	132
Know, Norma C	154	Lad, Mehetabel	7, 40, 73	Lanagan, Eunice	141
Knowles, Cora	154	Ladd, Dorryty	59	Lancaster, Annie F	9
Knowles, Mary F	220	Ladd, Elizabeth	64	Lancaster, Carrie	74
Knowles, Rebecca A	190	Ladd, Gladys	191	Lancaster, Pamela A	87
Knowlton, Diane C	152	Ladd, Joanna	48	Lancey, Janice A	188
Knox, Julia	204,213	Ladd, Mabel G	191	Lancey, Lisa M	162
Koahk, Annie	244	Ladd, Mary	21, 58	Landers, Catherine	148
Kohlauff, Carol M	98	Ladd, Olla M	34	Landers, Katherine	197
Kohlauff, Nancie L	89	Ladd, Susanna	2	Landers, Sandra E	126
Kopoulos, Clara G	189	Ladd, Wilkie L	197	Landregon, Mary	205
Koravos, Joanne	96	Ladware, Mary	47	Landrigan, Sheila M	192
Kortebien, Anna	245	Lafayette, Diane	91,108,166	Landry, Ruth E	119
Kotuli, Bernice B	118	Lafayette, Kimberly	92,139	Landry, Sharon E	176
Kouns, Dayna L	185	LaFlamme, Josephine	87	Lane, Edna E	186
Koza, Catherine	207	LaFlamme, Rhea M	114	Lane, Lucetta J	168
Kraft, Eula	228	LaFleche, Paula J	126,199	Lane, Mabel C	139
Kramer, Florence M	176	Lafleche, Donna M	136	Lane, Marion	184
Kramer, Katherine M	118	LaFleur, Myra L	116	Lane, Mary	255
Kreamer, Anne E	198	LaFleur, Rose M	122	Lane, Nellie M	197
Krebs, Linda A	128	LaFoe, Linda L	177	Lane, Ruth	210

Reynolds, Helen	151	Ringer, Ida	130	Robinson, Lucy	3, 36
Reynolds, Joanne N	174	Ringer, Letitia	107,174	Robinson, Marjorie D	91
Reynolds, Lillian	200	Riopel, Michele	123,194	Robinson, Mary	67, 76, 220
Reynolds, Mabel	46,152	Ripley, Frances T	172	Robinson, Nancy	64
Reynolds, Marilyn J	179	Rishel, Marietta C	227	Robinson, Pearl	96
Reynolds, Mary	62,209	Ristaino, Annie	151,199	Robinson, Polly	64
Reynolds, Myrtle	193	Ritchie, Gloria J	169	Robinson, Sarah	43
Reynolds, Rita A	184	Ritchie, Judith T	124	Robinson, Sheila A	90
Rhodes, Joyce K	121	Ritter, Sue J	115	Robinson, Susie H	31, 67
Rhuda, Julie M	97	Rizya, Joan F	157	Robinson, Zelma J	168
Ricaurricco, Nancy	188	Rizzo, Anna D	195	Roche, Pauline	151
Rice, Isabella	176	Rizzo, Jean M	154	Rochemont, Loomora G	48
Rice, Mary	249	Roach, Mary F	200	Rochmont, Caroline	36
Rich, Clara E	150	Robbins Ann L	123	Rochussen, Virginia J	185
Rich, Eliza E	57	Robbins, Mary	48	Rock, Barbara F	115,179
Richards, Carol W	181	Robbins, Mildred	136	Rock, Emma	192
Richards, Elizabeth	180	Roberts, Anne F	183	Rock, Florence	219
Richards, Florence	136	Roberts, Debra L	140	Rock, Isadora	73
Richards, Jean	158,160	Roberts, Eleanor A	88	Rock, Lunnena	248
Richards, Linda A	93,142	Roberts, Karen N	109,168	Rockey, Naomi L	165
Richards, Lydia	260	Roberts, Linda M	169	Roden, Jennie	225
Richards, Mary	163	Roberts, Mary E	198,257	Rodgers, Harriet M	174
Richardson, Alice	134,156	Roberts, Ruth C	190	Rodham, Kathryn L	181
Richardson, Annie	245	Roberts, Sarah	70	Rodriques, Ruth H	104
Richardson, Bonnie J	199	Roberts, Susan H	188	Roe, Bessie	221
Richardson, Dorcas	18	Roberts, Theresa M	193	Roels, Clarina B	115
Richardson, Nellie	174	Robertson, Azelma M	172	Roger, Beatrice	203
Richardson, Patricia A	121	Robey, Lydia	43	Rogers, Alice M	64, 196
Richmond, Catherine	153	Robey, Lydia	9	Rogers, Brenda L	90
Richter, Joan M	123	Robichaud, Patricia A	121	Rogers, Cora B	61
Ricker, Grace	236	Robidou, Patricia L	95	Rogers, Dorothy M	192
Ricker, Joan A	129	Robie, Madeline L	99,150	Rogers, Ellen A	51
Ricker, Pauline	143	Robillard, Amilda	218	Rogers, Flora L	134
Rickwall, Louise M	187	Robillard, Evangeline	177	Rogers, Josephine	107,144,
Riel, Malizzie S	138	Robinson, Abby S	49	Rogers, Lois D	91
Rietzel, Helena G	150	Robinson, Betty	62	Rogers, Nellie (Ellen)	15, 16
Riley, Debora M	152	Robinson, Beverly	162	Rogers, Olive A	64
Riley, Deborah Jo	148	Robinson, Blanche	144,214	Rogers, Patricia J	171
Riley, Eleanor M	182	Robinson, Cynthia A	123	Rogers, Sadie	190
Riley, Raymah H	162	Robinson, Eleanor M	120	Rogers, Theresa	132
Riley, Shirley M	188	Robinson, Elisabeth	52	Rogge, Bertha	150
Rimmer, Margaret	160	Robinson, Eliza	19	Rohr, Marilee	179
Rines, Beth A	98	Robinson, Emily	237	Rois, Elisabeth	228
Rines, Sarah	217	Robinson, Gladys	112,174	Rokes, Nellie A	142
Ring, Elizabeth	49	Robinson, Josephine	43, 49,	Rollins, Christie L	169
Ring, Mary	45	217		Rollins, Ella	218

www.ingramcontent.com/pod-product-compliance
Lightning Source LLC
Chambersburg PA
CBHW071837270326
41929CB00013B/2026